THE LITURGY DOCUMENTS

FOUNDATIONAL DOCUMENTS
ON THE ORIGINS AND IMPLEMENTATION
OF *SACROSANCTUM CONCILIUM*

VOLUME THREE

THE LITURGY DOCUMENTS

FOUNDATIONAL DOCUMENTS
ON THE
ORIGINS AND IMPLEMENTATION OF
SACROSANCTUM CONCILIUM

Volume Three

LITURGY
TRAINING
PUBLICATIONS

Nihil Obstat
Very Reverend Daniel A. Smilanic, JCD
Vicar for Canonical Services
Archdiocese of Chicago
March 25, 2013

Imprimatur
Reverend Monsignor John F. Canary, STL, DMIN
Vicar General
Archdiocese of Chicago
March 25, 2013

The *Nihil Obstat* and *Imprimatur* are declarations that the material herein is free from doctrinal or moral error, and thus is granted permission to publish in accordance with c. 827. No legal responsibility is assumed by the grant of this permission. No implication is contained herein that those who have granted the *Nihil Obstat* and *Imprimatur* agree with the content, opinions, or statements expressed.

Library of Congress Control Number: 2012940317

16   15   14   13   1   2   3   4

ISBN: 978-1-61671-101-6

LD3V1

The Church earnestly desires that all the faithful be led to that full, conscious, and active participation in liturgical celebrations called for by the very nature of the liturgy. Such participation by the Christian people as "a chosen race, a royal priesthood, a holy nation, God's own people" (1 Pt 2:9; see 2:4–5) is their right and duty by reason of their baptism.

In the reform and promotion of the liturgy, this full and active participation by all the people is the aim to be considered before all else. For it is the primary and indispensable source from which the faithful are to derive the true Christian spirit. . . .

—*Sacrosanctum Concilium*, 14

CONTENTS

ABBREVIATIONS

Many texts listed here appear in *Documents on the Liturgy, 1963–1979: Conciliar, Papal and Curial Texts* (DOL) (Collegeville, MN: The Liturgical Press, 1982). This list is not all-inclusive of liturgical documents promulgated before and after the Second Vatican Council.

AAS	*Acta Apostolicae Sedis*
ADA	*Abhinc duos annos*
AG	*Ad gentes divinitus*
BB	Book of Blessings
BCDW	Bishops' Committee on Divine Worship
BCL	Bishops' Committee on the Liturgy
BG	Book of the Gospels
BLS	Built of Living Stones: Art, Architecture, and Worship
c.; cc.	canon; canons
CB	Ceremonial of Bishops
CCC	Catechism of the Catholic Church
CCCB	Canadian Conference of Catholic Bishops
CCEC	Code of Canons of the Eastern Churches (*Codex canonum Ecclesiarum orientalium*)
CCL	*Corpus christianorum,* Series Latina
CD	*Christus Dominus*
CDF	Congregation for the Doctrine of the Faith
CDWDS	Congregation for Divine Worship and the Discipline of the Sacraments
CEILT	Criteria for the Evaluation of Inclusive Language Translations of Scriptural Texts Proposed for Liturgical Use
CHP	The Church at Prayer: A Holy Temple of the Lord
CI	Christian Initiation, General Introduction
CIC	1983 Code of Canon Law (*Codex Iuris Canonici*)
1917 CIC	1917 Code of Canon Law (*Codex Iuris Canonici*)

CMBVM(L)	Collection of Masses of the Blessed Virgin Mary: Lectionary
CMBVM(M)	Collection of Masses of the Blessed Virgin Mary: Missal
CP	*Comme le prévoit*
CR	Congregation of Rites
CSEL	*Corpus Scriptorum Ecclesiasticorum Latinorum*
CSL	Constitution on the Sacred Liturgy
CSP	Chirograph of the Supreme Pontiff
CT	*Catechesi tradendae*
DA	*Divino afflatu*
DD	*Dies Domini*
DCS	*Divini cultus sanctitatem*
DE	Directory for the Application of Principles and Norms on Ecumenism
DedCh	Dedication of a Church and an Altar
DMC	Directory for Masses with Children
DOL	Documents on the Liturgy (ICEL)
DSCAP	Directory on Sunday Celebrations in the Absence of a Priest
DSV	*De solemni vigilia paschali instauranda*
DV	*Dei Verbum*
EACW	Environment and Art in Catholic Worship
EE	*Ecclesia de Eucharistia*
EM	*Eucharisticum mysterium*
FYH	Fulfilled in Your Hearing: The Homily in the Sunday Assembly
GCSPD	Guidelines for the Celebration of the Sacraments with Persons with Disabilities

GILOH	General Instruction of the Liturgy of the Hours		OE	*Orientalium Ecclesiarum*
GIRM	The General Instruction of the Roman Missal		OEx	*Ordo Exsequiarum*, 1969
			OT	*Optatam totius*
GMEF	God's Mercy Endures Forever: Guidelines on the Presentation of Jews and Judaism in Catholic Preaching		PCS	Pastoral Care of the Sick: Rites of Anointing and Viaticum
			PG	*Patrologiae cursus completus: Series Graeca*
GS	*Gaudium et spes*			
GSF	Gathered in Steadfast Faith: Statement of the Bishops' Committee on Liturgy on Sunday Worship in the Absence of a Priest		PGR	Plenty Good Room: The Spirit and Truth of African American Catholic Worship
			PL	*Patrologiae cursus completus: Series Latina*
HCWEOM	Holy Communion and Worship of the Eucharist Outside Mass		PO	*Presbyterorum Ordinis*
			PS	*Paschale solemnitatis*
HLS	This Holy and Living Sacrifice: Directory for the Celebration and Reception of Communion under Both Kinds		RBC	Rite of Baptism for Children
			RC/ RConf	Rite of Confirmation
			RCIA	Rite of Christian Initiation of Adults
IO	*Inter Oecumenici*			
IST	In Spirit and Truth: Black Catholic Reflections on the Order of Mass		RM/ RomM	The Roman Missal
			RMarr	Rite of Marriage
			RP	Roman Pontifical
LA	*Liturgiam authenticam*		RPen	Rite of Penance
LG	*Lumen gentium*		RS	*Redemptionis sacramentum*
LHSOI	*Liturgicus hebdomadae sanctae Ordo instauratur*		RT	*Ratio translationis*
			SacCar	*Sacramentum caritatis*
LI	*Liturgicae instaurationes*		SacCom	*Sacram Communionem*
LM	Lectionary for Mass		SC	*Sacrosanctum Concilium*
LMT	Liturgical Music Today		SCAP	Sunday Celebrations in the Absence of a Priest
MC	*Mirae caritatis*			
MCC	*Mystici Corporis Christi*		SCC	To Speak as a Christian Community: Pastoral Message on Inclusive Language
MCW	Music in Catholic Worship			
MD	*Mediator Dei*			
MS	*Musicam sacram*		SCh	*Sources chrétiennes*
MSD	*Musicae sacrae disciplina*		SL	*Sacram Liturgiam*
MSSL	*De Musica sacra et sacra Liturgia*		SS	*Spiritus et Sponsa*
			STL	Sing to the Lord: Music in Divine Worship
n.; nn.	number; numbers			
NCCB	National Conference of Catholic Bishops		TAA	*Tres abhinc annos*
			TLS	*Tra le sollecitudini*
NDRHC	Norms for the Distribution and Reception of Holy Communion Under Both Kinds in the Dioceses of the United States of America		UNLY	Universal Norms on the Liturgical Year and the General Roman Calendar
			UR	*Unitatis redintegratio*
			USCCB	United States Conference of Catholic Bishops
NSC	National Statutes on the Catechumenate			
			VL	*Varietates legitimae*
OCF	Order of Christian Funerals		VQA	*Vicesimus quintus annus*

FOREWORD
THE PROPER CONTEXT FOR UNDERSTANDING
SACROSANCTUM CONCILIUM

Francis Cardinal George, OMI
Archbishop of Chicago

The most important religious event of the twentieth century was the Second Vatican Ecumenical Council, which had its first session on October 11, 1962, and its final session on December 8, 1965. One cannot fully appreciate this historic gathering without also studying what led up to it and immediately followed upon it.

In his address at the solemn opening of the Second Vatican Council, Pope John XXIII outlined the purpose of the Council:

- To guard and teach more efficaciously the sacred deposit of Christian doctrine passed down to us through the centuries;

- To address the new conditions and new forms of life, which provide new challenges and avenues for the Catholic apostolate;

- To deal with errors by making use of the medicine of mercy, demonstrating the validity of Church teaching rather than simply condemning fallacious teachings and opinions;

- To find new ways to express the substance of the ancient doctrine of the Deposit of Faith;

- To promote the unity of the Christian and the human families.[1]

Gathered for the opening of the Council were cardinals, patriarchs, archbishops, bishops, and religious superior generals from the farthest corners of the earth, numbering around 2,600 prelates. To this number were added theologians and other expert consultants, swelling the number of participants to over 3,000. In addition, media coverage of the Council and its numerous committee meetings also assured that the Council's decisions would be scrutinized. Sometimes, they were also misinterpreted by the world community.

The Second Vatican Council was called a pastoral council because its purpose was not to examine Church teaching directly, but to see what could be changed in the Church in order to place her in better dialogue with a world headed for self-destruction. The Council was missionary in its purpose. In order to save the world from itself, the Church would have to open dialogue on all fronts. This "opening of the windows" had a great impact on the way we live and worship as a Catholic community.

---

1. Floyd Anderson, *The Council Daybook, Vatican II, Session 1 and Session 2*, Washington: National Catholic Welfare Conference, 1965, pp. 26–28.

The first constitution[2] passed by the Second Vatican Council was *Sacrosanctum Concilium* (December 4, 1963). If the Church is to be correctly related to the world, she must first be rightly related to God. Worship establishes that relationship. As with all the Council documents, *Sacrosanctum Concilium* must be understood in light of a full century of efforts made by popes, Roman congregations, bishops, and scholars to foster a greater appreciation of the true nature of the liturgy and its importance in the life of the Church. In order to properly interpret *Sacrosanctum Concilium*, one needs to study these efforts, which are preserved in many of the documents contained in this third volume of *The Liturgy Documents*.

The Council wanted to foster greater participation in the liturgy, both interiorly in spirit and exteriorly in actions. The Council called for preserving the elements of the rite that come to us from apostolic times but adapting them so that the language and the actions of the Mass would make it easier for all the baptized to take part in them. The goal of liturgical reform was to have the Mass, in a sense, speak for itself.

The reform of the liturgical rites placed particular emphasis on Scripture. It also called for liturgical music in vernacular languages, as appropriate. It mandated homiletic preaching as integral to the rite itself. It made clear the connection between the worship of God and action for justice and peace and charity in the world that God created and his Son died to save. Many of these goals had been addressed by popes, bishops, Roman congregations, and scholars throughout the twentieth century.

The Council sought to emphasize continuity of liturgical reforms with the authentic traditions of liturgy and prayer inherited from the past. While the Eucharist is the summit of the Church's worship of God, the Council also encouraged popular devotions to the Blessed Virgin Mary, to the reserved Sacrament of the Altar, to the saints in the liturgical calendar, and popular participation in the celebration of the Liturgy of the Hours. The Council saw its call for liturgical renewal as being in continuity with, not a radical departure from, past tradition.

The goal of deeper and more authentic participation in the liturgy is to imbue all believers with a sense of time centered on the mysteries of Christ's life, Death, and Resurrection. Liturgical time keeps us living in the Kingdom of God, even as we work out our salvation within this world's temporal rhythms. The Mass bridges the gap between earth and heaven. We recall this fact each time we celebrate Mass and the priest holds up the consecrated host and chalice filled with the Precious Blood, saying: "Behold the Lamb of God. / Behold him who takes away the sins of the world. / Happy are those who are called to the Supper of the Lamb."

Often when people who were alive at the time of Vatican II speak of "the changes" brought about by the Council, they emphasize the external changes that came about in worship: Mass celebrated in the vernacular, altars moved

---

2. Apostolic constitutions are the most solemn and important documents issued by a pope and the Vatican Council with binding force upon the entire universal Church. Vatican II issued four constitutions: *Dei Verbum* (*Dogmatic Constitution on Divine Revelation*), *Lumen gentium* (*Dogmatic Constitution on the Church*), *Gaudium et spes* (*Pastoral Constitution on the Church in the Modern World*), and *Sacrosanctum Concilium* (*Constitution on the Sacred Liturgy*).

away from the back wall of the church in order to celebrate Mass facing the people, the use of a presidential chair, the removal of altar railings, congregational singing and participation in the responses formerly done by the servers and the choir, receiving Holy Communion while standing with a choice of receiving in the hand or on the tongue, receiving Communion from the chalice, less ringing or no ringing of bells during Mass, greater emphasis on Baptism and the use of immersion pools, the introduction of Reconciliation rooms with the option of face-to-face confession, the reintroduction of the permanent diaconate, the widespread use of male and female extraordinary ministers of Holy Communion and readers at Mass, increased use of the Anointing of the Sick (no longer called "Extreme Unction"), and the translation of all the liturgical books into the vernacular. A lot of change took place in a very short period of time, often without suitable and sufficient catechesis.

Because of the disruption in the Church's life with the first wave of "liturgical changes," a slow, deliberate, and extensive catechesis of the Catholic faithful was called for before introducing the new translation of the third edition of the post-Conciliar Roman Missal. The changes in the way we worship were themselves sound, but they needed to be understood in their proper ecclesial context. Most of all, they had to be seen as invitations to full, conscious, and informed participation in the liturgy by all the baptized.

Especially in the first half of the twentieth century, active participation in the liturgy and in Catholic action went hand in hand. In many documents on the Sacred Liturgy and the apostolate, there was a call to baptized Catholics not only to participate actively in the Eucharist but to exercise fully their Baptism by actively participating in the mission of the Church in the world. The connection between the work of liturgy and actions for social justice was made explicit by many popes, bishops, and theologians throughout the twentieth century.

On December 20, 1928, the apostolic constitution of Pope Pius XI on Divine Worship, *Divini cultus sanctitatem*, affirmed active participation in the liturgy in these words: "It is most important that when the faithful assist at the sacred ceremonies, . . . they should not be merely detached and silent spectators, but, filled with a deep sense of the beauty of the liturgy, they should sing alternatively with the clergy or choir, as it is prescribed."[3] In this way, the faithful can be formed in the true Christian spirit necessary for active participation in the Church's mission in the world.

On May 15, 1931, in the encyclical on the reconstruction of the social order, *Quadragesimo anno*, Pius XI called for a return to an organic conception of society as a solution for the problems besetting the world. In article 190 of this encyclical, Pius XI makes this claim:

> And so, then only will true cooperation be possible for a single common good when the constituent parts of society deeply feel themselves members of one great family and children of the same Heavenly Father; nay, that they are one body in Christ, "but severally members one of another," so that "if one member suffers anything, all the members suffer with it."[4]

---

3. *Divini cultus sanctitatem* (DCS), 9.
4. *Quadragesimo anno* (QA), 137.

The privileged place where we can experience such solidarity and reciprocal cooperation is in the liturgy, the source and center of our spiritual lives. The renewal of the world and the renewal of the liturgy were very closely related in the mind of Pope Pius XI and his successor, Pope Pius XII.

Even before Pope Pius XII began to speak of the liturgy as a corporate action of the entire Mystical Body, Head and members, theologians had made the connection between what Catholics did in church at worship and the way they lived in the world. Ideally, participation in the Mass gave baptized Catholics the desire to bring the redemptive influence of Christ in the Eucharist to bear upon the world. The apostolate then was seen as an extension of the altar, of the self-giving celebrated in the Eucharist and made evident in the world. In the liturgy and in the lay apostolate the same dynamic is at work: the creation of apostles according to the pattern of Christ's life.

Unfortunately, the liaison between liturgy and social justice began to weaken as the Liturgical Movement and the Social Justice Movement in the Catholic Church began to go in separate directions. With the instructions of Pius XII regarding the use of the vernacular in the liturgy, the appearance of bilingual (Latin-English) ritual books, the encouragement of the use of vernacular hymns, and the shortening of the Communion fast, the leadership of the liturgical movement sometimes appeared to be more concerned with reforming the texts of the liturgy than with reforming the life of society. However, this connection was not lost in the documents of the Second Vatican Council.

After the Second Vatican Council, there was, in most quarters, an enthusiastic embrace of the vernacular liturgy. There was also, in some quarters, a rejection of anything that was branded "old-fashioned" or "out of date." This led to abuses creeping into the celebration of the liturgy and the addition to or subtraction of elements of the liturgy without approval by Rome or the local Ordinary. A fundamental misreading by some of the intent of the constitutions, decrees, and guidelines of the Council led to corrective action on the part of the Holy Father, the Congregation for Divine Worship and the Discipline of the Sacraments, Episcopal Conferences, and local Ordinaries.

Pope Paul VI, Pope John Paul II, and Pope Benedict XVI have all written extensively on what constitutes the correct interpretation of *Sacrosanctum Concilium* and of the numerous Council documents and the decrees that have been issued since the conclusion of the Council. The editors of this volume have selected a few of the more important liturgical documents from the period after the Council up to the present in order to preserve the proper context in which a correct interpretation of *Sacrosanctum Concilium* can be understood.

I am grateful to the editors of Liturgy Training Publications for preserving basic documents that led up to and immediately followed the promulgation of *Sacrosanctum Concilium*. The introductions provided for each of these documents summarize their main points and give historical background for a better understanding of the context from which they came. In the past fifty years, we have made considerable progress in the renewal of the liturgy and of the life of the Church. Yet, there is always more that needs to be accomplished.

In many ways, the Second Vatican Council is yet to be "received," yet to be fully understood and implemented. The call for a New Evangelization is a call to implement the Council in its fullest sense. The Spirit is always ahead of us, of course, so there is a renewal of faith and of holiness going on each day. We see it especially in new movements and communities and in the renewed generosity of spirit among faith-filled people. God does not work on our timelines, but he is always generous. If we pray for a renewal of the faith, the gift will be given.

PASTORAL INTRODUCTION
AN OVERVIEW OF LITURGICAL REFORM

FROM THE COUNCIL OF TRENT TO THE SECOND VATICAN COUNCIL

Rev. Robert L. Tuzik

Special Assistant to Francis Cardinal George, OMI

Sacrosanctum Concilium (SC) was the first document of the Second Vatican Council. The Council Fathers met at various sessions between 1962–1965. The Council Fathers formed the Conciliar Commissions which met between sessions to prepare documents (constitutions and decrees) that would be voted upon at the Council. In addition the bishops from individual conferences would meet in between sessions to discuss their reaction to the various documents and proposals being addressed by the Council.

For many people today, SC is remembered for its call for "full, conscious and active participation in the celebration of the liturgy"[1] and its approval of a wider use of the vernacular in the liturgy.[2] However, there is far more depth to the vision and reforms of the liturgy called for in SC.

At times, we forget the history of liturgical renewal and reform, which led to the promulgation of SC. In this essay, we will trace the major events and documents (especially papal documents) that led to the approval of SC fifty years ago.

THE ECUMENICAL COUNCIL OF TRENT

The Council of Trent met in three sessions: 1545–1547, 1551, and from 1562–1563. While the Council of Trent is primarily known for doctrinal reforms and the defense of Orthodox teachings in light of the challenges made by the Protestant Reformation, this Council also had a profound impact on liturgical practice in the Western Church.

The Council of Trent mandated that a single *Missale Romanum* be used in most, if not all, the Western Churches. Prior to Trent, many places (for example, Italy, Germany, and France) had local rites similar to those found in Roman liturgical books; however, these local rites incorporated cultural adaptations unique to the particular regions. While Roman Eucharistic Prayer I, or the Roman Canon, was perhaps the most popular Eucharistic Prayer in use, there were many Eucharistic Prayers allowed in the celebration of the liturgy prior to the Council of Trent. At this time, there was amazing variety in the celebration of the liturgy, but not all the variations were appropriate.

Before the invention of the printing press by Johannes Gutenberg (about 1440), all liturgical books were hand-copied manuscripts, which included numerous copyists' errors. The copyists also felt free to adapt the Missal to fit the customs and traditions of his region. Every country, diocese, and sometimes even

---

1. *Sacrosanctum Concilium* (SC), 14.
2. See ibid., 36.

every parish, had its own way of celebrating Mass, although these variations did retain the traditional format of the liturgy: Introductory Rite, Scripture readings, Offertory or Preparation Rite, Prayer of Consecration, distribution of Holy Communion, and a Concluding Rite.[3] The way each part of the Mass was celebrated varied a good deal from place to place. Especially worrisome were prayers that had been added to the hand-copied texts, which were of doubtful orthodoxy. Because of the variations and the questionable texts, there was an obvious need for greater uniformity. The purpose of the Council of Trent was to preserve Orthodox teachings in the celebration of the liturgy. Because of the invention of the printing press, it was now possible for the Church to publish one Missal, thus, unifying the liturgical celebrations of the Western Church. This task was left to a special Commission appointed at end of the Council of Trent.

The Council Fathers of Trent believed that stronger regulation of the liturgy was required in order to clear up the numerous abuses that it identified in the celebration of the liturgy. The Preparatory Commission of the Council of Trent drew up a long list of abuses that needed to be corrected:

- Priests celebrating Mass so close together in the churches that their voices conflicted with one another;
- The celebration of other Masses during Solemn Mass (which would be considered the principle celebration of the day);
- Too many Masses being celebrated with no pastoral need;
- Masses celebrated without assistants;
- No one, not even the ministers, receiving Holy Communion at Mass;
- The rivalry of processions of the Blessed Sacrament from different churches, which break out into brawls;
- Priests quickly waving numerous Signs of the Cross over the host and chalice, as if these signs contained the power of consecration;
- Elevating the chalice by placing it on top of the priest's head;
- The laying of half-corrupt cadavers or body parts of saints on the altar during Mass;
- People bringing their dogs, falcons, and hawks with them to worship;
- Visitors wandering through the choir while the Liturgy of the Hours was being chanted by monks or nuns.[4]

In short, proper decorum and a well-instructed appreciation for the Sacred Mysteries was lacking in both priests and people.

In order to meet the doctrinal and liturgical challenges that the Church faced, Pope Pius V decided that it would be best if one Roman Missal was approved and used throughout the Western Church. An exception was made for those

---

3. Cheslyn Jones, Geoffrey Wainwright, Edward Yarnold, sj, and Paul Bradshaw, Eds., *The Study of the Liturgy, Revised Edition*, New York: Oxford University Press, 1992, p. 286.

4. See Joseph M. Powers, *Eucharistic Theology*, New York: Herder and Herder, 1967, p. 32. This list can be found in the introduction materials published with the Missal of Pope Pius V in 1570.

regions and religious orders that could demonstrate an uninterrupted custom of 200 years for their current rite (for example, the Mozarabic or Old Spanish liturgy). Otherwise, the liturgy of the city of Rome in its early centuries was to be the norm for worship in the Western Church.

Unfortunately, the Commission that produced the 1570 Missal of Pope Pius V chose to use a Missal from 1474. This Missal reflected the tradition of the Roman Curia in the thirteenth century. It was not the return to these sources that the Council of Trent intended. Knowledge of the history of the liturgy only went as far back as the eleventh or tenth centuries at best. Many important manuscripts preserved in libraries, cathedrals, and monasteries had yet to be discovered. Even the so-called *Greogorian Sacramentary* from the Vatican Library was not what it claimed to be. This particular Sacramentary demonstrated the influence of the Gallican (French) Church and the *Gelasian Sacramentary*, which most scholars today identify as the earliest extent Sacramentary in existence, written around 750.

Prior to the Council of Trent, religious orders (for example, Cistercians, Carthusians, Premonstratensians) had begun to regulate the Order of Mass. The Franciscans, who catechized much of Europe, brought with them a Franciscan Missal based on the *Missale secundum usum romanae curiae* (or the Missal according to the use of the Roman Curia). This Curial Missal reflected the liturgy celebrated in the Roman basilicas of the thirteenth century (around the time of Pope Innocent III). Because of the Franciscans, this Curial Missal began to be the predominant ritual book for Mass in use in the Western Church. When Pius V imposed the Missal on the Western Church, many regions were already quite familiar with the basic Order of Mass found in 1570 *Missale Romanum*.

CONGREGATION OF SACRED RITES

In 1588, Pope Sixtus V established the Congregation of Sacred Rites for the purpose of carrying out the decrees of the Council of Trent and implementing the use of the 1570 Missal of Pius V with its specific rubrics (or rules) for celebrating the liturgy. For the first time in the history of the Church, there was now a central authority whose responsibility was to regulate the liturgy and its celebration in the many Churches using the Western Rite. Where there had been greater diversity in the celebration of the liturgy, one set of texts and one set of rules were now expected to be followed by everyone in the Western Church.

The Council of Trent froze the celebration of the liturgy in a style dominated by the clergy with little active participation from the people. Trent allowed the private Mass to become the normal experience of worship. The Mass was celebrated by one priest with at best only a handful of the laity present. From 1200 on, the priest took over the roles of deacon, lector, choir, and congregation during private Masses. Since the priest did all the ministerial parts, there was no need for a separate book of Scriptures (or Lectionary). Instead, the 1570 Missal included the Scripture readings. Since many people did not understand the true nature of the liturgical celebration, they began to see the Mass as a way to adore Christ's presence in the sacred species and an opportunity to say one's private devotional prayers, rather than pray the Mass with the priest. No wonder the celebration of saints' days began to take the place of the Sunday liturgy. Saints were local heroes whom the people could readily identify themselves with, whereas the usual celebration of Sunday Mass often failed to engage their attention.

While the reforms of the Council of Trent met the doctrinal challenges of the Protestant Reformation and cleaned up the abuses present in the celebration of the liturgy in the sixteenth century, it also departed from the ancient tradition of the Holy Fathers found in such works as St. Justin Martyrs' *Apology* (c. 155) or the *Apostolic Tradition* of St. Hippolytus (c. 200). The ancient writings of the Church Fathers refer to a much different experience of worship: full and active participation by the laity; the involvement of lectors, deacons, cantors, choirs; Mass said facing the people; and the allowance of local variations (or cultural adaptations) in the liturgy.

DOM PROSPER GUÉRANGER, OSB

For several centuries, the Church suffered the loss of her musical tradition because of the increasing popularity of the Low Mass, which was dominated by the priest, and the Solemn Mass, which was dominated by trained choirs replacing the active participation of the congregation, Fortunately, in 1832, Dom Propser Guéranger, OSB, refounded the Benedictine Abbey of Solesmes as a monastery dedicated to the study and recovery of authentic Gregorian Chant (which was less complex and easier to sing than the difficult polyphonic chants in use in the nineteenth century). Solesmes became a center of liturgical renewal. Guéranger's book on the liturgical year, *L' Année Liturgique* rekindled a fresh new interest in the study of the liturgy. Benedictine monks were now becoming leaders in liturgical scholarship and renewal. Guéranger was the first to use the title "Liturgical Movement" to describe the revival of liturgical studies and the growing interest in understanding and improving participation in the liturgy.

RENEWED INTEREST IN PATRISTIC AND BIBLICAL STUDIES

It would be remiss to not mention the renewed interest that Catholic scholars had in the writings of the Fathers of the Church and in the study of the Bible in the nineteenth century. While Protestant theologians had created new vernacular translations of the Scriptures, the Catholic Church had lagged behind in supporting such interests. With the acceptance of Guéranger's call to study the history of the liturgy, there developed a renewed acceptance of Catholic biblical and patristic studies. These influences led to greater papal encouragement about the importance of active participation in the liturgy.

The movement toward restoring active participation in the liturgy by the laity received a major boost when Pope Pius X issued his famous document, *Tra le sollecitudini* (1903). One line in particular was quoted over and over again by leaders in the Liturgical Movement: "It being our ardent desire to see the true Christian spirit restored in every respect and be preserved by all the faithful, we deem it necessary to provide before everything else for the sanctity and dignity of the temple, in which the faithful assembly for the object of acquiring this spirit from its foremost and indispensable fount, which is the active participation in the holy mysteries and in the public and solemn prayer of the

Church."[5] The pope goes on to explain that he is referring to his desire to restore the singing of Gregorian Chant by the people: "Gregorian chant . . . is . . . the chant proper to the Roman Church, the only chant she has inherited from the ancient fathers, which she has jealously guarded for centuries in her liturgical codices, which she directly proposes to the faithful as her own, which she prescribes exclusively for some parts of the liturgy, and which the most recent studies have so happily restored to their integrity and purity."[6]

DOM LAMBERT BEAUDUIN, OSB

In 1909, a Catholic conference was held in Malines, Belgium, which most scholars view as the inauguration of the modern Liturgical Movement. A young priest, Dom Lambert Beauduin, OSB, from the Benedictine monastery at Mont Cesar in Belgium spoke at the conference expressing his conviction that the liturgy is the center of the piety of the Church! In November of 1909, he began to publish a liturgical journal, *Questions liturgiques et paroissales.* In June of 1910, Beauduin spoke at the first Liturgical Week held at Mont Cesar. He explained the goal of the Liturgical Movement was "to restore Christian spirituality (and) the means proposed was the restoration of the parochial High Mass on Sunday, with full participation."[7]

Beauduin's most famous work is his book, *L'pieté de l'eglise* (1914) or *Liturgy: The Life of the Church*, as titled in the 1926 English translation. In the chapter "The Sad Consequences of the Present Condition," Beauduin enumerates the results of the failure to maintain the liturgy as the center of true Christian piety: individualism, abandonment of prayer, deviations of piety, a secular spirit, and a lack of support for hierarchical life. He later expresses the goal of the Liturgical Movement as active participation of all Christian people in the Mass by understanding and following the rites and texts. He calls for singing by the congregation at the community's Solemn Mass on Sunday. He wants to restore Sunday Vespers (Evening Prayer) and Compline as true parish celebrations. He also speaks of the need to study the rites of all the sacraments and share this knowledge with others.[8] It's amazing how many of the recommendations Beauduin makes in his book are still being made to Catholics today.

Another interesting emphasis in Beauduin's writings is his belief that a greater appreciation of the mystery of the Incarnation leads to a deeper understanding and appreciation of the dignity of human life. He maintained that a renewed appreciation of the Church as the Body of Christ would lead to the development of stronger Christian communities both at worship and in the world. He also believed that a deeper understanding of the sacrifice of Christ on Calvary would lead to a living out of the Eucharistic sacrifice in real life. He was convinced that a renewal of the liturgy would lead to a renewal of the whole life of the Church. In many ways, his beliefs have found a new voice in *Sacrosanctum Concilium*.

---

5. *Tra le sollecitudini* (TLS), paragraph 3 of the document's introductory paragraphs.

6. Ibid., 3.

7. Sonya Quitsland, *Beauduin: A Prophet Vindicated*, New York: Newman Press, 1973, p. 19.

8. Lambert Beauduin, *Liturgy, the Life of the Church*, translated by Virgil Michel, OSB, Collegeville, MN: Liturgical Press, 1926, pp. 44–46.

Beaudin's belief that there is a close connection between liturgy and life was nothing new. In fact, in the social encyclicals of Pope Leo XIII this theme is often found. For example, in his encyclical, *Mirae caritatis: On the Most Holy Eucharist*, Leo XIII deplored the "frequent disturbances and strifes between class and class: arrogance, oppression, fraud on the part of the more powerful: misery, envy, and turbulence among the poor."[9] The remedy for such evils was to live the Eucharist, which Christ gave us as a symbol of unity and charity, a symbol of that Body of which he is the head. As Leo XIII says:

> Very beautiful and joyful too is the spectacle of Christian brotherhood and social equality which is afforded when men of all conditions, gentle and simple, rich and poor, learned and unlearned, gather round the holy altar, all sharing alike in this heavenly banquet.[10]

This theme of the Eucharist as an expression of the Body of Christ will continue to grow in importance, until it triumphs in 1943 in the great encyclical of Pius XII, *Mystici Corporis Christi*.

POPE PIUS X (1903–1914)

Along with encouragement for the laity to more actively participate in the liturgy, there was also encouragement for the laity to take a more active part in the apostolate. On February 2, 1904, Pope Pius X in his encyclical, *Ad diem illum*, spoke of the gifts of all members of the Mystical Body. He said these gifts are given for the increase or "up building of itself (the Mystical Body) in charity."[11] On June 11, 1905, Pius X affirmed the doctrine of Catholic action, whereby all members of the Mystical Body are called to cooperate in putting the teachings of the Church:

> Into execution first in themselves, and then to co-operate effectively in making others put them into practice, each one according to the grace he has received from God, according to his state and office, and according to the zeal that burns in his heart. Here we wish simply to mention the many works of zeal that are being carried out for the good of the Church, of society, and of individuals, and which are commonly referred to as Catholic Action.[12]

Consequently, since the beginning of the twentieth century there has been a clear mandate for the laity to participate in the apostolic work of the Church.

---

9. *Mirae caritatis*, 11.

10. Ibid., 11.

11. Pius X, *Ad diem illum*, in Emile Mersch, *The Whole Christ: the Historical Development of the Doctrine of the Mystical Body in Scripture and Tradition*, translated by John R. Kelly, Milwaukee: Bruce Publishing Company, 1938, p. 568.

12. Pius X, *Il forno proposito*, *op.cit.*, p. 568–569.

The liturgical and social justice movements in the Church grew up together in the late nineteenth and early twentieth centuries. The liturgy was often viewed as embodying the model of what the world needed to achieve: to become one people united in justice, peace, and love.

A key leader of the social justice movement was Fr. Joseph Cardijn, a socially minded Belgian priest who, in 1919, founded a group that he called the "Young Trade Unionists." In 1924, he changed the name of the group to *Jeunesse Ouvriére Chrétienne* (JOC) or the "Young Christian Workers." This movement became known as the Jocists. By 1938, there were 500,000 European members. By 1967, there were over two million members in sixty-nine countries. While Cardijn's group was initially met with suspicion and resistance from society and from officials in the Catholic Church, the group eventually received the blessing of Pope Pius XI in 1925. In fact, Pius XI saw membership in the JOC as an effective way to involve people in Catholic action.

Cardijn's methodology was summarized in the well-known phrase: "See, Judge, Act." First, *see* or examine a concrete situation in your community or society that cries out for Christian involvement in order to preserve or restore a just social order. Second, *judge* the situation by applying principles learned from the Gospel accounts, Catholic teaching, and the liturgy. Third, *act* or take actions to resolve the situation in a way that is charitable, honest, and just. This methodology served as the basis for the Young Christian Workers, the Young Christian Students, and the Catholic Family Movement in the United States. These three groups are known as the Specialized Lay Apostolate.

The format for the weekly meetings of the Specialized Lay Apostolate gave prominence to the study of the liturgy in the 1940s and 1950s. They began with a short Gospel discussion, followed by a discussion of the liturgy (the Mass, Sunday, the liturgical year, the implications of a Mystical Body ecclesiology, baptismal spirituality, Confirmation as the sacrament of Catholic action, the connection between liturgy and social justice, and so on). They engaged in a short inquiry of social problems and Catholic approaches to deal with these problems. The application of the "See, Judge, Act" method took place under the direction of their pastor in union with their bishop. Consequently, the JOC was in harmony with Pius XI's definition of Catholic action as lay participation in the apostolate of the hierarchy.

The document on the laity from the Second Vatican Council, *Apostolicam actuositatem* (promulgated November 18, 1965) includes a section on the "Apostolate of the Like towards Like." This section clearly draws upon the key insight found in Jocist methodology that young workers should minister to young workers, young students should minister to young students, or like ministers to like. Article 13 explains the impact of such apostolic activity in this powerful statement:

> The apostolate in one's social environment: that is the attempt to infuse with the christian spirit the mentality and behavior, laws and structures of the community in which one lives. So much is it the special work and responsibility of lay people that it cannot be properly carried out by any others. In this area lay people can conduct the apostolate of the like

towards like. There the witness of their life is completed by the witness of their word. It is amid the surroundings of their work that they are best qualified to be of help to their brothers and sisters, in the surroundings of their profession, of their study, leisure or local group.[13]

When it comes to implementing Pius XI's call for lay participation in Catholic action, Europe was at least ten years or more ahead of similar efforts in the United States. The Specialized Lay Apostolate really didn't take hold in the United States until the late 1930s and early 1940s. However, Catholics in the United States were determined to catch up in a big way.

PIUS XI (1922–1939)

Pius XI is known for making the connection between active participation in the liturgy and Catholic action. In his apostolic constitution, *Divini cultus sancti-tatem* (December 20, 1928), Pius XI states:

> There is thus a close connection between dogma and the sacred liturgy, and between Christian worship and the sanctification of the faithful. . . . It is most important that when the faithful assist at the sacred ceremonies, or when pious sodalities take part with the clergy in a procession, they should not be merely detached and silent spectators, but, filled with a deep sense of the beauty of the liturgy, should sing alternately with the clergy or the choir, as it is prescribed.[14]

Pius XI challenged all Christians to avoid being mere "detached and silent spectators"[15] but actively participate both in the liturgy and Catholic action.

In 1931, Pius XI made this call to active participation in the apostolate based on his concept of an organic conception of society, which would attend to the world's problems, "only [then] will true cooperation be possible for a single common good, when the constituent parts of society deeply feel themselves members of one great family and children of the same Heavenly Father; nay, that they are one body in Christ. . . ."[16] Of course, the privileged place to experience this unity is in the celebration of the liturgy.

In 1934, Pius XI explained the sacramental basis for his call to active participation in the apostolate in these words:

> The very sacraments of Baptism and Confirmation impose . . . this apostolate of Catholic action . . . since through (them) we become members of the Church, or of the Mystical Body of Christ, and among the members of this body . . . there must be solidarity of interests and reciprocal communication of life.[17]

Hence, it should not be surprising to hear *Sacrosanctum Concilium*, 14, also make this connection:

---

13. *Apostolicam actuositatem* (AA), 13.
14. *Divini cultus sanctitatem* (DCS), 9.
15. Ibid.
16. *Quadragesimo anno* (QA), 137.
17. Pius X, quoted in Ellard, *Christian Life and Worship, op.cit.*, p. 382.

The Church earnestly desires that all the faithful be led to that full, conscious, and active participation in liturgical celebrations called for by the very nature of the liturgy. Such participation by the Christian people as "a chosen race, a royal priesthood, a holy nation, God's own people" (1 Pt 2:9; see 2:4–5) is their right and duty by reason of their baptism.[18]

For this connection between active participation in the liturgy and active participation in the apostolate was one that many popes had worked to make throughout the twentieth century.

In *Mit brennender Sorge* (March 14, 1937), Pope Pius XI called for the closest union of the apostolate with the liturgy:

It is not enough to be a member of the Church of Christ, one needs to be a living member, in spirit and in truth, i.e., living in the state of grace and in the presence of God, either in innocence or in sincere repentance. If the Apostle of the nations, the vase of election, chastised his body and brought it into subjection: lest perhaps, when he had preached to others, he himself should become a castaway (1 *Cor.* ix. 27), could anybody responsible for the extension of the Kingdom of God claim any other method but personal sanctification? Only thus can we show to the present generation, and to the critics of the Church that "the salt of the earth," the leaven of Christianity has not decayed, but is ready to give the men of today—prisoners of doubt and error, victims of indifference, tired of their Faith and straying from God—the spiritual renewal they so much need. A Christianity which keeps a grip on itself, refuses every compromise with the world, takes the commands of God and the Church seriously, preserves its love of God and of men in all its freshness, such a Christianity can be, and will be, a model and a guide to a world which is sick to death and clamors for directions, unless it be condemned to a catastrophe that would baffle the imagination.[19]

It is this connection between participation in the liturgy and participation in Catholic action that motivated liturgical pioneers in Europe and the United States. They were not simply interested in encouraging the assembly's responses at Mass, (for example, *Et cum spiritu tuo*, Amen, and so on), encouraging chant and congregational singing, restoring Sunday as the original feast day, and other rubrical reforms. They were interested in a total reform of the life of the Church and society.

Pius XI made this point clear in a personal letter, *Ex officiosis literris*, sent on November 10, 1933 to Cardinal Manuel Gonçalves Cerejeira, Patriarch of Lisbon. Pius XI states: "In reality, . . . it is the sacraments of baptism and confirmation themselves that impose, among other obligations, that of the apostolate, of spiritual assistance to our neighbor."[20] Each member of the Mystical Body is called to share the life of the Trinity, the life that Christ came to earth

---

18. *Sacrosanctum Concilium* (SC), 14.

19. *Mit brennender Sorge* (MBS), 19.

20. Pius XI, "Ex officiosis literris," sent on November 10, 1933 to Cardinal Cerejeira, Patriarch of Lisbon and cited in Theodore M. Hesburgh, *The Theology of Catholic Action*, Notre Dame: Ave Maria Press, 1946, p. 32.

to bring to humanity, with those "who do not possess it, or who possess it only in a too feeble measure, or only in appearance."[21] In fact, you could say the apostolate as a sign or a proof of the fact that we share divine life in Christ as members of his Mystical Body.

VIRGIL MICHEL, OSB

No treatment of the history of the liturgical renewal in the United States prior to Vatican II would be complete without mentioning the extraordinary work done by a monk of St. John's Abbey in Collegeville, Minnesota, Virgil Michel, OSB. Michel was the bridge over which the key insights of the European Liturgical Movement travelled to this country. Like his European mentors, he too saw a connection between liturgy and social justice, communal prayer, and apostolic work. In 1924, he studied at Sant'Anselmo in Rome, where his professor was none other than Dom Lambert Beauduin, the famous liturgist and monk of Mont Cesar in Belgium.

Virgil Michel founded *Orate Fratres* (later called *Worship*) magazine in 1926. He translated into English many of the great works of European liturgists. He began a project called "The Popular Liturgical Library" in order to publish the work of American liturgists. Eventually, this led to the establishment of The Liturgical Press which is one of the foremost publishers of liturgical, theological, and pastoral resources in the United States. Michel's main concern was the spirit or theology of the liturgy not liturgical rubrics. He believed in active participation both in the liturgy and in the apostolate.

In the 1930s, Michel was among the first to foster the spread of the Dialogue Mass, in which the assembly made the responses and sang the chants. By the late 1930s, he had begun to speak openly about the merits of using the vernacular in the Mass. He also supported evening Masses, which had been out of fashion for centuries. He encouraged the laity to celebrate the Liturgy of the Hours. Liturgical Press eventually published *A Short Breviary* for lay use in 1941. Michel kept in touch with the major leaders of liturgical renewal in the United States: Martin Hellriegel, Gerald Ellard, Michael Mathis, H.A. Reinhold, Reynold Hillenbrand, and many others. He encouraged American liturgists to organize National Study Weeks like those taking place in Europe. Michel died in 1938 at the age of fifty; however, he laid a strong foundation for others to build upon in the coming years.

NATIONAL LITURGICAL STUDY WEEKS

In January 1940, the Benedictine Liturgical Conference, a voluntary organization of American Benedictine abbots, was founded at St. Procopius Priory in Lisle, Illinois (outside of Chicago). Its first project was to sponsor a National Liturgical Week, which took place in Chicago through October 21–25, 1950. The theme was "The Living Parish: Active and Intelligent Participation of the Laity in the Liturgy of the Catholic Church." Msgr. Reynold Hillenbrand, the well-known liturgist, social activist, and rector of St. Mary of the Lake Seminary was selected as the keynote speaker. The National Liturgical Weeks succeeded in

---

21. Ibid.

gathering together people from across the country interested in liturgical renewal. Those attending brought the new ideas back to their dioceses and parishes.

The National Study Weeks succeeded in obtaining Episcopal sponsorship, an important factor in making the recommendations of the speakers at the study days acceptable to a larger audience. In the 1940s, the influence of Popes Pius XI and Pius XII were very strong in the United States. Bishops began to speak about the liturgy as "the Mystical Body of Christ at worship."[22] Proper celebration of the liturgy was looked upon as a means of strengthening and elevating Catholic life and leading to effective Catholic action. People like Msgr. Reynold Hillenbrand organized a liturgical summer school at St. Mary of the Lake Seminary from July 14 to August 1, 1941, exposing a whole new generation of priests to the ideals of the liturgical and social justice movements. When these priests returned to their parishes, they began to implement the Dialogue Mass and gave new impetus to the assembly singing the chants for worship. Involvement in the Specialized Lay Apostolate also resulted in exposure to the ideals of the Liturgical Movement at these liturgical summer schools.

The abbots who were part of the Benedictine Liturgical Conference believed that a wider sponsorship of the National Liturgical Weeks was needed. And so, they dissolved the Benedictine Liturgical Conference on September 8, 1943, and turned its future over to the American Liturgical Advisory Committee, which eventually became known as the Liturgical Conference. In order to appreciate how great an impact the Liturgical Conference had on peoples' understanding of the liturgy in the United States, below is a list of the themes of the various National Liturgical Weeks from their beginning in 1940:

- 1940: The Living Parish, Active and Intelligent Participation of the Laity in the Liturgy
- 1941: The Living Parish, One in Worship, Charity, and Action
- 1942: The Praise of God
- 1943: Sacrifice
- 1944: Liturgy and Catholic Life
- 1945: Catholic Liturgy in Peace and Reconstruction
- 1946: The Family in Christ
- 1947: Christ's Sacrifice and Ours
- 1948: The New Man in Christ
- 1949: Sanctification of Sunday
- 1950: For Pastors and People: the Divine Office and the Mass
- 1951: The Priesthood of Christ
- 1952: The New Easter Vigil
- 1953: St. Pius X and Social Worship

---

22. See *Mediator Dei* (MD), 20; see also *Mystici Corporis Christi* (MCC), 82–83.

- 1954: Mary in the Liturgy

- 1955: The New Ritual: Liturgy and Social Order

What you will notice in the preceding list of topics is how "traditional" sounding the themes were. Absent from this list is the encouragement of replacing Latin with vernacular translations in the liturgy; noticeable, however, is the growing prevalence of more liturgical topics in the 1950s (for example, the restored Easter Vigil). Since social activists began to feel a bit left out of the agenda for these weeks, there began to be a split in the leadership of the liturgical and social justice movements in the 1950s in the United States. This is unfortunate, since it also led to a diminished audience for the ideals of the Liturgical Movement.

MICHAEL MATHIS, CSC

Another great American liturgical pioneer that influenced the spread of the ideals of the Liturgical Movement in the United States was Holy Cross priest, Michael Mathis, CSC. His first love was in the missionary apostolate of his religious order. However, a gift of the first volume of European scholar Pius Parsch's *The Church's Year of Grace* moved Mathis to develop his interest in the liturgy. Parsch provided a rich biblical and Patristic commentary on the various feasts and seasons of the liturgical year. It caused Mathis to wonder if his understanding of the liturgy was simply too rubrical and superficial. And so, he began to study early Church writings, the history of the liturgy, church architecture and music, and papal statements regarding the connection between liturgy and the apostolate. This appealed to Mathis's strong missionary sense, which he brought to his study of the liturgy. In fact, he even called the Missal "the best primer for the understanding of Christian teaching on the missions."[23]

In 1937, Mathis was asked to organize discussion groups for students at the University of Notre Dame on the work of the missions. His study groups met daily to study the Missal, celebrate a Dialogue Mass, and meditate daily on the texts of the Mass and Divine Office in order to build up the students' spiritual lives and encourage these students to live the insights and values discovered in prayer. Eventually, he settled on Matins as a vehicle for the study of the liturgy. He explains:

> My object, first, is to make available to a greater number of the faithful the rich and varied prayer forms which the church has given us to praise God, to deepen our understanding and appreciation of divine revelation, and to seek, especially in the Mass of the Faithful, special graces whereby we may be helped to translate into action the lessons taught. Secondly, I wish to show how the church has selected from sacred scripture and tradition and hagiography appropriate passages to illustrate the lessons she teaches on each of these feasts and the motherly exhortation she gives to put these into practice.[24]

---

23. Michael Mathis, CSC, "The Real Stuff" in *Apostolic Perspectives: A Quarterly Devoted to the Apostolate of the Church* 1958, p. 3.

24. Michael Mathis, CSC, "The Vigil Service" in *Education and the Liturgy: 18th North American Liturgical Week*, 1957 Elsberry, MO: The Liturgical Conference, 1958, p. 158.

Mathis's approach, which was to draw inspiration from the actual texts of the liturgy itself and to connect the liturgical celebration to the way we live our lives in the world, was very positively received by his students and the participants in our National Liturgical Study Weeks.

Mathis is probably best known for his founding of a School of Liturgy at the University of Notre Dame. He talked about this with the members of his order beginning in 1940. Finally, in 1947, part of his dream became a reality when an undergraduate program in liturgy was opened as a summer school session. A graduate school was approved in 1948 and the School of Liturgy won a permanent place among the university's academic programs. For years, dioceses in the United States have depended on graduates from the university's liturgy program to provide liturgical leadership to the priests and people of their dioceses. With the support of liturgical education and the need for liturgical commissions after the publication of *Sacrosanctum Concilium,* Notre Dame's School of Liturgy provided many of the skilled leaders needed to guide the introduction of the vernacular Missal of Paul VI and the revised rites for all the sacraments that had been approved by Rome. Consequently, Mathis's School of Liturgy has certainly played a major role in implementing the ideals of the Liturgical Movement in the United States.

PIUS XII

Many of the liturgical pioneers in Europe and the United States rejoiced when, in 1943, Pius XII issued his encyclical *Mystici Corporis Christi.* It was soon followed up in 1947 with the encyclical *Mediator Dei.* In the past, liturgy was described as "the social exercise of the virtue of religion or the public worship of the Church."[25] As such, this understanding of liturgy was shaped by individualistic approaches that treated the liturgy as merely a matter of ceremony and rubrics. Passive participation in the liturgy all too often turned the liturgy into a backdrop for personal devotion, thus hindering the full impact of divine grace and the experience of being a baptized member of the Mystical Body. *Mystici Corporis Christi* and *Mediator Dei* helped our liturgical leaders to shift the emphasis from individualism and private devotion to the social ("unitive") and public ("communal") nature of true worship.

A powerful statement on the social nature of the Eucharist is included in *Mystici Corporis Christi,* 83:

> The Sacrament of the Eucharist is itself a striking and wonderful figure of the unity of the Church, if we consider how in the bread to be consecrated many grains go to form one whole, and that in it the very Author of supernatural grace is given to us, so that through Him we may receive the spirit of charity in which we are bidden to live now no longer our own life but the life of Christ, and to love the Redeemer Himself in all the members of His social Body.[26]

---

25. See Robert Tuzik, *Reynold Hillenbrand: The Reform of the Catholic Liturgy and the Call to Social Action* (Chicago: Hillenbrand Books, 2010), pp. 120–130.

26. *Mystici Corporis Christi* (MCC), 83.

And so, a powerful, visionary encyclical by Pius XII begins to have its impact on our understanding of liturgy and life.

Apparently, Pius XII felt that more needed to be said about the importance of the liturgy in preserving the true Christian spirit among God's people. His landmark encyclical *Mediator Dei* gave us a definition of liturgy that moved beyond the popular understanding of liturgy as simply rubrics and ceremony. Pius XII states:

> The sacred liturgy is, consequently, the public worship which our Redeemer as Head of the Church renders to the Father, as well as the worship which the community of the faithful renders to its Founder, and through Him to the heavenly Father. It is, in short, the worship rendered by the Mystical Body of Christ in the entirety of its Head and members.[27]

This definition of liturgy as "the worship rendered by the Mystical Body of Christ" clearly brings out the unitive or social aspects of communal worship. However, the pope is not finished in exploring the effects of the liturgy.

Where in the past, participation in the liturgy was seen mostly in terms of achieving personal sanctification, Pius XII wanted to move beyond this personal dimension to explore the communal implications of worship:

> Not only through her ministers but with the help of the faithful individually, who have imbibed in this fashion the spirit of Christ, the Church endeavors to permeate with this same spirit the life and labors of men—their private and family life, their social, even economic and political life—that all who are called God's children may reach more readily the end He has proposed for them.[28]

> In the spiritual life, consequently, there can be no opposition between the action of God, who pours forth His grace into men's hearts so that the work of the redemption may always abide, and the tireless collaboration of man, who must not render vain the gift of God.[29]

While God does his part in nourishing our life of faith in the liturgy, we too must do our part in using wisely the gifts he has given us in the world. For in the liturgy and in the lay apostolate the same dynamic is at work: the creation of apostles according to the pattern of Christ's life.

Pius XII reintroduced the concept of lay participation in the priesthood of Christ later on in *Mediator Dei*:

> By the waters of baptism, as by common right, Christians are made members of the Mystical Body of Christ the Priest, and by the "character" which is imprinted on their souls, they are appointed to give worship to God. Thus they participate, according to their condition, in the priesthood of Christ.[30]

---

27. *Mediator Dei* (MD), 20.
28. Ibid., 34.
29. Ibid., 36.
30. Ibid., 88.

In the past, talk about participation in the common priesthood was looked upon as too Protestant an idea, almost denying the special nature of the Sacrament of Holy Orders. Fortunately, times were changing and Catholic biblical, Patristic, and liturgical studies were beginning to have their impact on official teaching.

USE OF THE VERNACULAR IN THE LITURGY

Pius XII gave further indication that a new openness to liturgical reform was dawning in the Church in regard to use of the vernacular:

> The use of the Latin language, customary in a considerable portion of the Church, is a manifest and beautiful sign of unity, as well as an effective antidote for any corruption of doctrinal truth. In spite of this, the use of the mother tongue in connection with several of the rites may be of much advantage to the people. But the Apostolic See alone is empowered to grant this permission.[31]

The reference above is to the use of bilingual rituals that contain the Rites of Baptism, the Reception of Converts, Extreme Unction (now called the Anointing of the Sick), the Funeral Rite, the Celebration of Marriage, the Churching of a Mother, and various blessings for example, blessings of Marriage anniversaries.

In 1948, Germany was the first country to receive permission to translate ritual text into the vernacular. Other countries quickly followed Germany's lead. In 1954, the bilingual version of the Roman Ritual was approved for use in the United States. Even before the interest in pursuing the use of bilingual rituals, groups were formed to study the use of the vernacular in the liturgy. At the Liturgical Week in Denver, Colorado (October 14–17, 1946), various liturgical pioneers met and founded the St. Jerome Society "to study in accordance with the teachings of the Catholic Church and with due regard of ecclesiastical authority, the possibilities of a greater use of the vernacular in the liturgical rites of the Church."[32] This finely nuanced statement of purpose reflects the fears that openly studying the use of the vernacular in worship would lead to the introduction of Protestant ideas of worship into the Catholic Church. Consequently, the first studies in the United States on the use of the vernacular required great patience and tact.

THE VERNACULAR SOCIETY

From its beginning in 1946, the St. Jerome Society based its goals on those of the English Vernacular Society. The English Vernacular Society had three important goals:

- Provide a vernacular ritual for the Rites of Baptism, Churching of Women, Marriage, Visitation of the Sick, Reception of Convert, administration of the last sacraments, funerals, and blessings;

---

31. Ibid., 60.
32. *The English Liturgist: A Bulletin issued to Members of the English Vernacular Society*, December, 1948, no. 8, p. 8. Note that the statement of purpose of the St. Jerome Society is almost identical to that of the English Vernacular Society in England.

- Provide vernacular versions of Vespers, Compline, the blessing of candles, ashes, palms, and an extension of the vernacular prayers and hymns used at Benediction;

- Foster the use of the Dialogue Mass and the vernacular in the liturgy.[33]

Because *Mediator Dei* encouraged the use of the vernacular in worship, the United States leaders of the St. Jerome Society felt it safe to identify themselves more openly with the goals of the English Vernacular Society. And so, on July 25, 1948 they changed their name from the St. Jerome Society to the Vernacular Society. However, suspicion and hostility accompanied the work of the Vernacular Society for many years to come.

The labors of countless numbers of liturgical leaders in studying the history of the liturgy began to bear fruit in the 1950s. For many years, it had been obvious to everyone that the Easter Vigil was meant to be a "night vigil." Having a light service at 10:00 AM in the morning didn't make sense. Moreover, the Easter Vigil was also the privileged time when adult converts would be baptized and received into the Church. Why not reintroduce the Easter Vigil as a night vigil and encourage the Baptism of converts during this Mass? There is obviously plenty of historical precedent for this change. And so, liturgical leaders rejoiced when, on February 9, 1951 the Sacred Congregation of Rites issued a Decree Restoring the Easter Vigil and "bringing back the Easter Vigil to its primitive splendor and of assigning to it the time observed in the beginning, that is, the early hours of the night preceding Resurrection Sunday."[34]

In the apostolic constitution, *Christus Dominus* (January 6, 1953), Pius XII traced the historical evolution of fasting before receiving Holy Communion. In 1953, the custom was to fast from midnight until one received Holy Communion. However, because many people found this practice deterred them from receiving Holy Communion and because there was a need for a reawakened devotion toward the Eucharist, Pius XII decreed:

- Water does not break the Eucharistic fast.

- The sick may take their medicine before receiving Holy Communion.

- Priests celebrating Mass at a later hour, after hard work, or a long journey, may drink something (but not alcohol) in addition to water. However, they must abstain from drink for at least an hour before receiving Holy Communion.

- Laity, due to hard work, fatigue from a long journey, or other serious inconvenience, may drink something (but not alcohol) in addition to water. However, they must abstain from drink for at least an hour before receiving Holy Communion.

---

33. These three goals are found in a membership brochure published by the Vernacular Society in 1949.

34. *Decree Restoring the Easter Vigil*, February 9, 1951 in Megivern, *op.cit.*, p. 128.

- When participating in an evening Mass, priests and people are to fast for three hours from solid food and alcoholic drinks, and for one hour as to nonalcoholic drink.[35]

And so, the easing of the norms for the Eucharistic fast occurred long before the calling of the Second Vatican Council.

On December 25, 1955, Pius XII issued a major encyclical on sacred music, *Musicae sacrae disciplina*. Most commentators consider it to be a masterpiece on the subject of sacred music and religious art. Pius XII explains the dignity and lofty character of sacred music in these words:

> The dignity and lofty purpose of sacred music consists in the fact that its lovely melodies and splendor beautify and embellish the voices of the priest who offers Mass and of the Christian people who praise the Sovereign God. Its special power and excellence should lift up to God the minds of the faithful who are present. It should make the liturgical prayers of the Christian community more alive and fervent so that everyone can praise and beseech the Triune God more powerfully, more intently and more effectively.[36]

Notice the way the pope refers to the "liturgical prayers of the Christian community." Pius XII obviously has been influenced by the movement to more active and intelligent participation of the laity in the liturgy.

What is most encouraging for people who wanted to see more of the vernacular introduced into the liturgy were the comments of Pius XII about the value of religious hymns in the vernacular. Pius XII says:

> The tunes of these hymns, which are often sung in the language of the people, are memorized with almost no effort or labor. The mind grasps the words and the music. They are frequently repeated and completely understood. Hence, even boys and girls, learning these sacred hymns at a tender age, are greatly helped by them to know, appreciate and memorize the truths of the faith. Therefore, they also serve as a kind of catechism . . . They give a kind of religious grandeur to their more solemn assemblies and gatherings. They bring pious joy, sweet consolation and spiritual progress to Christian families themselves. Hence, these popular hymns are of great help to the Catholic apostolate and should be carefully cultivated and promoted.[37]

That the Second Vatican Council would approve the expanded use of the vernacular in the liturgy came as no surprise to people who had been following closely the teachings of Pius XII.

While Pius XII used this encyclical to encourage people to join in singing the Latin chants, he also knew that popular hymns based on the liturgy were often sung in the vernacular after the priest recited the words in Latin. In Germany, they had many such hymns. Pius XII felt that it would be prudent to allow this custom to continue, although he basically favored people learning to

---

35. *Christus Dominus*, in Megivern, *op. cit.*, p. 135.
36. *Musicae sacrae disciplina* (MSD), 31.
37. Ibid., 37.

sing the Mass Propers in Latin. However, the vernacular was not to be used at Solemn Masses without the express permission of the Holy See.

After identifying the organ as holding the highest place in instruments used at the liturgy, Pius XII also approved of the use of other instruments "to give great help in attaining the lofty purpose of sacred music, so long as they play nothing profane, nothing clamorous or strident, and nothing at variance with the sacred services or the dignity of the place."[38] He goes on to mention violins and other instruments that use the bow because "when they are played by themselves or with other stringed instruments or with the organ, they express the joyous and sad sentiments of the soul with an indescribable power."[39]

On September 22, 1956, in his *Address on the Liturgical Movement to the International Congress on Pastoral Liturgy*, Pope Pius XII not only endorses many of the ideals of the Liturgical Movement, but provides a fine summary of the Church's current position on liturgical renewal.

First, the pope praises the influence of the Liturgical Movement on the celebration of the liturgy:

> If the position of the liturgical movement today is compared to that of thirty years ago, undeniable progress in its extent and in its depth becomes evident. Interest in the liturgy, practical accomplishments, and the active participation of the faithful have undergone a development which would then have been difficult to anticipate.[40]

Pius XII reaches this conclusion:

> The liturgical movement has appeared as a sign of God's providential dispositions for the present day, as a movement of the Holy Spirit in His Church, intended to bring men closer to those mysteries of the faith and treasures of grace which derive from active participation of the faithful in liturgical life.[41]

Here you can find the immediate predecessor to *Sacrosanctum Concilium*'s call for "full, conscious, active participation"[42] in the sacred mysteries.

Here are a few of the key points Pius XII makes in his 1956 address:

- Liturgy is a vital function of the whole Church, and not simply of a group or of a limited movement.

- The solemn ceremonies of the liturgy is a profession of faith in action.

- At the heart of the liturgy is the celebration of the Eucharist, the sacrifice and the repast (or meal).

- All the faithful ought to love and value the liturgy, take part in it, but remember that the work of the Church extends beyond it.

---

38. Ibid., 59.

39. Ibid.

40. *Address on the Liturgical Movement to the International Congress on Pastoral Liturgy*, second paragraph in Megivern, *op. cit.*, pp. 161–177.

41. Ibid., sixth paragraph in Megivern, *op. cit.*, p. 162.

42. See Megivern, *op. cit.*, pp. 161–162; see also SC, 14.

- The liturgy is an action of Christ *(actio Christi)*.

- The Eucharist is the real presence of Christ *(praesentia Christi)*.

- The liturgy teaches us that Christ is God *(Christus Deus)* by remembering his infinite and divine majesty *(Infinita et Divina Maiestas Christi)*.

- In liturgical matters, one must avoid two exaggerated viewpoints concerning the past: blind attachment and utter contempt. The liturgy contains immutable (or unchangeable) elements, a sacred content that transcends time, but changeable, transitory, and occasionally even defective elements.

- The liturgy stamps a characteristic mark on the life of the Church, even on the whole religious attitude of the day. Especially noteworthy is the active and conscientious participation of the faithful at liturgical functions.

- Today's liturgy involves a concern for progress, but also for conservation and defense. It returns to the past, but does not slavishly imitate. It creates new elements in the ceremonies themselves, in using the vernacular, in popular chant and in the building of churches.[43]

Consequently, the bishops at the Second Vatican Council had a very strong base of support for the insights contained in *Sacrosanctum Concilium*. Chief among them was the amazing work on the liturgy done by Pope Pius XII, as is evidenced in the preceding address.

CONCLUSION

I have attempted to share with you some of the highlights of the history of the liturgy from the time of the Council of Trent up to the calling of the Vatican Council and the approval of *Sacrosanctum Concilium* on December 4, 1963. The bishops who approved *Sacrosanctum Concilium* were not simply interested in liturgical renewal, but in a renewal of the whole life of the Church. They rightly concluded in SC 10 that:

> The liturgy is the summit toward which the activity of the Church is directed; at the same time it is the fount from which all the Church's power flows. For the aim and object of apostolic works is that all who are made children of God by faith and baptism should come together to praise God in the midst of his Church, to take part in the sacrifice, and to eat the Lord's Supper.[44]

With the preceding historical introduction as a guide, I hope you will reread *Sacrosanctum Concilium* and observe the numerous ways in which it has drawn upon the work of the leaders of the liturgical and social justice movements, especially the writings of the popes from the time of Leo XIII to the present.

---

43. Ibid., Megivern, *op. cit.*, p. 176.
44. SC, 10.

MIRAE CARITATIS
ON THE
MOST HOLY EUCHARIST

ENCYCLICAL LETTER
POPE LEO XIII
MAY 28, 1902

AN OVERVIEW OF *MIRAE CARITATIS*

Jakob K. Rinderknecht

The last century has seen many changes in everyday Catholic life, particularly in the area of liturgical practice. The importance of frequent Communion among these changes should not be undervalued. Robert Taft has described the shift as a "great pastoral victory that has turned around fifteen centuries of devotional history in fifty years."[1] Despite his strong language, this is no exaggeration. As Taft points out, the Church had worried about infrequent reception of the Eucharist for quite a long time; concern that the faithful were not receiving the Eucharist frequently enough appears first in a Homily of St. John Chrysostom.[2] Perhaps the most radical of such worries was manifested in the Fourth Lateran Council's (1213) institution of the "Easter duty," to receive the Sacraments of Reconciliation and Eucharist at least once a year, a requirement confirmed by the Council of Trent in 1551. The fact that these councils felt the need to require such an infrequent reception testifies to their belief that even this low standard was not being met.

Various trends within the nineteenth century gave the popes further cause for concern, especially the legacy of Jansenism. This movement had been officially condemned and largely overcome during the nineteenth century, but it had left its mark on Catholic culture. One of these long-term effects was a strengthening of the habit of infrequent Communion. The Jansenists had emphasized both the Real Presence and the extreme sinfulness of human beings, underwriting a common belief that an exceedingly high moral bar had to be reached before one could receive the sacrament, far beyond the absence of mortal sin. In common practice, Eucharistic devotion took the place of Holy Communion, as most people believed themselves to be unworthy of receiving the Eucharist. Popes throughout the nineteenth century and into the twentieth sought to build on the Eucharistic devotion that was already central to Catholic practice and encouraging Catholics to frequently receive the Eucharist.

The experience of the contemporary Church shows them to have been successful. Most Catholics receive the Eucharist regularly, many daily. Much of the credit for the change is rightly given to Pope Pius X, who gave permission for daily Communion in the absence of mortal sin in his *motu proprio, Sacra Tridentina Synodus* (December 20, 1905). This *motu proprio* built on the foundation laid by his predecessors. For example, Pius IX had twice issued encyclicals recommending more frequent Communion among the faithful, in December 1849 and March 1856.

Leo XIII had also waged a steady campaign to encourage regular reception throughout his pontificate, which lasted from 1878–1903. The legislative steps

---

1. Robert Taft, "The Frequency of the Celebration of the Eucharist Throughout History," *Between Memory and Hope: Readings on the Liturgical Year* (Collegeville, MN: The Liturgical Press, 2000); p. 92.

2. *In Heb 10, hom 17, 4. Patrologiae Graeca* (PG), volume 63, 131.

he took are themselves demonstrations of how far the Church had to go. He ruled, for example, that superiors of religious orders could not restrict the dates on which their confreres could receive the Eucharist and ruled such provisions within already existing constitutions to be without force. Near the end of his pontificate, on May 28, 1902, Leo issued the encyclical *Mirae caritatis*, regarding the frequent reception of the Eucharist. This encyclical laid the immediate groundwork for Pius X's declaration three years later. Pope Pius went one step beyond his predecessor in allowing "daily" Communion where Leo had encouraged "frequent" Communion.

That Pope Leo encouraged the faithful to commune in the form of an encyclical is unsurprising. Over the course of the twenty five years of his pontificate, he wrote more than eighty encyclicals on topics ranging from civil marriage law to freemasonry, from devotion to St. Joseph to the study of Scripture, including eleven on the Rosary. A frequent subject within his encyclical corpus is the relationship of the Church to the world. His encyclical *Rerum novarum* (1891), regarding capital and labor, is an especially clear example of this; it is usually the source from which interpreters of Leo XIII read his sense of the Church's public role. At the end of his pontificate, Leo XIII authored three encyclicals on devotion, which shed unique light on the question. The encyclical *Mirae caritatis* may be a less-often engaged source, but it clearly demonstrates the importance that liturgical practice played in Leo XIII's understanding of the Church's place in the world.

The late nineteenth century was a tumultuous era, torn by political realignments and competing ideologies. The Papal States had been lost in the decade before Leo's election and he lived out his entire pontificate in a Vatican that was under siege by the kingdom of Italy. The political influence of the Catholic Church was waning across Europe as secular governments were set up, often with explicit legal bans to the involvement of the Church in public life. When Leo XIII was able to engage these governments profitably, it was usually because of the intervention of dedicated Catholics in positions of power. A case in point would be his skillful use of the Center Party, Catholic representatives in the Reichstag. Because the Center Party controlled a decisive bloc of votes, the pope was able to keep Otto von Bismarck at the bargaining table to regularize the situation of Catholics within the Empire. He managed to achieve his goal in 1887, winning many of the concessions he sought. The personal Catholic commitments of these politicians allowed the pope to make his case to Bismarck and improve the lives of German Catholics.

In a sense, Leo XIII was a relative moderate among nineteenth and early-twentieth century popes. Of course, he believed that the Church was the divine authority that the world required, but his political experience led him to propose more subtle methods of wielding that authority in practice. He had voted with the majority at Vatican I in favor of infallibility, but he recognized that the theologically grounded authority of the papacy did not convince non-Catholic rulers. Therefore, his manner of engaging these powers did not focus on the public authority of the See of Rome and its bishop. Instead, he sought to diagnose the malaise of modernity in terms they would recognize and propose a vision of personal religious practice as its antidote. He laid out this vision in three general encyclicals published near the end of his life. These are *Annum sacram*

("On Consecration to the Sacred Heart"), issued May 25, 1899; *Tametsi futura* ("On Jesus Christ the Redeemer"), issued November 1, 1900; and *Mirae caritatis*. MC explicitly ties the three letters together, as making up one trajectory.[3]

The first of these encyclicals was issued in preparation for the Holy Year of 1900. In it, the pope asks that the whole Church join him in consecrating the entire world to the Sacred Heart of Jesus on June 9–11, 1899. He hoped that the consecration would produce three effects: first, it would strengthen and win grace for all those who consecrate themselves; second, it would win God's grace of infused charity for those who "neglect His law and its precepts"[4]; and third, it would implore the same gifts for those who have not yet received the Gospel.

The themes throughout AS are the promises of grace that Christ has made to those consecrated to the Sacred Heart and the necessity of such grace for the proper functioning of society. In particular, he hoped that the consecration would win grace for those in charge of nation-states, allowing them to recognize Christ's universal lordship, and drop the "wall . . . between the Church and civil society,"[5] which stood in defiance of divine law.

These themes were developed more fully in *Tametsi futura*, if in a somewhat more hopeful tone. Having experienced the Holy Year and seen the many pilgrims who had made their way to Rome, the pontiff was hopeful that God's grace was having an effect on the political realm. Nevertheless, looking at the state of politics, he could see that there were still a growing number of problems exemplified by the expanding numbers of socialists, anarchists, and freemasons.

Leo XIII recognized that the leaders of nations seek their people's good according to what they know. Therefore catechesis took center stage. In this encyclical he attempted to teach these leaders that nations, like individuals, need Christ. While in the first devotional encyclical he had attended to those who had not heard the Word of Christ, seeking to benefit them by consecrating the whole world to the Sacred Heart, in the second he focused on the secular leadership of the nations and their quest for a human-scale solution to the problems of society. If only these leaders were able to willingly accept Christ's right to reign over the world, he suggested, a right order would be established in which all of the modern problems would be overcome.

Again, the theme of catechesis is central; it is the bishops' duty to teach the world about Christ and his just claim to rule. If they do this well it may yet bring forth an increase of faith in the world. Because faith is God's gift to humans, it can only be given to individuals but its effects on society reach far beyond the individual. When Christ's kingship is recognized, Leo taught, people are able to live in the social forms that God intended and social harmony results.

It is in this context that the pope sets his third encyclical on devotion, *Mirae caritatis*. Within an overriding encouragement to more frequent reception of the Eucharist, he considers the Eucharist under four titles, "The Source of Life" (4–6), "The Mystery of Faith (7–10), "The Bond of Charity" (11–16), and "The Sacrifice of the Mass" (17–18). Like each of the two previous devotional encyclicals, this letter articulates how Eucharistic reception provides God's

---

3. See *Mirae caritatis* (MC), 1.

4. *Annum sacrum* (AS), 9.

5. Ibid., 10.

grace to the believer and therefore to the social body. MC develops the relationship of the supernatural to the natural he had earlier proposed in *Tametsi futura* along the same trajectory. The foundation of the Church changed everything in the world by an influx of grace such that once "'the goodness and kindness of God our Savior appeared,' . . . there at once burst forth a certain creative force which issued in a new order of things and pulsed through all the veins of society, civil and domestic."[6]

Without the influx of grace mediated by the Church, the world is incapable of functioning properly. He makes this claim repeatedly throughout the letter, under the various titles of the Eucharist: the Eucharist is the supernatural food of the soul, on which our renewed lives are dependent[7]; it is the miracle by which that faith is strengthened that can remake society[8]; it is the means by which the grace of indwelling charity is given, allowing society to be properly re-oriented in Christ[9]; finally, it is the sacrifice that wins God's favor for a world mired in sin.[10] The grace that the Eucharist produces is always infused into the individual Christian. However, it is never just for that individual. If there is a leitmotif running throughout the three encyclicals, it is that the commonweal is impossible unless it is grounded in a proper relationship to God and strengthened by God's grace made present in individual Christians.

The individual sense of Eucharistic grace in the encyclical does not rule out its effects on the public work of the Church as a social body. For Leo, receiving the Eucharist allows the Church to be the social body Christ calls it to be. Where MC is cited, this is the sense in which its teaching will be received. For example, it is in the context of considering the Eucharist as the spiritual food of the community of the faithful that Pope John Paul II mentions MC in his encyclical *Ecclesia de Eucharistia*.[11]

One could argue that it is precisely the success of Leo XIII and Pius X's movement to encourage frequent reception of the Eucharist that allowed the greater liturgical renewal of the last century, including the emphasis on the Eucharist as an ecclesial action. The watchwords of the movement have reminded the Church that the Mass is the "source and summit of the christian life,"[12] manifested in "fully conscious, and active participation in liturgical celebrations."[13] These hopes presume a Church in which reception of the Eucharist is central to Catholic life. While this encyclical did not in itself change the course of Church history, it was an important moment in the renewal that would bear much fruit in the coming century.

---

6. MC, paragraph 4; citing Titus 3:4.

7. See ibid., 5.

8. See ibid., 8.

9. See ibid., 15.

10. See ibid., 17.

11. See *Ecclesia de Eucharistia (EE)*, 9.

12. *Lumen gentium* (LG), 11.

13. *Sacrosanctum Concilium* (SC), 10 and LG, 14.

MIRAE CARITATIS
ENCYCLICAL LETTER OF POPE LEO XIII
ON THE MOST HOLY EUCHARIST

MAY 28, 1902

To Our Venerable Brethren, the Patriarchs, Primates, Archbishops, Bishops, and other Local Ordinaries, having Peace and Communion with the Holy See.

Venerable Brethren, Health and Apostolic Benediction,

To examine into the nature and to promote the effects of those manifestations of His wondrous love which, like rays of light, stream forth from Jesus Christ—this, as befits Our sacred office, has ever been, and this, with His help, to the last breath of Our life will ever be Our earnest aim and endeavour. For, whereas Our lot has been cast in an age that is bitterly hostile to justice and truth, we have not failed, as you have been reminded by the apostolic letter which we recently addressed to you, to do what in us lay, by Our instructions and admonitions, and by such practical measures as seemed best suited for their purpose, to dissipate the contagion of error in its many shapes, and to strengthen the sinews of the Christian life. Among these efforts of Ours there are two in particular, of recent memory, closely related to each other, from the recollection whereof we gather some fruit of comfort, the more seasonable by reason of the many causes of sorrow that weigh us down. One of these is the occasion on which We directed, as a thing most desirable, that the entire human race should be consecrated by a special act to the Sacred Heart of Christ our Redeemer; the other that on which We so urgently exhorted all those who bear the name Christian to cling loyally to Him Who, by divine ordinance, is "the Way, the Truth, and the Life," not for individuals alone bur for every rightly constituted society. And now that same apostolic charity, ever watchful over the vicissitudes of the Church, moves and in a manner compels Us to add one thing more, in order to fill up the measure of what We have already conceived and carried out. This is, to commend to all Christians, more earnestly than heretofore, the all-holy Eucharist, forasmuch as it is a divine gift proceeding from the very Heart of the Redeemer, Who "with desire desireth" this singular mode of union with men, a gift most admirably adapted to be the means whereby the salutary fruits of His redemption may be distributed. Indeed We have not failed in the past, more than once, to use Our authority and to exercise Our zeal in this behalf. It gives Us much pleasure to recall to mind that We have officially approved, and

---

* Please note that this is an older English translation. A more contemporary translation was not available at the time of this printing. This older translation has been included in this collection because of the document's important connection with the history of the Liturgical Movement.

enriched with canonical privileges, not a few institutions and confraternities having for their object the perpetual adoration of the Sacred Host; that We have encouraged the holding of Eucharistic Congresses, the results of which have been as profitable as the attendance at them has been numerous and distinguished; that We have designated as the heavenly patron of these and similar undertakings St. Paschal Baylon, whose devotion to the mystery of the Eucharist was so extraordinary.

2.　　Accordingly, Venerable Brethren, it has seemed good to Us to address you on certain points connected with this same mystery, for the defence and honour of which the solicitude of the Church has been so constantly engaged, for which Martyrs have given their lives, which has afforded to men of the highest genius a theme to be illustrated by their learning, their eloquence, their skill in all the arts; and this We will do in order to render more clearly evident and more widely known those special characteristics by virtue of which it is so singularly adapted to the needs of these our times. It was towards the close of His mortal life that Christ our Lord left this memorial of His measureless love for men, this powerful means of support "for the life of the world" (St. John vi., 52). And precisely for this reason, We, being so soon to depart from this life, can wish for nothing better than that it may be granted to us to stir up and foster in the hearts of all men the dispositions of mindful gratitude and due devotion towards this wondrous Sacrament, wherein most especially lie, as We hold, the hope and the efficient cause of salvation and of that peace which all men so anxiously seek.

3.　　Some there are, no doubt, who will express their surprise that for the manifold troubles and grievous afflictions by which our age is harassed We should have determined to seek for remedies and redress in this quarter rather than elsewhere, and in some, perchance, Our words will excite a certain peevish disgust. But this is only the natural result of pride; for when this vice has taken possession of the heart, it is inevitable that Christian faith, which demands a most willing docility, should languish, and that a murky darkness in regard of divine truths should close in upon the mind; so that in the case of many these words should be made good: "Whatever things they know not, they blaspheme" (St. Jude, 10). We, however, so far from being hereby turned aside from the design which We have taken in hand, are on the contrary determined all the more zealously and diligently to hold up the light for the guidance of the well disposed, and, with the help of the united prayers of the faithful, earnestly to implore forgiveness for those who speak evil of holy things.

THE SOURCE OF LIFE

4.　　To know with an entire faith what is the excellence of the Most Holy Eucharist is in truth to know what that work is which, in the might of His mercy, God, made man, carried out on behalf of the human race. For as a right faith teaches us to acknowledge and to worship Christ as the sovereign cause of our salvation, since He by His wisdom, His laws, His ordinances, His example, and by the shedding of His blood, made all things new; so the same faith likewise teaches us to acknowledge Him and to worship Him as really present in the Eucharist, as verily abiding through all time in the midst of men, in order that as their Master, their Good Shepherd, their most acceptable Advocate with the Father, He may impart to them of His own inexhaustible abundance the benefits of that redemption which He has accomplished. Now if any one will seriously consider the benefits which flow from the Eucharist he will understand that conspicuous and chief among them all is that in which the rest, without exception, are included; in a word it is for men the source of life, of that life which best deserves the name. "The bread which I will give is my flesh, for the life of the world" (St. John vi., 52). In more than one way, as We have elsewhere declared, is Christ "the life." He Himself declared that the reason of His advent among men was this, that He might bring them the assured fulness of a more than merely human life. "I am come that they may have life, and may have it more abundantly" (St. John x., 10). Everyone is aware that no sooner had "the goodness and kindness of God our Saviour appeared" (Tit. iii., 4), than there at once burst forth a certain creative force which issued in a new order of things and pulsed through all the veins of society, civil and domestic. Hence arose new relations between man and man; new rights and new duties, public and private; henceforth a new direction was given to government, to education, to the arts; and most important of all, man's thoughts and energies were turned towards religious truth and the pursuit of holiness. Thus was life communicated to man, a life truly heavenly and divine. And thus we are to account for those expressions which so often occur in Holy Writ, "the tree of life," "the word of life," "the book of life," "the crown of life," and particularly "the bread of life."

5.   But now, since this life of which We are speaking bears a definite resemblance to the natural life of man, as the one draws its nourishment and strength from food, so also the other must have its own food whereby it may be sustained and augmented. And here it will be opportune to recall to mind on what occasion and in what manner Christ moved and prepared the hearts of men for the worthy and due reception of the living bread which He was about to give them. No sooner had the rumour spread of the miracle which He had wrought on the shores of the lake of Tiberias, when with the multiplied loaves He fed the multitude, than many forthwith flocked to Him in the hope that they, too, perchance, might be the recipients of like favour. And, just as He had taken occasion from the water which she had drawn from the well to stir up in the Samaritan woman a thirst for that "water which springeth up unto life everlasting" (St. John iv., 14), so now Jesus availed Himself of this opportunity to excite in the minds of the multitude a keen hunger for the bread "which endureth unto life everlasting" (St. John vi., 27). Or, as He was careful to explain to them, was the bread which He promised the same as that heavenly manna which had been given to their fathers during their wanderings in the desert, or again the same as that which, to their amazement, they had recently received from Him; but He was Himself that bread: "I," said He, "am the bread of life" (St. John vi., 48). And He urges this still further upon them all both by invitation and by precept: "if any man shall eat of this bread, he shall live for ever; and the bread which I will give is my flesh, for the life of the world" (St. John vi., 52). And in these other words He brings home to them the gravity of the precept: "Amen, Amen, I say to you, unless you shall eat the flesh of the Son of Man and drink His blood, you shall not have life in you" (St. John vi., 54). Away then with the widespread but most

mischievous error of those who give it as their opinion that the reception of the Eucharist is in a manner reserved for those narrow-minded persons (as they are deemed) who rid themselves of the cares of the world in order to find rest in some kind of professedly religious life. For this gift, than which nothing can be more excellent or more conducive to salvation, is offered to all those, whatever their office or dignity may be, who wish–as every one ought to wish–to foster in themselves that life of divine grace whose goal is the attainment of the life of blessedness with God.

6.   Indeed it is greatly to be desired that those men would rightly esteem and would make due provision for life everlasting, whose industry or talents or rank have put it in their power to shape the course of human events. But alas! we see with sorrow that such men too often proudly flatter themselves that they have conferred upon this world as it were a fresh lease of life and prosperity, inasmuch as by their own energetic action they are urging it on to the race for wealth, to a struggle for the possession of commodities which minister to the love of comfort and display. And yet, whithersoever we turn, we see that human society, if it be estranged from God, instead of enjoying that peace in its possessions for which it had sought, is shaken and tossed like one who is in the agony and heat of fever; for while it anxiously strives for prosperity, and trusts to it alone, it is pursuing an object that ever escapes it, clinging to one that ever eludes the grasp. For as men and states alike necessarily have their being from God, so they can do nothing good except in God through Jesus Christ, through whom every best and choicest gift has ever proceeded and proceeds. But the source and chief of all these gifts is the venerable Eucharist, which not only nourishes and sustains that life the desire whereof demands our most strenuous efforts, but also enhances beyond measure that dignity of man of which in these days we hear so much. For what can be more honourable or a more worthy object of desire than to be made, as far as possible, sharers and partakers in the divine nature? Now this is precisely what Christ does for us in the Eucharist, wherein, after having raised man by the operation of His grace to a supernatural state, he yet more closely associates and unites him with Himself. For there is this difference between the food of the body and that of the soul, that whereas the former is changed into our substance, the latter changes us into its own; so that St. Augustine makes Christ Himself say: "You shall not change Me into yourself as you do the food of your body, but you shall be changed into Me" (confessions 1. vii., c. x.).

THE MYSTERY OF FAITH

7.   Moreover, in this most admirable Sacrament, which is the chief means whereby men are engrafted on the divine nature, men also find the most efficacious help towards progress in every kind of virtue. And first of all in faith. In all ages faith has been attacked; for although it elevates the human mind by bestowing on it the knowledge of the highest truths, yet because, while it makes known the existence of divine mysteries, it yet leaves in obscurity the mode of their being, it is therefore thought to degrade the intellect. But whereas in past times particular articles of faith have been made by turns the object of attack; the seat of war has since been enlarged and extended, until it has come to this, that men deny altogether that there is anything above and beyond nature. Now

nothing can be better adapted to promote a renewal of the strength and fervour of faith in the human mind than the mystery of the Eucharist, the "mystery of faith," as it has been most appropriately called. For in this one mystery the entire supernatural order, with all its wealth and variety of wonders, is in a manner summed up and contained: "He hath made a remembrance of His wonderful works, a merciful and gracious Lord; He hath given food to them that fear Him" (Psalm cx, 4–5). For whereas God has subordinated the whole supernatural order to the Incarnation of His Word, in virtue whereof salvation has been restored to the human race, according to those words of the Apostle; "He hath purposed . . . to re-establish all things in Christ, that are in heaven and on earth, in Him" (Eph. i., 9–10), the Eucharist, according to the testimony of the holy Fathers, should be regarded as in a manner a continuation and extension of the Incarnation. For in and by it the substance of the incarnate Word is united with individual men, and the supreme Sacrifice offered on Calvary is in a wondrous manner renewed, as was signified beforehand by Malachy in the words: "In every place there is sacrifice, and there is offered to My name a pure oblation" (Mal. i., II). And this miracle, itself the very greatest of its kind, is accompanied by innumerable other miracles; for here all the laws of nature are suspended; the whole substance of the bread and wine are changed into the Body and the Blood; the species of bread and wine are sustained by the divine power without the support of any underlying substance; the Body of Christ is present in many places at the same time, that is to say, wherever the Sacrament is consecrated. And in order that human reason may the more willingly pay its homage to this great mystery, there have not been wanting, as an aid to faith, certain prodigies wrought in His honour, both in ancient times and in our own, of which in more than one place there exist public and notable records and memorials. It is plain that by this Sacrament faith is fed, in it the mind finds its nourishment, the objections of rationalists are brought to naught, and abundant light is thrown on the supernatural order.

8. But that decay of faith in divine things of which We have spoken is the effect not only of pride, but also of moral corruption. For if it is true that a strict morality improves the quickness of man's intellectual powers, and if on the other hand, as the maxims of pagan philosophy and the admonitions of divine wisdom combine to teach us, the keenness of the mind is blunted by bodily pleasures, how much more, in the region of revealed truths, do these same pleasures obscure the light of faith, or even, by the just judgment of God, entirely extinguish it. For these pleasures at the present day an insatiable appetite rages, infecting all classes as with an infectious disease, even from tender years. Yet even for so terrible an evil there is a remedy close at hand in the divine Eucharist. For in the first place it puts a check on lust by increasing charity, according to the words of St. Augustine, who says, speaking of charity, "As it grows, lust diminishes; when it reaches perfection, lust is no more" (De diversis quaestionibus, lxxxiii., q. 36). Moreover the most chaste flesh of Jesus keeps down the rebellion of our flesh, as St. Cyril of Alexandria taught, "For Christ abiding in us lulls to sleep the law of the flesh which rages in our members" (Lib. iv., c. ii., in Joan., vi., 57). Then too the special and most pleasant fruit of the Eucharist is that which is signified in the words of the prophet: "What is the good thing of Him," that is, of Christ, "and what is His beautiful thing, but the corn of the

elect and the wine that engendereth virgins" (Zach. ix., 17), producing, in other words, that flower and fruitage of a strong and constant purpose of virginity which, even in an age enervated by luxury, is daily multiplied and spread abroad in the Catholic Church, with those advantages to religion and to human society, wherever it is found, which are plain to see.

9.   To this it must be added that by this same Sacrament our hope of everlasting blessedness, based on our trust in the divine assistance, is wonderfully strengthened. For the edge of that longing for happiness which is so deeply rooted in the hearts of all men from their birth is whetted even more and more by the experience of the deceitfulness of earthly goods, by the unjust violence of wicked men, and by all those other afflictions to which mind and body are subject. Now the venerable Sacrament of the Eucharist is both the source and the pledge of blessedness and of glory, and this, not for the soul alone, but for the body also. For it enriches the soul with an abundance of heavenly blessings, and fills it with a sweet joy which far surpasses man's hope and expectations; it sustains him in adversity, strengthens him in the spiritual combat, preserves him for life everlasting, and as a special provision for the journey accompanies him thither. And in the frail and perishable body that divine Host, which is the immortal Body of Christ, implants a principle of resurrection, a seed of immortality, which one day must germinate. That to this source man's soul and body will be indebted for both these boons has been the constant teaching of the Church, which has dutifully reaffirmed the affirmation of Christ: "He that eateth my flesh and drinketh my blood hath everlasting life; and I will raise him up at the last day" (St. John vi., 55).

10.   In connection with this matter it is of importance to consider that in the Eucharist, seeing that it was instituted by Christ as "a perpetual memorial of His Passion" (*Opusc.* lvii. *Offic. de festo Corporis Christi*), is proclaimed to the Christian the necessity of a salutary self-chastisement. For Jesus said to those first priests of His: "Do this in memory of Me" (Luke xxii, 18); that is to say, do this for the commemoration of My pains, My sorrows, My grievous afflictions, My death upon the Cross. Wherefore this Sacrament is at the same time a Sacrifice, seasonable throughout the entire period of our penance; and it is likewise a standing exhortation to all manner of toil, and a solemn and severe rebuke to those carnal pleasures which some are not ashamed so highly to praise and extol: "As often as ye shall eat this bread, and drink this chalice, ye shall announce the death of the Lord, until He come" (1 Cor. xi., 26).

THE BOND OF CHARITY

11.   Furthermore, if anyone will diligently examine into the causes of the evils of our day, he will find that they arise from this, that as charity towards God has grown cold, the mutual charity of men among themselves has likewise cooled. Men have forgotten that they are children of God and brethren in Jesus Christ; they care for nothing except their own individual interests; the interests and the rights of others they not only make light of, but often attack and invade. Hence frequent disturbances and strifes between class and class: arrogance, oppression, fraud on the part of the more powerful: misery, envy, and turbulence

among the poor. These are evils for which it is in vain to seek a remedy in leg-islation, in threats of penalties to be incurred, or in any other device of merely human prudence. Our chief care and endeavour ought to be, according to the admonitions which We have more than once given at considerable length, to secure the union of classes in a mutual interchange of dutiful services, a union which, having its origin in God, shall issue in deeds that reflect the true spirit of Jesus Christ and a genuine charity. This charity Christ brought into the world, with it He would have all hearts on fire. For it alone is capable of affording to soul and body alike, even in this life, a foretaste of blessedness; since it restrains man's inordinate self-love, and puts a check on avarice, which "is the root of all evil" (1 Tim. vi., 10). And whereas it is right to uphold all the claims of justice as between the various classes of society, nevertheless it is only with the effica-cious aid of charity, which tempers justice, that the "equality" which St. Paul commended (2 Cor. viii., 14), and which is so salutary for human society, can be established and maintained. This then is what Christ intended when he insti-tuted this Venerable Sacrament, namely, by awakening charity towards God to promote mutual charity among men. For the latter, as is plain, is by its very nature rooted in the former, and springs from it by a kind of spontaneous growth. Nor is it possible that there should be any lack of charity among men, or rather it must needs be enkindled and flourish, if men would but ponder well the char-ity which Christ has shown in this Sacrament. For in it He has not only given a splendid manifestation of His power and wisdom, but "has in a manner poured out the riches of His divine love towards men" (Conc. Trid., Sess. XIIL, *De Euch.* c. ii.). Having before our eyes this noble example set us by Christ, Who bestows on us all that He has assuredly we ought to love and help one another to the utmost, being daily more closely united by the strong bond of brotherhood. Add to this that the outward and visible elements of this Sacrament supply a singu-larly appropriate stimulus to union. On this topic St. Cyprian writes: "In a word the Lord's sacrifice symbolises the oneness of heart, guaranteed by a persever-ing and inviolable charity, which should prevail among Christians. For when our Lord calls His Body bread, a substance which is kneaded together out of many grains, He indicates that we His people, whom He sustains, are bound together in close union; and when He speaks of His Blood as wine, in which the juice pressed from many clusters of grapes is mingled in one fluid, He likewise indicates that we His flock are by the commingling of a multitude of persons made one" (Ep. 96 *ad Magnum* n. 5 (a1.6)). In like manner the angelic Doctor, adopting the sentiments of St. Augustine (Tract. xxxvi., *in Joan.* nn. 13, 17), writes: "Our Lord has bequeathed to us His Body and Blood under the form of substances in which a multitude of things have been reduced to unity, for one of them, namely bread, consisting as it does of many grains is yet one, and the other, that is to say wine, has its unity of being from the confluent juice of many grapes; and therefore St. Augustine elsewhere says: 'O Sacrament of mercy, O sign of unity, O bond of charity!' " (*Summ. Theol.* P. IIL, q. lxxix., a.l.). All of which is confirmed by the declaration of the Council of Trent that Christ left the Eucharist in His Church "as a symbol of that unity and charity whereby He would have all Christians mutually joined and united . . . a symbol of that one body of which He is Himself the head, and to which He would have us, as mem-bers attached by the closest bonds of faith, hope, and charity" (Conc. Trid., Sess.

XIIL, *De Euchar.*, c. ii.). The same idea had been expressed by St. Paul when he wrote: "For we, being many, are one bread, one body, all we who partake of the one bread" (I Cor. x., 17). Very beautiful and joyful too is the spectacle of Christian brotherhood and social equality which is afforded when men of all conditions, gentle and simple, rich and poor, learned and unlearned, gather round the holy altar, all sharing alike in this heavenly banquet. And if in the records of the Church it is deservedly reckoned to the special credit of its first ages that "the multitude of the believers had but one heart and one soul" (Acts iv., 32), there can be no shadow of doubt that this immense blessing was due to their frequent meetings at the Divine table; for we find it recorded of them: "They were persevering in the doctrine of the Apostles and in the communion of the breaking of bread" (Acts ii., 42).

12.   Besides all this, the grace of mutual charity among the living, which derives from the Sacrament of the Eucharist so great an increase of strength, is further extended by virtue of the Sacrifice to all those who are numbered in the Communion of Saints. For the Communion of Saints, as everyone knows, is nothing but the mutual communication of help, expiation, prayers, blessings, among all the faithful, who, whether they have already attained to the heavenly country, or are detained in the purgatorial fire, or are yet exiles here on earth, all enjoy the common franchise of that city whereof Christ is the head, and the constitution is charity. For faith teaches us, that although the venerable Sacrifice may be lawfully offered to God alone, yet it may be celebrated in honour of the saints reigning in heaven with God Who has crowned them, in order that we may gain for ourselves their patronage. And it may also be offered–in accordance with an apostolic tradition–for the purpose of expiating the sins of those of the brethren who, having died in the Lord, have not yet fully paid the penalty of their transgressions.

13.   That genuine charity, therefore, which knows how to do and to suffer all things for the salvation and the benefit of all, leaps forth with all the heat and energy of a flame from that most holy Eucharist in which Christ Himself is present and lives, in which He indulges to the utmost. His love towards us, and under the impulse of that divine love ceaselessly renews His Sacrifice. And thus it is not difficult to see whence the arduous labours of apostolic men, and whence those innumerable designs of every kind for the welfare of the human race which have been set on foot among Catholics, derive their origin, their strength, their permanence, their success.

14.   These few words on a subject so vast will, we doubt not, prove most helpful to the Christian flock, if you in your zeal, Venerable Brethren, will cause them to be expounded and enforced as time and occasion may serve. But indeed a Sacrament so great and so rich in all manner of blessings can never be extolled as it deserves by human eloquence, nor adequately venerated by the worship of man. This Sacrament, whether as the theme of devout meditation, or as the object of public adoration, or best of all as a food to be received in the utmost purity of conscience, is to be regarded as the centre towards which the spiritual life of a Christian in all its ambit gravitates; for all other forms of devotion,

whatsoever they may be, lead up to it, and in it find their point of rest. In this mystery more than in any other that gracious invitation and still more gracious promise of Christ is realised and finds its daily fulfilment: "Come to me all ye that labour and are heavily burdened, and I will refresh you" (St. Matt. xi., 28).

15.   In a word this Sacrament is, as it were, the very soul of the Church; and to it the grace of the priesthood is ordered and directed in all its fulness and in each of its successive grades. From the same source the Church draws and has all her strength, all her glory, her every supernatural endowment and adornment, every good thing that is here; wherefore she makes it the chiefest of all her cares to prepare the hearts of the faithful for an intimate union with Christ through the Sacrament of His Body and Blood, and to draw them thereto. And to this end she strives to promote the veneration of the august mystery by surrounding it with holy ceremonies. To this ceaseless and ever watchful care of the Church our Mother, our attention is drawn by that exhortation which was uttered by the holy Council of Trent, and which is so much to the purpose that for the benefit of the Christian people We here reproduce it in its entirety. "The Holy Synod admonishes, exhorts, asks and implores by the tender mercy of our God, that all and each of those who bear the name of Christian should at last unite and find peace in this sign of unity, in this bond of charity, in this symbol of concord; and that, mindful of the great majesty and singular love of Jesus Christ our Lord, Who gave His precious life as the price of our salvation, and His flesh for our food, they should believe and revere these sacred mysteries of His Body and Blood with such constancy of unwavering faith, with such interior devotion and worshipful piety, that they may be in condition to receive frequently that supersubstantial bread, and that it may be to them the life of their souls and keep their mind in soundness of faith; so that strengthened with its strength they may be enabled after the journey of this sorrowful pilgrimage to reach the heavenly country, there to see and feed upon that bread of angels which here they eat under the sacramental veils" (Conc. Trid., Sess. XXII, c. vi).

16.   History bears witness that the virtues of the Christian life have flourished best wherever and whenever the frequent reception of the Eucharist has most prevailed. And on the other hand it is no less certain that in days when men have ceased to care for this heavenly bread, and have lost their appetite for it, the practice of Christian religion has gradually lost its force and vigour. And indeed it was a needful measure of precaution against a complete falling away that Innocent III, in the Council of the Lateran, most strictly enjoined that no Christian should abstain from receiving the communion of the Lord's Body at least in the solemn paschal season. But it is clear that this precept was imposed with regret, and only as a last resource; for it has always been the desire of the Church that at every Mass some of the faithful should be present and should communicate. "The holy Synod would wish that in every celebration of the Mass some of the faithful should take part, not only by devoutly assisting thereat, but also by the sacramental reception of the Eucharist, in order that they might more abundantly partake of the fruits of this holy Sacrifice" (conc. Trid., Sess. XIII. *de Euchar.* c. viii).

17.   Most abundant, assuredly, are the salutary benefits which are stored up in this most venerable mystery, regarded as a Sacrifice; a Sacrifice which the Church is accordingly wont to offer daily "for the salvation of the whole world." And it is fitting, indeed in this age it is specially important, that by means of the united efforts of the devout, the outward honour and the inward reverence paid to this Sacrifice should be alike increased. Accordingly it is our wish that its manifold excellence may be both more widely known and more attentively considered. There are certain general principles the truth of which can be plainly perceived by the light of reason; for instance, that the dominion of God our Creator and Preserver over all men, whether in their private or in their public life, is supreme and absolute; that our whole being and all that we possess, whether individually or as members of society, comes from the divine bounty; that we on our part are bound to show to God, as our Lord, the highest reverence, and, as He is our greatest benefactor, the deepest gratitude. But how many are there who at the present day acknowledge and discharge these duties with full and exact observance? In no age has the spirit of contumacy and an attitude of defiance towards God been more prevalent than in our own; an age in which that unholy cry of the enemies of Christ: "We will not have this man to rule over us" (Luke xix., 14), makes itself more and more loudly heard, together with the utterance of that wicked purpose: "let us make away with Him" (Jer. xi., II); nor is there any motive by which many are hurried on with more passionate fury, than the desire utterly to banish God not only from the civil government, but from every form of human society. And although men do not everywhere proceed to this extremity of criminal madness, it is a lamentable thing that so many are sunk in oblivion of the divine Majesty and of His favours, and in particular of the salvation wrought for us by Christ. Now a remedy must be found for this wickedness on the one hand, and this sloth on the other, in a general increase among the faithful of fervent devotion towards the Eucharistic Sacrifice, than which nothing can give greater honour, nothing be more pleasing, to God. For it is a divine Victim which is here immolated; and accordingly through this Victim we offer to the most blessed Trinity all that honour which the infinite dignity of the Godhead demands; infinite in value and infinitely acceptable is the gift which we present to the Father in His only-begotten son; so that for His benefits to us we not only signify our gratitude, but actually make an adequate return.

18.   Moreover there is another twofold fruit which we may and must derive from this great Sacrifice. The heart is saddened when it considers what a flood of wickedness, the result—as We have said—of forgetfulness and contempt of the divine Majesty, has inundated the world. It is not too much to say that a great part of the human race seems to be calling down upon itself the anger of heaven; though indeed the crop of evils which has grown up here on earth is already ripening to a just judgment. Here then is a motive whereby the faithful may be stirred to a devout and earnest endeavour to appease God the avenger of sin, and to win from Him the help which is so needful in these calamitous times. And they should see that such blessings are to be sought principally by means of this Sacrifice. For it is only in virtue of the death which Christ suffered that

men can satisfy, and that most abundantly, the demands of God's justice, and can obtain the plenteous gifts of His clemency. And Christ has willed that the whole virtue of His death, alike for expiation and impetration, should abide in the Eucharist, which is no mere empty commemoration thereof, but a true and wonderful though bloodless and mystical renewal of it.

19.   To conclude, we gladly acknowledge that it has been a cause of no small joy to us that during these last years a renewal of love and devotion towards the Sacrament of the Eucharist has, as it seems, begun to show itself in the hearts of the faithful; a fact which encourages us to hope for better times and a more favourable state of affairs. Many and varied, as we said at the commencement, are the expedients which an inventive piety has devised; and worthy of special mention are the confraternities instituted either with the object of carrying out the Eucharistic ritual with greater splendour, or for the perpetual adoration of the venerable Sacrament by day and night, or for the purpose of making repara-tion for the blasphemies and insults of which it is the object. But neither We nor you, Venerable Brethren, can allow ourselves to rest satisfied with what has hitherto been done; for there remain many things which must be further devel-oped or begun anew, to the end that this most divine of gifts this greatest of mysteries, may be better understood and more worthily honoured and revered, even by those who already take their part in the religious services of the Church. Wherefore, works of this kind which have been already set on foot must be ever more zealously promoted; old undertakings must be revived wherever perchance they may have fallen into decay; for instance, Confraternities of the holy Eucharist, intercessory prayers before the blessed Sacrament exposed for the veneration of the faithful, solemn processions, devout visits to God's tabernacle, and other holy and salutary practices of some kind; nothing must be omitted which a pru-dent piety may suggest as suitable. But the chief aim of our efforts must be that the frequent reception of the Eucharist may be everywhere revived among Catholic peoples. For this is the lesson which is taught us by the example, already referred to, of the primitive Church, by the decrees of Councils, by the authority of the Fathers and of the holy men in all ages. For the soul, like the body, needs fre-quent nourishment; and the holy Eucharist provides that food which is best adapted to the support of its life. Accordingly all hostile prejudices, those vain fears to which so many yield, and their specious excuses from abstaining from the Eucharist, must be resolutely put aside; for there is question here of a gift than which none other can be more serviceable to the faithful people, either for the redeeming of time from the tyranny of anxious cares concerning perishable things, or for the renewal of the Christian spirit and perseverance therein. To this end the exhortations and example of all those who occupy a prominent position will powerfully contribute, but most especially the resourceful and diligent zeal of the clergy. For priests, to whom Christ our Redeemer entrusted the office of consecrating and dispensing the mystery of His Body and Blood, can assuredly make no better return for the honour which has been conferred upon them, than by promoting with all their might the glory of his Eucharist, and by inviting and drawing the hearts of men to the health-giving springs of this great Sacrament and Sacrifice, seconding hereby the longings of His most Sacred Heart.

20.   May God grant that thus, in accordance with Our earnest desire, the excellent fruits of the Eucharist may daily manifest themselves in greater abundance, to the happy increase of faith, hope, and charity, and of all Christian virtues; and may this turn to the recovery and advantage of the whole body politic; and may the wisdom of God's most provident charity, Who instituted this mystery for all time "for the life of the world," shine forth with an ever brighter sight.

21.   Encouraged by such hopes as these, Venerable Brethren, We, as a presage of the divine liberality and as a pledge of our own charity, most lovingly bestow on each of you, and on the clergy and flock committed to the care of each, our Apostolic Benediction.

Given at Rome, at St. Peter's on the 28th day of May, being the Vigil of the Solemnity of Corpus Christi, in the year 1902, of Our Pontificate the five and twentieth.

LEO XIII

TRA LE SOLLECITUDINI
ON SACRED MUSIC

MOTU PROPRIO
POPE PIUS X
NOVEMBER 22, 1903

AN OVERVIEW OF *TRA LE SOLLECITUDINI*

Rev. Anthony Ruff, OSB

Pope Pius X issued the document on sacred music, *Tra le sollecitudini* (TLS), on November 22, 1903. The title of this *motu proprio* is usually cited in the Italian language of the original; it later appeared in Latin as *Inter pastoralis officii*. Although *motu proprio* ("on his own initiative") refers to the manner in which a pope issues a document, music history sources sometimes refer to TLS as if *motu proprio* were the title of the document.

TLS was a landmark document for Catholic sacred music in the twentieth and twenty-first centuries. It was a powerful motor of reform, even as its implementation met with strong resistance in some quarters. It set the terms of the discussion for succeeding decades until the Second Vatican Council, where teachings of TLS were both affirmed and transformed in the light of the Council's reformist principles.

There is no mistaking the perceived abuse against which TLS thundered: the invasion into the sacred temple of what were considered secular and profane styles of music. Through the course of the eighteenth and nineteenth centuries, European church music increasingly incorporated compositional styles from the concert hall, opera house, and theater. The Romantic era brought about ever more dramatic expressions of creativity, with bravura vocal solos and more extensive instrumentation. To put music back in its proper place, TLS says that music is the "humble handmaid"[1] of the liturgy.

At the same time, as a reaction against Romantic culture, the notion arose in the second half of the nineteenth century of a "lost holiness." Reform movements sought to retrieve the sacredness of ancient music—especially Gregorian chant and choral polyphony in the style of Palestrina of the sixteenth century. The social and political backdrop of these movements was the secularization of states after the French Revolution and the Napoleonic wars. The quest for a "Catholic" and "holy" sound was part of a larger quest for Catholic identity within changed social circumstances.

The Benedictine monks of Solesmes Abbey in France were leaders in the revival of Gregorian chant. The influential Cecilian reform movements in Germany and other countries strongly fought against "secular" music in church, especially orchestral music. While some in Europe were reviving long-lost Renaissance choral literature, the Cecilians focused more on their own choral compositions, mostly forgotten today, which were written in mediocre imitation of Palestrina.

With TLS, Pope Pius X affirmed nineteenth-century movements for the reform of Catholic Church music and their Romantic notion of "sacred music." He also affirmed the Solesmes-led revival of Gregorian chant. Shortly after issuing TLS he entrusted to the Solesmes monks the work of editing the official chant books.

---

1. *Tra le sollecitudini* (TLS), 23.

Especially influential was the famous statement of the three qualities of authentic sacred music: holiness (or sanctity), goodness of form (or artistic quality), and universality.[2] The first quality, understood negatively, excludes anything profane in the music or the manner it is rendered. Holiness assumes that music has intrinsic, ontological qualities, apart from its cultural context or the function it performs. The second quality, goodness of form, is an aesthetic judgment about beauty and craftsmanship. It assumes that there are objective standards for musical quality. The third quality, universality, is said to arise spontaneously from the first two qualities. Music that is truly holy and of high artistic quality is said to have universal application and enjoy universal affirmation. Much discussion and dispute ensued after TLS about the meaning and application of these three qualities.

There is no mistaking the European focus of TLS, written at a time when the adherents of the Catholic Church were almost entirely Europeans and Americans of European descent. The three qualities of music are conceived with European presuppositions about what is sacred and secular in music, which standards are used to evaluate music, and which nations and cultures are taken into account in understanding universality. Many challenging multicultural issues had not yet arisen, issues that would arise in the course of the twentieth century as the Catholic faith expanded in non-Western cultures.

TLS upholds Gregorian chant as the highest model of sacred music that best exemplifies the three qualities of holiness, beauty, and universality. The principle is given that any other genre of music is sacred and liturgical to the extent that its ethos is similar to Gregorian chant.[3]

After Gregorian chant, TLS affirms the classic polyphony of the Roman school.[4] This refers especially to the music of Palestrina, who is the first major Western composer whose music remained in uninterrupted use after his death (1594). Roman school music written after Palestrina is in imitation of his style.

It had become customary since the early seventeenth century for composers to write in two compositional styles, *prima prattica* and *seconda prattica*. The first practice, also called *stile antico*, was a conscious imitation of classical polyphony and used especially in penitential seasons. The second practice kept pace with the broader evolution of Western art music. Composers devoted most of their interest to contemporary music in the second practice, with the liturgy and the music hall influencing each other. The symbiosis between Church and secular culture was to last for a couple centuries, and it reached a high point in the Viennese orchestral Church music of Mozart, Haydn, Beethoven, and Schubert. Then the evolution of Western art music increasingly began to be seen as problematic by Church figures. This is why TLS is rather skeptical of what it calls "modern music," which is admitted to the liturgy only when it exhibits excellence, sobriety, and gravity.[5] Modern music, especially theatrical (that is, operatic) music of Italy, is seen as almost entirely profane and unsuited for the liturgy.

---

2. See TLS, 2.
3. See ibid., 3.
4. See ibid., 4.
5. See ibid., 4.

After upholding Gregorian chant and classic polyphony as models of holiness, TLS treats other genres of sacred music, listing them in descending order according to their similarity to Gregorian chant. TLS permits organ music, which is subordinate to the vocal quality of Gregorian chant and classic polyphony.[6]

Limited use of wind instruments is permitted with the proper ecclesiastical permission, provided that the music is in "grave and suitable style."[7] Just as the organ is subordinate to the human voice, so the wind instruments must conform to the style of organ music. TLS prohibits piano, drums, cymbals, and bells,[8] and TLS by its silence prohibits stringed instruments. This was meant to exclude the tradition of Viennese orchestral music from liturgical use.

TLS permits bands to play in processions outside of church, provided nothing profane is played. The only permission for vernacular texts in TLS is found in the suggestion that bands accompany spiritual songs (outside the church building) sung in Latin or vernacular.[9] The document explicitly forbade any vernacular singing in the liturgy.[10]

TLS indicates the liturgical choir to be a clerical institution, ideally consisting entirely of clerics at least in minor orders.[11] Laymen, who of course were the vast majority of men in church choirs, were understood to be substitutes for ecclesiastical singers. Because women were understood to be incapable of exercising a liturgical office, they are entirely excluded from the choir. The document advises that choir schools for boys be founded, even in country parishes.[12]

"Active participation" (*partecipazione attiva* in the original) is mentioned briefly in the introduction to the document. It admonishes that Gregorian chant be restored to the people so that they might again take an active part in the liturgy.[13] The theme of active participation is not otherwise emphasized in TLS, but it was to become a tremendously important theme in succeeding decades. The entire twentieth century Liturgical Movement based its efforts for active participation in TLS, and so the *motu proprio* can be considered the founding document of the Liturgical Movement.

Because TLS was so sweeping in its condemnation of deeply ingrained practices, it was perhaps to be expected that its reception be controversial. Many reformist individuals and organizations were heartened and encouraged by TLS, and many others were newly drawn to the reformist cause. Congregational singing of Latin chant, for example, the Ordinary of the Mass, increased greatly. But some leading composers and music critics were openly and publicly critical of TLS. When Pope Pius XI issued *Divini cultus sanctitatem* in 1928 to commemorate the twenty-fifth anniversary of TLS, he both praised the improvements made and deplored that TLS was not being observed in some places.

---

6. See ibid., 15.

7. Ibid., 20.

8. See ibid., 19.

9. See ibid., 21.

10. See ibid., 7.

11. See ibid., 12–13.

12. See ibid., 27.

13. See ibid., 3.

The prohibition of orchestral church music was not well-received in Austria and Bavaria, and the pope himself soon granted an exception to the Austrian emperor on this point. The prohibition on vernacular singing was resisted in German-speaking and Slavic countries, where the custom for centuries was to sing vernacular hymns alongside or in replacement of Latin propers at High Mass. Many bishops were sympathetic to vernacular hymnody and permitted or even encouraged it. By 1943 Rome officially granted permission for Germany (which then included Austria) to continue the long-standing practice of singing vernacular hymns at Latin High Mass.

Although boy choirs were founded and all-male choirs were formed at the encouragement of TLS, the long-standing custom of women singing in choirs continued in most places. Church officials oftentimes tolerated or tacitly approved the practice. Women were officially admitted to the choir under Pius XII in 1955.

Subsequent papal and curial documents built upon TLS as they responded to changing circumstances. These later Roman documents all maintained the distinction between sacred and secular music, and they affirmed Gregorian chant and classic polyphony as the preferred genres of sacred music. But openness to modern styles of music increased, and under Pius XII stringed instruments became permissible in 1955.

An important development in the understanding of the holiness of music took place under Pius XII in 1955,[14] and then was taken into the liturgy constitution *Sacrosanctum Concilium* (SC) of the Second Vatican Council. SC states "sacred music will be the more holy the more closely it is joined to the liturgical rite."[15] This statement defines holiness in terms of ritual function, rather than understanding holiness as an intrinsic or ontological quality of music. The 1967 instruction *Musicam sacram* (MS) says "music is 'sacred' insofar as it is composed for the celebration of divine worship and possesses integrity of form."[16] Universality is not included. In his *Chirography* on sacred music in 2003 on the hundredth anniversary of TLS, Pope John Paul II retrieved the three qualities of holiness, sound form, and universality from Pius X, but placed them in the broader context of ritual function, assembly participation, and inculturation of the liturgy so as to draw on the strengths of all cultures.

As the Liturgical Movement grew in the decades leading up to the Second Vatican Council, papal teaching increasingly emphasized active participation, which was first mentioned in TLS. Encouragement for congregational vernacular singing—for example, at Low Mass where the Ordinary and Proper were not sung—grew increasingly strong. Singing vernacular hymns at Mass, not foreseen in TLS, was increasingly praised in subsequent papal documents.

TLS was important for articulating basic principles of Catholic Church music for succeeding decades. Under later popes, the criticism of secular and profane music gradually became less severe, and openness to modern styles of music increased. Stringed instruments became permissible under Pius XII in 1955, which signaled the official readmission of Viennese orchestral music to the liturgy. But in faithfulness to TLS, later Roman documents all maintained

---

14. See *Musicae sacrae disciplina* (MSD), 34.

15. *Sacrosanctum Concilium* (SC), 112.

16. *Musicam sacram* (MS), 4.

the distinction between sacred and secular music, and they all affirmed Gregorian chant and classic polyphony as the preferred genres of sacred music. This shows that subsequent papal and curial documents built upon TLS as they responded to changing circumstances.

TRA LE SOLLECITUDINI
MOTU PROPRIO OF POPE ST. PIUS X
ON THE RESTORATION OF CHURCH MUSIC

NOVEMBER 22, 1903

Chief amongst the anxieties of the pastoral office, not only of this Supreme Chair, which we, although unworthy, occupy through the inscrutable disposition of Providence, but of every local church, is without doubt that of maintaining and promoting the decorum of the house of God where the august mysteries of religion are celebrated, and where the Christian people assemble to receive the grace of the sacraments, to be present at the holy sacrifice of the altar, to adore the august sacrament of the Lord's Body and to join in the common prayer of the Church in the public and solemn liturgical offices. Nothing then should take place in the temple calculated to disturb or even merely to diminish the piety and devotion of the faithful, nothing that may give reasonable cause for disgust or scandal, nothing, above all, which directly offends the decorum and the sanctity of the sacred function and is thus unworthy of the house of prayer and of the majesty of God.

We do not deal separately with the abuses which may occur in this matter. Today our attention is directed to one of the most common of them, one of the most difficult to eradicate and the existence of which is sometimes to be deplored even when everything else is deserving of the highest praise—the beauty and sumptuousness of the temple, the splendor and the accurate order of the ceremonies, the attendance of the clergy, the gravity and piety of the officiating ministers. Such is the abuse in connection with sacred chant and music. And, indeed, whether it is owing to the nature of this art, fluctuating and variable as it is in itself, or to the successive changes in tastes and habits in the course of time, or the sad influence exercised on sacred art by profane and theatrical art, or the pleasure that music directly produces, and that is not always easily kept within the proper limits, or finally to the many prejudices on the matter so lightly introduced and so tenaciously maintained even among responsible and pious persons, there is a continual tendency to deviate from the right rule, fixed by the end for which art is admitted to the service of worship and laid down very clearly in the ecclesiastical canons, in the ordinances of the general and provincial councils, in the prescriptions which have on various occasions emanated from the Sacred Roman congregations, and from our predecessors, the sovereign pontiffs.

It is pleasing to us to be able to acknowledge with real satisfaction the large amount of good that has been done in this respect during the last decades in this our fair city of Rome, and in many churches in our country, but in a more special way among some nations in which excellent men, full of zeal for the worship of God, have, with the approval of this Holy See and under the direction of the Bishops, united in flourishing societies and restored sacred music to the fullest honor in nearly all their churches and chapels. Still the good work that has been done is very far indeed from being common to all, and when we consult our own personal experience and take into account the great number of complaints that have reached us from all quarters during the short time that has elapsed since it pleased the Lord to elevate our humble person to the summit of the Roman pontificate, we consider it our first duty, without further delay, to raise our voice at once in reproof and condemnation of all that is out of harmony with the right rule above indicated, in the functions of worship and in the performance of the ecclesiastical offices. It being our ardent desire to see the true Christian spirit restored in every respect and be preserved by all the faithful, we deem it necessary to provide before everything else for the sanctity and dignity of the temple, in which the faithful assembly for the object of acquiring this spirit from its foremost and indispensable fount, which is the active participation in the holy mysteries and in the public and solemn prayer of the Church. And it is vain to hope that the blessing of heaven will descend abundantly upon us for this purpose when our homage to the Most High, instead of ascending in the odor of sweetness, puts into the hand of the Lord the scourges with which the Divine Redeemer once drove the unworthy profaners from the temple. Wherefore, in order that no one in the future may be able to plead in excuse that he did not clearly understand his duty, and that all vagueness may be removed from the interpretation of some things which have already been commanded, we have deemed it expedient to point out briefly the principles regulating sacred music in the functions of public worship, and to gather together in the function of public worship, and to gather together in a general survey the principal prescriptions of the Church against the more common abuses in this matter. We, therefore, publish, *motu proprio* and with sure knowledge, our present "instruction" to which, as "to a juridical code of sacred music," we desire the fullness of our Apostolic authority that the force of law be given, and we impose its scrupulous observance on all by this document in our own handwriting.

INSTRUCTION ON SACRED MUSIC

1. General Principles

1.   Sacred music, as an integral part of the solemn liturgy, participates in its general object, which is the glory of God and the sanctification and edification of the faithful. It tends to increase the decorum and the splendor of the ecclesiastical ceremonies, and since its principal office is to clothe with befitting melody the liturgical text proposed for the understanding of the faithful its proper end is to add greater efficacy to the text, in order that by means of it the faithful may be the more easily moved to devotion and better disposed to receive the fruits of grace associated with the celebration of the most holy mysteries.

2.   Sacred music should consequently possess, in the highest degree, the qualities proper to the liturgy, and precisely sanctity and goodness of form from which spontaneously springs its other character, universality.

It must be holy, and must, accordingly, exclude all profanity not only in itself, but in the manner in which it is presented by those who execute it.

It must be true art, for otherwise it will be impossible for it to exercise on the minds of those who her it that efficacy which the Church aims at obtaining in admitting into her liturgy the art of musical sounds.

But it must, at the same time, be universal in this sense, that while every nation is permitted to admit into its ecclesiastical compositions those special forms which in a certain manner constitute the specific character of its native music, still these forms must be subordinated in such a manner to the general characteristics of sacred music that nobody of another nation may receive, on hearing them, an impression other than good.

2. The Kinds of Sacred Music

3.   These qualities are possessed in the highest degree by the Gregorian chant, which is, consequently, the chant proper to the Roman Church, the only Chant she has inherited from the ancient fathers, which she has jealously guarded for centuries in her liturgical codices, which she directly proposes to the faithful as her own, which she prescribes exclusively for some parts of the liturgy, and which the most recent studies have so happily restored to their integrity and purity.

Upon these grounds the Gregorian chant has always been regarded as the supreme model for sacred music, so that the following rule may be safely laid down: The more closely a composition for church approaches in its movement, inspiration and savor the Gregorian form, the more sacred and liturgical it is; and the more out of harmony it is with that supreme model, the less worthy it is of the temple.

The ancient traditional Gregorian chant must, therefore, be largely restored in the functions of public worship, and everybody must take for certain that an ecclesiastical function loses nothing of its solemnity when it is accompanied by no other music except them.

Efforts must especially be made to restore the use of the Gregorian chant by the people, so that the faithful may again take a more active part in the ecclesiastical offices, as they were wont to do in ancient times.

4.   The qualities mentioned are also possessed in an excellent degree by the classic polyphony, especially of the Roman school, which reached its greatest perfection in the fifteenth century, owing to the works of Pierluigi da Palestrina, and continued subsequently to produce compositions of excellent quality from the liturgical and musical standpoint. The classic polyphony approaches pretty closely to the Gregorian chant, the supreme model of all sacred music, and hence it has been found worthy of a place side by side with the Gregorian chant in the more solemn functions of the Church, such as those of the Pontifical chapel. This, too, must therefore be restored largely in ecclesiastical functions, especially in the more important basilicas, in cathedrals and in the churches and chapels of seminaries and other ecclesiastical institutions in which the necessary means are usually not lacking.

5.   The Church has always recognized and favored the progress of the arts, admitting to the service of worship everything good and beautiful discovered by genius in the course of ages—always, however, with due regard to the liturgical laws. Consequently modern music is also admitted in the Church, since it, too, furnishes compositions of such excellence, sobriety and gravity that they are in no way unworthy of the liturgical functions.

But as modern music has come to be devoted mainly to profane uses, greater care must be taken with regard to it, in order that the musical compositions of modern style which are admitted in the Church may contain nothing profane, be free from reminiscences of motifs adopted in the theatres and be not fashioned even in their external forms after the manner of profane pieces.

6.   Amongst the various kinds of modern music that which appears less suitable for accompanying the functions of public worship is the theatrical style, which was in the greatest vogue, especially in Italy, during the last century. This of its very nature is diametrically opposed to the Gregorian chant and the classic polyphony, and therefore to the most important law of all good music. Besides the intrinsic structure, the rhythm and what is known as the "conventionalism" of this style adapt themselves but badly to the exigencies of true liturgical music.

3. The Liturgical Text

7.   The language of the Roman Church is Latin. It is therefore forbidden to sing anything whatever in the vernacular in solemn liturgical functions—much more to sing in the vernacular the variable or common parts of the Mass and Office.

8.   The texts that may be rendered in music, and the order in which they are to be rendered, being determined for every liturgical function, it is not lawful to confuse this order or to change the prescribed texts for others, selected at will, or to omit them either entirely or even in part, unless when the rubrics allow that some versicles are simply recited in choir. However, it is permissible, according to the custom of the Roman Church, to sing a motet to the Blessed Sacrament after the "Benedictus" in a Solemn Mass. It is also permitted, after the offertory prescribed for the Mass has been sung, to execute during the time that remains a brief motet to words approved by the Church.

9.   The liturgical text must be sung as it is in the books without alteration or inversion of the words, without undue repetition, without breaking syllables and always in a manner intelligible to the faithful who listen.

4. External Form of the Sacred Compositions

10.   The different parts of the Mass and the Office must retain, even musically, that particular concept and form which ecclesiastical tradition has assigned to them, and which is admirably expressed in the Gregorian chant. Different, therefore, must be the method of composing an introit, a gradual, an antiphon, a psalm, a hymn, a *Gloria in Excelsis*.

11. In particular the following rules are to be observed:

a) The Kyrie, Gloria, Credo, etc., of the Mass must preserve the unity of composition proper to their text. It is not lawful, therefore, to compose them in separate pieces, in such a way as that each of such pieces may form a complete composition in itself, and be capable of being detached from the rest and substituted by another.

b) In the office of vespers it should be the rule to follow the *Caerimoniale Episcoporum*, which prescribes the Gregorian chant for the psalmody and permits figured music for the versicles of the *Gloria Patri* and the hymn.

It will nevertheless be lawful on the greater solemnities to alternate the Gregorian Chant of the choir with the so called *falsibordoni* or with verses similarly composed in a proper manner.

It may be also allowed sometimes to render the single psalms in their entirety in music, provided the form proper to psalmody be preserved in such compositions; that is to say, providing the singers seem to be psalmodizing among themselves, either with new motifs or with those taken from the Gregorian chant, or based upon it.

The psalms known as *di concerto* are, therefore, forever excluded and prohibited.

c) In the hymns of the Church the traditional form of the hymn is preserved. It is not lawful, therefore, to compose, for instance a *Tantum Ergo* in such wise that the first strophe presents a romanza, a cavatina, an adagio and the *Genitori* an allegro.

d) The antiphons of the vespers must be as rule rendered with the Gregorian melody proper to each. Should they, however, in some special case be sung in figured music, they must never have either the form of a concert melody or the fullness of a motet or a cantata.

4. The Singers

12. With the exception of the melodies proper to the celebrant at the altar and to the ministers, which must be always sung only in Gregorian chant, and without the accompaniment of the organ, all the rest of the liturgical chant belongs to the choir of levites, and, therefore, singers in church, even when they are laymen, are really taking the place of the ecclesiastical choir. Hence the music rendered by them must, at least for the greater part, retain the character of choral music.

By this it is not to be understood that solos are entirely excluded. But solo singing hould never predominate in such a way as to have the greater part of the liturgical chant executed in that manner; rather should it have the character of hint or a melodic projection, and be strictly bound up with the rest of the choral composition.

13.   On the same principle it follows that singers in church have a real liturgical office, and that therefore women, as being incapable of exercising such an office, cannot be admitted to form part of the choir or of the musical chapel. Whenever, then, it is desired to employ the acute voice of sopranos or contraltos, these parts must be taken by boys, according to the most ancient usage of the Church.

14.   Finally, only those are to be admitted to form part of the musical chapel of a church who are men of known piety and probity of life, and these should by their modest and devout bearing during the liturgical functions show that they are worthy of the holy office they exercise. It will also be fitting that singers while singing in church wear the ecclesiastical habit and surplice, and that they be hidden behind grating when the choir is excessively open to the public gaze.

6. Organ and Instruments

15.   Although the music proper to the Church is purely vocal music, music with the accompaniment of the organ is also permitted. In some special cases, within due limits and within the proper regards, other instruments may be allowed, but never without the special license of the ordinary, according to the prescriptions of the *Caerimoniale Episcoporum*.

16.   As the chant school should always have the principal place, the organ or instruments should merely sustain and never overwhelm it.

17.   It is not permitted to have the chant preceded by long preludes or to interrupt it with intermezzo pieces.

18.   The sound of the organ as an accompaniment to the chant in preludes, interludes and the like must not be only governed by the special nature of the instruments, but must participate in all the qualities proper to sacred music as above enumerated.

19.   The employment of the piano is forbidden in church, as is also that of noisy or frivolous instruments such as drums, cymbals, bells and the like.

20.   It is strictly forbidden to have bands play in church, and only in a special case and with the consent of the ordinary will it be permissible to admit a number of wind instruments, limited, judicious and proportioned to the size of the place—provided the composition and accompaniment to be executed be written in a grave and suitable style, and similar in all respects to that proper to the organ.

21.   In processions outside the church the ordinary may give permission for a band, provided no profane pieces are executed. It would be desirable in such cases that the band confine itself to accompanying some spiritual canticle sung in Latin or in the vernacular by the singers and the pious associations which take part in the procession.

7. The Length of the Liturgical Chant

22.   It is not lawful to keep the priest at the altar waiting on account of the chant or the music for a length of time not allowed by the liturgy. According to the ecclesiastical prescriptions the Sanctus of the Mass should be over before the elevation, and therefore the priest must have regard to the singers. The Gloria and the Credo ought, according to the Gregorian tradition, to be relatively short.

23.   In general, it must be considered to be a very grave abuse when the liturgy in ecclesiastical functions is made to appear secondary to and in a manner at the service of the music, for the music is merely a part of the liturgy and its humble handmaid.

8. Principal Means

24.   For the exact execution of what has been herein laid down, the bishops, if they have not already done so, are to institute in their dioceses a special commission composed of persons really competent in sacred music, and to this commission let them entrust in the manner they find most suitable the task of watching over the music executed in their churches. Nor are they to see merely that the music is good in itself, but also that it is adapted to the powers of the singers and be always well executed.

25.   In seminaries of clerics and in ecclesiastical institutions let the above-mentioned traditional Gregorian Chant be cultivated by all with diligence and love, according to the Tridentine prescriptions, and let the superiors be liberal of encouragement and praise towards their young subjects. In like manner let a *Schola Cantorum* be established, whenever possible, among the clerics for the execution of sacred polyphony and of good liturgical music.

26.   In the ordinary lessons of liturgy, morals, canon law given to the students of theology, let care be taken to touch on those points which regard more directly the principles and laws of sacred music, and let an attempt be made to complete the doctrine with some particular instruction in the esthetic side of the sacred art, so that the clerics may not leave the seminary ignorant of all those notions, necessary as they are for complete ecclesiastical culture.

27.   Let care be taken to restore, at least in the principal churches, the ancient *Scholae Cantorum* as has been done with excellent fruit in a great many places. It is not difficult for a zealous clergy to institute such *scholae* even in the minor country churches—nay, in them they will find a very easy means for gathering round them both the children and the adults, to their own profit and the edification of the people.

28.   Let efforts be made to support and promote in the best way possible the higher schools of sacred music where these already exist, and to help in founding them where they do not. It is of the utmost importance that the Church itself provide for the instruction of its masters, organists and singers, according to the true principles of sacred art.

9. Conclusion

29.   Finally, it is recommended to choirmasters, singers, members of the clergy, superiors of seminaries, ecclesiastical institutions and religious communities, parish priests and rectors of churches, canons of collegiate churches and cathedrals, and above all, to the diocesan ordinaries to favor with all zeal these prudent reforms, long desired and demanded with united voice by all; so that the authority of the Church which herself has repeatedly proposed them, and now inculcates them, may not fall into contempt.

Given from our Apostolic Palace at the Vatican on the day of the Virgin and Martyr, St. Cecilia, November 22, 1903, in the first year of our Pontificate.

PIUS X, POPE

DIVINO AFFLATU
THE REFORM OF THE ROMAN BREVIARY

APOSTOLIC CONSTITUTION
POPE PIUS X
NOVEMBER 1, 1911

ABHINC DUOS ANNOS
ON THE INTERIM REFORM
OF THE LITURGY

POPE PIUS X
MOTU PROPRIO
OCTOBER 23, 1913

AN OVERVIEW OF *DIVINO AFFLATU* AND *ABHINC DUOS ANNOS*

Michael R. Prendergast

The Roman Breviary is the title of the book obligatorily used for celebrating the Divine Office (Liturgy of the Hours) in the Roman Rite. The Office was first revised by Pope Pius V with the apostolic constitution, *Quod a nobis* on July 9, 1568. The reform of *The Roman Breviary* by Pope Pius X was promulgated with the apostolic constitution *Divino afflatu* on November 1, 1911 and the Church was called to embrace these changes with the *motu proprio, Abhinc duos annos* on October 23, 1913. The Office again underwent revisions by Pope Paul VI with the post-Conciliar apostolic constitution *Canticum laudis* on November 1, 1970.

Divino afflatu was significant as one of the first steps in the Liturgical Movement of the twentieth century to reform the Breviary. From the beginning of the Church, the psalms had cultivated the piety of the faithful, taught the Church to pray, strengthened virtue, and consoled the suffering. The weekly recitation of the psalter was the ancient law of the Church for her clergy, and it was preserved throughout consecutive revisions of the Breviary. The current office had been rendered practically impossible to pray because of the increase of saints' feasts. The observances of the saints had overshadowed Sunday and ferial offices and so some psalms were never recited, and others were repeated with wearisome duplication. The Holy Father received petitions from bishops requesting that the weekly recitation of the psalter be restored without increasing the burden of the limited number of clergy. A commission was assigned to satisfy that demand by lessening the burden placed upon clerics, without detracting from the veneration given to the saints. In the meantime, Pius made certain rubrical changes to insure the regular reading of the Scripture lessons, and to restore to their place of privilege the ancient Masses of the Sundays and especially the Lenten ferias.

Divino afflatu consists of only nine paragraphs. Pius X references SS. Basil and Augustine who both speak of the importance of the use of psalmody in "praising or morning, rejoicing in hope or yearning for accomplishment."[1] Pius X also looked to the writings of St. Athanasius who referred to the psalms as a "mirror in which he (one) may contemplate himself (themselves) and the movements of his (one's) soul."[2] Pius X recognized the work of his predecessors St. Pius V, Clement VII, and Urban VIII who contributed to the revision of *The Roman Breviary* during their pontificates.

Pius X laments the number of saints that had been added to the calendar and notes that in honor of their feasts "the offices of the Sundays and ferias are hardly ever heard."[3] The Holy Father wanted to see the entire psalter prayed dur-

---

1. *Divino afflatu* (DA), paragraph 2.
2. Ibid.
3. Ibid., paragraph 4.

ing the course of the week so that "by changing and varying the psalmody and the chant for the different hours, its desire is renewed and its attention restored."[4]

Several bishops from throughout the world had contacted the Apostolic See requesting that the ancient custom of reciting the whole of the psalter within a week's time be restored in such a way that a great burden would not be placed on the clergy "whose labors in the vineyard of the sacred ministry are now increased owing to the diminution in the number of laborers."[5] Pius X himself wished the whole of the psalter to be prayed within a week so that "the burden of the divine office may become not more oppressive, but actually lighter."[6] Pius X set about putting in charge a number of learned scholars to put into place a "new arrangement of the psaltery."[7]

The Holy Father instituted two immediate changes to the rubrics:

1. "the recitation of the divine office due honor, by their more frequent use, be restored to the appointed lessons of sacred Scripture with the responsories of the season;" and

2. the "most ancient Masses of the Sundays during the year and of the ferias, especially those of Lent, recover their rightful place."[8]

Pius X, at the outset of his apostolic constitution, abolishes "the order of the psaltery as it is at present in the Roman breviary, and we absolutely forbid the use of it after the 1st day of January of the year 1913."[9] Pius X gave immediate permission to the Church to use the new psalter upon its publication.

Divino afflatu allowed for the recitation of all 150 Psalms. In order to restore the ancient ideal of reciting all the psalms every week, the *motu proprio* changed the rubrics for lower-ranking feasts of saints. The arrangement of the psalms was done in such a way that the Divine Office would not take a greater amount of time for the priest to recite. *Divino afflatu* restored the ancient ideal without creating an additional burden for the clergy, and at the same time, introduced variety into the psalms for Lauds, Prime, Terce, Sext, None, and Compline.

Pope Pius X ordered a number of changes that were proposed by a committee of liturgical scholars whom he appointed, and were adopted by the Congregation of Rites. The Holy Father had requested the changes to take place after January 1, 1913 but the changes to the rite were not formally put into effect until October 23, 1913 with the *motu proprio, Abhinc duos annos.*

In *Abhinc duos annos*, Pope Pius X called on the entire Church to embrace the changes outlined by *Divino afflatu* and emphasized that the "new psalter be used more often, that the Sundays be observed more conscientiously, that provisions be made for the inconvenience of transferred offices, and that certain other changes be effected which seem to be justified."[10] Pius X had hoped to take on a total revision of the office but this did not come to pass. He was, however,

---

4. Ibid.
5. Ibid., paragraph 5.
6. Ibid.
7. Ibid.
8. Ibid., paragraph 6.
9. Ibid., paragraph 7.
10. *Abhinc duos annos* (ADA), paragraph 4.

able to accomplish his main goal of creating a new psalter. The changes made to the Office made it necessary to modify the *Missale Romanum* as well. These changes were promulgated with the 1920 typical edition of the Missal promulgated by Pius X's successor, Pope Benedict XV.

The main goal that Pius X achieved in his revision of the Breviary was a completely new arrangement of the psalms, distributing them or, when too long, dividing them so as to have approximately the same number of verses in each day's office. This change was made with a view to restoring the original use of the liturgy provided for the chant or recitation of the entire psalter each week. Thus Pius X was able to correct the concern about the multiplication of saints' days that the had made celebration of Sundays and ferias, and consequently the use of certain psalms, very rare.

Years later, Pope Pius XII also appointed a special commission to undertake a revision of the Breviary, which allowed for the use of a new translation of the psalms from the Hebrew. In 1955, Pius XII consulted with the bishops about introducing the revisions to the Breviary but they were not implemented until further revisions were made by Pope John XXIII in 1960.

The liturgy of the Church is living and is always undergoing changes and revisions so as to meet the people of God on their pilgrim journey. Pius X, Pius XII, and John XXIII understood this principle as they worked to include revisions to the prayer of the Church.

After repeated revisions of the Breviary, which we now know as the Liturgy of the Hours, a new Council (Vatican II) would be called and proceed with further changes. As the Church begins her day and ends her day in prayer, she participates in the sacrifice of praise that happens through all ages. Let us open our lips and proclaim God's praise.

DIVINO AFFLATU
APOSTOLIC CONSTITUTION OF POPE ST. PIUS X

NOVEMBER 1, 1911

It is beyond question that the psalms composed under divine inspiration, which are collected in the sacred books, have from the beginning of the Church not only contributed wonderfully to foster the piety of the faithful offering the sacrifice of praise always to God, that is to say, the fruit of lips confessing to his name (Heb 13:15), but have also had a conspicuous part, from custom introduced under the old law, in the sacred liturgy itself and in the divine office. Hence, as Basil says, that natural voice of the Church (*Homil. In Ps.* I, no. 2), and the psalmody called by our predecessor Urban VIII (in *Divinam psalmodiam*) the daughter of her hymnody which is constantly sung before the throne of God and the Lamb, and which, according to Athanasius, teaches the men whose chief care is the divine worship the manner in which God is to be praised and the words in which they are fitly to confess him *(Epist. ad Marcellinum in interpret. Psalmor* no. 10). Augustine beautifully says on the subject: "That God may be praised well by man, God himself has praised himself; and since he has been pleased to praise himself man has found the way to praise him (*In Psalm, cxliv.* no. 1).

Besides, there is in the Psalms a certain wonderful power for stimulating zeal in men's minds for all the virtues. For although all our Scripture, both Old and New, is divinely inspired and useful for doctrine, as is written, the Book of Psalms, like a paradise containing in itself (the fruits) all the others, gives forth songs, and with them also shows its own songs in psalmody (*cantus edit, et proprios insuper cum ipsis inter psallendum exhibet*). Such are the words of Athanasius (*Epist. ad Marcell.* op. cit. no. 2), who rightly adds in the same place: "To me it seems that the psalms for him who sings them are as a mirror in which he may contemplate himself and the movements of his soul, and, under this influence, recite them" (*op. cit.* no. 12). Hence, Augustine says in his *Confessions*: "How I wept in hymns and canticles, deeply moved by the voices of your sweetly sounding Church! These voices poured into my ears and truth became clear in my heart and then feelings of piety grew warm within me and my tears flowed and it was well with me for them" (book IX, ch. 6). For who can fail to be stirred by those numerous passages of the psalms which proclaim so loudly the immense majesty of God, his omnipotence, his ineffable justice or goodness or clemency, and his other infinite praises? Who can fail to be so inspired with similar feelings by those thanksgivings for benefits received from God, or by those so trustful prayers for benefits received from God, or by those so trustful prayers for benefits desired, or those cries of the penitent soul for its sins? Who is not stirred to admiration by the Psalmist as he recounts the acts of divine goodness toward the people of Israel and the whole race of man and when he hands down the dogmas of heavenly wisdom? Who is not kindled with love by the picture of Christ the Redeemer lovingly shadowed forth whose voice Augustine heard in all the psalms, praising or morning, rejoicing in hope or yearning for accomplishment? (*In Ps. xlii.*, no. I.)

With good reason was provision made long ago, by decrees of the Roman pontiffs, by canons of the councils, and by monastic laws, that members of both branches of the clergy should chant or recite the entire psaltery every week. And this same law, handed down from antiquity, our predecessors St. Pius V, Clement VIII and Urban VIII religiously observed in revising the Roman breviary. Even at present the psaltery should be recited in its entirety within the week were it not that owing to the changed condition of things such recitation is frequently hindered.

For in the course of time there has been a constant increase among the faithful in the number of those whom the Church, after their mortal life, has been accustomed to count among the denizens of heaven and to set before the Christian people as patrons and models. In their honor the offices of the saints began to be gradually extended until it has come about that the offices of the Sundays and ferias are hardly ever heard, and thus neglect has fallen on not a few Psalms, albeit these are, no less than the others, as Ambrose says (*Enarrat, in Ps. i.*, no. 9), "the benediction of the people, the praise of God, the praising of the multitude, the rejoicing of all, the speech of all, the voice of the Church, the resounding confession of faith, the full devotion of authority, the joy of liberty, the cry of gladness, the echo of joy." More than once serious complaints have been made by prudent and pious men about this omission, on the ground that owing to it those in sacred orders have been deprived of so many admirable aids for praising the Lord and expressing the inmost feelings of the soul, and that it has left them without that desirable variety in praying so highly necessary for our weakness in supplicating worthily, attentively and devoutly. For, as Basil has it, "the soul, in some strange way, frequently grows torpid in sameness, and what should be present to it becomes absent; whereas by changing and varying the psalmody and the chant for the different hours, its desire is renewed and its attention restored (*Regulae fusius tractatae*, q. 37, no. 5.)

No wonder, then, that a great many bishops in various parts of the world have sent expressions of their opinions on this matter to the Apostolic See, and especially in the Vatican Council when they asked, among other things, that the ancient custom of reciting the whole psaltery within the week might be restored as far as possible, but in such a way that the burden should not be made any heavier for the clergy, whose labors in the vineyard of the sacred ministry are now increased owing to the diminution in the number of the laborers. These petitions and wishes, which were our own, too, before we assumed the pontificate, and also the appeals which have since come from others of our venerable brothers and from pious men, we have decided should be granted—but with care, so that from the reciting of the entire psaltery within the week no diminution in the cultus of the saints may follow, on the one hand, and on the other, that the burden of the divine office may become not more oppressive, but actually lighter. Wherefore, after having suppliantly implored the Father of Lights and asked for the assistance of holy prayers on the matter, following in the first steps of our predecessor, we chose a number of learned and active men with the task of studying and consulting together in order to find some way, which might meet our wishes, for putting the idea into execution. In fulfillment of the charge entrusted to them they elaborated a new arrangement of the psaltery, and this having been approved by the cardinals of H. R. C. belonging to the Congregation of Sacred Rites, we have ratified it as being in entire harmony with our own mind, in all things, that is, as regards the order and partition of the psalms, the antiphons, versicles, hymns with their rubrics and rules, and we have ordered an authentic edition of it to be set up in our Vatican printing press and then published.

As the arrangement of the psaltery has a certain intimate connection with all the divine office and the liturgy, it will be clear to everybody that by what we have decreed we have taken the first step to the emendation of the Roman breviary and the missal, but for this we shall appoint shortly a special council or commission. Meanwhile, now that the occasion presents itself, we have decided to make some changes at present, as is prescribed in the accompanying rubrics; and first among them that in the recitation of the divine office due honor, by their more frequent use, be restored to the appointed lessons of sacred Scripture with the responsories of the season, and, second, that in the sacred liturgy those most ancient Masses of the Sundays during the year and of the ferias, especially those of Lent, recover their rightful place.

Therefore, by the authority of these letters, we first of all abolish the order of the psaltery as it is at present in the Roman breviary, and we absolutely forbid the use of it after the 1st day of January of the year 1913. From that day in all the churches of the secular and regular clergy, in the monasteries, orders, congregations and institutes of religious, by all and several who by office or custom recite the canonical hours according to the Roman breviary issued by St. Pius V and revisited by Clement VIII, Urban VIII and Leo XIII, we order the religious observance of the new arrangement of the psaltery in the form in which we have approved it and decreed its publication by the Vatican printing press. At the same time we proclaim the penalties prescribed in law against all who fail in their office of reciting the canonical hours everyday; all such are to know that they shall not be satisfying this grave duty unless they use this our disposition of the psaltery.

We command, therefore, all the patriarchs, archbishops, bishops, abbots and other prelates of churches, not excepting even the cardinal archpriests of the patriarchal basilicas of the city, to take care to introduce at the appointed time into their respective dioceses, churches or monasteries, the psaltery with the rules and rubrics as arranged by us; and the psaltery and these rules and rubrics we order to be also inviolately used and observed by all others who are under the obligation of reciting or chanting the canonical hours. In the meantime it shall be lawful for everybody and for the chapters themselves, provided the majority of a chapter be in favor, to use duly the new order of the psaltery immediately after its publication.

This we publish, declare, sanction, decreeing that these our letters always are and shall be valid and effective, notwithstanding apostolic constitutions and ordinances, general and special, and everything else whatsoever to the contrary. Wherefore, let nobody infringe or temerariously oppose this page of our abolition, revocation, permission, ordinance, precept, statute, indult, mandate and will. But if anybody shall presume to attempt this let him know that he will incur the indignation of almighty God and of his apostles the blessed Peter and Paul.

Given at Rome at St. Peter's in the year of the incarnation of the Lord 1911, on November the first, the feast of All Saints, in the ninth year of our pontificate.

A. CARDINAL AGLIARDI, CHANCELLOR OF H. R. C.

FR. SEB. CARDINAL MARTINELLI, PREFECT TO THE S. C. R.

VISA
M. RIGGI, C. A., NOT.

ABHINC DUOS ANNOS
MOTU PROPRIO OF POPE PIUS X

OCTOBER 23, 1913

Two years ago, in publishing Our Apostolic Constitution, *Divino Afflatu*, We had especially in sight the recitation, as far as possible in its entirety, of the Psalter on weekdays, and the restoration of the ancient Sunday offices. But Our mind was occupied with many other projects—some mere plans, others already on the way to realization—relating to the reform in the Roman Breviary.

However, because of the numerous difficulties preventing Us from executing them, We had to postpone them for a more favorable moment. To change the composition of the Breviary to make it in accordance with Our desires, that is, to give it a finished perfection in every part, would involve:

- restoring the calendar of the Universal Church to its original arrangement and style, retaining meanwhile the splendid richness which the marvelous fruitfulness of the Church, the Mother of Saints, has brought to bear upon it;

- utilizing appropriate passages of Scripture, of the Fathers and Doctors, after having reestablished the authentic text;

- prudently correcting the lives of the Saints according to documentary evidence;

- perfecting the arrangement of numerous points of the liturgy, eliminating superfluous elements.

But in the judgment of wise and learned persons, all this would require considerable work and time. For this reason, many years will have to pass before this type of liturgical edifice, composed with intelligent care for the Spouse of Christ to express her piety and faith, can appear purified of the imperfections brought by time, newly resplendent with dignity and fitting order.

In the meantime, through correspondence and conversations with a number of bishops, We have learned of their urgent desire—shared by many priests—to find in the Breviary, together with the new arrangement of the Psalter and its rubrics, all the changes which already have come or which might come with this new Psalter.

They have repeatedly asked Us, indeed they have repeatedly manifested their earnest desire that the new psalter be used more often, that the Sundays be observed more conscientiously, that provision be made for the inconvenience of transferred offices, and that certain other changes be effected which seem to be justified.

Because they are grounded in objectivity and completely conform to Our desire, we have agreed to these requests and We believe that the moment has come to grant them.

DIVINI CULTUS SANCTITATEM
THE HOLINESS OF
DIVINE LITURGY

APOSTOLIC CONSTITUTION
PIUS XI
DECEMBER 20, 1928

AN OVERVIEW OF *DIVINI CULTUS SANCTITATEM*

S. Judith M. Kubicki, CSSF

THE APOSTOLIC CONSTITUTION

Pius XI wrote the apostolic constitution, *Divini cultus sanctitatem* (DCS) (December 20, 1928), to commemorate the twenty-fifth anniversary of Pius X's *motu proprio*, *Tra le sollecitudini* (TLS) (November 22, 1903). This apostolic constitution reiterates and amplifies several key principles promulgated in the 1903 *motu proprio*, including the importance of active participation, the primacy of the voice (clergy, choirs, and congregation) in worship, the appropriateness of the organ, and the pre-eminence of Gregorian chant and sacred music.

An apostolic constitution is the most solemn form of a document issued by a pope in his own name. It may deal with both doctrinal and disciplinary matters regarding either the universal or a particular Church. The introduction to DCS makes several references to history and the Church's tradition regarding public prayer and her liturgical chants. In reviewing the works of his predecessors, Pius XI affirms that they had been as solicitous to safeguard the liturgy and preserve it from adulteration, as they had been to provide accurate expression of the dogmas of faith.

The primary focus of DCS is promoting the observance of prescriptions concerning Gregorian chant and sacred music in order to promote the piety and active participation of the faithful. In addition, its reformist agenda hopes to remove the secular or theatrical influences that had gradually crept into worship.

SIGNIFICANT LITURGICAL CHANGES

DCS does not offer significant changes to earlier liturgical documents. For the most part, it re-emphasizes the principles of TLS with some amplification. The introduction to DCS emphasizes the prescriptive nature of TLS when it observes that the "wise laws" of the 1903 document "have not been fully observed."[1] It strongly urges "scrupulous"[2] observance and obedience to the earlier work. Regarding education in Gregorian chant and sacred music, DCS restates earlier principles and makes more specific points regarding seminary curriculum, choir schools for boys, and music's major role in prayer. It also makes special mention of the Pontifical Institute of Sacred Music, urging bishops to send their best seminarians to study there.[3]

---

1. *Divini cultus sanctitatem* (DCS), introductory paragraph 5.
2. Ibid., introductory paragraph 6.
3. Ibid., 11.

DCS (1928) is part of an important series of documents about the role of liturgical music that appear over six decades, from TLS (1903) to *Sacrosanctum Concilium* (SC, 1963). Other writings, and finally SC, pick up on many of the themes of DCS, including its reiteration of Pius X's promotion of active participation of the entire congregation. By reiterating this principle, DCS intimates that it has not been observed in actual practice in most places. SC 115 reiterates the importance of education and training in liturgy and sacred music expressed in DCS and other documents. There is one addition, however. SC 115 encourages the establishment of higher institutes of sacred music wherever possible, not just in Rome.

DCS is very clear in its position regarding the genres or styles of music and use of instruments appropriate to the Sacred Liturgy. SC both affirms and builds on DCS, adding new perspectives. Gregorian chant and sacred music (polyphony as exemplified by Palestrina) is clearly endorsed as the ideal.[4] However, other kinds of sacred music are by no means excluded.[5] In addition, religious singing and the musical traditions of people in mission lands are to be given suitable roles. This includes the use of instruments other than the organ.[6]

HISTORICAL CONTEXT

When Pius XI wrote DCS, several developments were occurring both within the Church and in the broader world of music. Within the Church, these included theological renewal, a social action movement, a Catholic Action association, a biblical study movement, an ecumenical movement, and a liturgical movement.[7] Furthermore, the musical world had moved beyond Palestrina in terms of both genre and musical texture. DCS does not mention classical polyphony composed after Palestrina as had TLS. Paragraph five of DCS's introduction laments the use of music inappropriate for worship on the occasion of the centenaries of the death of Beethoven (1927) and of Schubert (1928). This has been interpreted as an implicit rejection of the Viennese classical school of church music.[8] Pius XI is highly critical of these performances "which, however excellent, are entirely out of keeping with the sacredness of the place and of the liturgy."[9]

Pius XI admits that his document was influenced by requests emerging from musical congresses, especially the one that met in Rome. While the requests are not specified, the topics covered suggest that complaints had been made regarding the lack of faithful observance to many elements of TLS. In fact, little progress had been made in promoting the active participation of the faithful through the necessary training in singing chant in most places. Furthermore, Pius XI's insistence that liturgical regulations are more than suggestions or

---

4. See *Sacrosanctum Concilium* (SC), 116–117.

5. See ibid., 116.

6. See ibid., 118–120.

7. James Hansen, "Divini Cultus (On Divine Worship)," in *The Song of the Assembly: Pastoral Music in Practice* (Portland, OR: Pastoral Press), p. 5.

8. Anthony Ruff, osb. *Sacred Music and Liturgical Reform: Treasures and Transformations* (Chicago, IL: Hillenbrand Books, 2007), pp. 289–290.

9. DCS, introductory paragraph 4.

optional guidelines suggests that, generally, they had not been seriously implemented on many levels.

The Church, under papal leadership, was working to preserve the treasury of Gregorian chant and sacred polyphony at the beginning of the twentieth century. At the same time, the cultures of various peoples, both in the West and in other areas where the Church was growing, were developing new styles of musical performance, both vocally and instrumentally. Trying to keep these out of the liturgy was an uphill battle.

IMPACT ON THE LIFE OF THE CHURCH

While DCS did not propose significant changes to previous papal legislation regarding liturgical music, it did keep the ideals of active participation, the essential role of music in worship, and the necessity of advanced education in music and liturgy, especially for clergy, in the forefront of the Church's imagination. Its strong preference for the organ as sole liturgical instrument (in addition to the human voice) likely abated efforts in some places to expand instrumental resources. Nevertheless, the insistent affirmation of the active participation of the people in DCS indicates the growing influence of the Liturgical Movement and points to its fuller implementation at the Second Vatican Council.

DIVINI CULTUS SANCTITATEM
APOSTOLIC CONSTITUTION OF POPE PIUS XI

DECEMBER 20, 1928

Since the Church has received from Christ her Founder the office of safeguarding the sanctity of divine worship, it is certainly incumbent upon her, while leaving intact the substance of the Sacrifice and the sacraments, to prescribe ceremonies, rites, formulas, prayers and chant for the proper regulation of that august public ministry, so rightly called the liturgy, or the eminently "sacred action." For the liturgy is indeed a sacred thing, since by it we are raised to God and united to Him, thereby professing our faith and our deep obligation to Him for the benefits we have received and the help of which we stand in constant need. There is thus a close connection between dogma and the sacred liturgy, and between Christian worship and the sanctification of the faithful. Hence Pope Celestine I saw the standard of faith expressed in the sacred formulas of the liturgy. "The rule of our faith," he says, "is indicated by the law of our worship. When those who are set over the Christian people fulfill the function committed to them, they plead the cause of the human race in the sight of God's clemency, and pray and supplicate in conjunction with the whole Church."

These public prayers, called at first "the work of God" and later "the divine office" or the daily "debt" which man owes to God, used to be offered both day and night in the presence of a great concourse of the faithful. From the earliest times the simple chants which graced the sacred prayers and the liturgy gave a wonderful impulse to the piety of the people. History tells us how in the ancient basilicas, where bishop, clergy and people alternately sang the divine praises, the liturgical chant played no small part in converting many barbarians to Christianity and civilization. It was in the churches that heretics came to understand more fully the meaning of the communion of saints; thus the Emperor Valens, an Arian, being present at Mass celebrated by St. Basil, was overcome by an extraordinary seizure and fainted. At Milan St. Ambrose was accused by heretics of attracting the crowds by means of liturgical chants, and it was due to these that St. Augustine made up his mind to become a Christian. It was in the churches, finally, where practically the whole city formed a great joint choir, that the workers, builders, artists, sculptors and writers gained from the liturgy that deep knowledge of theology which is so apparent in the monuments of the Middle Ages.

No wonder, then, that the Roman Pontiffs have been so solicitous to safeguard and protect the liturgy. They have used the same care in making laws for the regulation of the liturgy, in preserving it from adulteration, as they have in giving accurate expression to the dogmas of the faith. This is the reason why the Fathers made both spoken and written commentary upon the liturgy or "the law of worship"; for this reason the Council of Trent ordained that the liturgy should be expounded and explained to the faithful.

In our times too, the chief object of Pope Pius X, in the Motu proprio which he issued twenty-five years ago, making certain prescriptions concerning Gregorian chant and sacred music, was to arouse and foster a Christian spirit in the faithful, by wisely excluding all that might ill befit the sacredness and majesty of our churches. The faithful come to church in order to derive piety from its chief source, by taking an active part in the venerated mysteries and the public solemn prayers of the Church. It is of the utmost importance, therefore, that anything that is used to adorn the liturgy should be controlled by the Church, so that the arts may take their proper place as most noble ministers in sacred worship. Far from resulting in a loss to art, such an arrangement will certainly make for the greater splendor and dignity of the arts that are used in the Church. This has been especially true of sacred music. Wherever the regulations on this subject have been carefully observed, a new life has been given to this delightful art, and the spirit of religion has prospered; the faithful have gained a deeper understanding of the sacred liturgy, and have taken part with greater zest in the ceremonies of the Mass, in the singing of the psalms and the public prayers. Of this we ourself had happy experience when, in the first year of our pontificate, we celebrated Solemn Mass in the Vatican Basilica to the noble accompaniment of a choir of clerics of all nationalities, singing in Gregorian chant.

It is, however, to be deplored that these most wise laws in some places have not been fully observed, and therefore their intended results not obtained. We know that some have declared these laws, though so solemnly promulgated, were not binding upon their obedience. Others obeyed them at first, but have since come gradually to give countenance to a type of music which should be altogether banned from our churches. In some cases, especially when the memory of some famous musician was being celebrated, the opportunity has been taken of performing in church certain works which, however excellent, should never have been performed there, since they were entirely out of keeping with the sacredness of the place and of the liturgy.

In order to urge the clergy and faithful to a more scrupulous observance of these laws and directions which are to be carefully obeyed by the whole Church, we think it opportune to set down here something of the fruits of our experience during the last twenty-five years. This we do the more willingly because in this year we celebrate not only the memory of the reform of sacred music to which we have referred, but also the centenary of the monk Guido of Arezzo. Nine hundred years ago Guido, at the bidding of the pope, came to Rome and produced his wonderful invention,[1] whereby the ancient and traditional liturgical chants might be more easily published, circulated and preserved intact for posterity—to the great benefit and glory of the Church and of art. It was in the Lateran Palace that Gregory the Great, having made his famous collection of the traditional treasures of plainsong, editing them with additions of his own,

---

1. That is, the system of staff-notation—Tr.

had wisely founded his great *Schola* in order to perpetuate the true interpretation of the liturgical chant. It was in the same building that the monk Guido gave a demonstration of his marvelous invention before the Roman clergy and the Roman pontiff himself. The pope, by his approbation and high praise of it, was responsible for the gradual spread of the new system throughout the whole world, and thus for the great advantages that accrued therefrom to musical art in general.

We wish, then, to make certain recommendations to the bishops and ordinaries, whose duty it is, since they are the custodians of the liturgy, to promote ecclesiastical art. We are thus acceding to the requests which, as a result of many musical congresses and especially that recently held at Rome, have been made to us by not a few bishops and learned masters in the musical art. To these we accord due need of praise; and we ordain that the following directions, as hereunder set forth, with the practical methods indicated, be put into effect.

1.   All those who aspire to the priesthood, whether in seminaries or in religious houses, from their earliest years are to be taught Gregorian chant and sacred music. At that age they are able more easily to learn to sing, and to modify, if not entirely to overcome, any defects in their voices, which in later years would be quite incurable. Instruction in music and singing must be begun in the elementary, and continued in the higher classes. In this way, those who are about to receive sacred orders, having gradually experienced in chant, will be able during their theological course quite easily to undertake the higher and "esthetic" study of plainsong and sacred music, of polyphony and the organ, concerning which the clergy certainly ought to have a thorough knowledge.

2.   In seminaries, and in other houses of study for the formation of the clergy, both secular and regular, there should be a frequent and almost daily lecture or practice—however short—in Gregorian chant and sacred music. If this is carried out in the spirit of the liturgy, the students will find it a relief rather than a burden to their minds, after the study of the more exacting subjects. Thus a more complete education of both branches of the clergy in liturgical music will result in the restoration to its former dignity and splendor of the choral office, a most important part of divine worship; moreover, the *scholae* and choirs will be invested again with their ancient glory.

3.   Those who are responsible for and engaged in divine worship in basilicas and cathedrals, in collegiate and conventual churches of religious, should use all their endeavors to see that the choral office is carried out duly—i.e. in accordance with the prescriptions of the Church. And this, not only as regards the precept of reciting the divine office "worthily, attentively and devoutly," but also as regards the chant. In singing the psalms attention should be paid to the right tone, with its appropriate mediation and termination, and a suitable pause at the asterisk; so that every verse of the psalms and every strophe of the hymns may be sung by all in perfect time together. If this were rightly observed, then all who worthily sing the psalms would signify their unity of intention in worshipping God and, as one side of the choir sings in answer to the other, would

seem to emulate the ever-lasting praise of the Seraphim who cried one to the other "Holy, Holy, Holy."

4.   Lest anyone in future should invent easy excuses for exempting himself from obedience to the law of the Church, let every chapter and religious community deal with these matters at meetings held for the purpose; and just as formerly there used to be a *Cantor* or director of the choir, so in future let one be chosen from each chapter or choir of religious, whose duty it will be to see that the rules of the liturgy and of choral chant are observed and, both individually and generally, to correct the faults of the choir. In this connection it should be observed that, according to the ancient discipline of the Church and the constitutions of chapters still in force, all those at least who are bound to office in choir are obliged to be familiar with Gregorian chant. And the Gregorian chant which is to be used in every church, of whatever order, is the text which, revised according to the ancient manuscripts, has been authentically published by the Church from the Vatican press.

5.   We wish here to recommend, to those whom it may concern, the formation of choirs. These in the course of time came to replace the ancient *scholae* and were established in the basilicas and greater churches especially for the singing of polyphonic music. Sacred polyphony, We may here remark, is rightly held second only to Gregorian chant. We are desirous, therefore, that such choirs, as they flourished from the fourteenth to the sixteenth century, should now also be created anew and prosper, especially in churches where the scale on which the liturgy is carried out demands a greater number and a more careful selection of singers.

6.   Choir schools for boys should be established not only for the greater churches and cathedrals, but also for smaller parish churches. The boys should be taught by the choirmaster to sing properly, so that, in accordance with the ancient custom of the Church, they may sing in the choir with the men, especially as in polyphonic music the highest part, the *cantus*, ought to be sung by boys. Choirboys, especially in the sixteenth century, have given us masters of polyphony: first and foremost among them the great Palestrina.

7.   As we have learned that in some places an attempt is being made to reintroduce a type of music which is not entirely in keeping with the performance of the sacred office, particularly owing to the excessive use made of musical instruments, we hereby declare that singing with orchestral accompaniment is not regarded by the Church as a more perfect form of music or as more suitable for sacred purposes. Voices, rather than instruments, ought to be heard in the church: the voices of the clergy, the choir and the congregation. Nor should it be deemed that the Church, in preferring the human voice to any musical instrument, is obstructing the progress of music; for no instrument, however perfect, however excellent, can surpass the human voice in expressing human thought, especially when it is used by the mind to offer up prayer and praise to almighty God.

8.   The traditionally appropriate musical instrument of the Church is the organ, which, by reason of its extraordinary grandeur and majesty, has been considered a worthy adjunct to the liturgy, whether for accompanying the chant or, when the choir is silent, for playing harmonious music at the prescribed times. But here too must be avoided that mixture of the profane with the sacred which, through the fault partly of organmakers and partly of certain performers who are partial to the singularities of modern music, may result eventually in diverting this magnificent instrument from the purpose for which it is intended. We wish, within the limits prescribed by the liturgy, to encourage the development of all that concerns the organ; but we cannot but lament the fact that, as in the case of certain types of music which the Church has rightly forbidden in the past, so now attempts are being made to introduce a profane spirit into the Church by modern forms of music; which forms, if they begin to enter in, the Church would likewise be bound to condemn. Let our churches resound with organ music that gives expression to the majesty of the edifice and breathes the sacredness of the religious rites; in this way will the art both of those who build the organs and of those who play them flourish afresh, and render effective service to the sacred liturgy.

9.   In order that the faithful may more actively participate in divine worship, let them be made once more to sing the Gregorian chant, so far as it belongs to them to take part in it. It is most important that when the faithful assist at the sacred ceremonies, or when pious sodalities take part with the clergy in a procession, they should not be merely detached and silent spectators, but, filled with a deep sense of the beauty of the liturgy, should sing alternately with the clergy or the choir, as it is prescribed. If this is done, then it will no longer happen that the people either make no answer at all to the public prayers—whether in the language of the liturgy or in the vernacular—or at best utter the responses in a low and subdued manner.

10.   Let the clergy, both secular and regular, under the lead of their bishops and ordinaries, devote their energies either directly or through other trained teachers, to instructing the people in the liturgy and in music, as being matters closely associated with Christian doctrine. This will be best effected by teaching liturgical chant in schools, pious confraternities and similar associations. Religious communities of men or women should devote particular attention to the achievement of this purpose in the various educational institutions committed to their care. Moreover, we are confident that this object will be greatly furthered by those societies which, under the control of ecclesiastical authority, are striving to reform sacred music according to the laws of the Church.

11.   To achieve all that we hope for in this matter numerous trained teachers will be required. And in this connection we accord due praise to all the schools and institutes throughout the Catholic world which, by giving careful instruction in these subjects, are forming good and suitable teachers. But we have a special word of commendation for the Pontifical Higher School of Sacred Music, founded in Rome in the year 1910. This school, which was greatly encouraged by Pope Benedict XV and was by him endowed with new privileges, is most

particularly favored by us; for we regard it as a precious heritage left to us by two sovereign pontiffs, and we therefore wish to recommend it in a special way to all the bishops.

We are well aware that the fulfillment of these injunctions will entail great trouble and labor. But do we not all know how many artistic works our forefathers, undaunted by difficulties, have handed down to posterity, imbued as they were with pious zeal and with the spirit of the liturgy? Nor is this to be wondered at; for anything that is the fruit of the interior life of the Church surpasses even the most perfect works of this world. Let the difficulties of this sacred task, far from deterring, rather stimulate and encourage the bishops of the Church, who, by their universal and unfailing obedience to our behests, will render to the sovereign bishop a service most worthy of their episcopal office.

These things we command, declare and sanction, decreeing that this apostolic constitution be now and in the future firm, valid and efficacious, that it obtain full and complete effect, all things to the contrary notwithstanding. Let no man therefore infringe this constitution by us promulgated, nor dare to contravene it.

Given at St. Peter's, Rome, on the fiftieth anniversary of our ordination to the priesthood, the twentieth day of December in the year 1928, the seventh of our pontificate.

ANDREAS CARDINAL FRUHWIRTH
CANCELLARIUS S.R.E.

CAMILLUS CARDINAL LAURENTI
S.R.C. PRO-PRAEFECTUS

JOSEPHUS WILPERT
DECANUS COLL. PROTON. APOSTOLICORUM

DOMINICUS SPOLVERINI
PROTONOTARIUS APOSTOLICUS

MYSTICI CORPORIS CHRISTI
ON THE
MYSTICAL BODY OF CHRIST

ENCYCLICAL
POPE PIUS XII
JUNE 29, 1943

AN OVERVIEW OF *MYSTICI CORPORIS CHRISTI*

Rev. Richard Fragomeni

The year 1943 was marked with significant worldwide disorder. The Second World War was raging and the Nazi concentration camps were in full force. Nations around the globe were in political upheaval, as the social order rapidly changed with the redefinition of power and control and national boundaries. In such a disordered time, the reigning Roman Pontiff, Pius XII, published on June 29, 1943 his fourth encyclical, *Mystici Corporis Christi* (MCC). Giving official credence to an image of the Church that was current in theological circles of time,[1] it is addressed to the patriarchs, primates, archbishops, bishops, and other local ordinaries, who enjoy communion with the pope. As the Greek origin of the word *encyclical* suggests—a circular letter—MCC was circulated among these hierarchs alone. This was the ordinary custom of the era. Papal encyclicals were addressed to hierarchs, who would, in turn, be charged with the task of implementation of the content by study and dissemination among the presbyters and people in their charge. It was with the writings of Pope John XXIII that encyclicals began to be consistently addressed to the whole Church and to others, who, while not members of the Church, would be considered by the pope significant addressees of the pope's message. Addressing a wider audience than simply the hierarchs has now become the customary way of designating the readership of these papal missives.

This essay will introduce the reader to MCC. It proceeds in two parts. First, an overview of the document is offered to acquaint the reader with the major themes of the text. Second, certain observations and questions about the encyclical are given as a way of prompting the reader to think about the implications of MCC for liturgical practice in the twenty-first century.

An Overview of Mystici Corporis Christi

The Latin text of MCC, found on the Vatican website, has no section headings to assist the reader in understanding the topical flow of the text. The paragraphs are numbered, however.

When one reads the text, certain paragraphs seem to flow in such a way as to create an outline of the message that is presented. When MCC was first published in English, several such outlines were created. What follows here is informed by the outline of the encyclical, offered by the National Catholic Welfare Conference in its 1943 publication of the translated English text:[2]

---

1. See Emil Mersche, *The Theology of the Mystical Body,* translated by C. Vollert (St. Louis, MO: Herder, 1951). First appeared in French, 1933.

2. Please note that the National Catholic Welfare Conference is now the United States Conference of Catholic Bishops.

INTRODUCTION

In paragraphs 1 to 11 of MCC, a general introduction is given. The reasons why the pontiff writes this encyclical are offered. At the start, there is the acknowledgment that the world is in turbulent times and that what is needed is faith in God's providence:

> For We know that if all the sorrows and calamities of these stormy times, by which countless multitudes are being sorely tried, are accepted from God's hands with calm submission, they naturally lift souls above the passing things of earth to those of heaven that abide forever, and arouse a certain secret thirst and intense desire for spiritual things.[3]

The gift of the Holy Spirit is acknowledged and the recognition that in the Spirit, the Church is a source of admiration to the world because of the unity it demonstrates in a time of war and division, nation against nation. To this end, the doctrine of the Mystical Body of Christ will offer inspiration even to those not part of the Church.[4]

In paragraph 8, the chief reason for the writing of the encyclical is offered:

> But the chief reason for Our present exposition of this sublime doctrine is Our solicitude for the souls entrusted to Us. Much indeed has been written on this subject; and We know that many today are turning with greater zest to a study which delights and nourishes Christian piety. This, it would seem, is chiefly because a revived interest in the sacred liturgy, the more widely spread custom of frequent Communion, and the more fervent devotion to the Sacred Heart of Jesus practiced today, have brought many souls to a deeper consideration of the unsearchable riches of Christ which are preserved in the Church.[5]

For the pontiff the document is prompted toward a continuing encouragement to engage in the depth of the mysteries of Christ in both the liturgy and in popular religious practices.

PART I

After these introductory paragraphs, the first major part of the encyclical, paragraphs 12 to 66, develops the theology of the Church as the Mystical Body of Christ.

---

3. *Mystici Corporis Christi* (MCC), 4.
4. See ibid., 5–6.
5. Ibid., 8.

The beginning paragraphs of this section, 12 to 24, encompass a variety of subjects: The Church is a body that is one, undivided and visible; she is constituted both organically and hierarchically and endowed with the sacraments as a means to salvation; and she is composed of individual members, who have been baptized and possess the true faith. While the Church is a society and a social body, she has a transcendent nature to her as the Body of Christ.

This continues with an extended exposition of the Church as the Body of Christ.[6] This exposition begins with the claim that Christ is the founder of the Body by his preaching of the Gospel, by his suffering on the Cross, and by the giving of the Spirit at Pentecost. Thus, Christ is also the Head of the Body by reason of his preeminence:

> And first of all it is clear that the Son of God and of the Blessed Virgin is to be called the head of the Church by reason of His singular preeminence. For the Head is in the highest place. But who is in a higher place than Christ God, who as the Word of the Eternal Father must be acknowledged to be the "firstborn of every creature?" Who has reached more lofty heights than Christ Man who, though born of the Immaculate Virgin, is the true and natural Son of God, and in virtue of His miraculous and glorious resurrection, a resurrection triumphant over death, has become the "firstborn of the dead?"[7]

In this preeminence, Christ also governs the Church both invisibly and visibly by the pope who has been appointed by Christ. The claim is made that Christ and the pontiff constitute one only Head of the Body:

> That Christ and His Vicar constitute one only Head is the solemn teaching of Our predecessor of immortal memory Boniface VIII in the Apostolic Letter Unam Sanctam; and his successors have never ceased to repeat the same.[8]

In such a claim, the assertion is made that the invisible Head of the Body is made visible so that the haven of eternal salvation may be easily seen and found by all seekers of truth.

The remainder of this section elaborates an ecclesiology grounded in an understating of Christ and the Holy Spirit. While Christ is the Head of the Body, the Holy Spirit, flowing throughout the members of the Body, is the Soul of the Church.

> Finally, while by His grace He provides for the continual growth of the Church, He yet refuses to dwell through sanctifying grace in those members that are wholly severed from the Body. This presence and activity of the Spirit of Jesus Christ is tersely and vigorously described by Our predecessor of immortal memory Leo XIII in his Encyclical Letter Divinum Illud in these words: "Let it suffice to say that, as Christ is the Head of the Church, so is the Holy Spirit her soul."[9]

---

6. See ibid., 25–59.

7. Ibid., 36.

8. Ibid., 40.

9. Ibid., 57.

Paragraphs 60 to 66 specifically offer the rationale for the Church being the "Mystical" Body of Christ. After speaking of the physical Body of Christ, born of the Virgin, and of the Body of the Church, which is a social body, whose Head and Ruler is Christ and his Vicar, the encyclical moves into a deliberate proposition: the Church is more than a social body, as the Body of Christ she is a Mystical Body. Again, the Holy Spirit is portrayed as the essential force that enlivens the Church and distinguishes her from any other social, moral, or juridical body. The unifying gift of the Spirit of God fills and unifies the Church as the Mystical Body. In this, the Church is portrayed as more than a structure of hierarchical power, it is a living Mystical Body, a communion in Christ of all the members.

PART II

With paragraph 67, the second part of MCC begins and extends to paragraph 84. The union of the faithful with Christ is addressed with some proofs based on tradition for such closeness and communion. The end of this communion is identified: "the continual sanctifying of the members of the Body for the glory of God and of the Lamb what was slain."[10] The working of the Spirit is again emphasized and the holiness of the community is raised up as the noble end of the communion.

The movement, indwelling, and action of the Spirit is even more strongly acknowledged:

> This communication of the Spirit of Christ is the channel through which all the gifts, powers, and extraordinary graces found superabundantly in the Head as in their source flow into all the members of the Church, and are perfected daily in them according to the place they hold in the Mystical Body of Jesus Christ. Thus the Church becomes, as it were, the filling out and the complement of the Redeemer, while Christ in a sense attains through the Church a fullness in all things.[11]

Acknowledging that the Eucharist is the symbol of unity among the members of the Mystical Body, he acknowledges the importance of the sacred minister, the priest, who acts as a "viceregent not only of our Savior but of the whole Mystical Body and of each of the faithful."[12]

This second part concludes reminding the reader of the "sad and anxious times through which we are passing," and extolling the more frequent reception and reverence for the Eucharist, "which not infrequently makes Christians into heroes."[13]

---

10. Ibid., 68.
11. Ibid., 77.
12. Ibid., 82.
13. Ibid., 84.

The pastoral exhortation of Part III is a series of practical ways in which the members of the Mystical Body of Christ can come to authentic clarity of word and action in the world.

First, the document identifies certain errors that impact the spiritual life of Christians: false mysticism and quietism.

Second, the encyclical encourages frequent confession. In this regard, young clergy are admonished to encourage the faithful to confess their venial sins, and not simply their mortal sins. The reason for this practice of frequent confession is given:

> By it genuine self-knowledge is increased, Christian humility grows, bad habits are corrected, spiritual neglect and tepidity are resisted, the conscience is purified, the will strengthened, a salutary self-control is attained, and grace is increased in virtue of the Sacrament itself. Let those, therefore, among the younger clergy who make light of or lessen esteem for frequent confession realize that what they are doing is alien to the Spirit of Christ and disastrous for the Mystical Body of our Savior.[14]

Third, prayer of all kinds is encouraged: petitionary prayer and prayer to Christ. Of note, is the encouragement to practice mental prayer, the custom and practice of many holy men and women.

There continues with an exhortation to love the Church. The hidden and mysterious union of Christ with the members of the Church offers an incentive to love the Mystical Body:

> For nothing more glorious, nothing nobler, nothing surely more honorable can be imagined than to belong to the One, Holy Catholic, Apostolic and Roman Church, in which we become members of One Body as venerable as it is unique; are guided by one supreme Head; are filled with one divine Spirit; are nourished during our earthly exile by one doctrine and one heavenly Bread, until at last we enter into the one, unending blessedness of heaven.[15]

The faithful are encouraged to love the liturgy and the sacraments, the solemn ceremonies, the chant, the devotions, the sacramentals, and exercises of piety. These can become the source of consolation and hope in troubled times.

In return for such consolation that is offered, the faithful are also encouraged to love and obey the legitimate authority of those to whom they are entrusted in the church: the clergy, bishops, and the pope.

Loving and caring for the poor and the weak is held up as an essential part of Christian living. Here, Christ is given as the exemplar of such love and charity:

> In order to guard against the gradual weakening of that sincere love which requires us to see our Savior in the Church and in its members, it is most fitting that we should look to Jesus Himself as a perfect model of love for the Church.[16]

---

14. Ibid., 88.
15. Ibid., 91.
16. Ibid., 95.

At the end of Part III, the encyclical asks for continuous prayer for rulers of nations and for the members of the Church, especially for bishops and priests, priestly vocations, and for those who are being instructed for Baptism. Prayers for those who are not yet members of the Church are also encouraged.

Religious freedom, socially, and the freedom to choose a religious path, individually, are to be respected and protected. And a final word of encouragement is given to those who suffer, so that they may bear suffering and offer it to God:

> With the heart of a father We exhort all those who from whatever cause are plunged in grief and anguish to lift their eyes trustfully to heaven and to offer their sorrows to Him who will one day reward them abundantly. Let them all remember that their sufferings are not in vain, but that they will turn to their own immense gain and that of the Church, if to this end they bear them with patience.[17]

CONCLUSION

MCC concludes with paragraphs 110–113. In this conclusion, the Blessed Virgin Mary is invoked: "May she throw about the Church today, as in times gone by, the mantle of her protection and obtain from God that now at least the Church and all mankind may enjoy more peaceful days."[18]

Some Observations and Questions

While MCC does not directly deal with liturgical practice and norms, it, nevertheless, sets up an ecclesial vision that becomes the matrix for liturgical renewal that is developed later in Pius XII's 1947 encyclical, *Mediator Dei*, and in the liturgical renewal of the Second Vatican Council.

This matrix enriches the Catholic imagination from perceiving the Church as a Perfect Society, *Societas Perfecta*, simply a social body, where the hierarchical structure is identified as the Church, into a Mystical Body, where organically all are part of the Body of Christ.

The document's emphasis on the Holy Spirit working in the Church reintroduces an interest in the Spirit's operation in the life of the community and in the sacraments. The presence of the Holy Spirit becomes part of the ecclesial matrix and opens the way for the re-introduction of the Spirit in epiclesis prayers over offerings and community that is introduced by the revised liturgical texts of the Second Vatican Council.

This vision is then taken into the Second Vatican Council and becomes an essential element in the renewal of the liturgical rites. The baptismal priesthood, also called the royal priesthood, together with the ordained or ministerial priesthood, are engaged together in liturgy as the "source and summit of the Christian life."[19]

---

17. Ibid., 107.
18. Ibid., 111.
19. *Lumen gentium* (LG), 11.

Since World War II was raging at the time of its promulgation, MCC did not seem to be widely received in the Church. However, after the war, together with both *Divino afflante spiritu*, issued by Pius XII a few months after MCC, on September 30, 1943, which opened the door to historical critical methods in biblical studies and translations, and with *Mediator Dei*, this trio of texts opened up new modes of liturgical participation for the faithful. This included the revision of the liturgies of Holy Week and what is called the "Dialogue Mass."

Shortly after in Europe, the National Lay Apostolic Group and was formed after the First World Congress for the Apostolate of the Laity held in Rome in October 1951.

In 1972, Pope Paul VI in his, *motu proprio, Ministeria quaedam*, reconfigured the liturgical ministries of the Roman Church, making both lector and acolyte lay ministries. While consigning these officially over to men only, the function of these ministries continue to be shared by both laymen and laywomen.

The ecclesial matrix established by MCC brought forward a debate during the Second Vatican Council: Is the Church of Christ identified with the Roman Catholic Church, as written in MCC, or does the Church of Christ subsist in the Roman Catholic Church, as written in *Lumen gentium*? And, what does "subsist" actually mean?

This raises ecumenical questions, the questions concerning the salvation of non-Catholics, as well as the liturgical participation of Catholics and non-Catholics together. The matrix brought forward the acceptance by the Roman Catholic Church of the Baptisms of non-Catholics. No longer conditionally baptizing them, but receiving them as brothers and sisters, the interest developed in a common Lectionary, common prayer texts, and inter-Communion.

There is but one inconsistency that could be pointed out: in view of MCC's theological vision of ecclesial communion in the Spirit, which deepens relationships with all humanity, especially those in distress, why was there no explicit, forceful and official papal denouncing of the Holocaust, reaching its pinnacle of destruction at the time this encyclical was published? This is a curious question. In the renewal of the Liturgy, since the Second Vatican Council, a clearer link between the liturgy of the Church and the works of justice and charity has been made, to the point of declaring that any celebration of the Eucharist not linked to just and charitable action is inauthentic. [20]

MCC was a watershed document. Promulgated during a time of disruption and fear, it offered a hope of order and a narrative of a mystical world, where God is all in all. To this end it served the Church and offered a fresh image of the Body of Christ in its fullness in a darkened time. It was the freshness of this image that laid the groundwork for the renewal of the liturgy and for the gratefulness this author feels to Pius XII.

---

20. *Mane Nobiscum Domine*, 28.

MYSTICI CORPORIS CHRISTI
ENCYCLICAL OF POPE PIUS XII
ON THE MYSTICAL BODY OF CHRIST

TO OUR VENERABLE BRETHREN, PATRIARCHS, PRIMATES, ARCHBISHOPS, BISHOPS, AND OTHER LOCAL ORDINARIES ENJOYING PEACE AND COMMUNION WITH THE APOSTOLIC SEE

Venerable Brethren,
Health and Apostolic Benediction.

The doctrine of the Mystical Body of Christ, which is the Church,[1] was first taught us by the Redeemer Himself. Illustrating as it does the great and inestimable privilege of our intimate union with so exalted a Head, this doctrine by its sublime dignity invites all those who are drawn by the Holy Spirit to study it, and gives them, in the truths of which it proposes to the mind, a strong incentive to the performance of such good works as are conformable to its teaching. For this reason, We deem it fitting to speak to you on this subject through this Encyclical Letter, developing and explaining above all, those points which concern the Church Militant. To this We are urged not only by the surpassing grandeur of the subject but also by the circumstances of the present time.

2.   For We intend to speak of the riches stored up in this Church which Christ purchased with His own Blood,[2] and whose members glory in a thorn-crowned Head. The fact that they thus glory is a striking proof that the greatest joy and exaltation are born only of suffering, and hence that we should rejoice if we partake of the sufferings of Christ, that when His glory shall be revealed we may also be glad with exceeding joy.[3]

3.   From the outset it should be noted that the society established by the Redeemer of the human race resembles its divine Founder, who was persecuted, calumniated and tortured by those very men whom He had undertaken to save. We do not deny, rather from a heart filled with gratitude to God We admit, that even in our turbulent times there are many who, though outside the fold of Jesus Christ, look to the Church as the only haven of salvation; but We are also aware that the Church of God not only is despised and hated maliciously by those who shut their eyes to the light of Christian wisdom and miserably return to the teachings, customs and practices of ancient paganism, but is ignored and neglected,

---

1. Cf. *Col.* I, 24.
2. *Acts*, XX, 28.
3. Cf. I Peter, IV, 13.

and even at times looked upon as irksome by many Christians who are allured by specious error or caught in the meshes of the world's corruption. In obedience, therefore, Venerable Brethren, to the voice of Our conscience and in compliance with the wishes of many, We will set forth before the eyes of all and extol the beauty, the praises, and the glory of Mother Church to whom, after God, we owe everything.

4. And it is to be hoped that Our instructions and exhortations will bring forth abundant fruit in the souls of the faithful in the present circumstances. For We know that if all the sorrows and calamities of these stormy times, by which countless multitudes are being sorely tried, are accepted from God's hands with calm submission, they naturally lift souls above the passing things of earth to those of heaven that abide forever, and arouse a certain secret thirst and intense desire for spiritual things. Thus, urged by the Holy Spirit, men are moved, and as it were, impelled to seek the kingdom of God with greater diligence; for the more they are detached from the vanities of this world and from inordinate love of temporal things, the more apt they will be to perceive the light of heavenly mysteries. But the vanity and emptiness of earthly things are more manifest today than perhaps at any other period, when Kingdoms and States are crumbling, when enormous quantities of goods and all kinds of wealth are being sunk in the depths of the sea, and cities, towns and fertile fields are strewn with massive ruins and defiled with the blood of brothers.

5. Moreover, We trust that Our exposition of the doctrine of the Mystical Body of Christ will be acceptable and useful to those also who are without the fold of the Church, not only because their good will toward the Church seems to grow from day to day, but also because, while before their eyes nation rises up against nation, kingdom against kingdom, and discord is sown everywhere together with the seeds of envy and hatred, if they turn their gaze to the Church, if they contemplate her divinely-given unity–by which all men of every race are united to Christ in the bond of brotherhood–they will be forced to admire this fellowship in charity, and with the guidance and assistance of divine grace will long to share in the same union and charity.

6. There is a special reason too, and one most dear to Us, which recalls this doctrine to Our mind and with it a deep sense of joy. During the year that has passed since the twenty-fifth anniversary of Our Episcopal consecration, We have had the great consolation of witnessing something that has made the image of the Mystical Body of Jesus Christ stand out most clearly before the whole world. Though a long and deadly war has pitilessly broken the bond of brotherly union between nations, We have seen Our children in Christ, in whatever part of the world they happened to be, one in will and affection, lift up their hearts to the common Father, who, carrying in his own heart the cares and anxieties of all, is guiding the barque of the Catholic Church in the teeth of a raging tempest. This is a testimony to the wonderful union existing among Christians; but it also proves that, as Our paternal love embraces all peoples, whatever their nationality and race, so Catholics the world over, though their countries may have drawn the sword against each other, look to the Vicar of Jesus Christ as to

the loving Father of them all, who, with absolute impartiality and incorruptible judgment, rising above the conflicting gales of human passions, takes upon himself with all his strength the defense of truth, justice and charity.

7.   We have been no less consoled to know that with spontaneous generosity a fund has been created for the erection of a church in Rome to be dedicated to our saintly predecessor and patron, Eugene I. As this temple, to be built by the wish and through the liberality of all the faithful, will be a lasting memorial of this happy event, so We desire to offer this Encyclical Letter in testimony of Our gratitude. It tells of those living stones which rest upon the living corner-stone, which is Christ, and are built together into a holy temple, far surpassing any temple built by hands, into a habitation of God in the Spirit.[4]

8.   But the chief reason for Our present exposition of this sublime doctrine is Our solicitude for the souls entrusted to Us. Much indeed has been written on this subject; and We know that many today are turning with greater zest to a study which delights and nourishes Christian piety. This, it would seem, is chiefly because a revived interest in the sacred liturgy, the more widely spread custom of frequent Communion, and the more fervent devotion to the Sacred Heart of Jesus practiced today, have brought many souls to a deeper consideration of the unsearchable riches of Christ which are preserved in the Church. Moreover, recent pronouncements on Catholic Action, by drawing closer the bonds of union between Christians and between them and the ecclesiastical hierarchy and especially the Roman Pontiff, have undoubtedly helped not a little to place this truth in its proper light. Nevertheless, while We can derive legitimate joy from these considerations, We must confess that grave errors with regard to this doctrine are being spread among those outside the true Church, and that among the faithful, also, inaccurate or thoroughly false ideas are being disseminated which turn minds aside from the straight path of truth.

9.   For while there still survives a false *rationalism*, which ridicules anything that transcends and defies the power of human genius, and which is accompanied by a cognate error, the so-called *popular naturalism*, which sees and wills to see in the Church nothing but a juridical and social union, there is on the other hand a false *mysticism* creeping in, which, in its attempt to eliminate the immovable frontier that separates creatures from their Creator, falsifies the Sacred Scriptures.

10.   As a result of these conflicting and mutually antagonistic schools of thought, some, through vain fear, look upon so profound a doctrine as something dangerous, and so they shrink from it as from the beautiful but forbidden fruit of paradise. But this is not so. Mysteries revealed by God cannot be harmful to men, nor should they remain as treasures hidden in a field, useless. They have been given from on high precisely to help the spiritual progress of those who study them in a spirit of piety. For, as the Vatican Council teaches, "reason illumined by faith, if it seeks earnestly, piously and wisely, does attain under God, to a certain and most helpful knowledge of mysteries, by considering their analogy

---

4. Cf. *Eph.*, II, 21–22; I *Peter*, II, 5.

with what it knows naturally, and their mutual relations, and their common relations with man's last end," although, as the same holy Synod observes, reason, even thus illumined, "is never capable of understanding those mysteries as it does those truths which forms its proper object."[5]

11.   After pondering all this long and seriously before God We consider it part of Our pastoral duty to explain to the entire flock of Christ through this Encyclical Letter the doctrine of the Mystical Body of Christ and of the union in this Body of the faithful with the divine Redeemer; and then, from this consoling doctrine, to draw certain lessons that will make a deeper study of this mystery bear yet richer fruits of perfection and holiness. Our purpose is to throw an added ray of glory on the supreme beauty of the Church; to bring out into fuller light the exalted supernatural nobility of the faithful who in the Body of Christ are united with their Head; and finally, to exclude definitely the many current errors with regard to this matter.

12.   When one reflects on the origin of this doctrine, there come to mind at once the words of the Apostle: "Where sin abounded, grace did more abound."[6] All know that the father of the whole human race was constituted by God in so exalted a state that he was to hand on to his posterity, together with earthly existence, the heavenly life of divine grace. But after the unhappy fall of Adam, the whole human race, infected by the hereditary stain, lost their participation in the divine nature,[7] and we were all "children of wrath."[8] But the all-merciful God "so loved the world as to give His only-begotten Son,"[9] and the Word of the Eternal Father with the same divine love assumed human nature from the race of Adam—but as an innocent and spotless nature—so that He, as the new Adam, might be the source whence the grace of the Holy Spirit should flow unto all the children of the first parent. Through the sin of the first man they had been excluded from adoption as children of God; through the Word incarnate, made brothers according to the flesh of the only-begotten Son of God, they received also the power to become the sons of God.[10] As He hung upon the Cross, Christ Jesus not only appeased the justice of the Eternal Father which had been violated, but He also won for us, His brethren, an ineffable flow of graces. It was possible for Him of Himself to impart these graces to mankind directly; but He willed to do so only through a visible Church made up of men, so that through her all might cooperate with Him in dispensing the graces of Redemption. As the Word of God willed to make use of our nature, when in excruciating agony He would redeem mankind, so in the same way throughout the centuries He makes use of the Church that the work begun might endure.[11]

---

5. Sessio III; *Const. de fide cath.*, c. 4.

6. *Rom.*, V, 20.

7. Cf. II *Peter*, I, 4.

8. *Eph.*, II, 3.

9. *John*, III, 16.

10. Cf. *John*, I, 12.

11. Cf. Vat. Council, *Const. de Eccl.*, prol.

13.   If we would define and describe this true Church of Jesus Christ—which is the One, Holy, Catholic, Apostolic and Roman Church[12]—we shall find nothing more noble, more sublime, or more divine than the expression "the Mystical Body of Christ"—an expression which springs from and is, as it were, the fair flowering of the repeated teaching of the Sacred Scriptures and the Holy Fathers.

14.   That the Church is a body is frequently asserted in the Sacred Scriptures. "Christ," says the Apostle, "is the Head of the Body of the Church."[13] If the Church is a body, it must be an unbroken unity, according to those words of Paul: "Though many we are one body in Christ."[14] But it is not enough that the Body of the Church should be an unbroken unity; it must also be something definite and perceptible to the senses as Our predecessor of happy memory, Leo XIII, in his Encyclical *Satis Cognitum* asserts: "the Church is visible because she is a body."[15] Hence they err in a matter of divine truth, who imagine the Church to be invisible, intangible, a something merely "pneumatological" as they say, by which many Christian communities, though they differ from each other in their profession of faith, are united by an invisible bond.

15.   But a body calls also for a multiplicity of members, which are linked together in such a way as to help one another. And as in the body when one member suffers, all the other members share its pain, and the healthy members come to the assistance of the ailing, so in the Church the individual members do not live for themselves alone, but also help their fellows, and all work in mutual collaboration for the common comfort and for the more perfect building up of the whole Body.

16.   Again, as in nature a body is not formed by any haphazard grouping of members but must be constituted of organs, that is of members, that have not the same function and are arranged in due order; so for this reason above all the Church is called a body, that it is constituted by the coalescence of structurally united parts, and that it has a variety of members reciprocally dependent. It is thus the Apostle describes the Church when he writes: "As in one body we have many members, but all the members have not the same office: so we being many are one body in Christ, and everyone members one of another."[16]

17.   One must not think, however, that this ordered or "organic" structure of the body of the Church contains only hierarchical elements and with them is complete; or, as an opposite opinion holds, that it is composed only of those who enjoy charismatic gifts—though members gifted with miraculous powers will never be lacking in the Church. That those who exercise sacred power in this Body are its chief members must be maintained uncompromisingly. It is through them, by commission of the Divine Redeemer Himself, that Christ's apostolate as Teacher, King and Priest is to endure. At the same time, when the Fathers of

---

12. Cf. *ibidem, Const. de fide cath.*, c. 1.
13. *Col.*, I, 18.
14. *Rom.*, XII, 5.
15. Cf. *A.S.S.*, XXVIII, p. 710.
16. *Rom.*, XII, 4.

the Church sing the praises of this Mystical Body of Christ, with its ministries, its variety of ranks, its officers, it conditions, its orders, its duties, they are thinking not only of those who have received Holy Orders, but of all those too, who, following the evangelical counsels, pass their lives either actively among men, or hidden in the silence of the cloister, or who aim at combining the active and contemplative life according to their Institute; as also of those who, though living in the world, consecrate themselves wholeheartedly to spiritual or corporal works of mercy, and of those in the state of holy matrimony. Indeed, let this be clearly understood, especially in our days, fathers and mothers of families, those who are godparents through Baptism, and in particular those members of the laity who collaborate with the ecclesiastical hierarchy in spreading the Kingdom of the Divine Redeemer occupy an honorable, if often a lowly, place in the Christian community, and even they under the impulse of God and with His help, can reach the heights of supreme holiness, which, Jesus Christ has promised, will never be wanting to the Church.

18.   Now we see that the human body is given the proper means to provide for its own life, health and growth, and for that of all its members. Similarly, the Savior of mankind out of His infinite goodness has provided in a wonderful way for His Mystical Body, endowing it with the Sacraments, so that, as though by an uninterrupted series of graces, its members should be sustained from birth to death, and that generous provision might be made for the social needs of the Church. Through the waters of Baptism those who are born into this world dead in sin are not only born again and made members of the Church, but being stamped with a spiritual seal they become able and fit to receive the other Sacraments. By the chrism of Confirmation, the faithful are given added strength to protect and defend the Church, their Mother, and the faith she has given them. In the Sacrament of Penance a saving medicine is offered for the members of the Church who have fallen into sin, not only to provide for their own health, but to remove from other members of the Mystical Body all danger of contagion, or rather to afford them an incentive to virtue, and the example of a virtuous act.

19.   Nor is that all; for in the Holy Eucharist the faithful are nourished and strengthened at the same banquet and by a divine, ineffable bond are united with each other and with the Divine Head of the whole Body. Finally, like a devoted mother, the Church is at the bedside of those who are sick unto death; and if it be not always God's will that by the holy anointing she restore health to the mortal body, nevertheless she administers spiritual medicine to the wounded soul and sends new citizens to heaven—to be her new advocates—who will enjoy forever the happiness of God.

20.   For the social needs of the Church Christ has provided in a particular way by the institution of two other Sacraments. Through Matrimony, in which the contracting parties are ministers of grace to each other, provision is made for the external and duly regulated increase of Christian society, and, what is of greater importance, for the correct religious education of the children, without which this Mystical Body would be in grave danger. Through Holy Orders men are set aside and consecrated to God, to offer the Sacrifice of the Eucharistic

Victim, to nourish the flock of the faithful with the Bread of Angels and the food of doctrine, to guide them in the way of God's commandments and counsels and to strengthen them with all other supernatural helps.

21.   In this connection it must be borne in mind that, as God at the beginning of time endowed man's body with most ample power to subject all creatures to himself, and to increase and multiply and fill the earth, so at the beginning of the Christian era, He supplied the Church with the means necessary to overcome the countless dangers and to fill not only the whole world but the realms of heaven as well.

22.   Actually only those are to be included as members of the Church who have been baptized and profess the true faith, and who have not been so unfortunate as to separate themselves from the unity of the Body, or been excluded by legitimate authority for grave faults committed. "For in one spirit" says the Apostle, "were we all baptized into one Body, whether Jews or Gentiles, whether bond or free."[17] As therefore in the true Christian community there is only one Body, one Spirit, one Lord, and one Baptism, so there can be only one faith.[18] And therefore, if a man refuse to hear the Church, let him be considered—so the Lord commands—as a heathen and a publican.[19] It follows that those who are divided in faith or government cannot be living in the unity of such a Body, nor can they be living the life of its one Divine Spirit.

23.   Nor must one imagine that the Body of the Church, just because it bears the name of Christ, is made up during the days of its earthly pilgrimage only of members conspicuous for their holiness, or that it consists only of those whom God has predestined to eternal happiness. It is owing to the Savior's infinite mercy that place is allowed in His Mystical Body here below for those whom, of old, He did not exclude from the banquet.[20] For not every sin, however grave it may be, is such as of its own nature to sever a man from the Body of the Church, as does schism or heresy or apostasy. Men may lose charity and divine grace through sin, thus becoming incapable of supernatural merit, and yet not be deprived of all life if they hold fast to faith and Christian hope, and if, illumined from above, they are spurred on by the interior promptings of the Holy Spirit to salutary fear and are moved to prayer and penance for their sins.

24.   Let every one then abhor sin, which defiles the mystical members of our Redeemer; but if anyone unhappily falls and his obstinacy has not made him unworthy of communion with the faithful, let him be received with great love, and let eager charity see in him a weak member of Jesus Christ. For, as the Bishop of Hippo remarks, it is better "to be cured within the Church's community than to be cut off from its body as incurable members."[21] "As long as a member still

---

17. I *Cor.*, XII, 13.
18. Cf. *Eph.*, IV, 5.
19. Cf. *Matth.*, XVIII, 17.
20. Cf. *Matth.*, IX, 11; *Mark*, II, 16; *Luke*, XV, 2.
21. August., *Epist.*, CLVII, 3, 22: Migne, *P.L.*, XXXIII, 686.

forms part of the body there is no reason to despair of its cure; once it has been cut off, it can be neither cured nor healed."[22]

25.   In the course of the present study, Venerable Brethren, we have thus far seen that the Church is so constituted that it may be likened to a body. We must now explain clearly and precisely why it is to be called not merely a body, but the Body of Jesus Christ. This follows from the fact that our Lord is the Founder, the Head, the Support and the Savior of this Mystical Body.

26.   As We set out briefly to expound in what sense Christ founded His social Body, the following thought of Our predecessor of happy memory, Leo XIII, occurs to Us at once: "The Church which, already conceived, came forth from the side of the second Adam in His sleep on the Cross, first showed Herself before the eyes of men on the great day of Pentecost."[23] For the Divine Redeemer began the building of the mystical temple of the Church when by His preaching He made known His Precepts; He completed it when he hung glorified on the Cross; and He manifested and proclaimed it when He sent the Holy Ghost as Paraclete in visible form on His disciples.

27.   For while fulfilling His office as preacher He chose Apostles, sending them as He had been sent by the Father[24]—namely, as teachers, rulers, instruments of holiness in the assembly of the believers; He appointed their Chief and His Vicar on earth;[25] He made known to them all things and whatsoever He had heard from His Father;[26] He also determined that through Baptism[27] those who should believe would be incorporated in the Body of the Church; and finally, when He came to the close of His life, He instituted at the Last Supper the wonderful Sacrifice and Sacrament of the Eucharist.

28.   That He completed His work on the gibbet of the Cross is the unanimous teaching of the holy Fathers who assert that the Church was born from the side of our Savior on the Cross like a new Eve, mother of all the living.[28] "And it is now," says the great St. Ambrose, speaking of the pierced side of Christ, "that it is built, it is now that it is formed, it is now that it is . . . molded, it is now that it is created . . . Now it is that arises a spiritual house, a holy priesthood."[29] One who reverently examines this venerable teaching will easily discover the reasons on which it is based.

29.   And first of all, by the death of our Redeemer, the New Testament took the place of the Old Law which had been abolished; then the Law of Christ together with its mysteries, enactments, institutions, and sacred rites was ratified for the

---

22. August., *Serm.*, CXXXVII, 1: Migne, P.L., XXXVIII, 754.
23. Encycl. *Divinum Illud*: A.S.S., XXIX, p. 649.
24. *John*, XVII, 18.
25. Cf. *Matth.*, XVI, 18–19.
26. *John*, XV, 15; XVII, 8 and 14.
27. Cf. *John*, III, 5.
28. Cf. *Gen.*, III, 20.
29. Ambrose, *In Luc*, II, 87: Migne, P.L., XV, 1585.

whole world in the blood of Jesus Christ. For, while our Divine Savior was preaching in a restricted area—He was not sent but to the sheep that were lost of the House of Israel[30]—the Law and the Gospel were together in force;[31] but on the gibbet of His death Jesus made void the Law with its decrees[32] fastened the handwriting of the Old Testament to the Cross,[33] establishing the New Testament in His blood shed for the whole human race.[34] "To such an extent, then," says St. Leo the Great, speaking of the Cross of our Lord, "was there effected a transfer from the Law to the Gospel, from the Synagogue to the Church, from the many sacrifices to one Victim, that, as Our Lord expired, that mystical veil which shut off the innermost part of the temple and its sacred secret was rent violently from top to bottom."[35]

30.   On the Cross then the Old Law died, soon to be buried and to be a bearer of death,[36] in order to give way to the New Testament of which Christ had chosen the Apostles as qualified ministers;[37] and although He had been constituted the Head of the whole human family in the womb of the Blessed Virgin, it is by the power of the Cross that our Savior exercises fully the office itself of Head of His Church. "For it was through His triumph on the Cross," according to the teaching of the Angelic and Common Doctor, "that He won power and dominion over the gentiles";[38] by that same victory He increased the immense treasure of graces, which, as He reigns in glory in heaven, He lavishes continually on His mortal members; it was by His blood shed on the Cross that God's anger was averted and that all the heavenly gifts, especially the spiritual graces of the New and Eternal Testament, could then flow from the fountains of our Savior for the salvation of men, of the faithful above all; it was on the tree of the Cross, finally, that He entered into possession of His Church, that is, of all the members of His Mystical Body; for they would not have been united to this Mystical Body through the waters of Baptism except by the salutary virtue of the Cross, by which they had been already brought under the complete sway of Christ.

31.   But if our Savior, by His death, became, in the full and complete sense of the word, the Head of the Church, it was likewise through His blood that the Church was enriched with the fullest communication of the Holy Spirit, through which, from the time when the Son of Man was lifted up and glorified on the Cross by His sufferings, she is divinely illumined. For then, as Augustine notes,[39] with the rending of the veil of the temple it happened that the dew of the Paraclete's gifts, which heretofore had descended only on the fleece, that is on

---

30. Cf. *Matth.*, XV, 24.

31. Cf. St. Thos., I–II, q. 103, a. 3, ad 2.

32. Cf. *Eph.*, II, 15.

33. Cf. *Col.*, II, 14.

34. Cf. *Matth.*, XXVI, 28; I *Cor.*, XI, 25.

35. Leo the Great, *Serm.*, LXVIII, 3: Migne, P.L. LIV, 374.

36. Jerome and Augustine, *Epist.* CXII, 14 and CXVI, 16: Migne, P.L., XXII, 924 and 943; St. Thos., I–II, q. 103, a. 3, ad 2; a. 4; ad 1; Council of Flor. *pro Jacob.*: Mansi, XXXI, 1738.

37. Cf. II *Cor.*, III, 6.

38. Cf. St. Thos. III, q. 42, a. 1.

39. Cf. *De pecc. orig.*, XXV, 29: Migne, P.L., XLIV, 400.

the people of Israel, fell copiously and abundantly (while the fleece remained dry and deserted) on the whole earth, that is on the Catholic Church, which is confined by no boundaries of race or territory. Just as at the first moment of the Incarnation the Son of the Eternal Father adorned with the fullness of the Holy Spirit the human nature which was substantially united to Him, that it might be a fitting instrument of the Divinity in the sanguinary work of the Redemption, so at the hour of His precious death He willed that His Church should be enriched with the abundant gifts of the Paraclete in order that in dispensing the divine fruits of the Redemption she might be, for the Incarnate Word, a powerful instrument that would never fail. For both the juridical mission of the Church, and the power to teach, govern and administer the Sacraments, derive their supernatural efficacy and force for the building up of the Body of Christ from the fact that Jesus Christ, hanging on the Cross, opened up to His Church the fountain of those divine gifts, which prevent her from ever teaching false doctrine and enable her to rule them for the salvation of their souls through divinely enlightened pastors and to bestow on them an abundance of heavenly graces.

32.   If we consider closely all these mysteries of the Cross, those words of the Apostle are no longer obscure, in which he teaches the Ephesians that Christ, by His blood, made the Jews and Gentiles one "breaking down the middle wall of partition . . . in his flesh" by which the two peoples were divided; and that He made the Old Law void "that He might make the two in Himself into one new man," that is, the Church, and "might reconcile both to God in one Body by the Cross."[40]

33.   The Church which He founded by His Blood, He strengthened on the Day of Pentecost by a special power, given from heaven. For, having solemnly installed in his exalted office him whom He had already nominated as His Vicar, He had ascended into Heaven; and sitting now at the right hand of the Father He wished to make known and proclaim His Spouse through the visible coming of the Holy Spirit with the sound of a mighty wind and tongues of fire.[41] For just as He Himself when He began to preach was made known by His Eternal Father through the Holy Spirit descending and remaining on Him in the form of a dove,[42] so likewise, as the Apostles were about to enter upon their ministry of preaching, Christ our Lord sent the Holy Spirit down from Heaven, to touch them with tongues of fire and to point out, as by the finger of God, the supernatural mission and office of the Church.

34.   That this Mystical Body which is the Church should be called Christ's is proved in the second place from the fact that He must be universally acknowledged as its actual Head. "He," as St. Paul says, "is the Head of the Body, the Church."[43] He is the Head from whom the whole body perfectly organized, "groweth and maketh increase unto the edifying of itself."[44]

---

40. Cf. *Eph.*, II, 14–16.
41. Cf. *Acts*, II, 1–4.
42. Cf. *Luke*, III, 22; *Mark*, I, 10.
43. *Col.*, I, 18.
44. Cf. *Eph.*, IV, 16; *Col.*, II, 19.

35.   You are familiar, Venerable Brethren, with the admirable and luminous language used by the masters of Scholastic Theology and chiefly by the Angelic and Common Doctor, when treating this question; and you know that the reasons advanced by Aquinas are a faithful reflection of the mind and writings of the Holy Fathers, who moreover merely repeated and commented on the inspired word of Sacred Scripture.

36.   However for the good of all We wish to touch on this point briefly. And first of all it is clear that the Son of God and of the Blessed Virgin is to be called the head of the Church by reason of His singular preeminence. For the Head is in the highest place. But who is in a higher place than Christ God, who as the Word of the Eternal Father must be acknowledged to be the "firstborn of every creature?"[45] Who has reached more lofty heights than Christ Man who, though born of the Immaculate Virgin, is the true and natural Son of God, and in virtue of His miraculous and glorious resurrection, a resurrection triumphant over death, has become the "firstborn of the dead?"[46] Who finally has been so exalted as He, who as "the one mediator of God and men"[47] has in a most wonderful manner linked earth to heaven, who, raised on the Cross as on a throne of mercy, has drawn all things to Himself,[48] who, as the Son of Man chosen from among thousands, is beloved of God beyond all men, all angels and all created things?[49]

37.   Because Christ is so exalted, He alone by every right rules and governs the Church; and herein is yet another reason why He must be likened to a head. As the head is the "royal citadel" of the body[50]—to use the words of Ambrose—and all the members over whom it is placed for their good[51] are naturally guided by it as being endowed with superior powers, so the Divine Redeemer holds the helm of the universal Christian community and directs its course. And as to govern human society signifies to lead men to the end proposed by means that are expedient, just and helpful,[52] it is easy to see how our Savior, model and ideal of good Shepherds,[53] performs all these functions in a most striking way.

38.   While still on earth, He instructed us by precept, counsel and warning in words that shall never pass away, and will be spirit and life[54] to all men of all times. Moreover He conferred a triple power on His Apostles and their successors, to teach, to govern, to lead men to holiness, making this power, defined by special ordinances, rights and obligations, the fundamental law of the whole Church.

39.   But our Divine Savior governs and guides the Society which He founded directly and personally also. For it is He who reigns within the minds and hearts

---

45. *Col.*, I, 15.

46. *Col.*, I, 18; *Apoc.*, I, 5.

47. I *Tim.*, II, 5.

48. Cf. *John*, XII, 32.

49. Cf. Cyr. Alex., *Comm. in Ioh.* I, 4: Migne, P.G., LXXIII, 69; St. Thos., I, q. 20, a. 4, ad 1.

50. Hexaem., VI, 55: Migne, P.L., XIV, 265.

51. Cf. August., *De agon. Christi*, XX, 22: Migne, P.L., XL, 301.

52. Cf. St. Thos., I, q. 22, a. 1–4.

53. Cf. *John*, X, 1-18; I *Peter*, V, 1–5.

54. Cf. *John* VI, 63.

of men, and bends and subjects their wills to His good pleasure, even when rebellious. "The heart of the King is in the hand of the Lord; whithersoever he will, he shall turn it."[55] By this interior guidance He the Shepherd and Bishop of our souls,"[56] not only watches over individuals but exercises His providence over the universal Church, whether by enlightening and giving courage to the Church's rulers for the loyal and effective performance of their respective duties, or by singling out from the body of the Church—especially when times are grave—men and women of conspicuous holiness, who may point the way for the rest of Christendom to the perfecting of His Mystical Body. Moreover from Heaven Christ never ceases to look down with especial love on His spotless Spouse so sorely tried in her earthly exile; and when He sees her in danger, saves her from the tempestuous sea either Himself or through the ministry of His angels,[57] or through her whom we invoke as Help of Christians, or through other heavenly advocates, and in calm and tranquil waters comforts her with the peace "which surpasseth all understanding."[58]

40.   But we must not think that He rules only in a hidden[59] or extraordinary manner. On the contrary, our Redeemer also governs His Mystical Body in a visible and normal way through His Vicar on earth. You know, Venerable Brethren, that after He had ruled the "little flock"[60] Himself during His mortal pilgrimage, Christ our Lord, when about to leave this world and return to the Father, entrusted to the Chief of the Apostles the visible government of the entire community He had founded. Since He was all wise He could not leave the body of the Church He had founded as a human society without a visible head. Nor against this may one argue that the primacy of jurisdiction established in the Church gives such a Mystical Body two heads. For Peter in view of his primacy is only Christ's Vicar; so that there is only one chief Head of this Body, namely Christ, who never ceases Himself to guide the Church invisibly, though at the same time He rules it visibly, through him who is His representative on earth. After His glorious Ascension into Heaven this Church rested not on Him alone, but on Peter, too, its visible foundation stone. That Christ and His Vicar constitute one only Head is the solemn teaching of Our predecessor of immortal memory Boniface VIII in the Apostolic Letter *Unam Sanctam*;[61] and his successors have never ceased to repeat the same.

41.   They, therefore, walk in the path of dangerous error who believe that they can accept Christ as the Head of the Church, while not adhering loyally to His Vicar on earth. They have taken away the visible head, broken the visible bonds of unity and left the Mystical Body of the Redeemer so obscured and so maimed, that those who are seeking the haven of eternal salvation can neither see it nor find it.

---

55. *Proverbs*, XXI, 1.
56. Cf. I *Peter*, II, 25.
57. Cf. *Acts*, VIII, 26; IX, 1–19; X, 1-7; XII, 3–10.
58. *Philipp.*, IV, 7.
59. Cf. Leo XIII, *Satis Cognitum*: A.S.S., XXVIII, 725.
60. *Luke*, XII, 32.
61. Cf. *Corp. Iur. Can.*, Extr. Comm., I, 8, 1.

42.   What we have thus far said of the Universal Church must be understood also of the individual Christian communities, whether Oriental or Latin, which go to make up the one Catholic Church. For they, too, are ruled by Jesus Christ through the voice of their respective Bishops. Consequently, Bishops must be considered as the more illustrious members of the Universal Church, for they are united by a very special bond to the divine Head of the whole Body and so are rightly called "principal parts of the members of the Lord;"[62] moreover, as far as his own diocese is concerned, each one as a true Shepherd feeds the flock entrusted to him and rules it in the name of Christ.[63] Yet in exercising this office they are not altogether independent, but are subordinate to the lawful authority of the Roman Pontiff, although enjoying the ordinary power of jurisdiction which they receive directly from the same Supreme Pontiff. Therefore, Bishops should be revered by the faithful as divinely appointed successors of the Apostles,[64] and to them, even more than to the highest civil authorities should be applied the words: "Touch not my anointed one!"[65] For Bishops have been anointed with the chrism of the Holy Spirit.

43.   That is why We are deeply pained when We hear that not a few of Our Brother Bishops are being attacked and persecuted not only in their own persons, but—what is more cruel and heartrending for them—in the faithful committed to their care, in those who share their apostolic labors, even in the virgins consecrated to God; and all this, merely because they are a pattern of the flock from the heart[66] and guard with energy and loyalty, as they should, the sacred "deposit of faith"[67] confided to them; merely because they insist on the sacred laws that have been engraved by God on the souls of men, and after the example of the Supreme Shepherd defend their flock against ravenous wolves. Such an offence We consider as committed against Our own person and We repeat the noble words of Our Predecessor of immortal memory Gregory the Great: "Our honor is the honor of the Universal Church; Our honor is the united strength of Our Brethren; and We are truly honored when honor is given to each and every one."[68]

44.   Because Christ the Head holds such an eminent position, one must not think that he does not require the help of the Body. What Paul said of the human organism is to be applied likewise to the Mystical Body: "The head cannot say to the feet: I have no need of you."[69] It is manifestly clear that the faithful need the help of the Divine Redeemer, for He has said: "Without me you can do nothing,"[70] and according to the teaching of the Apostle every advance of this Mystical Body towards its perfection derives from Christ the Head.[71] Yet this,

62. Gregory the Great, *Moral.*, XIV, 35, 43: Migne, P.L., LXXV, 1062.
63. Cf. Vat. Council, *Const. de Eccl.*, Cap. 3.
64. Cf. Cod. *Iur. Can.*, can. 329, 1.
65. I *Paral.*, XVI, 22; *Ps.*, CIV, 15.
66. Cf. I *Peter*, V, 3.
67. Cf. I *Tim.*, VI, 20.
68. Cf. Ep. *ad Eulog.*, 30: Migne, *P.L.*, LXXVII, 933.
69. I *Cor.*, XII, 21.
70. *John*, XV, 5.
71. Cf. *Eph.*, IV, 16; *Col.*, II, 19.

also, must be held, marvelous though it may seem: Christ has need of His members. First, because the person of Jesus Christ is represented by the Supreme Pontiff, who in turn must call on others to share much of his solicitude lest he be overwhelmed by the burden of his pastoral office, and must be helped daily by the prayers of the Church. Moreover as our Savior does not rule the Church directly in a visible manner, He wills to be helped by the members of His Body in carrying out the work of redemption. That is not because He is indigent and weak, but rather because He has so willed it for the greater glory of His spotless Spouse. Dying on the Cross He left to His Church the immense treasury of the Redemption, towards which she contributed nothing. But when those graces come to be distributed, not only does He share this work of sanctification with His Church, but He wills that in some way it be due to her action. This is a deep mystery, and an inexhaustible subject of meditation, that the salvation of many depends on the prayers and voluntary penances which the members of the Mystical Body of Jesus Christ offer for this intention and on the cooperation of pastors of souls and of the faithful, especially of fathers and mothers of families, a cooperation which they must offer to our Divine Savior as though they were His associates.

45.   To the reasons thus far adduced to show that Christ our Lord should be called the Head of the Society which is His Body there may be added three others which are closely related to one another.

46.   We begin with the similarity which we see existing between Head and body, in that they have the same nature; and in this connection it must be observed that our nature, although inferior to that of the angels, nevertheless through God's goodness has risen above it: "For Christ," as Aquinas says, "is Head of the angels; for even in His humanity He is superior to angels . . . Even as man He illumines the angelic intellect and influences the angelic will. But in respect to similarity of nature Christ is not Head of the angels, because He did not take hold of the angels—to quote the Apostle—but of the seed of Abraham."[72] And Christ not only took our nature; He became one of our flesh and blood with a frail body that could suffer and die. But "If the Word emptied himself taking the form of a slave,"[73] it was that He might make His brothers according to the flesh partakers of the divine nature,[74] through sanctifying grace in this earthly exile, in heaven through the joys of eternal bliss. For the reason why the only-begotten Son of the Eternal Father willed to be a son of man was that we might be made conformed to the image of the Son of God[75] and be renewed according to the image of Him who created us.[76] Let all those, then, who glory in the name of Christian, look to our Divine Savior as the most exalted and the most perfect exemplar of all virtues; but let them also, by careful avoidance of sin and assiduous practice of virtue, bear witness by their conduct to

---

72. *Comm. in ep.ad Eph* ., Cap. 1, lect. 8; *Hebr.*, II, 16–17.
73. *Phillipp.*, II, 7.
74. Cf. II *Peter*, I, 4.
75. Cf. *Rom.*, VIII, 29.
76. Cf. *Col.*, III, 10.

His teaching and life, so that when the Lord shall appear they may be like unto Him and see Him as He is.[77]

47.   It is the will of Jesus Christ that the whole body of the Church, no less than the individual members, should resemble Him. And we see this realized when, following in the footsteps of her Founder, the Church teaches, governs, and offers the divine Sacrifice. When she embraces the evangelical counsels she reflects the Redeemer's poverty, obedience and virginal purity. Adorned with institutes of many different kinds as with so many precious jewels, she represents Christ deep in prayer on the mountain, or preaching to the people, or healing the sick and wounded and bringing sinners back to the path of virtue—in a word, doing good to all. What wonder then, if, while on this earth she, like Christ, suffer persecutions, insults and sorrows.

48.   Christ must be acknowledged Head of the Church for this reason too, that, as supernatural gifts have their fullness and perfection in Him, it is of this fullness that His Mystical Body receives. It is pointed out by many of the Fathers, that as the head of our mortal body is the seat of all the senses, while the other parts of our organism have only the sense of touch, so all the powers that are found in Christian society, all the gifts, all the extraordinary graces, attain their utmost perfection in the Head, Christ. "In Him it hath well pleased *the Father* that all fullness should dwell."[78] He is gifted with those supernatural powers that accompany the hypostatic union, since the Holy spirit dwells in Him with a fullness of grace than which no greater can be imagined. To Him has been given "power over all flesh";[79] "all the treasures of wisdom and knowledge are in Him"[80] abundantly. The knowledge which is called "vision" He possesses with such clarity and comprehensiveness that it surpasses similar celestial knowledge found in all the saints of heaven. So full of grace and truth is He that of His inexhaustible fullness we have all received.[81]

49.   These words of the disciple whom Jesus loved lead us to the last reason why Christ our Lord should be declared in a very particular way Head of His Mystical Body. As the nerves extend from the head to all parts of the human body and give them power to feel and to move, in like manner our Savior communicates strength and power to His Church so that the things of God are understood more clearly and are more eagerly desired by the faithful. From Him streams into the body of the Church all the light with which those who believe are divinely illumined, and all the grace by which they are made holy as He is holy.

50.   Christ enlightens His whole Church, as numberless passages from the Sacred Scriptures and the holy Fathers prove. "No man hath seen God at any time: the only-begotten Son who is in the bosom of the Father he hath declared

---

77. Cf. I *John*, III, 2.
78. *Col.*, I, 19.
79. Cf. *John*, XVII, 2.
80. Cf. *Col.*, II, 3.
81. Cf. *John*, I, 14–16.

him"[82] Coming as a teacher from God[83] to give testimony to the truth[84] He shed such light upon the nascent apostolic Church that the Prince of the Apostles exclaimed: "Lord, to whom shall we go? Thou hast the words of eternal life";[85] from heaven He assisted the evangelists in such a way that as members of Christ they wrote what they had learned, as it were, at the dictation of the Head.[86] And as for us today, who linger on in this earthly exile, He is still the author of faith as in our heavenly home He will be its finisher.[87] It is He who imparts the light of faith to believers; it is He who enriches pastors and teachers and above all His Vicar on earth with the supernatural gifts of knowledge, understanding and wisdom, so that they may loyally preserve the treasury of faith, defend it vigorously, and explain it and confirm it with reverence and devotion. Finally, it is He who, though unseen, presides at the Councils of the Church and guides them.[88]

51.   Holiness begins from Christ; and Christ is its cause. For no act conducive to salvation can be performed unless it proceeds from Him as from its supernatural source. "Without me," He says, "you can do nothing."[89] If we grieve and do penance for our sins if, with filial fear and hope, we turn again to God, it is because He is leading us. Grace and glory flow from His inexhaustible fullness. Our Savior is continually pouring out His gifts of counsel, fortitude, fear and piety, especially on the leading members of His Body, so that the whole Body may grow ever more and more in holiness and integrity of life. When the Sacraments of the Church are administered by external rite, it is He who produces their effect in souls.[90] He nourishes the redeemed with His own flesh and blood and thus calms the turbulent passions of the soul; He gives increase of grace and prepares future glory for souls and bodies. All these treasures of His divine goodness He is said to bestow on the members of His Mystical Body, not merely because He, as the Eucharistic Victim on earth and the glorified Victim in heaven, through His wounds and His prayers pleads our cause before the Eternal Father, but because He selects, He determines, He distributes every single grace to every single person "according to the measure of the giving of Christ."[91] Hence it follows that from our Divine Redeemer as from a fountainhead "the whole body, being compacted and fitly joined together, by what every joint supplieth according to the operation in the measure of every part, maketh increase of the body, into the edifying of itself in charity."[92]

52.   These truths which We have expounded, Venerable Brethren, briefly and succinctly tracing the manner in which Christ our Lord wills that His abundant

---

82. Cf. *John*, I, 18.
83. Cf. *John*, III, 2.
84. Cf. *John*, XVIII, 37.
85. Cf. *John*, VI, 68.
86. Cf. August., *De cons. evang.*, I, 35, 54; Migne, *P.L.*, XXXIV, 1070.
87. Cf. *Hebr.*, XII, 2.
88. Cf. Cyr. Alex., *Ep*, 55 *de Symb.*; Migne, *P.G.*, LXXVII, 293.
89. Cf. *John*, XV, 5.
90. Cf. St. Thos., III, q. 64, a.3.
91. *Eph.*, IV, 7.
92. *Eph.*, IV, 16; cf. *Col.*, II, 19.

graces should flow from His fullness into the Church, in order that she should resemble Him as closely as possible, help not a little to explain the third reason why the social Body of the Church should be honored by the name of Christ—namely, that our Savior Himself sustains in a divine manner the society which He founded.

53.   As Bellarmine notes with acumen and accuracy,[93] this appellation of the Body of Christ is not to be explained solely by the fact that Christ must be called the Head of His Mystical Body, but also by the fact that He so sustains the Church, and so in a certain sense lives in the Church, that she is, as it were, another Christ. The Doctor of the Gentiles, in his letter to the Corinthians, affirms this when, without further qualification, he calls the Church "Christ,"[94] following no doubt the example of his Master who called out to him from on high when he was attacking the Church: "Saul, Saul, why persecutest thou me?"[95] Indeed, if we are to believe Gregory of Nyssa, the Church is often called simply "Christ" by the Apostle;[96] and you are familiar Venerable Brethren, with that phrase of Augustine: "Christ preaches Christ."[97]

54.   Nevertheless this most noble title of the Church must not be so understood as if that ineffable bond by which the Son of God assumed a definite human nature belongs to the universal Church; but it consists in this, that our Savior shares prerogatives peculiarly His own with the Church in such a way that she may portray, in her whole life, both exterior and interior, a most faithful image of Christ. For in virtue of the juridical mission by which our Divine Redeemer sent His Apostles into the world, as He had been sent by the Father,[98] it is He who through the Church baptizes, teaches, rules, looses, binds, offers, sacrifices.

55.   But in virtue of that higher, interior, and wholly sublime communication, with which We dealt when We described the manner in which the Head influences the members, Christ our Lord wills the Church to live His own supernatural life, and by His divine power permeates His whole Body and nourishes and sustains each of the members according to the place which they occupy in the body, in the same way as the vine nourishes and makes fruitful the branches which are joined to it.[99]

56.   If we examine closely this divine principle of life and power given by Christ, insofar as it constitutes the very source of every gift and created grace, we easily perceive that it is nothing else than the Holy Spirit, the Paraclete, who proceeds from the Father and the Son, and who is called in a special way, the "Spirit of Christ" or the "Spirit of the Son."[100] For it was by this Breath of grace and

---

93. Cf. *De Rom. Pont.*, I, 9; *De Concil.*, II, 19.

94. Cf. I *Cor.*, XII, 12.

95. Cf. *Acts*, IX, 4; XXII, 7; XXVI, 14.

96. Cf. Greg. Nyss., *De vita Moysis*: Migne, *P.G.*, XLIV, 385.

97. Cf. *Serm.*,CCCLIV, 1: Migne, *P.L.*, XXXIX, 1563.

98. Cf. *John*, XXVII, 18, and XX, 21.

99. Cf. Leo XIII, *Sapientiae Christianae*: A.S.S., XXII, 392; *Satis Cognitum: ibidem*, XXVIII, 710.

100. *Rom*, VIII, 9; II *Cor.* III, 17; *Gal.* IV, 6.

truth that the Son of God anointed His soul in the immaculate womb of the Blessed Virgin; this Spirit delights to dwell in the beloved soul of our Redeemer as in His most cherished shrine; this Spirit Christ merited for us on the Cross by shedding His Own Blood; this Spirit He bestowed on the Church for the remission of sins, when He breathed on the Apostles;[101] and while Christ alone received this Spirit without measure,[102] to the members of the Mystical Body He is imparted only according to the measure of the giving of Christ from Christ's own fullness.[103] But after Christ's glorification on the Cross, His Spirit is communicated to the Church in an abundant outpouring, so that she, and her individual members, may become daily more and more like to our Savior. It is the Spirit of Christ that has made us adopted sons of God[104] in order that one day "we all beholding the glory of the Lord with open face may be transformed into the same image from glory to glory."[105]

57.   To this Spirit of Christ, also, as to an invisible principle is to be ascribed the fact that all the parts of the Body are joined one with the other and with their exalted Head; for He is entire in the Head, entire in the Body, and entire in each of the members. To the members He is present and assists them in proportion to their various duties and offices, and the greater or less degree of spiritual health which they enjoy. It is He who, through His heavenly grace, is the principle of every supernatural act in all parts of the Body. It is He who, while He is personally present and divinely active in all the members, nevertheless in the inferior members acts also through the ministry of the higher members. Finally, while by His grace He provides for the continual growth of the Church, He yet refuses to dwell through sanctifying grace in those members that are wholly severed from the Body. This presence and activity of the Spirit of Jesus Christ is tersely and vigorously described by Our predecessor of immortal memory Leo XIII in his Encyclical Letter *Divinum Illud* in these words: "Let it suffice to say that, as Christ is the Head of the Church, so is the Holy Spirit her soul."[106]

58.   If that vital principle, by which the whole community of Christians is sustained by its Founder, be considered not now in itself, but in the created effects which proceed from it, it consists in those heavenly gifts which our Redeemer, together with His Spirit, bestows on the Church, and which He and His Spirit, from whom come supernatural light and holiness, make operative in the Church. The Church, then, no less than each of her holy members can make this great saying of the Apostle her own: "And I live, now not I; but Christ liveth in me."[107]

59.   What We have said concerning the "mystical Head"[108] would indeed be incomplete if We were not at least briefly to touch on this saying of the same

---

101. Cf. *John*, XX, 22.
102. Cf. *John*, III, 34.
103. Cf. *Eph.*, I, 8; IV, 7.
104. Cf. *Rom*, VIII, 14–17; *Gal.*, IV, 6–7.
105. Cf. II *Cor.*, III, 18.
106. *A.S.S.*, XXIX, p. 650.
107. *Gal.*, II, 20.
108. Cf. Ambrose, *De Elia et ieiun.*,10, 36–37, et *In Psalm.* 118, *serm.* 20, 2; Migne, P.L., XIV, 710 et XV, 1483.

Apostle: "Christ is the Head of the Church: He is the savior of his Body."[109] For in these words we have the final reason why the Body of the Church is given the name of Christ, namely, that Christ is the Divine Savior of this Body. The Samaritans were right in proclaiming Him "Savior of the world;"[110] for indeed He most certainly is to be called the "Savior of all men," even though we must add with Paul: "especially of the faithful,"[111] since, before all others, He has purchased with His Blood His members who constitute the Church.[112] But as We have already treated this subject fully and clearly when speaking of the birth of the Church on the Cross, of Christ as the source of life and the principle of sanctity, and of Christ as the support of His Mystical Body, there is no reason why We should explain it further; but rather let us all, while giving perpetual thanks to God, meditate on it with a humble and attentive mind. For that which our Lord began when hanging on the Cross, he continues unceasingly amid the joys of heaven: "Our Head," says St. Augustine, "intercedes for us: some members He is receiving, others He is chastising, others cleansing, others consoling, others creating, others calling, others recalling, others correcting, others renewing."[113] But it is for us to cooperate with Christ in this work of salvation, "from one and through one saved and saviors."[114]

60.   And now, Venerable Brethren, We come to that part of Our explanation in which We desire to make clear why the Body of Christ, which is the Church, should be called mystical. This name, which is used by many early writers, has the sanction of numerous Pontifical documents. There are several reasons why it should be used; for by it we may distinguish the Body of the Church, which is a Society whose Head and Ruler is Christ, from His physical Body, which, born of the Virgin Mother of God, now sits at the right hand of the Father and is hidden under the Eucharistic veils; and, that which is of greater importance in view of modern errors, this name enables us to distinguish it from any other body, whether in the physical or the moral order.

61.   In a natural body the principle of unity unites the parts in such a manner that each lacks in its own individual subsistence; on the contrary, in the Mystical Body the mutual union, though intrinsic, links the members by a bond which leaves to each the complete enjoyment of his own personality. Moreover, if we examine the relations existing between the several members and the whole body, in every physical, living body, all the different members are ultimately destined to the good of the whole alone; while if we look to its ultimate usefulness, every moral association of men is in the end directed to the advancement of all in general and of each single member in particular; for they are persons. And thus—to return to Our theme—as the Son of the Eternal Father came down from heaven for the salvation of us all, He likewise established the body of the Church and enriched it with the divine Spirit to ensure that immortal souls

109. *Eph.*, V, 23.
110. *John*, IV, 42.
111. Cf. I *Tim.*, IV, 10.
112. *Acts*, XX, 28.
113. *Enarr. in Ps.*, LXXXV, 5; Migne, P.L., XXXVII, 1085.
114. Clem. Alex., *Strom.*, VII, 2; Migne, P.G. IX, 413.

should attain eternal happiness according to the words of the Apostle: "All things are yours; and you are Christ's; and Christ is God's."[115] For the Church exists both for the good of the faithful and for the glory of God and of Jesus Christ whom He sent.

62. But if we compare a mystical body with a moral body, it is to be noted that the difference between them is not slight; rather it is very considerable and very important. In the moral body the principle of union is nothing else than the common end, and the common cooperation of all under the authority of society for the attainment of that end; whereas in the Mystical Body of which We are speaking, this collaboration is supplemented by another internal principle, which exists effectively in the whole and in each of its parts, and whose excellence is such that of itself it is vastly superior to whatever bonds of union may be found in a physical or moral body. As We said above, this is something not of the natural but of the supernatural order; rather it is something in itself infinite, uncreated: the Spirit of God, who, as the Angelic Doctor says, "numerically one and the same, fills and unifies the whole Church."[116]

63. Hence, this word in its correct signification gives us to understand that the Church, a perfect society of its kind, is not made up of merely moral and juridical elements and principles. It is far superior to all other human societies;[117] it surpasses them as grace surpasses nature, as things immortal are above all those that perish.[118] Such human societies, and in the first place civil Society, are by no means to be despised or belittled; but the Church in its entirety is not found within this natural order, any more than the whole man is encompassed within the organism of our mortal body.[119] Although the juridical principles, on which the Church rests and is established, derive from the divine constitution given to it by Christ and contribute to the attaining of its supernatural end, nevertheless that which lifts the Society of Christians far above the whole natural order is the Spirit of our Redeemer who penetrates and fills every part of the Church's being and is active within it until the end of time as the source of every grace and every gift and every miraculous power. Just as our composite mortal body, although it is a marvelous work of the Creator, falls far short of the eminent dignity of our soul, so the social structure of the Christian community, though it proclaims the wisdom of its divine Architect, still remains something inferior when compared to the spiritual gifts which give it beauty and life, and to the divine source whence they flow.

64. From what We have thus far written, and explained, Venerable Brethren, it is clear, We think, how grievously they err who arbitrarily claim that the Church is something hidden and invisible, as they also do who look upon her as a mere human institution possessing a certain disciplinary code and external

---

115. I *Cor.*, III, 23; Pius XI, *Divini Redemptoris*: A.A.S., 1937, p. 80.
116. *De Veritate*, q. 29, a. 4, c.
117. Cf. Leo XIII, *Sapientiae Christianae*: A.S.S., XXII, p. 392.
118. Cf. Leo XIII, *Satis Cognitum*: A.S.S., XXVIII, p. 724.
119. Cf. *Ibidem*, p. 710.

ritual, but lacking power to communicate supernatural life.[120] On the contrary, as Christ, Head and Exemplar of the Church "is not complete, if only His visible human nature is considered . . . , or if only His divine, invisible nature . . . , but He is one through the union of both and one in both . . . so is it with His Mystical Body"[121] since the Word of God took unto Himself a human nature liable to sufferings, so that He might consecrate in His blood the visible Society founded by Him and "lead man back to things invisible under a visible rule."[122]

65.   For this reason We deplore and condemn the pernicious error of those who dream of an imaginary Church, a kind of society that finds its origin and growth in charity, to which, somewhat contemptuously, they oppose another, which they call juridical. But this distinction which they introduce is false: for they fail to understand that the reason which led our Divine Redeemer to give to the community of man He founded the constitution of a Society, perfect of its kind and containing all the juridical and social elements—namely, that He might perpetuate on earth the saving work of Redemption,[123]—was also the reason why He willed it to be enriched with the heavenly gifts of the Paraclete. The Eternal Father indeed willed it to be the "kingdom of the Son of his predilection;"[124] but it was to be a real kingdom in which all believers should make Him the entire offering of their intellect and will,[125] and humbly and obediently model themselves on Him, Who for our sake "was made obedient unto death."[126] There can, then, be no real opposition or conflict between the invisible mission of the Holy Spirit and the juridical commission of Ruler and Teacher received from Christ, since they mutually complement and perfect each other—as do the body and soul in man—and proceed from our one Redeemer who not only said as He breathed on the Apostles "Receive ye the Holy Spirit,"[127] but also clearly commanded: "As the Father hath sent me, I also send you;"[128] and again: "He that heareth you, heareth me."[129]

66.   And if at times there appears in the Church something that indicates the weakness of our human nature, it should not be attributed to her juridical constitution, but rather to that regrettable inclination to evil found in each individual, which its Divine Founder permits even at times in the most exalted members of His Mystical Body, for the purpose of testing the virtue of the Shepherds no less than of the flocks, and that all may increase the merit of their Christian faith. For, as We said above, Christ did not wish to exclude sinners from His Church; hence if some of her members are suffering from spiritual maladies, that is no reason why we should lessen our love for the Church, but

---

120. Cf. *Ibidem*, p. 710.
121. Cf. *Ibidem*, p. 710.
122. St. Thos., *De Veritate*, q. 29, a. 4, ad 9.
123. Vat. Council, Sess. IV, *Const. dogm. de Eccl.*, prol.
124. Col., I, 13.
125. Vat. Council, Sess. III, *Const. de fide Cath.*, Cap. 3.
126. *Philipp.*, II, 8.
127. *John*, XX, 22.
128. *John*, XX, 21.
129. *Luke*, X, 16.

rather a reason why we should increase our devotion to her members. Certainly the loving Mother is spotless in the Sacraments by which she gives birth to and nourishes her children; in the faith which she has always preserved inviolate; in her sacred laws imposed on all; in the evangelical counsels which she recommends; in those heavenly gifts and extraordinary grace through which with inexhaustible fecundity,[130] she generates hosts of martyrs, virgins and confessors. But it cannot be laid to her charge if some members fall, weak or wounded. In their name she prays to God daily: "Forgive us our trespasses;" and with the brave heart of a mother she applies herself at once to the work of nursing them back to spiritual health. When, therefore, we call the Body of Jesus Christ "mystical," the very meaning of the word conveys a solemn warning. It is a warning that echoes in these words of St. Leo: "Recognize, O Christian, your dignity, and being made a sharer of the divine nature go not back to your former worthlessness along the way of unseemly conduct. Keep in mind of what Head and of what Body you are a member."[131]

67.   Here, Venerable Brethren, We wish to speak in a very special way of our union with Christ in the Body of the Church, a thing which is, as Augustine justly remarks, sublime, mysterious and divine;[132] but for that very reason it often happens that many misunderstand it and explain it incorrectly. It is at once evident that this union is very close. In the Sacred Scriptures it is compared to the chaste union of man and wife, to the vital union of branch and vine, and to the cohesion found in our body.[133] Even more, it is represented as being so close that the Apostle says: "He (Christ) is the Head of the Body of the Church,"[134] and the unbroken tradition of the Fathers from the earliest times teaches that the Divine Redeemer and the Society which is His Body form but one mystical person, that is to say to quote Augustine, the whole Christ.[135] Our Savior Himself in His sacerdotal prayer did not hesitate to liken this union to that wonderful unity by which the Son is in the Father, and the Father in the Son.[136]

68.   Our union in and with Christ is first evident from the fact that, since Christ wills His Christian community to be a Body which is a perfect Society, its members must be united because they all work together towards a single end. The nobler the end towards which they strive, and the more divine the motive which actuates this collaboration, the higher, no doubt, will be the union. Now the end in question is supremely exalted; the continual sanctifying of the members of the Body for the glory of God and of the Lamb that was slain.[137] The motive is altogether divine: not only the good pleasure of the Eternal Father, and the most earnest wish of our Savior, but the interior inspiration and impulse of the Holy Spirit in our minds and hearts. For if not even the smallest act conducive

---

130. Cf. Vat. Council, Sess. III, *Const. de fide Cath.*, Cap 3.
131. *Serm.*, XXI, 3: Migne, P.L., LIV, 192–193.
132. Cf. August., *Contra Faust.*, 21, 8: Migne, P.L., XLII, 392.
133. Cf. *Eph.*, V, 22-23; *John*, XV, 1–5; *Eph.*, IV, 16.
134. *Col.*, I, 18.
135. Cf. *Enar. in Ps.*, XVII, 51 and XC, II, 1: Migne, P.L., XXXVI, 154, and XXXVII, 1159.
136. *John*, XVII, 21–23.
137. *Apoc.*, V, 12–13.

to salvation can be performed except in the Holy Spirit, how can countless multitudes of every people and every race work together harmoniously for the supreme glory of the Triune God, except in the power of Him, who proceeds from the Father and the Son in one eternal act of love?

69.   Now since its Founder willed this social body of Christ to be visible, the cooperation of all its members must also be externally manifest through their profession of the same faith and their sharing the same sacred rites, through participation in the same Sacrifice, and the practical observance of the same laws. Above all, it is absolutely necessary that the Supreme Head, that is, the Vicar of Jesus Christ on earth, be visible to the eyes of all, since it is He who gives effective direction to the work which all do in common in a mutually helpful way towards the attainment of the proposed end. As the Divine Redeemer sent the Paraclete, the Spirit of Truth, who in His name[138] should govern the Church in an invisible way, so, in the same manner, He commissioned Peter and his successors to be His personal representatives on earth and to assume the visible government of the Christian community.

70.   These juridical bonds in themselves far surpass those of any other human society, however exalted; and yet another principle of union must be added to them in those three virtues, Christian faith, hope and charity, which link us so closely to each other and to God.

71.   "One Lord, one faith,"[139] writes the Apostle: the faith, that is, by which we hold fast to God, and to Jesus Christ whom He has sent.[140] The beloved disciple teaches us how closely this faith binds us to God: "Whosoever shall confess that Jesus is the Son of God, God abideth in him, and he in God."[141] This Christian faith binds us no less closely to each other and to our divine Head. For all we who believe, "having the same spirit of faith,"[142] are illumined by the same light of Christ, nourished by the same Food of Christ, and live under the teaching authority of Christ. If the same spirit of faith breathes in all, we are all living the same life "in the faith of the Son of God who loved us and delivered himself for us."[143] And once we have received Christ, our Head, through an ardent faith so that He dwells within our hearts,[144] as He is the author so He will be the finisher of our faith.[145]

72.   As by faith on this earth we hold fast to God as the Author of truth, so by Christian hope we long for Him as the fount of blessedness, "looking for the blessed hope and coming of the glory of the great God."[146] It is because of this

---

138. Cf. *John*, XIV, 16 and 26.
139. *Eph.*, IV, 5.
140. Cf. *John*, XVII, 3.
141. I *John*, IV, 15.
142. II *Cor.*, IV, 13.
143. Cf. *Gal.*, II, 20.
144. Cf. *Eph.*, III, 17.
145. Cf. *Hebr.*, XII, 2.
146. *Tit.*, II, 13.

universal longing for the heavenly Kingdom that we do not desire a permanent home here below, but seek for one above,[147] and because of our yearning for the glory on high that the Apostle of the Gentiles did not hesitate to say: "One Body and one Spirit, as you are called in one hope of your calling;"[148] nay rather that Christ in us is our hope of glory.[149]

73.   But if the bonds of faith and hope, which bind us to our Redeemer in His Mystical Body are weighty and important, those of charity are certainly no less so. If even in the natural order the love of friendship is something supremely noble, what shall we say of that supernatural love, which God infuses in our hearts? "God is charity and he that abideth in charity abideth in God and God in him."[150] The effect of this charity—such would seem to be God's law—is to compel Him to enter into our loving hearts to return love for love, as He said: "If anyone love me . . . , my Father will love him and we will come to him and will make our abode with him."[151] Charity then, more than any other virtue binds us closely to Christ. How many children of the Church, on fire with this heavenly flame, have rejoiced to suffer insults for Him, and to face and overcome the hardest trials, even at the cost of their lives and the shedding of their blood. For this reason our Divine Savior earnestly exhorts us in these words: "Abide in my love." And as charity, if it does not issue effectively in good works, is something altogether empty and unprofitable, He added immediately: "If you keep my commandments you shall abide in my love; as I have also kept my Father's commandments and do abide in His love."[152]

74.   But, corresponding to this love of God and of Christ, there must be love of the neighbor. How can we claim to love the Divine Redeemer, if we hate those whom He has redeemed with His precious blood, so that He might make them members of His Mystical Body? For that reason the beloved disciple warns us: "If any man say: 'I love God' and hates his brother, he is a liar. For he that loveth not his brother whom he seeth, how can he love God whom he seeth not? And this commandment we have from God, that he who loveth God loveth his brother also."[153] Rather it should be said that the more we become "members one of another"[154] "mutually careful, one for another,"[155] the closer we shall be united with God and with Christ; as, on the other hand, the more ardent the love that binds us to God and to our divine Head, the closer we shall be united to each other in the bonds of charity.

75.   Now the only-begotten Son of God embraced us in His infinite knowledge and undying love even before the world began. And that He might give a visible

---

147. Cf. *Hebr.*, XIII, 14.
148. *Eph.*, IV, 4.
149. Cf. *Col.*, I, 27.
150. I *John*, IV, 16.
151. *John*, XIV, 28.
152. *John*, XV, 9–10.
153. I *John*, IV, 20–21.
154. *Rom.*, XII, 5.
155. I *Cor.*, XII, 25.

and exceedingly beautiful expression to this love, He assumed our nature in hypostatic union: hence—as Maximus of Turin with a certain unaffected simplicity remarks—"in Christ our own flesh loves us."[156] But the knowledge and love of our Divine Redeemer, of which we were the object from the first moment of His Incarnation, exceed all that the human intellect can hope to grasp. For hardly was He conceived in the womb of the Mother of God, when He began to enjoy the Beatific Vision, and in that vision all the members of His Mystical Body were continually and unceasingly present to Him, and He embraced them with His redeeming love. O marvelous condescension of divine love for us! O inestimable dispensation of boundless charity! In the crib, on the Cross, in the unending glory of the Father, Christ has all the members of the Church present before Him and united to Him in a much clearer and more loving manner than that of a mother who clasps her child to her breast, or than that with which a man knows and loves himself.

76.   From all that We have hitherto said, you will readily understand, Venerable Brethren, why Paul the Apostle so often writes that Christ is in us and we in Christ. In proof of which, there is this other more subtle reason. Christ is in us through His Spirit, whom He gives to us and through whom He acts within us in such a way that all the divine activity of the Holy Spirit within our souls must also be attributed to Christ.[157] "If a man hath not the Spirit of Christ, he is none of his," says the Apostle, "but if Christ be in you . . . , the spirit liveth because of justification."[158]

77.   This communication of the Spirit of Christ is the channel through which all the gifts, powers, and extraordinary graces found superabundantly in the Head as in their source flow into all the members of the Church, and are perfected daily in them according to the place they hold in the Mystical Body of Jesus Christ. Thus the Church becomes, as it were, the filling out and the complement of the Redeemer, while Christ in a sense attains through the Church a fullness in all things.[159] Herein we find the reason why, according to the opinion of Augustine already referred to, the mystical Head, which is Christ, and the Church, which here below as another Christ shows forth His person, constitute one new man, in whom heaven and earth are joined together in perpetuating the saving work of the Cross: Christ We mean, the Head and the Body, the whole Christ.

78.   For indeed We are not ignorant of the fact that his profound truth—of our union with the Divine Redeemer and in particular of the indwelling of the Holy Spirit in our souls—is shrouded in darkness by many a veil that impedes our power to understand and explain it, both because of the hidden nature of the doctrine itself, and of the limitations of our human intellect. But We know, too, that from well-directed and earnest study of this doctrine, and from the clash of diverse opinions and the discussion thereof, provided that these are regulated by the love of truth and by due submission to the Church, much light will be

---

156. *Serm.* XXIX: Migne, P.L., LVII, 594.
157. Cf. St. Thos., *Comm. in Ep. and Eph.*, Cap. II, lect. 5.
158. *Rom.*, VIII, 9–10.
159. Cf. St. Thos., *Comm. in Ep. ad Eph.*, Cap I, lect. 8.

gained, which, in its turn will help to progress in kindred sacred sciences. Hence, We do not censure those who in various ways, and with diverse reasonings make every effort to understand and to clarify the mystery of this our wonderful union with Christ. But let all agree uncompromisingly on this, if they would not err from truth and from the orthodox teaching of the Church: to reject every kind of mystic union by which the faithful of Christ should in any way pass beyond the sphere of creatures and wrongly enter the divine, were it only to the extent of appropriating to themselves as their own but one single attribute of the eternal Godhead. And, moreover, let all hold this as certain truth, that all these activities are common to the most Blessed Trinity, insofar as they have God as supreme efficient cause.

79.   It must also be borne in mind that there is question here of a hidden mystery, which during this earthly exile can only be dimly seen through a veil, and which no human words can express. The Divine Persons are said to indwell inasmuch as they are present to beings endowed with intelligence in a way that lies beyond human comprehension, and in a unique and very intimate manner which transcends all created nature, these creatures enter into relationship with Them through knowledge and love.[160] If we would attain, in some measure, to a clearer perception of this truth, let us not neglect the method strongly recommended by the Vatican Council[161] in similar cases, by which these mysteries are compared one with another and with the end to which they are directed, so that in the light which this comparison throws upon them we are able to discern, at least partially, the hidden things of God.

80.   Therefore, Our most learned predecessor Leo XIII of happy memory, speaking of our union with Christ and with the Divine Paraclete who dwells within us, and fixing his gaze on that blessed vision through which this mystical union will attain its confirmation and perfection in heaven says: "This wonderful union, or indwelling properly so-called, differs from that by which God embraces and gives joy to the elect only by reason of our earthly state."[162] In that celestial vision it will be granted to the eyes of the human mind strengthened by the light of glory, to contemplate the Father, the Son, and the Holy Spirit in an utterly ineffable manner, to assist throughout eternity at the processions of the Divine Persons, and to rejoice with a happiness like to that with which the holy and undivided Trinity is happy.

81.   It seems to Us that something would be lacking to what We have thus far proposed concerning the close union of the Mystical Body of Jesus Christ with its Head, were We not to add here a few words on the Holy Eucharist, by which this union during this mortal life reaches, as it were, a culmination.

82.   By means of the Eucharistic Sacrifice Christ our Lord willed to give the faithful a striking manifestation of our union among ourselves and with our divine Head, wonderful as it is and beyond all praise. For in this Sacrifice the

---

160. Cf. St. Thos., I, q. 43, a.3.
161. Sess. III. *Const. de fide Cath.*, Cap. 4.
162. Cf. *Divinum Illud:* A.S.S., XXIX, p. 653.

sacred minister acts as the viceregent not only of our Savior but of the whole Mystical Body and of each one of the faithful. In this act of Sacrifice through the hands of the priest, by whose word alone the Immaculate Lamb is present on the altar, the faithful themselves, united with him in prayer and desire, offer to the Eternal Father a most acceptable victim of praise and propitiation for the needs of the whole Church. And as the Divine Redeemer, when dying on the Cross, offered Himself to the Eternal Father as Head of the whole human race, so "in this clean oblation"[163] He offers to the heavenly Father not only Himself as Head of the Church, but in Himself His mystical members also, since He holds them all, even those who are weak and ailing, in His most loving Heart.

83.   The Sacrament of the Eucharist is itself a striking and wonderful figure of the unity of the Church, if we consider how in the bread to be consecrated many grains go to form one whole,[164] and that in it the very Author of supernatural grace is given to us, so that through Him we may receive the spirit of charity in which we are bidden to live now no longer our own life but the life of Christ, and to love the Redeemer Himself in all the members of His social Body.

84.   As then in the sad and anxious times through which we are passing there are many who cling so firmly to Christ the Lord hidden beneath the Eucharistic veils that neither tribulation, nor distress, nor famine, nor nakedness, nor danger, nor persecution, nor the sword can separate them from His love,[165] surely no doubt can remain that Holy Communion which once again in God's providence is much more frequented even from early childhood, may become a source of that fortitude which not infrequently makes Christians into heroes.

85.   If the faithful, Venerable Brethren, in a spirit of sincere piety understand these things accurately and hold to them steadfastly, they will the more easily avoid those errors which arise from an irresponsible investigation of this difficult matter, such as some have made not without seriously endangering Catholic faith and disturbing the peace of souls.

86.   For there are some who neglect the fact that the Apostle Paul has used metaphorical language in speaking of this doctrine, and failing to distinguish as they should the precise and proper meaning of the terms the physical body, the social body, and the Mystical Body, arrive at a distorted idea of unity. They make the Divine Redeemer and the members of the Church coalesce in one physical person, and while they bestow divine attributes on man, they make Christ our Lord subject to error and to human inclination to evil. But Catholic faith and the writings of the holy Fathers reject such false teaching as impious and sacrilegious; and to the mind of the Apostle of the Gentiles it is equally abhorrent, for although he brings Christ and His Mystical Body into a wonderfully intimate union, he nevertheless distinguishes one from the other as Bridegroom from Bride.[166]

---

163. *Mal.*, I, 11.
164. Cf. *Didache*, IX, 4.
165. Cf. *Rom.*, VIII, 35.
166. Cf. *Eph.*, V, 22–23.

87.   No less far from the truth is the dangerous error of those who endeavor to deduce from the mysterious union of us all with Christ a certain unhealthy *quietism*. They would attribute the whole spiritual life of Christians and their progress in virtue exclusively to the action of the Divine Spirit, setting aside and neglecting the collaboration which is due from us. No one, of course, can deny that the Holy Spirit of Jesus Christ is the one source of whatever supernatural powers enters into the Church and its members. For "The Lord will give grace and glory" as the Psalmist says.[167] But that men should persevere constantly in their good works, that they should advance eagerly in grace and virtue, that they should strive earnestly to reach the heights of Christian perfection and at the same time to the best of their power should stimulate others to attain the same goal,—all this the heavenly Spirit does not will to effect unless they contribute their daily share of zealous activity. "For divine favors are conferred not on those who sleep, but on those who watch," as St. Ambrose says.[168] For if in our mortal body the members are strengthened and grow through continued exercise, much more truly can this be said of the social Body of Jesus Christ in which each individual member retains his own personal freedom, responsibility, and principles of conduct. For that reason he who said: "I live, now not I, but Christ liveth in me"[169] did not at the same time hesitate to assert: "His (God's) grace in me has not been void, but I have labored more abundantly than all they: yet not I, but the grace of God with me."[170] It is perfectly clear, therefore, that in these false doctrines the mystery which we are considering is not directed to the spiritual advancement of the faithful but is turned to their deplorable ruin.

88.   The same result follows from the opinions of those who assert that little importance should be given to the frequent confession of venial sins. Far more important, they say, is that general confession which the Spouse of Christ, surrounded by her children in the Lord, makes each day by the mouth of the priest as he approaches the altar of God. As you well know, Venerable Brethren, it is true that venial sins may be expiated in many ways which are to be highly commended. But to ensure more rapid progress day by day in the path of virtue, We will that the pious practice of frequent confession, which was introduced into the Church by the inspiration of the Holy Spirit, should be earnestly advocated. By it genuine self-knowledge is increased, Christian humility grows, bad habits are corrected, spiritual neglect and tepidity are resisted, the conscience is purified, the will strengthened, a salutary self-control is attained, and grace is increased in virtue of the Sacrament itself. Let those, therefore, among the younger clergy who make light of or lessen esteem for frequent confession realize that what they are doing is alien to the Spirit of Christ and disastrous for the Mystical Body of our Savior.

89.   There are others who deny any impetratory power to our prayers, or who endeavor to insinuate into men's minds the idea that prayers offered to God in private should be considered of little worth, whereas public prayers which are

---

167. *Ps.*, LXXXIII, 12.
168. *Expos. Evang. sec. Luc.*, IV, 49; Migne. P.L. XV, 1626.
169. *Gal.*, II, 20.
170. I *Cor.*, XV, 10.

made in the Name of the Church are those which really matter, since they proceed from the Mystical Body of Christ. This opinion is false; for the divine Redeemer is most closely united not only with His Church, which is His Beloved Spouse, but also with each and every one of the faithful, and He ardently desires to speak with them heart to heart, especially after Holy Communion. It is true that public prayer, inasmuch as it is offered by Mother Church, excels any other kind of prayer by reason of her dignity as Spouse of Christ; but no prayer, even the most private, is lacking in dignity or power, and all prayer is of the greatest help to the Mystical Body in which, through the Communion of Saints, no good can be done, no virtue practiced by the individual members, which does not redound also to the salvation of all. Neither is a man forbidden to ask for himself particular favors even for this life merely because he is a member of this Body, provided he is always resigned to the divine will; for the members retain their own personality and remain subject to their own individual needs.[171] Moreover, how highly all should esteem mental prayer is proved not only by ecclesiastical documents, but also by the custom and practice of the saints.

90.   Finally, there are those who assert that our prayers should be directed not to the person of Jesus Christ, but rather to God, or to the Eternal Father through Christ, since our Savior as Head of His Mystical Body is only "Mediator of God and men."[172] But this certainly is opposed not only to the mind of the Church and to Christian usage, but to truth. For to speak exactly, Christ is Head of the universal Church as He exists at once in both of His natures[173] moreover He Himself has solemnly declared: "If you shall ask me anything in my name, that I will do."[174] For although prayers are very often directed to the Eternal Father through the only-begotten Son, especially in the Eucharistic Sacrifice—in which Christ, at once Priest and Victim, exercises in a special manner the office of Mediator—nevertheless not infrequently even in this Sacrifice, prayers are addressed to the Divine Redeemer also; for all Christians must clearly know and understand that the man Jesus Christ is also the Son of God and God Himself. And thus, when the Church Militant offers her adoration and prayers to the Immaculate Lamb, the Sacred Victim, her voice seems to reecho the never-ending chorus of the Church Triumphant: "To him that sitteth on the throne and to the Lamb benediction and honor and glory and power forever and ever."[175]

91.   Venerable Brethren, in Our exposition of this mystery which embraces the hidden union of us all with Christ, We have thus far, as Teacher of the Universal Church, illumined the mind with the light of truth, and Our pastoral office now requires that We provide an incentive for the heart to love this Mystical Body with that ardor of charity which is not confined to thoughts and words, but which issues in deeds. If those who lived under the Old Law could sing of their earthly city: "If I forget thee, O Jerusalem, let my right hand be forgotten; let my tongue cleave to my jaws if I do not remember thee, if I make not Jerusalem

---

171. Cf. St. Thos., II–II, q. 83, a. 5 et 6.
172. I *Tim.*, II, 5.
173. Cf. St. Thos., *De Veritate*, q. 29, a. 4, c.
174. *John*, XIV, 14.
175. *Apoc.*, V, 13.

the beginning of my joy,"[176] how much greater then should be the joy and exultation that should fill our hearts who dwell in a City built on the holy mountain of living and chosen stones, "Jesus Christ himself being the chief cornerstone."[177] For nothing more glorious, nothing nobler, nothing surely more honorable can be imagined than to belong to the One, Holy Catholic, Apostolic and Roman Church, in which we become members of One Body as venerable as it is unique; are guided by one supreme Head; are filled with one divine Spirit; are nourished during our earthly exile by one doctrine and one heavenly Bread, until at last we enter into the one, unending blessedness of heaven.

92. But lest we be deceived by the angel of darkness who transforms himself into an angel of light,[178] let this be the supreme law of our love: to love the Spouse of Christ as Christ willed her to be, and as He purchased her with His blood. Hence, not only should we cherish exceedingly the Sacraments with which holy Mother Church sustains our life, the solemn ceremonies which she celebrates for our solace and our joy, the sacred chant and the liturgical rites by which she lifts our minds up to heaven, but also the sacramentals and all those exercises of piety by which she consoles the hearts of the faithful and sweetly imbues them with the Spirit of Christ. As her children, it is our duty, not only to make a return to her for her maternal goodness to us, but also to respect the authority which she has received from Christ in virtue of which she brings into captivity our understanding unto the obedience of Christ.[179] Thus we are commanded to obey her laws and her moral precepts, even if at times they are difficult to our fallen nature; to bring our rebellious body into subjection through voluntary mortification; and at times we are warned to abstain even from harmless pleasures. Nor does it suffice to love this Mystical Body for the glory of its divine Head and for its heavenly gifts; we must love it with an effective love as it appears in this our mortal flesh—made up, that is, of weak human elements, even though at times they are little fitted to the place which they occupy in this venerable body.

93. In order that such a solid and undivided love may abide and increase in our souls day by day, we must accustom ourselves to see Christ Himself in the Church. For it is Christ who lives in His Church, and through her, teaches, governs, and sanctifies; it is Christ also who manifests Himself differently in different members of His society. If the faithful strive to live in a spirit of lively faith, they will not only pay due honor and reverence to the more exalted members of this Mystical Body, especially those who according to Christ's mandate will have to render an account of our souls,[180] but they will take to their hearts those members who are the object of our Savior's special love: the weak, We mean, the wounded, and the sick who are in need of material or spiritual assistance; children whose innocence is so easily exposed to danger in these days, and whose young hearts can be molded as wax; and finally the poor, in helping

---

176. *Ps.*, CXXXVI, 5–6.
177. *Eph.*, II, 20; I *Peter*, II, 4–5.
178. Cf. II *Cor.*, XI, 14.
179. Cf. II *Cor.*, X, 5.
180. Cf. *Hebr.*, XIII, 17.

whom we recognize as it were, through His supreme mercy, the very person of Jesus Christ.

94.   For as the Apostle with good reason admonishes us: "Those that seem the more feeble members of the Body are more necessary; and those that we think the less honorable members of the Body, we surround with more abundant honor."[181] Conscious of the obligations of Our high office We deem it necessary to reiterate this grave statement today, when to Our profound grief We see at times the deformed, the insane, and those suffering from hereditary disease deprived of their lives, as though they were a useless burden to Society; and this procedure is hailed by some as a manifestation of human progress, and as something that is entirely in accordance with the common good. Yet who that is possessed of sound judgment does not recognize that this not only violates the natural and the divine law[182] written in the heart of every man, but that it outrages the noblest instincts of humanity? The blood of these unfortunate victims who are all the dearer to our Redeemer because they are deserving of greater pity, "cries to God from the earth."[183]

95.   In order to guard against the gradual weakening of that sincere love which requires us to see our Savior in the Church and in its members, it is most fitting that we should look to Jesus Himself as a perfect model of love for the Church.

96.   And first of all let us imitate the breadth of His love. For the Church, the Bride of Christ, is one; and yet so vast is the love of the divine Spouse that it embraces in His Bride the whole human race without exception. Our Savior shed His Blood precisely in order that He might reconcile men to God through the Cross, and might constrain them to unite in one body, however widely they may differ in nationality and race. True love of the Church, therefore, requires not only that we should be mutually solicitous one for another[184] as members and sharing in their suffering[185] but likewise that we should recognize in other men, although they are not yet joined to us in the body of the Church, our brothers in Christ according to the flesh, called, together with us, to the same eternal salvation. It is true, unfortunately, especially today, that there are some who extol enmity, hatred and spite as if they enhanced the dignity and the worth of man. Let us, however, while we look with sorrow on the disastrous consequences of this teaching, follow our peaceful King who taught us to love not only those who are of a different nation or race,[186] but even our enemies.[187] While Our heart overflows with the sweetness of the teaching of the Apostle of the Gentiles, We extol with him the length, and the breadth, and the height, and the depth of the

---

181. I *Cor.*, XII, 22–23.
182. Cf. Decree of the Holy Office, 2 Dec. 1940: A.A.S., 1940, p. 553.
183. Cf. *Gen.*, IV, 10.
184. Cf. *Rom.*, XII, 5; I *Cor.*, XII, 25.
185. Cf. I *Cor.*, XII, 26.
186. Cf. *Luke*, X, 33–37.
187. Cf. *Luke*, VI, 27–35; *Matth.*,V, 44–48.

charity of Christ,[188] which neither diversity of race or customs can diminish, nor trackless wastes of the ocean weaken, nor wars, whether just or unjust, destroy.

97.   In this gravest of hours, Venerable Brethren, when bodies are racked with pain and souls are oppressed with grief, every individual must be aroused to this supernatural charity so that, by the combined efforts of all good men, striving to outdo each other in pity and mercy—We have in mind especially, those who are engaged in any kind of relief work—the immense needs of mankind, both spiritual and corporal, may be alleviated, and the devoted generosity, the inexhaustible fruitfulness of the Mystical Body of Jesus Christ, may shine resplendently throughout the whole world.

98.   As the vastness of the charity with which Christ loved His Church is equalled by its constant activity, we all, with the same assiduous and zealous charity must love the Mystical Body of Christ. Now from the moment of His Incarnation, when he laid the first foundations of the Church, even to His last mortal breath, our Redeemer never ceased for an instant, though He was the Son of God, to labor unto weariness in order to establish and strengthen His Church, whether by giving us the shining example of His holiness, or by preaching, or conversing, or gathering and instructing disciples. And so We desire that all who claim the Church as their mother, should seriously consider that not only the clergy and those who have consecrated themselves to God in the religious life, but the other members of the Mystical Body of Jesus Christ as well have, each in his degree, the obligation of working hard and constantly for the building up and increase of this Body. We wish this to be borne in mind especially by members of Catholic Action who assist the Bishops and the priests in their apostolic labors—and to their praise be it said, they do realize it—and also by those members of pious associations which work for the same end. There is no one who does not realize their energetic zeal is of the highest importance and of the greatest weight especially in the present circumstances.

99.   In this connection We cannot pass over in silence the fathers and mothers of families to whom our Savior has entrusted the youngest members of His Mystical Body. We plead with them most earnestly, for the love of Christ and the Church, to take the greatest possible care of the children confided to them, and to protect them from the snares of every kind into which they can be lured so easily today.

100.   Our Redeemer showed His burning love for the Church especially by praying for her to His heavenly Father. To recall but a few examples: everyone knows, Venerable Brethren, that just before the Crucifixion He prayed repeatedly for Peter,[189] for the other Apostles,[190] for all who, through the preaching of the holy Gospel would believe in Him.[191]

---

188. Cf. *Eph.*, III, 18.
189. Cf. *Luke*, XXII, 32.
190. Cf. *John*, XVII, 9–19.
191. Cf. *John*, XVII, 20–23.

101. After the example of Christ we too should pray daily to the Lord of the harvest to send laborers into His harvest.[192] Our united prayer should rise daily to heaven for all the members of the Mystical Body of Jesus Christ; first for Bishops who are responsible in a special way for their respective dioceses; then for priests and religious, both men and women, who have been called to the service of God, and who, at home and in the foreign missions, are protecting, increasing, and advancing the Kingdom of the Divine Redeemer. No member of this venerated Body must be forgotten in this common prayer; and let there be a special remembrance of those who are weighed down with the sorrows and afflictions of this earthly exile, as also for the suffering souls in Purgatory. Neither must those be neglected who are being instructed in Christian doctrine, so that they may be able to receive baptism without delay.

102. Likewise, We must earnestly desire that this united prayer may embrace in the same ardent charity both those who, not yet enlightened by the truth of the Gospel, are still outside the fold of the Church, and those who, on account of regrettable schism, are separated from Us, who though unworthy, represent the person of Jesus Christ on earth. Let us then re-echo that divine prayer of our Savior to the heavenly Father: "That they all may be one, as thou, Father, in me, and I in thee, that they also may be one in us; that the world may believe that thou hast sent me."[193]

103. As you know, Venerable Brethren, from the very beginning of Our Pontificate, We have committed to the protection and guidance of heaven those who do not belong to the visible Body of the Catholic Church, solemnly declaring that after the example of the Good Shepherd We desire nothing more ardently than that they may have life and have it more abundantly.[194] Imploring the prayers of the whole Church We wish to repeat this solemn declaration in this Encyclical Letter in which We have proclaimed the praises of the "great and glorious Body of Christ"[195] and from a heart overflowing with love We ask each and every one of them to correspond to the interior movements of grace, and to seek to withdraw from that state in which they cannot be sure of their salvation.[196] For even though by an unconscious desire and longing they have a certain relationship with the Mystical Body of the Redeemer, they still remain deprived of those many heavenly gifts and helps which can only be enjoyed in the Catholic Church. Therefore may they enter into Catholic unity and, joined with Us in the one, organic Body of Jesus Christ, may they together with us run on to the one Head in the Society of glorious love.[197] Persevering in prayer to the Spirit of love and truth, We wait for them with open and outstretched arms to come not to a stranger's house, but to their own, their father's home.

---

192. Cf. *Matth.*, IX, 38; *Luke*, X, 2.
193. *John*, XVII, 21.
194. Cf. Encyclical Letter, *Summi Pontificatus*: A.A.S., 1939, p. 419.
195. Iren., *Adv. Haer.*, IV, 33, 7: Migne, P.G., VII, 1076.
196. Cf. Pius IX, *Iam Vos Omnes*, 13 Sept. 1868: Act. Conc. Vat., C.L.VII, 10.
197. Cf. Gelas. I, *Epist.*, XIV: Migne, P.L. LIX, 89.

104. Though We desire this unceasing prayer to rise to God from the whole Mystical Body in common, that all the straying sheep may hasten to enter the one fold of Jesus Christ, yet We recognize that this must be done of their own free will; for no one believes unless he wills to believe.[198] Hence they are most certainly not genuine Christians[199] who against their belief are forced to go into a church, to approach the altar and to receive the Sacraments; for the "faith without which it is impossible to please God"[200] is an entirely free "submission of intellect and will."[201] Therefore, whenever it happens, despite the constant teaching of this Apostolic See,[202] that anyone is compelled to embrace the Catholic faith against his will, Our sense of duty demands that We condemn the act. For men must be effectively drawn to the truth by the Father of light through the Spirit of His beloved Son, because, endowed as they are with free will, they can misuse their freedom under the impulse of mental agitation and base desires. Unfortunately many are still wandering far from the Catholic truth, being unwilling to follow the inspirations of divine grace, because neither they[203] nor the faithful pray to God with sufficient fervor for this intention. Again and again We beg all we ardently love the Church to follow the example of the Divine Redeemer and to give themselves constantly to such prayer.

105. And likewise, above all in the present crisis, it seems to Us not only opportune but necessary that earnest supplications should be offered for kings, princes, and for all those who govern nations and are thus in a position to assist the Church by their protecting power, so that, the conflict ended, "peace, the work of justice"[204] under the impulse of divine charity may emerge from out this raging tempest and be restored to wearied man, and that holy Mother Church "may lead a quiet and peaceable life in all piety and chastity."[205] We must plead with God to grant that the rulers of nations may love wisdom,[206] so that the severe judgment of the Holy Spirit may never fall on them: "Because being ministers of His Kingdom you have not judged rightly, not kept the law of Justice, nor walked according to the will of God; horribly and speedily will he appear to you; for a most severe judgment shall be for them that bear rule. For to him that is little, mercy shall be granted; but the mighty shall be mightily tormented. For God will not except any man's person, neither will he stand in awe of any man's greatness; for he made the little and the great, and he hath equally care of all. But a greater punishment is ready for the more mighty. To you, therefore, O Kings, these are my words, that you may learn wisdom and not fall from it."[207]

---

198. Cf. August., *In Ioann. Ev. tract.*, XXVI, 2: Migne, P.L. XXX, 1607.

199. Cf. August., *Ibidem*.

200. *Hebr.*, XI, 6.

201. Vat. Counc. *Const. de fide Cath.*, Cap. 3.

202. Cf. Leo XIII, *Immortale Dei*: A.S.S., XVIII, pp. 174–175; *Cod. Iur. Can.*, c. 1351.

203. Cf. August., *Ibidem*.

204. *Is.*, XXXII,17.

205. Cf. I *Tim.*, II, 2.

206. Cf. *Wis.*, VI, 23.

207. *Ibidem*, VI, 4–10.

106. Moreover, Christ proved His love for His spotless Bride not only at the cost of immense labor and constant prayer, but by His sorrows and His sufferings which He willingly and lovingly endured for her sake. "Having loved His own . . . He loved them unto the end."[208] Indeed it was only at the price of His Blood that He purchased the Church.[209] Let us then follow gladly in the blood-stained footsteps of our King, for this is necessary to ensure our salvation: "For if we have been planted together in the likeness of His Resurrection"[210] and "if we be dead with him, we shall live also with Him."[211] Also our zealous love for the Church demands it, and our brotherly love for the souls she brings forth to Christ. For although our Savior's cruel passion and death merited for His Church an infinite treasure of graces, God's inscrutable providence has decreed that these graces should not be granted to us all at once; but their greater or lesser abundance will depend in no small part on our own good works, which draw down on the souls of men a rain of heavenly gifts freely bestowed by God. These heavenly gifts will surely flow more abundantly if we not only pray fervently to God, especially by participating every day if possible in the Eucharistic Sacrifice; if we not only try to relieve the distress of the needy and of the sick by works of Christian charity, but if we also set our hearts on the good things of eternity rather than on the passing things of this world; if we restrain this mortal body by voluntary mortification, denying it what is forbidden, and by forcing it to do what is hard and distasteful; and finally, if we humbly accept as from God's hands the burdens and sorrows of this present life. Thus, according to the Apostle, "we shall fill up those things that are wanting of the sufferings of Christ in our flesh for His Body, which is the Church."[212]

107. As We write these words there passes before Our eyes, alas, an almost endless throng of unfortunate beings for whom We shed tears of sorrow; sick, poor, disabled, widows, orphans, and many not infrequently languishing even unto death on account of their own painful trials or those of their families. With the heart of a father We exhort all those who from whatever cause are plunged in grief and anguish to lift their eyes trustfully to heaven and to offer their sorrows to Him who will one day reward them abundantly. Let them all remember that their sufferings are not in vain, but that they will turn to their own immense gain and that of the Church, if to this end they bear them with patience. The daily use of the offering made by the members of the Apostleship of Prayer will contribute very much to make this intention more efficacious and We welcome this opportunity of recommending this Association highly, as one which is most pleasing to God.

108. There never was a time, Venerable Brethren, when the salvation of souls did not impose on all the duty of associating their sufferings with the torments of our Divine Redeemer. But today that duty is more clear than ever, when a gigantic conflict has set almost the whole world on fire and leaves in its wake

---

208. *John*, XIII, 1.
209. Cf. *Acts*, XX, 28.
210. *Rom.*, VI, 5.
211. II *Tim.* II, 11.
212. Cf. *Col.*, I, 24.

so much death, so much misery, so much hardship; in the same way today, in a special manner, it is the duty of all to fly from vice, the attraction of the world, the unrestrained pleasures of the body, and also from worldly frivolity and vanity which contribute nothing to the Christian training of the soul nor to the gaining of Heaven. Rather let those weighty words of Our immortal predecessor Leo the Great be deeply engraven upon our minds, that by Baptism we are made flesh of the Crucified:[213] and that beautiful prayer of St. Ambrose: "Carry me, Christ, on the Cross, which is salvation to the wanderers, sole rest for the wearied, wherein alone is life for those who die."[214]

109. Before concluding, We cannot refrain from again and again exhorting all to love holy Mother Church with a devoted and active love. If we have really at heart the salvation of the whole human family, purchased by the precious Blood, we must offer every day to the Eternal Father our prayers, works and sufferings, for her safety and for her continued and ever more fruitful increase. And while the skies are heavy with storm clouds, and exceeding great dangers threaten the whole of human Society and the Church herself, let us commit ourselves and all that we have to the Father of Mercies, crying out: "Look down, we beseech Thee, Lord, on this Thy family, for which our Lord Jesus Christ did not hesitate to be betrayed into the hands of evil men and to undergo the torment of the Cross."[215]

110. Venerable Brethren, may the Virgin Mother of God hear the prayers of Our paternal heart—which are yours also—and obtain for all a true love of the Church—she whose sinless soul was filled with the divine spirit of Jesus Christ above all other created souls, who "in the name of the whole human race" gave her consent "for a spiritual marriage between the Son of God and human nature."[216] Within her virginal womb Christ our Lord already bore the exalted title of Head of the Church; in a marvelous birth she brought Him forth as the source of all supernatural life, and presented Him newly born, as Prophet, King and Priest to those who, from among Jews and Gentiles, were the first to come to adore Him. Furthermore, her only Son, condescending to His mother's prayer in "Cana of Galilee," performed the miracle by which "his disciples believed in Him."[217] It was she, the second Eve, who, free from all sin, original or personal, and always more intimately united with her Son, offered Him on Golgotha to the Eternal Father for all the children of Adam, sin-stained by his unhappy fall, and her mother's rights and her mother's love were included in the holocaust. Thus she who, according to the flesh, was the mother of our Head, through the added title of pain and glory became, according to the Spirit, the mother of all His members. She it was through her powerful prayers obtained that the spirit of our Divine Redeemer, already given on the Cross, should be bestowed, accompanied by miraculous gifts, on the newly founded Church at Pentecost; and finally, bearing with courage and confidence the tremendous burden of her sorrows and desolation, she, truly the Queen of Martyrs, more than all the faithful

213. Cf. *Serm.*, LXIII, 6; LXVI, 3: Migne, P.L., LIV, 357 and 366.
214. *In Ps.*, 118, XXII, 30: Migne, P.L., XV, 1521.
215. *Office for Holy Week.*
216. St. Thos., III, q. 30, a.1, c.
217. *John*, II, 11.

"filled up those things that are wanting of the sufferings of Christ . . . for His Body, which is the Church";[218] and she continues to have for the Mystical Body of Christ, born of the pierced Heart of the Savior,[219] the same motherly care and ardent love with which she cherished and fed the Infant Jesus in the crib.

111.   May she, then, the most holy Mother of all the members of Christ,[220] to whose Immaculate Heart We have trustfully consecrated all mankind, and who now reigns in heaven with her Son, her body and soul refulgent with heavenly glory—may she never cease to beg from Him that copious streams of grace may flow from its exalted Head into all the members of the Mystical Body. May she throw about the Church today, as in times gone by, the mantle of her protection and obtain from God that now at least the Church and all mankind may enjoy more peaceful days.

112.   Confiding in this sublime hope, from an overflowing heart We impart to you, one and all, Venerable Brethren, and to the flocks entrusted to your care, as a pledge of heavenly graces and a token of Our special affection, the Apostolic Benediction.

Given at Rome, at St. Peter's on the twenty-ninth day of June, the Feast of the Holy Apostles Peter and Paul, in the year 1943, the fifth of Our Pontificate.

PIUS XII

---

218. *Col.*, I, 24.
219. Cf. *Vesper hymn of Office of the Sacred Heart.*
220. Cf. Pius X, *Ad Diem Illum*: A.A.S., XXXVI, p. 453.

MEDIATOR DEI
ON THE
SACRED LITURGY

ENCYCLICAL
POPE PIUS XII
NOVEMBER 29, 1947

AN OVERVIEW OF *MEDIATOR DEI*
David W. Fagerberg

Pius XII served as pope during the turbulent years of 1939 to 1958. He became pope six months before Germany invaded Poland, and died three years into Khrushchev's term in the Soviet Union. He issued forty-one encyclicals during his pontificate, nine more than all his successors in the previous fifty years combined. An encyclical is a circular letter (from the Greek *kyklos*, meaning *circle*) that is addressed by the pope to a particular audience of bishops. Many reflected the state of affairs: on the unity of human society, prayers for social and world peace, prayers for peace in Palestine, on a program for combating atheistic propaganda, on the promotion of Catholic missions, on the persecuted Eastern Church in Bulgaria, and lamenting the use of force in Hungary. And in the midst of this social and political upheaval, Pius XII issued his influential encyclicals on theological and ecclesiastical matters: *Mystici Corporis Christi* in 1943; *Divino afflante spiritu* in 1943; *Musicae sacrae* in 1955; and, of concern to us here, *Mediator Dei* in 1947.

The Liturgical Movement had been underway for a century, or for three decades, depending on which of the two customary dates you choose for its origin. Some date it to Prosper Guéranger, named abbot of Solesmes in 1837, for his revival of chant and for authoring nine of the fifteen volumes of *The Liturgical Year*. Others date it to Lambert Beauduin's 1909 talk at the National Congress of Catholic Works in Belgium. But these are only arbitrary and convenient dates for marking a tide that was rising on many fronts. We will not be able to do it justice here, but we do want to confirm the impression that Pius XII wrote about a movement that was already in progress.

Historical studies into the origins of Christian worship began early. Fernand Cabrol and Henri Leclercq co-authored the *Dictionary of Christian Archeology and Liturgy* in 1903. Father Louis Duchesne published his study on Christian worship in 1904. Numerous Benedictine abbeys contributed to the Liturgical Movement at centers like Solesmes, Maredsous, Beuron, Maria Laach, and Mont Cesar. The last named began a periodical entitled *Liturgical Life* in 1909, and held the first liturgical day in 1910. Maria Laach's abbot, Ildefons Herwegen, convened a liturgical conference for laypeople in 1914, and in 1921 appointed Odo Casel editor of the *Yearbook for Liturgical Science*. Among Casel's 300 works, his book on the mystery of Christian worship appeared in 1932. Anton Baumstark began writing in 1923 about the historical development of liturgy, and became the father of the comparative study method. In Austria, the Augustinian Pius Parsch began a commentary on the liturgical year in 1923. Maurice de La Taille's influential three volumes on the sacrifice of the Mass, published in 1921, is being rediscovered today. In 1924, a young American Benedictine monk named Virgil Michel attended a course taught by Beauduin, and transplanted the movement to his abbey, St. John's in Collegeville, Minnesota, where he founded the Liturgical Press and began the journal *Oratre Fratres* in

1926. Josef Jungmann is best known for his historical study on the Mass, but he started out in 1936 by connecting liturgy with catechetics.

At the papal level, Pius X promulgated *Tra le sollecitudini* in 1903, which contained the first use of the expression *actuosa participatio*. "It being our ardent desire to see the true Christian spirit restored in every respect and be preserved by all the faithful, we deem it necessary to provide before everything else for the sanctity and dignity of the temple, in which the faithful assembly for the object of acquiring this spirit from its foremost and indispensable fount, which is the active participation in the holy mysteries and in the public and solemn p rayer of the Church."[1] In 1910 he discouraged postponing first Holy Communion beyond age seven in *Quam singulari*. Pius XI echoes this in *Divini cultus sanctitatem* (1928): "It is most important that when the faithful assist at the sacred ceremonies, or when pious sodalities take part with the clergy in a procession, they should not be merely detached and silent spectators, but, filled with a deep sense of the beauty of the liturgy. . . ."

We hardly do justice to a review of the Liturgical Movement in these two brief paragraphs. Our only intention was to say that the pot was bubbling: experiments with vernacular liturgies had been requested, liturgies in the round were being tried, connections were being explored between liturgy and spirituality, as well as to the welter of social movements of the day. Was the liturgical reform going in the right direction? Was it on solid ground? Was it congruent with tradition? Was it going too fast? Was it going too slow? These must have been among Pius XII's questions. How did he approach them?

There is a summary of his approach in paragraph 10 of *Mediator Dei* (MD), and it is crucial to interpreting the encyclical: "Let not the apathetic or half-hearted imagine, however, that We agree with them when We reprove the erring and restrain the overbold. No more must the imprudent think that we are commending them when We correct the faults of those who are negligent and sluggish." Should the critics of the Liturgical Movement think they have won when the pope reproves the erring and restrains the overbold? No. Should those who want to push the envelope still further think they have won when the pope corrects the negligent and sluggish? No. Pius XII avoids pitting one side against the other, he avoids casting the questions in win/lose terms, he avoids blanket approval and blanket condemnation. Doing so will require looking at issues with specificity, and making distinctions—it is not enough to be right, because maybe someone is right for the wrong reason; it is not enough to be wrong, because maybe someone is wrong for the right reason. There are paradoxes at work in this encyclical, paradoxes that should prevent either the left or right from claiming their prejudices are uncritically confirmed. Often the pope is interested in identifying the flip sides of the same mistake.

Pius XII provides one of the best definitions of liturgy ever in article 20: "The sacred liturgy is, consequently, the public worship which our Redeemer as Head of the Church renders to the Father, as well as the worship which the community of the faithful renders to its Founder, and through Him to the heavenly Father. It is, in short, the worship rendered by the Mystical Body of Christ in the entirety of its Head and members." Liturgy is (a) Christ's worship of the

---

1. Introductory paragraph from *Tra la Sollecitudini*.

Father, (b) our worship of Christ, and (c) worship made by Christ and ourselves to the Father. The holy Trinity is involved in liturgy.

There are no chapter divisions in this document; the paragraphs simply go by like cars on a railway track. But some of them look alike. This is a personal and unofficial arrangement:

OUTLINE

The practical applications concern such things as devotion, confession, asceticism and piety, adornment of the Church, music, fine arts, liturgies that are sacred, noble, universal, and so on.

Reading *Mediator Dei* is like listening in on one end of a telephone conversation: we hear the pope's reply, but not the original comment. Apparently there were arguments being made by both the imprudent and the apathetic that Pius XII wanted to interpret, balance, and clarify. Let us examine four of these by way of example.

First, concerning *lex orandi* someone appears to have been saying that the sacred liturgy is a kind of proving ground for their theories, and if something "works" in liturgy ("when it is found to have produced fruits of piety and sanctity"), then the Church is obliged to declare their teaching sound. This is how one group has interpreted the phrase *lex orandi, lex credendi*. Pius XII replies, "But this is not what the Church teaches and enjoins."[2] The ecclesiastical hierarchy has always organized, regulated, and enriched divine worship, modifying what was not fitting and adding what would increase the honor paid to Christ

---

2. *Mediator Dei* (MD), 47.

and instruct the Christian people.[3] One must not make liturgical experimentation a parallel magisterium.

Second, concerning historical studies, someone appears to have been saying that having traced everything back to their origins, we should mimic the liturgies of an earlier era, down to turning the altar back into a table, forbidding the use of sacred images and statues, redesigning the crucifix to exclude the suffering Christ, and rejecting polyphonic music. Pius XII replies, "assuredly it is a wise and most laudable thing to return in spirit and affection to the sources of the sacred liturgy . . . But it is neither wise nor laudable to reduce everything to antiquity by every possible device."[4] He thinks this way of acting would revive exaggerated and senseless antiquarianism.[5]

Third, concerning active participation, Pius XII's comments are spread throughout the document. His main assertion is that worship must be both interior and exterior, because people are a composite of soul and body. "The chief element of divine worship must be interior. . . . The sacred liturgy requires, however, that both of these elements be intimately linked with each other. This recommendation the liturgy itself is careful to repeat, as often as it prescribes an exterior act of worship."[6] Therefore, the encyclical uses "participate" to refer to both. On the one hand, by interior participation Christians should purify their hearts,[7] become more like their divine head,[8] and it is their duty at Mass to transform their hearts, block out every trace of sin, and strengthen whatever promotes supernatural life through Christ.[9] On the other hand, everyone's baptismal character appoints them to give worship to God,[10] liturgical scholarship has shown that the Christian community is in duty bound to participate in the liturgical rites,[11] and not in an inert and negligent fashion, either,[12] therefore, the pope praises those who strive to make the Christian people more familiar with the *Missale Romanum* with the idea of getting them to take part more easily and fruitfully, and he urges instruction of the faithful so that they may devoutly participate in the Eucharistic sacrifice.[13] Participation in liturgy must be interior as well as exterior, exterior as well as interior.

Fourth, concerning priesthood and the laity, the imprudent had taken the baptismal priesthood of the laity to mean that they were involved in the consecration, and the apathetic reacted that the laity were not involved in the sacrifice of the Mass in any way. Pius XII tells them both that to avoid error we must "define the exact meaning of the word 'offer.'"[14] On the one hand, he clearly defines the role of the priest. "The people . . . can in no way possess the sacerdotal

3. See ibid., 49.
4. Ibid., 62.
5. See ibid., 64.
6. Ibid., 24.
7. See ibid., 35.
8. See ibid., 78.
9. See ibid., 100.
10. See ibid., 88.
11. See ibid., 5.
12. See ibid., 80.
13. See ibid., 201.
14. Ibid., 92.

power"[15]; "the unbloody immolation at the words of consecration . . . is performed by the priest and by him alone"; the fact that the people do a visible liturgical rite does not prove they have the same kind of priesthood, "for this is the privilege only of the minister who has been divinely appointed to this office."[16] On the other hand, he clearly defines the role of the laity. "However, it must also be said that the faithful do offer the divine Victim, though in a different sense"[17]; he quotes Pope Innocent III as saying "not only do the priests offer the sacrifice, but also all the faithful," and Bellarmine as saying "the whole Church consents in the oblation made by Christ, and offers it along with Him"[18]; and in his own words he says, "Hence the whole Church can rightly be said to offer up the victim through Christ"[19] because the priest is representing Christ in the Mystical Body. "Now the sacrifice of the New Law signifies that supreme worship by which the principal Offerer himself, who is Christ, and, in union with Him and through Him, all the members of the Mystical Body pay God the honor and reverence that are due to Him."[20]

At the end of the encyclical, Pius XII asks those receiving it to guard their flocks against three sources of deception: false mysticism, dangerous humanism, or an exaggerated zeal for antiquity in matters liturgical. Another table of contents could be constructed by identifying errors that arise from them. For example:

- The sacred liturgy is merely the outward or visible part of worship, or the list of laws and prescriptions from the hierarchy.[21]

- Christian piety must be centered on the Mystical Body without regard for the personal or subjective.[22]

- There is some sort of opposition between the action of God and the collaboration of man.[23]

- In the New Testament the word "priesthood" means only the baptized, and the power Christ gave to his Apostles at the Last Supper applies directly to the entire Christian Church.[24]

- Private Masses are disapproved because they depart from the ancient way of offering the sacrifice.[25]

- The Mass should not be celebrated unless the faithful communicate.[26]

---

15. Ibid., 84.
16. Ibid., 92 and 93.
17. Ibid., 85.
18. Ibid., 86.
19. Ibid., 93.
20. Ibid.
21. See ibid., 25.
22. See ibid., 29.
23. See ibid., 36.
24. See ibid., 83.
25. See ibid., 95.
26. See ibid., 114.

- When Mass has ended, a person should not remain in prayer because this is a private act and not to the good of the community.[27]

- Attention should be not be paid to the historic Christ, only the glorified Christ.[28]

- There is an opposition between the sacred liturgy and other exercises of piety.[29]

- We may take it on ourselves to reform the exercises of piety and reduce them completely to the methods and norms of liturgical rites.[30]

Calling the twentieth century's liturgical development tumultuous would not have to be taken pejoratively. The scholarship brought so much to the table that it was a time of great excitement, joyousness, boisterous rediscovery. Beauduin was said to have burst into class one day and say, "I've just realized that the liturgy is the center of the piety of the church!" But there can be pejorative overtones, too: unrestrained, turbulent, confused, disorderly. Pius XII poured oil on the waters. A more reactionary personality might have been harsher and sought to shut down the renewal altogether. Instead, he asked everyone involved to make sure that when they picked up a new truth, and a renewed truth, they did not drop any of the traditional truths. G. K. Chesterton described this as the difference between reforming things and deforming them, and it turns on one simple principle. Imagine an institution of law as a fence or gate erected across a road. "The more modern type of reformer goes gaily up to it and says, 'I don't see the use of this; let us clear it away.' To which the more intelligent type of reformer will do well to answer: 'if you don't see the use of it, I certainly won't let you clear it away. Go away and think. Then, when you can come back and tell me that you do see the use of it, I may allow you to destroy it."[31]

An unconscious prejudice we carry is to think that being nearer to an event gives a more accurate understanding of it. If that be so (and it is not always) let us notice that *Mediator Dei* was written sixteen years before *Sacrosanctum Concilium*, and we now stand fifty years away from it.[32] There is congruence between them. *Mediator Dei* says "The sacred liturgy does, in fact, include the divine as well as human elements. The former, instituted as they have been by God, cannot be changed in any way by men. But the human components admit of various modifications, as the needs of the age, circumstance and the good of souls may require. . . ."[33] And *Sacrosanctum Concilium* begins by saying that the desire of the entire Second Vatican Council, not this document only, is to "impart an ever-increasing vigor to the Christian life of the faithful; to adapt

---

27. See ibid., 123.

28. See ibid., 162.

29. See ibid., 173.

30. See ibid., 184.

31. G. K. Chesterton, *The Thing: Why I am a Catholic*, "The Drift from Domesticity," in vol. III of *G. K. Chesterton: Collected Works* (San Francisco: Ignatius Press, 1990), 157.

32. At the time of this printing, the Church was approaching the fiftieth anniversary of the promulgation of *Sacrosanctum Concilium*.

33. MD, 50.

more suitably to the needs of our own times those institutions which are subject to change. . . ."[34]

The human components can change, the divine elements cannot. At the transition to practical applications, Pius XII summarized those elements. "Such is the nature and the object of the sacred liturgy: it treats of the Mass, the sacraments, the divine office; it aims at uniting our souls with Christ and sanctifying them through the divine Redeemer in order that Christ be honored and, through Him and in Him, the most Holy Trinity, *Glory be to the Father and to the Son and to the Holy Ghost.*"[35]

---

34. *Sacrosanctum Concilium* (SC), 1.
35. MD, 171.

MEDIATOR DEI
ENCYCLICAL OF POPE PIUS XII
ON THE SACRED LITURGY

TO THE VENERABLE BRETHREN, THE PATRIARCHS, PRIMATES, ARCHBISHOPS, BISHOPS, AND OTHER ORDINARIES IN PEACE AND COMMUNION WITH THE APOSTOLIC SEE

Venerable Brethren,
Health and Apostolic Benediction.

Mediator between God and men[1] and High Priest who has gone before us into heaven, Jesus the Son of God[2] quite clearly had one aim in view when He undertook the mission of mercy which was to endow mankind with the rich blessings of supernatural grace. Sin had disturbed the right relationship between man and his Creator; the Son of God would restore it. The children of Adam were wretched heirs to the infection of original sin; He would bring them back to their heavenly Father, the primal source and final destiny of all things. For this reason He was not content, while He dwelt with us on earth, merely to give notice that redemption had begun, and to proclaim the long-awaited Kingdom of God, but gave Himself besides in prayer and sacrifice to the task of saving souls, even to the point of offering Himself, as He hung from the cross, a Victim unspotted unto God, to purify our conscience of dead works, to serve the living God.[3] Thus happily were all men summoned back from the byways leading them down to ruin and disaster, to be set squarely once again upon the path that leads to God. Thanks to the shedding of the blood of the Immaculate Lamb, now each might set about the personal task of achieving his own sanctification, so rendering to God the glory due to Him.

2.   But what is more, the divine Redeemer has so willed it that the priestly life begun with the supplication and sacrifice of His mortal body should continue without intermission down the ages in His Mystical Body which is the Church. That is why He established a visible priesthood to offer everywhere the clean oblation[4] which would enable men from East to West, freed from the shackles of sin, to offer God that unconstrained and voluntary homage which their conscience dictates.

---

1. 1 Tim. 2:5.
2. Cf. Heb. 4:14.
3. Cf. Heb. 9:14.
4. Cf. Mal.1:11.

3.   In obedience, therefore, to her Founder's behest, the Church prolongs the priestly mission of Jesus Christ mainly by means of the sacred liturgy. She does this in the first place at the altar, where constantly the sacrifice of the cross is represented[5] and with a single difference in the manner of its offering, renewed.[6] She does it next by means of the sacraments, those special channels through which men are made partakers in the supernatural life. She does it, finally, by offering to God, all Good and Great, the daily tribute of her prayer of praise. "What a spectacle for heaven and earth," observes Our predecessor of happy memory, Pius XI, "is not the Church at prayer! For centuries without interruption, from midnight to midnight, the divine psalmody of the inspired canticles is repeated on earth; there is no hour of the day that is not hallowed by its special liturgy; there is no state of human life that has not its part in the thanksgiving, praise, supplication and reparation of this common prayer of the Mystical Body of Christ which is His Church!"[7]

4.   You are of course familiar with the fact, Venerable Brethren, that a remarkably widespread revival of scholarly interest in the sacred liturgy took place towards the end of the last century and has continued through the early years of this one. The movement owed its rise to commendable private initiative and more particularly to the zealous and persistent labor of several monasteries within the distinguished Order of Saint Benedict. Thus there developed in this field among many European nations, and in lands beyond the seas as well, a rivalry as welcome as it was productive of results. Indeed, the salutary fruits of this rivalry among the scholars were plain for all to see, both in the sphere of the sacred sciences, where the liturgical rites of the Western and Eastern Church were made the object of extensive research and profound study, and in the spiritual life of considerable numbers of individual Christians.

5.   The majestic ceremonies of the sacrifice of the altar became better known, understood and appreciated. With more widespread and more frequent reception of the sacraments, with the beauty of the liturgical prayers more fully savored, the worship of the Eucharist came to be regarded for what it really is: the fountain-head of genuine Christian devotion. Bolder relief was given likewise to the fact that all the faithful make up a single and very compact body with Christ for its Head, and that the Christian community is in duty bound to participate in the liturgical rites according to their station.

6.   You are surely well aware that this Apostolic See has always made careful provision for the schooling of the people committed to its charge in the correct spirit and practice of the liturgy; and that it has been no less careful to insist that the sacred rites should be performed with due external dignity. In this connection We ourselves, in the course of our traditional address to the Lenten preachers of this gracious city of Rome in 1943, urged them warmly to exhort their respective hearers to more faithful participation in the eucharistic sacrifice. Only a short while previously, with the design of rendering the prayers of

---

5. Cf. Council of Trent Sess. 22, c. 1.

6. Cf. *ibid.*, c. 2.

7. Encyclical Letter *Caritate Christi*, May 3, 1932.

the liturgy more correctly understood and their truth and unction more easy to perceive, We arranged to have the Book of Psalms, which forms such an important part of these prayers in the Catholic Church, translated again into Latin from their original text.[8]

7.　But while We derive no little satisfaction from the wholesome results of the movement just described, duty obliges Us to give serious attention to this "revival" as it is advocated in some quarters, and to take proper steps to preserve it at the outset from excess or outright perversion.

8.　Indeed, though we are sorely grieved to note, on the one hand, that there are places where the spirit, understanding or practice of the sacred liturgy is defective, or all but inexistent, We observe with considerable anxiety and some misgiving, that elsewhere certain enthusiasts, over-eager in their search for novelty, are straying beyond the path of sound doctrine and prudence. Not seldom, in fact, they interlard their plans and hopes for a revival of the sacred liturgy with principles which compromise this holiest of causes in theory or practice, and sometimes even taint it with errors touching Catholic faith and ascetical doctrine.

9.　Yet the integrity of faith and morals ought to be the special criterion of this sacred science, which must conform exactly to what the Church out of the abundance of her wisdom teaches and prescribes. It is, consequently, Our prerogative to commend and approve whatever is done properly, and to check or censure any aberration from the path of truth and rectitude.

10.　Let not the apathetic or half-hearted imagine, however, that We agree with them when We reprove the erring and restrain the overbold. No more must the imprudent think that we are commending them when We correct the faults of those who are negligent and sluggish.

11.　If in this encyclical letter We treat chiefly of the Latin liturgy, it is not because We esteem less highly the venerable liturgies of the Eastern Church, whose ancient and honorable ritual traditions are just as dear to Us. The reason lies rather in a special situation prevailing in the Western Church, of sufficient importance, it would seem, to require this exercise of Our authority.

12.　With docile hearts, then, let all Christians hearken to the voice of their Common Father, who would have them, each and every one, intimately united with him as they approach the altar of God, professing the same faith, obedient to the same law, sharing in the same Sacrifice with a single intention and one sole desire. This is a duty imposed, of course, by the honor due to God. But the needs of our day and age demand it as well. After a long and cruel war which has rent whole peoples asunder with its rivalry and slaughter, men of good will are spending themselves in the effort to find the best possible way to restore peace to the world. It is, notwithstanding, Our belief that no plan or initiative can offer better prospect of success than that fervent religious spirit and zeal by

---

8. Cf. Apostolic Letter (Motu Proprio) *In cotidianis precibus*, March 24, 1945.

which Christians must be formed and guided; in this way their common and whole-hearted acceptance of the same truth, along with their united obedience and loyalty to their appointed pastors, while rendering to God the worship due to Him, makes of them one brotherhood: "for we, being many, are one body: all that partake of one bread."[9]

13.   It is unquestionably the fundamental duty of man to orientate his person and his life towards God. "For He it is to whom we must first be bound, as to an unfailing principle; to whom even our free choice must be directed as to an ultimate objective. It is He, too, whom we lose when carelessly we sin. It is He whom we must recover by our faith and trust."[10] But man turns properly to God when he acknowledges His Supreme majesty and supreme authority; when he accepts divinely revealed truths with a submissive mind; when he scrupulously obeys divine law, centering in God his every act and aspiration; when he accords, in short, due worship to the One True God by practicing the virtue of religion.

14.   This duty is incumbent, first of all, on men as individuals. But it also binds the whole community of human beings, grouped together by mutual social ties: mankind, too, depends on the sovereign authority of God.

15.   It should be noted, moreover, that men are bound by his obligation in a special way in virtue of the fact that God has raised them to the supernatural order.

16.   Thus we observe that when God institutes the Old Law, He makes provision besides for sacred rites, and determines in exact detail the rules to be observed by His people in rendering Him the worship He ordains. To this end He established various kinds of sacrifice and designated the ceremonies with which they were to be offered to Him. His enactments on all matters relating to the Ark of the Covenant, the Temple and the holy days are minute and clear. He established a sacerdotal tribe with its high priest, selected and described the vestments with which the sacred ministers were to be clothed, and every function in any way pertaining to divine worship.[11] Yet this was nothing more than a faint foreshadowing[12] of the worship which the High Priest of the New Testament was to render to the Father in heaven.

17.   No sooner, in fact, "is the Word made flesh"[13] than he shows Himself to the world vested with a priestly office, making to the Eternal Father an act of submission which will continue uninterruptedly as long as He lives: "When He cometh into the world he saith. . . 'behold I come . . . to do Thy Will.'"[14] This act He was to consummate admirably in the bloody Sacrifice of the Cross: "It

---

9. 1 Cor. 10:17.
10. Saint Thomas, *Summa Theologica*, IIa IIa3 q. 81, art. 1.
11. Cf. Book of Leviticus.
12. Cf. Heb.10:1.
13. John, 1:14.
14. Heb.10:5–7.

is in this will we are sanctified by the oblation of the Body of Jesus Christ once."[15] He plans His active life among men with no other purpose in view. As a child He is presented to the Lord in the Temple. To the Temple He returns as a grown boy, and often afterwards to instruct the people and to pray. He fasts for forty days before beginning His public ministry. His counsel and example summon all to prayer, daily and at night as well. As Teacher of the truth He "enlighteneth every man"[16] to the end that mortals may duly acknowledge the immortal God, "not withdrawing unto perdition, but faithful to the saving of the soul."[17] As Shepherd He watches over His flock, leads it to life-giving pasture, lays down a law that none shall wander from His side, off the straight path He has pointed out, and that all shall lead holy lives imbued with His spirit and moved by His active aid. At the Last Supper He celebrates a new Pasch with solemn rite and ceremonial, and provides for its continuance through the divine institution of the Eucharist. On the morrow, lifted up between heaven and earth, He offers the saving sacrifice of His life, and pours forth, as it were, from His pierced Heart the sacraments destined to impart the treasures of redemption to the souls of men. All this He does with but a single aim: the glory of His Father and man's ever greater sanctification.

18.   But it is His will, besides, that the worship He instituted and practiced during His life on earth shall continue ever afterwards without intermission. For he has not left mankind an orphan. He still offers us the support of His powerful, unfailing intercession, acting as our "advocate with the Father."[18] He aids us likewise through His Church, where He is present indefectibly as the ages run their course: through the Church which He constituted "the pillar of truth"[19] and dispenser of grace, and which by His sacrifice on the cross, He founded, consecrated and confirmed forever.[20]

19.   The Church has, therefore, in common with the Word Incarnate the aim, the obligation and the function of teaching all men the truth, of governing and directing them aright, of offering to God the pleasing and acceptable sacrifice; in this way the Church re-establishes between the Creator and His creatures that unity and harmony to which the Apostle of the Gentiles alludes in these words: "Now, therefore, you are no more strangers and foreigners; but you are fellow citizens with the saints and domestics of God, built upon the foundation of the apostles and prophets, Jesus Christ Himself being the chief corner-stone; in whom all the building, being framed together, groweth up into a holy temple in the Lord, in whom you also are built together in a habitation of God in the Spirit."[21] Thus the society founded by the divine Redeemer, whether in her

---

15. *Ibid.* 10:10.
16. John, 1:9.
17. Heb. 10:39.
18. Cf. 1 John, 2:1.
19. Cf. 1 Tim. 3:15.
20. Cf. Boniface IX, *Ab origine mundi*, October 7, 1391; Callistus III, *Summus Pontifex*, January 1, 1456; Pius II, *Triumphans Pastor*, April 22, 1459; Innocent XI, *Triumphans Pastor*, October 3, 1678.
21. Eph. 2:19–22.

doctrine and government, or in the sacrifice and sacraments instituted by Him, or finally, in the ministry, which He has confided to her charge with the outpouring of His prayer and the shedding of His blood, has no other goal or purpose than to increase ever in strength and unity.

20.   This result is, in fact, achieved when Christ lives and thrives, as it were, in the hearts of men, and when men's hearts in turn are fashioned and expanded as though by Christ. This makes it possible for the sacred temple, where the Divine Majesty receives the acceptable worship which His law prescribes, to increase and prosper day by day in this land of exile of earth. Along with the Church, therefore, her Divine Founder is present at every liturgical function: Christ is present at the august sacrifice of the altar both in the person of His minister and above all under the eucharistic species. He is present in the sacraments, infusing into them the power which makes them ready instruments of sanctification. He is present, finally, in prayer of praise and petition we direct to God, as it is written: "Where there are two or three gathered together in My Name, there am I in the midst of them."[22] The sacred liturgy is, consequently, the public worship which our Redeemer as Head of the Church renders to the Father, as well as the worship which the community of the faithful renders to its Founder, and through Him to the heavenly Father. It is, in short, the worship rendered by the Mystical Body of Christ in the entirety of its Head and members.

21.   Liturgical practice begins with the very founding of the Church. The first Christians, in fact, "were persevering in the doctrine of the apostles and in the communication of the breaking of bread and in prayers."[23] Whenever their pastors can summon a little group of the faithful together, they set up an altar on which they proceed to offer the sacrifice, and around which are ranged all the other rites appropriate for the saving of souls and for the honor due to God. Among these latter rites, the first place is reserved for the sacraments, namely, the seven principal founts of salvation. There follows the celebration of the divine praises in which the faithful also join, obeying the behest of the Apostle Paul, "In all wisdom, teaching and admonishing one another in psalms, hymns and spiritual canticles, singing in grace in your hearts to God."[24] Next comes the reading of the Law, the prophets, the gospel and the apostolic epistles; and last of all the homily or sermon in which the official head of the congregation recalls and explains the practical bearing of the commandments of the divine Master and the chief events of His life, combining instruction with appropriate exhortation and illustration of the benefit of all his listeners.

22.   As circumstances and the needs of Christians warrant, public worship is organized, developed and enriched by new rites, ceremonies and regulations, always with the single end in view, "that we may use these external signs to keep us alert, learn from them what distance we have come along the road, and by them be heartened to go on further with more eager step; for the effect will

---

22. Matt. 18:20.
23. Acts 2:42.
24. Col. 3:16.

be more precious the warmer the affection which precedes it."[25] Here then is a better and more suitable way to raise the heart to God. Thenceforth the priesthood of Jesus Christ is a living and continuous reality through all the ages to the end of time, since the liturgy is nothing more nor less than the exercise of this priestly function. Like her divine Head, the Church is forever present in the midst of her children. She aids and exhorts them to holiness, so that they may one day return to the Father in heaven clothed in that beauteous raiment of the supernatural. To all who are born to life on earth she gives a second, supernatural kind of birth. She arms them with the Holy Spirit for the struggle against the implacable enemy. She gathers all Christians about her altars, inviting and urging them repeatedly to take part in the celebration of the Mass, feeding them with the Bread of angels to make them ever stronger. She purifies and consoles the hearts that sin has wounded and soiled. Solemnly she consecrates those whom God has called to the priestly ministry. She fortifies with new gifts of grace the chaste nuptials of those who are destined to found and bring up a Christian family. When as last she has soothed and refreshed the closing hours of this earthly life by holy Viaticum and extreme unction, with the utmost affection she accompanies the mortal remains of her children to the grave, lays them reverently to rest, and confides them to the protection of the cross, against the day when they will triumph over death and rise again. She has a further solemn blessing and invocation for those of her children who dedicate themselves to the service of God in the life of religious perfection. Finally, she extends to the souls in purgatory, who implore her intercession and her prayers, the helping hand which may lead them happily at last to eternal blessedness in heaven.

23.   The worship rendered by the Church to God must be, in its entirety, interior as well as exterior. It is exterior because the nature of man as a composite of body and soul requires it to be so. Likewise, because divine Providence has disposed that "while we recognize God visibly, we may be drawn by Him to love of things unseen."[26] Every impulse of the human heart, besides, expresses itself naturally through the senses; and the worship of God, being the concern not merely of individuals but of the whole community of mankind, must therefore be social as well. This obviously it cannot be unless religious activity is also organized and manifested outwardly. Exterior worship, finally, reveals and emphasizes the unity of the mystical Body, feeds new fuel to its holy zeal, fortifies its energy, intensifies its action day by day: "for although the ceremonies themselves can claim no perfection or sanctity in their own right, they are, nevertheless, the outward acts of religion, designed to rouse the heart, like signals of a sort, to veneration of the sacred realities, and to raise the mind to meditation on the supernatural. They serve to foster piety, to kindle the flame of charity, to increase our faith and deepen our devotion. They provide instruction for simple folk, decoration for divine worship, continuity of religious practice. They make it possible to tell genuine Christians from their false or heretical counterparts."[27]

---

25. Saint Augustine, *Epist. 130, ad Probam*, 18.
26. Roman Missal, Preface for Christmas.
27. Giovanni Cardinal Bona, *De divina psalmodia*, c. 19, par. 3, 1.

24.   But the chief element of divine worship must be interior. For we must always live in Christ and give ourselves to Him completely, so that in Him, with Him and through Him the heavenly Father may be duly glorified. The sacred liturgy requires, however, that both of these elements be intimately linked with each another. This recommendation the liturgy itself is careful to repeat, as often as it prescribes an exterior act of worship. Thus we are urged, when there is question of fasting, for example, "to give interior effect to our outward observance."[28] Otherwise religion clearly amounts to mere formalism, without meaning and without content. You recall, Venerable Brethren, how the divine Master expels from the sacred temple, as unworthily to worship there, people who pretend to honor God with nothing but neat and well-turned phrases, like actors in a theater, and think themselves perfectly capable of working out their eternal salvation without plucking their inveterate vices from their hearts.[29] It is, therefore, the keen desire of the Church that all of the faithful kneel at the feet of the Redeemer to tell Him how much they venerate and love Him. She wants them present in crowds—like the children whose joyous cries accompanied His entry into Jerusalem—to sing their hymns and chant their song of praise and thanksgiving to Him who is King of Kings and Source of every blessing. She would have them move their lips in prayer, sometimes in petition, sometimes in joy and gratitude, and in this way experience His merciful aid and power like the apostles at the lakeside of Tiberias, or abandon themselves totally, like Peter on Mount Tabor, to mystic union with the eternal God in contemplation.

25.   It is an error, consequently, and a mistake to think of the sacred liturgy as merely the outward or visible part of divine worship or as an ornamental ceremonial. No less erroneous is the notion that it consists solely in a list of laws and prescriptions according to which the ecclesiastical hierarchy orders the sacred rites to be performed.

26.   It should be clear to all, then, that God cannot be honored worthily unless the mind and heart turn to Him in quest of the perfect life, and that the worship rendered to God by the Church in union with her divine Head is the most efficacious means of achieving sanctity.

27.   This efficacy, where there is question of the eucharistic sacrifice and the sacraments, derives first of all and principally from the act itself (*ex opere operato*). But if one considers the part which the Immaculate Spouse of Jesus Christ takes in the action, embellishing the sacrifice and sacraments with prayer and sacred ceremonies, or if one refers to the "sacramentals" and the other rites instituted by the hierarchy of the Church, then its effectiveness is due rather to the action of the church (*ex opere operantis Ecclesiae*), inasmuch as she is holy and acts always in closest union with her Head.

28.   In this connection, Venerable Brethren, We desire to direct your attention to certain recent theories touching a so-called "objective" piety. While these theories attempt, it is true, to throw light on the mystery of the Mystical Body,

---

28. Roman Missal, Secret for Thursday after the Second Sunday of Lent.
29. Cf. Mark, 7:6 and Isaiah, 29:13.

on the effective reality of sanctifying grace, on the action of God in the sacraments and in the Mass, it is nonetheless apparent that they tend to belittle, or pass over in silence, what they call "subjective," or "personal" piety.

29.   It is an unquestionable fact that the work of our redemption is continued, and that its fruits are imparted to us, during the celebration of the liturgy, notable in the august sacrifice of the altar. Christ acts each day to save us, in the sacraments and in His holy sacrifice. By means of them He is constantly atoning for the sins of mankind, constantly consecrating it to God. Sacraments and sacrifice do, then, possess that "objective" power to make us really and personally sharers in the divine life of Jesus Christ. Not from any ability of our own, but by the power of God, are they endowed with the capacity to unite the piety of members with that of the head, and to make this, in a sense, the action of the whole community. From these profound considerations some are led to conclude that all Christian piety must be centered in the mystery of the Mystical Body of Christ, with no regard for what is "personal" or "subjective, as they would have it. As a result they feel that all other religious exercises not directly connected with the sacred liturgy, and performed outside public worship should be omitted.

30.   But though the principles set forth above are excellent, it must be plain to everyone that the conclusions drawn from them respecting two sorts of piety are false, insidious and quite pernicious.

31.   Very truly, the sacraments and the sacrifice of the altar, being Christ's own actions, must be held to be capable in themselves of conveying and dispensing grace from the divine Head to the members of the Mystical Body. But if they are to produce their proper effect, it is absolutely necessary that our hearts be properly disposed to receive them. Hence the warning of Paul the Apostle with reference to holy communion, "But let a man first prove himself; and then let him eat of this bread and drink of the chalice."[30] This explains why the Church in a brief and significant phrase calls the various acts of mortification, especially those practiced during the season of Lent, "the Christian army's defenses."[31] They represent, in fact, the personal effort and activity of members who desire, as grace urges and aids them, to join forces with their Captain–"that we may discover . . . in our Captain," to borrow St. Augustine's words, "the fountain of grace itself."[32] But observe that these members are alive, endowed and equipped with an intelligence and will of their own. It follows that they are strictly required to put their own lips to the fountain, imbibe and absorb for themselves the life-giving water, and rid themselves personally of anything that might hinder its nutritive effect in their souls. Emphatically, therefore, the work of redemption, which in itself is independent of our will, requires a serious interior effort on our part if we are to achieve eternal salvation.

32.   If the private and interior devotion of individuals were to neglect the august sacrifice of the altar and the sacraments, and to withdraw them from the stream

---

30. 1 Cor.11:28.

31. Roman Missal, Ash Wednesday; Prayer after the imposition of ashes.

32. *De praedestinatione sanctorum*, 31.

of vital energy that flows from Head to members, it would indeed be sterile, and deserve to be condemned. But when devotional exercises, and pious practices in general, not strictly connected with the sacred liturgy, confine themselves to merely human acts, with the express purpose of directing these latter to the Father in heaven, of rousing people to repentance and holy fear of God, of weaning them from the seductions of the world and its vice, and leading them back to the difficult path of perfection, then certainly such practices are not only highly praiseworthy but absolutely indispensable, because they expose the dangers threatening the spiritual life; because they promote the acquisition of virtue; and because they increase the fervor and generosity with which we are bound to dedicate all that we are and all that we have to the service of Jesus Christ. Genuine and real piety, which the Angelic Doctor calls "devotion," and which is the principal act of the virtue of religion–that act which correctly relates and fitly directs men to God; and by which they freely and spontaneously give themselves to the worship of God in its fullest sense[33]–piety of this authentic sort needs meditation on the supernatural realities and spiritual exercises, if it is to be nurtured, stimulated and sustained, and if it is to prompt us to lead a more perfect life. For the Christian religion, practiced as it should be, demands that the will especially be consecrated to God and exert its influence on all the other spiritual faculties. But every act of the will presupposes an act of the intelligence, and before one can express the desire and the intention of offering oneself in sacrifice to the eternal Godhead, a knowledge of the facts and truths which make religion a duty is altogether necessary. One must first know, for instance, man's last end and the supremacy of the Divine Majesty; after that, our common duty of submission to our Creator; and, finally, the inexhaustible treasures of love with which God yearns to enrich us, as well as the necessity of supernatural grace for the achievement of our destiny, and that special path marked out for us by divine Providence in virtue of the fact that we have been united, one and all, like members of a body, to Jesus Christ the Head. But further, since our hearts, disturbed as they are at times by the lower appetites, do not always respond to motives of love, it is also extremely helpful to let consideration and contemplation of the justice of God provoke us on occasion to salutary fear, and guide us thence to Christian humility, repentance and amendment.

33.　But it will not do to possess these facts and truths after the fashion of an abstract memory lesson or lifeless commentary. They must lead to practical results. They must impel us to subject our senses and their faculties to reason, as illuminated by the Catholic faith. They must help to cleanse and purify the heart, uniting it to Christ more intimately every day, growing ever more to His likeness, and drawing from Him the divine inspiration and strength of which it stands in need. They must serve as increasingly effective incentives to action: urging men to produce good fruit, to perform their individual duties faithfully, to give themselves eagerly to the regular practice of their religion and the energetic exercise of virtue. "You are Christ's, and Christ is God's."[34] Let everything, therefore, have its proper place and arrangement; let everything be "theocentric,"

---

33. Cf. Saint Thomas, *Summa Theologica*, II^a II^{a3}, q. 82, art. 1.
34. Cf. 1 Cor. 3:23.

so to speak, if we really wish to direct everything to the glory of God through the life and power which flow from the divine Head into our hearts: "Having therefore, brethren, a confidence in the entering into the holies by the blood of Christ, a new and living way which He both dedicated for us through the veil, that is to say, His flesh, and a high priest over the house of God; let us draw near with a true heart, in fullness of faith, having our hearts sprinkled from an evil conscience and our bodies washed with clean water, let us hold fast the confession of our hope without wavering . . . and let us consider one another, to provoke unto charity and to good works."[35]

34.   Here is the source of the harmony and equilibrium which prevails among the members of the Mystical Body of Jesus Christ. When the Church teaches us our Catholic faith and exhorts us to obey the commandments of Christ, she is paving a way for her priestly, sanctifying action in its highest sense; she disposes us likewise for more serious meditation on the life of the divine Redeemer and guides us to profounder knowledge of the mysteries of faith where we may draw the supernatural sustenance, strength and vitality that enable us to progress safely, through Christ, towards a more perfect life. Not only through her ministers but with the help of the faithful individually, who have imbibed in this fashion the spirit of Christ, the Church endeavors to permeate with this same spirit the life and labors of men—their private and family life, their social, even economic and political life—that all who are called God's children may reach more readily the end He has proposed for them.

35.   Such action on the part of individual Christians, then, along with the ascetic effort promoting them to purify their hearts, actually stimulates in the faithful those energies which enable them to participate in the august sacrifice of the altar with better dispositions. They now can receive the sacraments with more abundant fruit, and come from the celebration of the sacred rites more eager, more firmly resolved to pray and deny themselves like Christians, to answer the inspirations and invitation of divine grace and to imitate daily more closely the virtues of our Redeemer. And all of this not simply for their own advantage, but for that of the whole Church, where whatever good is accomplished proceeds from the power of her Head and redounds to the advancement of all her members.

36.   In the spiritual life, consequently, there can be no opposition between the action of God, who pours forth His grace into men's hearts so that the work of the redemption may always abide, and the tireless collaboration of man, who must not render vain the gift of God.[36] No more can the efficacy of the external administration of the sacraments, which comes from the rite itself (*ex opere operato*), be opposed to the meritorious action of their ministers of recipients, which we call the agent's action (*opus operantis*). Similarly, no conflict exists between public prayer and prayers in private, between morality and contemplation, between the ascetical life and devotion to the liturgy. Finally, there is no

---

35. Heb. 10:19–24.
36. Cf. 2 Cor. 6:1.

opposition between the jurisdiction and teaching office of the ecclesiastical hierarchy, and the specifically priestly power exercised in the sacred ministry.

37. Considering their special designation to perform the liturgical functions of the holy sacrifice and divine office, the Church has serious reason for prescribing that the ministers she assigns to the service of the sanctuary and members of religious institutes betake themselves at stated times to mental prayer, to examination of conscience, and to various other spiritual exercises.[37] Unquestionably, liturgical prayer, being the public supplication of the illustrious Spouse of Jesus Christ, is superior in excellence to private prayers. But this superior worth does not at all imply contrast or incompatibility between these two kinds of prayer. For both merge harmoniously in the single spirit which animates them, "Christ is all and in all."[38] Both tend to the same objective: until Christ be formed in us.[39]

38. For a better and more accurate understanding of the sacred liturgy another of its characteristic features, no less important, needs to be considered.

39. The Church is a society, and as such requires an authority and hierarchy of her own. Though it is true that all the members of the Mystical Body partake of the same blessings and pursue the same objective, they do not all enjoy the same powers, nor are they all qualified to perform the same acts. The divine Redeemer has willed, as a matter of fact, that His Kingdom should be built and solidly supported, as it were, on a holy order, which resembles in some sort the heavenly hierarchy.

40. Only to the apostles, and thenceforth to those on whom their successors have imposed hands, is granted the power of the priesthood, in virtue of which they represent the person of Jesus Christ before their people, acting at the same time as representatives of their people before God. This priesthood is not transmitted by heredity or human descent. It does not emanate from the Christian community. It is not a delegation from the people. Prior to acting as representative of the community before the throne of God, the priest is the ambassador of the divine Redeemer. He is God's vice-gerent in the midst of his flock precisely because Jesus Christ is Head of that body of which Christians are the members. The power entrusted to him, therefore, bears no natural resemblance to anything human. It is entirely supernatural. It comes from God. "As the Father hath sent me, I also send you[40] . . . he that heareth you heareth me[41] . . . go ye into the whole world and preach the gospel to every creature; he that believeth and is baptized shall be saved."[42]

---

37. Cf. Code of Canon Law, can. 125, 126, 565, 571, 595, 1367.
38. Col. 3:11.
39. Cf. Gal. 4:19.
40. John, 20:21.
41. Luke, 10:16.
42. Mark, 16:15–16.

41.   That is why the visible, external priesthood of Jesus Christ is not handed down indiscriminately to all members of the Church in general, but is conferred on designated men, through what may be called the spiritual generation of holy orders.

42.   This latter, one of the seven sacraments, not only imparts the grace appropriate to the clerical function and state of life, but imparts an indelible "character" besides, indicating the sacred ministers' conformity to Jesus Christ the Priest and qualifying them to perform those official acts of religion by which men are sanctified and God is duly glorified in keeping with the divine laws and regulations.

43.   In the same way, actually that baptism is the distinctive mark of all Christians, and serves to differentiate them from those who have not been cleansed in this purifying stream and consequently are not members of Christ, the sacrament of holy orders sets the priest apart from the rest of the faithful who have not received this consecration. For they alone, in answer to an inward supernatural call, have entered the august ministry, where they are assigned to service in the sanctuary and become, as it were, the instruments God uses to communicate supernatural life from on high to the Mystical Body of Jesus Christ. Add to this, as We have noted above, the fact that they alone have been marked with the indelible sign "conforming" them to Christ the Priest, and that their hands alone have been consecrated "in order that whatever they bless may be blessed, whatever they consecrate may become sacred and holy, in the name of our Lord Jesus Christ"[43] Let all, then, who would live in Christ flock to their priests. By them they will be supplied with the comforts and food of the spiritual life. From them they will procure the medicine of salvation assuring their cure and happy recovery from the fatal sickness of their sins. The priest, finally, will bless their homes, consecrate their families and help them, as they breathe their last, across the threshold of eternal happiness.

44.   Since, therefore, it is the priest chiefly who performs the sacred liturgy in the name of the Church, its organization, regulation and details cannot but be subject to Church authority. This conclusion, based on the nature of Christian worship itself, is further confirmed by the testimony of history.

45.   Additional proof of this indefeasible right of the ecclesiastical hierarchy lies in the circumstances that the sacred liturgy is intimately bound up with doctrinal propositions which the Church proposes to be perfectly true and certain, and must as a consequence conform to the decrees respecting Catholic faith issued by the supreme teaching authority of the Church with a view to safeguarding the integrity of the religion revealed by God.

46.   On this subject We judge it Our duty to rectify an attitude with which you are doubtless familiar, Venerable Brethren. We refer to the error and fallacious reasoning of those who have claimed that the sacred liturgy is a kind of proving ground for the truths to be held of faith, meaning by this that the Church is

---

43. Roman Pontifical, Ordination of a priest: anointing of hands.

obliged to declare such a doctrine sound when it is found to have produced fruits of piety and sanctity through the sacred rites of the liturgy, and to reject it otherwise. Hence the epigram, *"Lex orandi, lex credendi"*—the law for prayer is the law for faith.

47.   But this is not what the Church teaches and enjoins. The worship she offers to God, all good and great, is a continuous profession of Catholic faith and a continuous exercise of hope and charity, as Augustine puts it tersely. "God is to be worshipped," he says, "by faith, hope and charity."[44] In the sacred liturgy we profess the Catholic faith explicitly and openly, not only by the celebration of the mysteries, and by offering the holy sacrifice and administering the sacraments, but also by saying or singing the credo or Symbol of the faith—it is indeed the sign and badge, as it were, of the Christian—along with other texts, and likewise by the reading of holy scripture, written under the inspiration of the Holy Ghost. The entire liturgy, therefore, has the Catholic faith for its content, inasmuch as it bears public witness to the faith of the Church.

48.   For this reason, whenever there was question of defining a truth revealed by God, the Sovereign Pontiff and the Councils in their recourse to the "theological sources," as they are called, have not seldom drawn many an argument from this sacred science of the liturgy. For an example in point, Our predecessor of immortal memory, Pius IX, so argued when he proclaimed the Immaculate Conception of the Virgin Mary. Similarly during the discussion of a doubtful or controversial truth, the Church and the Holy Fathers have not failed to look to the age-old and age-honored sacred rites for enlightenment. Hence the well-known and venerable maxim, *"Legem credendi lex statuat supplicandi"*—let the rule for prayer determine the rule of belief.[45] The sacred liturgy, consequently, does not decide or determine independently and of itself what is of Catholic faith. More properly, since the liturgy is also a profession of eternal truths, and subject, as such, to the supreme teaching authority of the Church, it can supply proofs and testimony, quite clearly, of no little value, towards the determination of a particular point of Christian doctrine. But if one desires to differentiate and describe the relationship between faith and the sacred liturgy in absolute and general terms, it is perfectly correct to say, *"Lex credendi legem statuat supplicandi"*—let the rule of belief determine the rule of prayer. The same holds true for the other theological virtues also, *"In . . . fide, spe, caritate continuato desiderio semper oramus"*—we pray always, with constant yearning in faith, hope and charity.[46]

49.   From time immemorial the ecclesiastical hierarchy has exercised this right in matters liturgical. It has organized and regulated divine worship, enriching it constantly with new splendor and beauty, to the glory of God and the spiritual profit of Christians. What is more, it has not been slow—keeping the substance of the Mass and sacraments carefully intact—to modify what it deemed not altogether fitting, and to add what appeared more likely to increase the honor

---

44. *Enchiridion*, c. 3.
45. *De gratia Dei* "Indiculus."
46. Saint Augustine, *Epist. 130, ad Probam*, 18.

paid to Jesus Christ and the august Trinity, and to instruct and stimulate the Christian people to greater advantage.[47]

50.   The sacred liturgy does, in fact, include divine as well as human elements. The former, instituted as they have been by God, cannot be changed in any way by men. But the human components admit of various modifications, as the needs of the age, circumstance and the good of souls may require, and as the ecclesiastical hierarchy, under guidance of the Holy Spirit, may have authorized. This will explain the marvelous variety of Eastern and Western rites. Here is the reason for the gradual addition, through successive development, of particular religious customs and practices of piety only faintly discernible in earlier times. Hence likewise it happens from time to time that certain devotions long since forgotten are revived and practiced anew. All these developments attest the abiding life of the immaculate Spouse of Jesus Christ through these many centuries. They are the sacred language she uses, as the ages run their course, to profess to her divine Spouse her own faith along with that of the nations committed to her charge, and her own unfailing love. They furnish proof, besides, of the wisdom of the teaching method she employs to arouse and nourish constantly the "Christian instinct."

51.   Several causes, really have been instrumental in the progress and development of the sacred liturgy during the long and glorious life of the Church.

52.   Thus, for example, as Catholic doctrine on the Incarnate Word of God, the eucharistic sacrament and sacrifice, and Mary the Virgin Mother of God came to be determined with greater certitude and clarity, new ritual forms were introduced through which the acts of the liturgy proceeded to reproduce this brighter light issuing from the decrees of the teaching authority of the Church, and to reflect it, in a sense so that it might reach the minds and hearts of Christ's people more readily.

53.   The subsequent advances in ecclesiastical discipline for the administering of the sacraments, that of penance for example; the institution and later suppression of the catechumenate; and again, the practice of eucharistic communion under a single species, adopted in the Latin Church; these developments were assuredly responsible in no little measure for the modification of the ancient ritual in the course of time, and for the gradual introduction of new rites considered more in accord with prevailing discipline in these matters.

54.   Just as notable a contribution to this progressive transformation was made by devotional trends and practices not directly related to the sacred liturgy, which began to appear, by God's wonderful design, in later periods, and grew to be so popular. We may instance the spread and ever mounting ardor of devotion to the Blessed Eucharist, devotion to the most bitter passion of our Redeemer, devotion to the most Sacred Heart of Jesus, to the Virgin Mother of God and to her most chaste spouse.

---

47. Cf. Constitution *Divini cultus*, December 20, 1928.

55.   Other manifestations of piety have also played their circumstantial part in this same liturgical development. Among them may be cited the public pilgrimages to the tombs of the martyrs prompted by motives of devotion, the special periods of fasting instituted for the same reason, and lastly, in this gracious city of Rome, the penitential recitation of the litanies during the "station" processions, in which even the Sovereign Pontiff frequently joined.

56.   It is likewise easy to understand that the progress of the fine arts, those of architecture, painting and music above all, has exerted considerable influence on the choice and disposition of the various external features of the sacred liturgy.

57.   The Church has further used her right of control over liturgical observance to protect the purity of divine worship against abuse from dangerous and imprudent innovations introduced by private individuals and particular churches. Thus it came about–during the 16th century, when usages and customs of this sort had become increasingly prevalent and exaggerated, and when private initiative in matters liturgical threatened to compromise the integrity of faith and devotion, to the great advantage of heretics and further spread of their errors– that in the year 1588, Our predecessor Sixtus V of immortal memory established the Sacred Congregation of Rites, charged with the defense of the legitimate rites of the Church and with the prohibition of any spurious innovation.[48] This body fulfills even today the official function of supervision and legislation with regard to all matters touching the sacred liturgy.[49]

58.   It follows from this that the Sovereign Pontiff alone enjoys the right to recognize and establish any practice touching the worship of God, to introduce and approve new rites, as also to modify those he judges to require modification.[50] Bishops, for their part, have the right and duty carefully to watch over the exact observance of the prescriptions of the sacred canons respecting divine worship.[51] Private individuals, therefore, even though they be clerics, may not be left to decide for themselves in these holy and venerable matters, involving as they do the religious life of Christian society along with the exercise of the priesthood of Jesus Christ and worship of God; concerned as they are with the honor due to the Blessed Trinity, the Word Incarnate and His august mother and the other saints, and with the salvation of souls as well. For the same reason no private person has any authority to regulate external practices of this kind, which are intimately bound up with Church discipline and with the order, unity and concord of the Mystical Body and frequently even with the integrity of Catholic faith itself.

59.   The Church is without question a living organism, and as an organism, in respect of the sacred liturgy also, she grows, matures, develops, adapts and accommodates herself to temporal needs and circumstances, provided only that the integrity of her doctrine be safeguarded. This notwithstanding, the temerity

---

48. Constitution *Immensa*, January 22, 1588.
49. Code of Canon Law, can. 253.
50. Cf. Code of Canon Law, can. 1257.
51. Cf. Code of Canon Law, can. 1261.

and daring of those who introduce novel liturgical practices, or call for the revival of obsolete rites out of harmony with prevailing laws and rubrics, deserve severe reproof. It has pained Us grievously to note, Venerable Brethren, that such innovations are actually being introduced, not merely in minor details but in matters of major importance as well. We instance, in point of fact, those who make use of the vernacular in the celebration of the august eucharistic sacrifice; those who transfer certain feast-days—which have been appointed and established after mature deliberation—to other dates; those, finally, who delete from the prayerbooks approved for public use the sacred texts of the Old Testament, deeming them little suited and inopportune for modern times.

60.   The use of the Latin language, customary in a considerable portion of the Church, is a manifest and beautiful sign of unity, as well as an effective antidote for any corruption of doctrinal truth. In spite of this, the use of the mother tongue in connection with several of the rites may be of much advantage to the people. But the Apostolic See alone is empowered to grant this permission. It is forbidden, therefore, to take any action whatever of this nature without having requested and obtained such consent, since the sacred liturgy, as We have said, is entirely subject to the discretion and approval of the Holy See.

61.   The same reasoning holds in the case of some persons who are bent on the restoration of all the ancient rites and ceremonies indiscriminately. The liturgy of the early ages is most certainly worthy of all veneration. But ancient usage must not be esteemed more suitable and proper, either in its own right or in its significance for later times and new situations, on the simple ground that it carries the savor and aroma of antiquity. The more recent liturgical rites likewise deserve reverence and respect. They, too, owe their inspiration to the Holy Spirit, who assists the Church in every age even to the consummation of the world.[52] They are equally the resources used by the majestic Spouse of Jesus Christ to promote and procure the sanctity of man.

62.   Assuredly it is a wise and most laudable thing to return in spirit and affection to the sources of the sacred liturgy. For research in this field of study, by tracing it back to its origins, contributes valuable assistance towards a more thorough and careful investigation of the significance of feast-days, and of the meaning of the texts and sacred ceremonies employed on their occasion. But it is neither wise nor laudable to reduce everything to antiquity by every possible device. Thus, to cite some instances, one would be straying from the straight path were he to wish the altar restored to its primitive tableform; were he to want black excluded as a color for the liturgical vestments; were he to forbid the use of sacred images and statues in Churches; were he to order the crucifix so designed that the divine Redeemer's body shows no trace of His cruel sufferings; and lastly were he to disdain and reject polyphonic music or singing in parts, even where it conforms to regulations issued by the Holy See.

63.   Clearly no sincere Catholic can refuse to accept the formulation of Christian doctrine more recently elaborated and proclaimed as dogmas by the Church,

---

52. Cf. Matt. 28:20.

under the inspiration and guidance of the Holy Spirit with abundant fruit for souls, because it pleases him to hark back to the old formulas. No more can any Catholic in his right senses repudiate existing legislation of the Church to revert to prescriptions based on the earliest sources of canon law. Just as obviously unwise and mistaken is the zeal of one who in matters liturgical would go back to the rites and usage of antiquity, discarding the new patterns introduced by disposition of divine Providence to meet the changes of circumstances and situation.

64. This way of acting bids fair to revive the exaggerated and senseless antiquarianism to which the illegal Council of Pistoia gave rise. It likewise attempts to reinstate a series of errors which were responsible for the calling of that meeting as well as for those resulting from it, with grievous harm to souls, and which the Church, the ever watchful guardian of the "deposit of faith" committed to her charge by her divine Founder, had every right and reason to condemn.[53] For perverse designs and ventures of this sort tend to paralyze and weaken that process of sanctification by which the sacred liturgy directs the sons of adoption to their Heavenly Father of their souls' salvation.

65. In every measure taken, then, let proper contact with the ecclesiastical hierarchy be maintained. Let no one arrogate to himself the right to make regulations and impose them on others at will. Only the Sovereign Pontiff, as the successor of Saint Peter, charged by the divine Redeemer with the feeding of His entire flock,[54] and with him, in obedience to the Apostolic See, the bishops "whom the Holy Ghost has placed . . . to rule the Church of God,"[55] have the right and the duty to govern the Christian people. Consequently, Venerable Brethren, whenever you assert your authority—even on occasion with wholesome severity—you are not merely acquitting yourselves of your duty; you are defending the very will of the Founder of the Church.

66. The mystery of the most Holy Eucharist which Christ, the High Priest instituted, and which He commands to be continually renewed in the Church by His ministers, is the culmination and center, as it were, of the Christian religion. We consider it opportune in speaking about the crowning act of the sacred liturgy, to delay for a little while and call your attention, Venerable Brethren, to this most important subject.

67. Christ the Lord, "Eternal Priest according to the order of Melchizedek,"[56] "loving His own who were of the world,"[57] "at the last supper, on the night He was betrayed, wishing to leave His beloved Spouse, the Church, a visible sacrifice such as the nature of men requires, that would re-present the bloody sacrifice offered once on the cross, and perpetuate its memory to the end of time, and whose salutary virtue might be applied in remitting those sins which we daily

---

53. Cf. Pius VI, Constitution *Auctorem fidei*, August 28, 1794, nn. 31–34, 39, 62, 66, 69–74.
54. Cf. John, 21:15–17.
55. Acts, 20:28.
56. Ps.109:4.
57. John, 13:1.

commit, . . . offered His body and blood under the species of bread and wine to God the Father, and under the same species allowed the apostles, whom he at that time constituted the priests of the New Testament, to partake thereof; commanding them and their successors in the priesthood to make the same offering."[58]

68.   The august sacrifice of the altar, then, is no mere empty commemoration of the passion and death of Jesus Christ, but a true and proper act of sacrifice, whereby the High Priest by an unbloody immolation offers Himself a most acceptable victim to the Eternal Father, as He did upon the cross. "It is one and the same victim; the same person now offers it by the ministry of His priests, who then offered Himself on the cross, the manner of offering alone being different."[59]

69.   The priest is the same, Jesus Christ, whose sacred Person His minister represents. Now the minister, by reason of the sacerdotal consecration which he has received, is made like to the High Priest and possesses the power of performing actions in virtue of Christ's very person.[60] Wherefore in his priestly activity he in a certain manner "lends his tongue, and gives his hand" to Christ.[61]

70.   Likewise the victim is the same, namely, our divine Redeemer in His human nature with His true body and blood. The manner, however, in which Christ is offered is different. On the cross He completely offered Himself and all His sufferings to God, and the immolation of the victim was brought about by the bloody death, which He underwent of His free will. But on the altar, by reason of the glorified state of His human nature, "death shall have no more dominion over Him,"[62] and so the shedding of His blood is impossible; still, according to the plan of divine wisdom, the sacrifice of our Redeemer is shown forth in an admirable manner by external signs which are the symbols of His death. For by the "transubstantiation" of bread into the body of Christ and of wine into His blood, His body and blood are both really present: now the eucharistic species under which He is present symbolize the actual separation of His body and blood. Thus the commemorative representation of His death, which actually took place on Calvary, is repeated in every sacrifice of the altar, seeing that Jesus Christ is symbolically shown by separate symbols to be in a state of victimhood.

71.   Moreover, the appointed ends are the same. The first of these is to give glory to the Heavenly Father. From His birth to His death Jesus Christ burned with zeal for the divine glory; and the offering of His blood upon the cross rose to heaven in an odor of sweetness. To perpetuate this praise, the members of the Mystical Body are united with their divine Head in the eucharistic sacrifice,

---

58. Council of Trent, Sess. 22, c. 1.

59. *Ibid.*, c. 2.

60. Cf. Saint Thomas, *Summa Theologica*, III^a, q. 22, art. 4.

61. Saint John Chrysostom, *In Joann. Hom.*, 86:4.

62. Rom. 6:9.

and with Him, together with the Angels and Archangels, they sing immortal praise to God[63] and give all honor and glory to the Father Almighty.[64]

72.   The second end is duly to give thanks to God. Only the divine Redeemer, as the eternal Father's most beloved Son whose immense love He knew, could offer Him a worthy return of gratitude. This was His intention and desire at the Last Supper when He "gave thanks."[65] He did not cease to do so when hanging upon the cross, nor does He fail to do so in the august sacrifice of the altar, which is an act of thanksgiving or a "eucharistic" act; since this "is truly meet and just, right and availing unto salvation."[66]

73.   The third end proposed is that of expiation, propitiation and reconciliation. Certainly, no one was better fitted to make satisfaction to Almighty God for all the sins of men than was Christ. Therefore, He desired to be immolated upon the cross "as a propitiation for our sins, not for ours only but also for those of the whole world"[67] and likewise He daily offers Himself upon our altars for our redemption, that we may be rescued from eternal damnation and admitted into the company of the elect. This He does, not for us only who are in this mortal life, but also "for all who rest in Christ, who have gone before us with the sign of faith and repose in the sleep of peace;"[68] for whether we live, or whether we die "still we are not separated from the one and only Christ."[69]

74.   The fourth end, finally, is that of impetration. Man, being the prodigal son, has made bad use of and dissipated the goods which he received from his heavenly Father. Accordingly, he has been reduced to the utmost poverty and to extreme degradation. However, Christ on the cross "offering prayers and supplications with a loud cry and tears, has been heard for His reverence."[70] Likewise upon the altar He is our mediator with God in the same efficacious manner, so that we may be filled with every blessing and grace.

75.   It is easy, therefore, to understand why the holy Council of Trent lays down that by means of the eucharistic sacrifice the saving virtue of the cross is imparted to us for the remission of the sins we daily commit.[71]

76.   Now the Apostle of the Gentiles proclaims the copious plenitude and the perfection of the sacrifice of the cross, when he says that Christ by one oblation has perfected for ever them that are sanctified.[72] For the merits of this sacrifice, since they are altogether boundless and immeasurable, know no limits; for they are meant for all men of every time and place. This follows from the fact that

63. Cf. Roman Missal, Preface.

64. Cf. *Ibid.*, Canon.

65. Mark, 14:23.

66. Roman Missal, Preface.

67. 1 John, 2:2.

68. Roman Missal, Canon of the Mass.

69. Saint Augustine, *De Trinit.*, Book XIII, c. 19.

70. Heb. 5:7.

71. Cf. Sess. 22, c. 1.

72. Cf. Heb. 10:14.

in this sacrifice the God-Man is the priest and victim; that His immolation was entirely perfect, as was His obedience to the will of His eternal Father; and also that He suffered death as the Head of the human race: "See how we were bought: Christ hangs upon the cross, see at what a price He makes His purchase . . . He sheds His blood, He buys with His blood, He buys with the blood of the Spotless Lamb, He buys with the blood of God's only Son. He who buys is Christ; the price is His blood; the possession bought is the world."[73]

77.   This purchase, however, does not immediately have its full effect; since Christ, after redeeming the world at the lavish cost of His own blood, still must come into complete possession of the souls of men. Wherefore, that the redemption and salvation of each person and of future generations unto the end of time may be effectively accomplished, and be acceptable to God, it is necessary that men should individually come into vital contact with the sacrifice of the cross, so that the merits, which flow from it, should be imparted to them. In a certain sense it can be said that on Calvary Christ built a font of purification and salvation which He filled with the blood He shed; but if men do not bathe in it and there wash away the stains of their iniquities, they can never be purified and saved.

78.   The cooperation of the faithful is required so that sinners may be individually purified in the blood of the Lamb. For though, speaking generally, Christ reconciled by His painful death the whole human race with the Father, He wished that all should approach and be drawn to His cross, especially by means of the sacraments and the eucharistic sacrifice, to obtain the salutary fruits produced by Him upon it. Through this active and individual participation, the members of the Mystical Body not only become daily more like to their divine Head, but the life flowing from the Head is imparted to the members, so that we can each repeat the words of St. Paul, "With Christ I am nailed to the cross: I live, now not I, but Christ liveth in me."[74] We have already explained sufficiently and of set purpose on another occasion, that Jesus Christ "when dying on the cross, bestowed upon His Church, as a completely gratuitous gift, the immense treasure of the redemption. But when it is a question of distributing this treasure, He not only commits the work of sanctification to His Immaculate Spouse, but also wishes that, to a certain extent, sanctity should derive from her activity."[75]

79.   The august sacrifice of the altar is, as it were, the supreme instrument whereby the merits won by the divine Redeemer upon the cross are distributed to the faithful: "as often as this commemorative sacrifice is offered, there is wrought the work of our Redemption."[76] This, however, so far from lessening the dignity of the actual sacrifice on Calvary, rather proclaims and renders more manifest its greatness and its necessity, as the Council of Trent declares.[77] Its daily immolation reminds us that there is no salvation except in the cross of

73. Saint Augustine, *Enarr. in Ps.* 147, n. 16.

74. Gal. 2:19-20.

75. Encyclical Letter, *Mystici Corporis*, June 29, 1943.

76. Roman Missal, Secret of the Ninth Sunday after Pentecost.

77. Cf. Sess. 22, c. 2. and can. 4.

our Lord Jesus Christ[78] and that God Himself wishes that there should be a continuation of this sacrifice "from the rising of the sun till the going down thereof,"[79] so that there may be no cessation of the hymn of praise and thanksgiving which man owes to God, seeing that he required His help continually and has need of the blood of the Redeemer to remit sin which challenges God's justice.

80.   It is, therefore, desirable, Venerable Brethren, that all the faithful should be aware that to participate in the eucharistic sacrifice is their chief duty and supreme dignity, and that not in an inert and negligent fashion, giving way to distractions and day-dreaming, but with such earnestness and concentration that they may be united as closely as possible with the High Priest, according to the Apostle, "Let this mind be in you which was also in Christ Jesus."[80] And together with Him and through Him let them make their oblation, and in union with Him let them offer up themselves.

81.   It is quite true that Christ is a priest; but He is a priest not for Himself but for us, when in the name of the whole human race He offers our prayers and religious homage to the eternal Father; He is also a victim and for us since He substitutes Himself for sinful man. Now the exhortation of the Apostle, "Let this mind be in you which was also in Christ Jesus," requires that all Christians should possess, as far as is humanly possible, the same dispositions as those which the divine Redeemer had when He offered Himself in sacrifice: that is to say, they should in a humble attitude of mind, pay adoration, honor, praise and thanksgiving to the supreme majesty of God. Moreover, it means that they must assume to some extent the character of a victim, that they deny themselves as the Gospel commands, that freely and of their own accord they do penance and that each detests and satisfies for his sins. It means, in a word, that we must all undergo with Christ a mystical death on the cross so that we can apply to ourselves the words of St. Paul, "With Christ I am nailed to the cross."[81]

82.   The fact, however, that the faithful participate in the eucharistic sacrifice does not mean that they also are endowed with priestly power. It is very necessary that you make this quite clear to your flocks.

83.   For there are today, Venerable Brethren, those who, approximating to errors long since condemned[82] teach that in the New Testament by the word "priesthood" is meant only that priesthood which applies to all who have been baptized; and hold that the command by which Christ gave power to His apostles at the Last Supper to do what He Himself had done, applies directly to the entire Christian Church, and that thence, and thence only, arises the hierarchical priesthood. Hence they assert that the people are possessed of a true priestly power, while the priest only acts in virtue of an office committed to him by the community. Wherefore, they look on the eucharistic sacrifice as a "concelebration,"

---

78. Cf. Gal. 6:14.
79. Mal. 1:11.
80. Phil. 2:5.
81. Gal. 2:19.
82. Cf. Council of Trent, Sess. 23. c. 4.

in the literal meaning of that term, and consider it more fitting that priests should "concelebrate" with the people present than that they should offer the sacrifice privately when the people are absent.

84.   It is superfluous to explain how captious errors of this sort completely contradict the truths which we have just stated above, when treating of the place of the priest in the Mystical Body of Jesus Christ. But we deem it necessary to recall that the priest acts for the people only because he represents Jesus Christ, who is Head of all His members and offers Himself in their stead. Hence, he goes to the altar as the minister of Christ, inferior to Christ but superior to the people.[83] The people, on the other hand, since they in no sense represent the divine Redeemer and are not mediator between themselves and God, can in no way possess the sacerdotal power.

85.   All this has the certitude of faith. However, it must also be said that the faithful do offer the divine Victim, though in a different sense.

86.   This has already been stated in the clearest terms by some of Our predecessors and some Doctors of the Church. "Not only," says Innocent III of immortal memory, "do the priests offer the sacrifice, but also all the faithful: for what the priest does personally by virtue of his ministry, the faithful do collectively by virtue of their intention."[84] We are happy to recall one of St. Robert Bellarmine's many statements on this subject. "The sacrifice," he says "is principally offered in the person of Christ. Thus the oblation that follows the consecration is a sort of attestation that the whole Church consents in the oblation made by Christ, and offers it along with Him."[85]

87.   Moreover, the rites and prayers of the eucharistic sacrifice signify and show no less clearly that the oblation of the Victim is made by the priests in company with the people. For not only does the sacred minister, after the oblation of the bread and wine when he turns to the people, say the significant prayer: "Pray brethren, that my sacrifice and yours may be acceptable to God the Father Almighty;"[86] but also the prayers by which the divine Victim is offered to God are generally expressed in the plural number: and in these it is indicated more than once that the people also participate in this august sacrifice inasmuch as they offer the same. The following words, for example, are used: "For whom we offer, or who offer up to Thee . . . We therefore beseech thee, O Lord, to be appeased and to receive this offering of our bounded duty, as also of thy whole household. . . We thy servants, as also thy whole people . . . do offer unto thy most excellent majesty, of thine own gifts bestowed upon us, a pure victim, a holy victim, a spotless victim."[87]

---

83. Cf. Saint Robert Bellarmine, *De Missa, 2, c.4.*

84. *De Sacro Altaris Mysterio,* 3:6.

85. *De Missa,* 1, c. 27.

86. Roman Missal, Ordinary of the Mass.

87. *Ibid.,* Canon of the Mass.

88.   Nor is it to be wondered at, that the faithful should be raised to this dignity. By the waters of baptism, as by common right, Christians are made members of the Mystical Body of Christ the Priest, and by the "character" which is imprinted on their souls, they are appointed to give worship to God. Thus they participate, according to their condition, in the priesthood of Christ.

89.   In every age of the Church's history, the mind of man, enlightened by faith, has aimed at the greatest possible knowledge of things divine. It is fitting, then, that the Christian people should also desire to know in what sense they are said in the canon of the Mass to offer up the sacrifice. To satisfy such a pious desire, then, We shall here explain the matter briefly and concisely.

90.   First of all the more extrinsic explanations are these: it frequently happens that the faithful assisting at Mass join their prayers alternately with those of the priest, and sometimes—a more frequent occurrence in ancient times—they offer to the ministers at the altar bread and wine to be changed into the body and blood of Christ, and, finally, by their alms they get the priest to offer the divine victim for their intentions.

91.   But there is also a more profound reason why all Christians, especially those who are present at Mass, are said to offer the sacrifice.

92.   In this most important subject it is necessary, in order to avoid giving rise to a dangerous error, that we define the exact meaning of the word "offer." The unbloody immolation at the words of consecration, when Christ is made present upon the altar in the state of a victim, is performed by the priest and by him alone, as the representative of Christ and not as the representative of the faithful. But it is because the priest places the divine victim upon the altar that he offers it to God the Father as an oblation for the glory of the Blessed Trinity and for the good of the whole Church. Now the faithful participate in the oblation, understood in this limited sense, after their own fashion and in a twofold manner, namely, because they not only offer the sacrifice by the hands of the priest, but also, to a certain extent, in union with him. It is by reason of this participation that the offering made by the people is also included in liturgical worship.

93.   Now it is clear that the faithful offer the sacrifice by the hands of the priest from the fact that the minister at the altar, in offering a sacrifice in the name of all His members, represents Christ, the Head of the Mystical Body. Hence the whole Church can rightly be said to offer up the victim through Christ. But the conclusion that the people offer the sacrifice with the priest himself is not based on the fact that, being members of the Church no less than the priest himself, they perform a visible liturgical rite; for this is the privilege only of the minister who has been divinely appointed to this office: rather it is based on the fact that the people unite their hearts in praise, impetration, expiation and thanksgiving with prayers or intention of the priest, even of the High Priest himself, so that in the one and same offering of the victim and according to a visible sacerdotal rite, they may be presented to God the Father. It is obviously necessary that the external sacrificial rite should, of its very nature, signify the internal worship of the heart. Now the sacrifice of the New Law signifies that supreme worship

by which the principal Offerer himself, who is Christ, and, in union with Him and through Him, all the members of the Mystical Body pay God the honor and reverence that are due to Him.

94.   We are very pleased to learn that this teaching, thanks to a more intense study of the liturgy on the part of many, especially in recent years, has been given full recognition. We must, however, deeply deplore certain exaggerations and over-statements which are not in agreement with the true teaching of the Church.

95.   Some in fact disapprove altogether of those Masses which are offered privately and without any congregation, on the ground that they are a departure from the ancient way of offering the sacrifice; moreover, there are some who assert that priests cannot offer Mass at different altars at the same time, because, by doing so, they separate the community of the faithful and imperil its unity; while some go so far as to hold that the people must confirm and ratify the sacrifice if it is to have its proper force and value.

96.   They are mistaken in appealing in this matter to the social character of the eucharistic sacrifice, for as often as a priest repeats what the divine Redeemer did at the Last Supper, the sacrifice is really completed. Moreover, this sacrifice, necessarily and of its very nature, has always and everywhere the character of a public and social act, inasmuch as he who offers it acts in the name of Christ and of the faithful, whose Head is the divine Redeemer, and he offers it to God for the holy Catholic Church, and for the living and the dead.[88] This is undoubtedly so, whether the faithful are present—as we desire and commend them to be in great numbers and with devotion—or are not present, since it is in no wise required that the people ratify what the sacred minister has done.

97.   Still, though it is clear from what We have said that the Mass is offered in the name of Christ and of the Church and that it is not robbed of its social effects though it be celebrated by a priest without a server, nonetheless, on account of the dignity of such an august mystery, it is our earnest desire—as Mother Church has always commanded—that no priest should say Mass unless a server is at hand to answer the prayers, as canon 813 prescribes.

98.   In order that the oblation by which the faithful offer the divine Victim in this sacrifice to the heavenly Father may have its full effect, it is necessary that the people add something else, namely, the offering of themselves as a victim.

99.   This offering in fact is not confined merely to the liturgical sacrifice. For the Prince of the Apostles wishes us, as living stones built upon Christ, the cornerstone, to be able as "a holy priesthood, to offer up spiritual sacrifices, acceptable to God by Jesus Christ."[89] St. Paul the Apostle addresses the following words of exhortation to Christians, without distinction of time, "I beseech you therefore, . . . that you present your bodies, a living sacrifice, holy, pleasing unto God,

---

88. Roman Missal, Canon of the Mass.
89. 1 Peter, 2:5.

your reasonable service."[90] But at that time especially when the faithful take part in the liturgical service with such piety and recollection that it can truly be said of them: "whose faith and devotion is known to Thee,"[91] it is then, with the High Priest and through Him they offer themselves as a spiritual sacrifice, that each one's faith ought to become more ready to work through charity, his piety more real and fervent, and each one should consecrate himself to the furthering of the divine glory, desiring to become as like as possible to Christ in His most grievous sufferings.

100. This we are also taught by those exhortations which the Bishop, in the Church's name, addresses to priests on the day of their ordination, "Understand what you do, imitate what you handle, and since you celebrate the mystery of the Lord's death, take good care to mortify your members with their vices and concupiscences."[92] In almost the same manner the sacred books of the liturgy advise Christians who come to Mass to participate in the sacrifice: "At this . . . altar let innocence be in honor, let pride be sacrificed, anger slain, impurity and every evil desire laid low, let the sacrifice of chastity be offered in place of doves and instead of the young pigeons the sacrifice of innocence."[93] While we stand before the altar, then, it is our duty so to transform our hearts, that every trace of sin may be completely blotted out, while whatever promotes supernatural life through Christ may be zealously fostered and strengthened even to the extent that, in union with the immaculate Victim, we become a victim acceptable to the eternal Father.

101. The prescriptions in fact of the sacred liturgy aim, by every means at their disposal, at helping the Church to bring about this most holy purpose in the most suitable manner possible. This is the object not only of readings, homilies and other sermons given by priests, as also the whole cycle of mysteries which are proposed for our commemoration in the course of the year, but it is also the purpose of vestments, of sacred rites and their external splendor. All these things aim at "enhancing the majesty of this great Sacrifice, and raising the minds of the faithful by means of these visible signs of religion and piety, to the contemplation of the sublime truths contained in this sacrifice."[94]

102. All the elements of the liturgy, then, would have us reproduce in our hearts the likeness of the divine Redeemer through the mystery of the cross, according to the words of the Apostle of the Gentiles, "With Christ I am nailed to the cross. I live, now not I, but Christ liveth in me."[95] Thus we become a victim, as it were, along with Christ to increase the glory of the eternal Father.

103. Let this, then, be the intention and aspiration of the faithful, when they offer up the divine Victim in the Mass. For if, as St. Augustine writes, our mystery

---

90. Rom. 12:1.

91. Roman Missal, Canon of the Mass.

92. Roman Pontifical, Ordination of a priest.

93. *Ibid.*, Consecration of an altar, Preface.

94. Cf. Council of Trent, Sess. 22, c. 5.

95. Gal. 2:19–20.

is enacted on the Lord's table, that is Christ our Lord Himself,[96] who is the Head and symbol of that union through which we are the body of Christ[97] and members of His Body;[98] if St. Robert Bellarmine teaches, according to the mind of the Doctor of Hippo, that in the sacrifice of the altar there is signified the general sacrifice by which the whole Mystical Body of Christ, that is, all the city of the redeemed, is offered up to God through Christ, the High Priest:[99] nothing can be conceived more just or fitting than that all of us in union with our Head, who suffered for our sake, should also sacrifice ourselves to the eternal Father. For in the sacrament of the altar, as the same St. Augustine has it, the Church is made to see that in what she offers she herself is offered.[100]

104. Let the faithful, therefore, consider to what a high dignity they are raised by the sacrament of baptism. They should not think it enough to participate in the eucharistic sacrifice with that general intention which befits members of Christ and children of the Church, but let them further, in keeping with the spirit of the sacred liturgy, be most closely united with the High Priest and His earthly minister, at the time the consecration of the divine Victim is enacted, and at that time especially when those solemn words are pronounced, "By Him and with Him and in Him is to Thee, God the Father almighty, in the unity of the Holy Ghost, all honor and glory for ever and ever";[101] to these words in fact the people answer, "Amen." Nor should Christians forget to offer themselves, their cares, their sorrows, their distress and their necessities in union with their divine Savior upon the cross.

105. Therefore, they are to be praised who, with the idea of getting the Christian people to take part more easily and more fruitfully in the Mass, strive to make them familiar with the "Roman Missal," so that the faithful, united with the priest, may pray together in the very words and sentiments of the Church. They also are to be commended who strive to make the liturgy even in an external way a sacred act in which all who are present may share. This can be done in more than one way, when, for instance, the whole congregation, in accordance with the rules of the liturgy, either answer the priest in an orderly and fitting manner, or sing hymns suitable to the different parts of the Mass, or do both, or finally in high Masses when they answer the prayers of the minister of Jesus Christ and also sing the liturgical chant.

106. These methods of participation in the Mass are to be approved and recommended when they are in complete agreement with the precepts of the Church and the rubrics of the liturgy. Their chief aim is to foster and promote the people's piety and intimate union with Christ and His visible minister and to arouse those internal sentiments and dispositions which should make our hearts become like to that of the High Priest of the New Testament. However, though they show

96. Cf. *Serm.* 272.
97. Cf. 1 Cor. 12:27.
98. Cf. Eph. 5:30.
99. Cf. Saint Robert Bellarmine, *De Missa*, 2, c. 8.
100. Cf. *De Civitate Dei*, Book 10, c. 6.
101. Roman Missal, Canon of the Mass.

also in an outward manner that the very nature of the sacrifice, as offered by the Mediator between God and men,[102] must be regarded as the act of the whole Mystical Body of Christ, still they are by no means necessary to constitute it a public act or to give it a social character. And besides, a "dialogue" Mass of this kind cannot replace the high Mass, which, as a matter of fact, though it should be offered with only the sacred ministers present, possesses its own special dignity due to the impressive character of its ritual and the magnificence of its ceremonies. The splendor and grandeur of a high Mass, however, are very much increased if, as the Church desires, the people are present in great numbers and with devotion.

107. It is to be observed, also, that they have strayed from the path of truth and right reason who, led away by false opinions, make so much of these accidentals as to presume to assert that without them the Mass cannot fulfill its appointed end.

108. Many of the faithful are unable to use the Roman missal even though it is written in the vernacular; nor are all capable of understanding correctly the liturgical rites and formulas. So varied and diverse are men's talents and characters that it is impossible for all to be moved and attracted to the same extent by community prayers, hymns and liturgical services. Moreover, the needs and inclinations of all are not the same, nor are they always constant in the same individual. Who, then, would say, on account of such a prejudice, that all these Christians cannot participate in the Mass nor share its fruits? On the contrary, they can adopt some other method which proves easier for certain people; for instance, they can lovingly meditate on the mysteries of Jesus Christ or perform other exercises of piety or recite prayers which, though they differ from the sacred rites, are still essentially in harmony with them.

109. Wherefore We exhort you, Venerable Brethren, that each in his diocese or ecclesiastical jurisdiction supervise and regulate the manner and method in which the people take part in the liturgy, according to the rubrics of the missal and in keeping with the injunctions which the Sacred Congregation of Rites and the Code of canon law have published. Let everything be done with due order and dignity, and let no one, not even a priest, make use of the sacred edifices according to his whim to try out experiments. It is also Our wish that in each diocese an advisory committee to promote the liturgical apostolate should be established, similar to that which cares for sacred music and art, so that with your watchful guidance everything may be carefully carried out in accordance with the prescriptions of the Apostolic See.

110. In religious communities let all those regulations be accurately observed which are laid down in their respective constitutions, nor let any innovations be made which the superiors of these communities have not previously approved.

111. But however much variety and disparity there may be in the exterior manner and circumstances in which the Christian laity participate in the Mass and other liturgical functions, constant and earnest effort must be made to unite

---

102. Cf. 1 Tim. 2:5.

the congregation in spirit as much as possible with the divine Redeemer, so that their lives may be daily enriched with more abundant sanctity, and greater glory be given to the heavenly Father.

112. The august sacrifice of the altar is concluded with communion or the partaking of the divine feast. But, as all know, the integrity of the sacrifice only requires that the priest partake of the heavenly food. Although it is most desirable that the people should also approach the holy table, this is not required for the integrity of the sacrifice.

113. We wish in this matter to repeat the remarks which Our predecessor Benedict XIV makes with regard to the definitions of the Council of Trent: "First We must state that none of the faithful can hold that private Masses, in which the priest alone receives holy communion, are therefore unlawful and do not fulfill the idea of the true, perfect and complete unbloody sacrifice instituted by Christ our Lord. For the faithful know quite well, or at least can easily be taught, that the Council of Trent, supported by the doctrine which the uninterrupted tradition of the Church has preserved, condemned the new and false opinion of Luther as opposed to this tradition."[103] "If anyone shall say that Masses in which the priest only receives communion, are unlawful, and therefore should be abolished, let him be anathema."[104]

114. They, therefore, err from the path of truth who do not want to have Masses celebrated unless the faithful communicate; and those are still more in error who, in holding that it is altogether necessary for the faithful to receive holy communion as well as the priest, put forward the captious argument that here there is question not of a sacrifice merely, but of a sacrifice and a supper of brotherly union, and consider the general communion of all present as the culminating point of the whole celebration.

115. Now it cannot be over-emphasized that the eucharistic sacrifice of its very nature is the unbloody immolation of the divine Victim, which is made manifest in a mystical manner by the separation of the sacred species and by their oblation to the eternal Father. Holy communion pertains to the integrity of the Mass and to the partaking of the august sacrament; but while it is obligatory for the priest who says the Mass, it is only something earnestly recommended to the faithful.

116. The Church, as the teacher of truth, strives by every means in her power to safeguard the integrity of the Catholic faith, and like a mother solicitous for the welfare of her children, she exhorts them most earnestly to partake fervently and frequently of the richest treasure of our religion.

117. She wishes in the first place that Christians—especially when they cannot easily receive holy communion—should do so at least by desire, so that with

103. Encyclical Letter *Certiores effecti*, November 13, 1742, par. 1.
104. Council of Trent, Sess. 22, can. 8.

renewed faith, reverence, humility and complete trust in the goodness of the divine Redeemer, they may be united to Him in the spirit of the most ardent charity.

118. But the desire of Mother Church does not stop here. For since by feasting upon the bread of angels we can by a "sacramental" communion, as we have already said, also become partakers of the sacrifice, she repeats the invitation to all her children individually, "Take and eat. . . Do this in memory of Me"[105] so that "we may continually experience within us the fruit of our redemption"[106] in a more efficacious manner. For this reason the Council of Trent, reechoing, as it were, the invitation of Christ and His immaculate Spouse, has earnestly exhorted "the faithful when they attend Mass to communicate not only by a spiritual communion but also by a sacramental one, so that they may obtain more abundant fruit from this most holy sacrifice."[107] Moreover, our predecessor of immortal memory, Benedict XIV, wishing to emphasize and throw fuller light upon the truth that the faithful by receiving the Holy Eucharist become partakers of the divine sacrifice itself, praises the devotion of those who, when attending Mass, not only elicit a desire to receive holy communion but also want to be nourished by hosts consecrated during the Mass, even though, as he himself states, they really and truly take part in the sacrifice should they receive a host which has been duly consecrated at a previous Mass. He writes as follows: "And although in addition to those to whom the celebrant gives a portion of the Victim he himself has offered in the Mass, they also participate in the same sacrifice to whom a priest distributes the Blessed Sacrament that has been reserved; however, the Church has not for this reason ever forbidden, nor does she now forbid, a celebrant to satisfy the piety and just request of those who, when present at Mass, want to become partakers of the same sacrifice, because they likewise offer it after their own manner, nay more, she approves of it and desires that it should not be omitted and would reprehend those priests through whose fault and negligence this participation would be denied to the faithful."[108]

119. May God grant that all accept these invitations of the Church freely and with spontaneity. May He grant that they participate even every day, if possible, in the divine sacrifice, not only in a spiritual manner, but also by reception of the august sacrament, receiving the body of Jesus Christ which has been offered for all to the eternal Father. Arouse Venerable Brethren, in the hearts of those committed to your care, a great and insatiable hunger for Jesus Christ. Under your guidance let the children and youth crowd to the altar rails to offer themselves, their innocence and their works of zeal to the divine Redeemer. Let husbands and wives approach the holy table so that nourished on this food they may learn to make the children entrusted to them conformed to the mind and heart of Jesus Christ.

120. Let the workers be invited to partake of this sustaining and never failing nourishment that it may renew their strength and obtain for their labors an

---

105. 1 Cor. 11:24.
106. Roman Missal, Collect for Feast of Corpus Christi.
107. Sess. 22, c. 6.
108. Encyclical Letter *Certiores effecti*, par. 3.

everlasting recompense in heaven; in a word, invite all men of whatever class and compel them to come in;[109] since this is the bread of life which all require. The Church of Jesus Christ needs no other bread than this to satisfy fully our souls' wants and desires, and to unite us in the most intimate union with Jesus Christ, to make us "one body,"[110] to get us to live together as brothers who, breaking the same bread, sit down to the same heavenly table, to partake of the elixir of immortality.[111]

121. Now it is very fitting, as the liturgy otherwise lays down, that the people receive holy communion after the priest has partaken of the divine repast upon the altar; and, as we have written above, they should be commended who, when present at Mass, receive hosts consecrated at the same Mass, so that it is actually verified, "that as many of us, as, at this altar, shall partake of and receive the most holy body and blood of thy Son, may be filled with every heavenly blessing and grace."[112]

122. Still sometimes there may be a reason, and that not infrequently, why holy communion should be distributed before or after Mass and even immediately after the priest receives the sacred species—and even though hosts consecrated at a previous Mass should be used. In these circumstances—as we have stated above—the people duly take part in the eucharistic sacrifice and not seldom they can in this way more conveniently receive holy communion. Still, though the Church with the kind heart of a mother strives to meet the spiritual needs of her children, they, for their part, should not readily neglect the directions of the liturgy and, as often as there is no reasonable difficulty, should aim that all their actions at the altar manifest more clearly the living unity of the Mystical Body.

123. When the Mass, which is subject to special rules of the liturgy, is over, the person who has received holy communion is not thereby freed from his duty of thanksgiving; rather, it is most becoming that, when the Mass is finished, the person who has received the Eucharist should recollect himself, and in intimate union with the divine Master hold loving and fruitful converse with Him. Hence they have departed from the straight way of truth, who, adhering to the letter rather than the sense, assert and teach that, when Mass has ended, no such thanksgiving should be added, not only because the Mass is itself a thanksgiving, but also because this pertains to a private and personal act of piety and not to the good of the community.

124. But, on the contrary, the very nature of the sacrament demands that its reception should produce rich fruits of Christian sanctity. Admittedly the congregation has been officially dismissed, but each individual, since he is united with Christ, should not interrupt the hymn of praise in his own soul, "always returning thanks for all in the name of our Lord Jesus Christ to God the Father."[113]

---

109. Cf. Luke, 14:23.
110. 1 Cor. 10:17.
111. Cf. Saint Ignatius Martyr, *Ad Eph.* 20.
112. Roman Missal, Canon of the Mass.
113. Eph. 5:20.

The sacred liturgy of the Mass also exhorts us to do this when it bids us pray in these words, "Grant, we beseech thee, that we may always continue to offer thanks[114] . . . and may never cease from praising thee."[115] Wherefore, if there is no time when we must not offer God thanks, and if we must never cease from praising Him, who would dare to reprehend or find fault with the Church, because she advises her priests[116] and faithful to converse with the divine Redeemer for at least a short while after holy communion, and inserts in her liturgical books, fitting prayers, enriched with indulgences, by which the sacred ministers may make suitable preparation before Mass and holy communion or may return thanks afterwards? So far is the sacred liturgy from restricting the interior devotion of individual Christians, that it actually fosters and promotes it so that they may be rendered like to Jesus Christ and through Him be brought to the heavenly Father; wherefore this same discipline of the liturgy demands that whoever has partaken of the sacrifice of the altar should return fitting thanks to God. For it is the good pleasure of the divine Redeemer to hearken to us when we pray, to converse with us intimately and to offer us a refuge in His loving Heart.

125. Moreover, such personal colloquies are very necessary that we may all enjoy more fully the supernatural treasures that are contained in the Eucharist and according to our means, share them with others, so that Christ our Lord may exert the greatest possible influence on the souls of all.

126. Why then, Venerable Brethren, should we not approve of those who, when they receive holy communion, remain on in closest familiarity with their divine Redeemer even after the congregation has been officially dismissed, and that not only for the consolation of conversing with Him, but also to render Him due thanks and praise and especially to ask help to defend their souls against anything that may lessen the efficacy of the sacrament and to do everything in their power to cooperate with the action of Christ who is so intimately present. We exhort them to do so in a special manner by carrying out their resolutions, by exercising the Christian virtues, as also by applying to their own necessities the riches they have received with royal Liberality. The author of that golden book *The Imitation of Christ* certainly speaks in accordance with the letter and the spirit of the liturgy, when he gives the following advice to the person who approaches the altar, "Remain on in secret and take delight in your God; for He is yours whom the whole world cannot take away from you."[117]

127. Therefore, let us all enter into closest union with Christ and strive to lose ourselves, as it were, in His most holy soul and so be united to Him that we may have a share in those acts with which He adores the Blessed Trinity with a homage that is most acceptable, and by which He offers to the eternal Father supreme praise and thanks which find an harmonious echo throughout the heavens and the earth, according to the words of the prophet, "All ye works of the Lord, bless

---

114. Roman Missal, Postcommunion for Sunday within the Octave of Ascension.
115. *Ibid.*, Postcommunion for First Sunday after Pentecost.
116. Code of Canon Law, can. 810.
117. Book IV, c. 12.

the Lord."[118] Finally, in union with these sentiments of Christ, let us ask for heavenly aid at that moment in which it is supremely fitting to pray for and obtain help in His name.[119] For it is especially in virtue of these sentiments that we offer and immolate ourselves as a victim, saying, "make of us thy eternal offering."[120]

128. The divine Redeemer is ever repeating His pressing invitation, "Abide in Me."[121] Now by the sacrament of the Eucharist, Christ remains in us and we in Him, and just as Christ, remaining in us, lives and works, so should we remain in Christ and live and work through Him.

129. The Eucharistic Food contains, as all are aware, "truly, really and substantially the Body and Blood together with soul and divinity of our Lord Jesus Christ."[122] It is no wonder, then, that the Church, even from the beginning, adored the body of Christ under the appearance of bread; this is evident from the very rites of the august sacrifice, which prescribe that the sacred ministers should adore the most holy sacrament by genuflecting or by profoundly bowing their heads.

130. The Sacred Councils teach that it is the Church's tradition right from the beginning, to worship "with the same adoration the Word Incarnate as well as His own flesh,"[123] and St. Augustine asserts that, "No one eats that flesh, without first adoring it," while he adds that "not only do we not commit a sin by adoring it, but that we do sin by not adoring it."[124]

131. It is on this doctrinal basis that the cult of adoring the Eucharist was founded and gradually developed as something distinct from the sacrifice of the Mass. The reservation of the sacred species for the sick and those in danger of death introduced the praiseworthy custom of adoring the blessed Sacrament which is reserved in our churches. This practice of adoration, in fact, is based on strong and solid reasons. For the Eucharist is at once a sacrifice and a sacrament; but it differs from the other sacraments in this that it not only produces grace, but contains in a permanent manner the Author of grace Himself. When, therefore, the Church bids us adore Christ hidden behind the eucharistic veils and pray to Him for spiritual and temporal favors, of which we ever stand in need, she manifests living faith in her divine Spouse who is present beneath these veils, she professes her gratitude to Him and she enjoys the intimacy of His friendship.

---

118. Dan. 3:57.
119. Cf. John 16: 3.
120. Roman Missal, Secret for Mass of the Most Blessed Trinity.
121. John, 15:4.
122. Council of Trent, Sess. 13, can. 1.
123. Second Council of Constantinople, *Anath, de trib. Capit.*, can. 9; compare Council of Ephesus, *Anath. Cyrill*, can 8. Cf. Council of Trent, Sess. 13, can. 6; Pius VI Constitution *Auctorem fidei*, n. 61.
124. Cf. *Enarr in Ps.* 98:9.

132. Now, the Church in the course of centuries has introduced various forms of this worship which are ever increasing in beauty and helpfulness: as, for example, visits of devotion to the tabernacles, even every day; benediction of the Blessed Sacrament; solemn processions, especially at the time of Eucharistic Congress, which pass through cities and villages; and adoration of the Blessed Sacrament publicly exposed. Sometimes these public acts of adoration are of short duration. Sometimes they last for one, several and even for forty hours. In certain places they continue in turn in different churches throughout the year, while elsewhere adoration is perpetual day and night, under the care of religious communities, and the faithful quite often take part in them.

133. These exercises of piety have brought a wonderful increase in faith and supernatural life to the Church militant upon earth and they are reechoed to a certain extent by the Church triumphant in heaven which sings continually a hymn of praise to God and to the Lamb "who was slain."[125] Wherefore, the Church not merely approves these pious practices, which in the course of centuries have spread everywhere throughout the world, but makes them her own, as it were, and by her authority commends them.[126] They spring from the inspiration of the liturgy and if they are performed with due propriety and with faith and piety, as the liturgical rules of the Church require, they are undoubtedly of the very greatest assistance in living the life of the liturgy.

134. Nor is it to be admitted that by this Eucharistic cult men falsely confound the historical Christ, as they say, who once lived on earth, with the Christ who is present in the august Sacrament of the altar, and who reigns glorious and triumphant in heaven and bestows supernatural favors. On the contrary, it can be claimed that by this devotion the faithful bear witness to and solemnly avow the faith of the Church that the Word of God is identical with the Son of the Virgin Mary, who suffered on the cross, who is present in a hidden manner in the Eucharist and who reigns upon His heavenly throne. Thus, St. John Chrysostom states: "When you see It [the Body of Christ] exposed, say to yourself: Thanks to this body, I am no longer dust and ashes, I am no more a captive but a freeman: hence I hope to obtain heaven and the good things that are there in store for me, eternal life, the heritage of the angels, companionship with Christ; death has not destroyed this body which was pierced by nails and scourged, . . . this is that body which was once covered with blood, pierced by a lance, from which issued saving fountains upon the world, one of blood and the other of water. . . This body He gave to us to keep and eat, as a mark of His intense love."[127]

135. That practice in a special manner is to be highly praised according to which many exercises of piety, customary among the faithful, and with benediction of the blessed sacrament. For excellent and of great benefit is that custom which makes the priest raise aloft the Bread of Angels before congregations with heads bowed down in adoration, and forming with It the sign of the cross implores the

125. Apoc. 5:12, cp. 7:10.
126. Cf. Council of Trent, Sess. 13, c. 5 and can. 6.
127. *In I ad Cor.*, 24:4.

heavenly Father to deign to look upon His Son who for love of us was nailed to the cross, and for His sake and through Him who willed to be our Redeemer and our brother, be pleased to shower down heavenly favors upon those whom the immaculate blood of the Lamb has redeemed.[128]

136. Strive then, Venerable Brethren, with your customary devoted care so the churches, which the faith and piety of Christian peoples have built in the course of centuries for the purpose of singing a perpetual hymn of glory to God almighty and of providing a worthy abode for our Redeemer concealed beneath the eucharistic species, may be entirely at the disposal of greater numbers of the faithful who, called to the feet of their Savior, hearken to His most consoling invitation, "Come to Me all you who labor and are heavily burdened, and I will refresh you."[129] Let your churches be the house of God where all who enter to implore blessings rejoice in obtaining whatever they ask[130] and find there heavenly consolation.

137. Only thus can it be brought about that the whole human family settling their differences may find peace, and united in mind and heart may sing this song of hope and charity, "Good Pastor, truly bread—Jesus have mercy on us—feed us, protect us—bestow on us the vision of all good things in the land of the living."[131]

138. The ideal of Christian life is that each one be united to God in the closest and most intimate manner. For this reason, the worship that the Church renders to God, and which is based especially on the eucharistic sacrifice and the use of the sacraments, is directed and arranged in such a way that it embraces by means of the divine office, the hours of the day, the weeks and the whole cycle of the year, and reaches all the aspects and phases of human life.

139. Since the divine Master commanded "that we ought always to pray and not to faint,"[132] the Church faithfully fulfills this injunction and never ceases to pray: she urges us in the words of the Apostle of the Gentiles, "by him Jesus let us offer the sacrifice of praise always to God."[133]

140. Public and common prayer offered to God by all at the same time was customary in antiquity only on certain days and at certain times. Indeed, people prayed to God not only in groups but in private houses and occasionally with neighbors and friends. But soon in different parts of the Christian world the practice arose of setting aside special times for praying, as for example, the last hour of the day when evening set in and the lamps were lighted; or the first, heralded, when the night was coming to an end, by the crowing of the cock and the rising of the morning star. Other times of the day, as being more suitable for prayer are indicated in Sacred Scripture, in Hebrew customs or in keeping with

---

128. Cf. 1 Peter, 1:19.
129. Matt. 11:28.
130. Cf. Roman Missal, Collect for Mass for the Dedication of a Church.
131. Roman Missal, Sequence *Lauda Sion* in Mass for Feast of Corpus Christi.
132. Luke, 18:1.
133. Heb. 13:15.

the practice of everyday life. According to the acts of the Apostles, the disciples of Jesus Christ all came together to pray at the third hour, when they were all filled with the Holy Ghost;[134] and before eating, the Prince of the Apostles went up to the higher parts of the house to pray, about the sixth hour;[135] Peter and John "went up into the Temple at the ninth hour of prayer"[136] and at "midnight Paul and Silas praying . . . praised God."[137]

141. Thanks to the work of the monks and those who practice asceticism, these various prayers in the course of time become ever more perfected and by the authority of the Church are gradually incorporated into the sacred liturgy.

142. The divine office is the prayer of the Mystical Body of Jesus Christ, offered to God in the name and on behalf of all Christians, when recited by priests and other ministers of the Church and by religious who are deputed by the Church for this.

143. The character and value of the divine office may be gathered from the words recommended by the Church to be said before starting the prayers of the office, namely, that they be said "worthily, with attention and devotion."

144. By assuming human nature, the Divine Word introduced into this earthly exile a hymn which is sung in heaven for all eternity. He unites to Himself the whole human race and with it sings this hymn to the praise of God. As we must humbly recognize that "we know not what we should pray for, as we ought, the Spirit Himself asketh for us with unspeakable groanings."[138] Moreover, through His Spirit in us, Christ entreats the Father, "God could not give a greater gift to men . . . [Jesus] prays for us, as our Priest; He prays in us as our Head; we pray to Him as our God . . . we recognize in Him our voice and His voice in us . . . He is prayed to as God, He prays under the appearance of a servant; in heaven He is Creator; here, created though not changed, He assumes a created nature which is to be changed and makes us with Him one complete man, head and body."[139]

145. To this lofty dignity of the Church's prayer, there should correspond earnest devotion in our souls. For when in prayer the voice repeats those hymns written under the inspiration of the Holy Ghost and extols God's infinite perfections, it is necessary that the interior sentiment of our souls should accompany the voice so as to make those sentiments our own in which we are elevated to heaven, adoring and giving due praise and thanks to the Blessed Trinity; "so let us chant in choir that mind and voice may accord together."[140] It is not merely a question of recitation or of singing which, however perfect according to norms of music and the sacred rites, only reaches the ear, but it is especially a question

---

134. Cf. Acts, 2:1-15.
135. *Ibid.*, 10:9.
136. *Ibid.*, 3:1.
137. *Ibid.*, 16:25.
138. Rom. 8:26.
139. Saint Augustine, *Enarr. in Ps.* 85, n. 1.
140. Saint Benedict, *Regula Monachorum*, c. 19.

of the ascent of the mind and heart to God so that, united with Christ, we may completely dedicate ourselves and all our actions to Him.

146. On this depends in no small way the efficacy of our prayers. These prayers in fact, when they are not addressed directly to the Word made man, conclude with the phrase "though Jesus Christ our Lord." As our Mediator with God, He shows to the heavenly Father His glorified wounds, "always living to make intercessions for us."[141]

147. The Psalms, as all know, form the chief part of the divine office. They encompass the full round of the day and sanctify it. Cassiodorus speaks beautifully about the Psalms as distributed in his day throughout the divine office: "With the celebration of matins they bring a blessing on the coming day, they set aside for us the first hour and consecrate the third hour of the day, they gladden the sixth hour with the breaking of bread, at the ninth they terminate our fast, they bring the evening to a close and at nightfall they shield our minds from darkness."[142]

148. The Psalms recall to mind the truths revealed by God to the chosen people, which were at one time frightening and at another filled with wonderful tenderness; they keep repeating and fostering the hope of the promised Liberator which in ancient times was kept alive with song, either around the hearth or in the stately temple; they show forth in splendid light the prophesied glory of Jesus Christ: first, His supreme and eternal power, then His lowly coming to this terrestrial exile, His kingly dignity and priestly power and, finally, His beneficent labors, and the shedding of His blood for our redemption. In a similar way they express the joy, the bitterness, the hope and fear of our hearts and our desire of loving God and hoping in Him alone, and our mystic ascent to divine tabernacles.

149. "The psalm is . . . a blessing for the people, it is the praise of God, the tribute of the nation, the common language and acclamation of all, it is the voice of the Church, the harmonious confession of faith, signifying deep attachment to authority; it is the joy of freedom, the expression of happiness, an echo of bliss."[143]

150. In an earlier age, these canonical prayers were attended by many of the faithful. But this gradually ceased, and, as We have already said, their recitation at present is the duty only of the clergy and of religious. The laity have no obligation in this matter. Still, it is greatly to be desired that they participate in reciting or chanting vespers sung in their own parish on feast days. We earnestly exhort you, Venerable Brethren, to see that this pious practice is kept up, and that wherever it has ceased you restore it if possible. This, without doubt, will produce salutary results when vespers are conducted in a worthy and fitting manner and with such helps as foster the piety of the faithful. Let the public and private observance of the feasts of the Church, which are in a special way

---

141. Heb. 7:25.
142. *Explicatio in Psalterium*, Preface. Text as found in Migne, Parres Larini, 70:10. But some are of the opinion that part of this passage should not be attributed to Cassiodorus.
143. Saint Ambrose, *Enarr in Ps.* 1, n. 9.

dedicated and consecrated to God, be kept inviolable; and especially the Lord's day which the Apostles, under the guidance of the Holy Ghost, substituted for the sabbath. Now, if the order was given to the Jews: "Six days shall you do work; in the seventh day is the sabbath, the rest holy to the Lord. Every one that shall do any work on this day, shall die;"[144] how will these Christians not fear spiritual death who perform servile work on feast-days, and whose rest on these days is not devoted to religion and piety but given over to the allurements of the world? Sundays and holydays, then, must be made holy by divine worship, which gives homage to God and heavenly food to the soul. Although the Church only commands the faithful to abstain from servile work and attend Mass and does not make it obligatory to attend evening devotions, still she desires this and recommends it repeatedly. Moreover, the needs of each one demand it, seeing that all are bound to win the favor of God if they are to obtain His benefits. Our soul is filled with the greatest grief when We see how the Christian people of today profane the afternoon of feast days; public places of amusement and public games are frequented in great numbers while the churches are not as full as they should be. All should come to our churches and there be taught the truth of the Catholic faith, sing the praises of God, be enriched with benediction of the blessed sacrament given by the priest and be strengthened with help from heaven against the adversities of this life. Let all try to learn those prayers which are recited at vespers and fill their souls with their meaning. When deeply penetrated by these prayers, they will experience what St. Augustine said about himself: "How much did I weep during hymns and verses, greatly moved at the sweet singing of thy Church. Their sound would penetrate my ears and their truth melt my heart, sentiments of piety would well up, tears would flow and that was good for me."[145]

151.   Throughout the entire year, the Mass and the divine office center especially around the person of Jesus Christ. This arrangement is so suitably disposed that our Savior dominates the scene in the mysteries of His humiliation, of His redemption and triumph.

152.   While the sacred liturgy calls to mind the mysteries of Jesus Christ, it strives to make all believers take their part in them so that the divine Head of the mystical Body may live in all the members with the fullness of His holiness. Let the souls of Christians be like altars on each one of which a different phase of the sacrifice, offered by the High priest, comes to life again, as it were: pains and tears which wipe away and expiate sin; supplication to God which pierces heaven; dedication and even immolation of oneself made promptly, generously and earnestly; and, finally, that intimate union by which we commit ourselves and all we have to God, in whom we find our rest. "The perfection of religion is to imitate whom you adore."[146]

153.   By these suitable ways and methods in which the liturgy at stated times proposes the life of Jesus Christ for our meditation, the Church gives us examples

---

144. Exod. 31:15.
145. *Confessions*, Book 9, c. 6.
146. Saint Augustine, *De Civitate Dei*, Book 8, c. 17.

to imitate, points out treasures of sanctity for us to make our own, since it is fitting that the mind believes what the lips sing, and that what the mind believes should be practiced in public and private life.

154. In the period of Advent, for instance, the Church arouses in us the consciousness of the sins we have had the misfortune to commit, and urges us, by restraining our desires and practicing voluntary mortification of the body, to recollect ourselves in meditation, and experience a longing desire to return to God who alone can free us by His grace from the stain of sin and from its evil consequences.

155. With the coming of the birthday of the Redeemer, she would bring us to the cave of Bethlehem and there teach that we must be born again and undergo a complete reformation; that will only happen when we are intimately and vitally united to the Word of God made man and participate in His divine nature, to which we have been elevated.

156. At the solemnity of the Epiphany, in putting before us the call of the Gentiles to the Christian faith, she wishes us daily to give thanks to the Lord for such a blessing; she wishes us to seek with lively faith the living and true God, to penetrate deeply and religiously the things of heaven, to love silence and meditation in order to perceive and grasp more easily heavenly gifts.

157. During the days of Septuagesima and Lent, our Holy Mother the Church over and over again strives to make each of us seriously consider our misery, so that we may be urged to a practical emendation of our lives, detest our sins heartily and expiate them by prayer and penance. For constant prayer and penance done for past sins obtain for us divine help, without which every work of ours is useless and unavailing.

158. In Holy Week, when the most bitter sufferings of Jesus Christ are put before us by the liturgy, the Church invites us to come to Calvary and follow in the blood-stained footsteps of the divine Redeemer, to carry the cross willingly with Him, to reproduce in our own hearts His spirit of expiation and atonement, and to die together with Him.

159. At the Paschal season, which commemorates the triumph of Christ, our souls are filled with deep interior joy: we, accordingly, should also consider that we must rise, in union with the Redeemer, from our cold and slothful life to one of greater fervor and holiness by giving ourselves completely and generously to God, and by forgetting this wretched world in order to aspire only to the things of heaven: "If you be risen with Christ, seek the things that are above . . . mind the things that are above."[147]

160. Finally, during the time of Pentecost, the Church by her precept and practice urges us to be more docile to the action of the Holy Spirit who wishes us to

147. Col.3:1–2.

be on fire with divine love so that we may daily strive to advance more in virtue and thus become holy as Christ our Lord and His Father are holy.

161. Thus, the liturgical year should be considered as a splendid hymn of praise offered to the heavenly Father by the Christian family through Jesus, their perpetual Mediator. Nevertheless, it requires a diligent and well-ordered study on our part to be able to know and praise our Redeemer ever more and more. It requires a serious effort and constant practice to imitate His mysteries, to enter willingly upon His path of sorrow and thus finally share His glory and eternal happiness.

162. From what We have already explained, Venerable Brethren, it is perfectly clear how much modern writers are wanting in the genuine and true liturgical spirit who, deceived by the illusion of a higher mysticism, dare to assert that attention should be paid not to the historic Christ but to a "pneumatic" or glorified Christ. They do not hesitate to assert that a change has taken place in the piety of the faithful by dethroning, as it were, Christ from His position; since they say that the glorified Christ, who liveth and reigneth forever and sitteth at the right hand of the Father, has been overshadowed and in His place has been substituted that Christ who lived on earth. For this reason, some have gone so far as to want to remove from the churches images of the divine Redeemer suffering on the cross.

163. But these false statements are completely opposed to the solid doctrine handed down by tradition. "You believe in Christ born in the flesh," says St. Augustine, "and you will come to Christ begotten of God."[148] In the sacred liturgy, the whole Christ is proposed to us in all the circumstances of His life, as the Word of the eternal Father, as born of the Virgin Mother of God, as He who teaches us truth, heals the sick, consoles the afflicted, who endures suffering and who dies; finally, as He who rose triumphantly from the dead and who, reigning in the glory of heaven, sends us the Holy Paraclete and who abides in His Church forever; "Jesus Christ, yesterday and today, and the same forever."[149] Besides, the liturgy shows us Christ not only as a model to be imitated but as a master to whom we should listen readily, a Shepherd whom we should follow, Author of our salvation, the Source of our holiness and the Head of the Mystical Body whose members we are, living by His very life.

164. Since His bitter sufferings constitute the principal mystery of our redemption, it is only fitting that the Catholic faith should give it the greatest prominence. This mystery is the very center of divine worship since the Mass represents and renews it every day and since all the sacraments are most closely united with the cross.[150]

165. Hence, the liturgical year, devotedly fostered and accompanied by the Church, is not a cold and lifeless representation of the events of the past, or a

---

148. Saint Augustine, *Enarr. in Ps.* 123, n. 2.
149. Heb. 13:8.
150. Saint Thomas, *Summa Theologica* III^a, q. 49 and q. 62, art. 5.

simple and bare record of a former age. It is rather Christ Himself who is ever living in His Church. Here He continues that journey of immense mercy which He lovingly began in His mortal life, going about doing good,[151] with the design of bringing men to know His mysteries and in a way live by them. These mysteries are ever present and active not in a vague and uncertain way as some modern writers hold, but in the way that Catholic doctrine teaches us. According to the Doctors of the Church, they are shining examples of Christian perfection, as well as sources of divine grace, due to the merit and prayers of Christ; they still influence us because each mystery brings its own special grace for our salvation. Moreover, our holy Mother the Church, while proposing for our contemplation the mysteries of our Redeemer, asks in her prayers for those gifts which would give her children the greatest possible share in the spirit of these mysteries through the merits of Christ. By means of His inspiration and help and through the cooperation of our wills we can receive from Him living vitality as branches do from the tree and members from the head; thus slowly and laboriously we can transform ourselves "unto the measure of the age of the fullness of Christ."[152]

166. In the course of the liturgical year, besides the mysteries of Jesus Christ, the feasts of the saints are celebrated. Even though these feasts are of a lower and subordinate order, the Church always strives to put before the faithful examples of sanctity in order to move them to cultivate in themselves the virtues of the divine Redeemer.

167. We should imitate the virtues of the saints just as they imitated Christ, for in their virtues there shines forth under different aspects the splendor of Jesus Christ. Among some of these saints the zeal of the apostolate stood out, in others courage prevailed even to the shedding of blood, constant vigilance marked others out as they kept watch for the divine Redeemer, while in others the virginal purity of soul was resplendent and their modesty revealed the beauty of Christian humility; there burned in all of them the fire of charity towards God and their neighbor. The sacred liturgy puts all these gems of sanctity before us so that we may consider them for our salvation, and "rejoicing at their merits, we may be inflamed by their example."[153] It is necessary, then, to practice "in simplicity innocence, in charity concord, in humility modesty, diligence in government, readiness in helping those who labor, mercy in serving the poor, in defending truth, constancy, in the strict maintenance of discipline justice, so that nothing may be wanting in us of the virtues which have been proposed for our imitation. These are the footprints left by the saints in their journey homeward, that guided by them we might follow them into glory."[154] In order that we may be helped by our senses, also, the Church wishes that images of the saints be displayed in our churches, always, however, with the same intention "that we imitate the virtues of those whose images we venerate."[155]

---

151. Cf. Acts, 10:38.
152. Eph. 4:13.
153. Roman Missal, Collect for Third Mass of Several Martyrs outside Paschaltide.
154. Saint Bede the Venerable, *Hom. subd. 70* for Feast of All Saints.
155. Roman Missal, Collect for Mass of Saint John Damascene.

168. But there is another reason why the Christian people should honor the saints in heaven, namely, to implore their help and "that we be aided by the pleadings of those whose praise is our delight."[156] Hence, it is easy to understand why the sacred liturgy provides us with many different prayers to invoke the intercession of the saints.

169. Among the saints in heaven the Virgin Mary Mother of God is venerated in a special way. Because of the mission she received from God, her life is most closely linked with the mysteries of Jesus Christ, and there is no one who has followed in the footsteps of the Incarnate Word more closely and with more merit than she: and no one has more grace and power over the most Sacred Heart of the Son of God and through Him with the Heavenly Father. Holier than the Cherubim and Seraphim, she enjoys unquestionably greater glory than all the other saints, for she is "full of grace,"[157] she is the Mother of God, who happily gave birth to the Redeemer for us. Since she is therefore, "Mother of mercy, our life, our sweetness and our hope," let us all cry to her "mourning and weeping in this vale of tears,"[158] and confidently place ourselves and all we have under her patronage. She became our Mother also when the divine Redeemer offered the sacrifice of Himself; and hence by this title also, we are her children. She teaches us all the virtues; she gives us her Son and with Him all the help we need, for God "wished us to have everything through Mary."[159]

170. Throughout this liturgical journey which begins anew for us each year under the sanctifying action of the Church, and strengthened by the help and example of the saints, especially of the Immaculate Virgin Mary, "let us draw near with a true heart, in fullness of faith having our hearts sprinkled from an evil conscience, and our bodies washed with clean water,"[160] let us draw near to the "High Priest"[161] that with Him we may share His life and sentiments and by Him penetrate "even within the veil,"[162] and there honor the heavenly Father for ever and ever.

171. Such is the nature and the object of the sacred liturgy: it treats of the Mass, the sacraments, the divine office; it aims at uniting our souls with Christ and sanctifying them through the divine Redeemer in order that Christ be honored and, through Him and in Him, the most Holy Trinity, *Glory be to the Father and to the Son and to the Holy Ghost.*

172. In order that the errors and inaccuracies, mentioned above, may be more easily removed from the Church, and that the faithful following safer norms may be able to use more fruitfully the liturgical apostolate, We have deemed it

---

156. Saint Bernard, *Sermon 2 for Feast of All Saints.*
157. Luke, 1:28.
158. "Salve Regina."
159. Saint Bernard, *In Nativ. B.M.V.,* 7.
160. Heb. 10:22.
161. *Ibid.,* 10:21.
162. *Ibid.,* 6:19.

opportune, Venerable Brethren, to add some practical applications of the doctrine which We have explained.

173. When dealing with genuine and solid piety We stated that there could be no real opposition between the sacred liturgy and other religious practices, provided they be kept within legitimate bounds and performed for a legitimate purpose. In fact, there are certain exercises of piety which the Church recommends very much to clergy and religious.

174. It is Our wish also that the faithful, as well, should take part in these practices. The chief of these are: meditation on spiritual things, diligent examination of conscience, enclosed retreats, visits to the blessed sacrament, and those special prayers in honor of the Blessed Virgin Mary among which the rosary, as all know, has pride of place.[163]

175. From these multiple forms of piety, the inspiration and action of the Holy Spirit cannot be absent. Their purpose is, in various ways, to attract and direct our souls to God, purifying them from their sins, encouraging them to practice virtue and, finally, stimulating them to advance along the path of sincere piety by accustoming them to meditate on the eternal truths and disposing them better to contemplate the mysteries of the human and divine natures of Christ. Besides, since they develop a deeper spiritual life of the faithful, they prepare them to take part in sacred public functions with greater fruit, and they lessen the danger of liturgical prayers becoming an empty ritualism.

176. In keeping with your pastoral solicitude, Venerable Brethren, do not cease to recommend and encourage these exercises of piety from which the faithful, entrusted to your care, cannot but derive salutary fruit. Above all, do not allow—as some do, who are deceived under the pretext of restoring the liturgy or who idly claim that only liturgical rites are of any real value and dignity—that churches be closed during the hours not appointed for public functions, as has already happened in some places: where the adoration of the august sacrament and visits to our Lord in the tabernacles are neglected; where confession of devotion is discouraged; and devotion to the Virgin Mother of God, a sign of "predestination" according to the opinion of holy men, is so neglected, especially among the young, as to fade away and gradually vanish. Such conduct most harmful to Christian piety is like poisonous fruit, growing on the infected branches of a healthy tree, which must be cut off so that the life-giving sap of the tree may bring forth only the best fruit.

177. Since the opinions expressed by some about frequent confession are completely foreign to the spirit of Christ and His Immaculate Spouse and are also most dangerous to the spiritual life, let Us call to mind what with sorrow We wrote about this point in the encyclical on the Mystical Body. We urgently insist once more that what We expounded in very serious words be proposed by you for the serious consideration and dutiful obedience of your flock, especially to students for the priesthood and young clergy.

---

163. Cf. Code of Canon Law, Can. 125.

178. Take special care that as many as possible, not only of the clergy but of the laity and especially those in religious organizations and in the ranks of Catholic Action, take part in monthly days of recollection and in retreats of longer duration made with a view to growing in virtue. As We have previously stated, such spiritual exercises are most useful and even necessary to instill into souls solid virtue, and to strengthen them in sanctity so as to be able to derive from the sacred liturgy more efficacious and abundant benefits.

179. As regards the different methods employed in these exercises, it is perfectly clear to all that in the Church on earth, no less in the Church in heaven, there are many mansions,[164] and that asceticism cannot be the monopoly of anyone. It is the same spirit who breatheth where He will,[165] and who with differing gifts and in different ways enlightens and guides souls to sanctity. Let their freedom and the supernatural action of the Holy Spirit be so sacrosanct that no one presume to disturb or stifle them for any reason whatsoever.

180. However, it is well known that the spiritual exercise according to the method and norms of St. Ignatius have been fully approved and earnestly recommended by Our predecessors on account of their admirable efficacy. We, too, for the same reason have approved and commended them and willingly do We repeat this now.

181. Any inspiration to follow and practice extraordinary exercises of piety must most certainly come from the Father of Lights, from whom every good and perfect gift descends;[166] and, of course, the criterion of this will be the effectiveness of these exercises in making the divine cult loved and spread daily ever more widely, and in making the faithful approach the sacraments with more longing desire, and in obtaining for all things holy due respect and honor. If on the contrary, they are an obstacle to principles and norms of divine worship, or if they oppose or hinder them, one must surely conclude that they are not in keeping with prudence and enlightened zeal.

182. There are, besides, other exercises of piety which, although not strictly belonging to the sacred liturgy, are, nevertheless, of special import and dignity, and may be considered in a certain way to be an addition to the liturgical cult; they have been approved and praised over and over again by the Apostolic See and by the bishops. Among these are the prayers usually said during the month of May in honor of the Blessed Virgin Mother of God, or during the month of June to the most Sacred Heart of Jesus: also novenas and triduums, stations of the cross and other similar practices.

183. These devotions make us partakers in a salutary manner of the liturgical cult, because they urge the faithful to go frequently to the sacrament of penance, to attend Mass and receive communion with devotion, and, as well, encourage

---

164. Cf. John, 14:2.
165. John, 3:8.
166. Cf. James, 1:17.

them to meditate on the mysteries of our redemption and imitate the example of the saints.

184. Hence, he would do something very wrong and dangerous who would dare to take on himself to reform all these exercises of piety and reduce them completely to the methods and norms of liturgical rites. However, it is necessary that the spirit of the sacred liturgy and its directives should exercise such a salutary influence on them that nothing improper be introduced nor anything unworthy of the dignity of the house of God or detrimental to the sacred functions or opposed to solid piety.

185. Take care then, Venerable Brethren, that this true and solid piety increases daily and more under your guidance and bears more abundant fruit. Above all, do not cease to inculcate into the minds of all that progress in the Christian life does not consist in the multiplicity and variety of prayers and exercises of piety, but rather in their helpfulness towards spiritual progress of the faithful and constant growth of the Church universal. For the eternal Father "chose us in Him [Christ] before the foundation of the world that we should be holy and unspotted in His sight."[167] All our prayers, then, and all our religious practices should aim at directing our spiritual energies towards attaining this most noble and lofty end.

186. We earnestly exhort you, Venerable Brethren, that after errors and falsehoods have been removed, and anything that is contrary to truth or moderation has been condemned, you promote a deeper knowledge among the people of the sacred liturgy so that they more readily and easily follow the sacred rites and take part in them with true Christian dispositions.

187. First of all, you must strive that with due reverence and faith all obey the decrees of the Council of Trent, of the Roman Pontiffs, and the Sacred Congregation of Rites, and what the liturgical books ordain concerning external public worship.

188. Three characteristics of which Our predecessor Pius X spoke should adorn all liturgical services: sacredness, which abhors any profane influence; nobility, which true and genuine arts should serve and foster; and universality, which, while safeguarding local and legitimate custom, reveals the catholic unity of the Church.[168]

189. We desire to commend and urge the adornment of churches and altars. Let each one feel moved by the inspired word, "the zeal of thy house hath eaten me up";[169] and strive as much as in him lies that everything in the church, including vestments and liturgical furnishings, even though not rich nor lavish, be perfectly clean and appropriate, since all is consecrated to the Divine Majesty. If we have previously disapproved of the error of those who would wish to outlaw images from churches on the plea of reviving an ancient tradition, We now

---

167. Eph. 1:4.
168. Cf. Apostolic Letter (Motu Proprio) *Tra le sollecitudini*, November 22, 1903.
169. Ps. 68:9; John, 2:17.

deem it Our duty to censure the inconsiderate zeal of those who propose for veneration in the Churches and on the altars, without any just reason, a multitude of sacred images and statues, and also those who display unauthorized relics, those who emphasize special and insignificant practices, neglecting essential and necessary things. They thus bring religion into derision and lessen the dignity of worship.

190. Let us recall, as well, the decree about "not introducing new forms of worship and devotion."[170] We commend the exact observance of this decree to your vigilance.

191. As regards music, let the clear and guiding norms of the Apostolic See be scrupulously observed. Gregorian chant, which the Roman Church considers her own as handed down from antiquity and kept under her close tutelage, is proposed to the faithful as belonging to them also. In certain parts of the liturgy the Church definitely prescribes it;[171] it makes the celebration of the sacred mysteries not only more dignified and solemn but helps very much to increase the faith and devotion of the congregation. For this reason, Our predecessors of immortal memory, Pius X and Pius XI, decree—and We are happy to confirm with Our authority the norms laid down by them—that in seminaries and religious institutes, Gregorian chant be diligently and zealously promoted, and moreover that the old *Scholae Cantorum* be restored, at least in the principal churches. This has already been done with happy results in not a few places.[172]

192. Besides, "so that the faithful take a more active part in divine worship, let Gregorian chant be restored to popular use in the parts proper to the people. Indeed it is very necessary that the faithful attend the sacred ceremonies not as if they were outsiders or mute onlookers, but let them fully appreciate the beauty of the liturgy and take part in the sacred ceremonies, alternating their voices with the priest and the choir, according to the prescribed norms. If, please God, this is done, it will not happen that the congregation hardly ever or only in a low murmur answer the prayers in Latin or in the vernacular."[173] A congregation that is devoutly present at the sacrifice, in which our Savior together with His children redeemed with His sacred blood sings the nuptial hymn of His immense love, cannot keep silent, for "song befits the lover"[174] and, as the ancient saying has it, "he who sings well prays twice." Thus the Church militant, faithful as well as clergy, joins in the hymns of the Church triumphant and with the choirs of angels, and, all together, sing a wondrous and eternal hymn of praise to the most Holy Trinity in keeping with words of the preface, "with whom our voices, too, thou wouldst bid to be admitted."[175]

---

170. Supreme Sacred Congregation of the Holy Office, Decree of May 26, 1937.
171. Cf. Pius X, Apostolic Letter (Motu Proprio) *Tra le sollectitudini.*
172. Cf. Pius X, *loc. cit.*; Pius XI, Constitution *Divini cultus,* 2, 5.
173. Pius XI, Constitution *Divini cultus,* 9.
174. Saint Augustine, *Serm. 336,* n. 1.
175. Roman Missal, Preface.

193. It cannot be said that modern music and singing should be entirely excluded from Catholic worship. For, if they are not profane nor unbecoming to the sacredness of the place and function, and do not spring from a desire of achieving extraordinary and unusual effects, then our churches must admit them since they can contribute in no small way to the splendor of the sacred ceremonies, can lift the mind to higher things and foster true devotion of soul.

194. We also exhort you, Venerable Brethren, to promote with care congregational singing, and to see to its accurate execution with all due dignity, since it easily stirs up and arouses the faith and piety of large gatherings of the faithful. Let the full harmonious singing of our people rise to heaven like the bursting of a thunderous sea[176] and let them testify by the melody of their song to the unity of their hearts and minds,[177] as becomes brothers and the children of the same Father.

195. What We have said about music, applies to the other fine arts, especially to architecture, sculpture and painting. Recent works of art which lend themselves to the materials of modern composition, should not be universally despised and rejected through prejudice. Modern art should be given free scope in the due and reverent service of the church and the sacred rites, provided that they preserve a correct balance between styles tending neither to extreme realism nor to excessive "symbolism," and that the needs of the Christian community are taken into consideration rather than the particular taste or talent of the individual artist. Thus modern art will be able to join its voice to that wonderful choir of praise to which have contributed, in honor of the Catholic faith, the greatest artists throughout the centuries. Nevertheless, in keeping with the duty of Our office, We cannot help deploring and condemning those works of art, recently introduced by some, which seem to be a distortion and perversion of true art and which at times openly shock Christian taste, modesty and devotion, and shamefully offend the true religious sense. These must be entirely excluded and banished from our churches, like "anything else that is not in keeping with the sanctity of the place."[178]

196. Keeping in mind, Venerable Brethren, pontifical norms and decrees, take great care to enlighten and direct the minds and hearts of the artists to whom is given the task today of restoring or rebuilding the many churches which have been ruined or completely destroyed by war. Let them be capable and willing to draw their inspiration from religion to express what is suitable and more in keeping with the requirements of worship. Thus the human arts will shine forth with a wondrous heavenly splendor, and contribute greatly to human civilization, to the salvation of souls and the glory of God. The fine arts are really in conformity with religion when "as noblest handmaids they are at the service of divine worship."[179]

---

176. Saint Ambrose, *Hexameron*, 3:5, 23.
177. Cf. Acts, 4:32.
178. Code of Canon Law, can. 1178.
179. Pius XI, Constitution *Divini cultus*.

197. But there is something else of even greater importance, Venerable Brethren, which We commend to your apostolic zeal, in a very special manner. Whatever pertains to the external worship has assuredly its importance; however, the most pressing duty of Christians is to live the liturgical life, and increase and cherish its supernatural spirit.

198. Readily provide the young clerical student with facilities to understand the sacred ceremonies, to appreciate their majesty and beauty and to learn the rubrics with care, just as you do when he is trained in ascetics, in dogma and in a canon law and pastoral theology. This should not be done merely for cultural reasons and to fit the student to perform religious rites in the future, correctly and with due dignity, but especially to lead him into closest union with Christ, the Priest, so that he may become a holy minister of sanctity.

199. Try in every way, with the means and helps that your prudence deems best, that the clergy and people become one in mind and heart, and that the Christian people take such an active part in the liturgy that it becomes a truly sacred action of due worship to the eternal Lord in which the priest, chiefly responsible for the souls of his parish, and the ordinary faithful are united together.

200. To attain this purpose, it will greatly help to select carefully good and upright young boys from all classes of citizens who will come generously and spontaneously to serve at the altar with careful zeal and exactness. Parents of higher social standing and culture should greatly esteem this office for their children. If these youths, under the watchful guidance of the priests, are properly trained and encouraged to fulfill the task committed to them punctually, reverently and constantly, then from their number will readily come fresh candidates for the priesthood. The clergy will not then complain—as, alas, sometimes happens even in Catholic places—that in the celebration of the august sacrifice they find no one to answer or serve them.

201. Above all, try with your constant zeal to have all the faithful attend the eucharistic sacrifice from which they may obtain abundant and salutary fruit; and carefully instruct them in all the legitimate ways we have described above so that they may devoutly participate in it. The Mass is the chief act of divine worship; it should also be the source and center of Christian piety. Never think that you have satisfied your apostolic zeal until you see your faithful approach in great numbers the celestial banquet which is a sacrament of devotion, a sign of unity and a bond of love.[180]

202. By means of suitable sermons and particularly by periodic conferences and lectures, by special study weeks and the like, teach the Christian people carefully about the treasures of piety contained in the sacred liturgy so that they may be able to profit more abundantly by these supernatural gifts. In this matter, those who are active in the ranks of Catholic Action will certainly be a help to you, since they are ever at the service of the hierarchy in the work of promoting the kingdom of Jesus Christ.

---

180. Cf. Saint Augustine, *Tract. 26 in John 13*.

203. But in all these matters, it is essential that you watch vigilantly lest the enemy come into the field of the Lord and sow cockle among the wheat;[181] in other words, do not let your flocks be deceived by the subtle and dangerous errors of false mysticism or quietism—as you know We have already condemned these errors;[182] also do not let a certain dangerous "humanism" lead them astray, nor let there be introduced a false doctrine destroying the notion of Catholic faith, nor finally an exaggerated zeal for antiquity in matters liturgical. Watch with like diligence lest the false teaching of those be propagated who wrongly think and teach that the glorified human nature of Christ really and continually dwells in the "just" by His presence and that one and numerically the same grace, as they say, unites Christ with the members of His Mystical Body.

204. Never be discouraged by the difficulties that arise, and never let your pastoral zeal grow cold. "Blow the trumpet in Sion . . . call an assembly, gather together the people, sanctify the Church, assemble the ancients, gather together the little ones, and them that suck at the breasts,"[183] and use every help to get the faithful everywhere to fill the churches and crowd around the altars so that they may be restored by the graces of the sacraments and joined as living members to their divine Head, and with Him and through Him celebrate together the august sacrifice that gives due tribute of praise to the Eternal Father.

205. These, Venerable Brethren, are the subjects We desired to write to you about. We are moved to write that your children, who are also Ours, may more fully understand and appreciate the most precious treasures which are contained in the sacred liturgy: namely, the eucharistic sacrifice, representing and renewing the sacrifice of the cross, the sacraments which are the streams of divine grace and of divine life, and the hymn of praise, which heaven and earth daily offer to God.

206. We cherish the hope that these Our exhortations will not only arouse the sluggish and recalcitrant to a deeper and more correct study of the liturgy, but also instill into their daily lives its supernatural spirit according to the words of the Apostle, "extinguish not the spirit."[184]

207. To those whom an excessive zeal occasionally led to say and do certain things which saddened Us and which We could not approve, we repeat the warning of St. Paul, "But prove all things, hold fast that which is good."[185] Let Us paternally warn them to imitate in their thoughts and actions the Christian doctrine which is in harmony with the precepts of the immaculate Spouse of Jesus Christ, the mother of saints.

208. Let Us remind all that they must generously and faithfully obey their holy pastors who possess the right and duty of regulating the whole life, especially

---

181. Cf. Matt. 13:24–25.
182. Encyclical letter *Mystici Corporis*.
183. Joel, 2:15–16.
184. I Thess. 5:19.
185. *Ibid.*, 5:21.

the spiritual life, of the Church. "Obey your prelates and be subject to them. For they watch as being to render an account of your souls; that they may do this with joy and not with grief."[186]

209. May God, whom we worship, and who is "not the God of dissension but of peace,"[187] graciously grant to us all that during our earthly exile we may with one mind and one heart participate in the sacred liturgy which is, as it were, a preparation and a token of that heavenly liturgy in which we hope one day to sing together with the most glorious Mother of God and our most loving Mother, "To Him that sitteth on the throne, and to the Lamb, benediction and honor, and glory and power for ever and ever."[188]

210. In this joyous hope, We most lovingly impart to each and every one of you, Venerable Brethren, and to the flocks confided to your care, as a pledge of divine gifts and as a witness of Our special love, the apostolic benediction.

Given at Castel Gandolfo, near Rome, on the 20th day of November in the year 1947, the 9th of Our Pontificate.

PIUS XII

---

186. Heb. 13:17.
187. 1 Cor.14:33.
188. Apoc. 5:13.

THE DECREES
ON THE
RENEWAL OF HOLY WEEK

DE SOLEMNI VIGILIA
PASCHALI INSTAURANDA

DECREE RESTORING EASTER VIGIL

SACRED CONGREGATION OF RITES
FEBRUARY 9, 1951

LITURGICUS HEBDOMADAE
SANCTAE ORDO INSTAURATUR

THE RESTORATION OF
THE HOLY WEEK ORDER

DECREE AND INSTRUCTION OF
THE SACRED CONGREGATION OF RITES
NOVEMBER 16, 1955

CIRCA ORDINEM HEBDOMADAE
SANCTAE INSTAURATUM

THE RESTORED ORDER OF HOLY WEEK

ORDINANCES AND DECLARATIONS OF
THE SACRED CONGREGATION OF RITES
FEBRUARY 1, 1957

AN OVERVIEW OF THE DECREES ON THE RENEWAL OF HOLY WEEK

Corinna Laughlin

One of the firstfruits of Pope Pius XII's encyclical *Mediator Dei*, in which the Church officially embraced the Liturgical Movement, was the restoration of the liturgies of Holy Week. Like *Mediator Dei* before them, and *Sacrosanctum Concilium* after them, these decrees emphasize liturgical research as a guiding principle for restoration of the liturgy, and the participation of the faithful as the key value to be sought in reform.

The decrees were prepared by a special commission of scholars assembled by Pope Pius XII in 1948, and chaired by the head of the Sacred Congregation of Rites, Cardinal Clemente Micara, until 1953, and thereafter by Cardinal Gaetano Cicognani, who replaced him. The commission was discontinued on July 8, 1960, to be replaced, three days later, with the Preparatory Commission of the Second Vatican Council, which included many of the same members.[1]

BEGINNINGS: THE RESTORATION OF THE EASTER VIGIL

De solemni vigilia paschali instauranda appeared on February 9, 1951. The word *instauranda* means "restoration" or "repair," but as we will see, there are significant elements of reform in this decree as well.

The brief introduction points to the dramatic changes in the Easter Vigil over the centuries, as the celebration was gradually moved back from the early hours of Easter morning, to the evening before, and finally to the morning of Holy Saturday, and as "modifications were introduced to the detriment of the primitive symbolism."[2] But in the present day, "development in researches on ancient liturgy"[3] has given the Church a glimpse of the "primitive splendor"[4] of the Easter Vigil, and a longing to restore it. Changing the time of the celebration is the first and most important step. By moving the Vigil back to its proper time, late in the evening of Holy Saturday, the ancient texts and rites will have even deeper meaning, and there will be a signal pastoral benefit as well, by "facilitating the presence of numerous faithful."[5]

The decree also includes the revised rubrics for the Vigil. In addition to the time of the celebration, several other ancient practices are restored. The lighting

---

1. See Bugnini, Annibale [Archbishop]. *The Reform of the Liturgy, 1948–1975.* Translated by Matthew J. O'Connell, (Collegeville, MN: The Liturgical Press, 1990), p. 9.

2. *De solemni vigilia paschali instauranda*. Please note that the translation of this document included in this collection does not include article numbers. The complete Latin text, of which no official full-English translation exists, is available at the Vatican website in the *Acta Apostolica Sedis* for 1951, available at: www.vatican.va/archive/aas/documents/AAS%2043%20%5b1951%5d%20-%20ocr.pdf, pp. 128–137; accessed November 26, 2012.

3. Ibid.

4. Ibid.

5. Ibid.

of candles by the assembly returns, as does their participation in the procession following the Paschal candle. And there are some significant changes, intended to foster the participation of the faithful. Thus, the number of Old Testament readings is reduced from twelve to four (only with the 1970 Missal would it be increased to seven[6]), and a brand new element is added in the renewal of baptismal promises for the assembly—a revision made even more striking by the additional note that the vernacular may be used at the discretion of the bishop.

The restoration of the Easter Vigil was a watershed moment for the Liturgical Movement, as long-held principles bore fruit not only in words, but in the liturgy itself. Godfrey Diekmann, OSB called the reform of the Vigil "extraordinarily significant,"[7] and observed that it "was done precisely in order to make possible a better understanding and a greater degree of participation by the faithful."[8] Liturgist Pius Parsch thanked Pope Pius XII for giving Holy Saturday back to the Church as "the most calm and quiet day of the entire Church year, a day broken by no liturgical function."[9] He went on to claim some credit for the restoration of the Vigil:

> It is a restoration that is in part due to our efforts. For in its various editions *Das Jahr des Heiles* during more than a quarter century has stood at the door of the Father of Christendom like the importunate friend in the Gospel story until an answer was finally given. Even the last edition still expressed our wish: "It is one of the great objectives of the liturgical movement to restore to the Catholic world the Easter Vigil service, the 'mother of all vigils,' as St. Augustine called it. The unliturgical spirit and mentality of the last centuries has deprived us of the holiest of all nights; the liturgical spirit of our day will correct this error."[10]

De solemni vigilia paschali instauranda provided the restored Easter Vigil on an experimental basis. Local bishops, and religious congregations of men, were encouraged, but not required, to celebrate the Vigil according to the new rubrics, and to share their experiences with the Sacred Congregation for Rites. The response was so positive—Annibale Bugnini calls it "an explosion of joy throughout the Church"[11]—that work on the restoration of the entirety of Holy Week immediately began.

THE RESTORATION OF HOLY WEEK

Liturgicus hebdomadae sanctae Ordo instauratur, "The Restoration of the Holy Week Order," appeared on November 16, 1955. Unlike the 1951 decree on the Vigil, this decree is binding on all "who follow the Roman rite,"[12] beginning

---

6. Martimort, A.G. *The Church at Prayer, Volume IV: The Liturgy and Time*, (Collegeville, MN: The Liturgical Press, 1986), p. 41.

7. Hughes, Kathleen, Ed. *How Firm a Foundation: Voices of the Early Liturgical Movement*, (Chicago, IL: Liturgy Training Publications, 1990), p. 93.

8. Ibid.

9. Parsch, Pius. *The Church's Year of Grace, Volume II: Septuagesima to Holy Saturday*, (Collegeville, MN: The Liturgical Press, 1962), p. 337.

10. Ibid., pp. 337–338.

11. Bugnini, p. 10.

12. *Liturgicus hebdomadae sanctae Ordo instauratur*, prescription 1.

with Holy Week of 1956. ("Other Latin rites are bound to follow only the time established in the new ordo for the liturgical services"[13]—the fact that this is the only element required of all liturgical traditions is another indication of the importance of the shift in the start times of the various liturgies.)

The document begins with a fairly extensive history of the Church's celebration of Easter. It began with "a special three-day period,"[14] that is, Friday, Saturday, and Sunday, and then added Holy Thursday and Palm Sunday—"thus there arose a special liturgical week . . . enriched with exceptionally complete and sacred ceremonies,"[15] all closely related to the Gospel narratives.

But with time, and "for various pertinent reasons"[16] changes began to be introduced. Not only the Vigil but all the services of Holy Week were moved to the morning. The document uses strong language to describe the damage that was done: "The solemn liturgy of the Easter vigil . . . *lost* its original clarity and the meaning of its words and symbols when it was *torn* from its proper nocturnal setting. Moreover, Holy Saturday, with too early a recollection of the Easter gladness *intruding* into it, *lost* its original character."[17]

But the purity of the liturgies themselves is not the only concern here. With the changing "conditions of social life,"[18] most of the faithful no longer had the freedom to participate in the morning liturgies of the Triduum. Then, in 1642, Pope Urban VII declared that Thursday, Friday, and Saturday of Holy Week would no longer be Holydays of Obligation, but would rank simply as ferial days. As a result, attendance at these sacred liturgies declined even more, until "common and almost universal experience shows that these solemn and important liturgical services of the last three days of Holy Week are often conducted by the clergy in church buildings that are almost deserted."[19] And the absence of the faithful is cause for concern, because these liturgies are a source of grace, "endowed with a singular dignity, but also with a special sacramental force and efficacy for nourishing Christian life."[20] Here again, the presence and the understanding of the faithful are prime motivators in the restoration of Holy Week.

"At the Proper Time"

The second section of the decree is devoted to time, and the insistent refrain here is "at the proper time." Not only the principal liturgies of the Triduum, but the Liturgy of the Hours as well, must now be celebrated at their proper times. Thus, the Evening Mass of the Lord's Supper should begin "not before five o'clock or after eight o'clock,"[21] the Good Friday service at "approximately three o-clock . . . but not later than six o'clock"[22] and the Easter Vigil at about 11:00 PM. "Matins and lauds," the two morning offices, "are not anticipated but are

---

13. Ibid.
14. Ibid., introductory paragraphs.
15. Ibid.
16. Ibid.
17. Ibid., emphasis added.
18. Ibid., 5.
19. Ibid.
20. Ibid.
21. Ibid., prescription 7.
22. Ibid., prescription 8.

recited in the morning at the proper time."[23] While this sounds obvious enough, it is a change that would have a significant impact: Matins and Lauds were typically celebrated the evening before, and during Holy Week they had taken on a life of their own in the services known as Tenebrae.

Formerly, the Lenten fast ended at noon on Holy Saturday, and that day was spent in anticipation of Easter, with the Easter blessing of homes taking place on this day in many places. Now, the fast is extended until midnight of that day, and Holy Saturday becomes once again a day of anticipation and vigil.

Mystery and Meaning

The decree is accompanied by a practical "Instruction on the Correct Use of the Restored Ordo of Holy Week," and a final section "On the Solution of Certain Difficulties." The first section, about the need for "pastoral and ritual preparation," is perhaps the most intriguing. It emphasizes the duty of bishops to provide instruction for the priests "not only in the ritual observance of the restored ordo of Holy Week, but also in its liturgical meaning and its pastoral purpose."[24] It is not enough to know how to carry out these liturgies: priests need to understand what they are doing, and they need to help the faithful "properly to understand"[25] them as well, so that they can participate "both mentally and spiritually."[26] The document then gives brief notes on the key meaning of each of the principal liturgies of Holy Week: Palm Sunday is our "public testimony . . . to Christ the King;"[27] Holy Thursday is about love, and the people should especially be instructed on the "profound meaning" of the restored rite of the washing of feet;[28] on Good Friday, the people should recognize the connection between the suffering and Death of Christ and the sacrament we share, and thus the Communion Rite is restored, so that all may receive "the Lord's body which was given for all on this day;"[29] and Holy Saturday will require especially careful instruction so that people understand "the unique liturgical character"[30] of this day of waiting and meditation.

Sources of Tension

The restoration of Holy Week brought with it a change in emphasis. Popular devotions, which had long supplanted the liturgies themselves in the lives of the faithful, must now take second place. Bishops and priests are told "prudently to harmonize these customs, which appear to contribute to solid piety, with the restored ordo of Holy Week,"[31] and the faithful must come to realize "the supreme value of the sacred liturgy," greater than any devotion, "however good these may be."[32] One practice mentioned in the decree is the custom of visiting churches

23. Ibid., prescription 5.
24. Ibid., instruction 1.
25. Ibid.
26. Ibid.
27. Ibid., instruction 2a.
28. Ibid., instruction 2b.
29. Ibid., instruction 2c.
30. Ibid., instruction 2d.
31. Ibid., instruction 23.
32. Ibid.

on Holy Thursday, to pray before the altar of repose. With the change in the time of the liturgy from morning to evening, the number of hours available for adoration is significantly lessened—thus, "pastors and rectors of churches should warn the faithful in time about the public adoration of the holy Eucharist."[33]

The revisions to Holy Week would also cause some disruption to the sacramental practice in many areas. The faithful are urged to seek confession earlier in Holy Week, "especially in those places where it has been customary for the faithful to troop to confession on Holy Saturday evening and Easter Sunday morning."[34] The distribution of Holy Communion often took place at various times, after Mass or even outside of Mass entirely. This practice is tightened considerably—on Holy Thursday and Holy Saturday, Holy Communion "can be given only during Mass or immediately after it,"[35] and on Good Friday, only in the context of the liturgy, except for the sick and dying.

RESPONSES TO THE RESTORED RITES

On February 1, 1957, the Sacred Congregation of Rites issued *Circa Ordinem hebdomadae sanctae instauratum*. The document begins by remarking that "The liturgical restoration of Holy Week . . . was joyfully received by all and accomplished everywhere with the greatest pastoral success." But certain "practical difficulties" became clear after the first use of the restored rites in Holy Week of 1956. This third document provides additional details intended to bring greater integrity to the celebrations.

The restored Holy Week order provided for simple and solemn forms of the various liturgies. Now, the use of the solemn forms is strongly encouraged, and a reminder is added that even for the simple forms, additional ministers will be required, "either clerics or at least boys—a minimum of three for the Second Passion Sunday or Palm Sunday and for the Mass of the Lord's Supper; a minimum of four for the celebration of the liturgical service of Good Friday and for the Easter Vigil."[36] There is no room for liturgical minimalism in Holy Week! Other notes emphasize the integrity of the rites. Thus it is not permitted to bless palm branches outside of the liturgy.[37] The Transfer of the Blessed Sacrament may take place only in churches where the Good Friday liturgy will be observed[38] —emphasizing the link between the Eucharist and the Passion of the Lord. The conferral of Holy Orders—"tonsure or minor or major Orders"—may no longer take place during the Easter Vigil, as had previously been the case[39]—Baptism and our participation in the Paschal Mystery are the only focal points here.

CONCLUSION: LAYING A FOUNDATION FOR RENEWAL AND REFORM

More than a decade before the opening of the Council, liturgical renewal began in earnest with the restoration and reform of Holy Week. The values that drove

---

33. Ibid., instruction 10.

34. Ibid., instruction 2a.

35. Ibid., instruction 19.

36. *Circa Ordinem hebdomadae sanctae instauratum*, I.2.

37. Ibid., 2.5.

38. Ibid., 2.14.

39. Ibid., 5.22.

these decrees would emerge again in *Sacrosanctum Concilium* (SC): awareness of the historical development of the liturgy[40] and respect for the liturgies outside of the Roman Rite[41]; the power of the liturgy to form and teach[42]; the recognition that more is required in the celebration of the liturgy than merely following the rubrics[43]; the importance of the participation and understanding of the faithful[44]; the need for a variety of ministers to carry out the liturgy in its fullness[45]; the centrality of the Paschal Mystery in the life of the Church[46]; the value of the vernacular for the faithful.[47] While the liturgies of Holy Week would undergo additional reform and adaptation with the 1970 Missal, there is a deep and unmistakable continuity between these reforms and those of the Second Vatican Council.

---

40. See *Sacrosanctum Concilium* (SC) 21, 23.
41. Ibid., 3.
42. Ibid., 33.
43. Ibid., 11.
44. Ibid., 11, 14, 19.
45. Ibid., 28, 29.
46. Ibid., 102.
47. Ibid., 36.

DE SOLEMNI VIGILIA PASCHALI INSTAURANDA
DECREE RESTORING EASTER VIGIL

SACRED CONGREGATION OF RITES
FEBRUARY 9, 1951

Since early times the Church solemnly celebrates the Easter Vigil, which St. Augustine calls "the mother of all the holy vigils." This vigil was celebrated during the early hours of the morning preceding the Resurrection of Our Lord. But in the course of centuries and for various reasons, the celebration was put ahead, first to the early evening, then to the afternoon, and finally to the morning of Holy Saturday; at the same time some modifications were introduced to the detriment of the primitive symbolism.

However in our times, which are distinguished for development in researches on ancient liturgy, has witnessed the fulfillment of the ardent desire of bringing back the Easter Vigil to its primitive splendor and of assigning to it the time observed in the beginning, that is, the early hours of the night preceding Resurrection Sunday. In favor of such a return there is added a special motive of pastoral order: that of facilitating the presence of numerous faithful. In fact, as Holy Saturday is no longer a holyday, as it once was, the greater part of the faithful cannot assist at the sacred rite, if it takes place in the morning.

LITURGICUS HEBDOMADAE SANCTAE ORDO INSTAURATUR

THE RESTORATION OF THE HOLY WEEK ORDER

DECREE AND INSTRUCTION OF THE
SACRED CONGREGATION OF RITES
NOVEMBER 16, 1955

GENERAL DECREE

THE LITURGICAL ORDER OF HOLY WEEK IS RESTORED

From apostolic times holy Mother Church has taken care each year to celebrate the principal mysteries of our redemption, namely the passion, death and resurrection of our Lord Jesus Christ, with an absolutely singular commemoration.

At first the supreme moments of these mysteries, those of "the crucified, buried and risen" Christ (St. Augustine, *Ep.* 55, 14), were recalled in a special three-day period. Soon a solemn commemoration of the institution of the most holy Eucharist was added. Finally, on the Sunday immediately preceding the passion, a liturgical celebration of the triumphant messianic entry of our Lord and King into the Holy City was added. Thus there arose a special liturgical week which, by reason of the greatness of the mysteries celebrated, was designated as "Holy" and was enriched with exceptionally complete and sacred ceremonies.

In the beginning these rites were performed on the same days of the week and at the same hours of the day that the sacred mysteries occurred. Thus, the institution of the holy Eucharist was recalled on Thursday evening by the solemn Mass of the Lord's Supper. On Friday there was a special liturgical function in the hours after noon, recalling the Lord's passion and death. Finally, on Holy Saturday night there began a solemn vigil which ended the following morning with the joy of the resurrection.

During the middle ages they began, for various pertinent reasons to set an earlier time for the performance of liturgical services on those days, so that toward the end of that period all of these liturgical services had been transferred to the morning. This did not take place without detriment to the liturgical meaning, nor without causing some confusion between the Gospel "narratives and the liturgical ceremonies attached to them. The solemn liturgy of the Easter vigil in particular lost its original clarity and the meaning of its words and symbols when it was torn from its proper nocturnal setting. Moreover, Holy Saturday, with too early a recollection of the Easter gladness intruding into it, lost its original character as a day of mourning for the burial of the Lord.

In more recent times another change, very serious from the pastoral point of view, took place. For many centuries, Thursday, Friday and Saturday of Holy Week were holy days of obligation, so that the Christian people, freed from servile works, could be present at the ceremonies taking place on those days. But in the course of the seventeenth century the Roman pontiffs themselves were compelled, because of the complete change in the conditions of social life, to reduce the number of the holy days of obligation. And so Urban VIII was compelled in his apostolic constitution *Universa per orbem* of September 24, 1642, to declare that the last three days of Holy Week were no longer holy days of obligation, and to classify them as working days.

Hence, the attendance of the faithful at these ceremonies necessarily decreased, especially because the services had long been moved back to the morning hours, when schools, factories and public business of every kind are usually open and functioning on working days throughout the world. As a matter of fact, common and almost universal experience shows that these solemn and important liturgical services of the last three days of Holy Week are often conducted by the clergy in church buildings that are almost deserted.

This is certainly to be regretted, since these liturgical services of Holy Week are endowed not only with a singular dignity, but also with a special sacramental force and efficacy for nourishing Christian life.

Nor can there be proper compensation for the loss of these liturgical functions through those pious devotional exercises which are usually called extra-liturgical and which are performed in the afternoon hours of these three days.

For these reasons during recent years experts on the liturgy, priests having the care of souls, and especially the bishops have sent earnest petitions to the Holy See begging that the liturgical functions of the last three days of Holy Week be restored to the hours after noon, as formerly, so that all the faithful might more easily be present at these services.

After carefully considering the matter, Pope Pius XII restored the liturgy of the sacred vigil of Easter in 1951. The celebration was to be held at the discretion of the ordinary and as an experiment.

This experiment was highly successful everywhere, as many ordinaries reported to the Holy See. These same ordinaries also renewed their petitions for a liturgical restoration for the other days of Holy Week, asking that the sacred functions be moved back to the evening hours as had been done in the case of the Easter vigil. Moreover, evening Masses, provided for in the apostolic constitution *Christus Domimis* of January 6, 1953, were being said everywhere and were attended by many. With all these things in mind Pope Pius XII commanded the Commission for the Restoration of the Liturgy established by him to examine the question of restoring the order of Holy Week and to propose a solution. After obtaining that answer, His Holiness decreed, as the seriousness of the affair demanded, that the entire question be subjected to a special examination by the Cardinals of the Sacred Congregation of Rites.

The cardinals gathered in an extraordinary session at the Vatican on July 19 of this year. They considered the matter thoroughly and voted unanimously that the restored ordo of Holy Week be approved and prescribed, subject to the approval of the Holy Father.

After all this had been reported in detail to the Holy Father by the undersigned Cardinal Prefect, His Holiness deigned to approve what the cardinals had decided.

Hence, by special mandate of the same Pope Pius XII, the Sacred Congregation of Rites has decreed the following:

I. THE RESTORED ORDER OF HOLY WEEK IS PRESCRIBED

1.   Those who follow the Roman rite are bound in the future to follow the restored ordo for Holy Week set forth in the original Vatican edition. Those who follow other Latin rites are bound to follow only the time established in the new ordo for the liturgical services.

2.   This new ordo must be followed from March 25, the second Sunday of Passiontide or Palm Sunday, 1956.

3.   Throughout all of Holy Week no commemoration is admitted and in the Mass *orationes imperatae*, no matter how they may have been ordered, are also forbidden.

II. ON THE PROPER HOURS FOR THE CELEBRATION OF THE SACRED LITURGY OF HOLY WEEK

On the Divine Office

4.   On the second Sunday of Passiontide or Palm Sunday, and on Monday, Tuesday and Wednesday of Holy Week the divine office is said at the usual hours.

5.   During the sacred triduum, that is, on the Thursday of the Lord's Supper, on Friday of the Lord's passion and death, and on Holy Saturday, the following rules are to be observed if the office is said *in choir* or *in common*.

Matins and lauds are not anticipated but are recited in the morning at the proper time. However, in churches where the Mass of the Chrism is being said on Holy Thursday morning, the matins and lauds of Holy Thursday can be anticipated.

The little hours are said at the proper time.

Vespers are omitted on Thursday and Friday, when the principal liturgical functions of those days take their place. On Holy Saturday, however, they are said after noon at the accustomed hour.

Compline is said after the evening liturgical functions on Thursday and Friday. On Holy Saturday it is omitted.

In *private recitations* of the office on these three days, all the canonical hours should be recited according to the rubrics.

On the Mass or the Principal Liturgical Function

6.   On Palm Sunday the solemn blessing and the procession of the palms are held in the morning at the accustomed hour. Where the office is said in choir, the proper time is after terce.

7.   On the Thursday of the Lord's Supper the Mass of the Chrism is celebrated after terce. The Mass of the Lord's Supper, however, is celebrated in the evening at the most convenient time, but not before five o'clock or after eight o'clock.

8.   On the Friday of the Lord's passion and death the solemn liturgical service is celebrated in the afternoon at approximately three o'clock. If there is some pastoral reason to do so, it is allowed to choose a later hour, but not later than six o'clock.

9.   The solemn Easter vigil is to be celebrated at a fitting time, one which will permit the solemn Mass of this vigil to begin about midnight of the night between Holy Saturday and Easter Sunday. Where the conditions of the faithful and of the place make it fitting in the judgment of the ordinary of the place to anticipate the hour for celebrating the vigil, this should not begin before twilight, or certainly not before sunset.

III. ON EXTENDING THE LENTEN ABSTINENCE AND FAST UNTIL THE MIDNIGHT OF HOLY SATURDAY

10.   The abstinence and fasting prescribed for Lent which, up until this time, according to canon 1252, § 4, ceased after noon on Holy Saturday, will in the future cease at midnight of the same Holy Saturday.

All things to the contrary notwithstanding.

INSTRUCTION

ON THE CORRECT USE OF THE RESTORED ORDO OF HOLY WEEK

Since it is the purpose of the restored ordo of Holy Week that, with the venerable liturgical services of these days restored to the hours that are proper and opportune, these liturgical services may be attended more easily, more devoutly and more fruitfully by the faithful, it is highly important that this salutary purpose be realized.

Hence it has seemed opportune to this Sacred Congregation of Rites to add to the general decree an instruction, by which the change to the new order may be made easier and the faithful may be led more securely to derive richer fruits from a living participation in the sacred ceremonies.

The knowledge and the observance of this instruction are obligatory for those whom it concerns.

I. ON THE PASTORAL AND RITUAL PREPARATION

1.   Local ordinaries should carefully see to it that priests, especially those who have the care of souls, be well instructed not only in the ritual observance of the restored ordo of Holy Week, but also in its liturgical meaning and its pastoral purpose.

They should likewise take care that the faithful also, during the holy season of Lent, be faithfully taught properly to understand the restored ordo of Holy Week, so that they may both mentally and spiritually participate in the services.

2.   The following are the chief points of instruction that should be given to the Christian people:

a) For Second Sunday of Passiontide, Called Palm Sunday

The faithful are to be urged to assist in greater numbers at the solemn procession of the palms, so as to give public testimony of their love and gratitude to Christ the King.

Moreover, the faithful should be admonished to approach the sacrament of penance in time during Holy Week. This admonition must be stressed especially in those places where it has been customary for the faithful to troop to confession on Holy Saturday evening and Easter Sunday morning. Let those who have the responsibility for souls zealously see to it that the faithful have ready access to the sacrament of penance during all of Holy Week and especially on the last three days of that week.

b) The Thursday of the Lord's Supper

The faithful should be taught about the love with which Christ the Lord, "on the day before he suffered," instituted the Eucharist, a sacrifice and sacrament, and an everlasting memorial of his passion, to be renewed unceasingly by the ministry of priests.

The faithful should also be urged to render due adoration to the Blessed Sacrament after the Mass of the Lord's Supper.

Where the washing of the feet, to show the Lord's commandment on charity, is performed in a church according to the rubrics of the restored ordo of Holy Week, the faithful should be instructed on the profound meaning of this sacred rite, and should be taught that it is only proper that they should abound in works of Christian charity on this day.

c) The Friday of the Lord's Passion and Death

The faithful should be brought to a right understanding of the unique liturgical services of this day. In these services, after the sacred readings and prayers, the passion of our Lord is solemnly sung, prayers are offered for the needs of the entire Church and of the human race, and the holy cross, the memorial of our redemption, is most devoutly adored by the Christian family, the clergy and the people. Finally, according to the rubrics of the restored ordo, and as was the custom for many centuries, all who wish to do so and who are properly prepared can go to holy communion, so that, devoutly receiving the Lord's body which was given for all on this day, they may receive richer fruits of the redemption.

The priests must emphasize the fact that on this most holy day the faithful should keep their minds piously recollected and should not forget the laws of abstinence and fasting.

d) For Holy Saturday and the Easter Vigil

First of all it is imperative that the faithful be carefully instructed about the unique liturgical character of Holy Saturday. This is a day of most intense sorrow, the day on which the Church tarries at the Lord's tomb, meditating on his Passion and death. While the altar remains stripped, the Church abstains from the sacrifice of the Mass until after the solemn vigil or the nocturnal wait for the resurrection, come the Easter joys, which overflow abundantly into the days that follow.

The intention and purpose of this vigil is to point out and to recall in the liturgical service how life and grace have come to us from the Lord's death. And so our Lord himself is presented under the symbol of the paschal candle as "the light of the world" (Jn 8:12), who has dispelled the darkness of our sins by the grace of his light. The *Exsultet* is sung, in which the splendor of the holy night of the resurrection is glorified. The wonderful works wrought by God under the old alliance, pale foreshadowings of the marvels done under the new covenant, are recalled. There is the blessing of the baptismal water, in which, "buried together with Christ" unto the death of sin, we rise again with the same Christ so that "we may walk in newness of life" (Rom 6:4). Then, by the renewal of our baptismal vows we promise to bear witness before all by our lives and our conduct to this grace which Christ has merited for us and which he confers upon us in baptism. Finally, after we have implored the intercession of the Church triumphant, the sacred vigil ends with the solemn Mass of the resurrection.

3.   No less necessary is the ritual preparation for the sacred ceremonies of Holy Week. Hence, all the things that are required for the devout and becoming performance of the liturgical services of Holy Week must be carefully prepared and put in order. The sacred ministers and the others who take part in the services, whether clerics or laymen, especially the boys, should be thoroughly instructed on what they are to do.

II. ANNOTATIONS TO CERTAIN RUBRICS OF THE ORDO OF HOLY WEEK

a) For the Entire Week

4.   Where there is a sufficient number of sacred ministers, the sacred services of Holy Week should be conducted with all the splendor of the sacred rites. Where there are not enough sacred ministers, the simple rite should be used, observing the special rubrics as noted in their proper places.

5.   Whenever in the restored ordo of Holy Week the words "as in the Roman breviary" occur, everything is to be taken from this liturgical book, observing the norms set forth in the general decree of the Sacred Congregation of Rites "On Reducing the Rubrics to a Simpler Form," issued March 23, 1955.

6.   During all of Holy Week, that is, from the second Sunday of Passiontide or Palm Sunday up to the Mass of the Easter vigil inclusive, in the Mass (and on Friday in the solemn liturgical service), whenever the function is solemn, that is, performed with sacred ministers, the celebrant is to omit whatever the deacon, the subdeacon or the lector sing or read in the performance of their own parts of the ceremony.

b) For the Second Sunday of Passiontide or Palm Sunday

7.   In the blessing and the procession, palm or olive branches, or the branches of other trees, may be used. These branches may, in accordance with local custom, be prepared by the faithful themselves and brought by them into the church, or they may be distributed to the faithful after they are blessed.

c) For the Thursday of the Lord's Supper

8.   As is prescribed in the Roman missal, a suitable place should be prepared in some chapel or at some altar of the church for the solemn reposition of the sacrament. This should as far as possible be becomingly ornamented with veils and lights.

9.   In accordance with the decrees of the Sacred Congregation of Rites concerning abuses which are to be avoided or removed in the preparation of this place, a severity consonant with the liturgy of these days is definitely recommended.

10.   Pastors and rectors of churches should warn the faithful in time about the public adoration of the holy Eucharist. This is to be begun as soon as the Mass of the Lord's Supper has ended, and is to be continued at least until midnight, when the memory of the Lord's passion and death takes the place of the liturgical commemoration of the institution of the holy Eucharist.

d) For the Easter Vigil

11.   There is nothing to prevent the previous preparation, in colors or in some other way, of the marks to be incised on the paschal candle by the celebrant.

12.   It is fitting that the candles held by the clergy and by the people should remain lighted while the *Exsultet* is being sung and during the renewal of the baptismal vows.

13.   The container for the water that is to be blessed should be decorated in a fitting manner.

14.   If there are people to be baptized, especially if there are many, it is permissible to advance to a convenient time in the morning of the same day the ceremonies

of the Roman ritual which precede the actual administration of baptism, namely in the baptism of infants up to the words *"Credis in Deum"* [*Rituale Romanum*, tit. 3, ch. 2, no. 12] and in the baptism of adults up to the words *"Quis vocaris?"* (*Rituale Romanum*, tit. 3, ch. 4, no. 38).

15.   If it should happen that holy orders are also being conferred during this solemn vigil, the pontiff this night should put the final admonition (with the imposition of the so-called "duty) which, according to the *Pontificale Romanum*, should come after the pontifical blessing and before the last gospel, before the pontifical blessing.

16.   On the vigil of Pentecost, the lessons or prophecies, the blessing of the baptismal water, and the litanies are omitted. The mass, even when this is the conventual Mass or a solemn or sung Mass, is begun in the usual manner after the Confiteor has been said at the altar steps. It begins with the introit *"Cum sanctificatus fueris"* as is prescribed for private Masses in this same place in the Roman missal.

III. ON THE MASS, HOLY COMMUNION, AND THE EUCHARISTIC FAST DURING THESE THREE DAYS

17.   On the Thursday of the Lord's Supper, that very ancient tradition of the Roman Church must be observed according to which the celebration of private Masses is forbidden, and all priests and clerics are to assist at the Mass of the Lord's Supper and are encouraged to receive holy communion (see canon 862).

However, where pastoral reasons so require, the local ordinary may permit one or two low Masses in all churches and public oratories. In semi-public oratories there can be only one low Mass, this in order to give all the faithful the opportunity to assist at the sacrifice of the Mass and to receive the Lord's body on this day. These Masses are permitted only during the hours assigned for the celebration of the solemn Mass of the Lord's Supper (decree, 2, no. 7).

18.   On the Thursday of the Lord's Supper, holy communion may be distributed to the faithful only during the evening Masses or immediately after them. Likewise, on Holy Saturday it can be given only during Mass or immediately after it. The sick who are in danger of death are excepted from this rule.

19.   On the Friday of the Lord's passion and death, holy communion may be distributed only at the solemn liturgical services in the afternoon, except to the sick who are in danger of death.

20.   Priests who celebrate the Mass of the Easter vigil at the proper hour, that is, after midnight of the night between Saturday and Sunday, can also celebrate the Mass of the feast on Easter Sunday and, if they have the indult, they may celebrate twice or three times.

21.   Local ordinaries who celebrate the Mass for the consecration of the chrism in the morning of the Thursday of the Lord's Supper can also celebrate the solemn

Mass of the Lord's Supper the evening of that day. If they should wish to celebrate the solemn Easter vigil on Holy Saturday, they may but are not obliged to celebrate the solemn Mass on Easter Sunday itself.

22.   As regards the eucharistic fast, the norms of the apostolic constitution *Christus Dominus*, and the accompanying instruction of the Supreme Sacred Congregation of the Holy Office of January 6, 1953[1] are to be observed.

IV. ON THE SOLUTION OF CERTAIN DIFFICULTIES

23.   Since there are in various places and among various peoples many popular customs connected with the observance of Holy Week, local ordinaries and priests having the care of souls should seek prudently to harmonize these customs, which appear to contribute to solid piety, with the restored ordo of Holy Week. The faithful should also be taught the supreme value of the sacred liturgy, which always and especially today by its very nature far surpasses other kinds of devotions and customs, however good these may be.

24.   Where it has hitherto been the custom to bless homes on Holy Saturday, let the local ordinaries give proper directions so that this blessing may be given at a more convenient time either before or after Easter. The blessing should be given by the pastor or by another priest having the care of souls and delegated by the pastor. And they may take this opportunity paternally to visit the faithful entrusted to them and to take account of their spiritual condition (canon 462, 60).

25.   The ringing of the bells, which is prescribed for the beginning of the hymn *Gloria in excelsis* in the Mass of the Easter vigil, is to be done in this way:[2]

a) In places where there is only one church, the bells should be rung when the singing of this hymn begins.

b) In places where there are many churches, regardless of whether the ceremonies take place at the same time in all of them or not, the bells of all the churches should be rung at the same time as those of the cathedral church, or the mother church, or the principal church. Should there be doubt as to which is the mother church or the principal church, the ordinary of the place should be consulted.

---

1. *AAS* 45, 15.

2. The *AAS* mention here only the Mass of the Easter Vigil, whereas the text previously published in *L'Osservatore Romano* included in this provision also the ringing of the bells at the Gloria in the solemn evening Mass of Holy Thursday. Since the text of the *Acta* is the only official one, it is to be followed. This is confirmed by information privately obtained at the Sacred Congregation of Rites.

CIRCA ORDINEM HEBDOMADAE SANCTAE INSTAURATUM

THE RESTORED ORDER OF HOLY WEEK

ORDINANCES AND DECLARATIONS OF THE
SACRED CONGREGATION OF RITES

FEBRUARY 1, 1957

The liturgical restoration of Holy Week which was promulgated by the Sacred Congregation of Rites by the general decree *Maxima Redemptionis nostrae mysteria*, November 16, 1955,[1] has been received with universal joy and put into practice everywhere with great pastoral success.

However, some of the most excellent bishops, in the reports made to this Sacred Congregation, have indicated certain practical difficulties occasioned by various local and national conditions. To meet these difficulties, the pontifical commission of experts which prepared the restored order has, after mature reflection, drawn up these ordinances and declarations, in which is incorporated also the previous declaration made by this Sacred Congregation on March 15, 1956, regarding the celebration of the restored rites.[2] The general decree *Maxima Redemptionis nostrae mysteria*, and the Instruction of November 16, 1955, which was published with it, continue in force, with the exception of matters which are changed by the present document.

All this, which was reported in detail to His Holiness by the undersigned Cardinal Prefect, has been approved by His Holiness.

Accordingly, by special mandate of His Holiness Pius XII, by divine Providence Pope, the Sacred Congregation of Rites provides as follows:

I. THE USE OF THE SOLEMN OR OF THE SIMPLE RITE
IN CELEBRATING THE LITURGY OF HOLY WEEK

1.   In all churches and public and semi-public oratories where there is a sufficient number of sacred ministers, the sacred rites of Second Passion Sunday, or Palm Sunday, of Holy Thursday in *Cena Domini*, of Good Friday on the passion and death of our Lord, and of the paschal vigil, can be celebrated in the solemn form (declaration of March 15, 1956, no. 1, and instruction of November 16, 1955, no. 4).

---

1. *AAS* 47, 838.
2. *AAS* 48, 153.

2.   In churches and public and semi-public oratories where sacred ministers are not available, the simple rite may be used. But for performing this simple rite there must be a sufficient number of "servers," either clerics or at least boys, namely at least three for the Second Passion Sunday, or Palm Sunday, and for the Mass *in Cena Domini*, and at least four for the celebration of the liturgical action of Good Friday on the passion and death of our Lord, and of the paschal vigil. These "servers" must be carefully instructed as to what they have to do (instruction of November 16, 1955, no. 3). These two conditions, namely instruction of November 16, 1955, no. 3). These two conditions, namely a sufficient number of "servers" and their adequate preparation, are strictly required for performing the simple rite. Local ordinaries should see that these two conditions for the simple rite are exactly observed (declaration of March 15, 1956, no. 2).

3.   Where the liturgical actions of Holy Week are performed in the simple rite, if another priest or at least a deacon is available, there is no objection to having him, in the vestments of a deacon, sing the gospel when it occurs, or the history of the passion (but reserving the part of *Christus* to the celebrant), or the *praeconium paschale*, also lessons and invitations such as *Flectamus genua* and *Levate*, or *Benedicamus Domino*, or *Ite, Missa est*; in short, let him take the part of the deacon.

II. THE SECOND SUNDAY OF THE PASSION, OR PALM SUNDAY

4.   The solemn blessing of the palms and the procession, with the Mass which follows, are to be performed in the morning at the usual hour of the principal Mass, in choir after terce (see general decree of November 16, 1955, no. 6).

In churches where evening Masses are regularly celebrated with a large attendance of the faithful, the local ordinary can permit the blessing of the palms and the procession with the Mass which follows it to be celebrated in the evening, if there is a real pastoral reason for it, but in that case the blessing and procession are not to take place in the morning in those churches.

5.   It is not allowed to celebrate merely the blessing of the palms, not followed by the procession and Mass.

6.   The blessing of the palms can be done in another church from which the procession moves to the principal church for the celebration of the Mass (ordo, no. 17). Where there is no such other church, the blessing of the palms can be done in some other suitable place, even out of doors, in front of a sacred shrine or before the processional cross, provided the procession goes from there to the church for the celebration of Mass.

7.   Since it is scarcely possible for all the faithful to be present for the blessing of the palms, rectors of churches should see to it that blessed palms be ready in the sacristy or in some other suitable place, to be distributed to the faithful who were not in the procession.

III. HOLY THURSDAY *IN CENA DOMINI*

8.   The Mass of the Chrism is to be celebrated in the morning after terce; but the Mass in *Cena Domini* is to be celebrated in the evening, at a convenient hour, but not before four o'clock in the afternoon, nor after nine in the evening.

9.   Where a pastoral reason so requires, the local ordinary can permit one or two *low* Masses in all churches or pubic oratories, besides the principal Mass in *Cena Domini*; but in semi-public oratories, only one (see instruction of November 16, 1955, no. 17).

But if for any reason the principal Mass in *Cena Domini* cannot be celebrated even in the simple rite, the local ordinary for a pastoral reason can permit two *low* Masses to be celebrated in churches or public oratories, but only one in semi-public oratories (declaration of March 15, 1956, no. 4).

These low Masse are to be celebrated within the same hours as those assigned above in no. 8 for the Mass in *Cena Domini*.

10.   It is very desirable that even in the low Masses above mentioned (no. 9), the celebrant, after the gospel, should address the faithful briefly on the principal mysteries of the day.

11.   On Holy Thursday holy communion may be distributed to the faithful only at the principal Mass in *Cena Domini* and at all the other low Masses which the local ordinary has permitted, or immediately after the Masses.

12.   On this day holy communion may be brought to the sick in the morning or in the afternoon.

13.   To priests who have charge of two or more parishes, the local ordinary can permit bination of the Mass in *Cena Domini* (declaration of March 15, 1956, no. 6).

14.   Where the transfer and reposition of the most Blessed Sacrament on Holy Thursday takes place after the Mass in *Cena Domini*, even though it was celebrated in the simple form, it is strictly required that in the same church or oratory the afternoon liturgical action of Good Friday on the passion and death of our Lord be also celebrated (declaration of March 15, 1956, no. 3).

IV. GOOD FRIDAY ON THE PASSION AND DEATH OF OUR LORD

15.   On Good Friday on the passion and death of our Lord, the solemn liturgical action is celebrated in the afternoon about three o'clock; for a pastoral reason it may be begun at noon or later, but not after nine in the evening.

16.   To priests who have charge of two or more parishes, the local ordinary can permit the repetition of the liturgical action on the passion and death of our Lord, not however in the same parish, and always within the same hours as those specified above in no. 15 for the performance of that action (see declaration of March 15, 1956, no. 6).

17.   If the pastor or the rector of the church foresees that, owing to the great number of people, the adoration of the holy cross as prescribed in the order of Holy Week can scarcely be performed, or at least not without some loss of order and devotion, the ceremony may be done in the following way: after the clergy, if any are present, and the servers have made their adoration, the celebrant receives the cross from the hands of the servers and, standing at the top of the altar steps, in a few words invites the people to adore the cross, and then holds it aloft for a short time so that the faithful may adore it in silence.

18.   On Good Friday on the passion and death of our Lord, holy communion may be distributed only at the solemn afternoon liturgical action, except to persons in danger of death (see instruction of November 16, 1955, no. 19).

V. HOLY SATURDAY AND THE PASCHAL VIGIL

19.   As to the hour for celebrating the paschal vigil, the following rules are to be observed:

a) The proper hour is one which makes it possible for the Mass of the vigil to be begun about midnight between Holy Saturday and Easter Sunday (general decree of November 16, 1955, no. 9).

b) But where, in view of peculiar conditions of the people or of the place, for grave reasons of a public and pastoral nature it seems proper in the judgment of the local ordinary to anticipate the hour for celebrating the vigil, this may be done; but it may not be begun before twilight, or certainly not before sunset (see general decree of November 16, 1955, no. 9).

c) But the permission to anticipate the hour of the paschal vigil cannot be given by the local ordinary indiscriminately and in general for the whole diocese or district, but only for those churches or places where it is really necessary; moreover, it is preferable that the strictly proper hour be observed at least in the cathedral church, and in all other churches, especially those of religious, where this can be done without grave inconvenience.

20.   The paschal vigil can be celebrated also in churches or oratories where the functions of Holy Thursday and Good Friday did not take place; and it may likewise be omitted in churches and oratories where those functions were celebrated (declaration of March 15, 1956, no. 5).

21.   To priests who have charge of two or more parishes, the local ordinary can permit the bination of the Mass of the paschal vigil, not however in the same parish (declaration of March 15, 1956, no. 6).

22.   Since the paschal vigil has been restored to its original nocturnal setting, it is not appropriate to confer tonsure or minor or major orders at the Mass of this vigil.

All things to the contrary notwithstanding.

CHRISTUS DOMINUS
CONCERNING THE DISCIPLINE
TO BE OBSERVED WITH RESPECT
TO THE EUCHARISTIC FAST

APOSTOLIC CONSTITUTION
POPE PIUS XII
JANUARY 6, 1953

SACRAM COMMUNIONEM
FURTHER MODIFICATIONS
OF THE EUCHARISTIC FAST

MOTU PROPRIO
POPE PIUS XII
MARCH 19, 1957

AN OVERVIEW OF *CHRISTUS DOMINUS* AND *SACRAM COMMUNIONEM*

Deacon Francis L. Agnoli

In 1953, and again in 1957, Pope Pius XII relaxed the centuries-old practice of fasting before the reception of Holy Communion. In the twenty-first century, when—at least anecdotally[1]—the Eucharistic fast is no longer being generally observed, these seem to be fairly insignificant moments in the history of the Church. But, at the time, they were seen as momentous developments. Benedictine liturgical scholar, and future *peritus* (advisor) at the Second Vatican Council, Godfrey Diekmann, OSB, wrote this in response to the pope's initiative in 1953:

> In a word, the history of the Eucharistic fast presents a uniformity through the centuries that has few parallels. The discipline was rigid from very early times. Its obligatory nature was unquestioned, and allowed of but rare exceptions. In the light of these facts, the action of our Holy Father, by which for the good of souls discipline is made more clearly subordinate to the Sacrament which it should serve, is *an event of pastoral care of major historical moment.*[2]

BACKGROUND OF FASTING[3]

The practice of temporarily abstaining from food and/or drink, in whole or in part, is a ubiquitous religious practice. Historically, fasting has been undertaken for a variety of reasons. In ancient Israel, fasting was associated with repentance and supplication (especially in the face of disaster) as well as with mourning. In essence, fasting connoted an attitude of humility before God. Fasting was even used to assist in divination and the induction of visions. By the inter-testamental period,[4] fasting had come to be associated with individual and communal asceticism and religious devotion, and was usually coupled with almsgiving and prayer.

The primitive Church's approach to fasting reflected this Jewish background. It was some time before Christianity developed its own particular approach to fasting. Eventually, some Christian communities adopted particular fasting practices to set themselves apart from their Jewish neighbors.[5] Fasting as part of preparation for Baptism—undertaken by both catechumens and the

---

1. I can find no evidence that this question has been researched, including by the Center for Applied Research in the Apostolate (CARA).

2. Godfrey Diekmann, "Some Reflections on the Eucharistic Fast," *Worship* 27 no 4 (March 1953): p. 208. Italics mine.

3. See also John Muddiman, "Fast, Fasting," in *The Anchor Yale Bible Dictionary*, volume 2, ed. David Noel Freedman, Gary A. Herion, David F. Graf et al., (New York: Doubleday, 1992), 773–776 and Joan M. Nuth, "Fasting," *The New Dictionary of Catholic Spirituality*, electronic ed., ed. Michael Downey, (Collegeville, MN: Liturgical Press, 2000), 390–392.

4. The period between the end of the Old Testament and the beginning of the New Testament.

5. For example, the *Didache* (8:1) urges fasting on Wednesdays and Fridays, instead of on Mondays and Thursdays—when the "hypocrites" (Jews) fast.

community at large—was being practiced by the second century.[6] Over time, this period of pre-baptismal fasting expanded and eventually developed into part of the observance of Lent as a penitential season. Under Hellenistic influence, fasting in the early Christian community also came to reflect an emphasis on ascesis or disciplining the body—both as a way to defend against the influences of evil spirits as well as a way to "purify the mind for contemplation and communion with God."[7] By the Middle Ages, an additional theme had been appended to fasting: the joining of one's sacrifice to the sufferings of Christ.

THE HISTORY OF THE EUCHARISTIC FAST

It is with this background in mind that we can trace the development of the Eucharistic fast. The first clear evidence that we have for this fast comes from Augustine of Hippo, suggesting that by the late fourth or early fifth century the practice was well established. Clear evidence for a universal Eucharistic fast before this time is lacking, and to read its later development into Paul's admonition of the Corinthians (1 Corinthians 11:21, 33–34)—as did both Augustine (Ep. 54.6.8) and Pope Pius XII (*Christus Dominus*)—is anachronistic. However, the fact that Tertullian and Hippolytus mention that those who commune from the Eucharistic bread brought home from the Sunday liturgy ought to receive that bread before any other food suggests that fasting before Eucharist may have been practiced long before it was legislated.[8] Over time, the practice developed that one was to fast not only before Holy Communion, but before attending the Eucharist whether one was planning on communing or not.[9]

What motivated such a fast in the early Church? Diekmann saw in the origins of the Eucharistic fast a basic principle of the Christian life: "death to self and to sin is the only path to receiving an abundant outpouring of the divine life."[10] In other words, fasting prepares the communicant to receive the sacrament more fruitfully. However, Augustine maintained that the underlying reason for the fast, which he held was instituted by the Holy Spirit, is "for the honor of so great a sacrament."[11] It seems that by the time legislation was necessary to enforce the fast, the historical circumstances had also shifted: various Christological and anthropological controversies led to the divinity of Christ as well as the sinfulness of human beings being stressed.[12] As a result, an

---

6. Godfrey Diekmann points out that fasting before the reception of sacraments or sacramentals has a long history in the Church. He concludes: "All of this is simply another way of stating the classical Christian arguments motivating the [Eucharistic] fast: it overcomes Satan, it atones for sin, and it prepares for the coming of the Holy Ghost, the sanctifier." See "The Fast Ought Not Prevent Communion," *Worship* 27 no. 11 (Oct 1953): pp. 519–520.

7. Nuth, p. 390.

8. Diekmann, "Some Reflections on the Eucharistic Fast," p. 207.

9. Such was the practice until the 1300s (Diekmann, "Some Reflections on the Eucharistic Fast," 207).

10. Diekmann, "The Fast Ought Not Prevent Communion," p. 521.

11. Augustine of Hippo. Ep. 54.6.8.

12. Might the Christological controversies (such as Arianism) as well as the arguments against the Pelagians be the driving forces behind legislating the Eucharistic fast? In other words, if fasting was not universal (in practice if not in intent) before this time, did it become so as a response to these pressures?

over-emphasis on the reverence ("honor")[13] due the sacrament, as appropriate as it might be, had unforeseen and unintended consequences. Rather than fasting as an ascetical practice aimed at preparing one for a more fruitful reception of Holy Communion, fasting as reflective of a growing sense of unworthiness began to keep Christians away from the Eucharist.

THE LITURGICAL MOVEMENT,[14] POPE PIUS X, AND POPE PIUS XII

Such was the general attitude toward Eucharistic Communion until the papacy of Pius X. In 1903, the pope issued his *motu proprio, Tra le sollecitudini,* which included a reference in its introduction to the importance of the "active participation" of the faithful in the liturgy. The use of Pius X's phrase—"active participation"—was embraced by the Liturgical Movement, especially as attention turned from the monastic and scholarly to the parochial and popular. It was in this context that Pius X called for more frequent Communion (*Sacra Tridentina Synodus,* 1905) and lowered the age for first Holy Communion (*Quam singulari,* 1910). Pius X's intentions very quickly ran into a major challenge: the strict Eucharistic fast in place. Those desiring to receive Holy Communion were to fast from food and liquids, including water, from midnight. This observance was codified in the 1917 *Code of Canon Law,* canons 808[15] and 858.[16]

In the time between 1917 and 1953, especially in the context and aftermath of World War II, a number of indults allowing exceptions to the Eucharistic fast were granted. In addition to exceptions granted for reasons of health, these indults attempted to address how industrialization was rapidly changing the way people lived their daily lives and making the observation of the traditional fast from midnight more and more difficult. The end result was a confusing mosaic of rules governing the Eucharistic fast in various parts of the world. It was this combination of factors—the growing obstacles to more frequent Communion as well as the increasing lack of uniformity in practice—that prompted Pope Pius XII to act.

POPE PIUS XII: *CHRISTUS DOMINUS* (1953)

On January 6, 1953, Pope Pius XII issued his "Epiphany gift"[17]—the apostolic constitution, *Christus Dominus.* After briefly tracing the history of the Eucharistic

---

13. "The stomach should be empty of all other food out of reverence for the divine Guest to be received—that became more or less the *exclusive* motivation for the fast" (Diekmann, "The Fast Ought Not Prevent Communion," p. 522; emphasis in original).

14. See Virgil Funk, "Liturgical Movement, The (1830–1969)," in *The New Dictionary of Sacramental Worship,* electronic ed., ed. Peter E. Fink, 695–715. Collegeville, MN: Liturgical Press, 2000.

15. Canon 808: "It is not licit for priests to celebrate without having observed a natural fast from midnight." Translation from: Edward N. Peters, *The 1917 or Pio-Benedictine Code of Canon Law in English Translation with Extensive Scholarly Apparatus* (San Francisco: Ignatius Press, 2001), 293.

16. Canon 858: "§1. Whoever has not observed a natural fast from midnight cannot be admitted to the most holy Eucharist, unless danger of death urges, or it is necessary to avoid irreverence toward the sacrament. §2. Those who have been sick lying down for a month, however, without a certain hope of a speedy recovery, with the prudent advice of a confessor, can take the most holy Eucharist once or twice in a week even if beforehand they have taken some medicine or some liquid as a drink." Translation from Peters, 306.

17. Diekmann, "Some Reflections on the Eucharistic Fast," p. 205.

fast and the reasons for it,[18] the pope laid out his argument for allowing exceptions to the universal "law and custom dealing with the Eucharistic fast." For him, the overarching issue was that societal changes were making it more and more difficult for the faithful to receive Holy Communion if the fast from midnight was maintained. He specifically named the conditions that were creating obstacles to more frequent reception of the sacrament: decreasing numbers of priests, the realities encountered by missionaries, the working conditions and hours brought about by industrialization, increasing ease and frequency of travel, and illness. In addition, he mentioned the desire to make Holy Communion more accessible to mothers before they began their daily work at home as well as to children before school—who, if they wished to commune, would have to first go to Mass and then return home for breakfast before going on to their classes.

Christus Dominus includes six rules. First, it is made clear that the Eucharistic fast from midnight remained in force everywhere unless one of the conditions laid out in the document applied. Regardless, it was decreed that natural water no longer broke the fast. Second, the sick (on the advice of a confessor) could consume non-alcoholic beverages and medicine if needed. Third, if laboring under strenuous conditions, priests were to fast for only one hour before Mass; and, fourth, the ablutions (using only water) could be consumed by priests who said Mass two or three times in a day. Fifth, if a serious inconvenience arose (such as tiring work, late hour, or long journey), the faithful—on the advice of a confessor—could reduce the fast to one hour. Finally, local ordinaries were given the right to allow for Masses after 4 PM—in which case the fast was reduced to three hours from food and alcohol and one hour from non-alcoholic beverages.

These changes were enthusiastically welcomed among those promoting the liturgical renewal. It was clear that the Holy Father was putting "the good of souls"[19] first in doing what was necessary to make Communion more accessible. While warmly received, the pope's decrees were unevenly put into practice. Many, priests and laity alike, found the rules difficult to understand. In addition, in spite of the instruction accompanying *Christus Dominus*, debates soon arose concerning the proper interpretation of these new rules.[20] Because all previous indults had been abrogated, in some places the new constitution actually led to greater restrictions.[21] After a few years, it was not unusual to see calls for further simplification.

---

18. The Holy Father mentions the reverence owed to Christ as the primary reason for the fast. To these he adds (1) receiving the Eucharist fasting shows that the sacrament is our most important food; (2) the fast honors the Redeemer; (3) it fosters piety; and (4) the mind is more attentive to spiritual things if the body is not weighed down by food.

19. H. A. Reinhold, "The Eucharistic Decrees," *Worship* 27 no. 4 (March 1953): 189. See also Diekmann, "Some Reflections on the Eucharistic Fast," p. 208.

20. See John J. Reed, SJ, "Modified Discipline of the Eucharistic Fast," *Theological Studies* 14 no. 2 (June 1953): 215–241 and John J. Reed, SJ, "Select Questions on the Eucharistic Fast," *Theological Studies* 16 no. 1 (March 1955): 30–76.

21. For example, in some places, workers had been allowed solid food up to four hours before Holy Communion. Hilary Werts, SJ, "A Note on the Eucharistic Fast," *Theological Studies* 16 no 2 (June 1955): p. 275.

Those calls did not go unheeded. On March 19, 1957, at the request of bishops from around the world, Pope Pius XII, issued his apostolic letter *motu proprio*, *Sacram Communionem*, thereby reducing the Eucharistic fast for the entire Church to three hours from food and alcohol and one hour from non-alcoholic drinks. Water still would not break the fast. The sick were excused completely. Consultation with a confessor was no longer necessary; the shortened fast was not to be considered a concession for a few—but the law for all.[22] Importantly, the pope did urge Catholics to keep the fast from midnight if possible and, if not, to "compensate for the benefits received [from enjoying the concessions granted] by becoming illustrious examples of the Christian life, especially by works of penance and charity."[23]

CONCLUSIONS, CONTRIBUTIONS, AND CONNECTIONS TO *SACROSANCTUM CONCILUM*

From the vantage point of the twenty-first century, perhaps these changes made by Pope Pius XII seem fairly insignificant. But the comments by Godfrey Diekmann, OSB, that opened this article should not be lightly dismissed. These two documents from Pope Pius XII should be placed in the context of the Liturgical Movement, and so leading up to and informing *Sacrosanctum Concilium*. It was the pontiff's clear aim to reduce obstacles to more frequent Communion— and thereby encourage "active participation"[24] in that sense. As *Sacrosanctum Concilium* makes clear, the divine encounter takes place through "signs perceptible to the senses," not through passive attendance.[25] It is noteworthy that these changes were made at the behest of bishops from around the world, echoing *Sacrosanctum Concilium's* emphasis on collegiality and the central role that the bishop ought to play in regulating the liturgy in his diocese.[26] As Massimo Faggioli points out, *Sacrosanctum Concilium* puts forth an ecclesiology centered on the local Church (diocese), the People of God in a particular place and of a particular time.[27] Finally, and this should not be underestimated, the relaxation of such a long-standing traditional discipline gave clear indication that the Church *could* change—and, if the "good of souls" so demanded, *should* change.[28] The adjustment of the Eucharistic fast to life in the mid-twentieth century, as well as the other cautious liturgical changes that took place in the 1950s—such as the reforms of Holy Week and increasing, though still limited, permission for the use of the vernacular in certain places—opened the doors to the more comprehensive *aggiornamento* that was called for at Vatican II.

---

22. Alfredo Cardinal Ottaviani, Commentary accompanying *Sacram Communionem*, 1957.

23. Pius XII, Apostolic Letter *motu proprio, Sacram Communionem*, 1957.

24. See *Sacrosanctum Concilium*, 14, 19, 27, 30, 41, 50, 55, 113, 114, 121, and 124. See especially article 55, which states: "That more complete form of participation in the Mass which the faithful, after the priest's communion, receive the Lord's body from the same sacrifice, is strongly endorsed."

25. *Sacrosanctum Concilium*, 7.

26. *Sacrosanctum Concilium*, 22.1, 22.2, 25, 36.3, 36.4, 41, 45, 55, 57, 128. See Massimo Faggioli, *True Reform: Liturgy and Ecclesiology in* Sacrosanctum Concilium (Collegeville, MN: A Pueblo Book. The Liturgical Press, 2012), p. 73.

27. Faggioli, 75, 77, 81–87. He holds that there is an intimate connection between this ecclesiology and the Council's call for the active participation of all the faithful.

28. *Sacrosanctum Concilium* 23; Faggioli, pp. 109, 131.

CHRISTUS DOMINUS
APOSTOLIC CONSTITUTION OF POPE PIUS XII
NEW DISCIPLINE FOR THE EUCHARISTIC FAST
JANUARY 6, 1953

Christ the Lord "on the night in which He was betrayed"[1] when for the last time He celebrated the Pasch of the old law, after supper was finished,[2] took bread, and giving thanks, broke and gave to His disciples, saying: "This is my body, which shall be given up for you";[3] and in like manner he handed them the chalice, saying: "This is my blood of the new covenant, which is being shed for many";[4] "do this in remembrance of me."[5] From these passages of Holy Scripture it is completely evident that the divine redeemer wished to substitute for this final paschal celebration, in which a lamb was eaten according to the Hebrew rites, a new Pasch to endure to the end of the world, that is, the eating of the immaculate Lamb, who was to be immolated for the life of the world, so that the new Pasch of the new law should bring the ancient Passover to an end, and the shadow be dispelled by the reality.[6]

However, since this conjunction of the two suppers was designed to signify the transition from the old Pasch to the new, it is easy to see why the Church, in renewing the eucharistic sacrifice by command of the divine Redeemer in remembrance of him, could depart from the practice of the ancient love feast and introduce that of the eucharistic fast.

For from ancient times the custom developed of administering the Eucharist to the faithful fasting.[7] Toward the end of the fourth century, fasting was already prescribed by several councils for those who were going to celebrate the eucharistic sacrifice. Thus in the year 393 the Council of Hippo decreed: "Let the sacrament of the altar be celebrated only by those who are fasting";[8] a little later, that is, in the year 397, this precept was set forth in the same words by the Third Council of Carthage;[9] and by the beginning of the fifth century this custom was quite common and could be called immemorial. Hence St. Augustine states that

---

1. 1 Cor 11–23.
2. See Luke 22:20.
3. 1 Cor 11:24.
4. Mt 26:28.
5. See 1 Cor., 11:24–25.
6. See the hymn *Lauda Sion* in the Roman Missal.
7. See Pope Benedict XIV, *De Synodo Diocesana*, 6, ch. 8, no. 10.
8. Conc. Hipp., canon 28: Mansi 3, 923.
9. Conc. Carth. III, ch. 29: Mansi 3, 885.

the most holy Eucharist is always received fasting, and that this usage is observed throughout the world.[10]

Undoubtedly this practice was based on very serious reasons, among which may be mentioned first of all the circumstance which the apostle of the Gentiles deplores in speaking of the fraternal love feast of the Christians.[11] Abstinence from food and drink is in keeping with the profound reverence which we owe to the supreme majesty of Jesus Christ when we are about to receive him hidden under the eucharistic veils. Moreover, when we receive his most precious body and blood before taking any other food, we clearly show that it is the first and greatest nourishment by which our soul is supported and its holiness increased. Hence, the same St. Augustine reminds us: "It has pleased the Holy Spirit that in honor of so great a sacrament the body of the Lord should enter the mouth of a Christian before any other foods."[12]

Not only does this fast discharge the obligation of honor to the divine Redeemer, but it also fosters devotion; and so it can help to augment those most salutary fruits of holiness which Christ, the fountainhead and Author of all good, demands that we who are enriched by his grace bring forth.

Besides, everyone knows from experience that by the very laws of human nature, when the body is not burdened with food the mind is rendered more alert and is more strongly moved to meditate on that hidden and sublime mystery which is enacted in the soul as in a temple, to the increase of divine charity.

The solicitude of the Church for the observance of the eucharistic fast can be gathered also from the fact that she imposed severe penalties for the violation of this precept. Thus the Seventh Council of Toledo in the year 646 threatened with excommunication anyone who should celebrate Mass without fasting;[13] and in the year 572 the Third Council of Braga,[14] as well as in the year 585 the Second Council of Macon,[15] had already decreed that anyone who should be proved guilty of this act should be deposed from his office and dignity.

Nevertheless, as the centuries rolled by, diligent consideration was also given to the fact that at times it was expedient in view of special circumstances to relax somewhat this law of fasting as it affected the faithful. Accordingly, the Council of Constance in the year 1415, while reaffirming the sacrosanct law of fasting, also added a certain modification: ". . . the authority of the sacred canons and approved custom of the Church have prescribed and now prescribe that this sacrament must not be celebrated after supper, nor be received by the faithful not fasting, except in the case of illness or other necessity recognized or permitted by the law or by the Church."[16]

---

10. See St. Augustine, *Ep. LIV ad Ian.*, ch. 6; PL, 33, 203.
11. See 1 Cor 11–21 ff.
12. St. Augustine, *loc. cit.*
13. Conc. Tolet. VII, ch. 2; Mansi 10, 768.
14. Conc. Bracar. III, canon 10; Mansi 9, 841.
15. Conc. Matiscon. II, canon 6: Mansi 9, 952.
16. Conc. Constant. sess. 13 ; Mansi 27, 727.

It has seemed good to recall these things to mind so that all may understand that, although we have been induced by new conditions of time and circumstances to grant not a few faculties and permissions in this matter, nevertheless we intend by this apostolic letter to confirm the full force of the law and custom concerning the eucharistic fast; and that we also wish to remind those who are able to comply with that law, that they diligently continue to do so, so that only those who need these concessions may make use of them, according to their need.

We are filled with the sweetest consolation—and we are happy to mention it here, though briefly—when we behold devotion to the august Sacrament of the altar daily increasing not only in the souls of the faithful but also in the splendor of divine worship, a thing which has been very frequently shown in the public manifestations of the people. To this effect undoubtedly the solicitous attentions of the sovereign pontiffs have contributed not a little, especially in the case of Blessed Pius X who, calling upon all to renew the ancient custom of the Church, exhorted them to approach the table of the angels as frequently as possible and even daily if possible;[17] and, inviting also the little ones to this heavenly food, wisely decreed that the precept of confession and holy communion applied to each and every person who had attained the use of reason;[18] and this is also prescribed by the code of canon law.[19] Spontaneously and willingly responding to these wishes of the sovereign pontiffs, the faithful have come to holy communion in ever increasing numbers. And would that this hunger for the bread of heaven and thirst for the precious blood were enkindled in all men of every age and of every social rank!

It should be observed, however, that the times in which we live and their special conditions have introduced into common currency and the ordinary course of life many circumstances which occasion grave difficulties, apt to deter people from participating in the divine mysteries, if all most absolutely observe the law of the eucharistic fast as it has been observed up to the present time.

In the first place, obviously priests today are numerically unequal to the task of ministering to the growing necessities of the faithful. On feast days especially they must often put up with excessive labors, as they have to celebrate the eucharistic sacrifice at a late hour and not infrequently two or three times on the same day; and at times they must travel long distances in order that considerable sections of their flock may not be without Mass. Exhausting apostolic labors of this sort unquestionably undermine the health of priests, as they must not only celebrate Mass, explain the Gospel, hear confessions, teach catechism and attend to the other duties of their office, which demand of them more and more application and work, but must also carefully plan and provide the ways and means of combating the relentless assault which in these days has been launched on such a wide front and with such shrewdness and bitterness against God and his Church.

---

17. Decree of S.C. Sacr., *Sacra Tridentina Synodus*, December 20, 1905: *ASS* 38, 400; *Fontes* 6, no. 4326, 828.

18. Decree of S.C. Sacr., *Quam singulari*, August 8, 1910; *AAS* 2, 577, *Fontes* 5, no. 2103, 80.

19. Canon 863; see canon 854, § 5.

But our mind and heart go out above all to those who are working in distant countries far from their native land, and who have generously responded to that invitation and command of the divine Master: "Go, therefore, and make disciples of all nations."[20] We are speaking of the heralds of the Gospel who, enduring exhausting labors and conquering all the difficulties of communication, are striving with all their power to bring the light of the Christian religion to all according to their capacity, and to nourish their people, who often are but recent converts to the Catholic faith, with the bread of angels which fosters virtue and rekindles devotion.

In almost the same situation are those faithful who live in the many areas cared for by Catholic missionaries or in other places where they do not have their own resident priest, but must await until a late hour the arrival of another priest before they can participate in the eucharistic sacrifice and be nourished with the divine food.

Moreover, now that machines of every sort have been brought into general use, it very often happens that not a few workmen employed in factories, or in transportation, shipping or other public utilities, are occupied day and night on swing shifts, so that their weakened conditions sometimes compel them to take some nourishment, and thus they are prevented from approaching the eucharistic table fasting.

Mothers of families also are often unable to come to the holy table until they have attended to their household duties, which often demand many hours of work.

It also happens that in schools and academies for boys and girls there are very many who desire to answer that divine invitation: "Let the little children come to me,"[21] perfectly trusting that he who "feedeth among the lilies"[22] will guard the innocence of their souls and the purity of their lives against the enticements of youth and the snares of the world. And yet at times it is very difficult for them, before going to school, to go to church and there nourish themselves with the bread of angels and afterward return home to take their necessary nourishment.

Moreover, we must remember that today large numbers of people cross from place to place in the afternoon or early evening to take part in religious services or to attend meetings on social questions. If, then, it were permitted to celebrate on such occasions the eucharistic mystery, which is the living font of divine grace and incites the will to glow with the desire of virtue, there is no doubt that all could draw from this source the strength to adopt a thoroughly Christian way of thought and action and to obey just laws.

These special considerations may well be supplemented by others which are of universal application. Although in these our times medical science and the study of hygiene have made such progress and have contributed so much to

---

20. Mt 28: 19.
21. Mk 10:14.
22. Cant 2:16; 6:2.

diminishing the death rate, especially among the young, yet the conditions of modern life and the hardships resulting from the frightful wars of this century are such that they have to a great extent undermined constitutions and weakened physical health.

For these reasons and especially in order the better to promote the reawakened devotion toward the Eucharist, not a few bishops of various countries have respectfully petitioned by letter that this law of fasting be somewhat mitigated; and this Apostolic See has already graciously granted special faculties and permissions in this matter to the sacred ministers and to the faithful. In this connection we may recall the decree entitled *Post editum*, which was issued by the Sacred Congregation of the Council, December 7, 1906, for the sick;[23] and the letter of March 22, 1923 given to local ordinaries for priests, by the Supreme Sacred Congregation of the Holy Office.[24]

In these latter times the petitions of the bishops in this matter have been more frequent and more insistent and the faculties granted have been correspondingly greater, especially those bestowed at the time of the war. Without doubt, that is an excellent indication that there exist new, serious continuing and sufficiently general causes which make it exceedingly difficult in many circumstances both for priests to celebrate the eucharistic sacrifice and for the faithful to receive the bread of angels fasting.

Wherefore, in order to meet these grave inconveniences and difficulties and in order that diversity of indults may not lead to differences in practice, we think it necessary to decree a mitigation of the eucharistic fast in such a way that, as far as possible, even in the special conditions of time and place and persons, all may more easily be able to observe that law. In issuing this decree we are confident that we will be able to contribute much to the increase of devotion to the Eucharist, and thus better persuade and induce all to partake at the table of the angels, with an undoubted increase of glory to God and of holiness to the mystical body of Jesus Christ.

Accordingly, by our apostolic authority we decree and provide as follows:

1.   The law of the Eucharistic fast from midnight continues in force for all of those who are not in the special conditions which we are about to explain in this apostolic letter. However, for the future, it is to be a general and common principle for all, whether priests or faithful, that natural water does not break the eucharistic fast.

2.   The sick, even though not confined to bed, may with the prudent advice of a confessor take something by way of drink or of true medicine, exclusive of alcoholics. The same faculty is granted to priests who are ill yet intend to celebrate Mass.

3.   Priests who are going to celebrate either at a rather late hour, or after fatiguing work in the sacred ministry or after a long journey, may take something by

23. *ASS* 39, 603; *Fontes* 6, no. 4331, 843.
24. *AAS* 15, 151.

way of drink, exclusive of alcoholic beverages; however, they must abstain from such drink for at least the space of one hour before saying Mass.

4.   Those who say Mass twice or three times may take the ablutions, but in this case the ablutions are to consist of water only, without wine.

5.   In like manner the faithful, even though not ill, who because of serious inconvenience—that is, fatiguing work, the lateness of the hour at which alone they can receive holy communion, or a long journey which they must make—cannot approach the eucharistic table completely fasting, may, with the prudent advice of a confessor, for as long as the need lasts, take something by way of drink, exclusive of alcoholic beverages; however, they must abstain from such drink for at least the space of one hour before receiving communion.

6.   We grant to local ordinaries, if the circumstances demand it, the faculty to permit the celebration of Mass in the evening, as we have said, but with the understanding that the Mass shall not begin before four o'clock in the afternoon, on the following days: on holy days of obligation which are still in effect, or on those which were formerly observed; on the first Friday of each month; on the occasion of solemnities which are celebrated with a large concourse of people; and also, in addition to these days, once each week. The priest must observe the fast for three hours as to solid food and alcoholic drink, and for one hour as to nonalcoholic drink. During these Masses, moreover, the faithful may receive holy communion, observing the same rule as regards the eucharistic fast, and without prejudice to the prescription of canon 857.

In mission territories, considering the very special conditions which prevail there and because of which, generally speaking, it is rare for priests to be able to visit the distant stations, local ordinaries can grant to missionaries the same faculty also for other days of the week.

Local ordinaries, however, should carefully see to it that the every interpretation be avoided which would enlarge the faculties granted, and that all abuse and irreverence in this matter be precluded. For in bestowing these faculties which are demanded today by circumstances of persons, times and places, we wish most emphatically to confirm the importance, force and efficacy of the eucharistic fast for those who are about to receive the divine Redeemer hidden under the eucharistic veils. And moreover, as bodily inconvenience is diminished, the soul ought as far as possible to make up for it, either by interior penance or in other ways, according to the traditional practice of the Church which usually prescribes other works when it mitigates the obligation to fast. Therefore, those who make use of the faculties here granted should direct more fervent prayers to heaven, adore God, thank him and especially expiate their faults and implore new graces from above. Since all should clearly realize that the Eucharist was instituted by Jesus Christ "as an everlasting memorial of his passion,"[25] they should stir up in hearts those sentiments of Christian humility and Christian penance which meditation on the sufferings and death of the divine Redeemer

---

25. St. Thomas, *Opusc.* LVII, Office for the Feast of Corpus Christi, lect. IV: *Opera Omnia*, Rome, 1570, vol. XVII.

ought to arouse. Likewise, let all offer to the same divine Redeemer, ever immolating himself on the altar and thus renewing the greatest proof of his love, increased fruits of charity toward their neighbor. In this way certainly all will contribute to the daily better fulfillment of that saying of the apostle of the Gentiles: "The bread is one, we though many are one body, all of us who partake of the one bread."[26]

It is our will that all the decrees contained in this letter be established, ratified and valid, notwithstanding anything to the contrary, even though worthy of most special mention; and all other privileges and faculties which have been granted in any way whatsoever by the Holy See are hereby abolished, so that everywhere all persons may uniformly and duly this discipline.

All the provisions herein set forth shall be operative from the day of promulgation in the *Acta Apostolicae Sedis.*[27]

Given at Rome at St. Peter's, in the year of the Lord 1953, on the sixth day of January, the Epiphany of the Lord, in the fourteenth year of our pontificate.

---

26. 1 Cor 10:17.
27. The day of promulgation was January 16, 1953.

SACRAM COMMUNIONEM

MOTU PROPRIO OF POPE PIUS XII ON FURTHER MODIFICATIONS OF THE EUCHARISTIC FAST

MARCH 19, 1957

Early in 1953 We promulgated the Apostolic Constitution *Christus Dominus* in order that the faithful could receive Holy Communion frequently and satisfy more easily for precept for hearing Mass on holydays. By this Constitution We mitigated the severity of the Eucharistic fast and gave local ordinaries power to permit, under fixed conditions, the celebration of Mass and reception of Holy Communion in the afternoon.

We also defined the period during which one must fast before celebrating Mass or receiving Holy Communion after noon, as three hours preceding celebration or reception, for solid foods, and one hour for non-alcoholic beverages.

Inspired by the abundant benefits which resulted from this concession, the Bishops have extended their deepest thanks to Us, and many of them, for the greater good of their flocks, have asked Us in repeated and insistent requests to permit the daily celebration of Mass during the hours after noon. They also ask that We prescribe this same period of time for the fast when Mass is celebrated, or Holy Communion received, before noon.

Out of consideration for the notable changes which have occurred in working and office hours, and in social life generally, We have decided to fulfill the earnest requests of the Hierarchy, and therefore decree:

1.   Local Ordinaries, except for Vicars General without special mandate, are empowered to permit the daily celebration of Mass after noon if the spiritual good of a considerable number of the faithful demands it.

2.   The period for observing the Eucharistic fast by priests before Mass and by the faithful before Holy Communion—whether before or after noon—is reduced to three hours from solid food and alcoholic beverages, but to one hour from non-alcoholic beverages. The fast is not broken by drinking water.

3.   Those who celebrate Mass or receive Holy Communion at midnight or in the very early hours of the morning are bound to observe the Eucharistic fast according to the rules laid down above.

4.   The sick, even though they are not confined to bed, can consume non-alcoholic beverages and real and appropriate medicines, whether liquids or solids,

before celebrating Mass or receiving Holy Communion, without any restriction of time.

But We earnestly exhort priests and faithful who are able to do so, to preserve the venerable and ancient form of Eucharistic fast before Mass or Holy Communion.

Finally, all who enjoy these concessions are to endeavor seriously to compensate for the benefits received by becoming illustrious examples of the Christian life, especially by works of penance and charity.

The instructions contained in this Apostolic Letter, issued *motu proprio*, shall take effect from the twenty-fifth day of March, the feast of the Annunciation of the Blessed Virgin Mary.

Anything to the contrary notwithstanding, even though worthy of special mention.

Given at Rome, in St. Peter's, on the 19th day of March, on the feast of St. Joseph, Patron of the universal Church, in the year 1957, the 19th of Our Pontificate.

MUSICAE SACRAE DISCIPLINA

ON SACRED MUSIC

ENCYCLICAL
POPE PIUS XII
DECEMBER 25, 1955

DE MUSICA SACRA ET SACRA LITURGIA

ON SACRED MUSIC
AND SACRED LITURGY

INSTRUCTION
SACRED CONGREGATION FOR RITES
SEPTEMBER 3, 1958

AN OVERVIEW OF *MUSICAE SACRAE DISCIPLINA* AND *DE MUSICA SACRA ET SACRA LITURGIA*

Steven R. Janco

CONTEXT, CLASSIFICATION, AND TERMINOLOGY

We turn our attention to two documents issued in the 1950s, near the end of the pontificate of Pope Pius XII: the encyclical *Musicae sacrae disciplina* (MSD),[1] issued on December 25, 1955; and *De Musica sacra et sacra Liturgia* (MSSL), an instruction issued by the Sacred Congregation for Rites on September 3, 1958, just one month before the death of Pius XII on October 9.

While we cannot help but examine these pre-Vatican II documents through the lens of our own post-Vatican II liturgical experience, many of their contributions cannot readily be identified and appreciated unless we take into account the context in and for which they were written and the concerns addressed in documents that preceded them. Though issued in the years just before Pope John XXIII announced plans for the Second Vatican Council, both MSD and MSSL address the needs of the Roman Rite liturgy in use at the time, the Tridentine Mass celebrated in Latin, as well as its three modes of celebration: the Solemn High Mass (sung), the High Mass (sung), and the Low Mass (spoken). That being said, we must also acknowledge that the Liturgical Movement and the scholarship that accompanied it were already impacting the Church's liturgical life by this time. Pius XII devoted his lengthy 1947 encyclical *Mediator Dei* to the topic of liturgy, examining in detail the priestly role of the congregation in the Eucharistic liturgy and calling for greater participation of the faithful in liturgical celebration. Four years later, he called for the restoration of the Easter Vigil and began the work of reforming the other liturgies of Holy Week. The publication of these revised rites in 1955 was a significant moment in the life of the universal Church, a sign of the fruitfulness of liturgical scholarship, and a foreshadowing of more extensive reforms to come. MSD and MSSL were issued on the heels of these significant developments.

At the same time, in the 1950s the most authoritative ecclesiastical document devoted to music remained Pius X's *motu proprio, Tra le sollecitudini* (TLS), which was issued in 1903, more than fifty years earlier. TLS condemns what were perceived to be inappropriate theatrical and operatic influences on sacred music and calls for wider use of recently revised Gregorian chant volumes as a way to promote greater congregational participation in the liturgy. Though

---

1. The Vatican website titles this document *Musicae sacrae*, though it may be more widely known by the longer title employed in this overview. The longer title and its abbreviation (MSD) help to distinguish the document from others with similar titles and abbreviations.

MSD and MSSL move beyond TLS in many ways, its influence can readily be seen in the two later documents.

While it is important to interpret liturgical documents in light of earlier statements, examining older documents also affords the opportunity to see how their principles and prescriptions are affirmed, modified, or superseded in later statements. The reader may wish to keep in mind that MSD and MSSL were the most recent Vatican statements devoted to music and the liturgy when *Sacrosanctum Concilium* (SC, 1963) and *Musicam sacram* (MS, 1967) were being drafted.

It will be helpful to briefly examine the classification of MSD and MSSL. Issued as an encyclical and addressed to "Our Venerable Brethren, the Patriarchs, Primates, Archbishops, Bishops and other Local Ordinaries," MSD is principally a teaching document rather than a juridical one, exploring sacred music from historical, theological, and artistic perspectives—though it must be noted that MSD does reference prescriptions in TLS and discuss some specific norms and practices. MSSL was issued by the Sacred Congregation for Rites as an instruction, a document designed to provide guidance and direction for the interpretation and practical implementation of principles articulated in other documents—in this case *Mediator Dei* (MD) and MSD. MSSL is less philosophical and much more businesslike in tone, focusing on specific details rather than broader themes.

Before discussing these two documents individually, it will be useful to comment on terminology used in both. Both MSD and MSSL employ the then-customary term "sacred music" and both documents use the term in two ways. First, "sacred music" serves as an umbrella term that includes several distinct categories of music, including Gregorian chant, classical polyphony, modern sacred compositions, and vernacular hymnody. MSSL adds "religious music," pieces usually performed in concert whose theme or intent is "to arouse devotion and religious sentiments."[2] MSSL also devotes significant attention to organ music: accompaniments, pieces played "alone," and improvised music.

In addition to this broader usage, both documents at times employ the term "sacred music" when referring specifically to music used in the celebration of liturgy. Today most would use the term "liturgical music." One *does* find the term "liturgical music" in MSD, but it appears only once.[3]

MUSICAE SACRAE DISCIPLINA

Pope Pius XII's encyclical *Musicae sacrae disciplina* offers a comprehensive and positive overview of the role of music in Catholic worship. While paying tribute to the work of his predecessors, in particular TLS and the apostolic constitution *Divini cultus sanctitatem*, issued by Pius XI in 1928, Pius XII eschews the restrictive and corrective tone of these earlier documents and does not limit himself to repeating their prescriptions. From the outset, he expresses the hope that "the noble art of sacred music—adapted to contemporary conditions and in some way enriched—may ever more perfectly accomplish its mission."[4] He indicates that his "experience of pastoral life and the advances being made in the study of this

---

2. *De Musica sacra et sacra Liturgia* [MSSL], 10.
3. *Musicae sacrae disciplina* [MSD], 35.
4. Ibid., 3.

art"[5] have persuaded him that the time was right to issue a new document focused on music and the liturgy.

MSD opens expansively, stating that music is a gift from God, a gift given to people of every time and place. "Even among pagan peoples, sacred song and the art of music have been used to ornament and decorate religious ceremonies."[6] Having established that broad foundation, MSD provides an overview of the important role of song throughout the history of God's people, noting that "new forms of sacred chant" and "new types of songs" have been developed along the way.[7] Before moving on to discuss music in its liturgical context, MSD considers music in a broader, more philosophical exploration of art and the role of artists.

One significant contribution of MSD is that it moves beyond an understanding of sacred music principally as a way of clothing liturgical text "with suitable melody"[8] and explores more broadly "the manifold power and the apostolic effectiveness of sacred music."[9] Music has a "special power and excellence" that "should lift up to God the minds of the faithful. . . ."[10] One of the functions of sacred music is "accompanying and beautifying . . . liturgical ceremonies. . . ."[11] It makes liturgical prayers "more alive and fervent so that everyone can praise and beseech the Triune God more powerfully, more intently and more effectively."[12] The document notes that hymns, "born as they are from the most profound depths of the people's soul, deeply move the emotions and spirit and stir up pious sentiments."[13] And in a foreshadowing of SC's assertion that music is "the more holy the more closely it is joined to liturgical rite,"[14] MSD notes that "the dignity and force of sacred music are greater the closer music itself approaches to the supreme act of Christian worship, the Eucharistic sacrifice of the altar."[15]

While MSD affirms the qualities of sacred music outlined in TLS—holiness, goodness of form, and universality, the document is often cited for granting several new permissions that, while addressing "contemporary conditions," move beyond TLS. First, while TLS had prohibited the use of any instrument other than the organ, MSD opens the door to other possibilities. "Besides the organ, other instruments can be called upon to give great help in attaining the lofty purpose of sacred music. . . . "[16] Pius XII gives special mention to stringed instruments that "use the bow" because they "express the joyous and sad sentiments of the soul with an indescribable power."[17]

---

5. Ibid., 2.
6. Ibid., 6.
7. Ibid., 11.
8. Ibid., 1.
9. Ibid., 38.
10. Ibid., 35.
11. Ibid.
12. Ibid., 31.
13. Ibid., 63.
14. *Sacrosanctum Concilium* (SC), 112.
15. MSD, 34.
16. Ibid., 59.
17. Ibid.

Second, while TLS limits liturgical song to Gregorian chant, MSD includes popular religious song (especially hymns) as an additional category of sacred music and permits the singing of vernacular hymns during sung and spoken Masses.[18] Aimed at keeping the faithful "from attending the Holy Sacrifice like dumb and idle spectators,"[19] this new permission led to the familiar four-hymn formula that carried over to the Vatican II liturgy and proved problematic as focus shifted from singing *during* the liturgy to singing *the liturgy*.

Third, unlike TLS, MSD permits the inclusion of female singers in choirs, though officially *only* when enough male singers are not available. The document allows that "a group of men and women or girls, located in a place outside the sanctuary set apart for the exclusive use of this group, can sing the liturgical texts at Solemn Mass. . . ."[20] Though our contemporary sensibilities might view this as a demeaning concession, Pius XII here opens a significant door and demonstrates a shift in priorities. Effective liturgical celebration and quality music making are the main concern. Long-standing customs that stand in the way may be changed.

Pius laid a careful foundation for these shifts during his earlier survey of the history of congregational song. From the countless references to music in the Old Testament he chooses to include just two quotations. Both involve the use of musical instruments and one describes the musical leadership of a woman. After passing through the Red Sea, the people of Israel sang under the charismatic leadership of Miriam, who also danced and played a tambourine. When the ark was moved from the house of Abinadab to the city of David, "all Israel played before the Lord on all manner of instruments made of wood, on harps and lutes and timbrels and cornets and cymbals (2 Sam 6:5)."[21] From the New Testament Pius XII quotes Paul's Letter to the Ephesians, which mentions the singing of "hymns": "Be filled with the Spirit, speaking to one another in psalms and hymns and spiritual songs."[22] Pius points out specifically that Paul "indicates that this custom of singing hymns was in force in the assemblies of Christians when he says: 'When you come together each of you has a hymn.'"[23] By including these particular quotations, Pius XII seeks to demonstrate that he is not introducing new innovations, but rather recovering and reintroducing venerable ancient practices.

DE MUSICA SACRA ET SACRA LITURGIA

The instruction *De Musica sacra et sacra Liturgia* observes that "sacred music and sacred liturgy are so naturally inter-woven that laws cannot be made for the one without affecting the other."[24] From both MD and MSD the instruction claims to assemble "all the main points on sacred liturgy, sacred music, and the

---

18. Ibid., 62–64.

19. Ibid., 64.

20. Ibid., 74.

21. Ibid., 7.

22. Ephesians 5:18ff; cf. Colossians 3:16.

23. MSD, 8.

24. *De Musica sacra et sacra Liturgia* (MSSL), introductory paragraphs.

pastoral advantages of both."[25] Unlike the encyclicals it presumes to summarize, however, MSSL does not attempt to inspire or theologize. It clarifies definitions of terms and concepts found in the earlier documents, provides general norms, and applies principles to a wide range of liturgical and musical issues by promoting or forbidding specific practices.

MSSL addresses the discussion of congregational participation articulated in MD. Interior participation is fundamental and most important, while exterior participation makes the congregation's participation "more complete."[26] Active participation is "perfect" [27] when it includes reception of the Holy Eucharist. The document then recommends a series of practical steps that may introduced, little by little, to foster active participation in all three forms of the celebration of Mass: the Solemn High Mass, the High Mass, and the Low Mass—through singing in the case of the first two, and through both singing and speaking in the case of the Low Mass.

In the case of both forms of the sung Mass, three "degrees" of sung participation by the congregation are presented: 1. responses to dialogues (for example, *et cum spiritu tuo* [and with your spirit] and *Gloria tibi, Domine* [Glory to you, Lord]); 2. parts of the Ordinary (for example, *Kyrie, Sanctus-Benedictus, Agnus Dei*); 3. parts of the Proper of the Mass, "if those present are well trained in Gregorian chant."[28] As late as 1967, MS cites MSSL and lists these degrees of participation "for pastoral reasons degrees of solemnity for the sung Mass are proposed here in order that it will become easier, in accord with each congregation's capability, to make the celebration of Mass more solemn through the use of singing."[29] Whereas *The General Instruction of the Roman Missal* and *Sing to the Lord: Music in Divine Worship* will later suggest that the dialogues of the Mass are among the more *important* elements to be sung, it is clear in MSSL and later in MS that dialogues are listed first because they offer the *easiest* way to introduce congregational singing. Simpler elements that are repeated frequently are listed next. More complicated and variable propers are listed last.

Later in the document one comes across something rather unexpected: a discussion of "modern technology" and pastoral issues that it raises. One can assume from the following prohibition that some experimentation with a variety of technologies had been reported: "The use of automatic instruments and machines, such as the automatic organ, phonograph, radio, tape or wire recorders, and other similar machines, is absolutely forbidden in liturgical functions. . . ."[30] The use of movie projectors is also prohibited.

MSSL does not view all modern technology with suspicion, however. It provides guidelines for Masses that will be broadcast on television and radio. It permits the use of sound amplification systems for liturgical celebrations and for the first time recognizes the electronic organ as an option that may be "tolerated temporarily" in communities that cannot afford to install a pipe organ.[31]

---

25. Ibid.
26. Ibid., 22.
27. Ibid., 23.
28. Ibid., 25.
29. *Musicam sacram* (MS), 28.
30. MSSL, 71.
31. Ibid., 64.

The document permits the use of electronic carillon devices, but cautions that they may not be used as a substitute for genuine tower bells.

Though it does not address the issue of church architecture directly, MSSL had an impact on the design of some churches built in the late 1950s and early 1960s. MSSL surprised more than a few by calling for the organ and choir to be located near the main altar when possible. The document indicates that the location should be such that "the singers or musicians occupying a raised platform are not conspicuous to the congregation in the main body of the church."[32] A number of churches built during this time feature near or behind (or above) the sanctuary a recessed room or area for singers and instrumentalists that is separated from the main worship space by a grate or grill. While they were an attempt to address a specific recommendation, these ill-considered spaces created significant acoustic, visibility, and logistical problems that rendered them obstacles to effective liturgical celebration.

When we discuss the role of music in liturgical celebration since Vatican II, we rightly appeal to Chapter VI of *Sacrosanctum Concilium* as the charter of renewed focus on assembly song. But when one examines MSD and MSSL, it becomes clear that many of the chapter's key principles had already been established during the papacy of Pius XII. One wonders what Chapter VI might have looked like had Pius XII not presented his optimistic and forward-looking vision of liturgical music a few years earlier.

---

32. Ibid., 67.

MUSICAE SACRAE
ENCYCLICAL OF POPE PIUS XII
ON SACRED MUSIC

TO OUR VENERABLE BRETHREN, THE PATRIARCHS, PRIMATES, ARCHBISHOPS, BISHOPS, AND OTHER LOCAL ORDINARIES IN PEACE AND COMMUNION WITH THE APOSTOLIC SEE

Health and Apostolic Benediction.

1.   The subject of sacred music has always been very close to Our heart. Hence it has seemed appropriate to us in this encyclical letter to give an orderly explanation of the topic and also to answer somewhat more completely several questions which have been raised and discussed during the past decades. We are doing so in order that this noble and distinguished art may contribute more every day to greater splendor in the celebration of divine worship and to the more effective nourishment of spiritual life among the faithful.

2.   At the same time We have desired to grant what many of you, venerable brethren, have requested in our wisdom and also what has been asked by outstanding masters of this liberal art and distinguished students of sacred music at meetings devoted to the subject. The experience of pastoral life and the advances being made in the study of this art have persuaded Us that this step is timely.

3.   We hope, therefore, that what St. Pius X rightly decreed in the document which he accurately called the "legal code of sacred music"[1] may be confirmed and inculcated anew, shown in a new light and strengthened by new proofs. We hope that the noble art of sacred music—adapted to contemporary conditions and in some way enriched—may ever more perfectly accomplish its mission.

4.   Music is among the many and great gifts of nature with which God, in Whom is the harmony of the most perfect concord and the most perfect order, has enriched men, whom He has created in His image and likeness.[2] Together with the other liberal arts, music contributes to spiritual joy and the delight of the soul.

5.   On this subject St. Augustine has accurately written: "Music, that is the science or the sense of proper modulation, is likewise given by God's generosity to mortals having rational souls in order to lead them to higher things."[3]

---

1. Motu proprio, *Tra le sollecitudini*, Acta Pii X, I, 77.
2. Cf. *Gen.* 1. 26.
3. *Epis. 161. De origine animae hominis*, 1, 2; PL XXXIII, 725.

6.   No one, therefore, will be astonished that always and everywhere, even among pagan peoples, sacred song and the art of music have been used to ornament and decorate religious ceremonies. This is proved by many documents, both ancient and new. No one will be astonished that these arts have been used especially for the worship of the true and sovereign God from the earliest times. Miraculously preserved unharmed from the Red Sea by God's power, the people of God sang a song of victory to the Lord, and Miriam, the sister of Moses, their leader, endowed with prophetic inspiration, sang with the people while playing a tambourine.[4]

7.   Later, when the ark of God was taken from the house of Abinadab to the city of David, the king himself and "all Israel played before the Lord on all manner of instruments made of wood, on harps and lutes and timbrels and cornets and cymbals."[5] King David himself established the order of the music and singing used for sacred worship.[6] This order was restored after the people's return from exile and was observed faithfully until the Divine Redeemer's coming.

8.   St. Paul showed us clearly that sacred chant was used and held in honor from the very beginning in the Church founded by the Divine Redeemer when he wrote to the Ephesians: "Be filled with the Spirit, speaking to one another in psalms and hymns and spiritual songs."[7] He indicates that this custom of singing hymns was in force in the assemblies of Christians when he says: "When you come together each of you has a hymn."[8]

9.   Pliny testifies that the same thing held true after apostolic times. He writes that apostates from the Faith said that "this was their greatest fault or error, that they were accustomed to gather before dawn on a certain day and sing a hymn to Christ as if He were God."[9] These words of the Roman proconsul in Bithynia show very clearly that the sound of church singing was not completely silenced even in times of persecution.

10.   Tertullian confirms this when he says that in the assemblies of the Christians "the Scriptures are read, the psalms are sung, sermons are preached."[10]

11.   There are many statements of the fathers and ecclesiastical writers testifying that after freedom and peace had been restored to the Church the psalms and hymns of liturgical worship were in almost daily use. Moreover, new forms of sacred chant were gradually created and new types of songs were invented. These were developed more and more by the choir schools attached to cathedrals and other important churches, especially by the School of Singers in Rome.

---

4. Cf. *Ex.* 15. 1–20.
5. II *Sam.* 6. 5.
6. Cf. I *Para.* 23. 5; 25. 2–31.
7. *Eph.* 5. 18ff; cf. *Col.* 3. 16.
8. I *Cor.* 14. 26.
9. Pliny, *Epis.* X, 96–97.
10. Tertullian, *De anima*, ch. 9; PL II, 701; and *Apol.* 39; PL I, 540.

12.   According to tradition, Our predecessor of happy memory, St. Gregory the Great, carefully collected and wisely arranged all that had been handed down by the elders and protected the purity and integrity of sacred chant with fitting laws and regulations.

13.   From Rome, the Roman mode of singing gradually spread to other parts of the West. Not only was it enriched by new forms and modes, but a new kind of sacred singing, the religious song, frequently sung in the vernacular, was also brought into use.

14.   The choral chant began to be called "Gregorian" after St. Gregory, the man who revived it. It attained new beauty in almost all parts of Christian Europe after the 8th or 9th century because of its accompaniment by a new musical instrument called the "organ." Little by little, beginning in the 9th century, polyphonic singing was added to this choral chant. The study and use of polyphonic singing were developed more and more during the centuries that followed and were raised to a marvelous perfection under the guidance of magnificent composers during the 15th and 16th centuries.

15.   Since the Church always held this polyphonic chant in the highest esteem, it willingly admitted this type of music even in the Roman basilicas and in pontifical ceremonies in order to increase the glory of the sacred rites. Its power and splendor were increased when the sounds of the organ and other musical instruments were joined with the voices of the singers.

16.   Thus, with the favor and under the auspices of the Church the study of sacred music has gone a long way over the course of the centuries. In this journey, although sometimes slowly and laboriously, it has gradually progressed from the simple and ingenuous Gregorian modes to great and magnificent works of art. To these works not only the human voice, but also the organ and other musical instruments, add dignity, majesty and a prodigious richness.

17.   The progress of this musical art clearly shows how sincerely the Church has desired to render divine worship ever more splendid and more pleasing to the Christian people. It likewise shows why the Church must insist that this art remain within its proper limits and must prevent anything profane and foreign to divine worship, from entering into sacred music along with genuine progress, and perverting it.

18.   The Sovereign Pontiffs have always diligently fulfilled their obligation to be vigilant in this matter. The Council of Trent also forbids "those musical works in which something lascivious or impure is mixed with organ music or singing."[11] In addition, not to mention numerous other Sovereign Pontiffs, Our predecessor Benedict XIV of happy memory in an encyclical letter dated February 19, 1749, which prepared for a Holy Year and was outstanding for its great learning

---

11. Council of Trent, Session XXII: *Decretum de observandis et evitandis in celebratione Missae.*

and abundance of proofs, particularly urged Bishops to firmly forbid the illicit and immoderate elements which had arrogantly been inserted into sacred music.[12]

19.   Our predecessors Leo XII, Pius VII, Gregory XVI, Pius IX, and Leo XIII[13] followed the same line.

20.   Nevertheless it can rightly be said that Our predecessor of immortal memory, St. Pius X, made as it were the highest contribution to the reform and renewal of sacred music when he restated the principles and standards handed down from the elders and wisely brought them together as the conditions of modern times demanded.[14] Finally, like Our immediate predecessor of happy memory, Pius XI, in his Apostolic Constitution *Divini cultus sanctitatem (The Holiness of Divine Worship)*, issued December 20, 1929,[15] We ourself in the encyclical *Mediator Dei (On the Sacred Liturgy)*, issued November 20, 1947,[16] have enriched and confirmed the orders of the older Pontiffs.

21.   Certainly no one will be astonished that the Church is so vigilant and careful about sacred music. It is not a case of drawing up laws of aesthetics or technical rules that apply to the subject of music. It is the intention of the Church, however, to protect sacred music against anything that might lessen its dignity, since it is called upon to take part in something as important as divine worship.

22.   On this score sacred music obeys laws and rules which are no different from those prescribed for all religious art and, indeed, for art in general. Now we are aware of the fact that during recent years some artists, gravely offending against Christian piety, have dared to bring into churches works devoid of any religious inspiration and completely at variance with the right rules of art. They try to justify this deplorable conduct by plausible-looking arguments which they claim are based on the nature and character of art itself. They go on to say that artistic inspiration is free and that it is wrong to impose upon it laws and standards extraneous to art, whether they are religious or moral, since such rules seriously hurt the dignity of art and place bonds and shackles on the activity of an inspired artist.

23.   Arguments of this kind raise a question which is certainly difficult and serious, and which affects all art and every artist. It is a question which is not to be answered by an appeal to the principles of art or of aesthetics, but which must be decided in terms of the supreme principle of the final end, which is the inviolate and sacred rule for every man and every human act.

24.   The ordination and direction of man to his ultimate end—which is God—by absolute and necessary law based on the nature and the infinite perfection of God Himself is so solid that not even God could exempt anyone from it. This

---

12. Cf. encyclical letter of Benedict XIV *Annus qui*, Opera omnia (Prati edition, vol. 17, 1, page 16).

13. Cf. apostolic letter *Bonum est confiteri Domino*, August 2, 1828; Cf. *Bullarium Romanum*, Prati edition, ex Typ. Aldina, IX, 139ff.

14. Cf. *Acta Pii* X, I 75–87; *Acta Sanctae Sedis*, XXXVI (1903–1904) 329–39, 387–95.

15. Cf. AAS., XXI, 33ff.

16. Cf. AAS., XXXIX, 521–95.

eternal and unchangeable law commands that man himself and all his actions should manifest and imitate, so far as possible, God's infinite perfection for the praise and glory of the Creator. Since man is born to attain this supreme end, he ought to conform himself and through his actions direct all powers of his body and his soul, rightly ordered among themselves and duly subjected to the end they are meant to attain, to the divine Model. Therefore even art and works of art must be judged in the light of their conformity and concord with man's last end.

25.   Art certainly must be listed among the noblest manifestations of human genius. Its purpose is to express in human works the infinite divine beauty of which it is, as it were, the reflection. Hence that outworn dictum "art for art's sake" entirely neglects the end for which every creature is made. Some people wrongly assert that art should be exempted entirely from every rule which does not spring from art itself. Thus this dictum either has no worth at all or is gravely offensive to God Himself, the Creator and Ultimate End.

26.   Since the freedom of the artist is not a blind instinct to act in accordance with his own whim or some desire for novelty, it is in no way restricted or destroyed, but actually ennobled and perfected, when it is made subject to the divine law.

27.   Since this is true of works of art in general, it obviously applies also to religious and sacred art. Actually religious art is even more closely bound to God and the promotion of His praise and glory, because its only purpose is to give the faithful the greatest aid in turning their minds piously to God through the works it directs to their senses of sight and hearing. Consequently the artist who does not profess the truths of the faith or who strays far from God in his attitude or conduct should never turn his hand to religious art. He lacks, as it were, that inward eye with which he might see what God's majesty and His worship demand. Nor can he hope that his works, devoid of religion as they are, will ever really breathe the piety and faith that befit God's temple and His holiness, even though they may show him to be an expert artist who is endowed with visible talent. Thus he cannot hope that his works will be worthy of admission into the sacred buildings of the Church, the guardian and arbiter of religious life.

28.   But the artist who is firm in his faith and leads a life worthy of a Christian, who is motivated by the love of God and reverently uses the powers the Creator has given him, expresses and manifests the truths he holds and the piety he possesses so skillfully, beautifully and pleasingly in colors and lines or sounds and harmonies that this sacred labor of art is an act of worship and religion for him. It also effectively arouses and inspires people to profess the faith and cultivate piety.

29.   The Church has always honored and always will honor this kind of artist. It opens wide the doors of its temples to them because what these people contribute through their art and industry is a welcome and important help to the Church in carrying out its apostolic ministry more effectively.

30.   These laws and standards for religious art apply in a stricter and holier way to sacred music because sacred music enters more intimately into divine worship than many other liberal arts, such as architecture, painting and sculpture. These last serve to prepare a worthy setting for the sacred ceremonies. Sacred music, however, has an important place in the actual performance of the sacred ceremonies and rites themselves. Hence the Church must take the greatest care to prevent whatever might be unbecoming to sacred worship or anything that might distract the faithful in attendance from lifting their minds up to God from entering into sacred music, which is the servant, as it were, of the sacred liturgy.

31.   The dignity and lofty purpose of sacred music consists in the fact that its lovely melodies and splendor beautify and embellish the voices of the priest who offers Mass and of the Christian people who praise the Sovereign God. Its special power and excellence should lift up to God the minds of the faithful who are present. It should make the liturgical prayers of the Christian community more alive and fervent so that everyone can praise and beseech the Triune God more powerfully, more intently and more effectively.

32.   The power of sacred music increases the honor given to God by the Church in union with Christ, its Head. Sacred music likewise helps to increase the fruits which the faithful, moved by the sacred harmonies, derive from the holy liturgy. These fruits, as daily experience and many ancient and modern literary sources show, manifest themselves in a life and conduct worthy of a Christian.

33.   St. Augustine, speaking of chants characterized by "beautiful voice and most apt melody," says: "I feel that our souls are moved to the ardor of piety by the sacred words more piously and powerfully when these words are sung than when they are not sung, and that all the affections of our soul in their variety have modes of their own in song and chant by which they are stirred up by an indescribable and secret sympathy."[17]

34.   It is easy to infer from what has just been said that the dignity and force of sacred music are greater the closer sacred music itself approaches to the supreme act of Christian worship, the Eucharistic sacrifice of the altar. There can be nothing more exalted or sublime than its function of accompanying with beautiful sound the voice of the priest offering up the Divine Victim, answering him joyfully with the people who are present and enhancing the whole liturgical ceremony with its noble art.

35.   To this highest function of sacred music We must add another which closely resembles it, that is its function of accompanying and beautifying other liturgical ceremonies, particularly the recitation of the Divine Office in choir. Thus the highest honor and praise must be given to liturgical music.

36.   We must also hold in honor that music which is not primarily a part of the sacred liturgy, but which by its power and purpose greatly aids religion. This music is therefore rightly called religious music. The Church has possessed such

---

17. St. Augustine, *Confessions*, Book X, chap. 33, MPL, XXXII, 799ff.

music from the beginning and it has developed happily under the Church's auspices. As experience shows, it can exercise great and salutary force and power on the souls of the faithful, both when it is used in churches during non-liturgical services and ceremonies, or when it is used outside churches at various solemnities and celebrations.

37.   The tunes of these hymns, which are often sung in the language of the people, are memorized with almost no effort or labor. The mind grasps the words and the music. They are frequently repeated and completely understood. Hence even boys and girls, learning these sacred hymns at a tender age, are greatly helped by them to know, appreciate and memorize the truths of the faith. Therefore they also serve as a sort of catechism. These religious hymns bring pure and chaste joy to young people and adults during times of recreation. They give a kind of religious grandeur to their more solemn assemblies and gatherings. They bring pious joy, sweet consolation and spiritual progress to Christian families themselves. Hence these popular religious hymns are of great help to the Catholic apostolate and should be carefully cultivated and promoted.

38.   Therefore when We praised the manifold power and the apostolic effectiveness of sacred music, We spoke of something that can be a source of great joy and solace to all who have in any way dedicated themselves to its study and practice. All who use the art they possess to compose such musical compositions, to teach them or to perform them by singing or using musical instruments, undoubtedly exercise in many ways a true and genuine apostolate. They will receive from Christ the Lord the generous rewards and honors of apostles for the work they have done so faithfully.

39.   Consequently they should hold their work in high esteem, not only as artists and teachers of art, but also as ministers of Christ the Lord and as His helpers in the work of the apostolate. They should likewise show in their conduct and their lives the dignity of their calling.

40.   Since, as We have just shown, the dignity and effectiveness of sacred music and religious chant are so great, it is very necessary that all of their parts should be diligently and carefully arranged to produce their salutary results in a fitting manner.

41.   First of all the chants and sacred music which are immediately joined with the Church's liturgical worship should be conducive to the lofty end for which they are intended. This music—as our predecessor Pius X has already wisely warned us—"must possess proper liturgical qualities, primarily holiness and goodness of form; from which its other note, universality, is derived."[18]

42.   It must be *holy*. It must not allow within itself anything that savors of the profane nor allow any such thing to slip into the melodies in which it is expressed. The Gregorian chant which has been used in the Church over the course of so

---

18. *Acta Pii X*, loc. cit., 78.

many centuries, and which may be called, as it were, its patrimony, is gloriously outstanding for this holiness.

43.   This chant, because of the close adaptation of the melody to the sacred text, is not only most intimately conformed to the words, but also in a way interprets their force and efficacy and brings delight to the minds of the hearers. It does this by the use of musical modes that are simple and plain, but which are still composed with such sublime and holy art that they move everyone to sincere admiration and constitute an almost inexhaustible source from which musicians and composers draw new melodies.

44.   It is the duty of all those to whom Christ the Lord has entrusted the task of guarding and dispensing the Church's riches to preserve this precious treasure of Gregorian chant diligently and to impart it generously to the Christian people. Hence what Our predecessors, St. Pius X, who is rightly called the renewer of Gregorian chant,[19] and Pius XI[20] have wisely ordained and taught, We also, in view of the outstanding qualities which genuine Gregorian chant possesses, will and prescribe that this be done. In the performance of the sacred liturgical rites this same Gregorian chant should be most widely used and great care should be taken that it should be performed properly, worthily and reverently. And if, because of recently instituted feast days, new Gregorian melodies must be composed, this should be done by true masters of the art. It should be done in such a way that these new compositions obey the laws proper to genuine Gregorian chant and are in worthy harmony with the older melodies in their virtue and purity.

45.   If these prescriptions are really observed in their entirety, the requirements of the other property of sacred music—that property by virtue of which it should be an *example of true art*—will be duly satisfied. And if in Catholic churches throughout the entire world Gregorian chant sounds forth without corruption or diminution, the chant itself, like the sacred Roman liturgy, will have a characteristic of universality, so that the faithful, wherever they may be, will hear music that is familiar to them and a part of their own home. In this way they may experience, with much spiritual consolation, the wonderful unity of the Church. This is one of the most important reasons why the Church so greatly desires that the Gregorian chant traditionally associated with the Latin words of the sacred liturgy be used.

46.   We are not unaware that, for serious reasons, some quite definite exceptions have been conceded by the Apostolic See. We do not want these exceptions extended or propagated more widely, nor do We wish to have them transferred to other places without due permission of the Holy See. Furthermore, even where it is licit to use these exemptions, local Ordinaries and the other pastors should take great care that the faithful from their earliest years should learn at least the easier and more frequently used Gregorian melodies, and should know how

---

19. Letter to Card. Respighi, *Acta Pii X*, loc. cit. 68–74, see 73ff.; *Acta Sanctae Sedis*, XXXVI (1903–04), 325–29, 395–98, see 398.
20. Pius XI, apostolic constitution. *Divini cultus*, AAS, XXI (1929), 33ff.

to employ them in the sacred liturgical rites, so that in this way also the unity and the universality of the Church may shine forth more powerfully every day.

47.   Where, according to old or immemorial custom, some popular hymns are sung in the language of the people after the sacred words of the liturgy have been sung in Latin during the solemn Eucharistic sacrifice, local Ordinaries can allow this to be done "if, in the light of the circumstances of the locality and the people, they believe that (custom) cannot prudently be removed."[21] The law by which it is forbidden to sing the liturgical words themselves in the language of the people remains in force, according to what has been said.

48.   In order that singers and the Christian people may rightly understand the meaning of the liturgical words joined to the musical melodies, it has pleased Us to make Our own the exhortation made by the Fathers of the Council of Trent. "Pastors and all those who have care of souls," were especially urged that "often, during the celebration of Mass, they or others whom they delegate explain something about what is read in the Mass and, among other things, tell something about the mystery of this most holy sacrifice. This is to be done particularly on Sundays and holy days."[22]

49.   This should be done especially at the time when catechetical instruction is being given to the Christian people. This may be done more easily and readily in this age of ours than was possible in times past, because translations of the liturgical texts into the vernacular tongues and explanations of these texts in books and pamphlets are available. These works, produced in almost every country by learned writers, can effectively help and enlighten the faithful to understand and share in what is said by the sacred ministers in the Latin language.

50.   It is quite obvious that what We have said briefly here about Gregorian chant applies mainly to the Latin Roman Rite of the Church. It can also, however, be applied to a certain extent to the liturgical chants of other rites—either to those of the West, such as the Ambrosian, Gallican or Mozarabic, or to the various eastern rites.

51.   For as all of these display in their liturgical ceremonies and formulas of prayer the marvelous abundance of the Church, they also, in their various liturgical chants, preserve treasures which must be guarded and defended to prevent not only their complete disappearance, but also any partial loss or distortion.

52.   Among the oldest and most outstanding monuments of sacred music, the liturgical chants of the different eastern rites hold a highly important place. Some of the melodies of these chants, modified in accordance with the character of the Latin liturgy, had a great influence on the composition of the musical works of the Western Church itself. It is Our hope that the selection of sacred eastern rite hymns—which the Pontifical Institute of Oriental Studies, with the help of the Pontifical Institute of Sacred Music, is busily working to complete—

---

21. *Code of Canon Law*, Can. 5.
22. Council of Trent, Session XXII, *De Sacrificio Missae*, C. VIII.

will achieve good doctrinal and practical results. Thus eastern rite seminarians, well trained in sacred chant, can make a significant contribution to enhancing the beauty of God's house after they have been ordained priests.

53.   It is not Our intention in what We have just said in praise and commendation of the Gregorian chant to exclude sacred polyphonic music from the rites of the Church. If this polyphonic music is endowed with the proper qualities, it can be of great help in increasing the magnificence of divine worship and of moving the faithful to religious dispositions. Everyone certainly knows that many polyphonic compositions, especially those that date from the 16th century, have an artistic purity and richness of melody which render them completely worthy of accompanying and beautifying the Church's sacred rites.

54.   Although over the course of the centuries genuine polyphonic art gradually declined and profane melodies often crept into it, during recent decades the indefatigable labors of experts have brought about a restoration. The works of the old composers have been carefully studied and proposed as models to be imitated and rivaled by modern composers.

55.   So it is that in the basilicas, cathedrals and churches of religious communities these magnificent works of the old masters and the polyphonic compositions of more recent musicians can be performed, contributing greatly to the beauty of the sacred rite. Likewise We know that simpler but genuinely artistic polyphonic compositions are often sung even in smaller churches.

56.   The Church favors all these enterprises. As Our predecessor of immortal memory, St. Pius X, says, the Church "unceasingly encourages and favors the progress of the arts, admitting for religious use all the good and the beautiful that the mind of man has discovered over the course of the centuries, but always respecting the liturgical laws."[23]

57.   These laws warn that great prudence and care should be used in this serious matter in order to keep out of churches polyphonic music which, because of its heavy and bombastic style, might obscure the sacred words of the liturgy by a kind of exaggeration, interfere with the conduct of the liturgical service or, finally, lower the skill and competence of the singers to the disadvantage of sacred worship.

58.   These norms must be applied to the use of the organ or other musical instruments. Among the musical instruments that have a place in church the organ rightly holds the principal position, since it is especially fitted for the sacred chants and sacred rites. It adds a wonderful splendor and a special magnificence to the ceremonies of the Church. It moves the souls of the faithful by the grandeur and sweetness of its tones. It gives minds an almost heavenly joy and it lifts them up powerfully to God and to higher things.

---

23. *Acta Pii X*, loc. cit., 80.

59.   Besides the organ, other instruments can be called upon to give great help in attaining the lofty purpose of sacred music, so long as they play nothing profane, nothing clamorous or strident, and nothing at variance with the sacred services or the dignity of the place. Among these the violin and other musical instruments that use the bow are outstanding because, when they are played by themselves or with other stringed instruments or with the organ, they express the joyous and sad sentiments of the soul with an indescribable power. Moreover, in the encyclical *Mediator Dei*, We Ourselves gave detailed and clear regulations concerning the musical modes that are to be admitted into the worship of the Catholic religion.

60.   "For, if they are not profane or unbecoming to the sacredness of the place and function and do not spring from a desire to achieve extraordinary and unusual effects, then our churches must admit them, since they can contribute in no small way to the splendor of the sacred ceremonies, can lift the mind to higher things, and can foster true devotion of the soul."[24]

61.   It should hardly be necessary to add the warning that, when the means and talent available are unequal to the task, it is better to forego such attempts than to do something which would be unworthy of divine worship and sacred gatherings.

62.   As We have said before, besides those things that are intimately associated with the Church's sacred liturgy, there are also popular religious hymns which derive their origin from the liturgical chant itself. Most of these are written in the language of the people. Since these are closely related to the mentality and temperament of individual national groups, they differ considerably among themselves according to the character of different races and localities.

63.   If hymns of this sort are to bring spiritual fruit and advantage to the Christian people, they must be in full conformity with the doctrine of the Catholic faith. They must also express and explain that doctrine accurately. Likewise they must use plain language and simple melody and must be free from violent and vain excess of words. Despite the fact that they are short and easy, they should manifest a religious dignity and seriousness. When they are fashioned in this way these sacred canticles, born as they are from the most profound depths of the people's soul, deeply move the emotions and spirit and stir up pious sentiments. When they are sung at religious rites by a great crowd of people singing as with one voice, they are powerful in raising the minds of the faithful to higher things.

64.   As we have written above, such hymns cannot be used in Solemn High Masses without the express permission of the Holy See. Nevertheless at Masses that are not sung solemnly these hymns can be a powerful aid in keeping the faithful from attending the Holy Sacrifice like dumb and idle spectators. They can help to make the faithful accompany the sacred services both mentally and vocally and to join their own piety to the prayers of the priest. This happens

---

24. AAS, XXXIX (1947), 590.

when these hymns are properly adapted to the individual parts of the Mass, as We rejoice to know is being done in many parts of the Catholic world.

65.   In rites that are not completely liturgical religious hymns of this kind— when, as We have said, they are endowed with the right qualities—can be of great help in the salutary work of attracting the Christian people and enlightening them, in imbuing them with sincere piety and filling them with holy joy. They can produce these effects not only within churches, but outside of them also, especially on the occasion of pious processions and pilgrimages to shrines and at the time of national or international congresses. They can be especially useful, as experience has shown, in the work of instructing boys and girls in Catholic truth, in societies for youth and in meetings of pious associations.

66.   Hence We can do no less than urge you, venerable brethren, to foster and promote diligently popular religious singing of this kind in the dioceses entrusted to you. There is among you no lack of experts in this field to gather hymns of this sort into one collection, where this has not already been done, so that all of the faithful can learn them more easily, memorize them and sing them correctly.

67.   Those in charge of the religious instruction of boys and girls should not neglect the proper use of these effective aids. Those in charge of Catholic youth should make prudent use of them in the highly important work entrusted to them. Thus there will be hope of happily attaining what everyone desires, namely the disappearance of worldly songs which because of the quality of their melodies or the frequently voluptuous and lascivious words that go with them are a danger to Christians, especially the young, and their replacement by songs that give chaste and pure pleasure, that foster and increase faith and piety.

68.   May it thus come about that the Christian people begin even on this earth to sing that song of praise it will sing forever in heaven: "To Him who sits upon the throne, and to the Lamb, blessing and honor and glory and dominion forever and ever."[25]

69.   What we have written thus far applies primarily to those nations where the Catholic religion is already firmly established. In mission lands it will not be possible to accomplish all these things until the number of Christians has grown sufficiently, larger church buildings have been erected, the children of Christians properly attend schools established by the Church and, finally, until there is an adequate number of sacred ministers. Still We urgently exhort apostolic workers who are laboring strenuously in these extensive parts of the Lord's vineyard to pay careful attention to this matter as one of the serious problems of their ministry.

70.   Many of the peoples entrusted to the ministry of the missionaries take great delight in music and beautify the ceremonies dedicated to the worship of idols with religious singing. It is not prudent, then, for the heralds of Christ, the true God, to minimize or neglect entirely this effective help in their apostolate.

---

25. *Apoc.* 5. 13.

Hence the preachers of the Gospel in pagan lands should sedulously and willingly promote in the course of their apostolic ministry the love for religious song which is cherished by the men entrusted to their care. In this way these people can have, in contrast to their own religious music which is frequently admired even in cultivated countries, sacred Christian hymns in which the truths of the faith, the life of Christ the Lord and the praises of the Blessed Virgin Mary and the Saints can be sung in a language and in melodies familiar to them.

71. Missionaries should likewise be mindful of the fact that, from the beginning, when the Catholic Church sent preachers of the Gospel into lands not yet illumined by the light of faith, it took care to bring into those countries, along with the sacred liturgical rites, musical compositions, among which were the Gregorian melodies. It did this so that the people who were to be converted might be more easily led to accept the truths of the Christian religion by the attractiveness of these melodies.

72. So that the desired effect may be produced by what We have recommended and ordered in this encyclical, following in the footsteps of Our predecessors, you, venerable brethren, must carefully use all the aids offered by the lofty function entrusted to you by Christ the Lord and committed to you by the Church. As experience teaches, these aids are employed to great advantage in many churches throughout the Christian world.

73. First of all see to it that there is a good school of singers in the cathedral itself and, as far as possible, in other major churches of your dioceses. This school should serve as an example to others and influence them to carefully develop and perfect sacred chant.

74. Where it is impossible to have schools of singers or where there are not enough choir boys, it is allowed that "a group of men and women or girls, located in a place outside the sanctuary set apart for the exclusive use of this group, can sing the liturgical texts at Solemn Mass, as long as the men are completely separated from the women and girls and everything unbecoming is avoided. The Ordinary is bound in conscience in this matter."[26]

75. Great care must be taken that those who are preparing for the reception of sacred orders in your seminaries and in missionary or religious houses of study are properly instructed in the doctrine and use of sacred music and Gregorian chant according to the mind of the Church by teachers who are experts in this field, who esteem the traditional customs and teachings and who are entirely obedient to the precepts and norms of the Holy See.

76. If, among the students in the seminary or religious house of study, anyone shows remarkable facility in or liking for this art, the authorities of the seminary or house of study should not neglect to inform you about it. Then you may avail yourself of the opportunity to cultivate these gifts further and send him either to the Pontifical Institute of Sacred Music in Rome or to some other institution

---

26. Decrees of the Sacred Congregation of Rites, nos. 3964, 4201, 4231.

of learning in which this subject is taught, provided that the student manifests the qualities and virtues upon which one can base a hope that he will become an excellent priest.

77.   In this matter care must also be taken that local Ordinaries and heads of religious communities have someone whose help they can use in this important area which, weighed down as they are by so many occupations, they cannot easily take care of themselves.

78.   It would certainly be best if in diocesan Councils of Christian Art there were someone especially expert in the fields of religious music and chant who could carefully watch over what is being done in the diocese, inform the Ordinary about what has been done and what is going to be done, receive the Ordinary's commands and see that they are obeyed. If in any diocese there is one of these associations, which have been wisely instituted to foster sacred music and have been greatly praised and commended by the Sovereign Pontiffs, the Ordinary in his prudence may employ this association in the task of fulfilling responsibility.

79.   Pious associations of this kind, which have been founded to instruct the people in sacred music or for advanced study in this subject, can contribute greatly by words and example to the advance of sacred music.

80.   Help and promote such associations, venerable brethren, so that they may lead an active life, may employ the best and the most effective teachers, and so that, throughout the entire diocese, they may diligently promote the knowledge, love and use of sacred music and religious harmonies, with due observance of the Church's laws and due obedience to Ourselves.

81.   Moved by paternal solicitude, We have dealt with this matter at some length. We are entirely confident that you, venerable brethren, will diligently apply all of your pastoral solicitude to this sacred subject which contributes so much to the more worthy and magnificent conduct of divine worship.

82.   It is Our hope that whoever in the Church supervises and directs the work of sacred music under your leadership may be influenced by Our encyclical letter to carry on this glorious apostolate with new ardor and new effort, generously, enthusiastically and strenuously.

83.   Hence, We hope that this most noble art, which has been so greatly esteemed throughout the Church's history and which today has been brought to real heights of holiness and beauty, will be developed and continually perfected and that on its own account it will happily work to bring the children of the Church to give due praise, expressed in worthy melodies and sweet harmonies, to the Triune God with stronger faith, more flourishing hope and more ardent charity.

84.   May it produce even outside the walls of churches—in Christian families and gatherings of Christians—what St. Cyprian beautifully spoke of to Donatus, "Let the sober banquet resound with Psalms. And if your memory be good and your voice pleasant, approach this work according to custom. You give more

nourishment to those dearest to you if we hear spiritual things and if religious sweetness delights the ears."[27]

85.   In the meantime, buoyed up by the hope of richer and more joyous fruits which We are confident will come from this exhortation of Ours, as a testimony of Our good will and as an omen of heavenly gifts to each one of you, venerable brethren, to the flock entrusted to your care and to those who observe Our wishes and work to promote sacred music, with abundant charity, We impart the Apostolic Benediction.

Given at St. Peter's in Rome, December 25, on the feast of the Nativity of Our Lord Jesus Christ, in the year 1955, the 17th of Our Pontificate.

PIUS XII

---

27. St. Cyprian, *Letter to Donatus* (Letter 1, n. 16) PL, IV, 227.

DE MUSICA SACRA ET SACRA LITURGIA

INSTRUCTION ON SACRED MUSIC AND SACRED LITURGY

SACRED CONGREGATION FOR RITES
SEPTEMBER 3, 1958

INTRODUCTION

In our time the Supreme Pontiffs have issued three important documents on the subject of sacred music: the *Motu proprio Inter sollicitudines* of Saint Pius X, Nov. 22, 1903; the Apostolic constitution *Divini cultus* of Pius XI of happy memory, Dec. 20, 1928; and the encyclical *Musicæ sacræ disciplina* of the happily reigning Supreme Pontiff Pius XII, Dec. 25, 1955. Other papal documents have also been issued, along with decrees of the Sacred Congregation of Rites in regard to sacred music.

As everyone realizes, sacred music and sacred liturgy are so naturally interwoven that laws cannot be made for the one without affecting the other. Indeed in the papal documents, and the decrees of the Sacred Congregation of Rites we find materials common to both sacred music, and sacred liturgy.

Before his encyclical on sacred music, the Supreme Pontiff, Pius XII, issued another encyclical on the sacred liturgy, *Mediator Dei*,[1] which very clearly explains, and demonstrates the relation between liturgical doctrine, and pastoral needs. It has therefore been considered appropriate to put together from the above documents a special instruction containing all the main points on sacred liturgy, sacred music, and the pastoral advantages of both. In this way their directives may be more easily, and securely put into practice.

It is for this purpose that the present instruction has been prepared. Experts in sacred music, and the Pontifical Commission for the General Restoration of the Liturgy have given advice and assistance.

The organization of this instruction is as follows:

Chapter I: General Concepts (no. 1–10)

Chapter II: General Norms (no. 11–21)

Chapter III-1. Principal liturgical functions in which sacred music is used

---

1. November 20, 1947.

Chapter I explains a few general concepts; chapter II then takes up the general norms for the use of sacred music in the liturgy. With this background chapter III presents the entire subject of sacred music, and sacred liturgy in detail. Each section establishes its own general principles, and then applies them to particular cases.

CHAPTER I: GENERAL CONCEPTS

1.   "The sacred liturgy comprises the entire public worship of the Mystical Body of Jesus Christ, Head and members."[2] "Liturgical ceremonies" are sacred rites instituted by Jesus Christ or the Church; they are carried out by persons lawfully appointed, and according to the prescriptions of liturgical books approved by the Holy See; their purpose is to give due worship to God, the Saints, and the Blessed.[3] Any other services, whether performed inside or outside the church, are called "private devotions," even though a priest is present or conducts them.

2.   The holy sacrifice of the Mass is an act of worship offered to God in the name of Christ and the Church; of its nature, it is public, regardless of the place or manner of its celebration. Thus, the term "private Mass" should never be used.

3.   There are two kinds of Masses: the sung Mass ("*Missa in cantu*"), and the read Mass ("*Missa lecta*"), commonly called low Mass.

There are two kinds of sung Mass: one called a solemn Mass if it is celebrated with the assistance of other ministers, a deacon and a subdeacon; the other called a high Mass if there is only the priest celebrant who sings all the parts proper to the sacred ministers.

4.   "Sacred music" includes the following: a) Gregorian chant; b) sacred polyphony; c) modern sacred music; d) sacred organ music; e) hymns; and f) religious music.

5.   Gregorian chant, which is used in liturgical ceremonies, is the sacred music proper to the Roman Church; it is to be found in the liturgical books approved by the Holy See. This music has been reverently, and faithfully fostered, and developed from most ancient, and venerable traditions; and even in recent times new chants have been composed in the style of this tradition. This style of music has no need of organ or other instrumental accompaniment.

6.   Sacred polyphony is measured music which arose from the tradition of Gregorian chant. It is choral music written in many voiceparts, and sung without instrumental accompaniment. It began to flourish in the Latin Church in the Middle Ages, and reached its height in the art of Giovanni Pierluigi da Palestrina (1524–1594) in the latter half of the sixteenth century; distinguished musicians of our time still cultivate this art.

---

2. *Mediator Dei*, Nov. 20, 1947: AAS 39 [1947] 528–529.

3. Cf. canon 1256.

7.   Modern sacred music is likewise sung in many voiceparts, but at times with instrumental accompaniment. Its composition is of more recent date, and in a more advanced style, developed from the previous centuries. When this music is composed specifically for liturgical use it must be animated by a spirit of devotion, and piety; only on this condition can it be admitted as suitable accompaniment for these services.

8.   Sacred music for organ is music composed for the organ alone. Ever since the pipe organ came into use this music has been widely cultivated by famous masters of the art. If such music complies with the laws for sacred music, it is an important contribution to the beauty of the sacred liturgy.

9.   Hymns are songs which spontaneously arise from the religious impulses with which mankind has been endowed by its Creator. Thus they are universally sung among all peoples.

This music had a fine effect on the lives of the faithful, imbuing both their private, and social lives with a true Christian spirit.[4] It was encouraged from the earliest times, and in our day it is still to be recommended for fostering the piety of the faithful, and enhancing their private devotions. Even such music can, at times, be admitted to liturgical ceremonies (This music had a fine effect on the lives of the faithful, imbuing both their private, and social lives with a true Christian spirit).[5]

10. Religious music is any music which, either by the intention of the composer or by the subject or purpose of the composition, serves to arouse devotion, and religious sentiments. Such music "is an effective aid to religion."[6] But since it was not intended for divine worship, and was composed in a free style, it is not to be used during liturgical ceremonies.

CHAPTER II: GENERAL NORMS

11. This instruction is binding on all rites of the Latin Church. Thus, what is said of Gregorian chant applies to all the chants which are used in other Latin rites.

Sacred music is to be taken generally in this instruction as embracing both vocal and instrumental music. But at times it will be limited to instrumental music only, as will be clear from the context.

A church ordinarily means any sacred place; this includes a church in the strict sense, as well as public, semi-public, and private oratories; again the context itself may restrict the meaning to a church in the strict sense.

12. Liturgical ceremonies are to be carried out as indicated in the liturgical books approved by the Holy See; this applies to the universal Church, to particular

---

4. Cf. Eph 5:18–20; Col 3:16
5. *Musicæ sacræ disciplina*, Dec. 25, 1955; AAS 48 [1956] 13–14.
6. *Musicæ sacræ disciplina*, idem.

churches, and to religious communities.[7] Private devotions, however, may be conducted according to local or community customs if they have been approved by competent ecclesiastical authority.[8]

Liturgical ceremonies, and private devotions are not to be mixed; but if the situation allows, such devotions may either precede or follow a liturgical ceremony.

13. a) Latin is the language of liturgical ceremonies; however, the liturgical books mentioned above, if they have been approved for general use or for a particular place or community, may make use of another language for certain liturgical ceremonies, and in such cases, this will be explicitly stated. Any exceptions to the general rule of Latin will be mentioned later in this Instruction.

b) Special permission is needed for the use of the vernacular which is a word-for-word translation in the celebration of sung liturgical ceremonies.[9]

c) Individual exceptions to the exclusive use of Latin in liturgical ceremonies which have already been granted by the Holy See still remain in effect. These permissions are not to be modified in their meaning nor extended to other regions without authorization from the Holy See.

d) In private devotions any language more suited to the faithful may be used.

14. a) In sung Masses only Latin is to be used. This applies not only to the celebrant, and his ministers, but also to the choir or congregation.

"However, popular vernacular hymns may be sung at the solemn Eucharistic Sacrifice (sung Masses), after the liturgical texts have been sung in Latin, in those places where such a centenary or immemorial custom has obtained. Local ordinaries may permit the continuation of this custom 'if they judge that it cannot prudently be discontinued because of the circumstances of the locality or the people.'"[10]

b) At low Mass the faithful who participate directly in the liturgical ceremonies with the celebrant by reciting aloud the parts of the Mass which belong to them must, along with the priest and his server, use Latin exclusively.

But if, in addition to this direct participation in the liturgy, the faithful wish to add some prayers or popular hymns, according to local custom, these may be recited or sung in the vernacular.

c) It is strictly forbidden for the faithful in unison or for a commentator to recite aloud with the priest the parts of the Proper, Ordinary, and canon of the Mass. This prohibition extends to both Latin, and a vernacular word-for-word

---

7. Cf. canon 1257.
8. Cf. canon 1259.
9. Motu proprio *Inter sollicitudines* AAS 36 [1903–1904] 334; Decr. auth. S.R.C. 4121.
10. Cf. Canon 5. *Musicæ sacræ disciplina*: AAS 48 [1956] 16–17.

translation. Exceptions will be enumerated in paragraph 31. However, it is desirable that a lector read the Epistle and Gospel in the vernacular for the benefit of the faithful at low Masses on Sundays and feast days. Between the Consecration, and the *Pater noster* a holy silence is fitting.

SACRED PROCESSIONS

15.   In sacred processions conducted according to the liturgical books, only the language prescribed or permitted by these books should be used. In other processions, held as private devotions, the language more suited to the faithful may be used.

16.   Gregorian chant is the music characteristic of the Roman Church. Therefore, its use is not only permitted, but encouraged at all liturgical ceremonies above all other styles of music, unless circumstances demand otherwise. From this it follows that:

a) The language of Gregorian chant, because of its character as liturgical music, must be exclusively Latin.

b) The priest and his ministers must use only the Gregorian melodies given in the standard editions when they sing their parts according to the rubrics of the liturgical ceremonies. Any sort of instrumental accompaniment is forbidden.

This is binding also on choir, and congregation when they answer the chants of the priest or his ministers according to the rubrics.

c) Finally, if a particular indult has been granted for the priest, deacon, subdeacon, or lector to read solemnly the Epistle, Lesson, or Gospel in the vernacular after they have been chanted in their Gregorian melodies, they must be read in a loud and clear voice, without any attempt to imitate the Gregorian melodies.[11]

17.   When the choir is capable of singing it, sacred polyphony may be used in all liturgical ceremonies. This type of sacred music is especially appropriate for ceremonies celebrated with greater splendor, and solemnity.

18.   Modern sacred music may also be used in all liturgical ceremonies if it conforms to the dignity, solemnity, and sacredness of the service, and if there is a choir capable of rendering it artistically.

19.   Hymns may be freely used in private devotions. But in liturgical ceremonies the principles laid down in paragraphs 13–15 should be strictly observed.

20.   Religious music should be entirely excluded from all liturgical functions; however, such music may be used in private devotions. With regard to concerts in church, the principles stated below in paragraphs 54, and 55 are to be observed.

---

11. Cf. no. 96e.

21.   Everything which the liturgical books prescribe to be sung, either by the priest and his ministers, or by the choir or congregation, forms an integral part of the sacred liturgy. Therefore:

a) It is strictly forbidden to change in any way the sung text, to alter or omit words, or to introduce inappropriate repetitions. This applies also to compositions of sacred polyphony, and modern sacred music: each word should be clearly, and distinctly audible.

b) It is explicitly forbidden to omit either the whole or a part of any liturgical text unless the rubrics provide for such a change.

c) But if for some reason a choir cannot sing one or another liturgical text according to the music printed in the liturgical books, the only permissible substitution is this: that it be sung either recto tono, i.e., on a straight tone, or set to one of the psalm tones. Organ accompaniment may be used. Typical reasons for permitting such a change are an insufficient number of singers, or their lack of musical training, or even, at times, the length of a particular rite or chant.

CHAPTER III-1. PRINCIPAL LITURGICAL FUNCTIONS IN WHICH SACRED MUSIC IS USED

A. MASS

a. General principles regarding the participation of the faithful

22.   By its very nature, the Mass requires that all present take part in it, each having a particular function.

a) Interior participation is the most important; this consists in paying devout attention, and in lifting up the heart to God in prayer. In this way the faithful "are intimately joined with their High Priest . . . and together with Him, and through Him offer (the Sacrifice), making themselves one with Him."[12]

b) The participation of the congregation becomes more complete, however, when, in addition to this interior disposition, exterior participation is manifested by external acts, such as bodily position (kneeling, standing, sitting), ceremonial signs, and especially responses, prayers, and singing.

The Supreme Pontiff Pius XII, in his encyclical on the sacred liturgy, *Mediator Dei*, recommended this form of participation:

"Those who are working for the exterior participation of the congregation in the sacred ceremonies are to be warmly commended. This can be accomplished in more than one way. The congregation may answer the words of the priest, as prescribed by the rubrics, or sing hymns appropriate to the different

---

12. *Mediator Dei*, Nov. 20, 1947: AAS 39 [1947] 552.

parts of the Mass, or do both. Also, at solemn ceremonies, they may alternate in singing the liturgical chant."[13]

When the papal documents treat of "active participation" they are speaking of this general participation,[14] of which the outstanding example is the priest, and his ministers who serve at the altar with the proper interior dispositions, and carefully observe the rubrics, and ceremonies.

c) Active participation is perfect when "sacramental" participation is included. In this way "the people receive the Holy Eucharist not only by spiritual desire, but also sacramentally, and thus obtain greater benefit from this most holy Sacrifice."[15]

d) Since adequate instruction is necessary before the faithful can intelligently, and actively participate in the mass, it will help to note here a very wise law enacted by the Council of Trent: "This holy Council orders that pastors, and all those who are entrusted with the care of souls shall frequently give a commentary on one of the texts used at Mass, either personally or through others, and, in addition, explain some aspect of the mystery of this holy Sacrifice; this should be done especially on Sundays, and feast days in the sermon which follows the Gospel"[16] (or "when the people are being instructed in the catechism"[17]).

MORE PERFECT WORSHIP

23. The primary end of general participation is the more perfect worship of God, and the edification of the faithful. Thus the various means of congregational participation should be so controlled that there is no danger of abuse, and this end is effectively achieved.

b. Participation of the faithful in sung Mass

24. The more noble form of the Eucharistic celebration is the solemn Mass because in it the solemnities of ceremonies, ministers, and sacred music all combine to express the magnificence of the divine mysteries, and to impress upon the minds of the faithful the devotion with which they should contemplate them. Therefore, we must strive that the faithful have the respect due to this form of worship by properly participating in it in the ways described below.

25. In solemn Mass there are three degrees of the participation of the faithful:

a) First, the congregation can sing the liturgical responses. These are: *Amen; Et cum spiritu tuo; Gloria tibi, Domine; Habemus ad Dominum; Dignum et*

---

13. AAS 39 [1947] 560.

14. *Mediator Dei:* AAS 39 [1947] 530–537.

15. Council of Trent, Sess. 22, ch. 6; cf. also *Mediator Dei:* AAS 39 [1947] 565: "It is most appropriate, as the liturgy itself prescribes, for the people to come to holy Communion after the priest has received at the altar."

16. Council of Trent, Sess. 22, ch. 8.

17. *Musicæ sacræ disciplina:* AAS 48 [1956] 17.

justum est; Sed libera nos a malo; Deo gratias. Every effort must be made that the faithful of the entire world learn to sing these responses.

b) Secondly, the congregation can sing the parts of the Ordinary of the Mass: *Kyrie, eleison; Gloria in excelsis Deo; Credo; Sanctus-Benedictus; Agnus Dei.* Every effort must be made that the faithful learn to sing these parts, particularly according to the simpler Gregorian melodies. But if they are unable to sing all these parts, there is no reason why they cannot sing the easier ones: *Kyrie, eleison; Sanctus-Benedictus; Agnus Dei;* the choir, then, can sing the *Gloria,* and *Credo.*

RECOMMENDED CHANTS

In connection with this, the following Gregorian melodies, because of their simplicity, should be learned by the faithful throughout the world: the *Kyrie, eleison; Sanctus-Benedictus; Agnus Dei* of Mass XVI from the Roman Gradual; the *Gloria in excelsis Deo,* and *Ite, missa est-Deo gratias* of Mass XV; and either Credo I or Credo III. In this way it will be possible to achieve that most highly desirable goal of having the Christian faithful throughout the world manifest their common faith by active participation in the holy Sacrifice of the Mass, and by common and joyful song.[18]

c) Thirdly, if those present are well trained in Gregorian chant, they can sing the parts of the Proper of the Mass. This form of participation should be carried out particularly in religious congregations and seminaries.

26.   High Mass, too, has its special place, even though it lacks the sacred ministers, and the full magnificence of the ceremonies of solemn Mass, for it is nonetheless enriched with the beauty of chant, and sacred music.

It is desirable that on Sundays, and feast days the parish or principal Mass be a sung Mass.

What has been said above in paragraph 25 about the participation of the faithful in Solemn High Mass also applies to the High Mass.

27.   Also note the following points with regard to the sung Mass:

a) If the priest and his ministers go in procession by a long aisle, it would be permissible for the choir, after the singing of the Introit antiphon, and its psalm verse, to continue singing additional verses of the same psalm. The antiphon itself may be repeated after each verse or after every other verse; when the celebrant has reached the altar, the psalm ceases, and the Gloria Patri is sung, and finally the antiphon is repeated to conclude the *Introit* procession.

b) After the Offertory antiphon is sung, it is also allowed to sing the ancient Gregorian melodies of the original Offertory verses which once were sung after the antiphon.

---

18. *Musicæ sacræ disciplina*: AAS 48 [1956] 16.

But if the Offertory antiphon is taken from a psalm, it is then permitted to sing additional verses of this same psalm. In this case, too, the antiphon may be repeated after each verse of the psalm, or after every second verse; when the offertory rite is finished at the altar the psalm is ended with the *Gloria Patri*, and the antiphon is repeated. If the antiphon is not taken from a psalm, then any psalm suited to the feast may be used. Another possibility is that any Latin song may be used after the Offertory antiphon provided it is suited to the spirit of this part of the Mass. The singing should never last beyond the "Secret."

c) The proper time for the chanting of the Communion antiphon is while the priest is receiving the holy Eucharist. But if the faithful are also to go to Communion the antiphon should be sung while they receive. If this antiphon, too, is taken from a psalm, additional verses of this psalm may be sung. In this case, too, the antiphon is repeated after each, or every second verse of the psalm; when distribution of Communion is finished, the psalm is closed with the *Gloria Patri*, and the antiphon is once again repeated. If the antiphon is not taken from a psalm, any psalm may be used which is suited to the feast, and to this part of the mass.

After the Communion antiphon is sung, and the distribution of Communion to the faithful still continues, it is also permitted to sing another Latin song in keeping with this part of the Mass.

Before coming to Communion the faithful may recite the threefold *Domine, non sum dignus* together with the priest.

d) If the Sanctus-Benedictus are sung in Gregorian chant, they should be put together without interruption; otherwise, the Benedictus should be sung after the Consecration.

e) During the Consecration, the singing must stop, and there should be no playing of instruments; if this has been the custom, it should be discontinued.

f) Between the Consecration, and the *Pater Noster* a devout silence is recommended.

g) While the priest is giving the blessing to the faithful at the end of the Mass, there should be no organ playing; also, the celebrant must pronounce the words of the blessing so that all the faithful can understand them.

AT LOW MASS

c. Participation of the faithful in low Mass

28. Care must be taken that the faithful assist at low Mass, too, "not as strangers or mute spectators,"[19] but as exercising that kind of participation demanded by so great, and fruitful a mystery.

---

19. *Divini cultus*, Dec. 20, 1928: AAS 21 [1929] 40.

29.   The first way the faithful can participate in the low Mass is for each one, on his own initiative, to pay devout attention to the more important parts of the Mass (interior participation), or by following the approved customs in various localities (exterior participation).

Those who use a small missal, suitable to their own understanding, and pray with priest in the very words of the Church, are worthy of special praise. But all are not equally capable of correctly understanding the rites, and liturgical formulas; nor does everyone possess the same spiritual needs; nor do these needs remain constant in the same individual. Therefore, these people may find a more suitable or easier method of participation in the Mass when "they meditate devoutly on the mysteries of Jesus Christ, or perform other devotional exercises, and offer prayers which, though different in form from those of the sacred rites, are in essential harmony with them."[20]

In this regard, it must be noted that if any local custom of playing the organ during low Mass might interfere with the participation of the faithful, either by common prayer or song, the custom is to be abolished. This applies not only to the organ, but also to the harmonium or any other musical instrument which is played without interruption. Therefore, in such Masses, there should be no instrumental music at the following times:

a. After the priest reaches the altar until the Offertory;

b. From the first versicles before the Preface until the *Sanctus* inclusive;

c. From the Consecration until the *Pater Noster*, where the custom obtains;

d. From the *Pater Noster* to the *Agnus Dei* inclusive; at the Confiteor before the Communion of the faithful ; while the Postcommunion prayer is being said, and during the Blessing at the end of the Mass.

PRAYERS AND HYMNS

30.   The faithful can participate another way at the Eucharistic Sacrifice by saying prayers together or by singing hymns. The prayers and hymns must be chosen appropriately for the respective parts of the Mass, and as indicated in paragraph 14c.

31.   A final method of participation, and the most perfect form, is for the congregation to make the liturgical responses to the prayers of the priest, thus holding a sort of dialogue with him, and reciting aloud the parts which properly belong to them.

There are four degrees or stages of this participation:

a) First, the congregation may make the easier liturgical responses to the prayers of the priest: *Amen; Et cum spiritu tuo; Deo gratias; Gloria tibi Domine;*

---

20. *Mediator Dei,* AAS 39 [1947] 560–561.

Laus tibi, Christe; Habemus ad Dominum; Dignum et justum est; Sed libera nos a malo;

 b) Secondly, the congregation may also say prayers, which, according to the rubrics, are said by the server, including the *Confiteor*, and the triple *Domine non sum dignus* before the faithful receive Holy Communion;

 c) Thirdly, the congregation may say aloud with the celebrant parts of the Ordinary of the Mass: *Gloria in excelsis Deo; Credo; Sanctus-Benedictus; Agnus Dei;*

 d) Fourthly, the congregation may also recite with the priest parts of the Proper of the Mass: Introit, Gradual, Offertory, Communion. Only more advanced groups who have been well trained will be able to participate with becoming dignity in this manner.

32. Since the *Pater Noster* is a fitting, and ancient prayer of preparation for Communion, the entire congregation may recite this prayer in unison with the priest in low Masses; the Amen at the end is to be said by all. This is to be done only in Latin, never in the vernacular.

33. The faithful may sing hymns during low Mass, if they are appropriate to the various parts of the mass.

34. Where the rubrics prescribe the *clara voce*, the celebrant must recite the prayers loud enough so that the faithful can properly, and conveniently follow the sacred rites. This must be given special attention in a large church, and before a large congregation.

THE MASS IN CHOIR

d. Conventual Mass, or the Mass in Choir

35. The conventual Mass, among all other liturgical ceremonies, has a special dignity: this is the Mass which must be celebrated daily in connection with the Divine Office by those whom the Church obliges to choir service.

 For the Mass, together with the Divine Office, is the summit of all Christian worship; it is the fullness of praise offered daily to Almighty God in public, and external ceremony.

 Since, however, this perfection of public, and corporate worship cannot be realized daily in every church, it is performed vicariously by those who have the "choir obligation," and are deputed for this service. This is especially true of cathedral churches acting in the name of the entire diocese.

 Thus all "choir" ceremonies should be performed with special dignity and solemnity, making use of both chant and sacred music.

36. The conventual Mass should, therefore, be a solemn Mass, or at least a high Mass.

Even if particular laws or indults have dispensed from the solemnity of the "choir" Mass, the canonical hours are not to be recited during the conventual Mass. It would be more appropriate to celebrate a conventual low Mass according to the manner outlined in paragraph 31; however, any use of the vernacular is to be excluded.

THE CONVENTUAL MASS

37.   Regarding the conventual Mass, the following prescriptions are to be observed:

a) On each day only one conventual Mass is to be celebrated; this must correspond to the Office recited in choir unless the rubrics direct otherwise.[21] However, if there are pious foundations or other legitimate reasons which require more than one conventual Mass, they still remain in force.

b) The conventual Mass follows the rules of a sung or low Mass.

c) Unless the superior of a community decides that it should be said after *Sext* or *None*, and this only for a serious reason, the conventual Mass is to be said after Terce.

d) Conventual Masses "outside the choir," which until now were sometimes prescribed by the rubrics, are now abolished.

e) Assistance of priests in the Holy Sacrifice of the Mass, and so-called "synchronized" Masses.

38.   In the Latin Church sacramental concelebration is limited by law to two specifically stated cases. The Supreme Sacred Congregation of the Holy Office, in a decision of May 23, 1947,[22] declared invalid the concelebration of the sacrifice of the Mass by priests who do not pronounce the words of consecration, even though they wear the sacred vestments, and no matter what their intention may be. But when there are many priests gathered for a meeting, it is permissible "for only one of their number to celebrate a Mass at which the others (whether all of them or many) are present, and receive Holy Communion from one priest celebrant." However, "this is to be done only for a justifiable reason, and provided the Bishop has not forbidden it because of the danger that the faithful might think it strange;" also, the practice must not be motivated by the error, pointed out by the Supreme Pontiff Pius XII, which taught that "the celebration of one Mass at which a hundred priests devoutly assist is equal to a hundred Masses celebrated by a hundred priests."[23]

39.   So-called "synchronized" Masses, are, however, forbidden. These are Masses in which two or more priests simultaneously, on one or more altars, so time their celebration of Mass that all their words, and actions are pronounced, and performed together at one and the same time, even with the aid of modern instru-

---

21. *Additiones et variationes in rubricis Missalis*, ti. I, n. 4.

22. AAS 49 [1957] 370.

23. Cf. Address to Cardinals and Bishops, Nov. 2, 1954: AAS 46 [1954] 669–670; and Address to International Congress on Pastoral Liturgy at Assisi, Sep. 22, 1956: AAS 48 [1956] 716–717.

ments to assure absolute uniformity or "synchronization," particularly if many priests are celebrating.

B. DIVINE OFFICE

40.   The Divine Office is said either in choir, in common, or alone.

The Office is said in choir when it is recited by a community obliged by Church law to choir duty; it is said in common when recited by a community not bound to choir duty.

However it is said, whether in choir, in common, or alone, it must always be looked upon as an act of public worship offered to God in the name of the Church, if it said by persons deputed to this obligation by the Church.

41.   The Divine Office by its very nature is so constructed that it should be performed by mutually alternating voices; moreover, some parts even presuppose that they be sung.

42.   Thus the celebration of the Divine Office in choir must be retained, and promoted. Likewise, its performance in common, including the singing of at least some parts of the Office, is earnestly recommended when circumstances of places, persons, and time permit.

43.   The recitation of the psalms in choir or in common, whether sung in Gregorian chant or simply recited, should be performed in a solemn, and becoming manner; care should be taken that the proper tones, appropriate pauses, and perfect harmony be preserved.

44.   If the psalms of a particular canonical hour are to be sung, they should be sung at least partly according to the Gregorian tones; this may be done either with alternate psalms, or with alternate verses of the same psalm.

VESPERS WHEN POSSIBLE

45.   Where the ancient, and venerable custom of singing Vespers according to the rubrics together with the people on Sundays, and feast days is still practiced, it should be continued; where this is not done, it should be reintroduced, as far as possible, at least several times a year.

The local Ordinary should take care that the celebration of evening Masses does not interfere with the practice of singing Vespers on Sundays, and feast days. For evening Masses, which the local Ordinary may permit "for the spiritual good of a sizable number of the faithful,"[24] must not be at the expense of

---

24. Apostolic Constitution *Christus Dominus*, Jan. 6, 1953: AAS 45 [1953] 15–24; Instruction of the Supreme Congregation of the Holy Office, same day: AAS 45 [1953] 47–51; *Motu Proprio Sacram Communionem*, March 19, 1957: AAS 49 [1957] 177–178.

other liturgical services, and private devotions by which the people ordinarily sanctify the holy days.

Hence, the custom of singing Vespers or of holding private devotions with Benediction should be retained wherever such is done, even though evening Mass is celebrated.

46. In clerical seminaries, however, both diocesan and religious, at least part of the Divine Office should frequently be said in common; so far as possible it should be sung. On Sundays and feast days, Vespers at least must be sung.[25]

BENEDICTION

47. Benediction of the Blessed Sacrament is a true liturgical ceremony; hence it must be conducted in accordance with the "Roman Ritual," ti. X, ch V, no. 5.

Wherever an immemorial custom exists of imparting the Eucharistic Benediction in another way, the Ordinary may give his permission for the custom to continue; but it is recommended that the Roman custom of giving Benediction be prudently given preference.

CHAPTER III-2. KINDS OF SACRED MUSIC

A. SACRED POLYPHONY

48. Compositions of sacred polyphony, by the old masters as well as by contemporary artists, are not to be introduced into the liturgy unless it has first been established that, either in their original form or in arrangements, they comply fully with the ideals, and admonitions set forth in the encyclical *Musicæ sacræ disciplina*.[26] If there is any doubt, the diocesan commission on sacred music is to be consulted.

49. Ancient manuscripts of this music still lying about in archives should be uncovered, and if necessary, steps taken for their preservation. Musicologists should make critical editions of them as well as editions suitable for liturgical use.

B. MODERN SACRED MUSIC

50. Modern compositions of sacred music are only to be used during liturgical ceremonies if they conform to the spirit of the liturgy, and to the ideals of sacred music as laid down in the encyclical *Musicæ sacræ disciplina*.[27] Judgments in this matter are to be made by the diocesan commission of sacred music.

---

25. Cf. canon 1367, 3.
26. AAS 48 [1956] 18–20.
27. AAS 48 [1956] 19–20.

C. POPULAR RELIGIOUS SONG

51. Hymns ought to be highly encouraged, and fostered, for this form of music does much to imbue the Christian with a deep religious spirit, and to raise the thoughts of the faithful to the truths of our faith.

Hymns have their own part to play in all the festive solemnities of Christian life, whether public or of a more personal nature; they also find their part in the daily labors of the Christian. But they attain their ideal usefulness in all private devotions, whether conducted outside or inside the church. At times their use is even permitted during liturgical functions, in accord with the directions given above in paragraphs 13–15.

52. If hymns are to attain their purpose, their texts "must conform to the doctrine of the Catholic Church, plainly stating, and explaining it. The vocabulary should be simple, and free of dramatic, and meaningless verbiage. Their tunes, however brief, and easy, should evince a religious dignity and propriety."[28] Local Ordinaries should carefully see that these ideals are observed.

53. All who have the training should be encouraged to compile serviceable collections of these hymns which have been handed down either orally or in writing, even the most ancient, and to publish them for the use of the faithful, with the approval of the local Ordinary.

D. RELIGIOUS MUSIC

54. The type of music which inspires its hearers with religious sentiments, and even devotion, and yet, because of its special character cannot be used in liturgical functions, is nevertheless worthy of high esteem, and ought to be cultivated in its proper time. This music justly merits, therefore, the title "religious music".

55. The proper places for the performance of such music are concert halls, theaters, or auditoriums, but not the church, which is consecrated to the worship of God.

However, if none of these places are available, and the local Ordinary judges that a concert of religious music might be advantageous for the spiritual welfare of the faithful, he may permit a concert of this kind to be held in a church, provided the following provisions are observed:

a) The local Ordinary must give his permission for each concert in writing.

b) Requests for such permissions must also be in writing, stating the date of the concert, the compositions to be performed, the names of the directors (organist, and choral director), and the performers.

c) The local Ordinary is not to give this permission without first consulting the diocesan commission of sacred music, and perhaps other authorities

---

28. *Musicæ sacræ disciplina* (AAS 48 [1956] 20.

upon whose judgment he may rely, and then only if he knows that the music is not only outstanding for its true artistic value, but also for its sincere Christian spirit; he must also be assured that the performers possess the qualities to be mentioned below in paragraphs 97, and 98.

d) Before the concert, the Blessed Sacrament should be removed from the church, and reserved in one of the chapels, or even in the sacristy, is a respectful way. If this cannot be done, the audience should be told that the Blessed Sacrament is present in the church, and the pastor should see to it that there is no danger of irreverence.

e) The main body of the church is not to be used for selling admission tickets or distributing programs of the concert.

f) The musicians, singers, and audience should conduct themselves, and dress in a manner befitting the seriousness, and holiness of the sacred edifice in which they are present.

g) If circumstances permit, the concert should be concluded by some private devotion, or better still, with benediction of the Blessed Sacrament. In this way the devotion, and edification of the faithful, which was the purpose of the concert, will be crowned by a religious service.

CHAPTER III-3. BOOKS OF LITURGICAL CHANT

56.   The standard editions of the liturgical chant of the Roman Church are:

* Roman Gradual, with the Ordinary of the Mass;

* Roman Antiphonal, for the Day Hours;

* Offices of the Dead, Holy Week, and Christmas.

57.   All publication rights to the Gregorian melodies as they appear in the liturgical books approved by the Roman Church are the property of the Holy See.

58.   The following decrees of the Sacred Congregation of Rites remain in force: Instruction on the Publication, and Approval of Books Containing the Gregorian Liturgical Chant, Aug. 11, 1905;[29] Declaration Concerning the Publication and Approval of Books Containing the Gregorian Liturgical Chant, Feb. 14, 1906;[30] and the decree which treats of particular questions regarding the approval of books containing the chant for the "Propers" of certain dioceses, and religious congregations, issued Feb. 24, 1911.[31]

The rules established by the Sacred Congregation of Rites on Authorization to Publish Liturgical Books, Aug. 10, 1946,[32] also apply to books of liturgical chant.

---

29. Decr. Auth. SRC 4166.
30. Decr. Auth. SRC 4178.
31. Decr. Auth. SRC 4260.
32. AAS 38 [1946] 371–372.

59.   Thus, the authentic Gregorian chant is that which is published in the standard Vatican editions, or which has been approved by the Sacred Congregation of Rites for a particular church or religious community. Publishers who have this authorization are obliged, therefore, to reproduce both the melody, and the text exactly as approved in all details.

The rhythmic signs which have been inserted into some chant editions on private authority are permitted so long as they not alter the melodic line of the grouping of the notes, as they appear in the Vatican editions.

CHAPTER III-4. MUSICAL INSTRUMENTS AND BELLS

A. SOME GENERAL PRINCIPLES

60.   The following principles for the use of musical instruments in the sacred liturgy are to be recalled:

a) Because of the nature, sanctity, and dignity of the sacred liturgy, the playing of any musical instrument should be as perfect as possible. It would be preferable to omit the use of instruments entirely (whether it be the organ only, or any other instrument), than to play them in a manner unbecoming their purpose. As a general rule it is better to do something well, however modest, than to attempt something more elaborate without the proper means.

b) The difference between sacred, and secular music must be taken into consideration. Some musical instruments, such as the classic organ, are naturally appropriate for sacred music; others, such as string instruments which are played with a bow, are easily adapted to liturgical use. But there are some instruments which, by common estimation, are so associated with secular music that they are not at all adaptable for sacred use.

c) Finally, only instruments which are personally played by a performer are to be used in the sacred liturgy, not those which are played mechanically or automatically.

B. THE CLASSIC ORGAN AND SIMILAR INSTRUMENTS

61.   The principal musical instrument for solemn liturgical ceremonies of the Latin Church has been and remains the classic pipe organ.

62.   An organ destined for liturgical use, even if small, should be designed according to the norms of organ building, and be equipped with the type of pipes suitable for sacred use. Before it is to be used it should be properly blessed, and as a sacred object, receive proper care.

63.   Besides the classic organ, the harmonium or reed organ may also be used provided that its tonal quality, and volume are suitable for sacred use.

64.   As a substitute, the electronic organ may be tolerated temporarily for liturgical functions, if the means for obtaining even a small pipe organ are not available. In each case, however, the explicit permission of the local Ordinary is required. He, on his part, should consult the diocesan commission on sacred music, and others trained in this field, who can make suggestions for rendering such an instrument more suitable for sacred use.

65.   The musicians who play the instruments mentioned in paragraphs 61-64 should be sufficiently skilled in their art so that they can accompany the sacred chant or any other music, and can also play alone with appropriate skill. Indeed, since it is also often necessary to be able to improvise music suited to the various phases of the liturgical action, they should possess sufficient knowledge of, and capability in the techniques of organ playing , and of sacred music.

Organists should religiously care for the instruments entrusted to them. Whenever they are seated at the organ during sacred functions, organists should be conscious of the active part they are taking in glorifying God, and edifying the faithful.

66.   The organ playing, whether during liturgical functions or private devotions, should be carefully adapted to the liturgical season and feast day, to the nature of the rites and exercises themselves, and to their various parts.

67.   The organ should be located in a suitable place near the main altar, unless ancient custom or a special reason approved by the local Ordinary demand otherwise; but the location should be such that the singers or musicians occupying a raised platform are not conspicuous to the congregation in the main body of the church.

C. SACRED INSTRUMENTAL MUSIC

68.   Other instruments besides the organ, especially the smaller bowed instruments, may be used during the liturgical functions, particularly on days of greater solemnity. These may be used together with the organ or without it, for instrumental numbers or for accompanying the singing. However, the following rules derived from the principles stated above (no. 60) are to strictly observed:

a) the instruments are truly suitable for sacred use;

b) they are to be played with such seriousness, and religious devotion that every suggestion of raucous secular music is avoided, and the devotion of the faithful is fostered;

c) the director, organist, and other instrumentalists should be well trained in instrumental techniques, and the laws of sacred music.

69.   The local Ordinary, with the aid of his diocesan commission on sacred music, should see to it that these rules on the use of instruments during the sacred liturgy are faithfully observed. If need be, they should not hesitate to

issue special instructions in this regard as required by local conditions, and approved customs.

D. MUSICAL INSTRUMENTS, AND MECHANICAL DEVICES

70. Musical instruments which by common acception, and use are suitable only for secular music must be entirely excluded from all liturgical functions, and private devotions.

71. The use of automatic instruments and machines, such as the automatic organ, phonograph, radio, tape or wire recorders, and other similar machines, is absolutely forbidden in liturgical functions and private devotions, whether they are held inside or outside the church, even if these machines be used only to transmit sermons or sacred music, or to substitute for the singing of the choir or faithful, or even just to support it.

However, such machines may be used, even inside the church, but not during services of any kind, whether liturgical or private, in order to give the people a chance to listen to the voice of the Supreme Pontiff or the local Ordinary, or the sermons of others. These mechanical devices may be also be used to instruct the faithful in Christian doctrine or in the sacred chant or hymn singing; finally they may be used in processions which take place outside the church, as a means of directing, and supporting the singing of the people.

72. Loudspeakers may be used even during liturgical functions, and private devotions for the purpose of amplifying the living voice of the priest celebrant or the commentator, or others who, according to the rubrics or by order of the pastor, are expected to make their voices heard.

73. The use of any kind of projector, and particularly movie projectors, with or without sound track, is strictly forbidden in church for any reason, even if it be for a pious, religious, or charitable cause.

In constructing or remodeling meeting halls near the church or under it (if there is no other place), care must be taken that there is no direct entrance from the hall into the church, and that the noise from the hall, especially if it is going to be used for entertainments, shall in no way profane the holiness, and silence of the sacred place.

E. THE TRANSMISSION OF SACRED FUNCTIONS OVER RADIO AND TELEVISION

74. For any radio or television broadcast of liturgical functions or private devotions, the local Ordinary must give his express permission; this is required whether they are being held inside or outside the church. Before granting permission, the Ordinary must be sure that:

a) the singing and music fully comply with the laws of the liturgy, and sacred music;

b) in the case of a television broadcast, all those taking part in the ceremonies are so well instructed that the ceremonies may be carried out in full conformity with the rubrics, and with fitting dignity.

Standing permission may be granted by the local Ordinary for broadcasts to originate regularly from a particular church if, upon inquiry, he is certain that all the requirements will faithfully be met.

75. Television cameras should be kept out of the sanctuary as much as possible; they should never be located so close to the altar as to interfere with the sacred rites.

Cameramen and technicians should conduct themselves with the devotion becoming a sacred place and the rites, and not disturb the prayerful spirit of the congregation, especially at those moments which demand the utmost recollection.

76. Photographers in particular should observe these directives, since it is much easier for them to move about with their cameras.

77. Each pastor is to see to it that the prescriptions given in 75 and 76 are faithfully observed in his church. Local Ordinaries, moreover, shall not fail to issue more specific directives as circumstances require.

78. Since the very nature of a radio broadcast requires that the listeners be able to follow the action without interruption, a broadcast Mass will be more effective if the priest pronounces the words a little more loudly than demanded by the "low voice" of the rubrics, and correspondingly pronounces louder still the words to be said in a clear voice according to the rubrics; this is particularly desirable when there is no commentator. Then the listeners will be able to follow the entire Mass with no difficulty.

79. It is well to remind the radio and television audiences before the program that listening to the broadcast does not fulfill their obligation to attend Mass.

F. THE TIMES WHEN THE PLAYING OF MUSICAL INSTRUMENTS IS FORBIDDEN

80. The playing of the organ, and even more, of other instruments, is an embellishment of the sacred liturgy; for that reason they should be accommodated to the varying degrees of joy in different liturgical seasons, and feast days.

81. Accordingly, the playing of the organ, and all other instruments is forbidden for liturgical functions, except Benediction, during the following times:

a) Advent, from first Vespers of the first Sunday of Advent until None of the Vigil of Christmas;

b) Lent and Passiontide, from Matins of Ash Wednesday until the hymn Gloria in excelsis Deo in the Solemn Mass of the Easter Vigil;

c) the September Ember days if the ferial Mass and Office are celebrated;

d) in all Offices and Masses of the Dead.

82.   Only the organ may be used on the Sundays of *Septuagesima, Sexagesima,* and *Quinquagesima,* and on the ferial days following these Sundays.

83.   However, during the seasons, and days just mentioned, the following exceptions to the rule may be made:

a) the organ may be played, and other instruments used on holy days of obligation, and holidays (except Sundays), on the feasts of the principal local patron saint, the titular day, and the dedication anniversary of the local church, the titular or founders day of a religious congregation, and on the occasion of some extraordinary solemnity;

b) the organ only (including the harmonium or reed organ) may be used on the third Sunday of Advent, and the fourth Sunday of Lent, on Thursday of Holy Week during the Mass of Chrism, and during the solemn evening Mass of the Last Supper from the beginning to the end of the hymn *Gloria in excelsis Deo;*

c) the organ only may be used at Mass, and Vespers for the sole purpose of supporting the singing.

Local Ordinaries may determine more precisely the application of these prohibitions, and permissions according to the approved local or regional customs.

84.   Throughout the Sacred *Triduum,* from the midnight before Holy Thursday until the hymn *Gloria in excelsis Deo* of the Solemn Mass of the Easter Vigil, the organ or harmonium shall remain completely silent, excepting the instance mentioned in paragraph 83b.

This prohibition holds even for private devotions during the Sacred *Triduum;* no exceptions or contrary custom are to be tolerated.

85.   Pastors and others in charge must not fail to explain to the people the meaning of this liturgical silence. They should also take care that during these seasons, and particular days the other liturgical restrictions on decorating the altar are likewise observed.

G. BELLS

86.   The ancient and highly approved tradition of ringing bells in the Latin Church should be devotedly carried on by all who have this responsibility.

87.   Church bells may not be used until they have been solemnly consecrated, or at least blessed; thereafter, they should be treated with the care due to sacred objects.

88.   Approved customs, and the various ways of ringing bells, according to the occasion, should be carefully preserved. Local Ordinaries should set down the traditional, and customary practices, or prescribe them if there are none.

89.   Attachments designed to amplify the sound of the bells or to make them easier to ring, may be permitted by the local Ordinary after consultation with experts. If there is doubt the matter should be referred to the Sacred Congregation of Rites.

90.   Besides the various customary, and approved ways of ringing bells mentioned in paragraph 88 some places have an arrangement of smaller bells, hanging in a bell tower, for the purpose of ringing out various melodies. This is commonly called a carillon. It is to be entirely excluded from liturgical use. These small bells may not be consecrated or blessed according to the solemn rite in the Roman Pontifical, but they may receive a simple blessing.

91.   Every effort should be made to furnish all churches, public and semi-public oratories with at least one or two bells, even though they are small. But it is strictly forbidden to substitute any kind of machine or instrument which merely imitates or amplifies the sound of bells mechanically or automatically. Such machines may be used, however, as a carillon in accordance with what has been said above.

92.   The prescriptions of canons 1169, 1185, and 612 of the Code of Canon Law are to be exactly observed.

CHAPTER III-5. PERSONS HAVING PRINCIPAL FUNCTIONS IN SACRED MUSIC AND THE SACRED LITURGY

93.   The priest-celebrant is the presiding officer in all liturgical functions. All others participate in the service in their own proper manner. Thus:

a) Clerics present at a liturgical ceremony in the manner, and form prescribed by the rubrics, who fulfill the role of sacred or minor ministers or sing in the choir or *schola cantorum*, exercise a liturgical ministry which is direct, and proper to them by virtue of their ordination or elevation to the clerical state.

b) The laity also participate actively in the liturgy by virtue of their baptismal character which enables them, in their own way, to offer the divine Victim to God the Father with the priest in the holy sacrifice of the Mass itself.[33]

c) Therefore, laity of the male sex, whether boys, young men, or adults, when appointed by competent ecclesiastical authority to serve at the altar or to perform the sacred music, and when they fulfill this office in the manner, and form prescribed by the rubrics, exercise a liturgical ministry which is direct,

---

33. Cf. Mystici Corporis Christi, June 29, 1943; AAS 35 [1943] 232–233; *Mediator Dei*, Nov. 20, 1947: AAS 39 [1947] 555–556.

though delegated. If they are singers, they must be a part of the choir or *schola cantorum*.

94. In addition to observing the rubrics carefully, the priest celebrant and the sacred ministers should endeavor to execute their sung parts as correctly, distinctly, and artistically as possible.

95. When the ministers can be chosen for a liturgical function, preference should be given to those who have the greater singing ability, especially if it is a more solemn liturgical function or one which has more difficult chants, or is to be broadcast or televised.

THE COMMENTATOR

96. The active participation of the faithful can be more easily brought about with the help of a commentator, especially in holy Mass, and in some of the more complex liturgical ceremonies. At suitable times he should briefly explain the rites themselves, and the prayers of the priest and ministers; he should also direct the external participation of the congregation, that is, their responses, prayers, and singing. Such a commentator may be used if the following rules are observed:

a) The role of commentator should properly be carried out by a priest or at least a cleric. If none is available, a layman of good Christian character, and well instructed in his duties may fill the role. Women, however, may never act as commentator; in case of necessity, a woman would be permitted only to lead the prayers, and singing of the congregation.

b) If the commentator is a priest or a cleric, he should wear a surplice, and stand in the sanctuary or near the Communion rail, or at the lectern or pulpit. If he is a layman, he should stand in a convenient place in front of the congregation, but not in the sanctuary or in the pulpit.

c) The explanations and directions to be given by the commentator should be prepared in writing; they should be brief, clear, and to the point; they should be spoken at a suitable time, and in a moderate tone of voice; they should never interfere with the prayers of the priest who is celebrating. In short, they should be a real help, and not a hindrance to the devotion of the congregation.

d) In directing the prayers of the congregation, the commentator should recall the prescriptions given above in paragraph 14c.

e) In those places where the Holy See has permitted the reading of the Epistle and Gospel in the vernacular after the Latin text has been chanted, the commentator may not substitute for the celebrant, deacon, or subdeacon in reading them.

f) The commentator should follow the celebrant closely, and so accompany the sacred action that it is not delayed or interrupted, and the entire ceremony carried out with harmony, dignity, and devotion.

97.   Those who have a part in the sacred music—composers, organists, choir directors, singers, and instrumentalists—should above all be outstanding Christians, and give example to the rest of the faithful, conformable to their role as direct or indirect participants in the sacred liturgy.

98.   Besides excelling in Christian faith and morals, these persons must also possess the training necessary to fulfill their particular role of participation in the liturgy.

a) Composers of sacred music should have a thorough knowledge of the historical, dogmatic or doctrinal, practical, and rubrical aspects of the liturgy; they should know Latin; and finally they should be well trained in the art, and the history of both sacred, and secular music.

b) Organists, and choir directors should also have a comprehensive knowledge of the liturgy, and a sufficient understanding of Latin; and finally they should be well trained in their art, and able to carry out their role worthily, and competently.

c) Singers, both boys and adults, should be taught the meaning of the liturgical functions, and of the texts they sing insofar as they are capable of comprehending, for then their singing will be inspired by an understanding mind, and a loving heart, and be truly rendered as befits the service of an intelligent person. They should also be taught to pronounce the Latin words correctly, and distinctly. Pastors, and those directly in charge must see to it that good order, and true devotion reign in that part of the church occupied by the singers.

d) Instrumentalists who perform sacred music should not only be well trained in the techniques of their instruments, but should also know how to adapt them to the playing of sacred music. They should be well enough instructed in the sacred liturgy that their devotion will be evidenced by an artistic performance.

THE SCHOLA CANTORUM

99.   It is highly desirable that a choir or *schola cantorum* be established in all cathedral churches, in parish churches, and all other churches of importance where the liturgical functions can be carried out as described in paragraph 93a, and c.

100. Wherever such a choir cannot be organized, a choir of the faithful, either mixed or consisting only of women or girls, can be permitted. But such a choir should take its place outside the sanctuary or Communion rail. The men should be separated from the women or girls so that anything unbecoming may be avoided. Local Ordinaries are to issue precise regulations about these matters, and pastors are to see to their enforcement.[34]

---

34. Decr. Auth. SCR 3964, 4210, 4231, and the encyclical *Musicæ sacræ disciplina*: AAS [1956] 23.

101. It would be ideal, and worthy of commendation if organists, choir directors, singers, instrumentalists, and others engaged in the service of the Church, would contribute their talents for the love of God, and in the spirit of religious devotion, without salary; should they be unable to offer their services free of charge, Christian justice, and charity demand that the church give them a just wage, according to the recognized standards of the locality, and provisions of law.

102. The local Ordinary should, after consultation with the diocesan commission of sacred music, fix a scale of wages to be observed throughout the diocese for the various offices mentioned in the previous paragraph.

103. An adequate program of social security should also be set up for these persons in accordance with civil law; if the law makes no provisions, the local Ordinary himself should make regulations regarding social security.

CHAPTER III-6. DUTY TO CULTIVATE SACRED MUSIC AND SACRED LITURGY

A. TRAINING OF THE CLERGY, AND PEOPLE

104. Sacred music, and the liturgy are intimately bound together; sacred chant forms an integral part of the liturgy (no. 21), while hymns are used to a great extent in private devotions, and at times even during liturgical functions themselves (no. 19). For that reason, instruction in both sacred music, and sacred liturgy cannot be separated from each other: both belong to the life of the Christian, though in varying degree, depending upon one's own of life, and rank among the clergy, and faithful.

Hence, every Christian should have some instruction in the sacred liturgy, and sacred music, in accordance with his station in life.

105. The Christian family is the natural, and in fact, primary school of Christian education. It is in the family circle that the little children are first introduced to the knowledge, and life of a Christian. The aim of this first education should be that the children learn to take part in the private devotions, and even in the liturgical functions, particularly the Mass, as their age, and understanding enable them. Furthermore, they should begin to learn, and love the hymns sung both in the home, and in the church (cf. above, no. 9, 51-53).

106. In private or elementary schools the following directions should be observed:

a) If the schools are conducted by Catholics, and are free to set up their own programs, the school children are to be given additional training in sacred music, and hymns. Above all, they are to be more thoroughly instructed in the holy sacrifice of the mass, adapted to their own age level, and in the manner of participating in it; they should also be taught to sing the simpler Gregorian melodies.

b) If the schools are public, and subject to the laws of the state, the local Ordinaries should see to it that these children, too, are educated in the sacred liturgy, and the sacred chant.

107. This applies to an even greater degree to the intermediate or secondary schools, so that adolescents may acquire the maturity to lead a good social, and Christian life.

108. Universities, and colleges of arts and sciences, too, must strive to deepen and further this musical, and liturgical education. It is important that those who have completed higher studies, and who take upon themselves the responsibilities of public life, have a complete appreciation of all the aspects of Christian life. Thus all priests who have charge of university students should endeavor to imbue in them a deeper understanding of the sacred liturgy, and the sacred chant, both as to its theory, and its practice. If circumstances permit, they should use the forms of Mass participation described in paragraphs 26 and 31.

109. Young men aspiring to the priesthood need an even greater knowledge of the liturgy, and sacred music than do the faithful; wherefore, they should be given complete and sound instruction in both. Hence, everything prescribed by Canon Law in this matter,[35] or specifically ordered by competent authority, must be observed in every detail under serious obligation of conscience.[36]

110. Men and women religious, as well as members of Secular institutes, should be given a thorough and progressive formation in both the sacred liturgy, and the sacred chant, beginning with their probation and novitiate.

Competent instructors should be procured to teach, direct, and accompany the sacred chant in all the houses of these communities, and those dependent upon them. Religious superiors should see to it that the entire community is adequately trained in the chant, and not just select members.

111. Some churches, by their very nature, require that the sacred liturgy, and sacred music be carried out with special dignity, and solemnity. Such churches are the principal parish churches, collegiate and cathedral churches, and important centers of pilgrimages. Those attached to these churches, whether clergy, servers, or musicians, should diligently prepare themselves to perform the sacred chant, and carry out the liturgical functions in a pre-eminent fashion.

112. The foreign missions present special problems in the introduction, and adaptation of the sacred liturgy, and sacred chant.

A distinction must first be made between people who have their own culture, very rich, and in some instances going back for thousands of years, and people who still have not developed a high level of culture.

With this in mind, some general principles may be established:

---

35. Canon 1354, 1 and 3; 1365, 2.
36. Cf. especially the apostolic constitution *Divini cultus,* on the wide promotion of the liturgy, Gregorian chant, and sacred music, of Dec. 20, 1928: AAS 31 [1929] 33–41.

a) Missionary priests must be trained in the sacred liturgy, and sacred chant.

b) If the people to whom the priests are sent already have a highly developed musical culture, the missionaries should cautiously try to adapt this native music to sacred use. In particular, private devotions should be arranged so that the native faithful can use their own traditional language, and musical idiom to express their religious devotion. But the missionaries should remember that even the Gregorian melodies can sometimes easily be sung by native peoples, as experience has shown, because these melodies often bear close resemblances to their own native music.

c) But if the natives are of a less civilized race, then what has been said in paragraph "b" must be adapted to suit the capabilities, and character of these peoples. Where there is a good religious family life and community of spirit, the missionaries should be very careful not to extinguish it, but rather to rid it of superstitions, and imbue it with a true Christian spirit.

B. PUBLIC AND PRIVATE SCHOOLS OF SACRED MUSIC

113. Pastors and those in charge shall see to it that there are servers present, boys, young men, and even adults, for liturgical functions and private devotions. These servers should be noted for their devotion, well instructed in the ceremonies, and adequately trained in sacred music, and hymns.

114. The boy choir, an organization praised over and over by the Holy See,[37] is even more important to the performance of sacred music, and the singing of hymns.

It is desirable, and every effort should be made, that every church have its own boy choir. The boys should be thoroughly instructed in the sacred liturgy, and particularly in the art of singing with devotion.

DIOCESAN INSTITUTES

115. Moreover, it is recommended that every diocese have a school or institute of chant and organ where organists, choir directors, singers and instrumentalists can be properly trained.

In some cases a number of dioceses will prefer to collaborate in organizing such a school. Pastors and others in charge should be alert in detecting, and sending talented young men to these schools, and encourage them in their studies.

116. The great importance of academies and schools of higher learning which are established specifically for more comprehensive studies in sacred music must be recognized. The Pontifical Institute of Sacred Music in Rome, established by Saint Pius X, holds first place among these.

---

37. Apostolic constitution *Divini cultus:* AAS 21 [1929] 28; *Musicæ sacræ disciplina*: AAS 48 [1956] 23.

Local Ordinaries should send priests with special talent and a love for this art to such schools, particularly to the Pontifical Institute of Sacred Music in Rome.

117.   In addition to the schools established to teach sacred music, many societies, named after Saint Gregory or Saint Cecilia or other saints, have been founded to promote sacred music in various ways. The increase of such societies and their associations on a national or even international scale can do much to further the cause of sacred music.

118.   Since the time of Pius X, every diocese has been required to have a special commission of sacred music.[38] The members of this commission, both priests and laymen, specially selected for their knowledge, experience, and talent in the various kinds of sacred music, are to be appointed by the local Ordinary.

The Ordinaries of a number of dioceses may, if they wish, establish a joint commission.

Since sacred music is so closely bound with the liturgy and with sacred art, commissions of sacred art, and of the liturgy,[39] are also to be established in every diocese. These three commissions may meet together—at times it is even advisable—to work out their common problems by a mutual exchange of opinions and solutions.

Local Ordinaries should see to it that these commissions meet frequently, or as often as circumstances require. Moreover, the local Ordinary himself should occasionally preside at these meetings.

This instruction on sacred music, and the sacred liturgy was submitted to His Holiness Pope Pius XII by the undersigned Cardinal Prefect of the Sacred Congregation of Rites. His Holiness deigned to give his special approval and authority to all its prescriptions. He also commanded that it be promulgated, and be conscientiously observed by all to whom it applies.

Anything contrary to what is herein contained is no longer in force.

Issued at Rome, from the office of the Sacred Congregation of Rites, on the feast of Saint Pius X, Sept. 3, 1958.

C. CARD. CICOGNANI, PREFECT

+ A. CARINCI, ARCHBP. OF SELEUCIA, SECRETARY

---

38. Motu proprio *Inter sollicitudines*, Nov. 22, 1903: AAS 36 [1903–1904] no. 24; Decr. Auth. SRC 4121.

39. Circular letter of the Secretariate of State, Sep. 1, 1924, Prot. 34215; *Mediator Dei*, Nov. 20, 1947: AAS 39 [1947] 561–562.

ADDRESS OF POPE PIUS XII
TO THE
INTERNATIONAL CONGRESS
ON PASTORAL LITURGY

SEPTEMBER 22, 1956

AN OVERVIEW OF THE ADDRESS OF POPE PIUS XII TO THE INTERNATIONAL CONGRESS ON PASTORAL LITURGY

Rev. Msgr. Joseph DeGrocco

This address or allocution[1] of Pope Pius XII was given at the closing of the International Congress on Pastoral Liturgy held in Assisi from September 18–22, 1956. That Congress was held as a tribute to Pope Pius XII, in honor of the eight-ieth year of his life.[2] It was fitting to honor the pope in that way since he was held in such high regard by those who were involved in the Liturgical Movement. Not only did Pius XII undertake liturgical reforms as a part of his pontificate, but he is credited with providing leadership in making the Liturgical Movement "a *pastoral*-liturgical apostolate that is the pulse-beat of the Church's work for the salvation of souls."[3]

The concern for the general pastoral nature of, and the specific pastoral applications of the work being done by the Liturgical Movement is evidenced in the titles of the addresses presented at this Congress: "The Pastoral Idea in the History of the Liturgy" by Rev. Josef A. Jungmann, SJ; "The Pastoral Theology of the Encyclicals *Mystici Corporis* and *Mediator Dei*" by Rt. Rev. Bernard Capelle, OSB; "The Pastoral Value of the Word of God in the Sacred Liturgy," by Rev. Augustine Bea, SJ; and "Liturgical Renewal and the Renewal of Preaching" by Rev. A.M. Roguet, OP.[4]

The allocution gives the pope's approbation and approval to the ongoing work of the reform of the liturgy, while at the same time offering some cautions concerning excesses and abuses. This is typical of what we find in the writings of Pius XII regarding the liturgical reform—at the same time as he gives his approval, he calls for balance and restraint, as exemplified in his words at the very end of this address: "We sincerely desire the progress of the liturgical move-ment, and wish to help it, but it is also Our duty to forestall whatever might be a source of error or danger."

The allocution is structured under two main headings, "The Liturgy and the Church" and "The Liturgy and the Lord," and it is in the section "The Liturgy and the Church" that we see a discussion of the relationship between liturgy and ecclesiology, a discussion containing items similar to those the pope con-sidered in *Mediator Dei*. As we read these ideas written by Pius XII, we can look back on them from the perspective of the intervening years since 1956, and, by taking into consideration subsequent developments in liturgical theology and

---

1. An allocution is an address given by the pope that is pastoral, not doctrinal, in nature. It may be thought of as a kind of a non-homiletic exhortation.

2. *The Assisi Papers: Proceedings of the First International Congress of Pastoral Liturgy, Assisi-Rome, September 18-22, 1956,* (Collegeville, MN: The Liturgical Press, 1957, p. vi.

3. Ibid.

4. *Op.cit.*, xvii.

what was actually put forth in *Sacrosanctum Concilium*, we can see, as is typical of the pope's writings on the reform of the liturgy, a certain "back-and-forth" type of tension of ideas—we can find notions that are forward-moving and that will come to fruition at the Second Vatican Council, and, at the same time, we can see how those notions are not brought to their full conclusion, as his liturgical theology is still somewhat bound by his ecclesiology. Pius XII's ecclesiology would still have been a universalist ecclesiology where the Church is seen as acting only through its chief members, that is, only the ordained participate directly in the mission of the Church, and therefore in the liturgical action.

Thus, we can see behind it all a wrestling with the question of the relationship between the ordained, ministerial priesthood and the common priesthood of the baptized *vis-à-vis* the laity's participation in the liturgical act. The reform movement was putting forth the notion that all (ordained and lay) offered the sacrifice, and to a degree Pius XII is able to embrace this idea; for example, in this allocution he quotes article 5 of his encyclical, *Mediator Dei*, which states, "The Sacred Liturgy is the whole public worship of the Mystical Body of Jesus Christ, Head and members."[5] He also notes in the address how all the faithful "bring all that they have received from God, all the powers of their minds and hearts and of all their achievements." He further points out how "The contributions which are brought to the liturgy by the Hierarchy and by the faithful are not to be reckoned as two separate quantities, but represent the work of members of the same organism, which acts as a single living entity . . . [T]he liturgy is the work of the *Church whole and entire.*"

At the same time, however, he also clearly maintains that direct participation in the liturgical act is reserved to the priest alone. He reiterates what he wrote in his allocution of November 2, 1954, in article 12: "Thus the priest celebrant, putting on the person of Christ, alone offers sacrifice, and not the people, nor the clerics, nor even the priests who reverently assist. All, however, can and should take an active part in the sacrifice."[6] This is because he continues to isolate the essence of participation in the Eucharistic sacrifice solely as the power to consecrate. Yet, one of the theological fruits of the liturgical reform movement was the reintegration of the theological focal points of real presence, sacrifice, and communion in the theology of the Eucharist, to broaden the understanding of the liturgical act as something wider than simply the consecration.

To be sure, Pius XII wishes the faithful to fully, consciously, and actively participate in the action, but the question remains concerning the actual nature of that participation. For him, only the hierarchy has a "direct access" to the liturgical action (because it is centered in consecration alone), while the faithful do not. He is not at the point of saying, as *Sacrosanctum Concilium* will later say, that the faithful participate in the liturgical action by virtue of their Baptism[7] and that such participation is a direct participation "not only through the hands of the priest, but also with him."[8] Thus, for him, participation on the

---

5. *Mediator Dei*, 5; quoted in *Address of Pope Pius XII to the International Congress on Pastoral Liturgy*.

6. *Acta Ap. Sedis*, 1, c., p. 668; quoted in *Address of Pope Pius XII to the International Congress on Pastoral Liturgy*.

7. See *Sacrosanctum Concilium* (SC), 14.

8. Ibid., 48.

part of the faithful can still be a matter of "following their performance [that is, passively following the performance of the rites by the clergy] with fervor."[9]

Nonetheless, there is much in this allocution that lays the groundwork for the further development of the theology of liturgical participation. Pius XII points to the necessary connection between liturgy and life when he states that the faithful must receive the "truth and grace of Christ by means of the liturgy" and "transform them into values for life." We might see in that statement a connection with *Sacrosanctum Concilium's* statements that the liturgy is the source for the Christian life[10] and the "primary and indispensable source from which the faithful are to derive the true Christian spirit."[11] Furthermore, the pope's point that "public worship is not . . . the *whole Church*" and that worship does not "exhaust the field of her activities" sounds like a direct forerunner to *Sacrosanctum Concilium* 9, which points out that "The liturgy does not exhaust the entire activity of the Church." The fact that a life of faith and conversion, a daily dying and rising with the Lord, must be brought to the liturgy by the faithful is highlighted by both the pope's allocution and *Sacrosanctum Concilium*.

There are other points in this allocution that will be developed in subsequent years by liturgical theology, such as the nature of the real presence, the relationship between sacrifice and adoration, the placement of the tabernacle, and devotion to the Eucharist outside Mass. In these areas we have the presentation of ideas with which the liturgical reform movement, concerned with the more ecclesial and more dynamic aspects of the liturgy, as opposed to a more individualistic and pietistic approach, would have resonated well; for example, the pope pronounces in the allocution that "The altar is more important than the tabernacle, because on it is offered the Lord's sacrifice," and "One has a perfect right to distinguish between the offering or the sacrifice of the Mass and the *'cultus latreuticus'* offered to the God-Man hidden in the Eucharist." To be sure, some of the questions addressed in this allocution are still under discussion in our own time, such as the precise meaning of concelebration and the proper understanding of popular devotions to the Eucharist. One would have to consider such lack of finality regarding answers to these questions as something good and healthy, again pointing to the significance of the contributions made by Pius XII to the conversations of his day, conversations still relevant in our own.

This allocution, then, seeks to give further impetus to the liturgical movement by affirming its progress and steering it along a *via media*, which both respects the past and continues to move forward into the future. The pope reminds the liturgical reformers to "avoid two exaggerated viewpoints concerning the past: blind attachment and utter contempt." Interestingly, right after that, the next point he makes that "the liturgy contains immutable elements, a sacred content that transcends time; but changeable, transitory, occasionally even defective, elements are to be found there," a line which we see repeated almost *verbatim* in *Sacrosanctum Concilium* 21. This is another clear indication

---

9. Quote from *Address of Pope Pius XII to the International Congress on Pastoral Liturgy*; bracketed text added by author for further explanation. In *Mediator Dei*, 108, the pope allows that participation in Mass could include meditation on the mysteries of Christ or other pious prayers and exercises different from those of the Mass.

10. See SC, 10.

11. Ibid., 14.

of the pope's openness to the continuation of the work of the reform. He goes on to note how " . . . today's liturgy involves a concern for progress, but also for conservation and defense. It returns to the past, but does not slavishly imitate." Papal approval is further given as Pius XII deems the work being done in liturgical circles as "quite balanced," as, in his estimation, the scholars and others working in the reform "seek and study seriously, hold on to what is really worthwhile without, however, falling into excess." Those words give us a concise summary of this document's place as yet another element in the tapestry of events that continued to propel the liturgical reform movement forward and imbue it with life and momentum. As such, this allocution gives us an insight into the excitement that must have permeated the times, as dialogue, exchange and interaction were taking place between the Holy Father and those scholars and reformers who were on the "front lines" of research and participation in liturgical congresses.

ON THE LITURGICAL MOVEMENT

ADDRESS OF POPE PIUS XII TO THE INTERNATIONAL CONGRESS ON PASTORAL LITURGY

SEPTEMBER 22, 1956

You have asked Us to deliver an address upon the closing of the International Congress on Pastoral Liturgy which has just been held in Assisi. We readily accede to your request and bid you welcome.

If the position of the liturgical movement today is compared to that of thirty years ago, undeniable progress in its extent and in its depth becomes evident. Interest in the liturgy, practical accomplishments, and the active participation of the faithful have undergone a development which would then have been difficult to anticipate.

The chief driving force, both in doctrinal matters and in practical applications, came from the Hierarchy and, in particular, from Our saintly Predecessor, Pius X, who gave the liturgical movement a decisive impulse by his *Motu Proprio* of October 23, 1913, *"Abhinc duos annos."*[1]

The faithful received these directives gratefully and showed themselves ready to comply with them. Liturgists applied themselves to their task with zeal and, as a result, many interesting and rewarding projects were soon under way, although, at times, certain deviations had to be corrected by the Church's authority.

Of the many documents published on this subject in recent times, it will suffice for Us to mention three: The Encyclical *"Mediator Dei," "On the Liturgy,"* of November 20, 1947;[2] the new decree on Holy Week, dated November 16, 1955,[3] which has helped the faithful to achieve a better understanding and fuller participation in the love, sufferings and triumph of our Savior; and finally, the Encyclical *"De musica sacra"* of December 25, 1955.[4]

Thus the liturgical movement has appeared as a sign of God's providential dispositions for the present day, as a movement of the Holy Spirit in His Church, intended to bring men closer to those mysteries of the faith and treasures of grace which derive from the active participation of the faithful in liturgical life.

---

1. *Acta Ap. Sedis*, a. 5, 1913.
2. *Acta Ap. Sedis*, a. 39, 1947.
3. *Acta Ap. Sedis*, a. 47, 1955.
4. *Acta Ap. Sedis*, a. 48, 1956.

The Congress which is just concluding has had for its particular end a demonstration of the inestimable value of the liturgy in the sanctification of souls, and, consequently, in the Church's pastoral activity.

You have studied this aspect of the liturgy as it is revealed in history and has continued to be revealed. You have also seen how this aspect of the liturgy is founded in the nature of things, that is, how it is derived from essential elements of the liturgy.

Your Congress, then, included a study of historical developments, some reflections on existing conditions, and an examination both of objectives to be sought in the future and of means suitable for their attainment. After careful consideration of your program, We express Our hope that this new sowing of seed, added to those of the past, will produce rich harvests for the benefit of individuals and the whole Church.

In this address, instead of presenting to you in greater detail norms which the Holy See has already spoken sufficiently, We have decided it would be more useful to touch on a few important points which are actually under discussion in the field of liturgy and dogma, and which hold Our special interest. We shall group these considerations under two headings. These will be simple pointers rather than the express themes We propose to develop: The Liturgy and the Church, the Liturgy and the Lord.

I. THE LITURGY AND THE CHURCH

As we have said in the Encyclical *"Mediator Dei,"* the liturgy is a vital function of the whole Church, and not simply of a group or of a limited movement. "The Sacred Liturgy is the whole public worship of the Mystical Body of Jesus Christ, Head and members."[5]

The Mystical Body of our Lord lives on the truth of Christ and on the graces which flow through its members, giving them life and uniting them to one another and their Head. This is what St. Paul means when he says in the first Epistle to the Corinthians: *"All are yours, and you are Christ's, and Christ is God's."*[6] All then is directed toward God, His service, and His glory.

The Church, filled with the gifts and the life of God, devotes herself with a deep and spontaneous movement to the adoration and praise of the infinite God. Through the liturgy she renders to Him, as a corporate body, that worship which is His due.

To this unique liturgy, all the members, those clothed with episcopal power and those belonging to the body of the faithful, bring all that they have received from God, all the powers of their minds and hearts and all of their achievements. This is true, above all, of the Hierarchy, since it holds the *"depositum fidei"* and the *"depositum gratiae."*

---

5. *Acta Ap. Sedis*, a. 39, 1947.
6. I *Cor.* 3, 23.

From the *"depositum fidei,"* from the truth of Christ contained in Scripture and Tradition, the Hierarchy draws the great mysteries of the faith, in particular, those of the Trinity, the Incarnation, and the Redemption, and causes them to pass into the liturgy. But it would be difficult to find a truth the Christian faith which is not expressed in some manner in the liturgy, whether in readings from the Old and the New Testament during Holy Mass and the Divine Office, or in the riches which the mind and heart discover in the Psalms.

Moreover, the solemn ceremonies of the liturgy are a profession of faith in action. They give concrete expression to the great truths of the faith which concern the inscrutable designs of God's generosity and His inexhaustible benefits to men, the love and mercy of the heavenly Father for the world, the salvation for which He sent His Son and delivered Him to death.

It is thus that the Church communicates in abundance in the liturgy the treasures of the *"depositum fidei,"* of the truth of Christ.

Through the liturgy also are diffused the riches of the *"depositum gratiae"* which the Savior has transmitted to His Apostles: sanctifying grace, the virtues and gifts, the power to baptize, to confer the Holy Spirit, to forgive sins through the sacrament of Penance, and to ordain priests.

At the heart of the liturgy is the celebration of the Eucharist, the sacrifice and the repast. In the liturgy also are all the sacraments gathered up, and the Church, by means of the sacramentals, generously multiplies gifts of grace in the most varied circumstances.

The Hierarchy also extends its care to all that helps increase the beauty and dignity of liturgical ceremonies: the places of worship, their furnishing, the liturgical vestments, sacred music, and sacred art.

If the Hierarchy communicates the truth and the grace of Christ by means of the liturgy, the faithful on their side, have a duty to receive them, to give them their whole-hearted consent, to transform them into values for life. They accept all that is offered to them—the graces of the sacrifice of the altar, of the sacraments and sacramentals—not as mere passive recipients of the graces flowing over them, but cooperating in these graces with all their will and strength, and, above all, participating in the liturgical offices, or at least following their performance with fervor.

The laity have contributed in large measure, and by a constant effort to continue to contribute, to increase the external solemnity of worship, to build churches and chapels, to adorn them, to enhance the beauty of the liturgical ceremonies with all the splendors of sacred art.

The contributions which are brought to the liturgy by the Hierarchy and by the faithful are not to be reckoned as two separate quantities, but represent the work of members of the same organism, which acts as a single living entity. The shepherds and the flock, the teaching Church and the Church taught, form a single and unique body of Christ. So there is no reason for entertaining suspicion, rivalries, open or hidden opposition, either in one's thought or in one's manner of speaking and acting. Among members of the same body there ought to reign, before all else, harmony, union and cooperation. It is within this unity that the Church prays, makes it offering, grows in holiness. One can declare therefore with justice that the liturgy is the work of the *Church whole and entire.*

But We have to add: public worship is not on that account the *whole Church.* It does not exhaust the field of her activities.

Alongside public worship, which is that of the community, there is still place for private worship, which the individual pays to God in the secret of his heart or expresses by exterior acts. This private worship has as many variations as there are Christians, though it proceeds from the same faith and the same grace of Christ. The Church not only tolerates this kind of worship, but gives it full recognition and approval, without however raising it in any way to the primary position of liturgical worship.

But when We say that public worship does not exhaust the field of the Church's activities, We are thinking in particular of the tasks of teaching and of pastoral care, of the *"Tend the flock of God, which is among you."*[7]

We have recalled the role which the Magisterium, the depository of the truth of Christ, exercises through the liturgy. The influence of the governing power upon it is also evident. For it belongs to the Popes to give recognition to rites which are in force, to introduce any new practices, to establish rules for the manner of worship. It pertains to the Bishops to watch carefully that the prescriptions of canon law with regard to divine worship are observed.[8]

But the functions of teaching and control extend even beyond that. To ascertain this it is sufficient to glance at canon law and its statements concerning the Pope, the Roman Congregations, the Bishops, Councils, the Magisterium, and ecclesiastical discipline. The same conclusion may be reached by observing the life of the Church, and in Our two Allocutions of May 31 and November 2, 1954, on the threefold function of the Bishop, We expressly insisted on the extent of his obligations. They are not limited to teaching and government, but embrace also all other human activities in the measure in which religious and moral interests are involved.[9]

If then the duties and the interests of the Church on this point are universal, the priests and the faithful will be cautious in their manner of thinking and acting, lest they fall into narrowness of view or lack of understanding.

Our Encyclical *"Mediator Dei,"* has already corrected certain erroneous statements which were tending either to orientate religious and pastoral teaching into a form exclusively liturgical, or to raise obstacles to the liturgical movement because it was not understood.

In reality, there exists no objective difference between the end pursued by the liturgy and that of the other functions of the Church. As for differences of opinion, though they are genuine, they do not present insuperable obstacles.

---

7. *1 Peter.* 5, 2.
8. *Acta Ap. Sedis*, a. 39, 1947.
9. *Acta Ap. Sedis*, a. 46, 1954.

These considerations will suffice to show, We hope, that the liturgy is the work of the whole Church, and that all of the faithful, as members of the Mystical Body, ought to love and value it, and take part in it, while understanding that the tasks of the Church extend well beyond it.

II. THE LITURGY AND THE LORD

We wish to consider now in a special manner the liturgy of the Mass and the Lord Who in it is both Priest and Oblation. As some inaccuracies and some misunderstandings are coming to light here and there with regard to certain points, We shall say a word about the *"actio Christi,"* and about the *"praesentia Christi,"* and about the *"infinita et divina maiestas Christi."*

1. "ACTIO CHRISTI"

The liturgy of the Mass has for its end the expression through the senses of the grandeur of the mystery which is accomplished in it, and efforts are being made today which tend to make the faithful participate in as active and intelligent a manner as possible. Though this aim is justified, there is risk of lessening reverence if attention is distracted from the main action to direct it to the splendor of other ceremonies.

What is this main action of the Eucharistic sacrifice?

We have spoken explicitly of it in the Allocution of November 2, 1954.[10] We there cited first the teaching of the Council of Trent: *"In this divine sacrifice which takes place at Mass, the same Christ is present and is immolated in an unbloody manner, Who once on the altar of the Cross offered Himself in a bloody manner . . . For the victim is one and the same, now offering Himself through the ministry of priests, Who then offered Himself on the Cross; only the manner of offering is different."*[11]

And We continued in these words: *"Thus the priest-celebrant, putting on the person of Christ, alone offers sacrifice, and not the people, nor the clerics, nor even the priests who reverently assist. All, however, can and should take an active part in the sacrifice."*[12]

We then emphasized that, from a failure to distinguish between the participation of the celebrant in the fruits of the sacrifice of the Mass and the nature of the action which he performs, the conclusion was reached that *"the offering of one Mass, at which a hundred priests assist with religious devotion, is the same as a hundred Masses celebrated by a hundred priests."* Concerning this statement We said: *"It must be rejected as an erroneous opinion."*

And We added by way of explanation: *"With regard to the offering of the Eucharistic Sacrifice, the actions of Christ, the High Priest, are as many as are*

---

10. *Acta Ap. Sedis*, a. 46, 1954.

11. *Conc. Trid.*, Sess. XXII, cap. 2.

12. *Acta Ap. Sedis*, 1, c.

the priests celebrating, not as many as are the priests reverently hearing the Mass of a Bishop or a priest; for those present at the Mass in no sense sustain, or act in, the person of Christ sacrificing, but are to be compared to the faithful layfolk who are present at the Mass."[13]

On the subject of liturgical congresses, We remarked on the same occasion: "*These meetings sometimes follow a definite program, so that only one offers the Mass, and others (all or the majority) assist at this one Mass, and receive the Holy Eucharist during it from the hands of the celebrant. If this be done for a good and sound reason, . . . the practice is not to be opposed, so long as the error We have mentioned is not underlying it,*" that is to say, the error of equating the offering of a hundred Masses by a hundred priests to the offering of one Mass at which a hundred priests are devoutly present.

According to this, the central element of the Eucharistic Sacrifice is that in which Christ intervenes as "*se ipsum offerens*"—to adopt the words of the Council of Trent (Sess. XXII, cap. 2). That happens at the consecration when, in the very act of transubstantiation worked by the Lord,[14] the priest celebrant is "*personam Christi gerens.*"

Even if the consecration takes place without pomp and in all simplicity, it is the central point of the whole liturgy of the sacrifice, the central point of the "*actio Christi cuius personam gerit sacerdos celebrans,*" or "*sacerdotes concelebrantes*" in the case of a true concelebration.

Some recent events give Us the occasion to speak with precision on certain points regarding the matter. When the consecration of the bread and wine is validly brought about, the whole action of Christ is actually accomplished. Even if all that remains could not be completed, still, nothing essential is wanting to the Lord's oblation.

After the consecration is performed, the "*oblatio hostiae super altare positae*" can be accomplished by the priest celebrant, by the Church, by the other priests, by each of the faithful. But this action is not "*actio ipsius Christi per sacerdotem ipsius personam sustinentem et gerentem.*" In reality the action of the consecrating priest is the very action of Christ Who acts through His minister. In the case of a concelebration in the proper sense of the word, Christ, instead of acting through one minister, acts through several. On the other hand, in a merely ceremonial consecration, which could also be the act of a lay person, there is no question of simultaneous consecration, and this fact raises the important point: "What intention and what exterior action are required to have a true concelebration and simultaneous consecration?"

On this subject let Us recall what We said in our Apostolic Constitution "*Episcopalis Consecrationis*" of November 30, 1944.[15] We there laid down that in an episcopal consecration the two Bishops who accompany the consecrator must have the intention of consecrating the Bishop-Elect, and that, consequently,

---

13. *Acta Ap. Sedis*, 1. c.
14. Cf. *Conc. Trid.*, Sess. XIII, ch. 4 and 3.
15. *Acta Ap. Sedis*, a. 37, 1945.

they must perform the exterior actions and pronounce the words by which the power and the grace to transmit are signified and transmitted. It is, then, not sufficient for them to unite their wills with that of the chief consecrator, and to declare that they make his words and actions their own. They must themselves perform the actions and pronounce the essential words.

The same thing likewise happens in concelebration in the true sense. It is not sufficient to have and to indicate the will to make one's own the words and actions of the celebrant. The concelebrants must themselves say over the bread and the wine, "This is my Body," "This is my Blood." Otherwise, their concelebration is purely ceremonial.

And so it may not be affirmed that, "in the last analysis the only decisive question is to know in what measure personal participation, supported by the grace which one receives in the offering of worship, increases the participation in the cross and in the grace of Christ, Who unites us to Himself and with each other." This inaccurate manner of putting the question We have already rejected in the Allocution of November 2, 1954; but certain theologians still cannot reconcile themselves to it. We therefore repeat it: the decisive question (for concelebration as for the Mass of a single priest) is not to know the fruit the soul draws from it, but the nature of the act which is performed: does or does not the priest, as minister of Christ, perform *"actio Christi se ipsum sacrificantis et offerentis?"*

Likewise for the sacraments, it is not a question of knowing the fruit produced by them, but whether the essential elements of the sacramental sign (the performing of the sign by the minister himself who performs the gestures and pronounces the words with the intention *saltem faciendi quod facit ecclesia*) have been validly performed.

Likewise, in celebration and concelebration, one must see whether, along with the necessary interior intention, the celebrant completes the external action, and, above all, pronounces the words which constitute the *"actio Christi se ipsum sacrificantis et offerentis."* This is not verified when the priest does not pronounce over the bread and the wine our Lord's words: "This is my Body," "This is my Blood."

2. "PRAESENTIA CHRISTI"

Just as altar and sacrifice dominate liturgical worship, the life of Christ must be said to be completely dominated by the sacrifice of the Cross.

The Angel's words to His foster-father: *"He shall save his people from their sins,"*[16] those of John the Baptist: *"Behold the lamb of God, who takes away the sin of the world,"*[17] those of Christ Himself to Nicodemus: *"Even so must the Son of Man be lifted up, that those who believe in him . . . may have life everlasting,"*[18] to His disciples: *"But I have a baptism to be baptized with, and*

---

16. *Mt.* 1, 21.
17. *John*, 1, 29.
18. *John*, 3, 14–15.

how distressed I am until it is accomplished,[19] and the words especially which He spoke at the Last Supper and on Calvary, all show that the core of our divine Lord's life and thought was the Cross and the offering of Himself to the Father in order to reconcile men to God and to save them.

But is not He who offers sacrifice somehow greater than the sacrifice itself? So now we would like to speak to you about the Lord Himself, and first of all to call your attention to the fact that in the Eucharist the Church possesses the Lord, flesh and blood, body and soul and divinity. This is solemnly defined by the Council of Trent, in its thirteenth Session, canon 1. It suffices, moreover, to take the words pronounced by Jesus in their clear, literal, unambiguous meaning to arrive at the same conclusion: "Take and eat. This is my Body, which shall be given for you. Take and drink, this is my Blood, which shall be shed for you." And St. Paul uses the same clear and simple words in his first letter to the Corinthians.[20]

On this subject there is neither doubt nor divergence of opinion among Catholics. But as soon as speculative theology begins to discuss the manner in which Christ is present in the Eucharist, serious differences of opinion rise on a number of points. We do not wish to go into these speculative controversies. We would like, however, to point out certain limits and insist on a fundamental principle of interpretation whose neglect causes Us some anxiety.

Speculation must take as its norm that the literal meaning of scriptural texts, the faith and teaching of the Church, take precedence over a scientific system and theoretical considerations. Science must conform to revelation, not revelation to science. When a philosophical concept distorts the genuine meaning of a revealed truth, it is either inaccurate or being applied incorrectly.

This principle finds application in the doctrine of the real presence. Certain theologians, though they accept the Council's teaching on the real presence and transubstantiation, interpret the words of Christ and those of the Council in such a way that nothing more remains of the presence of Christ than a sort of envelope empty of its natural content.

In their opinion, what the species of bread and wine substantially and actually contain is "the Lord in heaven," with Whom the species have a so-called real and substantial relation of content and presence. Such a speculative interpretation raises serious objections when presented as one fully adequate, since the Christian sense of the faithful, the constant catechetical teaching of the Church, the terms of the Council, and above all the words of our Lord require that the Eucharist contain the Lord Himself.

The sacramental species are not the Lord, even if they have a so-called essential relation of container and presence contained with the substance of the heavenly Christ. The Lord said: "This is my Body! This is my Blood!" He did not say, "This is something apparent to the senses which signifies the presence of My Body and Blood."

---

19. *Luke*, 12, 50.
20. I *Cor.*, 11, 23–25.

No doubt He could effect that those perceptible signs of a true relation of presence should also be perceptible and efficacious sings of sacramental grace; but there is question here of the essential content of the "eucharistic species," not of their sacramental efficacy. Therefore it cannot be admitted that the theory We have just described gives full satisfaction to the words of Christ; that the presence of Christ in the Eucharist means nothing more; or that this theory is adequate to enable us to say in all truth of the Eucharist: "It is the Lord."[21]

Undoubtedly, the majority of the faithful is unable to grasp the difficult speculative problems and the attempts to explain the nature of Christ's presence. The Roman Catechism, moreover, advises against discussing such questions before the faithful,[22] but it neither mentions nor proposes the theory outlined above. Still less does it affirm that such a theory exhausts the meaning of Christ's words and gives them a full explanation. One can still search for scientific explanations and interpretations, but they must not, so to speak, drive Christ from the Eucharist and leave in the tabernacle only a Eucharistic species retaining a so-called real and essential relation with the true Lord Who is in Heaven.

It is surprising that those who are not satisfied with the theory We have just described should be listed as adversaries, among the non-scientific "physicists," or that there is no hesitation in saying, with regard to the so-called scientific conception of Christ's presence: "This truth is not for the masses."

To these considerations We must add some remarks concerning the tabernacle. Just as We said above: "The Lord is somehow greater than the altar and the sacrifice," so now We might say: "Is the tabernacle, where dwells the Lord Who has come down amongst His people, greater than altar and sacrifice?" The altar is more important than the tabernacle, because on it is offered the Lord's sacrifice. No doubt the tabernacle holds the "*Sacramentum permanens*;" but it is not an "*altare permanens*," for the Lord offers Himself in sacrifice only on the altar during the celebration of Holy Mass, not after or outside the Mass.

In the tabernacle, on the other hand, He is present as long as the consecrated species last, yet is not making a permanent sacrificial offering.

One has a perfect right to distinguish between the offering or the sacrifice of the Mass and the "*cultus latreuticus*" offered to the God-Man hidden in the Eucharist. A decision of the Sacred Congregation of Rites, dated July 7, 1927, severely limits exposition of the Blessed Sacrament during Mass.[23] But this is easily explained by a concern to keep habitually separate the act of sacrifice and the worship of simple adoration, in order that the faithful may clearly understand the characteristics proper to each.

Still an awareness of their unity is more important than a realization of their differences. It is one and the same Lord Who is immolated on the altar and honored in the tabernacle, and Who pours out His blessings from the tabernacle.

---

21. Cf. *John*, 21, 7.
22. Cf. *Catech. Rom.*, pars II, cap. IV, n. 43, sq.
23. *Acta Ap. Sedis*, a. 19, 1927.

A person who was thoroughly convinced of this would avoid many difficulties. He would be wary of exaggerating the significance of one to the detriment of the other, and of opposing decisions of the Holy See.

The Council of Trent has explained the disposition of soul required concerning the Blessed Sacrament: *"If anyone says that Christ, the only-begotten Son of God, is not to be adored in the holy sacrament of the Eucharist with the worship of latria, including the external worship, and that the sacrament, therefore, is not to be honored with extraordinary festive celebrations nor solemnly carried from place to place in processions according to the praiseworthy universal rite and custom of the holy Church: or that the sacrament is not to be publicly exposed for the people's adoration, and that those who adore it are idolators: let him be anathema."*[24]

"If anyone says that it is not permissible to keep the sacred Eucharist in a holy place, but that it must necessarily be distributed immediately after the consecration to those who are present; or that it is not permissible to carry the Eucharist respectfully to the sick: let him be anathema."[25]

He who clings wholeheartedly to this teaching has no thought of formulating objections against the presence of the tabernacle on the altar.

In the instruction of the Holy Office, *"De arte sacra,"* of June 30, 1952,[26] the Holy See insists, among other things, on this point: *"This Supreme Sacred Congregation strictly commands that the prescriptions of Canons 1268, #2, and 1269, #1, be faithfully observed: 'The Most Blessed Eucharist should be kept in the most distinguished and honorable place in the church, and hence as a rule at the main altar unless some other be considered more convenient and suitable for veneration and worship due to so great a Sacrament. . . . The Most Blessed Sacrament must be kept in an immovable tabernacle set in the middle of the altar.'"*[27]

There is question, not so much of the material presence of the tabernacle on the altar, as of a tendency to which We would like to call your attention, that of a lessening of esteem for the presence and action of Christ in the tabernacle. The sacrifice of the altar is held sufficient, and the importance of Him who accomplishes it is reduced.

Yet the person of our Lord must hold the central place in worship, for it is His person that unifies the relations of the altar and the tabernacle and gives them their meaning.

It is through the sacrifice of the altar, first of all, that the Lord becomes present in the Eucharist, and He is in the tabernacle only as a *"memoria sacrificii et passionis suae."*

---

24. *Conc. Trid.*, Sessio XIII, can. 6.
25. *Conc. Trid.*, l. c., can. 7.
26. *Acta Ap. Sedis*, a 44, 1952.
27. *Acta Ap. Sedis*, l, c.

To separate tabernacle from altar is to separate two things which by their origin and their nature should remain united.

Specialists will offer various opinions for solving the problem of so placing the tabernacle on the altar as not to impede the celebration of Mass when the priest is facing the congregation. The essential point is to understand that it is the same Lord present on the altar and in the tabernacle.

One might also stress the attitude of the Church regarding certain pious practices: visits to the Blessed Sacrament, which she earnestly recommends, the Forty Hours devotion or "perpetual adoration," the holy hour, the solemn carrying of Holy Communion to the sick, processions of the Blessed Sacrament. The most enthusiastic and convinced liturgist must be able to understand and appreciate what our Lord in the tabernacle means to the solidly pious faithful, be they unlearned or educated. He is their counselor, their consoler, their strength and refuge, their hope in life and in death.

Not satisfied simply with letting the faithful come to their Lord in the tabernacle, the liturgical movement, then, will strive to draw them even more.

3. "INFINITA ET DIVINA MAIESTAS CHRISTI"

The third and final point We would like to treat is that of the "infinita et divina Maiestas" of Christ, which the words "Christus Deus" expresses.

Certainly the Incarnate Word is Lord and Savior of men; but He is and remains the Word, the infinite God. In the Athanasian creed it is said: "Our Lord Jesus Christ, Son of God, is God and Man."

The humanity of Christ has a right also to the worship of "latria" because of its hypostatic union with the Word, but his divinity is the reason and source of this worship. And so, the divinity of Christ cannot remain on the outer edge of liturgical thought.

It is normal to go "ad Patrem per Christum," since Christ is Mediator between God and men. But He is not only Mediator; He is also within the Trinity, equal to the Father and the Holy Spirit. Let it suffice to recall the magnificent prologue of St. John's Gospel: "The Word was God. . . . All things were made through him, and without him nothing was made that has been made."[28] Christ is First and Last, Alpha and Omega.

At the end of the world, when all enemies shall have been overcome, and last of all, death itself, Christ, the Word subsisting in human nature, will give over the Kingdom to God His Father, and the Son will subject Himself to Him Who has subjected all to the son, so that "God may be all in all."[29]

Meditation on the "infinita, summa, divina Maiestas" of Christ can surely contribute to a deeper appreciation of the liturgy. That is why We wished to call your attention to this point.

---

28. *John*, 1, 1–3.
29. I *Cor.*, 15, 28.

In closing We would like to add two remarks on the "liturgy and the past" and the "liturgy and the present."

The Liturgy and the Past. In liturgical matters, as in many other fields, one must avoid two exaggerated viewpoints concerning the past: blind attachment and utter contempt. The liturgy contains immutable elements, a sacred content which transcends time; but changeable, transitory, occasionally even defective, elements are to be found there.

It seems to Us that the present day attitude of liturgical circles toward the past is quite balanced. They seek and study seriously, hold on to what is really worthwhile without, however, falling into excess. Yet here and there erroneous tendencies appear, resistances, enthusiasms or condemnations, whose concrete manifestations you know well, and which We briefly mentioned above.

The Liturgy and the Present. The Liturgy stamps a characteristic mark on the life of the Church, even on the whole religious attitude of the day. Especially noteworthy is the active conscientious participation of the faithful at liturgical functions.

From the Church's side, today's liturgy involves a concern for progress, but also for conservation and defense. It returns to the past, but does not slavishly imitate. It creates new elements in the ceremonies themselves, in using the vernacular, in popular chant and in the building of churches.

Yet it would be superfluous to call once more to mind that the Church has grave motives for firmly insisting that in the Latin rite the priest celebrating Mass has an absolute obligation to use Latin, and also, when Gregorian chant accompanies the Holy Sacrifice, that this be done in the Church's tongue.

For their part the faithful are careful to respond to the measures taken by the Church, but adopt divergent attitudes: some manifest promptness and enthusiasm, even at times a too lively fervor which provokes the intervention of authority. Others show indifference and even opposition. Thus are laid bare differences of temperament, and preferences for individual piety or for community worship.

Present day liturgy interests itself likewise in many special problems. Among these are the relation of the liturgy to the religious ideas of the world of today, contemporary culture, social questions, depth psychology.

This mere enumeration is enough to show you that the various aspects of today's liturgy not only arouse Our interest, but keep Our vigilance on alert. We sincerely desire the progress of the liturgical movement, and wish to help it, but it is also Our duty to forestall whatever might be a source of error or danger.

It is, however, a consolation and joy for Us to know that in these matters We can rely on your help and understanding.

May these considerations, along with the labors which occupied your attention these past days, produce abundant fruit and contribute to the attainment of the goal towards which the sacred liturgy is striving. In token of divine blessings, which We beg for you and the souls confided to you, We impart to you from Our heart Our Apostolic Benediction.

* *Reported in Osservatore Romano, September 24, 1956. French text. Translated based on one released by Vatican Press Office. Most of the quotations in this address were cited by the Holy Father in Latin but have been translated here. Latin phrases incorporated directly into the text of the address have been left in that language. This address was delivered to twelve hundred delegates to the International Congress on Pastoral Liturgy who had come to Rome by special train after their four day session at Assisi. About a hundred delegates from the United States were present.*

SACROSANCTUM CONCILIUM

CONSTITUTION ON THE SACRED LITURGY

SECOND VATICAN COUNCIL
DECEMBER 4, 1963

AN OVERVIEW OF *SACROSANCTUM CONCILIUM*

Rev. Msgr. Kevin Irwin

AUTHORITY OF *SACROSANCTUM CONCILIUM*

A major strength of the Catholic theological tradition is the opportunity, not to say necessity of making distinctions (for example, St. Thomas Aquinas in his *Summa Theologiae*). An important principle in interpreting documents from the Second Vatican Council is to be aware of a document's genre and the relative importance the Church assigns to that document precisely because of its genre. To assert that "the Vatican says . . ." may be a convenient way to introduce "breaking news" or any of a range of possible topics in documents and other sources. But it can be sloppy theologically and ignore the fact that there is a clear and definitive "hierarchy" that the Church itself assigns to its documents.

The text at hand, *Sacrosanctum Concilium* (SC; the *Constitution on the Sacred Liturgy*) from the Second Vatican Council, is a case in point. It is commonly held that among the "acts of the Holy See" as published (in Latin) in the Vatican's official organ *Acta Apostolicae Sedis* (AAS) the highest rank is ascribed to the "acts of the Second Vatican Council." The same *Acta* publishes papal documents and pronouncements and after the "solemn profession of faith" it ranks "acts for the beginning and conclusion of the Second Vatican Council" as of highest authority above such documents as "decretals," "encyclical letters," "apostolic exhortations," and so on.[1]

Then under the heading of documents of Vatican II the *Acta* ranks three kinds of documents that were promulgated from the Council. In "hierarchical" order they are "Constitutions," "Decrees," and "Declarations."[2] Given the ranking of Church documents it is clear that a Constitution from a general Church council like Vatican II ranks very high. Among the documents in this book, *The Liturgy Documents*, *Sacrosanctum Concilium* ranks the highest.[3]

---

1. See, Francis G. Morrisey, *The Canonical Significance of Papal and Curial Pronouncements.* (Washington, D.C.: Canon Law Society of America, 1978) 21–22. Also see, Francis A. Sullivan, *Creative Fidelity.* Weighing and Interpreting Documents of the Magisterium. (Eugene, OR.: Wipf and Stock, 2003.) Original The Paulist Press, 1996.

2. Ibid., 7 where he states: "It would seem that the Constitutions are addressed to the universal Church, while the Decrees are directed more specifically to a given category of the faithful or to a special form of apostolate, e.g. to the members of the Eastern Churches, to Bishops, religious and so forth. The Declarations are policy statements giving the ordinary teaching of the Church [e.g. On the Relation of the Church to Non Christian Religions, *Nostra aetate*]. . . ."

3. At the same time this is not to mitigate the authoritative teaching of all the Council's documents. For example, even though *Nostra Aetate*, is ranked in third place after Constitutions and Declarations, its assertions about the relations between Catholics and Jews opened the way for Pope John Paul II and others to foster strong and fruitful relations with non Christian religions.

Another aspect of the authority of a conciliar document (and most other Church documents) is that the officially promulgated Latin text is the official text. In an Internet world it is relatively easy to call up the Latin text of Vatican documents and their modern language translations.[4] Especially because we are two generations removed from the events of Vatican II it is important to be very attentive about what the text says precisely and exactly. Years ago the eyewitnesses at Vatican II could have helped us interpret words and phrases in the documents, which is simply not possible today.[5]

STRUCTURE OF *SACROSANCTUM CONCILIUM*

SC is divided into an introduction, seven chapters (unequal in length) and an appendix (on a proposed revision of the calendar for ecumenical purposes). Before delving into SC's seven chapters it is important to note its first four paragraphs, specifically their context and meaning. The Council's deliberations began in the fall 1962. SC was the first of its documents to be promulgated (in 1963). Therefore these paragraphs were the first ones from the Council that the Catholic Church and the wider world would read. The Council Fathers were well aware of this when they spoke first about the aims of the Council. (In fact the first two Latin words [which always comprise the Latin title of the document] of this *Constitution* are *Sacrosanctum Concilium*, "This sacred council," which itself sets up not only the *Constitution* but also the whole Council.) This important first paragraph states:

> In faithful obedience to tradition, the Council declares that the Church holds all lawfully acknowledged rites to be of equal right and dignity and wishes to preserve them in the future and to foster them in every way. The Council also desires that, where necessary, the rites be revised carefully in the light of sound tradition and that they be given new vigor to meet the circumstances and needs of modern times.[6]

It would be useful to return to this paragraph again and again when trying to appreciate what the aims of the Council itself were as well as the emphasis it places on the faithful's growing in the Christian life by means of the reform and promotion of the liturgy.

---

4. For example, the Latin text of *Sacrosanctum Concilium* is found at http://www.vatican.va/archive/hist_councils/ii_vatican_council/documents/vat-ii_const_19631204_sacrosanctum-concilium_lt.htm.

5. That there is a significant debate underway about how to interpret the documents of Vatican II is clear. Among a host of others see Giuseppe Alberigo. *History of Vatican II*. Five volumes. English language editor Joseph A. Komonchak. English edition edited by Joseph A. Komonchak. (Leuven: Peeters/Maryknoll: Orbis Books, 1995–2006), Giuseppe Alberigo, *A Brief History of Vatican II*. Condensed version of Conclusions from five volumes. Trans., Matthew Sherry. (Maryknoll: Orbis Books, 2006). *Herbert* Vorgrimler, ed, *Commentary on the Documents of Vatican II*. (New York: Herder and Herder, 1967–69). German original *Zweite Vatikanische Konzil. Dokumente und Kommentar*. Agostino Marchetto, *Il concilio ecumenico Vaticano II. Contrappunto per la storia*. (Roma: Libreria Editirice Vaticana, 2005), Roberto De Mattei, *Il concilio Vaticano II. Una storia mai scritta*. (Torino: Lindau, 2010), John O'Malley S.J., *What Happened at Vatican II* (Oxford University Press, 2008) and Massimo Faggioli, *Vatican II. The Battle for Meaning*. (NY/Mahwah: Paulist Press, 2012).

6. *Sacrosanctum Concilium* (SC), 4.

This is followed by a second paragraph that is rich theologically, especially its use of the important phrase from the Church's *lex orandi*, namely that it is in the liturgy that "the work of our redemption is accomplished." Again this is an assertion that deserves deep reflection as it sets our sights on why the liturgy is so important. The third and fourth paragraphs set up the rest of SC by directing that the rites will "be revised carefully in the light of sound tradition, and that they be given new vigor to meet the circumstances and needs of modern times."[7] The chapters of *Sacrosanctum Concilium* are noted below.

   I. General Principles for the Reform and Promotion of the Sacred Liturgy (the longest and most detailed of all the chapters) with the following subsections:

   A. The Nature of the Liturgy and Its Importance in the Church's Life

   B. The Promotion of Liturgical Instruction and Active Participation

   C. The Reform of the Sacred Liturgy

   D. The Promotion of Liturgical Life in Diocese and Parish

   E. The Promotion of Pastoral-Liturgical Action

   II. The Most Sacred Mystery of the Eucharist

   III. The Other Sacraments and the Sacramentals

   IV. The Divine Office

   V. The Liturgical Year

   VI. Sacred Music

   VII. Sacred Art and Sacred Furnishings

Certainly from a theological perspective Chapter One deserves serious study and reflection because it grounds the rest of the document and it guided the process of the reform of the rites of the liturgy. Among the most prominent assertions in SC is the importance of "active participation" in the liturgy. While adding up the number of times a word is used in any document and on that basis suggesting its importance can be very deceptive and skew the data, nonetheless the fact that the term "participation" is used sixteen times in *Sacrosanctum Concilium* and that its modifier is "active" on twelve of those occasions and "liturgical instruction and active participation" is cited as one of the three principles on which the restoration and promotion of the sacred liturgy is based is very significant.[8]

---

7. Ibid. That this paragraph has been seen as an interpretative key to the entire Council is upheld by a number of scholars, most notably Massimo Faggioli in "*Sacrosanctum concilium* and the Meaning of Vatican II," *Theological Studies* 71 (2010) pp. 437–52.

8. See SC, 14, 19, 27, 30, 41, 50, 113, 114, 121, 124 and the title preceding SC, 14.

Even while asserting the high importance to be given to SC it should be seen in continuity with Vatican documents that preceded and led to it. These include documents such as: Pope Pius X's *motu proprio, Tra le sollectitudini* (1903) on active participation in the liturgy, Pope Pius XII's encyclical *Mystici Corporis* (1943) on the Church, and his encyclical *Mediator Dei* on the sacred liturgy (1947). In addition there are the important changes in the liturgies of Holy Week (now called the Sacred Paschal Triduum) implemented by Pope Pius XII in the mid-1950s (first in experimental form in 1951, then promulgated in 1955 and celebrated in 1956). Each of these can be seen as "building blocks" of SC because they deal (in order) with participation, the nature of the Church, the nature of liturgy, and the revision of rites. That SC ushered in enormous changes in the liturgy is clear. What is equally clear is that the liturgy constitution set this direction but did not offer the last word on the reform of the liturgy, for example on the vernacular in the liturgy.[9] Here SC asserted that Latin is the language of the Roman liturgy, but it also gave local episcopal conferences the opening to request that (parts of and eventually all of) the liturgy can be celebrated in the vernacular.[10] These permissions were requested by episcopal conferences and approved by the Holy See and are normative and authoritative.

Especially in an era of some controversy over the reformed liturgy it is important to respect what this document said and then to follow up by researching subsequent Vatican documents on the liturgy (such as those contained in the rest of this book). For example, with regard to the Mass it is important to place the assertions of SC in Chapter Two in relation to what is asserted about the theology, structure, and protocols of the reformed Mass in *The General Instruction of the Roman Missal*, the *Lectionary for Mass*, and *The Roman Missal* itself (in their latest editions).

FIFTY YEARS LATER

Trying to assess the importance and impact of any of the documents from the Second Vatican Council after "only" fifty years can be a foolhardy and doomed project. The Church and her liturgy is always "a work in progress." However it would be (almost) universally claimed that the reform of the liturgy was among the most noticeable and well received achievements coming from the Council. At the same time with fifty years' hindsight it might be appropriate to offer a comment on how something that was a major emphasis in SC has come to be more nuanced in recent years—the notion of active participation.

The phrase "liturgical participation" is redundant. Liturgy is always about our *taking part*, our *participation* in the reality of God through Christ in the power of the Holy Spirit in the communion of the Church. By its nature the liturgy is the Church's privileged and guaranteed means of our participation in these sacred realities and events. The very term *anamnesis* means that we make memory together and in making memory we take part in what was once accomplished

---

9. See the commentary on this paragraph in Norman P. Tanner, *The Councils of the Church: A Short History.* (New York: Herder and Herder, 2001) pp. 100–101.

10. See SC, 36.

for our sakes and our salvation, in the present through Sacred Rites as we look for its fulfillment at the end of time. Here time—past, present, and future—intersect and eternity is experienced here and now.

The modifier "active" needs to be contextualized. The context for *Sacrosanctum Concilium* was the celebration of rites as revised after the Council of Trent or as in use up through 1962. This meant that the gathered assembly most often watched and observed what was occurring with some active participation through song and texts.[11] That the Council Fathers at Vatican II wanted to change that and increase "full, conscious and active participation in the sacred liturgy"[12] is clear. Where formerly the use of hand Missals (officially sanctioned by the Church in the last part of the nineteenth century) was an option now the use of a worship aid, or hymnal, or ritual book would be *de rigeur*. Being attentive and responding to what was occurring in and through the liturgy is now to be presumed.

Not all "active participation" means doing something externally. Obviously part of active participation in the liturgy is processing, singing, speaking, and engaging in ritual gestures, and so on, according to the principle that liturgical roles mean that we all do what we are asked to do, no more, no less. But a large part of "active participation" means being silent—listening and being attentive to what is going on as enacted by all the liturgy's ministers on our behalf and for our sakes. Critiques from as high a source as the papacy itself about the assembly celebrating itself and that the liturgy after the Second Vatican Council can be "too horizontal" are at issue here. The only caution I wish to add is that any critique of the excesses or misunderstandings of liturgical participation should never eclipse in any way the sacramental and incarnational principles and that mediatorship of salvation is through the actions of human beings. This is to say that by its nature liturgy involves the whole person: bodies, minds, emotions, and so on; and all our faculties: sight, sound, smell, taste, and touch. Any reevaluation of "active participation" must include the full engagement of all of these faculties. Liturgy should never be confused with the passivity of a theater or television audience. We are all the "actants" of the liturgy, there are not the performers and the audience. That is why "active participation" is a redundant phrase. I am concerned that some critiques of "active participation" make the rites of the liturgy superfluous provided that one is engaged in the Paschal Mystery. Liturgical rites are the Church's privileged way to do this.[13]

Liturgy is always enacted, celebrated, and engaged in. It is not done on behalf of others who are silent before it. Rethinking the meaning of "active participation" does not mean returning to the era of hand Missals to read along

---

11. It was a 1958 document from the Congregation of Rites (then so called) that fostered the gathered assembly's active participation in the "dialogue Mass" and in singing four hymns at Mass.

12. See SC, 14.

13. I noted above that there is a certain polarization that is possible today in interpreting the Council's documents, especially the Liturgy Constitution. Yet on the issue of "active participation" authors who take different positions on a number of things can and do come together on "participation" as a premise and basis for the reformed liturgy. See, among others, Annibale Bugnini, *The Reform of the Liturgy* 1948–75. Trans. Matthew O'Connell. (Collegeville, MN: The Liturgical Press, 1990) and Nicola Giampietro, *The Development of the Liturgical Reform As Seen by Cardinal Ferdinando Antonelli from 1948 to 1970*. (Fort Collins, CO: Roman Catholic Books, 2009).

and following along in a text with what the liturgy's ministers are saying and doing.[14]

Having taught this document for over three decades I find that I now spend far more time on Chapter One about the principles of the liturgy and its reform (outlined in subsequent chapters) than I did in the past. This is to say that I emphasize what SC says about the *theology* of the liturgy—about ecclesiology (among other things, liturgical roles, the hierarchical structure of the liturgy, the preference for communal celebrations of the liturgy), participation (as noted above), the notion of liturgical adaptation and inculturation in light of Chapter Nine of *The General Instruction of the Roman Missal*, eschatology ("the heavenly liturgy") and the breadth of the liturgy's rites emphasizing but not limited to the Eucharist.[15] In addition, I have found it important to teach what is asserted in the *Constitution's* footnotes. It is here that much of the breadth and depth of the liturgical scholarship on which SC is based can be found (including Patristic authors, citations from other Councils like Trent and citations from the Church's *lex orandi*). In addition, at the risk of oversimplifying, I would assert that we have a long way to go to implement what is requested in articles 15–16 on education about the Sacred Liturgy and an appropriate method for that study.

As a concluding reflection on liturgical participation, I invite the reader to reread and ponder the first paragraph of *Sacrosanctum Concilium* as well as the meaning(s) of the Prayer over the Offerings at the Evening Mass of the Lord's Supper:

> Grant us, O Lord, we pray,
> that we may participate worthily in these mysteries,
> for whenever the memorial of this sacrifice is celebrated
> the work of our redemption is accomplished.

---

14. See SC, 37–40.

15. Among others, see Fred McManus, "Active Participation: An Ongoing Assessment." *American Essays in Liturgy* (Collegeville, MN: The Liturgical Press, 1988) and *Actuosa Participatio. Conoscere, comprendere, e vivere la Liturgia. Studi in onore del Prof. Domenico Sartore.* Edited by Agostino Montan and Manlio Sodi. (Citta del Vaticano: Libreria Editrice Vaticana, 2002).

SACROSANCTUM CONCILIUM

CONSTITUTION ON THE SACRED LITURGY

1. This Sacred Council has several aims in view: it desires to impart an ever increasing vigor to the Christian life of the faithful; to adapt more suitably to the needs of our own times those institutions that are subject to change; to foster whatever can promote union among all who believe in Christ; to strengthen whatever can help to call the whole of humanity into the household of the Church. The Council therefore sees particularly cogent reasons for undertaking the reform and promotion of the liturgy.

2. For the liturgy, "making the work of our redemption a present actuality,"[1] most of all in the divine sacrifice of the eucharist, is the outstanding means whereby the faithful may express in their lives and manifest to others the mystery of Christ and the real nature of the true Church. It is of the essence of the Church to be both human and divine, visible yet endowed with invisible resources, eager to act yet intent on contemplation, present in this world yet not at home in it; and the Church is all these things in such wise that in it the human is directed and subordinated to the divine, the visible likewise to the invisible, action to contemplation, and this present world to that city yet to come which we seek.[2] While the liturgy daily builds up those who are within into a holy temple of the Lord, into a dwelling place for God in the Spirit,[3] to the mature measure of the fullness of Christ,[4] at the same time it marvelously strengthens their power to preach Christ and thus shows forth the Church to those who are outside as a sign lifted up among the nations,[5] under which the scattered children of God may be gathered together,[6] until there is one sheepfold and one shepherd.[7]

3. Wherefore the Council judges that the following principles concerning the promotion and reform of the liturgy should be called to mind and practical norms established.

Among these principles and norms there are some that can and should be applied both to the Roman Rite and also to all the other rites. The practical norms

---

1. RomM, prayer over the gifts, Holy Thursday and 2d Sunday in Ordinary Time.
2. See Heb 13:14.
3. See Eph 2:21–22.
4. See Eph 4:13.
5. See Is 11:12.
6. See Jn 11:52.
7. See Jn 10:16.

that follow, however, should be taken as applying only to the Roman Rite, except for those that, in the very nature of things, affect other rites as well.

4.   Lastly, in faithful obedience to tradition, the Council declares that the Church holds all lawfully acknowledged rites to be of equal right and dignity and wishes to preserve them in the future and to foster them in every way. The Council also desires that, where necessary, the rites be revised carefully in the light of sound tradition and that they be given new vigor to meet the circumstances and needs of modern times.

CHAPTER I
GENERAL PRINCIPLES FOR THE REFORM AND PROMOTION OF THE SACRED LITURGY

I. NATURE OF THE LITURGY AND ITS IMPORTANCE IN THE CHURCH'S LIFE

5.   God who "wills that all be saved and come to the knowledge of the truth" (1 Tm 2:4), "who in many and various ways spoke in times past to the fathers by the prophets" (Heb 1:1), when the fullness of time had come sent his Son, the Word made flesh, anointed by the Holy Spirit, to preach the Gospel to the poor, to heal the contrite of heart;[1] he is "the physician, being both flesh and of the Spirit,"[2] the mediator between God and us.[3] For his humanity, united with the person of the Word, was the instrument of our salvation. Therefore in Christ "the perfect achievement of our reconciliation came forth and the fullness of divine worship was given to us.[4]

The wonderful works of God among the people of the Old Testament were a prelude to the work of Christ the Lord. He achieved his task of redeeming humanity and giving perfect glory to God, principally by the paschal mystery of his blessed passion, resurrection from the dead, and glorious ascension, whereby "dying, he destroyed our death and, rising, he restored our life."[5] For it was from the side of Christ as he slept the sleep of death upon the cross that there came forth the sublime sacrament of the whole Church.[6]

6.   As Christ was sent by the Father, he himself also sent the apostles, filled with the Holy Spirit. Their mission was, first, by preaching the Gospel to every creature,[7] to proclaim that by his death and resurrection Christ has freed us from Satan's grip[8] and brought us into the Father's kingdom. But the work they

---

1. See Is 61:1; Lk 4:18.
2. Ignatius of Antioch, *To the Ephesians* 7, 2.
3. See 1 Tm 2:5.
4. *Sacramentarium Veronense* (ed. Mohlberg), no. 1265.
5. RomM, preface I of Easter.
6. RomM, prayer after the seventh reading, Easter Vigil.
7. See Mk 16:15.
8. See Acts 26:18.

preached they were also to bring into effect through the sacrifice and the sacraments, the center of the whole liturgical life. Thus by baptism all are plunged into the paschal mystery of Christ: they die with him, are buried with him, and rise with him;[9] they receive the spirit of adoption as children "in which we cry: Abba, Father" (Rom 8:15), and thus become true adorers whom the Father seeks.[10] In like manner, as often as they eat the supper of the Lord they proclaim the death of the Lord until he comes.[11] For that reason, on the very day of Pentecost when the Church appeared before the world, "those who received the word" of Peter "were baptized." And "they continued steadfastly in the teaching of the apostles and in the communion of the breaking of bread and in prayers . . . praising God and being in favor with all the people" (Acts 2:41–47). From that time onward the Church has never failed to come together to celebrate the paschal mystery: reading those things "which were in all the Scriptures concerning him" (Lk 24:27); celebrating the eucharist, in which "the victory and triumph of his death are again made present";[12] and at the same time giving thanks "to God for his inexpressible gift" (2 Cor 9:15) in Christ Jesus, "in praise of his glory" (Eph 1:12), through the power of the Holy Spirit.

7.   To accomplish so great a work, Christ is always present in his Church, especially in its liturgical celebrations. He is present in the sacrifice of the Mass, not only in the person of his minister, "the same now offering, through the ministry of priests, who formerly offered himself on the cross,"[13] but especially under the eucharistic elements. By his power he is present in the sacraments, so that when a man baptizes it is really Christ himself who baptizes.[14] He is present in his word, since it is he himself who speaks when the holy Scriptures are read in the Church. He is present, lastly, when the Church prays and sings, for he promised: "Where two or three are gathered together in my name, there am I in the midst of them" (Mt 18:20).

Christ always truly associates the Church with himself in this great work wherein God is perfectly glorified and the recipients made holy. The Church is the Lord's beloved Bride who calls to him and through him offers worship to the eternal Father.

Rightly, then, the liturgy is considered as an exercise of the priestly office of Jesus Christ. In the liturgy, by means of signs perceptible to the senses, human sanctification is signified and brought about in ways proper to each of these signs; in the liturgy the whole public worship is performed by the Mystical Body of Jesus Christ, that is, by the Head and his members.

From this it follows that every liturgical celebration, because it is an action of Christ the Priest and of his Body which is the Church, is a sacred action surpassing

---

9. See Rom 6:4; Eph 2:6; Col 3:1.

10. See Jn 4:23.

11. See 1 Cor 11:26.

12. Council of Trent, sess. 13, 11 Oct 1551, *Decree on the Holy Eucharist*, chap. 5.

13. Council of Trent, sess. 22, 17 Sept 1562, *Doctrine on the Holy Sacrifice of the Mass*, chap. 2.

14. See Augustine, *In Ioannis Evangelium Tractatus 6*, chap. 1, n. 7.

all others; no other action of the Church can equal its effectiveness by the same title and to the same degree.

8.   In the earthly liturgy we take part in a foretaste of that heavenly liturgy celebrated in the holy city of Jerusalem toward which we journey as pilgrims, where Christ is sitting at the right hand of God, a minister of the holies and of the true tabernacle;[15] we sing a hymn to the Lord's glory with the whole company of heaven; venerating the memory of the saints, we hope for some part and fellowship with them; we eagerly await the Savior, our Lord Jesus Christ, until he, our life, shall appear and we too will appear with him in glory.[16]

9.   The liturgy does not exhaust the entire activity of the Church. Before people can come to the liturgy they must be called to faith and to conversion: "How then are they to call upon him in whom they have not yet believed? But how are they to believe him whom they have not heard? And how are they to hear if no one preaches? And how are men to preach unless they be sent?" (Rom 10:14–15).

Therefore the Church announces the good tidings of salvation to those who do not believe, so that all may know the true God and Jesus Christ whom he has sent and may be converted from their ways, doing penance.[17] To believers, also, the Church must ever preach faith and penance, prepare them for the sacraments, teach them to observe all that Christ has commanded,[18] and invite them to all the works of charity, worship, and the apostolate. For all these works make it clear that Christ's faithful, though not of this world, are to be the light of the world and to glorify the Father in the eyes of all.

10.   Still, the liturgy is the summit toward which the activity of the Church is directed; at the same time it is the fount from which all the Church's power flows. For the aim and object of apostolic works is that all who are made children of God by faith and baptism should come together to praise God in the midst of his Church, to take part in the sacrifice, and to eat the Lord's Supper.

The liturgy in its turn moves the faithful, filled with "the paschal sacraments," to be "one in holiness";[19] it prays that "they may hold fast in their lives to what they have grasped by their faith";[20] the renewal in the eucharist of the covenant between the Lord and his people draws the faithful into the compelling love of Christ and sets them on fire. From the liturgy, therefore, particularly the eucharist, grace is poured forth upon us as from a fountain; the liturgy is the source for achieving in the most effective way possible human sanctification and God's glorification, the end to which all the Church's other activities are directed.

---

15. See Rv. 21:2; Col 3:1; Heb 8:2.
16. See Phil 3:20; Col 3:4.
17. See Jn 17:3; Lk 24:47; Acts 2:38.
18. See Mt 28:20.
19. RomM, prayer after communion, Easter Vigil.
20. RomM, opening prayer, Mass for Monday of Easter Week.

11.   But in order that the liturgy may possess its full effectiveness, it is necessary that the faithful come to it with proper dispositions, that their minds be attuned to their voices, and that they cooperate with divine grace, lest they receive it in vain.[21] Pastors must therefore realize that when the liturgy is celebrated something more is required than the mere observance of the laws governing valid and lawful celebration; it is also their duty to ensure that the faithful take part fully aware of what they are doing, actively engaged in the rite, and enriched by its effects.

12.   The spiritual life, however, is not limited solely to participation in the liturgy. Christians are indeed called to pray in union with each other, but they must also enter into their chamber to pray to the Father in secret;[22] further, according to the teaching of the Apostle, they should pray without ceasing.[23] We learn from the same Apostle that we must always bear about in our body the dying of Jesus, so that the life also of Jesus may be made manifest in our bodily frame.[24] This is why we ask the Lord in the sacrifice of the Mass that "receiving the offering of the spiritual victim," he may fashion us for himself "as an eternal gift."[25]

13.   Popular devotions of the Christian people are to be highly endorsed, provided they accord with the laws and norms of the Church, above all when they are ordered by the Apostolic See.

Devotions proper to particular Churches also have a special dignity if they are undertaken by mandate of the bishops according to customs or books lawfully approved.

But these devotions should be so fashioned that they harmonize with the liturgical seasons, accord with the sacred liturgy, are in some way derived from it, and lead the people to it, since, in fact, the liturgy, by its very nature far surpasses any of them.

II. PROMOTION OF LITURGICAL INSTRUCTION AND ACTIVE PARTICIPATION

14.   The Church earnestly desires that all the faithful be led to that full, conscious, and active participation in liturgical celebrations called for by the very nature of the liturgy. Such participation by the Christian people as "a chosen race, a royal priesthood, a holy nation, God's own people" (1 Pt 2:9; see 2:4–5) is their right and duty by reason of their baptism.

In the reform and promotion of the liturgy, this full and active participation by all the people is the aim to be considered before all else. For it is the primary and indispensable source from which the faithful are to derive the true

---

21. See 2 Cor 6:1.
22. See Mt 6:6.
23. See 1 Thes 5:17.
24. See 2 Cor 4:10–11.
25. RomM, prayer over the gifts, Saturday after the 2d, 4th, and 6th Sundays of Easter.

Christian spirit and therefore pastors must zealously strive in all their pastoral work to achieve such participation by means of the necessary instruction.

Yet it would be futile to entertain any hopes of realizing this unless, in the first place, the pastors themselves become thoroughly imbued with the spirit and power of the liturgy and make themselves its teachers. A prime need, therefore, is that attention be directed, first of all, to the liturgical formation of the clergy. Wherefore the Council has decided to enact what follows.

15.   Professors appointed to teach liturgy in seminaries, religious houses of study, and theological faculties must be thoroughly trained for their work in institutes specializing in this subject.

16.   The study of liturgy is to be ranked among the compulsory and major courses in seminaries and religious houses of studies; in theological faculties it is to rank among the principal courses. It is to be taught under its theological, historical, spiritual, pastoral, and canonical aspects. Moreover, other professors, while striving to expound the mystery of Christ and the history of salvation from the angle proper to each of their own subjects, must nevertheless do so in a way that will clearly bring out the connection between their subjects and the liturgy, as also the underlying unity of all priestly training. This consideration is especially important for professors of dogmatic, spiritual, and pastoral theology and for professors of holy Scripture.

17.   In seminaries and houses of religious, clerics shall be given a liturgical formation in their spiritual life. The means for this are: proper guidance so that they may be able to understand the sacred rites and take part in them whole-heartedly; the actual celebration of the sacred mysteries and of other, popular devotions imbued with the spirit of the liturgy. In addition they must learn how to observe the liturgical laws, so that life in seminaries and houses of religious may be thoroughly permeated by the spirit of the liturgy.

18.   Priests, both secular and religious, who are already working in the Lord's vineyard are to be helped by every suitable means to understand ever more fully what it is they are doing in their liturgical functions; they are to be aided to live the liturgical life and to share it with the faithful entrusted to their care.

19.   With zeal and patience pastors must promote the liturgical instruction of the faithful and also their active participation in the liturgy both internally and externally, taking into account their age and condition, their way of life, and their stage of religious development. By doing so, pastors will be fulfilling one of their chief duties as faithful stewards of the mysteries of God; and in this matter they must lead their flock not only by word but also by example.

20.   Radio and television broadcasts of sacred rites must be marked by discretion and dignity, under the leadership and direction of a competent person appointed for this office by the bishops. This is especially important when the service to be broadcast is the Mass.

III. THE REFORM OF THE SACRED LITURGY

21.   In order that the Christian people may more surely derive an abundance of graces from the liturgy, the Church desires to undertake with great care a general reform of the liturgy itself. For the liturgy is made up of immutable elements, divinely instituted, and of elements subject to change. These not only may but ought to be changed with the passage of time if they have suffered from the intrusion of anything out of harmony with the inner nature of the liturgy or have become pointless.

In this reform both texts and rites should be so drawn up that they express more clearly the holy things they signify and that the Christian people, as far as possible, are able to understand them with ease and to take part in the rites fully, actively, and as befits a community.

Wherefore the Council establishes tbe general norms that follow.

A. General Norms

22.   § 1. Regulation of the liturgy depends solely on the authority of the Church, that is, on the Apostolic See and, accordingly as the law determines, on the bishop.

§ 2. In virtue of power conceded by the law, the regulation of the liturgy within certain defined limits belongs also to various kinds of competent territorial bodies of bishops lawfully established.

§ 3. Therefore, no other person, not even if he is a priest, may on his own add, remove, or change anything in the liturgy.

23.   That sound tradition may be retained and yet the way remain open to legitimate progress, a careful investigation is always to be made into each part of the liturgy to be revised. This investigation should be theological, historical, and pastoral. Also the general laws governing the structure and meaning of the liturgy must be studied in conjunction with the experience derived from recent liturgical reforms and from the indults conceded to various places. Finally, there must be no innovations unless the good of the Church genuinely and certainly requires them; care must be taken that any new forms adopted should in some way grow organically from forms already existing.

As far as possible, marked differences between the rites used in neighboring regions must be carefully avoided.

24.   Sacred Scripture is of the greatest importance in the celebration of the liturgy. For it is from Scripture that the readings are given and explained in the homily and that psalms are sung; the prayers, collects, and liturgical songs are scriptural in their inspiration; it is from the Scriptures that actions and signs derive their meaning. Thus to achieve the reform, progress, and adaptation of the liturgy, it is essential to promote that warm and living love for Scripture to which the venerable tradition of both Eastern and Western rites gives testimony.

25.   The liturgical books are to be revised as soon as possible; experts are to be employed in this task and bishops from various parts of the world are to be consulted.

B. Norms Drawn from the Hierarchic and Communal Nature of the Liturgy

26.   Liturgical services are not private functions, but are celebrations belonging to the Church, which is the "sacrament of unity," namely, the holy people united and ordered under their bishops.[26]

Therefore liturgical services involve the whole Body of the Church; they manifest it and have effects upon it; but they also concern the individual members of the Church in different ways, according to their different orders, offices, and actual participation.

27.   Whenever rites, according to their specific nature, make provision for communal celebration involving the presence and active participation of the faithful, it is to be stressed that this way of celebrating them is to be preferred, as far as possible, to a celebration that is individual and, so to speak, private.

This applies with special force to the celebration of Mass and the administration of the sacraments, even though every Mass has of itself a public and social character.

28.   In liturgical celebrations each one, minister or layperson, who has an office to perform, should do all of, but only, those parts which pertain to that office by the nature of the rite and the principles of liturgy.

29.   Servers, readers, commentators, and members of the choir also exercise a genuine liturgical function. They ought to discharge their office, therefore, with the sincere devotion and decorum demanded by so exalted a ministry and rightly expected of them by God's people.

Consequently, they must all be deeply imbued with the spirit of the liturgy, in the measure proper to each one, and they must be trained to perform their functions in a correct and orderly manner.

30.   To promote active participation, the people should be encouraged to take part by means of acclamations, responses, psalmody, antiphons, and songs, as well as by actions, gestures, and bearing. And at the proper times all should observe a reverent silence.

31.   The revision of the liturgical books must ensure that the rubrics make provision for the parts belonging to the people.

32.   The liturgy makes distinctions between persons according to their liturgical function and sacred orders and there are liturgical laws providing for due honors to be given to civil authorities. Apart from these instances, no special

---

26. Cyprian, *On the Unity of the Catholic Church* 7; see *Letter* 66, n. 8, 3.

honors are to be paid in the liturgy to any private persons or classes of persons, whether in the ceremonies or by external display.

C. Norms Based on the Teaching and Pastoral Character of the Liturgy

33.   Although the liturgy is above all things the worship of the divine majesty, it likewise contains rich instruction for the faithful.[27] For in the liturgy God is speaking to his people and Christ is still proclaiming his gospel. And the people are responding to God by both song and prayer.

Moreover, the prayers addressed to God by the priest, who presides over the assembly in the person of Christ, are said in the name of the entire holy people and of all present. And the visible signs used by the liturgy to signify invisible divine realities have been chosen by Christ or the Church. Thus not only when things are read "that were written for our instruction" (Rom 15:4), but also when the Church prays or sings or acts, the faith of those taking part is nourished and their minds are raised to God, so that they may offer him their worship as intelligent beings and receive his grace more abundantly.

In the reform of the liturgy, therefore, the following general norms are to be observed.

34.   The rites should be marked by a noble simplicity; they should be short, clear, and unencumbered by useless repetitions; they should be within the people's powers of comprehension and as a rule not require much explanation.

35.   That the intimate connection between words and rites may stand out clearly in the liturgy:

1. In sacred celebrations there is to be more reading from holy Scripture and it is to be more varied and apposite.

2. Because the spoken word is part of the liturgical service, the best place for it, consistent with the nature of the rite, is to be indicated even in the rubrics; the ministry of preaching is to be fulfilled with exactitude and fidelity. Preaching should draw its content mainly from scriptural and liturgical sources, being a proclamation of God's wonderful works in the history of salvation, the mystery of Christ, ever present and active within us, especially in the celebration of the liturgy.

3. A more explicitly liturgical catechesis should also be given in a variety of ways. Within the rites themselves provision is to be made for brief comments, when needed, by the priest or a qualified minister; they should occur only at the more suitable moments and use a set formula or something similar.

4. Bible services should be encouraged, especially on the vigils of the more solemn feasts, on some weekdays in Advent and Lent, and on Sundays and holy days. They are particularly to be recommended in places where no priest is available; when this is the case, a deacon or some other person authorized by the bishop is to preside over the celebration.

---

27. See Council of Trent, sess. 22, 17 Sept 1562, *Doctrine on the Holy Sacrifice of the Mass*, chap. 8.

36.   § 1. Particular law remaining in force, the use of the Latin language is to be preserved in the Latin rites.

§ 2. But since the use of the mother tongue, whether in the Mass, the administration of the sacraments, or other parts of the liturgy, frequently may be of great advantage to the people, the limits of its use may be extended. This will apply in the first place to the readings and instructions and to some prayers and chants, according to the regulations on this matter to be laid down for each case in subsequent chapters.

§ 3. Respecting such norms and also, where applicable, consulting the bishops of nearby territories of the same language, the competent, territorial ecclesiastical authority mentioned in art. 22, §2 is empowered to decide whether and to what extent the vernacular is to be used. The enactments of the competent authority are to be approved, that is, confirmed by the Holy See.

§ 4. Translations from the Latin text into the mother tongue intended for use in the liturgy must be approved by the competent, territorial ecclesiastical authority already mentioned.

D. Norms for Adapting the Liturgy to the Culture and Traditions of Peoples

37.   Even in the liturgy the Church has no wish to impose a rigid uniformity in matters that do not affect the faith or the good of the whole community; rather, the Church respects and fosters the genius and talents of the various races and peoples. The Church considers with sympathy and, if possible, preserves intact the elements in these peoples' way of life that are not indissolubly bound up with superstition and error. Sometimes in fact the Church admits such elements into the liturgy itself, provided they are in keeping with the true and authentic spirit of the liturgy.

38.   Provisions shall also be made, even in the revision of liturgical books, for legitimate variations and adaptations to different groups, regions, and peoples, especially in mission lands, provided the substantial unity of the Roman Rite is preserved; this should be borne in mind when rites are drawn up and rubrics devised.

39.   Within the limits set by the *editio typica* of the liturgical books, it shall be for the competent, territorial ecclesiastical authority mentioned in art. 22, §2 to specify adaptations, especially in the case of the administration of the sacraments, the sacramentals, processions, liturgical language, sacred music, and the arts. This, however, is to be done in accord with the fundamental norms laid down in this Constitution.

40.   In some places and circumstances, however, an even more radical adaptation of the liturgy is needed and this entails greater difficulties. Wherefore:

1. The competent, territorial ecclesiastical authority mentioned in art. 22, §2, must, in this matter, carefully and prudently weigh what elements from the traditions and culture of individual peoples may be appropriately admitted into

divine worship. They are to propose to the Apostolic See adaptations considered useful or necessary that will be introduced with its consent.

2. To ensure that adaptations are made with all the circumspection they demand, the Apostolic See will grant power to this same territorial ecclesiastical authority to permit and to direct, as the case requires, the necessary preliminary experiments within certain groups suited for the purpose and for a fixed time.

3. Because liturgical laws often involve special difficulties with respect to adaptation, particularly in mission lands, experts in these matters must be employed to formulate them.

IV. PROMOTION OF LITURGICAL LIFE IN DIOCESE AND PARISH

41. The bishop is to be looked on as the high priest of his flock, the faithful's life in Christ in some way deriving from and depending on him.

Therefore all should hold in great esteem the liturgical life of the diocese centered around the bishop, especially in his cathedral church; they must be convinced that the preeminent manifestation of the Church is present in the full, active participation of all God's holy people in these liturgical celebrations, especially in the same eucharist, in a single prayer, at one altar at which the bishop presides, surrounded by his college of priests and by his ministers.[28]

42. But because it is impossible for the bishop always and everywhere to preside over the whole flock in his Church, he cannot do otherwise than establish lesser groupings of the faithful. Among these the parishes, set up locally under a pastor taking the place of the bishop, are the most important: in some manner they represent the visible Church established throughout the world.

And therefore both in attitude and in practice the liturgical life of the parish and its relationship to the bishop must be fostered among the faithful and clergy; efforts must also be made toward a lively sense of community within the parish, above all in the shared celebration of the Sunday Mass.

V. PROMOTION OF PASTORAL-LITURGICAL ACTION

43. Zeal for the promotion and restoration of the liturgy is rightly held to be a sign of the providential dispositions of God in our time, a movement of the Holy Spirit in his Church. Today it is a distinguishing mark of the Church's life, indeed of the whole tenor of contemporary religious thought and action.

So that this pastoral-liturgical action may become even more vigorous in the Church, the Council decrees what follows.

44. It is advisable that the competent, territorial ecclesiastical authority mentioned in art. 22, §2 set up a liturgical commission, to be assisted by experts in

---

28. See Ignatius of Antioch, *To the Magnesians*, 7; *To the Philadelphians*, 4; *To the Smyrnians*, 8.

liturgical science, music, art, and pastoral practice. As far as possible the commission should be aided by some kind of institute for pastoral liturgy, consisting of persons eminent in these matters and including the laity as circumstances suggest. Under the direction of the aforementioned territorial ecclesiastical authority, the commission is to regulate pastoral-liturgical action throughout the territory and to promote studies and necessary experiments whenever there is question of adaptations to be proposed to the Apostolic See.

45.   For the same reason every diocese is to have a commission on the liturgy, under the direction of the bishop, for promoting the liturgical apostolate.

Sometimes it may be advisable for several dioceses to form among themselves one single commission, in order to promote the liturgy by means of shared consultation.

46.   Besides the commission on the liturgy, every diocese, as far as possible, should have commissions for music and art.

These three commissions must work in closest collaboration; indeed it will often be best to fuse the three of them into one single commission.

CHAPTER II
THE MOST SACRED MYSTERY OF THE EUCHARIST

47.   At the Last Supper, on the night when he was betrayed, our Savior instituted the eucharistic sacrifice of his body and blood. He did this in order to perpetuate the sacrifice of the cross throughout the centuries until he should come again and in this way to entrust to his beloved Bride, the Church, a memorial of his death and resurrection: a sacrament of love, a sign of unity, a bond of charity,[1] a paschal banquet "in which Christ is eaten, the heart is filled with grace, and a pledge of future glory given to us."[2]

48.   The Church, therefore, earnestly desires that Christ's faithful, when present at this mystery of faith, should not be there as strangers or silent spectators; on the contrary, through a good understanding of the rites and prayers they should take part in the sacred service conscious of what they are doing, with devotion and full involvement. They should be instructed by God's word and be nourished at the table of the Lord's body; they should give thanks to God; by offering the immaculate Victim, not only through the hands of the priest, but also with him, they should learn to offer themselves as well; through Christ the Mediator,[3] they should be formed day by day into an ever more perfect unity with God and with each other, so that finally God may be all in all.

---

1. See Augustine, *In Ioannis Evangelium Tractatus 36*, chap. 6, n. 13.

2. Liturgy of the Hours, antiphon for Canticle of Mary, evening prayer II, feast of Corpus Christi.

3. See Cyril of Alexandria, *Commentary on the Gospel of John*, book 11, chap. 11–12.

49.   Thus, mindful of those Masses celebrated with the assistance of the faithful, especially on Sundays and holy days of obligation, the Council makes the following decrees in order that the sacrifice of the Mass, even in its ritual forms, may become pastorally effective to the utmost degree.

50.   The Order of Mass is to be revised in a way that will bring out more clearly the intrinsic nature and purpose of its several parts, as also the connection between them, and will more readily achieve the devout, active participation of the faithful.

For this purpose the rites are to be simplified, due care being taken to preserve their substance; elements that, with the passage of time, came to be duplicated or were added with but little advantage are now to be discarded; other elements that have suffered injury through accident of history are now, as may seem useful or necessary, to be restored to the vigor they had in the traditions of the Fathers.

51.   The treasures of the Bible are to be opened up more lavishly, so that a richer share in God's word may be provided for the faithful. In this way a more representative portion of holy Scripture will be read to the people in the course of a prescribed number of years.

52.   By means of the homily the mysteries of the faith and the guiding principles of the Christian life are expounded from the sacred text during the course of the liturgical year; as part of the liturgy itself therefore, the homily is strongly recommended; in fact, at Masses celebrated with the assistance of the people on Sundays and holy days of obligation it is not to be omitted except for a serious reason.

53.   Especially on Sundays and holy days of obligation there is to be restored, after the gospel and the homily, "the universal prayer" or "the prayer of the faithful." By this prayer, in which the people are to take part, intercession shall be made for holy Church, for the civil authorities, for those oppressed by various needs, for all people, and for the salvation of the entire world.[4]

54.   With art. 36 of this Constitution as the norm, in Masses celebrated with the people a suitable place may be allotted to their mother tongue. This is to apply in the first place to the readings and "the universal prayer," but also, as local conditions may warrant, to those parts belonging to the people.

Nevertheless steps should be taken enabling the faithful to say or to sing together in Latin those parts of the Ordinary of the Mass belonging to them.

Wherever a more extended use of the mother tongue within the Mass appears desirable, the regulation laid down in art. 40 of this Constitution is to be observed.

55.   That more complete form of participation in the Mass by which the faithful, after the priest's communion, receive the Lord's body from the sacrifice, is strongly endorsed.

---

4. See 1 Tm 2:1–2.

The dogmatic principles laid down by the Council of Trent remain intact.[5] In instances to be specified by the Apostolic See, however, communion under both kinds may be granted both to clerics and religious and to the laity at the discretion of the bishops, for example, to the ordained at the Mass of their ordination, to the professed at the Mass of their religious profession, to the newly baptized at the Mass following their baptism.

56.   The two parts that, in a certain sense, go to make up the Mass, namely, the liturgy of the word and the liturgy of the eucharist, are so closely connected with each other that they form but one single act of worship. Accordingly this Council strongly urges pastors that in their catechesis they insistently teach the faithful to take part in the entire Mass, especially on Sundays and holy days of obligation.

57.   § 1. Concelebration, which aptly expresses the unity of the priesthood, has continued to this day as a practice in the Church of both East and West. For this reason it has seemed good to the Council to extend permission for concelebration to the following cases:

    1. a. on Holy Thursday, both the chrism Mass and the evening Mass;

       b. Masses during councils, bishops' conferences, and synods;

       c. the Mass at the blessing of an abbot.

    2. Also, with permission of the Ordinary, who is the one to decide whether concelebration is opportune, to:

       a. the conventual Mass and the principal Mass in churches, when the needs of the faithful do not require that all the priests on hand celebrate individually;

       b. Masses celebrated at any kind of meeting of priests, whether secular or religious.

       § 2. 1. The regulation, however, of the discipline of concelebration in the diocese pertains to the bishop.

       2. This, however, does not take away the option of every priest to celebrate Mass individually, not, however, at the same time and in the same church as a concelebrated Mass or on Holy Thursday.

58.   A new rite for concelebration is to be drawn up and inserted into the Roman Pontifical and Roman Missal.

---

5. Council of Trent, sess. 21, *Doctrine on Communion under Both Species*, chap. 1–3.

CHAPTER III
THE OTHER SACRAMENTS AND THE SACRAMENTALS

59.   The purpose of the sacraments is to make people holy, to build up the Body of Christ, and, finally, to give worship to God; but being signs they also have a teaching function. They not only presuppose faith, but by words and objects they also nourish, strengthen, and express it; that is why they are called "sacraments of faith." They do indeed impart grace, but, in addition, the very act of celebrating them disposes the faithful most effectively to receive this grace in a fruitful manner, to worship God rightly, and to practice charity.

It is therefore of the highest importance that the faithful should readily understand the sacramental signs and should with great eagerness frequent those sacraments that were instituted to nourish the Christian life.

60.   The Church has, in addition, instituted sacramentals. These are sacred signs bearing a kind of resemblance to the sacraments: they signify effects, particularly of a spiritual kind, that are obtained through the Church's intercession. They dispose people to receive the chief effect of the sacraments and they make holy various occasions in human life.

61.   Thus, for well-disposed members of the faithful, the effect of the liturgy of the sacraments and sacramentals is that almost every event in their lives is made holy by divine grace that flows from the paschal mystery of Christ's passion, death, and resurrection, the fount from which all sacraments and sacramentals draw their power. The liturgy means also that there is hardly any proper use of material things that cannot thus be directed toward human sanctification and the praise of God.

62.   With the passage of time, however, certain features have crept into the rites of the sacraments and sacramentals that have made their nature and purpose less clear to the people of today; hence some changes have become necessary as adaptations to the needs of our own times. For this reason the Council decrees what follows concerning the revision of these rites.

63.   Because the use of the mother tongue in the administration of the sacraments and sacramentals can often be of considerable help for the people, this use is to be extended according to the following norms:

a.   With art. 36 as the norm, the vernacular may be used in administering the sacraments and sacramentals.

b.   Particular rituals in harmony with the new edition of the Roman Ritual shall be prepared without delay by the competent, territorial ecclesiastical authority mentioned in art. 22, §2 of this Constitution. These rituals are to be adapted, even in regard to the language employed, to the needs of the different regions. Once they have been reviewed by the Apostolic See, they are to be used in the regions for which they have been prepared. But those who draw up these rituals or particular collections of rites must not leave out the prefatory instructions for the individual rites in the Roman Ritual, whether the instructions are pastoral and rubrical or have some special social bearing.

64.   The catechumenate for adults, divided into several stages, is to be restored and put into use at the discretion of the local Ordinary. By this means the time of the catechumentate, which is intended as a period of well-suited instruction, may be sanctified by sacred rites to be celebrated at successive intervals of time.

65.   With art. 37–40 of this Constitution as the norm, it is lawful in mission lands to allow, besides what is part of Christian tradition, those initiation elements in use among individual peoples, to the extent that such elements are compatible with the Christian rite of initiation.

66.   Both of the rites for the baptism of adults are to be revised: not only the simpler rite, but also the more solemn one, with proper attention to the restored catechumenate. A special Mass "On the Occasion of a Baptism" is to be incorporated into the Roman Missal.

67.   The rite for the baptism of infants is to be revised and it should be suited to the fact that those to be baptized are infants. The roles as well as the obligations of parents and godparents should be brought out more clearly in the rite itself.

68.   The baptismal rite should contain alternatives, to be used at the discretion of the local Ordinary, for occasions when a very large number are to be baptized together. Moreover, a shorter rite is to be drawn up, especially in mission lands, for use by catechists, but also by the faithful in general, when there is danger of death and neither a priest nor a deacon is available.

69.   In place of the rite called the "Order of Supplying What Was Omitted in the Baptism of an Infant," a new rite is to be drawn up. This should manifest more clearly and fittingly that an infant who was baptized by the short rite has already been received into the Church.

Similarly, a new rite is to be drawn up for converts who have already been validly baptized; it should express that they are being received into the communion of the Church.

70.   Except during the Easter season, baptismal water may be blessed within the rite of baptism itself by use of an approved, shorter formulary.

71.   The rite of confirmation is also to be revised in order that the intimate connection of this sacrament with the whole of Christian initiation may stand out more clearly; for this reason it is fitting for candidates to renew their baptismal promises just before they are confirmed.

Confirmation may be conferred within Mass when convenient; as for the rite outside Mass, a formulary is to be composed for use as an introduction.

72.   The rite and formularies for the sacrament of penance are to be revised so that they more clearly express both the nature and effect of the sacrament.

73. "Extreme unction," which may also and more properly be called "anointing of the sick," is not a sacrament for those only who are at the point of death. Hence, as soon as any one of the faithful begins to be in danger of death from sickness or old age, the fitting time for that person to receive this sacrament has certainly already arrived.

74. In addition to the separate rites for anointing of the sick and for viaticum, a continuous rite shall be drawn up, structured so that the sick person is anointed after confessing and before receiving viaticum.

75. The number of the anointings is to be adapted to the circumstances; the prayers that belong to the rite of anointing are to be so revised that they correspond to the varying conditions of the sick who receive the sacrament.

76. Both the ceremonies and texts of the ordination rites are to be revised. The address given by the bishop at the beginning of each ordination or consecration may be in the vernacular.

When a bishop is consecrated, all the bishops present may take part in the laying on of hands.

77. The marriage rite now found in the Roman Ritual is to be revised and enriched in such a way that it more clearly signifies the grace of the sacrament and imparts a knowledge of the obligations of spouses.

"If any regions follow other praiseworthy customs and ceremonies when celebrating the sacrament of marriage, the Council earnestly desires that by all means these be retained."[1]

Moreover, the competent, territorial ecclesiastical authority mentioned in art. 22, §2 of this Constitution is free to draw up, in accord with art. 63, its own rite, suited to the usages of place and people. But the rite must always conform to the law that the priest assisting at the marriage must ask for and obtain the consent of the contracting parties.

78. Marriage is normally to be celebrated within Mass, after the reading of the gospel and the homily and before "the prayer of the faithful." The prayer for the bride, duly emended to remind both spouses of their equal obligation to remain faithful to each other, may be said in the vernacular.

But if the sacrament of marriage is celebrated apart from Mass, the epistle and gospel from the nuptial Mass are to be read at the beginning of the rite and the blessing is always to be given to the spouses.

79. The sacramentals are to be reviewed in the light of the primary criterion that the faithful participate intelligently, actively, and easily; the conditions of our own days must also be considered. When rituals are revised, in accord with art. 63, new sacramentals may also be added as the need for them becomes apparent.

---

1. Council of Trent, sess. 24, *Decree on Reform*, chap. 1. See also RomR, title 8, chap. 2, n. 6.

Reserved blessings shall be very few; reservations shall be in favor only of bishops and Ordinaries.

Let provision be made that some sacramentals, at least in special circumstances and at the discretion of the Ordinary, may be administered by qualified laypersons.

80.   The rite for the consecration to a life of virginity as it exists in the Roman Pontifical is to be revised.

A rite of religious profession and renewal of vows shall be drawn up with a view to achieving greater unity, simplicity, and dignity. Apart from exceptions in particular law, this rite should be adopted by those who make their profession or renewal of vows within Mass.

Religious profession should preferably be made within Mass.

81.   The rite of funerals should express more clearly the paschal character of Christian death and should correspond more closely to the circumstances and traditions of various regions. This applies also to the liturgical color to be used.

82.   The rite for the burial of infants is to be revised and a special Mass for the occasion provided.

CHAPTER IV
DIVINE OFFICE

83.   Christ Jesus, High Priest of the new and eternal covenant, taking human nature, introduced into this earthly exile the hymn that is sung throughout all ages in the halls of heaven. He joins the entire human community to himself, associating it with his own singing of this canticle of divine praise.

For he continues his priestly work through the agency of his Church, which is unceasingly engaged in praising the Lord and interceding for the salvation of the whole world. The Church does this not only by celebrating the eucharist, but also in other ways, especially by praying the divine office.

84.   By tradition going back to early Christian times, the divine office is so arranged that the whole course of the day and night is made holy by the praises of God. Therefore, when this wonderful song of praise is rightly performed by priests and others who are deputed for this purpose by the Church's ordinance or by the faithful praying together with the priest in the approved form, then it is truly the voice of a bride addressing her bridegroom; it is the very prayer that Christ himself, together with his Body, addresses to the Father.

85.   Hence all who render this service are not only fulfilling a duty of the Church, but also are sharing in the greatest honor of Christ's Bride, for by offering these praises to God they are standing before God's throne in the name of the Church, their Mother.

86.   Priests engaged in the sacred pastoral ministry will offer the praises of the hours with greater fervor the more vividly they realize that they must heed St. Paul's exhortation: "Pray without ceasing" (1 Thes 5:17). For the work in which they labor will effect nothing and bring forth no fruit except by the power of the Lord who said: "Without me you can do nothing" (Jn 15:5). That is why the apostles, instituting deacons, said: "We will devote ourselves to prayer and to the ministry of the word" (Acts 6:4).

87.   In order that the divine office may be better and more completely carried out in existing circumstances, whether by priests or by other members of the Church, the Council, carrying further the restoration already so happily begun by the Apostolic See, has seen fit to decree what follows concerning the office of the Roman Rite.

88.   Because the purpose of the office is to sanctify the day, the traditional sequence of the hours is to be restored so that once again they may be genuinely related to the hour of the day when they are prayed, as far as it is possible. Moreover, it will be necessary to take into account the modern conditions in which daily life has to be lived, especially by those who are called to labor in apostolic works.

89.   Therefore, when the office is revised, these norms are to be observed:

a. By the venerable tradition of the universal Church, lauds as morning prayer and vespers as evening prayer are the two hinges on which the daily office turns; hence they are to be considered as the chief hours and celebrated as such.

b. Compline is to be so composed that it will be a suitable prayer for the end of the day.

c. The hour known as matins, although it should retain the character of nocturnal praise when celebrated in choir, shall be adapted so that it may be recited at any hour of the day; it shall be made up of fewer psalms and longer readings.

d. The hour of prime is to be suppressed.

e. In choir the minor hours of terce, sext, and none are to be observed. But outside choir it will be lawful to choose whichever of the three best suits the hour of the day.

90.   The divine office, because it is the public prayer of the Church, is a source of devotion and nourishment also for personal prayer. Therefore priests and all others who take part in the divine office are earnestly exhorted in the Lord to attune their minds to their voices when praying it. The better to achieve this, let them take steps to improve their understanding of the liturgy and of the Bible, especially the psalms.

In revising the Roman office, its ancient and venerable treasures are to be so adapted that all those to whom they are handed on may more fully and readily draw profit from them.

91.   So that it may really be possible in practice to observe the course of the hours proposed in art. 89, the psalms are no longer to be distributed over just one week, but over some longer period of time.

The work of revising the psalter, already happily begun, is to be finished as soon as possible and is to take into account the style of Christian Latin, the liturgical use of psalms, including their being sung, and the entire tradition of the Latin Church.

92.   As regards the readings, the following shall be observed:

a. Readings from sacred Scripture shall be arranged so that the riches of God's word may be easily accessible in more abundant measure.

b. Readings excerpted from the works of the Fathers, doctors, and ecclesiastical writers shall be better selected.

c. The accounts of the martyrdom or lives of the saints are to be made to accord with the historical facts.

93.   To whatever extent may seem advisable, the hymns are to be restored to their original form and any allusion to mythology or anything that conflicts with Christian piety is to be dropped or changed. Also, as occasion arises, let other selections from the treasury of hymns be incorporated.

94.   That the day may be truly sanctified and the hours themselves recited with spiritual advantage, it is best that each of them be prayed at a time most closely corresponding to the true time of each canonical hour.

95.   In addition to the conventual Mass, communities obliged to choral office are bound to celebrate the office in choir every day. In particular:

a. Orders of canons, of monks and of nuns, and of other regulars bound by law or constitutions to choral office must celebrate the entire office.

b. Cathedral or collegiate chapters are bound to recite those parts of the office imposed on them by general or particular law.

c. All members of the above communities who are in major orders or are solemnly professed, except for lay brothers, are bound individually to recite those canonical hours which they do not pray in choir.

96.   Clerics not bound to office in choir, if they are in major orders, are bound to pray the entire office every day, either in common or individually, following the norms in art. 89.

97.   Appropriate instances are to be defined by the rubrics in which a liturgical service may be substituted for the divine office.

In particular cases and for a just reason Ordinaries may dispense their subjects wholly or in part from the obligation of reciting the divine office or may commute it.

98.   Members of any institute dedicated to acquiring perfection who, according to their constitutions, are to recite any parts of the divine office are thereby performing the public prayer of the Church.

They too perform the public prayer of the Church who, in virtue of their constitutions, recite any little office, provided this has been drawn up after the pattern of the divine office and duly approved.

99.   Since the divine office is the voice of the Church, that is, of the whole Mystical Body publicly praising God, those clerics who are not obliged to office in choir, especially priests who live together or who meet together for any purpose, are urged to pray at least some part of the divine office in common.

All who pray the divine office, whether in choir or in common, should fulfill the task entrusted to them as perfectly as possible: this refers not only to the internal devotion of their minds but also to their external manner of celebration.

It is advantageous, moreover, that the office in choir and in common be sung when there is an opportunity to do so.

100. Pastors should see to it that the chief hours, especially vespers, are celebrated in common in church on Sundays and the more solemn feasts. The laity, too, are encouraged to recite the divine office either with the priests, or among themselves, or even individually.

101. § 1. In accordance with the centuries-old tradition of the Latin rite, clerics are to retain the Latin language in the divine office. But in individual cases the Ordinary has the power of granting the use of a vernacular translation, prepared in accord with art. 36, to those clerics for whom the use of Latin constitutes a grave obstacle to their praying the office properly.

§ 2. The competent superior has the power to grant the use of the vernacular in the celebration of the divine office, even in choir, to nuns and to members of institutes dedicated to acquiring perfection, both men who are not clerics and women. The version, however, must be one that has been approved.

§ 3. Any cleric bound to the divine office fulfills his obligation if he prays the office in the vernacular together with a group of the faithful or with those mentioned in §2, provided the text of the translation has been approved.

CHAPTER V
THE LITURGICAL YEAR

102. The Church is conscious that it must celebrate the saving work of the divine Bridegroom by devoutly recalling it on certain days throughout the course of the year. Every week, on the day which the Church has called the Lord's Day, it keeps the memory of the Lord's resurrection, which it also celebrates once in the year, together with his blessed passion, in the most solemn festival of Easter.

Within the cycle of a year, moreover, the Church unfolds the whole mystery of Christ, from his incarnation and birth until his ascension, the day of Pentecost, and the expectation of blessed hope and of the Lord's return.

Recalling thus the mysteries of redemption, the Church opens to the faithful the riches of the Lord's powers and merits, so that these are in some way made present in every age in order that the faithful may lay hold on them and be filled with saving grace.

103. In celebrating this annual cycle of Christ's mysteries, the Church honors with special love Mary, the Mother of God, who is joined by an inseparable bond to the saving work of her Son. In her the Church holds up and admires the most excellent effect of the redemption and joyfully contemplates, as in a flawless image, that which the Church itself desires and hopes wholly to be.

104. The Church has also included in the annual cycle days devoted to the memory of the martyrs and the other saints. Raised up to perfection by the manifold grace of God and already in possession of eternal salvation, they sing God's perfect praise in heaven and offer prayers for us. By celebrating their passage from earth to heaven the Church proclaims the paschal mystery achieved in the saints, who have suffered and been glorified with Christ; it proposes them to the faithful as examples drawing all to the Father through Christ and pleads through their merits for God's favors.

105. Finally, in the various seasons of the year and according to its traditional discipline, the Church completes the formation of the faithful by means of devout practices for soul and body, by instruction, prayer, and works of penance and of mercy.

Accordingly the sacred Council has seen fit to decree what follows.

106. By a tradition handed down from the apostles and having its origin from the very day of Christ's resurrection, the Church celebrates the paschal mystery every eighth day, which, with good reason, bears the name of the Lord's Day or Sunday. For on this day Christ's faithful must gather together so that, by hearing the word of God and taking part in the eucharist, they may call to mind the passion, the resurrection, and the glorification of the Lord Jesus and may thank God, who "has begotten them again unto a living hope through the resurrection of Jesus Christ from the dead" (1 Pt 1:3). Hence the Lord's Day is the first holy day of all and should be proposed to the devotion of the faithful and taught to them in such a way that it may become in fact a day of joy and of freedom from

work. Other celebrations, unless they be truly of greatest importance, shall not have precedence over the Sunday, the foundation and core of the whole liturgical year.

107. The liturgical year is to be so revised that the traditional customs and usages of the sacred seasons are preserved or restored to suit the conditions of modern times; their specific character is to be retained, so that they duly nourish the devotion of the faithful who celebrate the mysteries of Christian redemption and above all the paschal mystery. If certain adaptations are considered necessary on account of local conditions, they are to be made in accordance with the provisions of art. 39 and 40.

108. The minds of the faithful must be directed primarily toward those feasts of the Lord on which the mysteries of salvation are celebrated in the course of the year. Therefore, the Proper of Seasons shall be given the precedence due to it over the feasts of the saints, in order that the entire cycle of the mysteries of salvation may be celebrated in the measure due to them.

109. Lent is marked by two themes, the baptismal and the penitential. By recalling or preparing for baptism and by repentance, this season disposes the faithful, as they more diligently listen to the word of God and devote themselves to prayer, to celebrate the paschal mystery. The baptismal and penitential aspects of Lent are to be given greater prominence in both the liturgy and liturgical catechesis. Hence:

a. More use is to be made of the baptismal features proper to the Lenten liturgy; some of those from an earlier era are to be restored as may seem advisable.

b. The same is to apply to the penitential elements. As regards catechesis, it is important to impress on the minds of the faithful not only the social consequences of sin but also the essence of the virtue of penance, namely, detestation of sin as an offense against God; the role of the Church in penitential practices is not to be neglected and the people are to be exhorted to pray for sinners.

110. During Lent penance should be not only inward and individual, but also outward and social. The practice of penance should be fostered, however, in ways that are possible in our own times and in different regions and according to the circumstances of the faithful; it should be encouraged by the authorities mentioned in art. 22.

Nevertheless, let the paschal fast be kept sacred. Let it be observed everywhere on Good Friday and, where possible, prolonged throughout Holy Saturday, as a way of coming to the joys of the Sunday of the resurrection with uplifted and welcoming heart.

111. The saints have been traditionally honored in the Church and their authentic relics and images held in veneration. For the feasts of the saints proclaim the wonderful works of Christ in his servants and display to the faithful fitting examples for their imitation.

Lest the feasts of the saints take precedence over the feasts commemorating the very mysteries of salvation, many of them should be left to be celebrated by a particular Church or nation or religious family; those only should be extended to the universal Church that commemorate saints of truly universal significance.

CHAPTER VI
SACRED MUSIC

112. The musical tradition of the universal Church is a treasure of inestimable value, greater even than that of any other art. The main reason for this preeminence is that, as sacred song closely bound to the text, it forms a necessary or integral part of the solemn liturgy.

Holy Scripture itself has bestowed praise upon sacred song[1] and the same may be said of the Fathers of the Church and of the Roman pontiffs, who in recent times, led by St. Pius X, have explained more precisely the ministerial function supplied by sacred music in the service of the Lord.

Therefore sacred music will be the more holy the more closely it is joined to the liturgical rite, whether by adding delight to prayer, fostering oneness of spirit, or investing the rites with greater solemnity. But the Church approves of all forms of genuine art possessing the qualities required and admits them into divine worship.

Accordingly, the Council, keeping the norms and precepts of ecclesiastical tradition and discipline and having regard to the purpose of sacred music, which is the glory of God and the sanctification of the faithful, decrees what follows.

113. A liturgical service takes on a nobler aspect when the rites are celebrated with singing, the sacred ministers take their parts in them, and the faithful actively participate.

As regards the language to be used, the provisions of art. 36 are to be observed; for the Mass, those of art. 54; for the sacraments, those of art. 63; for the divine office, those of art. 101.

114. The treasure of sacred music is to be preserved and fostered with great care. Choirs must be diligently developed, especially in cathedral churches; but bishops and other pastors of souls must be at pains to ensure that whenever a liturgical service is to be celebrated with song, the whole assembly of the faithful is enabled, in keeping with art. 28 and 30, to contribute the active participation that rightly belongs to it.

115. Great importance is to be attached to the teaching and practice of music in seminaries, in the novitiates and houses of study of religious of both sexes, and also in other Catholic institutions and schools. To impart this instruction, those in charge of teaching sacred music are to receive thorough training.

---

1. See Eph 5:19; Col 3:16.

It is recommended also that higher institutes of sacred music be established whenever possible.

Musicians and singers, especially young boys, must also be given a genuine liturgical training.

116. The Church acknowledges Gregorian chant as distinctive of the Roman liturgy; therefore, other things being equal, it should be given pride of place in liturgical services.

But other kinds of sacred music, especially polyphony, are by no means excluded from liturgical celebrations, provided they accord with the spirit of the liturgical service, in the way laid down in art. 30.

117. The *editio typica* of the books of Gregorian chant is to be completed and a more critical edition is to be prepared of those books already published since the reform of St. Pius X.

It is desirable also that an edition be prepared containing the simpler melodies for use in small churches.

118. The people's own religious songs are to be encouraged with care so that in sacred devotions as well as during services of the liturgy itself, in keeping with rubrical norms and requirements, the faithful may raise their voices in song.

119. In certain parts of the world, especially mission lands, people have their own musical traditions and these play a great part in their religious and social life. Thus, in keeping with art. 39 and 40, due importance is to be attached to their music and a suitable place given to it, not only in forming their attitude toward religion, but also in adapting worship to their native genius.

Therefore, when missionaries are being given training in music, every effort should be made to see that they become competent in promoting the traditional music of the people, both in schools and in sacred services, as far as may be practicable.

120. In the Latin Church the pipe organ is to be held in high esteem, for it is the traditional musical instrument that adds a wonderful splendor to the Church's ceremonies and powerfully lifts up the spirit to God and to higher things.

But other instruments also may be admitted for use in divine worship, with the knowledge and consent of the competent territorial authority and in conformity with art. 22, §2, art. 37 and art. 40. This applies, however, only on condition that the instruments are suitable, or can be made suitable, for sacred use, are in accord with the dignity of the place of worship, and truly contribute to the uplifting of the faithful.

121. Composers, filled with the Christian spirit, should feel that their vocation is to develop sacred music and to increase its store of treasures.

Let them produce compositions having the qualities proper to genuine sacred music, not confining themselves to works that can be sung only by large choirs, but providing also for the needs of small choirs and for the active participation of the entire assembly of the faithful.

The texts intended to be sung must always be consistent with Catholic teaching; indeed they should be drawn chiefly from holy Scripture and from liturgical sources.

CHAPTER VII
SACRED ART AND SACRED FURNISHINGS

122. The fine arts are deservedly ranked among the noblest activities of human genius and this applies especially to religious art and to its highest achievement, sacred art. These arts, by their very nature, are oriented toward the infinite beauty of God, which they attempt in some way to portray by the work of human hands. They are dedicated to advancing God's praise and glory to the degree that they center on the single aim of turning the human spirit devoutly toward God.

The Church has therefore always been the friend of the fine arts, has ever sought their noble help, and has trained artists with the special aim that all things set apart for use in divine worship are truly worthy, becoming, and beautiful, signs and symbols of the supernatural world. The Church has always regarded itself as the rightful arbiter of the arts, deciding which of the works of artists are in accordance with faith, with reverence, and with honored traditional laws and are thereby suited for sacred use.

The Church has been particularly careful to see that sacred furnishings worthily and beautifully serve the dignity of worship and has admitted changes in materials, design, or ornamentation prompted by the progress of the technical arts with the passage of time.

Wherefore it has pleased the Fathers to issue the following decrees on these matters.

123. The Church has not adopted any particular style of art as its very own but has admitted styles from every period, according to the proper genius and circumstances of peoples and the requirements of the many different rites in the Church. Thus, in the course of the centuries, the Church has brought into being a treasury of art that must be very carefully preserved. The art of our own days, coming from every race and region, shall also be given free scope in the Church, on condition that it serves the places of worship and sacred rites with the reverence and honor due to them. In this way contemporary art can add its own voice to that wonderful chorus of praise sung by the great masters of past ages of Catholic faith.

124. In encouraging and favoring art that is truly sacred, Ordinaries should strive after noble beauty rather than mere sumptuous display. This principle is to apply also in the matter of sacred vestments and appointments.

Let bishops carefully remove from the house of God and from other places of worship those works of artists that are repugnant to faith and morals and to

Christian devotion and that offend true religious sense either by their grotesqueness or by the deficiency, mediocrity, or sham in their artistic quality.

When churches are to be built, let great care be taken that they are well suited to celebrating liturgical services and to bringing about the active participation of the faithful.

125. The practice of placing sacred images in churches so that they may be venerated by the faithful is to be maintained. Nevertheless there is to be restraint regarding their number and prominence so that they do not create confusion among the Christian people or foster religious practices of doubtful orthodoxy.

126. When deciding on works of art, local Ordinaries shall give hearing to the diocesan commission on sacred art, and if need be, to others who are especially expert, as well as to the commissions referred to in art. 44, 45, and 46. Ordinaries must be very careful to see that sacred furnishings and valuable works of art are not disposed of or damaged, for they are the adornment of the house of God.

127. Bishops should have a special concern for artists, so as to imbue them with the spirit of sacred art and liturgy. This they may do in person or through competent priests who are gifted with a knowledge and love of art.

It is also recommended that schools or academies of sacred art to train artists be founded in those parts of the world where they seem useful.

All artists who, prompted by their talents, desire to serve God's glory in holy Church, should ever bear in mind that they are engaged in a kind of sacred imitation of God the Creator and are concerned with works intended to be used in Catholic worship, to uplift the faithful, and to foster their devotion and religious formation.

128. Along with the revision of the liturgical books, as laid down in art. 25, there is to be an early revision of the canons and ecclesiastical statutes regulating the supplying of material things involved in sacred worship. This applies in particular to the worthy and well-planned construction of places of worship, the design and construction of altars, the nobility, placement, and security of the eucharistic tabernacle, the practicality and dignity of the baptistry, the appropriate arrangement of sacred images and church decorations and appointments. Laws that seem less suited to the reformed liturgy are to be brought into harmony with it or else abolished; laws that are helpful are to be retained if already in use or introduced where they are lacking.

With art. 22 of this Constitution as the norm, the territorial bodies of bishops are empowered to make adaptations to the needs and customs of their different regions; this applies especially to the material and design of sacred furnishings and vestments.

129. During their philosophical and theological studies, clerics are to be taught about the history and development of sacred art and about the sound principles on which the production of its works must be grounded. In consequence they will be able to appreciate and preserve the Church's treasured monuments and

be in a position to offer good advice to artists who are engaged in producing works of art.

130. It is fitting that the use of pontifical insignia be reserved to those ecclesiastical persons who have either episcopal rank or some definite jurisdiction.

APPENDIX
DECLARATION OF THE SECOND VATICAN ECUMENICAL COUNCIL ON REVISION OF THE CALENDAR

131. The Second Vatican Ecumenical Council recognizes the importance of the wishes expressed by many on assigning the feast of Easter to a fixed Sunday and on an unchanging calendar and has considered the effects that could result from the introduction of a new calendar. Accordingly the Council issues the following declaration:

1. The Council is not opposed to the assignment of the feast of Easter to a particular Sunday of the Gregorian Calendar, provided those whom it may concern, especially other Christians who are not in communion with the Apostolic See, give their assent.

2. The Council likewise declares that it does not oppose measures designed to introduce a perpetual calendar into civil society.

Among the various systems being suggested to establish a perpetual calendar and to introduce it into civil life, only those systems are acceptable to the Church that retain and safeguard a seven-day week with Sunday and introduce no days outside the week, so that the present sequence of weeks is left intact, unless the most serious reasons arise. Concerning these the Apostolic See will make its own judgment.

The Fathers of the Council have given assent to all and to each part of the matters set forth in this Constitution. And together with the venerable Fathers, we, by the apostolic power given to us by Christ, approve, enact, and establish in the Holy Spirit each and all the decrees in this Constitution and command that what has been thus established in the Council be promulgated for the glory of God.

SACRAM LITURGIAM
ON PUTTING INTO EFFECT
SOME PRESCRIPTIONS OF THE
CONSTITUTION ON THE LITURGY

APOSTOLIC LETTER ISSUED
MOTU PROPRIO
POPE PAUL VI
JANUARY 25, 1964

AN OVERVIEW OF *SACRAM LITURGIAM*
Corinna Laughlin

Sacram Liturgiam (SL) has the distinction of being the first document on the liturgy to appear after the promulgation of *Sacrosanctum Concilium* (SC). It thus marks the earliest steps toward implementing the Second Vatican Council's liturgical reforms. This brief *motu proprio* lays out the plan for beginning the work of reform, and includes some specific directives on changes that may (or must) take place before the revision of the rites can occur. The *motu proprio* appeared on January 25, 1964, shortly following the decisive vote on *Sacrosanctum Concilium* on December 4, 1963 and the conclusion of the second session of the Second Vatican Council.

BACKGROUND

Pope Paul VI had hoped to be able to provide a short instruction indicating the elements of *Sacrosanctum Concilium* that could be implemented immediately before the end of the second session. In October 1963, several weeks before the final vote on *Sacrosanctum Concilium* took place, he asked Cardinal Giacomo Lercaro of Bologna to prepare a draft document. Lercaro in turn invited a group of liturgists to review *Sacrosanctum Concilium* and submit their thoughts for the first steps toward implementation. (Renowned liturgists Josef Jungmann, A. G. Martimort, and Frederick McManus, all of whom were serving as Council *periti*[1], were among those involved in this preliminary work.) Pope Paul VI was rightly concerned about two extremes of reaction to the Council's liturgical reforms: on the one hand, those who would leap into changes without sufficient guidance, and on the other, those who might take a lengthy *vacatio legis*[2] as an excuse to do nothing at all. The *motu proprio* would help rein in the former and prod the latter to action.

The final draft was submitted to Pope Paul VI on November 21. This did not allow sufficient time for the document to be completed and distributed before the end of the second session of the Council. In his closing address, Pope Paul VI both lauded the achievements of the Council and offered a word of caution, specifically about the liturgy. To attain the true ends of *Sacrosanctum Concilium*, he said:

> It is necessary that no attempt should be made to introduce into the official prayer of the Church private changes or singular rites, nor should anyone arrogate to himself the right to interpret arbitrarily the Constitution on the Liturgy which today we promulgate, before opportune and authoritative instructions are given. Furthermore the reforms which will be prepared by postconciliar bodies must first receive official approbation. The

---

1. *Periti* is Latin for "experts." In regards to the Second Vatican Council, it refers to the theologians who were consulted during the duration of the Council.

2. The period of time between when a law is first issued and when it legally takes effect.

nobility of ecclesiastical prayer and its musical expression throughout the world, is something no one would wish to disturb or to damage.[3]

Ultimately, the draft for the *motu proprio* underwent still more revision before it finally appeared six weeks after the Council Fathers had returned home, on January 25, 1964. The date chosen was significant: It was the fifth anniversary of the announcement of the Council by Pope John XXIII on January 25, 1959.

INTRODUCING THE WORK OF REFORM

Sacram Liturgiam consists of an explanatory introduction followed by eleven points, noting specific elements of *Sacrosanctum Concilium*, which either may or must be put into effect following the established *vacatio legis*.

The introduction of the document places the reforms of the liturgy in the context of history: Paul VI observes that it has been the concern of prior popes and of the bishops that the liturgy be "safeguarded, developed, and, where necessary, reformed."[4] This care for the liturgy is demonstrated by past legislation on liturgical matters, and most particularly by *Sacrosanctum Concilium*, approved by the bishops—as Paul VI takes care to point out—by a nearly unanimous vote.

Concern for the liturgy is not just one among many concerns facing Church leaders. Since our earthly liturgy is "a foretaste of that heavenly liturgy celebrated in the holy city of Jerusalem toward which we journey as pilgrims,"[5] our concern for the liturgy is really an expression of our eagerness to reach the heavenly city. The more earnest we are in our pilgrimage, the more eager we will be to seek more perfect worship, as "the hearts of the faithful . . . are therefore drawn, even compelled, to seek this holiness."[6]

Since the purpose of the liturgical reforms is first and foremost to assist this pilgrimage toward heaven, it is essential that it be undertaken without delay. All "the faithful, and especially priests"[7] are urged to study *Sacrosanctum Concilium* and to prepare themselves to implement its changes "wholeheartedly."[8] Bishops are enjoined to "immediate, intense effort" to help all the faithful to "grasp the innate power and value of the liturgy and at the same time participate devoutly, body and soul, in the rites of the Church."[9] There are to be no exceptions: the reforms of the liturgy demand that bishops, priests, and faithful plunge into a study of the liturgy adapted to "their age, particular state in life, and level of culture."[10] *Sacrosanctum Concilium* is for everyone.

As the *motu proprio* makes clear, *Sacrosanctum Concilium* is the beginning, not the end, of the reform of the liturgy. It would require an enormous amount of work to bring the precepts of this document to life in the Church.

---

3. Closing Address of Pope Paul VI at the Second Session, December 4, 1963. Reprinted in Xavier Rynne, *The Second Session: The Debates and Decrees of Vatican Council II*, September 29 to December 4, 1963, p. 369.

4. *Sacram Liturgiam* (SL), paragraph 1.

5. *Sacrosanctum Concilium* (SC), 8.

6. SL, paragraph 3.

7. Ibid., paragraph 4.

8. Ibid.

9. Ibid.

10. Ibid.

Sacram Liturgiam includes the very important announcement of "a special commission," charged with bringing about the reforms with "the wisdom and prudence required."[11] This group, called the Consilium, was of enormous importance to the reform of the liturgy. The group began to take shape in December 1963 and would eventually consist of about fifty members (bishops) assisted by about one hundred and fifty consultors (experts in various fields, primarily priests, but including some lay members as well).

IMMEDIATE IMPACT OF *SACROSANCTUM CONCILIUM*

Clearly, the work of the Consilium would take a considerable amount of time, but in the meantime the "anticipated fruits of grace"[12] of *Sacrosanctum Concilium* should not be withheld from the faithful. The *motu proprio* continues with a list of elements that can be implemented at once, as early as the month following the publication of the document—the First Sunday of Lent, February 16, 1964.

The first items[13] have to do with the clergy. In keeping with SC 15, 16, and 17, the *motu proprio* directs that liturgy should immediately be added to the course of study in seminaries and houses of religious formation. No time is to be wasted: "orderly and intense"[14] study of the liturgy should be available to future priests by the beginning of the next academic year.

As called for by *Sacrosanctum Concilium* (and, indeed, recommended in Pope Pius XII's 1947 encyclical *Mediator Dei*) a liturgical commission should be established in every diocese, as well as commissions on music and on art, though the three may be combined if necessary.

The next prescriptions[15] impact the assembly. The document's call for more preaching—Homilies on Sundays and feasts—is to be put into effect immediately. The Sacraments of Confirmation and Marriage are to be celebrated, whenever possible, within the Mass, following the Homily. In the case of weddings celebrated outside of Mass, the liturgy is to be expanded: "the epistle and gospel of the nuptial Mass are to be read in the vernacular"[16] and the nuptial blessing is to be included.

The next four articles[17] relate to the Divine Office. These are the changes that would have the most immediate impact on priests and religious. During the Council debates on the liturgy, a considerable amount of time had been dedicated to the Divine Office, which was based on a monastic model, and could be quite burdensome in its length for busy priests and religious living and working outside of a monastery. Pending the revision of the Office (Liturgy of the Hours), several changes are permitted. The Hour of Prime, which was one of the "little hours,"[18] usually joined to Lauds (Morning Prayer), may be omitted altogether, and those not bound by a monastic rule can choose from among the other

---

11. Ibid., paragraph 5.
12. Ibid., paragraph 6.
13. See ibid., I–II.
14. Ibid, I.
15. See ibid., III–V.
16. Ibid., V.
17. See ibid., VI–IX.
18. Ibid, VI.

"little hours"[19] of Terce, Sext, and None whichever is most suited to the time of day. Bishops are given permission to dispense the obligation to pray the Office under certain circumstances, for pastoral need, or even to substitute another form of prayer. Religious communities are free to pray the Office in keeping with their own tradition, whether "some part of the divine office or a little office."[20] If it is "structured like the divine office and duly approved,"[21] the community may receive permission to use it. Finally, the *motu proprio* emphasizes the use of the vernacular for the Divine Office,[22] even though it will take time for vernacular editions to be prepared.

Sacram Liturgiam ends with questions of authority and liturgical change. While *Sacrosanctum Concilium* gives considerable authority to the "various kinds of competent territorial bodies of bishops lawfully established,"[23] the *motu proprio* clarifies and limits this authority: "we decree that for the present these must be national bodies."[24] The document ends on a cautionary note, echoing SC 22 with a reminder that the Church—that is, "the Holy See and the bishop"[25]—alone has authority to regulate the reform of the liturgy, and "no other person, not even a priest" may add or take away anything from the liturgy.

CONCLUSION

The changes called for by *Sacram Liturgiam* are quite small, and reflect a cautious approach in the midst of the fervor of enthusiasm around the promulgation of *Sacrosanctum Concilium*. Reception of the *motu proprio* was mixed, and many changes were made to the text following its first release. The official version published in *Acta Apostolicae Sedis*, was quite different in a number of places from the first edition as it appeared in *L'Osservatore Romano*. For example, the first version indicated that vernacular texts were to be proposed (*propositas*) by the territorial groups of bishops, and recognized and approved by the Holy See (*recognoscendas atque probandas*). This was a move away from the provisions of *Sacrosanctum Concilium*, and the final corrected version, citing SC 36, states that the bishops will approve vernacular texts (*approbandas*), while the Holy See will review or confirm them (*probanda seu confirmanda*). The struggle between centralized authority and decentralization, which characterized many of the Council debates, continued to play out in the postconciliar documents, including *Sacram Liturgiam*—which can claim to be the very first.

---

19. Ibid.
20. Ibid., VIII.
21. Ibid., VIII.
22. See ibid., IX.
23. SC, 22 § 2.
24. SL, X.
25. Ibid., XI.

SACRAM LITURGIAM

ON PUTTING INTO EFFECT SOME PRESCRIPTIONS OF THE CONSTITUTION ON THE SACRED LITURGY

MOTU PROPRIO
PAUL VI
JANUARY 25, 1964

That the sacred liturgy be carefully safeguarded, developed, and, where necessary, reformed has been the concern of earlier popes, of ourself, and of the bishops of the Church. The many published documents on liturgical topics, known to all, confirm this. So does the Constitution on the Liturgy, approved with near unanimity by Vatican Council II in solemn session and promulgated 4 December 1963.

The concern for the liturgy rests on the fact that "in the earthly liturgy we take part in a foretaste of that heavenly liturgy celebrated in the holy city of Jerusalem toward which we journey as pilgrims, where Christ is sitting at the right hand of God, a minister of the holies and of the true tabernacle (see Rv 21:2; Col 3:1; Heb 8:2); we sing a hymn to the Lord's glory with the whole company of heaven; venerating the memory of the saints, we hope for some part and communion with them; we eagerly await the Savior, our Lord Jesus Christ, until he, our life, shall appear and we too will appear with him in glory (see Phil 3:20; Col 3:2)."[1]

The hearts of the faithful who so worship God, the source and exemplar of all holiness, are therefore drawn, even compelled, to seek this holiness and in this way to become in this earthly pilgrimage "seekers of holy Zion."[2]

Accordingly, our foremost concern is clearly that the faithful, and especially priests, dedicate themselves first of all to the study of the Constitution on the Liturgy and from this moment on prepare themselves to carry out its prescriptions wholeheartedly as soon as these take effect. Because by the very nature of the case the understanding and dissemination of liturgical laws must go into effect without delay, we earnestly exhort bishops of dioceses to an immediate, intense effort, aided by their sacred ministers, "the stewards of God's mysteries,"[3] so that their own faithful, in keeping with their age, particular state in life, and level of culture will grasp the innate power and value of the liturgy and at the same time participate devoutly, body and soul, in the rites of the Church.[4]

---

1. SC art. 8.
2. Hymn of lauds, feast of the Dedication of a Church.
3. 1 Cor 4:1.
4. See SC art. 19.

Many of the prescriptions of the Constitution clearly cannot be put into effect in a short period of time, since some of the rites must first be revised and new liturgical books prepared. In order that this work may be carried out in the wisdom and prudence required, we are setting up a special commission with the principal task of seeing that the prescriptions of the Constitution are put into effect.

Other norms of the Constitution, however, are applicable now; we desire their immediate observance, so that the faithful may no longer be without the anticipated fruits of grace.

By apostolic authority and *motu proprio*, therefore, we prescribe and decree that the following norms shall go into effect beginning with the First Sunday of Lent, 16 February 1964, the expiration date of the established *vacatio legis*.

I.   The norms in art. 15, 16, and 17 on the teaching of liturgy in seminaries, houses of study of religious, and theological faculties are to be incorporated into their programs of study in such a way that with the beginning of the next academic year students may devote themselves to liturgical studies in an orderly and intense way.

II.   In keeping with the norms of art. 45 and 46, in all dioceses there is to be a commission that is entrusted, under the bishop's direction, with the duty of increasing the knowledge and furthering the progress of the liturgy.

In this matter it may be advantageous for several dioceses to have a joint commission.

Each diocese should also, as far as possible, have two other commissions, one for music, the other for art.

In some dioceses it will often be advisable to merge the three commissions into one.

III.   On the date already established, the norms of art. 52 shall take effect, namely, that there be a homily during Mass on Sundays and holydays of obligation.

IV.   We direct the implementation of the part of art. 71 that permits the sacrament of confirmation to be celebrated, when convenient, within Mass after the reading of the gospel and the homily.

V.   Regarding art. 78, the sacrament of marriage is normally to be celebrated within Mass, after the gospel has been read and the homily given.

Should marriage be celebrated without a Mass, the following regulations, pending revision of the entire rite, are to be observed: at the beginning of the rite, following a brief instruction,[5] the epistle and gospel of the nuptial Mass are to be read in the vernacular; then the blessing found in the *Rituale Romanum*, tit. VIII, cap. III is always to be given to the spouses.

---

5. See SC art. 35, § 3.

VI.   Although the order for divine office has not yet been revised and reformed, in keeping with art. 89, those not bound by choral obligation now have our permission, from the expiration date of the *vacatio legis*, to omit the hour of prime and to choose from among the other little hours the one best suited to the time of day.

We make this concession with the full confidence that sacred ministers will not grow slack in devotion, but rather that, if they diligently carry out the duties of their priestly office for the love of God, they will see themselves as going through the day closely united in spirit with him.

VII.   Also in regard to the divine office, Ordinaries may, in particular cases and for just cause, dispense their subjects from the obligation, in whole or in part, or may replace it with something else.[6]

VIII. In regard also to recitation of the office, we declare that members of any institute of religious perfection who by reason of their own rule recite either some part of the divine office or a little office, structured like the divine office and duly approved, shall be counted as celebrating public prayer with the Church.[7]

IX.   To those bound to recite the divine office art. 101 of the Constitution grants the faculty—in various ways and for various classes of people—to use the vernacular instead of Latin. Therefore it seems advisable to make it clear that the various vernacular versions must be drawn up and approved by the competent, territorial ecclesiastical authority, as provided in art. 36, §§ 3 and 4; and that, as provided in art. 36, § 3, the acts of this authority require due approval, that is, confirmation, of the Holy See. This is the course to be taken whenever any Latin liturgical text is translated into the vernacular by the authority already mentioned.

X.   Whenever the Constitution (art. 22, § 2), entrusts regulation of the liturgy, within certain specified limits, to various types of competent, lawfully constituted, territorial assemblies of bishops, we decree that for the present these must be national bodies.

In such national assemblies, besides the residential bishops, all those mentioned in CIC can. 292 may participate and vote; coadjutor and auxiliary bishops may also be summoned to meetings.

Passage of lawful decrees in these bodies requires two-thirds of the votes, cast by secret ballot.

XI.   Finally, we want it understood that over and above the liturgical matters changed by this Apostolic Letter or made effective before the date established, regulation of the liturgy depends exclusively on the authority of the Church, i.e., of the Holy See and of the bishop in accordance with the law; therefore no

---

6. See SC art. 97.
7. See SC art. 98.

other person, not even a priest, may add, take away, or change anything in matters of liturgy.[8]

We order that all matters decreed by this Letter, issued *motu proprio*, are confirmed and established, anything to the contrary notwithstanding.

---

8. See SC art. 22, §§ 1 and 3.

INTER OECUMENICI
FIRST INSTRUCTION ON THE
ORDERLY CARRYING OUT
OF THE
CONSTITUTION ON THE SACRED LITURGY

SACRED CONGREGATION OF RITES,
CONSILIUM FOR THE IMPLEMENTATION OF THE
CONSTITUTION ON THE SACRED LITURGY
SEPTEMBER 26, 1964

AN OVERVIEW OF *INTER OECUMENICI*

Michael R. Prendergast

The first instruction issued after *Sacrosanctum Concilium* (SC), *Inter Oecumenici* (IO), received approval by Pope Paul VI on September 26, 1964. This instruction was prepared by the Consilium, a group of experts appointed by the Holy Father who were international, competent, collegial, and productive and whose mission was in support of a liturgy open to renewal. By the mandate of Pope Paul VI, the instruction was ordered to be published and faithfully observed by the Church, beginning on the First Sunday of Lent, March 7, 1965. The instruction makes it clear that spiritual formation is essential to the agenda of SC. "Necessary before all else . . . is the shared conviction that the Constitution on the Liturgy has as its objective not simply to change liturgical forms and texts but rather to bring to life the kind of formation of the faithful and ministry of pastors that will have their summit and source in the liturgy."[1] The liturgical apostolate demands the effort to respond to the requirements of fidelity to SC and to the new rubrics for the celebration of the sacraments.

Between the time SC was promulgated on December 4, 1963 and the first instruction on September 26, 1964 Pope Paul VI issued the *motu proprio, Sacrum Liturgiam (SL)*, on January 25, 1964. SL was a prelude to IO in that the Holy Father outlined eleven norms that could be observed immediately so that "the faithful may no longer be without the anticipated fruits of grace:"[2] These norms were to be implemented beginning on the First Sunday of Lent, February 16, 1964. These norms included:

- The teaching of liturgy in seminaries.[3]

- Bishops who regulate the liturgy within specific limits are to be territorial assemblies of bishops (national bodies).[4]

- Creation of a diocesan liturgical commission and a commission for music and art.[5]

- A Homily as part of Mass on Sundays and Holydays of Obligation.[6]

- Confirmation, celebrated following the Liturgy of the Word at Mass.[7]

- Marriage, celebrated during Mass along with the epistle, Gospel, and nuptial blessing being read in the vernacular.[8]

---

1. See *Sacrosanctum Concilium* (SC), 10; *Inter Oecumenici (IO)*, 5.
2. *Sacram Liturgiam* (SL), introductory paragraphs.
3. IO, 14–18.
4. Ibid., 20–31.
5. Ibid., 44–47.
6. Ibid., 53–55.
7. Ibid., 64–67.
8. Ibid., 70–75.

- Concern for the obligations and dispensations for the Liturgy of the Hours.[9]

- The design of churches and altars that facilitate the assembly's full participation in the liturgy.[10]

The Holy Father spoke of the liturgical reform to an assembly of Italian bishops in April 1964 who were experts on liturgical reform and to a consistory of cardinals in June 1964 on carrying out the reforms of the liturgy.

The first and practical instruction on the reform of the liturgy in the Roman Rite strongly emphasizes the liturgical formation of the clergy, seminarians, and laity. IO is an intermediary instruction, promogulated when various minor changes were made in the Mass. In 1964 the most significant changes were the restoration of concelebration and permission to celebrate the sacraments and most of the Mass in the vernacular. Mass facing the people also began to spread widely in most countries.

The instruction begins with an introduction outlining three key points: the nature of the instruction, principles to be kept in mind, and hope-filled results. This introduction calls for both pastors and the faithful to "deepen their understanding of its genuine spirit and with good will put it into practice,"[11] when celebrating the liturgy. The papal mandate attached to the instruction authorizes certain measures to go into effect immediately "before revision of the liturgical books."[12] The Holy Father suggested that the reform of the liturgy would be successful if the promotion of active participation proceeded "step by step in stages and if pastors present and explain it to them by means of the needed catechesis."[13] Central to the celebration of the liturgy is a "living experience of the paschal mystery"[14] and the celebration of the sacraments, sacramentals, and the liturgical year. The instruction speaks of the importance of "rightly linking pastoral activity with the liturgy and carrying out a pastoral liturgy not as if it were set apart and existing in isolation but as it is closely joined to other pastoral works," what the instruction calls a "close, living union between liturgy, catechesis, religious formation, and preaching."[15] Finally, the introduction calls on bishops and priests to "attach ever greater importance to their whole pastoral ministry as it is focused toward the liturgy."[16]

The instruction contains five chapters that parallel SC: "General Norms," "Mystery of the Eucharist," "The Other Sacraments and Sacramentals," "Divine Office," and "Designing Churches and Altars" and how to apply them.

There are thirty-eight paragraphs in the chapter of "General Norms." This part of the instruction lays out how the norms apply[17] including a strong endorsement

---

9. Ibid., 78–89.

10. Ibid., 90–99.

11. Ibid., 1.

12. Ibid., 3.

13. Ibid., 4.

14. Ibid., 6.

15. Ibid., 7.

16. Ibid., 8.

17. See ibid., 9–11.

that instruction and preparation of the faithful is required.[18] The following two sections of the instruction apply to the formation of clerics and their spiritual life. The instruction lays out the requirements for liturgical formation in seminaries and religious houses,[19] the ongoing education of clerics and the creation of institutes of pastoral liturgy.[20] All of the instruction should be applied to curriculum in seminaries and houses of study.[21] The instruction calls for celebrations of the liturgy to be carried out with "dignity,"[22] mentions the inclusion of a cantor and commentator,[23] and calls for sacred furnishings and vestments to have the "mark of genuine Christian art."[24] In regard to the liturgical formation of the clerics' spiritual life we find the call for the liturgy to be fully celebrated in the realm of spirituality and theology,[25] celebrated daily and on Sunday, and Holyday celebrations of the Mass should be sung and include a Homily.[26] The Hours of Lauds, Vespers, and Compline should be celebrated in common and when possible seminarians are encouraged to "sing evening prayer in the cathedral church."[27] Devotions are to "harmonize with the liturgy, in keeping with the Constitution."[28] This application should be applied to both men and women members of religious institutes.[29]

Section V of Chapter One concerns the liturgical formation of the faithful and their calling for their active participation "in keeping with their way of life, and stage of religious development."[30] The instruction calls for the assistance of lay religious associations to share "more fully in the Church's life" and work with their pastors to promote the liturgical life of the parish.[31]

The next twelve paragraphs address the competent authority in liturgical matters.[32] This section of the instruction lays out the way in which Conferences of Bishops (referred to as territories of bishops in the document) and local bishops regulate the liturgy, which is in "keeping with the norms and spirit of the Constitution on the Liturgy."[33] The section concludes with noting that local territorial bishops need approval "that is confirmation of the Holy See"[34] of local decrees.

---

18. See ibid., 10.
19. See ibid., 11a.
20. See ibid., 11c.
21. See ibid., 12.
22. Ibid., 13a.
23. See ibid., 13b.
24. Ibid., 13c.
25. See ibid., 14.
26. See ibid., 15.
27. Ibid., 16.
28. SC, 13.
29. See IO, 18.
30. SC, 19.
31. IO, 19; see SC, 42.
32. See IO, 20–31.
33. Ibid., 22.
34. Ibid., 31.

The instruction reminds the celebrant that "parts belonging to the choir of the people . . . are not said privately by the priest,"[35] and calls for liturgical services to "manifest a noble simplicity."[36] Two paragraphs are devoted to the importance of the Word of God[37] even in places without a resident priest. The next section on the translation of vernacular texts calls for consultation with "bishops of neighboring regions using the same language"[38] and that celebrations in the native tongue are appropriate "for people of a foreign language, especially for immigrants."[39] The chants to be used in the liturgy require the "approval by the competent, territorial ecclesiastical authority."[40]

The document calls for individual conferences of bishops to establish commissions that include experts in liturgical and pastoral matters[41] that will assist bishops "to promote pastoral-liturgical activity"[42] in an effective manner. Finally, diocesan liturgical commissions are to work to promote "pastoral-liturgical activity in the diocese."[43]

Chapter Two on the "Mystery of the Eucharist" includes thirteen paragraphs that focus on the Order of Mass; the readings and the chants of the Mass; the Homily; the Universal Prayer; and the use of the vernacular in the Mass. The first paragraphs are instructions to be observed by the priest celebrant including granting permission to pray the Lord's Prayer in the vernacular[44] and names "the formulary for distributing Holy Communion, Corpus Christi" but now calls for the signing of the communicant with the host to be omitted.[45] The instruction calls for the Liturgy of the Word to be proclaimed "facing the people"[46] from a lectern or "at the edge of the sanctuary."[47] The importance of the Homily in the Sunday Mass is stressed and is even "recommended, especially on some of the weekdays of Advent and Lent or on other occasions when the faithful come to church in large numbers."[48] The Homily is meant to have an "intimate connection with at least the principal seasons and feasts of the liturgical year, that is, with the mystery of redemption."[49] The Universal Prayer is to be introduced in places where it is not the custom and "a deacon, cantor, or other suitable minister may sing the intentions or intercessions."[50]

While Part V of this section on the "Mystery of the Eucharist" allows for the vernacular at the Mass, and personal Missals are still to include the "Latin

---

35. Ibid., 32.
36. Ibid., 36; see SC, 34.
37. See ibid., 37–38.
38. Ibid., 40c.
39. Ibid., 41.
40. Ibid, 42.
41. See ibid., 44.
42. Ibid., 46.
43. Ibid., 47a.
44. See ibid., 48g.
45. See ibid., 48i.
46. Ibid., 49.
47. Ibid, 49a.
48. Ibid., 53.
49. Ibid., 55; see SC, 102–104.
50. Ibid., 56.

text as well"[51] so that the people may sing or recite the ordinary parts of the Mass in Latin. The faithful may receive Holy Communion at the morning Mass of Christmas Day and Easter Sunday even if they had received Communion at Midnight Mass or at the Easter Vigil.[52]

Chapter Three is about "Other Sacraments and Sacramentals." Here the document speaks of the use of the vernacular[53]; removes certain elements from the rites of infant and adult Baptism[54]; allows for a continuous rite for the Anointing of the Sick with Viaticum and the celebration of the Sacrament of Confession[55]; calls for the Rite of Marriage to be celebrated within Mass (following a Homily) which "is never to be omitted"[56]; as well as the importance of the nuptial blessing.[57] This chapter concludes with a reference to the sacramentals[58] and continues to reserve certain blessings for the bishop.[59]

Chapter Four on the "Divine Office" addresses the reform of the Office. Those bound by choir are obligated to celebrate the Hours in community each day but may be dispensed from doing so "for a just reason."[60] The praying of the Office in the Latin language is highly valued.[61] Clerics who are granted the "right to use the vernacular: when celebrating the Liturgy of the Hours must use a Breviary that contains both Latin and the vernacular language of the cleric."[62]

Chapter V on the "Designing of Churches and Altars" ensures that in the building, restoration, or adaptation of churches the space is suited for active participation of the faithful[63] in the liturgical celebrations.[64] Each church is to have a freestanding main altar, "to permit walking around it and celebration facing the people."[65] The chair for the priest celebrant should avoid "any semblance of a throne."[66] Crosses and candlesticks used to be placed on the altar. The document now states crosses and candlesticks may "also be placed next to [the altar]."[67] The reservation of the Eucharist may be "in the middle of the main altar" or "in another, special and properly adorned part of the church."[68] The place of the organ and choir must show "that the singers and the organist form part of the united community."[69] The faithful are to take their place where they

---

51. Ibid., 57c.
52. Ibid., 60.
53. See ibid., 61.
54. See ibid., 62–63.
55. See ibid., 68.
56. Ibid., 70.
57. See ibid., 74a, d.
58. See SC, 79.
59. See IO, 77.
60. Ibid., 79.
61. See ibid., 85.
62. Ibid., 89.
63. See SC, 124.
64. See IO, 90.
65. Ibid., 91,
66. Ibid., 92.
67. Ibid., 95.
68. Ibid.
69. Ibid., 97.

will "assure their proper participation in the sacred rites"[70] but the custom of reserving places for special persons is to be suppressed.[71] The use of sound equipment so that all may hear is encouraged. The baptistery must also "clearly express the dignity of the sacrament of baptism and [be] a place well suited to communal celebrations."[72]

Changes introduced by *Inter Oecumenici*, such as the vernacular liturgy, the readings proclaimed facing the people and read by a layman, the omissions of the Gospel passage read at the end of Mass, and the prayers after Mass, the new formula for distributing Holy Communion, (*Corpus Christi*, "The Body of Christ"), are seen as the key practices that echo *Sacrosanctum Concilium's* call for full, conscious and active participation in the liturgy.[73]

---

70. Ibid., 98.
71. See SC, 32b.
72. Ibid., 99; see SC, 27.
73. See SC, 14.

INTER OECUMENICI
ON THE ORDERLY CARRYING OUT OF THE CONSTITUTION ON THE LITURGY
INSTRUCTION
SACRED CONGREGATION OF RITES, CONSILIUM FOR THE IMPLEMENTATION OF THE CONSTITUTION ON THE SACRED LITURGY SEPTEMBER 26, 1964

INTRODUCTION

I. NATURE OF THIS INSTRUCTION

1.   Among the Second Vatican Ecumenical Council's primary achievements must be counted the Constitution on the Liturgy, since it regulates the most exalted sphere of the Church's activity. The document will have ever richer effects as pastors and faithful alike deepen their understanding of its genuine spirit and with good will put it into practice.

2.   The Consilium, which Pope Paul VI established by the Motu Proprio *Sacram Liturgiam*, has promptly taken up its two appointed tasks: to carry out the directives of the Constitution and of *Sacram Liturgiam* and to provide the means for interpreting these documents and putting them into practice.

3.   That these documents should immediately be properly carried out everywhere and any possible doubts on interpretation removed are matters of the utmost importance. Therefore, by papal mandate, the Consilium has prepared the present Instruction. It sets out more sharply the functions of conferences of bishops in liturgical matters, explains more fully those principles stated in general terms in the aforementioned documents, and authorizes or mandates that those measures that are practicable before revision of the liturgical books go into effect immediately.

II. PRINCIPLES TO BE KEPT IN MIND

4.   The reason for deciding to put these things into practice now is that the liturgy may ever more fully satisfy the conciliar intent on promoting active participation of the faithful.

The faithful will more readily respond to the overall reform of the liturgy if this proceeds step by step in stages and if pastors present and explain it to them by means of the needed catechesis.

5.   Necessary before all else, however, is the shared conviction that the Constitution on the Liturgy has as its objective not simply to change liturgical forms and texts but rather to bring to life the kind of formation of the faithful and ministry of pastors that will have their summit and source in the liturgy (see SC art. 10). That is the purpose of the changes made up to now and of those yet to come.

6.   Pastoral activity guided toward the liturgy has its power in being a living experience of the paschal mystery, in which the Son of God, incarnate and made obedient even to the death of the cross, has in his resurrection and ascension been raised up in such a way that he communicates his divine life to the world. Through this life those who are dead to sin and conformed to Christ "may live no longer for themselves but for him who for their sake died and was raised" (2 Cor 5:15).

Faith and the sacraments of faith accomplish this, especially baptism (see SC art. 6) and the mystery of the eucharist (see SC art. 47), the center of the other sacraments and sacramentals (see SC art. 61) and of the cycle of celebrations that in the course of the year unfold Christ's paschal mystery (see SC art. 102–107).

7.   The liturgy, it is true, does not exhaust the entire activity of the Church (see SC art. 9); nevertheless the greatest care must be taken about rightly linking pastoral activity with the liturgy and carrying out a pastoral liturgy not as if it were set apart and existing in isolation but as it is closely joined to other pastoral works.

Especially necessary is a close, living union between liturgy, catechesis, religious formation, and preaching.

III. RESULTS TO BE HOPED FOR

8.   Bishops and their assistants in the priesthood should, therefore, attach ever greater importance to their whole pastoral ministry as it is focused toward the liturgy. Then the faithful themselves will richly partake of the divine life through sharing in the sacred celebrations and, changed into the leaven of Christ and the salt of the earth, will proclaim that divine life and pass it on to others.

CHAPTER 1

General Norms

I. HOW THE NORMS APPLY

9.   The practical norms, in the Constitution and in this Instruction, as well as practices this Instruction allows or mandates even before revision of the liturgical books, even if they are part of the Roman Rite, may be applied in other Latin rites, due regard being given to the provisions of law.

10.   Matters that this Instruction commits to the power of the competent, territorial ecclesiastical authority can and should be put into effect only by such authority through lawful decrees.

In every case the time and circumstances in which such decrees begin to take effect are to be stipulated, with a reasonable preceding interval (*vacatio*) provided for instruction and preparation of the faithful regarding their observance.

II. THE LITURGICAL FORMATION OF CLERICS (SC ART. 15–16 AND 18)

11.   Regarding the liturgical formation of the clergy:

a. In theological faculties there shall be a chair of liturgy so that all students may receive the requisite liturgical instruction; in seminaries and religious houses of studies local Ordinaries and major superiors shall see to it that as soon as possible there is a properly trained specialist in liturgy.

b. Professors appointed to teach liturgy shall be trained as soon as possible, in keeping with the norms of the Constitution art. 15.

c. For the continuing liturgical education of clerics, especially those already working in the Lord's vineyard, institutes in pastoral liturgy shall be set up wherever possible.

12.   The course in liturgy shall be of appropriate duration, to be fixed in the curriculum of studies by competent authority, and shall follow a method patterned on the norm of the Constitution art. 16.

13.   Liturgical celebrations shall be carried out as perfectly as possible. Therefore:

a. Rubrics shall be observed exactly and ceremonies carried out with dignity, under the careful supervision of superiors and with the required preparation beforehand.

b. Clerics shall frequently exercise the liturgical functions proper to their order, i.e., of deacon, subdeacon, acolyte, reader, as well as those of commentator and cantor.

c. Churches and chapels, all sacred furnishings and vestments shall bear the mark of genuine Christian art, including the contemporary.

III. LITURGICAL FORMATION OF THE CLERIC'S SPIRITUAL LIFE (SC ART. 17)

14.   In order that clerics may be trained for a full participation in liturgical celebrations and for a spiritual life deriving from them and to be shared later with others, the Constitution on the Liturgy shall be put into full effect in seminaries and religious houses of studies in keeping with the norms of the documents of the Holy See, the superiors and faculty all working together in harmony to achieve this goal. In order to guide clerics properly toward the liturgy: books are to be recommended on liturgy, especially in its theological and spiritual dimensions,

and made available in the library in sufficient numbers; there are to be meditations and conferences, drawn above all from the fonts of sacred Scripture and liturgy (see Const. art. 35, 2); and those communal devotions are to be observed that are in keeping with Christian customs and practice and are suited to the various seasons of the liturgical year.

15.   The eucharist, center of the whole spiritual life, is to be celebrated daily and with the use of different forms of celebration best suited to the condition of the participants.

On Sundays and on the other greater holydays a sung Mass shall be celebrated, with all who live in the house participating; there is to be a homily and, as far as possible, all who are not priests shall receive communion. Once the new rite has been published, concelebration is permitted for priests, especially on more solemn feasts, if pastoral needs do not require individual celebration.

At least on the great festivals it would be well for seminarians to participate in the eucharist gathered round the bishop in the cathedral church.

16.   Even if not yet bound by obligation to divine office, clerics should each day recite or sing in common lauds in the morning as morning prayer and vespers in the evening as evening prayer or compline at the end of the day. Superiors should, as far as possible, themselves take part in this common recitation. Sufficient time shall be provided in the daily schedule for clerics in sacred orders to pray the divine office.

At least on major festivals it would be well, when possible, for seminarians to sing evening prayer in the cathedral church.

17.   Religious devotions, arranged according to the laws or customs of each place or institute, shall be held in due esteem. Nevertheless, care should be taken that, especially if they are held in common, they harmonize with the liturgy, in keeping with the Constitution art. 13, and that they take into account the seasons of the liturgical year.

IV. LITURGICAL FORMATION OF MEMBERS OF RELIGIOUS INSTITUTES

18.   The foregoing articles on the liturgical formation of clerics' spiritual life are to be applied, with the required modifications, to both men and women members of religious institutes.

V. LITURGICAL FORMATION OF MEMBERS OF THE FAITHFUL (SC ART. 19)

19.   Pastors shall strive diligently and patiently to carry out the mandate of the Constitution on the liturgical formation of the faithful and on their active participation, both inward and outward, "in keeping with their age and condition, their way of life, and stage of religious development" (SC art. 19). They should be especially concerned about the liturgical formation and active participation of those involved in lay religious associations; such people have the responsibility of sharing more fully in the Church's life and of assisting their pastors in the effective promotion of parish liturgical life (see SC art. 42).

20.   Regulation of the liturgy belongs to the authority of the Church; no one, therefore, is to act on individual initiative in this matter, thereby, as might well happen, doing harm to the liturgy and to its reform under competent authority.

21.   The Holy See has the authority to reform and approve the general liturgical books; to regulate the liturgy in matters affecting the universal Church; to approve or confirm the *acta* and decisions of territorial authorities; and to accede to their proposals and requests.

22.   The bishop has the authority to regulate the liturgy within his own diocese, in keeping with the norms and spirit of the Constitution on the Liturgy, the decrees of the Holy See, and competent territorial authority.

23.   The various territorial assemblies of bishops that have responsibility for the liturgy by virtue of the Constitution art. 22 should for the time being be taken to mean one of the following:

    a. an assembly of all the bishops of a nation, in accordance with the norm of the Motu Proprio *Sacram Liturgiam* X;

    b. an assembly already lawfully constituted and consisting of the bishops— or of the bishops and other local Ordinaries—of several nations;

    c. an assembly yet to be constituted, with the permission of the Holy See, and consisting of the bishops—or of the bishops and local Ordinaries— of several nations, especially if the bishops in the individual nations are so few that it would be more advantageous for a group to be formed of those from various nations sharing the same language and culture.

If particular local conditions suggest another course, the matter should be referred to the Holy See.

24.   The following must be included in the call to any of the above-mentioned assemblies:

    a. residential bishops;

    b. abbots and prelates *nullius*;

    c. vicars and prefects apostolic;

    d. permanently appointed apostolic administrators of dioceses;

    e. all other local Ordinaries, except vicars general.

Coadjutor and auxiliary bishops may be called by the president, with the consent of the majority of the voting members of the assembly.

25.   Unless there is some other lawful provision for certain places and in view of special circumstances, the assembly must be convened:

   a. by the one who is the president, in the case of assemblies already lawfully constituted;

   b. in other cases, by the archbishop or bishop having right of precedence under the norm of law.

26.   The president, with the consent of the fathers, establishes the rules of order for dealing with issues and opens, transfers, extends, and adjourns the sessions of the assembly.

27.   A deliberative vote belongs to all those named in no. 24, including coadjutor and auxiliary bishops, unless the convening instrument expressly provides otherwise.

28.   Lawful enactment of decrees requires a two-thirds vote by secret ballot.

29.   The *acta* of the competent territorial authority, to be transmitted to the Holy See for approval, that is, confirmation, should include the following:

   a. the names of participants in the assembly;

   b. a report on matters dealt with;

   c. the outcome of the vote on each decree.

These *acta*, signed by the president and secretary of the assembly and stamped with a seal, shall be sent in duplicate to the Consilium.

30.   With regard to *acta* containing decrees on use of the vernacular and the manner of its introduction into the liturgy, the *acta*, following the Constitution on the Liturgy art. 36, § 3 and the Motu Proprio *Sacram Liturgiam* no. IX, should also contain:

   a. a list of the individual parts of the liturgy for which use of the vernacular has been decided;

   b. two copies of the liturgical texts prepared in the vernacular, one of which will be returned to the assembly of bishops;

   c. a brief report on the criteria used for the work of translation.

31.   The decrees of the territorial authority needing the approval, that is, confirmation, of the Holy See shall be promulgated and implemented only when they have received such approval, that is, confirmation.

32. Parts belonging to the choir or to the people and sung or recited by them are not said privately by the celebrant.

33. Nor are readings that are read or sung by the appropriate minister said privately by the celebrant.

VIII. DISCRIMINATION TO BE AVOIDED (SC ART. 32)

34. Individual bishops, or, if it seems advisable, regional or national conferences of bishops shall see to it that the Council's prohibition against preferential treatment of individuals or a social class either in the ceremonies or by outward display is respected in their territories.

35. In addition, pastors shall not neglect to ensure prudently and charitably that in the liturgical services and more especially in the celebration of Mass and the administration of the sacraments and sacramentals the equality of the faithful is clearly apparent and that any suggestion of moneymaking is avoided.

IX. SIMPLIFICATION OF CERTAIN RITES (SC ART. 34)

36. In order that liturgical services may manifest a noble simplicity more attuned to the spirit of the times:

   a. the celebrant and ministers shall bow to the choir only at the beginning and end of a service;

   b. incensation of the clergy, apart from those who are bishops, shall take place toward each side of the choir, with three swings of the censer;

   c. incensation shall be limited to the one altar where the liturgical rite is being celebrated;

   d. kissing of the hand and of objects presented or received shall be omitted.

X. CELEBRATIONS OF THE WORD OF GOD (SC ART. 35, § 4)

37. In places without a priest and where none is available for celebration of Mass on Sundays and holydays of obligation, a sacred celebration of the word of God with a deacon or even a properly appointed layperson presiding, shall be arranged, at the discretion of the local Ordinary.

The plan of such a celebration shall be almost the same as that of the liturgy of the word at Mass. Normally the epistle and gospel from the Mass of the day shall be read in the vernacular, with chants, especially from the psalms, before and between the readings. If the one presiding is a deacon, he shall give a homily; a nondeacon shall read a homily chosen by the bishop or the pastor. The whole celebration is to end with the universal prayer or prayer of the faithful and the Lord's Prayer.

38.　Celebrations of the word of God, to be promoted on the vigils of more solemn feast days, should also follow the structure of the liturgy of the word at Mass, although it is quite permissible to have but one reading.

Where there are several readings, their arrangement, for a clear perception of the progression of salvation history, should place the Old Testament reading before the one from the New Testament and should show the reading of the gospel to be the culmination of all.

39.　The diocesan liturgical commissions shall be responsible for suggesting and making available such resources as will ensure dignity and devotion in these celebrations of the word.

XI. VERNACULAR TRANSLATIONS OF LITURGICAL TEXTS (SC ART. 36 § 3)

40.　Vernacular translations of liturgical texts to be prepared in conformity with the norms of art. 36, § 3, will benefit from observing the following criteria.

 a. The basis of the translations is the Latin liturgical text. The version of the biblical passages should conform to the same Latin liturgical text. This does not, however, take away the right to revise that version, should it seem advisable, on the basis of the original text or of some clearer version.

 b. The liturgical commission mentioned in the Constitution art. 44 and in the present Instruction art. 44 is to have special responsibility for the preparation of translations of liturgical texts, with the institute of pastoral liturgy providing as much assistance as possible. But where there is no such commission, two or three bishops are to share responsibility for the translating; they are to choose experts, including the laity, in Scripture, liturgy, the biblical languages, Latin, the vernacular, and music. Sound translation of a liturgical text into the language of a people has to answer many requirements simultaneously.

 c. Where applicable, there should be consultation on translations with bishops of neighboring regions using the same language.

 d. In nations of several languages there should be a translation for each language, to be submitted to the bishops involved for careful examination.

 e. Special attention should be given to the high quality of books used for reading the liturgical text to the people in the vernacular, so that even the book's appearance may prompt greater reverence for the word of God and for sacred objects.

41.　Liturgical services held anywhere for people of a foreign language, especially for immigrants, members of a personal parish, or other like groups, may, with the consent of the local Ordinary, lawfully be celebrated in the native tongue of these faithful. Such celebrations are to conform to the limits for use of the vernacular and to the translation approved by the competent, territorial ecclesiastical authority for the language in question.

42.   Melodies for parts to be sung in the vernacular by celebrant and ministers must have the approval of the competent, territorial ecclesiastical authority.

43.   Particular liturgical books lawfully approved before the promulgation of the Constitution on the Liturgy and indults granted up to then, unless they conflict with the Constitution, remain in force until other dispositions are made as the reform of the liturgy is completed, in whole or in part.

XII. LITURGICAL COMMISSION OF THE ASSEMBLY OF BISHOPS (SC ART. 44)

44. The liturgical commission, which should be expeditiously established by the territorial authority, shall as far as possible be chosen from among the bishops themselves or at least include one of them, along with priests expert in liturgical and pastoral matters and designated by name for this office.

The members and consultants of the commission should ideally meet several times a year to deal with issues as a group.

45. The territorial authority may properly entrust the following to the commission:

a. to carry out studies and experiments in keeping with the norms of the Constitution art. 40, §§ 1 and 2;

b. to further practical initiatives for the whole region that will foster liturgical life and the application of the Constitution on the Liturgy;

c. to prepare studies and the resources required as a result of decrees of the plenary assembly of bishops;

d. to control pastoral liturgy in the whole nation, to see to the application of decrees of the plenary assembly, and to report on these matters to the assembly;

e. to further frequent consultation and promote collaboration with regional associations involved with Scripture, catechetics, pastoral care, music, and art, as well as with every kind of lay religious association.

46.   Members of the institute of pastoral liturgy, as well as experts called to assist the liturgical commission, shall be generous in aiding individual bishops to promote pastoral-liturgical activity more effectively in their territory.

47. The diocesan liturgical commission, under the direction of the bishop, has these responsibilities:

  a. to be fully informed on the state of pastoral-liturgical activity in the diocese;

  b. to carry out faithfully those proposals in liturgical matters made by the competent authority and to keep informed on the studies and programs taking place elsewhere in this field;

  c. to suggest and promote practical programs of every kind that may contribute to the advancement of liturgical life, especially in the interest of aiding priests laboring in the Lord's vineyard;

  d. to suggest, in individual cases or even for the whole diocese, timely, step-by-step measures for the work of pastoral liturgy, to appoint and to call upon people capable of helping priests in this matter as occasion arises, to propose suitable means and resources;

  e. to see to it that programs in the diocese designed to promote liturgy go forward with the cooperation and mutual help of other groups along the lines mentioned above (no. 45 e) regarding the liturgical commission of the assembly of bishops.

CHAPTER II

Mystery of the Eucharist

I. ORDO MISSAE (SC ART. 50)

48. Until reform of the entire *Ordo Missae*, the points that follow are to be observed:

  a. The celebrant is not to say privately those parts of the Proper sung or recited by the choir or the congregation.

  b. The celebrant may sing or recite the parts of the Ordinary together with the congregation or choir.

  c. In the prayers at the foot of the altar at the beginning of Mass Psalm 42 is omitted. All the prayers at the foot of the altar are omitted whenever there is another liturgical rite immediately preceding.

  d. In solemn Mass the subdeacon does not hold the paten but leaves it on the altar.

  e. In sung Masses the secret prayer or prayer over the gifts is sung and in other Masses recited aloud.

f. The doxology at the end of the canon, from *Per ipsum* through *Per omnia saecula saeculorum. R. Amen*, is to be sung or recited aloud. Throughout the whole doxology the celebrant slightly elevates the chalice with the host, omitting the signs of the cross, and genuflects at the end after the *Amen* response by the people.

g. In recited Masses the congregation may recite the Lord's Prayer in the vernacular along with the celebrant; in sung Masses the people may sing it in Latin along with the celebrant and, should the territorial ecclesiastical authority have so decreed, also in the vernacular, using melodies approved by the same authority.

h. The embolism after the Lord's Prayer shall be sung or recited aloud.

i. The formulary for distributing holy communion is to be, *Corpus Christi*. As he says these words, the celebrant holds the host slightly above the ciborium and shows it to the communicant, who responds: *Amen*, then receives communion from the celebrant, the sign of the cross with the host being omitted.

j. The last gospel is omitted; the Leonine Prayers are suppressed.

k. It is lawful to celebrate a sung Mass with only a deacon assisting.

l. It is lawful, when necessary, for bishops to celebrate a sung Mass following the form used by priests.

II. READINGS AND CHANTS BETWEEN READINGS (SC ART. 51)

49. In Masses celebrated with a congregation, the lessons, epistle, and gospel are to be read or sung facing the people:

a. at the lectern or at the edge of the sanctuary in solemn Masses;

b. at the altar, lectern, or the edge of the sanctuary—whichever is more convenient—in sung or recited Masses if sung or read by the celebrant; at the lectern or at the edge of the sanctuary if sung or read by someone else.

50. In nonsolemn Masses celebrated with the faithful participating a qualified reader or the server reads the lessons and epistles with the intervening chants; the celebrant sits and listens. A deacon or a second priest may read the gospel and he says the *Munda cor meum*, asks for the blessing, and, at the end, presents the Book of the Gospels for the celebrant to kiss.

51. In sung Masses, the lessons, epistle, and gospel, if in the vernacular, may simply be read.

52. For the reading or singing of the lessons, epistle, intervening chants, and gospel, the following is the procedure.

a. In solemn Masses the celebrant sits and listens to the lessons, the epistle, and chants. After singing or reading the epistle, the subdeacon goes to the celebrant for the blessing. At this point the celebrant, remaining seated, puts incense into the thurible and blesses it. During the singing of the *Alleluia* and verse or toward the end of other chants after the epistle, the celebrant rises to bless the deacon. From his place he listens to the gospel, kisses the Book of the Gospels, and, after the homily, intones the *Credo*, when prescribed. At the end of the *Credo* he returns to the altar with the ministers, unless he is to lead the prayer of the faithful.

b. The celebrant follows the same procedures in sung or recited Masses in which the lessons, epistle, intervening chants, and the gospel are sung or recited by the minister mentioned in no. 50.

c. In sung or recited Masses in which the celebrant sings or recites the gospel, during the singing or saying of the *Alleluia* and verse or toward the end of other chants after the epistle, he goes to the foot of the altar and there, bowing profoundly, says the *Munda cor meum*. He then goes to the lectern or to the edge of the sanctuary to sing or recite the gospel.

d. But in a sung or recited Mass if the celebrant sings or reads all the lessons at the lectern or at the edge of the sanctuary, he also, if necessary, recites the chants after the lessons and the epistle standing in the same place; then he says the *Munda cor meum*, facing the altar.

III. HOMILY (SC ART. 52)

53. There shall be a homily on Sundays and holydays of obligation at all Masses celebrated with a congregation, including conventual, sung, or pontifical Masses.

On days other than Sundays and holydays a homily is recommended, especially on some of the weekdays of Advent and Lent or on other occasions when the faithful come to church in large numbers.

54. A homily on the sacred text means an explanation, pertinent to the mystery celebrated and the special needs of the listeners, of some point in either the readings from sacred Scripture or in another text from the Ordinary or Proper of the day's Mass.

55. Because the homily is part of the liturgy for the day, any syllabus proposed for preaching within the Mass during certain periods must keep intact the intimate connection with at least the principal seasons and feasts of the liturgical year (see SC art. 102–104), that is, with the mystery of redemption.

IV. UNIVERSAL PRAYER OR PRAYER OF THE FAITHFUL (SC ART. 53)

56. In places where the universal prayer or prayer of the faithful is already the custom, it shall take place before the offertory, after the *Oremus*, and, for the time being, with formularies in use in individual regions. The celebrant is to

lead the prayer at either his chair, the altar, the lectern, or the edge of the sanctuary.

A deacon, cantor, or other suitable minister may sing the intentions or intercessions. The celebrant takes the introductions and concluding prayer, this being ordinarily the *Deus, refugium nostrum et virtus* (MR, Orationes diversae no. 20) or another prayer more suited to particular needs.

In places where the universal prayer or prayer of the faithful is not the custom, the competent territorial authority may decree its use in the manner indicated above and with formularies approved by that authority for the time being.

V. PART ALLOWED THE VERNACULAR IN MASS (SC ART. 54)

57.   For Masses, whether sung or recited, celebrated with a congregation, the competent, territorial ecclesiastical authority on approval, that is, confirmation, of its decisions by the Holy See, may introduce the vernacular into:

   a. the proclaiming of the lessons, epistle, and gospel; the universal prayer or prayer of the faithful;

   b. as befits the circumstances of the place, the chants of the Ordinary of the Mass, namely, the *Kyrie, Gloria, Credo, Sanctus-Benedictus, Agnus Dei*, as well as the introit, offertory, and communion antiphons and the chants between the readings;

   c. acclamations, greeting, and dialogue formularies, the *Ecce Agnus Dei, Domine, non sum dignus, Corpus Christi* at the communion of the faithful, and the Lord's Prayer with its introduction and embolism.

Missals to be used in the liturgy, however, shall contain besides the vernacular version the Latin text as well.

58.   The Holy See alone can grant permission for use of the vernacular in those parts of the Mass that the celebrant sings or recites alone.

59.   Pastors shall carefully see to it that the Christian faithful, especially members of lay religious institutes, also know how to recite or sing together in Latin, mainly with simple melodies, the parts of the Ordinary of the Mass proper to them.

VI. FACULTY OF REPEATING COMMUNION ON THE SAME DAY (SC ART. 55)

60.   The faithful who receive communion at the Mass of the Easter Vigil or the Midnight Mass of Christmas may receive again at the second Mass of Easter and at one of the Day Masses of Christmas.

CHAPTER III

The Other Sacraments and the Sacramentals

I. PART ALLOWED THE VERNACULAR (SC ART. 63)

61. The competent territorial authority, on approval, that is, confirmation, of its decisions by the Holy See, may introduce the vernacular for:

   a. the rites, including the essential sacramental forms, of baptism, confirmation, penance, anointing of the sick, marriage, and the distribution of holy communion;

   b. the conferral of orders: the address preliminary to ordination or consecration, the examination of the bishop-elect at an episcopal consecration, and the admonitions;

   c. sacramentals;

   d. rite of funerals.

Whenever a more extensive use of the vernacular seems desirable, the prescription of the Constitution art. 40 is to be observed.

II. ELEMENTS TO BE DROPPED IN THE RITE OF SUPPLYING CEREMONIES FOR A PERSON ALREADY BAPTIZED (SC ART. 69)

62. In the rite of supplying ceremonies in the case of a baptized infant, *Rituale Romanum* tit. II, cap. 6, the exorcisms in no. 6 (*Exi ab eo*), no. 10 (*Exorcizo te, immunde spiritus—Ergo, maledicte diabole*), and no. 15 (*Exorcizo te, omnis spiritus*) are to be dropped.

63. In the rite for supplying ceremonies in the case of a baptized adult, *Rituale Romanum* tit. II, cap. 6, the exorcisms in no. 5 (*Exi ab eo*), no. 15 (*Ergo, maledicte diabole*), no. 17 (*Audi, maledicte satana*), no. 19 (*Exorcizo te—Ergo, maledicte diabole*), no. 21 (*Ergo, maledicte diabole*), no. 23 (*Ergo, maledicte diabole*), no. 25 (*Exorcizo te—Ergo, maledicte diabole*), no. 31 (*Nec te latet*), and no. 35 (*Exi, immunde spiritus*) are to be dropped.

III. CONFIRMATION (SC ART. 71)

64. If confirmation is conferred within Mass, the Mass should be celebrated by the bishop himself; in this case he confers the sacrament clad in Mass vestments.

The Mass within which confirmation is conferred may be celebrated as a second-class votive Mass of the Holy Spirit.

65. After the gospel and homily, before the reception of confirmation, it is well for those being confirmed to renew their baptismal promises, according to the

rite in lawful use in individual regions, unless they have already done so before Mass.

66.   If the Mass is celebrated by someone else, the bishop should assist at the Mass in the vestments prescribed for the conferral of confirmation; they may be either of the color of the Mass or white. The bishop himself should give the homily and the celebrant should resume the Mass only after the conferral of confirmation.

67.   The conferral of confirmation follows the rite outlined in the *Pontificale Romanum*, but with a single sign of the cross at the words *In nomine Patris, et Filii, et Spiritus Sancti* that follow the formulary, *Signo te*.

IV. CONTINUOUS RITE FOR ANOINTING THE SICK AND *VIATICUM* (SC ART. 74)

68.   When the anointing of the sick and viaticum are administered at the same time, unless a continuous rite already exists in a local ritual, the sequence of the rite is to be as follows: after the sprinkling with holy water and the prayer upon entering the room as given in the rite of anointing, the priest should, if need be, hear the confession of the sick person, then administer the anointing and finally give viaticum, omitting the sprinkling with its formularies, the *Confiteor*, and the absolution. If, however, the apostolic blessing with plenary indulgence at the hour of death is also to be imparted, it shall be given immediately before the anointing; the sprinkling with its formularies, the *Confiteor*, and absolution are omitted.

V. LAYING ON OF HANDS IN THE CONSECRATION OF A BISHOP (SC ART. 76)

69.   At the consecration of a bishop all bishops present, clad in choral vesture, may participate in the laying on of hands. Only the consecrator and the two coconsecrators, however, pronounce the words, *Accipe Spiritum Sanctum*.

VI. RITE OF MARRIAGE (SC ART. 78)

70.   Unless there is some good, excusing reason, marriage shall be celebrated within Mass, after the gospel and homily. The homily is never to be omitted.

71.   Whenever marriage is celebrated within Mass, the *Missa votiva pro sponsis* shall always be celebrated, even in closed times, or a commemoration made from it, in keeping with the rubrics.

72.   As far as possible, the pastor himself or the one he delegates to assist at the marriage shall celebrate the Mass; if another priest assists at the marriage, the celebrant shall not continue the Mass until the rite of marriage has been completed.

The priest who only assists at the marriage but does not celebrate the Mass shall be vested in surplice and white stole and, if it is the local custom, also in cope; he shall also give the homily. But the celebrant is always to give the blessing after the *Pater noster* and before the *Placeat*.

73.   The nuptial blessing shall always be given within the Mass, even in closed times and even if one or both of the spouses is entering into a second marriage.

74.   In the celebration of marriage outside Mass:

a. At the beginning of the rite, in keeping with the Motu Proprio *Sacram Liturgiam* no. V, a brief instruction shall be given, not a homily but simply an introduction to the celebration of marriage (see SC art. 35, § 3). After the reading of the epistle and gospel from the *Missa pro sponsis*, there shall be a sermon or homily based on the sacred text (see SC art. 52). The order of the whole rite, then, is to be as follows: the brief instruction, reading of the epistle and gospel in the vernacular, homily, celebration of marriage, nuptial blessing.

b. For the reading of the epistle and gospel from the *Missa pro sponsis*, if there is no vernacular text approved by the competent territorial ecclesiastical authority, it is lawful for the time being to use a text approved by the local Ordinary.

c. Singing is allowed between the epistle and gospel. After the rite of marriage and before the nuptial blessing it is most desirable to have the prayer of the faithful in a form approved by the local Ordinary and incorporating intercessions for the spouses.

d. Even in closed times and even if one or both of the spouses is entering a second marriage, they are to receive the nuptial blessing, according to the formulary in the *Rituale Romanum* tit. VIII, cap. 3, unless local rituals provide a different one.

75.   If marriage is celebrated during closed times, the pastor shall advise the spouses to be mindful of the proper spirit of the particular liturgical season.

VII. SACRAMENTALS (SC ART. 79)

76.   For the blessing of candles on 2 February and of ashes on Ash Wednesday just one of the prayers for these in the *Missale Romanum* suffices.

77.   The blessings in the *Rituale Romanum* tit. IX, cap. 9, 10, 11, hitherto reserved, may be given by any priest, except for: the blessing of a bell for the use of a blessed church or oratory (cap. 9, no. 11); the blessing of the cornerstone of a church (cap. 9, no. 16); the blessing of a new church or public oratory (cap. 9, no. 17); the blessing of an antemensium (cap. 9, no. 21); the blessing of a new cemetery (cap. 9, no. 22); papal blessings (cap. 10, nos. 1–3); the blessing and erection of the stations of the cross (cap. 11, no. 1), reserved to the bishop.

CHAPTER IV

Divine Office

I. CELEBRATION OF DIVINE OFFICE BY THOSE BOUND TO CHOIR

78. Until reform of the divine office is completed:

    a. Communities of canons, monks, nuns, other regulars or religious bound to choir by law or constitutions must, in addition to the conventual Mass, celebrate the entire divine office daily in choir.

    Individual members of these communities who are in major orders or solemnly professed, except for lay brothers, are obliged, even if lawfully dispensed from choir, to private recitation each day of the hours they do not celebrate in choir.

    b. Cathedral and collegiate chapters must, besides the conventual Mass, celebrate in choir those parts of the office imposed on them by common or particular law.

    Individual chapter members, besides the canonical hours obligatory for all clerics in major orders (see SC art. 96 and 89), must recite in private the hours that are celebrated by their chapter.

    c. In mission regions, while preserving the religious or capitular choral discipline established by law, religious or capitulars who are lawfully absent from choir by reason of pastoral ministry may, with permission of the local Ordinary (not of his vicar general or delegate), use the concession granted by the Motu Proprio *Sacram Liturgiam* no. VI.

II. FACULTY OF DISPENSING FROM OR COMMUTING DIVINE OFFICE (SC ART. 97)

79. The faculty given all Ordinaries to dispense their subjects, in individual cases and for a just reason, from the obligation of the divine office in whole or in part or to commute it is also extended to major superiors of nonexempt clerical, religious institutes and of societies of common life.

III. LITTLE OFFICES (SC ART. 98)

80. No little office can be classified as conformed to the divine office if it does not consist of psalms, readings, hymns, and prayers or if it has no relationship to the hours of the day and the particular liturgical season.

81. But little offices already lawfully approved suffice for the time being as a sharing in the public prayer of the Church, provided their make-up meets the criteria just stated.

    For use as part of the public prayer of the Church, any new little office must have the approval of the Holy See.

82. The translation of the text of a little office into the vernacular for use as the public prayer of the Church must have the approval of the competent, territorial ecclesiastical authority, following approval, that is, confirmation, by the Holy See.

83. The Ordinary or major superior of the subject is the authority competent to grant use of the vernacular in the recitation of a little office to anyone bound to it by constitution or to dispense from or commute the obligation.

IV. DIVINE OFFICE OR LITTLE OFFICE CELEBRATED IN COMMON BY RELIGIOUS INSTITUTES (SC ART. 99)

84. The obligation of celebrating in common all or part of the divine office or a little office imposed by their constitution on members of institutes of perfection does not take away the faculty of omitting prime and of choosing from among the little hours the one best suited to the time of day (see Motu Proprio *Sacram Liturgiam* no. VI).

V. LANGUAGE FOR RECITATION OF DIVINE OFFICE (SC ART. 101)

85. In reciting the divine office in choir clerics are bound to retain the Latin language.

86. The faculty granted the Ordinary to allow use of the vernacular in individual cases by those clerics for whom the use of Latin constitutes a serious hindrance to fulfilling the obligation of the office is extended also to the major superiors of nonexempt, clerical religious institutes and of societies of common life.

87. The serious hindrance required for the concession of the faculty mentioned ought to be evaluated on the basis of the physical, moral, intellectual, and spiritual condition of the petitioner. Nevertheless, this faculty, conceded solely to make the recitation of the divine office easier and more devout, is not intended to lessen in any way the obligation of priests in the Latin rite to learn Latin.

88. The respective Ordinaries of the same language are to prepare and approve the translations of the divine office for the non-Roman rites. (For parts of the office shared with the Roman Rite, however, they are to use the version approved by competent territorial authority.) The Ordinaries are then to submit the translation for the Holy See's confirmation.

89. Breviaries for clerics who, according to the provisions of art. 101, § 2, have the right to use the vernacular for the divine office should contain the Latin text along with the vernacular.

CHAPTER V

Designing Churches and Altars to Facilitate Active Participation of the Faithful

I. DESIGN OF CHURCHES

90. In building new churches or restoring and adapting old ones every care is to be taken that they are suited to celebrating liturgical services authentically and that they ensure active participation by the faithful (see SC art. 124).

II. MAIN ALTAR

91. The main altar should preferably be freestanding, to permit walking around it and celebration facing the people. Its location in the place of worship should be truly central so that the attention of the whole congregation naturally focuses there.

Choice of materials for the construction and adornment of the altar is to respect the prescriptions of law.

The sanctuary area is to be spacious enough to accommodate the sacred rites.

III. CHAIR FOR CELEBRANT AND MINISTERS

92. In relation to the plan of the church, the chair for the celebrant and ministers should occupy a place that is clearly visible to all the faithful and that makes it plain that the celebrant presides over the whole community.

Should the chair stand behind the altar, any semblance of a throne, the prerogative of a bishop, is to be avoided.

IV. MINOR ALTARS

93. There are to be fewer minor altars and, where the design of the building permits, the best place for them is in chapels somewhat set apart from the body of the church.

V. ALTAR APPOINTMENTS

94. At the discretion of the Ordinary, the cross and candlesticks required on the altar for the various liturgical rites may also be placed next to it.

VI. RESERVATION OF THE EUCHARIST

95. The eucharist is to be reserved in a solid and secure tabernacle, placed in the middle of the main altar or on a minor, but truly worthy altar, or, in accord with lawful custom and in particular cases approved by the local Ordinary, also in another, special, and properly adorned part of the church.

It is lawful to celebrate Mass facing the people even on an altar where there is a small but becoming tabernacle.

96.   There should be a lectern or lecterns for the proclamation of the readings, so arranged that the faithful may readily see and hear the minister.

VIII. PLACE FOR CHOIR AND ORGAN

97.   The choir and organ shall occupy a place clearly showing that the singers and the organist form part of the united community of the faithful and allowing them best to fulfill their part in the liturgy.

IX. PLACE FOR THE FAITHFUL

98.   Special care should be taken that the place for the faithful will assure their proper participation in the sacred rites with both eyes and mind. Normally there should be benches or chairs for their use but, in keeping with the Constitution art. 32, the custom of reserving places for special persons is to be suppressed.

Care is also to be taken to enable the faithful not only to see the celebrant and other ministers but also to hear them easily, even by use of modern sound equipment.

X. BAPTISTERY

99.   In the construction and decoration of the baptistery great pains are to be taken to ensure that it clearly expresses the dignity of the sacrament of baptism and that it is a place well suited to communal celebrations (see SC art. 27).

This Instruction was prepared by the Consilium by mandate of Pope Paul VI, and presented to the Pope by Cardinal Giacomo Lercaro, President of the Consilium. After having carefully considered the Instruction, in consultation with the Consilium and the Congregation of Rites, Pope Paul in an audience granted to Cardinal Arcadio Maria Larraona, Prefect of the Congregation of Rites, gave it specific approval as a whole and in its parts, confirmed it by his authority, and ordered it to be published and faithfully observed by all concerned, beginning on the first Sunday of Lent, 7 March 1965.

MUSICAM SACRAM
ON MUSIC IN THE LITURGY

INSTRUCTION
SACRED CONGREGATION OF RITES
MARCH 5, 1967

AN OVERVIEW OF *MUSICAM SACRAM*

Rev. Anthony Ruff, osb

Musicam sacram was issued on February 9, 1967 with the approval of Pope Paul VI. It was prepared by the Consilium, the body officially responsible for carrying out the liturgical reform after the Second Vatican Council, with collaboration from the Sacred Congregation of Rites. The document was written to give assistance in the area of worship music for problems resulting from the liturgical reforms of the Second Vatican Council. It does not include all legislation on sacred music, but as article 3 says, it establishes "the principal norms that seem most needed at the present time."

The achievement of *Musicam sacram* is that it holds together two things: great respect for the musical heritage of the Church, and unflinching commitment to liturgical reform, even when this entails significant changes to preconciliar practice. It was issued at a time when the liturgy had already begun to be reformed by a flurry of Roman decrees, but before the reformed Order of Mass was promulgated in 1969. This explains why some of its specific prescriptions are written with the preconciliar liturgy in view, even though the document clearly anticipates the reformed liturgy in its principles and directives. It is not difficult to identify in the document the few *lacunae* or aspects later superseded—for example, the low ranking at article 31 of the "chants after a lesson" (now generally termed the "Responsorial Psalm") and Alleluia before the Gospel, before these elements received proper emphasis with the reformed Lectionary of 1970 and in the 1981 *General Introduction to the Lectionary*. *Musicam sacram* as a whole stands up very well in its articulation of the foundational principles of liturgical reform as applied to music.

The historical context for *Musicam sacram* includes the series of papal documents on music issued since *Tra le sollecitudini* (1903), and more proximately, the heated conflict that had reached a peak already before the Second Vatican Council as some traditional musicians strongly resisted liturgical reform. Annibale Bugnini, secretary of the Consilium, said that the lengthy drafting process of the document was a *via dolorosa* (way of suffering). This was because of heated disputes between liturgical reformers and some traditional musicians who saw the reform as a threat to traditional repertoire and practices. Pope Paul VI took a personal interest in the document, studying the opposing arguments and intervening to offer direction for the final form of the document.

Papal documents on music from 1903 until the Second Vatican Council showed both consistency in basic principles and significant evolution as the impetus for liturgical renewal grew. These documents consistently affirmed the distinction between sacred and secular styles of music, the latter inappropriate for liturgical use, and consistently stated that Gregorian chant is the highest model of sacred music. But as the twentieth century progressed, papal documents increasingly emphasized active participation of the people, showed increasing interest in vernacular hymnody—first outside the liturgy, then within it, and became less skeptical of modern styles of music.

On the complex philosophical question of whether to evaluate worship music according to its intrinsic qualities or according to its functional ability to fulfill its ritual purpose, the preconciliar papal documents seem to favor the former, whereby music is valued for its intrinsic qualities. *Tra le sollecitudini* in 1903 listed these qualities as holiness, goodness of form, and universality. At the same time, the preconciliar documents do state that sacred music must be subordinate to the liturgy.

An important development in the understanding of the "holiness" of music is seen in the 1955 document *Musicae sacrae disciplina*, which stated at article 34 that "the dignity and force of sacred music are greater the closer sacred music itself approaches . . . the Eucharistic sacrifice of the altar." This notion was taken into *Sacrosanctum Concilium* of the Second Vatican Council, where article 112 says that "sacred music will be the more holy the more closely it is joined to the liturgical rite." These statements define holiness in terms of ritual function, rather than understanding holiness as an intrinsic or ontological quality of music.

Musicam sacram employs the language of the preceding documents, but with significant developments and new emphases in the light of the reform principles of the Second Vatican Council. The distinction between sacred and secular music hardly figures in it, apart from the last-minute addition at article 4, which says that sacred music is music written for the liturgy that is endowed with holiness and goodness of form (*sanctitate et bonitate formarum*). The listing of the genres of sacred music at article 4 as "Gregorian chant, the several styles of polyphony, both ancient and modern; sacred music for organ and for other permitted instruments, and the sacred, i.e., liturgical or religious, music of the people" recalls the listing of genres in the preconciliar documents. But the emphasis throughout the document is not on pre-existent repertoires with intrinsic qualities, but much more on music which fits the structure of the reformed liturgy and enables the active participation of the people. As article 9 states, "The Church does not exclude any type of sacred music from liturgical services as long as the music matches the spirit of the service itself and the character of the individual parts and is not a hindrance to the required active participation of the people." The very title of the instruction, "On Music *In* the Liturgy," emphasizes the bond between music and ritual more than does the title of the 1958 instruction "on sacred music *and* sacred liturgy." Gregorian chant is accorded pride of place in *Musicam sacram*, following *Sacrosanctum Concilium*, but article 50 limits this primacy to liturgical services celebrated in Latin. Active participation, mentioned already in 1903 and increasingly emphasized in subsequent documents, is stressed repeatedly and emphatically as a fundamental principle, as is the case in *Sacrosanctum Concilium*.

Having put *Musicam sacram* in its historical context, we turn now to some particular issues, to examine how the document brings together respect for tradition and commitment to liturgical reform.

Given the strong emphasis on Gregorian chant in the preconciliar documents on sacred music, where Gregorian chant is always treated as the first and most important genre of sacred music, it is noteworthy that *Musicam sacram* affirms the value of Gregorian chant but does not particularly emphasize it. After the first mention of Gregorian chant at article 4b at the head of the list of genres of sacred music, chant is not treated again until article 50, after all the other principles of music in the liturgy have been laid out. As noted above, the primacy of Gregorian chant is limited to services celebrated in Latin at article 50, a narrowing of what is stated in *Sacrosanctum Concilium*. The ideal at article 33 that the assembly "have a part in singing the Proper of the Mass, especially by use of the simpler responses or other appropriate melodies" relativizes the value of the Gregorian chant propers, which are for trained choir and do not allow for assembly singing. Article 32 allows for hymns to replace the chant propers for the Entrance, Offertory, and Communion—a practice that has since led to the virtual disappearance of the chant propers, which probably was not intended by the instruction.

It is a basic principle of *Musicam sacram* that music derives its purpose and function from the liturgy itself. Article 6 calls for attentiveness to the "exact fidelity to the meaning and character of each part and of each song." As noted above, article 9 admits any genre of music that "matches the spirit of the service itself and the character of the individual parts." Article 53 directs that one first find which parts of the inherited treasury "best meet the requirements of the reformed liturgy," and then which parts can be adapted to meet these requirements. Those parts that "are incompatible with the nature of the liturgical service or with its proper pastoral celebration" might be transferred to other devotions or paraliturgical services. Such counsel shows that *Musicam sacram* puts forth new criteria for the evaluation of music, and assumes that not all inherited repertoire will meet those criteria.

Regarding active participation of the people, *Musicam sacram* article 15 uses the strong language of *Sacrosanctum Concilium*, article 14, in promoting "that full, conscious, and active participation in liturgical celebrations called for by the very nature of the liturgy. Such participation by the Christian people as "a chosen race, a royal priesthood, a holy nation, God's own people" (1 Pt 2:9; see 2:4–5) is their right and duty by reason of their baptism." Article 15 says that participation is first interior, and then external. This allows for participation both by listening to ministers or choir and by joining externally in congregational song. As much as the document affirms the importance of choirs and their singing for the people,[1] the statements on the choir repeatedly include admonitions that the people participate actively in song.

Article 5 states that "a liturgical service takes on a nobler aspect when the rites are celebrated with singing, the ministers of each rank take their parts in them, and the congregation actively participates." *Musicam sacram* offered, already in 1967, a visionary ideal of sung liturgy, which has only recently been taken up in the English-speaking world. This ideal is that dialogues between priests or minister and people are sung as a basic backdrop to the other sung elements such as acclamations and antiphons and hymns. The practice of sung liturgy was common to East and West in the first millennium, but was gradually lost in the West, where a distinction developed between "High Mass" (sung Mass) and "Low Mass" (recited Mass) and sung Mass became the exception. Although article 28 claims to retain the distinction between sung and recited Masses, articles 29–31 set forth degrees of participation that in fact undercut it.

---

1. See *Musicam sacram* (MS), 15c and 19–23.

Now there can be more or less singing at any liturgy, as resources allow—and as article 36 says, "any one of the parts of the Proper or the Ordinary in a low Mass may be sung." But articles 29–31 decree that one start with the first degree of sung dialogues when deciding which parts of the liturgy to sing.

The choir, variously called *chorus*, *cappella*, or *schola cantorum*, is strongly emphasized in *Musicam sacram*. According to article 19 its role is both to perform the parts that belong to it and to encourage active participation of the people. Article 20 wishes that choirs in prominent churches continue to cultivate the "priceless treasury of sacred music," and article 50c says that music for one or more voices should be "held in respect, encouraged, and used as the occasion suggests." Article 23 says that the choir is both part of the congregation and has a special role. Article 34 says that choral settings of the Ordinary of the Mass may be performed by choir alone, "as long as the people are not completely excluded from taking part in the singing"—presumably in other parts of the liturgy such as the dialogues or the responsorial psalm.[2] On the other hand, article 16 says that "the usage of entrusting to the choir alone the entire singing of the whole Proper and the whole Ordinary, to the complete exclusion of the people's participation in the singing, is to be deprecated."

In accord with its respect for traditional repertoire, *Musicam sacram* emphasizes the importance of beauty and musical quality, both in musical works and in their rendition. Article 59 admonishes composers that their additions to the treasury be "a truly worthy part" of the Church's musical heritage. Article 8 says that those known to be more excellent at singing are to be preferred, especially when a liturgy is broadcast. Cantors are to be "thoroughly trained" according to article 21. Article 24 states that choir members are to receive musical as well as liturgical and spiritual formation, in order to enhance the "dignity of the liturgical service." Article 63 admonishes that musical instruments be used for "the beauty of worship." Article 67 says that organists and musicians should "possess the skill to play properly the instrument entrusted to them," along with understanding the spirit of the liturgy.

Musicam sacram treats what is now called "inculturation" only briefly at article 61, which speaks of harmonizing indigenous musical traditions with the spirit of the liturgy, and articles 62 and 63, which speak of admitting instruments from local cultures and traditions that are compatible with the liturgy. *Musicam sacram* is focused mostly on European and Western questions of inherited repertoires, their cultivation and adaptation and further development, in the light of the demands of the reformed liturgy. For further guidance on questions of the relationship of liturgical music to cultural contexts, one should look to other documents such as the fourth instruction on *Sacrosanctum Concilium* on "Inculturation and the Roman Liturgy" of 1994, *Varietates legitimae*.

For the task it gives itself, *Musicam sacram* succeeds admirably. In its synthesis of inherited riches and their continuing development in the light of new demands, it stands as one of the hallmark documents of liturgical reform.

---

2. See ibid., 33.

MUSICAM SACRAM
ON MUSIC IN THE LITURGY

INSTRUCTION

SACRED CONGREGATION OF RITES
MARCH 5, 1967

PREFACE

1.   Sacred music is one of the elements of liturgical reform that Vatican Council II considered thoroughly. The Council explained the role of music in divine worship and set out many principles and rules in the Constitution on the Liturgy, which has an entire chapter on the subject.

2.   The recently begun reform of the liturgy is already putting the conciliar enactments into effect. The new norms relative to the faithful's active participation and the structuring of the rites, however, have given rise to some problems about music and its ministerial function. It seems necessary to solve these in order to bring out more clearly the meaning of the relevant principles of the Constitution on the Liturgy.

3.   By mandate of Pope Paul VI the Consilium has carefully examined these problems and drawn up the present Instruction. It is not a collection of all the legislation on sacred music, but a statement simply of the principal norms that seem most needed at the present time. The Instruction also stands as a continuation and complement of the earlier Instruction of the Congregation of Rites on the correct carrying out of the Constitution on the Liturgy, which was also prepared by the Consilium and issued 26 September 1964.

4.   The reasonable expectation is that in welcoming and carrying out these norms pastors, composers, and the faithful, will strive with one accord to achieve the genuine purpose of sacred music, "which is the glory of God and the sanctification of the faithful."[1]

    a. Music is "sacred" insofar as it is composed for the celebration of divine worship and possesses integrity of form.[2]

---

1. SC art. 112.
2. See St. Pius X, Motu Proprio *Tra le sollecitudini*, 22 Nov. 1903, no. 2: *Acta Sanctae Sedis* 36 (1903–04) 332.

b. The term "sacred music" here includes: Gregorian chant, the several styles of polyphony, both ancient and modern; sacred music for organ and for other permitted instruments, and the sacred, i.e., liturgical or religious, music of the people.[3]

I. GENERAL NORMS

5.　A liturgical service takes on a nobler aspect when the rites are celebrated with singing, the ministers of each rank take their parts in them, and the congregation actively participates.[4] This form of celebration gives a more graceful expression to prayer and brings out more distinctly the hierarchic character of the liturgy and the specific make-up of the community. It achieves a closer union of hearts through the union of voices. It raises the mind more readily to heavenly realities through the splendor of the rites. It makes the whole celebration a more striking symbol of the celebration to come in the heavenly Jerusalem.

Pastors are therefore to strive devotedly to achieve this form of celebration. They would do well even to adapt to congregational celebrations without singing the distribution of functions and parts that more properly belongs to sung services. They are to be particularly careful that there are enough necessary, qualified ministers and that the people's active participation is helped.

The truly successful preparation of a liturgical celebration is to be achieved through the cooperation, under the parish priest (pastor) or rector, of all who have a part in the rites themselves and in the pastoral and musical elements of the celebration.

6.　To give its true structure to the celebration of the liturgy requires, first, the proper assignment of functions and the kind of execution in which "each one, minister or layperson, who has an office to perform, does all of, but only, those parts which pertain to that office by the nature of the rite and the principles of liturgy."[5] But an additional requirement is exact fidelity to the meaning and character of each part and of each song. To achieve this end it is above all necessary that those parts which of their nature call for singing are in fact sung and in the style and form demanded by the parts themselves.

7.　The amount of singing determines the gradations between the most solemn form of liturgical celebrations, in which all the parts calling for singing are sung, and the most simple form, in which nothing is sung. For the choice of parts to be sung, those should be first that of their nature are more important and particularly those sung by the priest or other ministers and answered by the congregation or sung by the priest and congregation together. Later other parts, for the congregation alone or the choir alone, may be added gradually.

8.　Whenever a choice of people for a sung liturgical celebration is possible, those with musical talent should obviously be preferred. This is particularly the

---

3. See SCR, Instr. on sacred music and the liturgy, 3 Sept. 1958, no. 4: AAS 50 (1958) 633.
4. See SC art. 113.
5. SC art. 28.

case with the more solemn liturgical services, those involving more difficult music, or those to be broadcast on radio or television.[6]

When no such choice is possible and the priest or minister does not have the voice to sing properly, he may recite, audibly and clearly, one or other of the more difficult parts belonging to him. This, however, is not to be done merely to suit the personal preference of the priest or minister.

9. The choice of the style of music for a choir or congregation should be guided by the abilities of those who must do the singing. The Church does not exclude any type of sacred music from liturgical services as long as the music matches the spirit of the service itself and the character of the individual parts[7] and is not a hindrance to the required active participation of the people.[8]

10. It is advisable that there be as much suitable variety as possible in the forms of celebration and the degree of participation in proportion to the solemnity of the day and of the assembly, in order that the faithful will more willingly and effectively contribute their own participation.

11. The real solemnity of a liturgical service, it should be kept in mind, depends not on a more ornate musical style or more ceremonial splendor but on a worthy and reverent celebration. This means respect for the integrity of the rites, that is, carrying out each of the parts in keeping with its proper character. More ornate styles of singing and greater ceremonial splendor are obviously sometimes desirable, when they are possible. But it would be in conflict with the genuine solemnity of a liturgical service if such things were to cause any element of the service to be omitted, altered, or performed improperly.

12. The Apostolic See alone has authority to establish, in accord with the norms of tradition and particularly of the Constitution on the Liturgy, those general principles that stand as the foundation for sacred music. The various lawfully-constituted territorial bodies of bishops and the bishops themselves have authority to regulate sacred music within the already defined limits.[9]

II. THOSE WITH A ROLE IN LITURGICAL CELEBRATIONS

13. Liturgical services are celebrations of the Church, that is, of the holy people united in proper order under a bishop or priest.[10] In a liturgical service the priest and his ministers have a special place because of holy orders; the servers, reader, commentator, and choir members, because of the ministry they perform.[11]

14. Acting in the person of Christ, the priest presides over the gathered assembly. The prayers he sings or recites aloud are spoken in the name of the entire

---

6. See SCR, Instr. on sacred music and the liturgy, 3 Sept. 1958, no. 95: AAS 30 (1958) 656–657.
7. See SC art. 116.
8. See SC art. 28.
9. See SC art. 22.
10. See SC art. 26 and 41–42; LG no. 28.
11. See SC art. 29.

people of God and of all in the assembly;[12] therefore all present must listen to them with reverence.

15. The faithful carry out their proper liturgical function by offering their complete, conscious, and active participation. The very nature of the liturgy demands this and it is the right and duty of the Christian people by reason of their baptism.[13] This participation must be:

   a. internal, that is, the faithful make their thoughts match what they say and hear, and cooperate with divine grace;[14]

   b. but also external, that is, they express their inner participation through their gestures, outward bearing, acclamations, responses, and song.[15] The faithful are also to be taught that they should try to raise their mind to God through interior participation as they listen to the singing of ministers or choir.

16. A liturgical celebration can have no more solemn or pleasing feature than the whole assembly's expressing its faith and devotion in song. Thus an active participation that is manifested by singing should be carefully fostered along these lines:

   a. It should include especially the acclamations, responses to the greetings of the priest and the ministers and responses in litanies, the antiphons and psalms, the verses of the responsorial psalm, and other similar verses, hymns, and canticles.[16]

   b. Pertinent catechesis as well as actual practice should lead the people gradually to a more extensive and indeed complete participation in all the parts proper to them.

   c. Some of the congregational parts may be assigned to the choir alone, however, especially when the people are not yet sufficiently trained or melodies for part-singing are used. But the people are not to be excluded from the other parts proper to them. The practice of assigning the singing of the entire Proper and Ordinary of the Mass to the choir alone without the rest of the congregation is not to be permitted.

17. At the proper times a holy silence is also to be observed.[17] That does not mean treating the faithful as outsiders or mute onlookers at the liturgical service; it means rather making use of their own sentiments to bring them closer to the mystery being celebrated. Such sentiments are evoked by the word of God,

---

12. See SC art. 33.
13. See SC art. 14.
14. See SC art. 11.
15. See SC art. 30.
16. See SC art. 30.
17. See SC art. 30.

the songs and prayers, and the people's spiritual bond with the priest as he recites the parts belonging to the celebrant.

18.   Those of the faithful who are members of religious societies for the laity should receive special training in sacred song, in order that they may make an effective contribution to sustaining and furthering the congregation's participation.[18] But the training of all the people in this regard is to be carried out thoroughly and patiently as part of their complete liturgical formation. It should be suited to their age, condition, way of life, and stage of religious development and should begin from the very first years of their schooling in the primary grades.[19]

19.   Because of the liturgical ministry it exercises, the choir (*cappella musica; schola cantorum*) should be mentioned here explicitly.

The conciliar norms regarding reform of the liturgy have given the choir's function greater prominence and importance. The choir is responsible for the correct performance of the parts that belong to it, according to the differing types of liturgical assembly and for helping the faithful to take an active part in the singing. Therefore:

    a. Choirs are to be developed with great care, especially in cathedrals and other major churches, in seminaries, and in religious houses of study.

    b. In smaller churches as well a choir should be formed, even if there are only a few members.

20.   Over the centuries the choirs of basilicas, cathedrals, monasteries, and other major churches have won high praise because they have preserved and developed the priceless treasury of sacred music. By means of rules issued specifically for them and reviewed and approved by the Ordinary such choirs are to be continued in order to carry out liturgical celebrations with greater solemnity.

Nevertheless choir directors and parish priests (pastors) or rectors of churches are to ensure that the congregation always joins in the singing of at least the more simple parts belonging to them.

21.   Especially where even a small choir is not possible, there must be at least one or more cantors, thoroughly trained to intone at least the simpler chants that the congregation sings and to lead and sustain the singing.

Even in churches having a choir it is better for a cantor to be present for those celebrations that the choir cannot attend but that should be carried out with some degree of solemnity and thus with singing.

22.   Depending on the established customs of peoples and on other circumstances, a choir may be made up of men and boys, of all men or all boys, of both men and women, and, where the situation really requires, even of all women.

---

18. See SCR, Instr. InterOec, 26 Sept. 1964, nos. 19 and 59.
19. See SC art. 19. SCR, Instr. on sacred music and the liturgy, 3 Sept. 1958, nos. 106–108: AAS 50 (1958) 660.

23.   According to the design of the particular church, the place for the choir is to be such that:

  a. its status as a part of the community with a special function is clearly evident;

  b. the performance of its liturgical ministry is facilitated;[20]

  c. full, that is, sacramental, participation in the Mass remains convenient for each of the members.

When there are women members, the choir's place is to be outside the sanctuary.

24.   In addition to musical training, choir members should receive instruction on the liturgy and on spirituality. Then the results of the proper fulfillment of their liturgical ministry will be the dignity of the liturgical service and an example for the faithful, as well as the spiritual benefit of the choir members themselves.

25.   Diocesan, national, and international associations for sacred music, especially those approved and repeatedly endorsed by the Apostolic See, are to offer help for both the artistic and spiritual training of choirs.

26.   The priest, ministers, servers, choir members, and commentator are to sing or recite the parts assigned to them in a fully intelligible way, in order to make it easier and obvious for the congregation to respond when the rite requires. The priest and the ministers of every rank should join their own voices with those of the entire assembly in the parts belonging to the congregation.[21]

III. SINGING DURING MASS

27.   As far as possible, eucharistic celebrations with the people, especially on Sundays, should by preference take the form of a Mass with singing, even more than once in the same day.

28.   The distinction between the solemn, the high, and the low Mass, sanctioned by the 1958 Instruction (no. 3) remains in force, according to tradition and current law. But for pastoral reasons degrees of solemnity for the sung Mass are proposed here in order that it will become easier, in accord with each congregation's capability, to make the celebration of Mass more solemn through the use of singing.

These degrees must be so employed, however, that the first may always be used without the others, but the second and third never without the first. Thus all cases the faithful are to be brought to take part fully in the singing.

---

20. See SCR, InterOec no. 97.
21. See SCR, InterOec no. 48 b.

29. To the first degree belong:

    a. in the entrance rites
      • the priest's greeting and the congregation's response;
      • the opening prayer.

    b. in the liturgy of the word
      • the gospel acclamations.

    c. in the liturgy of the eucharist
      • the prayer over the gifts;
      • the preface, with the opening dialogue and the *Sanctus*;
      • the Lord's Prayer, with the invitation and embolism;
      • the greeting *May the peace of the Lord*;
      • the prayer after communion;
      • the final dismissal.

30. To the second degree belong:

    a. *Kyrie, Gloria, Agnus Dei*;

    b. profession of faith;

    c. general intercessions.

31. To the third degree belong:

    a. songs for the entrance procession and for communion;

    b. chants after a lesson or epistle;

    c. *Alleluia* before the gospel;

    d. songs for the presentation of the gifts;

    e. the Scripture readings, except when it seems better not to have them sung.

32. In some places there is the lawful practice, occasionally confirmed by indult, of substituting other songs for the entrance, offertory, and communion chants in the *Graduale*. At the discretion of the competent territorial authority this practice may be kept, on condition that the songs substituted fit in with those parts of the Mass, the feast, or the liturgical season. The texts of such songs must also have the approval of the same territorial authority.

33. The assembly of the faithful should, as far as possible, have a part in singing the Proper of the Mass, especially by use of the simpler responses or other appropriate melodies.

Of all the chants for the Proper the one coming between the readings as a gradual or responsorial psalm is particularly significant. It is intrinsically a part of the liturgy of the word and thus is to be sung with the whole assembly sitting, listening, and even, if possible, taking part.

34.   When there is to be part-singing for the chants of the Ordinary of the Mass, they may be sung by the choir alone in the customary way, that is, either a cappella or with instrumental accompaniment. The Congregation, however, must not be altogether left out of the singing for the Mass.

In other cases the chants of the Ordinary may be divided between choir and congregation or between one part of the congregation and another. The singing is then done by alternating verses or in any other way that takes in most of the entire text. It is important in any such arrangement, however, to attend to the following. Because it is a profession of faith, the *Credo* is best sung by all or else sung in a manner that allows the congregation's proper participation. Because it is an acclamation concluding the preface, the *Sanctus* should as a rule be sung by the entire assembly along with the priest. Because it accompanies the breaking of the bread, the *Agnus Dei* may be repeated as often as necessary, especially in concelebrations and it is appropriate as well for the congregation to have a part in it, at least by singing the final *Grant us peace*.

35.   The congregation should join the priest in singing the Lord's Prayer.[22] When it is in Latin, it is sung to the traditional melodies; the melodies for singing it in the vernacular must have the approval of the competent territorial authority.

36.   Any one of the parts of the Proper or the Ordinary in a low Mass may be sung. Sometimes it is even quite appropriate to have other songs at the beginning, at the presentation of the gifts, and at the communion, as well as at the end of Mass. It is not enough for these songs to be "eucharistic" in some way; they must be in keeping with the parts of the Mass and with the feast or liturgical season.

IV. SINGING THE DIVINE OFFICE

37.   Celebration of the divine office in song is more in keeping with the nature of this prayer and a sign of both higher solemnity and closer union of hearts in praising God. In keeping with the explicit wish of the Constitution on the Liturgy,[23] therefore, the singing of the office is strongly recommended to those who carry it out in choir or in common.

At least on Sundays and holydays it would be well for them to sing some part of the office, especially morning prayer and evening prayer, the two principal hours.

Other clerics living together in centers of study or coming together for retreats or for other meetings should take the opportunity to sanctify their assemblies through the singing of some parts of the divine office.

---

22. See SCR, Instr. InterOec no. 48 g.
23. See SC art. 99.

38.   In the singing of the divine office both the law in force for those bound to choir and particular indults remain unchanged. But the principle of "progressive" solemnity is applicable; namely, the parts that of their nature are more directly designed for singing (dialogues, hymns, verses, canticles) are sung and the other parts recited.

39.   The faithful are to be invited, and also instructed through proper catechesis, to celebrate some parts of the divine office together on Sundays and holydays, especially evening prayer or whatever other hours are customary in different places or groups. All the faithful, especially the better educated, are to be guided through proper instruction to use the psalms in their Christian meaning for prayer. In this way the faithful will be led gradually to a fuller appreciation and use of the Church's public prayer.

40.   Formation in the use of the psalms is particularly important for members of institutes professing the evangelical counsels, in order that they may possess a rich resource for nurturing their spiritual life. They should, if possible, celebrate the principal hours of the office, and even with singing, so that they will take part more completely in the public prayer of the Church.

41.   Clerics must retain Latin in the choral celebration of the office, in conformity with the norm of the Constitution on the Liturgy that is based on the centuries-old tradition of the Latin rite.[24]

The Constitution on the Liturgy,[25] however, also makes provision for the faithful, nuns, and other nonclerical members of institutes professing the evangelical counsels to use the vernacular in the office. Attention should therefore be given to providing melodies for the vernacular singing of the divine office.

V. SACRED MUSIC IN THE CELEBRATION OF THE SACRAMENTS AND SACRAMENTALS, IN SPECIAL SERVICES OF THE LITURGICAL YEAR, IN CELEBRATIONS OF THE WORD OF GOD, AND IN POPULAR DEVOTION

42.   The Council has stated as a principle that whenever rites according to their specific nature make provision for communal celebration involving the presence and active participation of the faithful, this way of celebrating them is to be preferred to a celebration that is individual and, so to speak, private.[26] From this it follows that singing becomes very important, in that it more strikingly expresses the "ecclesial" aspect of a celebration.

43.   Certain celebrations of the sacraments and sacramentals are particularly significant in the life of a parish community: confirmations, ordinations, marriages, the consecration of a church or altar, funerals, etc. As far as possible, therefore, they should be carried out with singing, so that even the solemnity of the

---

24. See SC art. 101, §1. SCR, Instr. InterOec no. 85.
25. See SC art. 101, §§2 and 3.
26. See SC art. 27.

rite may contribute to a greater pastoral effectiveness. Every precaution is to be taken, however, against introducing into a celebration under the guise of solemnity anything merely profane or out of keeping with divine worship; this applies particularly to marriages.

44.   Celebrations that have a distinctive character in the course of the liturgical year should also be marked by greater solemnity through singing. The rites of Holy Week should be given a unique solemnity; through the celebration of the paschal mystery these rites lead the faithful to the very center of the liturgical year and of the liturgy itself.

45.   Suitable melodies are also to be provided for the liturgy of the sacraments and sacramentals and for other special services of the liturgical year. These melodies are meant to favor a more solemn celebration even in the vernacular, in keeping with the norms of the competent authority and the capability of each liturgical assembly.

46.   Music also has great power to nurture the faithful's devotion in celebrations of the word of God and in popular devotions.

The model for celebrations of the word of God[27] should be the liturgy of the word at Mass.[28] Among the important resources for popular devotions are the psalms, musical works taken from the treasury of the past and the present, the religious songs of the people, the playing of the organ and other suitable instruments.

Musical pieces that no longer have a place in the liturgy, but have the power to touch religious feeling and to assist meditation on the sacred mysteries are very well suited for use in popular devotions and especially in celebrations of the word of God.[29]

VI. LANGUAGE FOR USE IN SUNG LITURGIES; PRESERVING THE TREASURY OF SACRED MUSIC

47.   According to the Constitution on the Liturgy, "particular law remaining in force, the use of the Latin language is to be preserved in the Latin rites."[30]

At the same time "use of the mother tongue . . . frequently may be of great advantage to the people."[31] Therefore "the competent ecclesiastical authority . . . is empowered to decide whether and to what extent the vernacular is to be used. . . . The *acta* of the competent authority are to be approved, that is, confirmed by the Apostolic See."[32]

---

27. See SCR, Instr. InterOec nos. 37–39.
28. See SCR, Instr. InterOec no. 37.
29. See no. 53 of this Instruction.
30. SC art. 36, §1.
31. SC art. 36, §2.
32. SC art. 36, §3.

These norms being observed exactly, there should be a wise use of the kind of participation that is best suited to the capabilities of each assembly.

Pastors should see to it that, in addition to the vernacular, "the faithful are also able to say or to sing together in Latin those parts of the Ordinary of the Mass belonging to them."[33]

48. Once the vernacular has been introduced into the Mass, local Ordinaries should determine whether it is advisable to retain one or more Masses in Latin, particularly sung Masses. This applies especially to great cities in churches with a large attendance of faithful using a foreign language.

49. The norms of the Congregation of Seminaries and Universities on liturgical formation in seminaries are to be observed in regard to use of Latin or of the vernacular in liturgical celebrations in a seminary.

The norms in the Motu Proprio *Sacrificium laudis*, 15 August 1966, and this Congregation's instruction on the language for religious in celebrating the divine office and the conventual or community Mass, 23 November 1965, are to be followed in their liturgical services by the members of institutes professing the evangelical counsels.

50. In liturgies to be celebrated in Latin:

a. Because it is proper to the Roman liturgy, Gregorian chant has pride of place, all other things being equal.[34] Proper use should be made of the melodies in the *editiones typicae* of this chant.

b. "It is desirable also that an edition be prepared containing simpler melodies for use in small churches."[35]

c. Other kinds of melodies, either for unison or part-singing and taken from the traditional repertoire or from new works, are to be held in respect, encouraged, and used as the occasion suggests.[36]

51. In view of local conditions, the pastoral good of the faithful, and the idiom of each language, parish priests (pastors) are to decide whether selections from the musical repertoire composed for Latin texts should be used not only for liturgies in Latin but also for those in the vernacular.

52. To preserve the treasury of sacred music and to encourage new styles of sacred song, "great importance is to be attached to the teaching and practice of music in seminaries, in the novitiates and houses of study of religious of both sexes, and also in other Catholic institutions and schools" and particularly in institutes of higher studies specifically established for this purpose.[37] Especially

---

33. SC art. 54. SCR, Instr. InterOec no. 59.
34. See SC art. 116.
35. SC art. 117.
36. See SC art. 116.
37. SC art. 115.

to be promoted are the study and use of Gregorian chant; its distinctive qualities make it an important foundation for a mastery of sacred music.

53.   New compositions are to conform faithfully to the principles and rules here set forth. "They are to have the qualities proper to genuine sacred music; they are not to be limited to works that can be sung only by large choirs, but are to provide also for the needs of small choirs and for the active participation of the entire assembly of the faithful."[38]

Those parts of the traditional treasury of music that best meet the requirements of the reformed liturgy are to receive attention first. Then experts are to study the possibility of adapting other parts to the same requirements. Finally, parts that are incompatible with the nature of the liturgical service or with its proper pastoral celebration are to be transferred to an appropriate place in popular devotions and particularly in celebrations of the word of God.[39]

VII. COMPOSING MUSICAL SETTINGS FOR VERNACULAR TEXTS

54.   Translators of texts to be set to music should take care to combine properly conformity to the Latin and adaptability to the music. They are to respect the idiom and grammar of the vernacular and the proper characteristics of the people. Composers of new melodies are to pay careful heed to similar guidelines, as well as the laws of sacred music.

The competent territorial authority must accordingly see to it that experts in music and in Latin and the vernacular form part of the commission charged with preparing translations and that their cooperation enters into the work from the very outset.

55.   The competent territorial authority will decide whether vernacular texts traditionally associated with certain melodies may be used, even though these texts do not correspond exactly to the approved translations of liturgical texts.

56.   Of special importance among the melodies to be composed for vernacular texts are those that belong to the priest and ministers for singing alone, together with the congregation, or in dialogue with the congregation. Composers of these melodies are to study whether the corresponding traditional melodies of the Latin liturgy may suggest melodies for use with the same texts in the vernacular.

57.   New melodies for the priest and ministers must receive the approval of the competent territorial authority.[40]

58.   The bodies of bishops concerned are to see to it that there is a single vernacular translation for a single language used in different regions. It is advisable also to have, as far as possible, one or more common melodies for the priest's and ministers' parts and for the congregation's acclamations and responses. This

---

38. SC art. 121.
39. See no. 46 of this Instruction.
40. See SCR, Instr. InterOec no. 42.

will foster a shared way for people of the same language to take part in the liturgy.

59. In their approach to a new work, composers should have as their motive the continuation of the tradition that provided the Church a genuine treasury of music for use in divine worship. They should thoroughly study the works of the past, their styles and characteristics; at the same time they should reflect on the new laws and requirements of the liturgy. The objective is that "any new form adopted should in some way grow organically from forms already existing"[41] and that new works will become a truly worthy part of the Church's musical heritage.

60. New melodies for the vernacular texts obviously require a period of testing in order to become firmly established. But their use in church purely for the sake of trying them out must be avoided, since that would be out of keeping with the holiness of the place, the dignity of the liturgy, and the devotion of the faithful.

61. The attempt to adapt sacred music in those areas that possess their own musical tradition, especially mission lands, requires special preparation on the part of musicians.[42] The issue is one of harmoniously blending a sense of the sacred the spirit, traditions, and expressions proper to the genius of those peoples. All involved must possess a sufficient knowledge of the Church's liturgy and musical tradition as well as of the language, the popular singing, and the other cultural expressions of the people for whom they labor.

VIII. SACRED INSTRUMENTAL MUSIC

62. Musical instruments either accompanying the singing or played alone can add a great deal to liturgical celebrations.

"The pipe organ is to be held in high esteem, for it is the traditional musical instrument that adds a wonderful splendor to the Church's ceremonies and powerfully lifts up the spirit to God and to higher things.

"But other instruments also may be admitted for use in divine worship, with the knowledge and consent of the competent territorial authority. . . . This may be done, however, only on condition that the instruments are suitable, or can be made suitable, for sacred use, are in accord with the dignity of the place of worship, and truly contribute to the uplifting of the faithful."[43]

63. One criterion for accepting and using musical instruments is the genius and traditions of the particular peoples. At the same time, however, instruments that are generally associated and used only with worldly music are to be absolutely barred from liturgical services and religious devotions.[44] All musical

---

41. SC art. 23.
42. See SC art. 119.
43. SC art. 120.
44. See SCR, Instr. on music and the sacred liturgy, 3 Sept. 1958, no. 70 (1958) 652.

instruments accepted for divine worship must be played in such a way as to meet the requirements of a liturgical service and to contribute to the beauty of worship and the building up of the faithful.

64.   Musical instruments as the accompaniment for singing have the power to support the voice, to facilitate participation, and to intensify the unity of the worshiping assembly. But their playing is not to drown out the voice so that the texts cannot be easily heard. Instruments are to be silent during any part sung by the priest or ministers by reason of their function.

65.   As accompaniment for the choir or congregation the organ and other lawfully acceptable instruments may be played in both sung and read Masses. Solo playing is allowed at the beginning of Mass, prior to the priest's reaching the altar, at the presentation of the gifts, at the communion, and at the end of Mass.

With the appropriate adaptations, the same rule may be applied for other liturgical services.

66.   Solo playing of musical instruments is forbidden during Advent, Lent, the Easter triduum, and at services and Masses for the dead.

67.   It is, of course, imperative that organists and other musicians be accomplished enough to play properly. But in addition they must have a deep and thorough knowledge of the significance of the liturgy. That is required in order that even their improvisations will truly enhance the celebration in accord with the genuine character of each of its parts and will assist the participation of the faithful.[45]

IX. COMMISSIONS IN CHARGE OF PROMOTING SACRED MUSIC

68.   Diocesan music commissions make an important contribution to the promotion of sacred music as part of the program of pastoral liturgy in the diocese.

As far as possible, therefore, every diocese is to have such a commission to work in close conjunction with the diocesan liturgical commission.

For greater efficiency it will be better in most cases to combine the two commissions into one, made up of experts in each field.

It is also strongly recommended that, when it is considered helpful, several dioceses establish a single commission to carry out a unified program in an entire region through a coordinated use of resources.

69.   The liturgical commission recommended for bodies of bishops[46] is also to have responsibility for music and should accordingly include musical experts in its membership. It would also be well for this commission to establish contacts not only with the diocesan commissions but also with other associations

---

45. See nos. 24–25 of this Instruction.
46. See SC art. 44.

of the region that are involved with sacred music. This applies also to the institutes of pastoral liturgy mentioned in the same article of the Constitution.

At an audience granted to Cardinal Arcadio M. Larraona, Prefect of this Congregation, 9 February 1967, Pope Paul VI approved the present Instruction, confirmed it by his authority, and commanded its publication, setting 14 May 1967, Pentecost Sunday, as its effective date.

All things to the contrary notwithstanding.

TRES ABHINC ANNOS
SECOND INSTRUCTION
ON THE ORDERLY CARRYING OUT
OF THE CONSTITUTION
ON THE LITURGY

SACRED CONGREGATION OF RITES
CONSILIUM FOR THE IMPLEMENTATION
OF THE
CONSTITUTION ON THE SACRED LITURGY
MAY 4, 1967

AN OVERVIEW OF *TRES ABHINC ANNOS*
Rev. Msgr. Richard B. Hilgartner

The years following the Second Vatican Council's call for a reform of the Church's liturgy are sometimes described as confusing times during which changes and experiments were being introduced constantly with little explanation or preparation. The real work of liturgical reform, however, was anything but random or chaotic. The very subtitle of the instruction, *Tres abhinc annos*, explains the purpose of the document. Issued by the Sacred Congregation of Rites on behalf of the Consilium with the approval of Pope Paul VI, it offered a number of particular initiatives and clarifications, and put forth a number of changes in the Order of the Mass and the other ritual books in order to continue the orderly carrying out of *Sacrosanctum Concilium (SC)*.

SC announced the intention of the Church to undertake a reform of the Roman liturgy primarily through the simplification of her rites and the reform of the liturgical books. SC itself, however, did not enact or announce any particular reforms. The official reform of the Church's liturgy, as outlined in broad terms in SC, began soon after it was promulgated on December 4, 1963. Pope Paul VI's *motu proprio, Sacram Liturgiam* (January 25, 1964), put in place the structure—the special commission known as the Consilium—to oversee the work of the reform.

The Consilium's first instruction, *Inter Oecumenici*, issued by the Congregation of Rites in September 1964, introduced a number of reforms and adaptations that could be introduced quickly into the liturgy. Those adaptations were put into effect in 1965. At the same time, the Consilium was putting into place an ordered plan for the reform of the various liturgical rites and books. Several different working groups prepared various studies and would eventually prepare drafts of the reformed liturgical books. The Consilium also received feedback and evaluations from bishops and Conferences of Bishops regarding the various elements being introduced and some of the experimental changes that were underway.

Tres abhinc annos continued what was effectively begun in *Inter Oecumenici*, introducing several particular changes and adaptations in anticipation of the promulgation of a reformed *Missale Romanum* and other liturgical books. The instruction itself stated that there were some reforms that ought to be introduced gradually, and these particular adaptations could be introduced through mere adjustments to rubrics without having to alter the rites or books themselves. Primarily addressing matters in the Order of Mass and in the Liturgy of the Hours, *Tres abhinc annos* dealt with questions of the choice of Mass texts, the Lectionary, the simplification of gestures and postures, the way in which the Canon of the Mass is recited, liturgical vesture, and the use of the vernacular.

Sacrosanctum Concilium called for a study and reform of the liturgical calendar in such a way that the principal seasons and feasts of the Paschal

Mystery have prominence[1] and that they are not obscured by observances of lesser importance. *Tres abhinc annos* addressed several areas of concern in regard to the choice of Mass texts, such as the use of Votive Masses. It also addressed the common practice of making use of more than one Collect at Mass, which was commonplace at the time. It suggested that only one Collect should normally be used. There were exceptions, however, such as in some Ritual Masses, in which a second Collect could be combined with the first, but with only one concluding formula for the oration. This move illustrates a move toward simplicity and the priorities outlined in the *Universal Norms on the Liturgical Year and the General Roman Calendar* in place today.

Related to the matter of the choice of Mass texts is the question of readings from Scripture. The revised *Lectionary for Mass*, promulgated in 1969, was the response to *Sacrosanctum Concilium*'s call for the inclusion of more Scripture in the liturgy: "The treasures of the Bible are to be opened up more lavishly . . . "[2]; and "In sacred celebrations there is to be more reading from holy Scripture and it is to be more varied and apposite."[3] In the meantime, *Tres abhinc annos* permitted the broader use of collections of weekday readings developed by Conferences of Bishops, thus applying the principle of *Sacrosanctum Concilium* gradually before introducing the full reformed order of readings.

One of the principles applied most broadly throughout the liturgical reform was the Council Fathers' call for the simplification of gestures and postures in the liturgy: "For this purpose the rites are to be simplified, due care being taken to preserve their substance; elements that, with the passage of time, came to be duplicated or were added with but little advantage are now to be discarded. . . ."[4]

The most extensive adaptations announced in *Tres abhinc annos* pertain to the modification of rubrics of the *Missale Romanum*. These include the elimination of repetitive tracings of the Sign of the Cross over the Eucharistic sacrifice (leaving only one) and the tracings of the Sign of the Cross with the paten, the host, and the chalice, as well as the elimination of some genuflections and kissing of the altar at various points in the Mass. There were several other modifications for the sake of simplicity as well. The custom of the priest's joining of thumb and forefinger after handling the consecrated host (in order to preserve any particles that may remain on one's fingers) was no longer required, nor was the use of the maniple (a band of silk or other fabric draped over the priest's left arm). Regarding the latter, though it was never officially abrogated but only made optional, it fell out of use because the maniple was not listed among the sacred vestments in the 1970 *Missale Romanum*.[5]

Sacrosantum Concilium's call for the active participation of the faithful in the liturgy[6] was already bearing fruit in some of the adaptations that had been introduced in *Inter Oecumenici*. "Christ's faithful, when present at the mystery of faith, should not be there as strangers or silent spectators; on the contrary,

---

1. See *Sacrosanctum Concilium* (SC), 102–111.

2. Ibid., 51.

3. Ibid., 35 §1.

4. Ibid., 50.

5. See *The General Instruction of the Roman Missal* (GIRM/1970), 297–299.

6. See SC, 14.

through a good understanding of the rites and prayers they should take part in the sacred service conscious of what they are doing, with devotion and full involvement."[7] *Tres abhinc annos* summarized reports of the success of such adaptations by noting the "increased, more aware, and intense participation of the faithful everywhere in the liturgy."[8] Furthermore, the *Constitution* goes on to say that the faithful participate in the action by offering the sacrifice together with the priest. Though the *Constitution* did not offer an explanation as to the relationship between the priest's offering and the faithful's offering, or suggest how this could be brought to bear in the liturgy, it was clear that hearing and understanding the liturgical action and making the various responses and acclamations would contribute to such participation. *Tres abhinc annos* suggested, therefore, that the Canon of the Mass could be prayed aloud.

Also in response to the Council's call for the active participation of the faithful in liturgical action, perhaps the most significant single element contained in the instruction is the expansion of the use of the vernacular in the celebration of the liturgy. In 1964, authorization had been given to allow the vernacular to be used for certain elements in the liturgy, including the Scripture readings, the Prayer of the Faithful, the chants of the Ordinary of the Mass, the chants of the Propers of the Mass, the dialogues and greetings, the Lord's Prayer (with its introduction and embolism), the formula for giving Holy Communion, and the orations. During the years that followed, more and more Conferences of Bishops were submitting vernacular translations for approval for use, many conferences had requested permission for expansion of the use of vernacular, and it was becoming clear that the need for this would only grow. The use of various vernacular languages had become an effective means to the "full, conscious, and active participation"[9] of the faithful in the sacred liturgy. *Tres abhinc annos* gave to Conferences of Bishops the authority to allow the vernacular for the Canon of the Mass, essentially extending the use of the vernacular to the entire Mass. In addition, the instruction extended the use of the vernacular to the entire rites of Holy Orders and to the readings of the Divine Office (Liturgy of the Hours).

A separate decree from the Sacred Congregation of Rites was issued on May 18, 1967[10] to promulgate particular changes in the Order of Mass in the *Missale Romanum*. These particular changes were effective with the issuance of the decree. While the Consilium was given the mandate of overseeing the liturgical reforms prompted by the Council, only the Sacred Congregation of Rites (later the Congregation for Divine Worship and the Discipline of the Sacraments) could actually effect any changes in the rites themselves. Since the Consilium reported directly to the pope, it was not necessarily accountable to the Congregation of Rites, and yet it depended on the Congregation to enact its work. This relationship was often complicated and led to problems of communication between the two groups, since each reported its work directly to the pope. When the Congregation of Rites was replaced with the new Congregation for Divine Worship

---

7. See ibid., 48.

8. *Tres abhinc annos*, introduction.

9. Ibid., 14.

10. Prot R. 21/967.

in 1970, the Consilium would be replaced by a special commission working with the Congregation to oversee the final work on the reformed rites.

Looking back at the adaptations introduced in *Tres abhinc annos* in light of the 1970 *Missale Romanum* of Pope Paul VI, one can see clearly the gradual development of the reformed rites: the use of the vernacular, the simplification of the rites (especially its gestures and postures), and the place of Scripture. One cannot help but notice the consistent trajectory from *Sacrosanctum Concilium* through the instructions *Inter Oecumenici* and *Tres abhinc annos* to the *Missale Romanum* of 1970. Even today, the goals of Second Vatican Council, as articulated in *Sacrosanctum Concilium* are evident in the celebration of the liturgy according to the third edition of *The Roman Missal* (2010). The prominence of Scripture, the "noble simplicity"[11] of the rites, and the "full, conscious, and active participation"[12] of the faithful in the celebration of those rites remain among the guiding principles for those who prepare and enact the celebration of the Mass and the sacraments of the Church.

---

11. SC, 34.
12. Ibid., 14.

TRES ABHINC ANNOS

ON THE ORDERLY CARRYING OUT OF THE CONSTITUTION ON THE LITURGY

INSTRUCTION
SACRED CONGREGATION OF RITES

CONSILIUM FOR THE IMPLEMENTATION OF THE
CONSTITUTION ON THE SACRED LITURGY
MAY 4, 1967

Three years ago the Instruction *Inter Oecumenici*, issued by the Congregation of Rites, 26 September 1964, established a number of adaptations for introduction into the sacred rites. These adaptations, the firstfruits of the general liturgical reform called for by the conciliar Constitution on the Liturgy, took effect on 7 March 1965.

Their rich yield is becoming quite clear from the many reports of bishops, which attest to an increased, more aware, and intense participation of the faithful everywhere in the liturgy, especially in the holy sacrifice of the Mass.

To increase this participation even more and to make the liturgical rites, especially the Mass, clearer and better understood, the same bishops have proposed certain other adaptations. Submitted first to the Consilium, the proposals have undergone careful examination and discussion by the Consilium and the Congregation of Rites.

At least for the moment, not every proposal can be sanctioned. Others, however, do seem worth putting into effect immediately, because pastoral considerations commend them and they seem to offer no hindrance to the definitive reform of the liturgy yet to come. Further, they seem advantageous for the gradual introduction of that reform and are feasible simply by altering rubrics, not the existing liturgical books.

On this occasion it seems necessary to recall to everyone's mind that capital principle of church discipline which the Constitution on the Liturgy solemnly confirmed. "Regulation of the liturgy depends solely on the authority of the Church. Therefore no other person, not even if he is a priest, may on his own add, take away, or change anything in the liturgy" (SC art. 22, §§ 2–3).

Ordinaries, both local and religious, should therefore be mindful of their grave duty before the Lord to watch carefully over observance of this norm, so important for church life and order. All ministers of sacred rites as well as all the faithful should also willingly conform to it.

Individual spiritual growth and well-being demand this, as do harmonious cooperation in the Lord and mutual good example among the faithful in any local community. It is required also by the serious responsibility of each community to cooperate for the good of the Church throughout the world, especially today when the good or evil that develops in local communities quickly has an impact on the fabric of the whole family of God.

All should heed the warning of the Apostle: "For God is not a God of discord but of peace" (1 Cor 14:33).

The following adaptations and changes are instituted to achieve the more specific actualization and measured progress of the liturgical reform.

I. OPTIONS IN THE TEXTS FOR MASS

1. Outside Lent, on days of class III, the Mass either of the office of the day or of the commemoration made at morning prayer may be celebrated. If the second is chosen, the color of the office of the day may be used, in keeping with the *Codex rubricarum* no. 323.

2. Once the conference of bishops in its own region has sanctioned an order of readings for weekdays in Masses with a congregation this may also be used for Masses celebrated without a congregation and the readings may be in the vernacular.

This order of readings for weekdays may be used on certain days of class II, to be indicated in the lectionary itself, and in all Masses of class III and IV, whether Masses of the season or of saints, or votive Masses not having their own, strictly proper readings, that is, those that mention the mystery or person being celebrated.

3. On weekdays in Ordinary Time, in the celebration of the Mass of the Sunday preceding, one of the Prayers for Various Needs or an opening prayer from the votive Masses for Various Needs may be taken from the Missal to replace the prayer of the Sunday Mass.

II. PRAYERS IN THE MASS

4. In the Mass only one prayer is to be said; depending on the rubrics, however, there is added before the single conclusion:

    a. the prayer proper to a rite (*Codex rubricarum* no. 447);

    the prayer from the Mass for the profession of men or women religious, displacing the Mass of the day (*Rubr. spec. Missalis*);

    the prayer from the votive Mass *Pro sponsis* displaced by the Mass of the day (*Codex rubricarum* no. 380).

    b. the prayer from the votive Mass of thanksgiving (*Codex rubricarum* no. 382 and *Rubr. spec. Missalis*);

the prayer for the anniversaries of the pope and the bishop (*Codex rubricarum* nos. 449–450);

the prayer for the anniversary of the priest's own ordination (*Codex rubricarum* nos. 451–452).

5.   If in the same Mass several prayers were to be required before the single conclusion, the only one added in fact is the one most in keeping with the celebration.

6.   Instead of an imperated prayer, the bishop may insert one or more intentions for particular needs into the general intercessions.

In them by decree of the conference of bishops intentions also may be included for civil rulers (now used in various forms in the different countries) and special intentions for the particular needs of a nation or region.

III. CHANGES IN THE ORDER OF MASS

7.   The celebrant genuflects only:

   a. on going to or leaving the altar if there is a tabernacle containing the blessed sacrament;

   b. after elevating the host and the chalice;

   c. after the doxology at the end of the canon;

   d. at communion, before the words *Panem caelestem accipiam;*

   e. after the communion of the faithful, when he has placed the remaining hosts in the tabernacle.

All other genuflections are omitted.

8.   The celebrant kisses the altar only: at the beginning of Mass, while saying the *Oramus te Domine,* or on going to the altar, if the prayers at the foot of the altar are omitted; at the end of Mass before the blessing and dismissal of the people.

The kissing of the altar is otherwise omitted.

9.   At the offertory, after offering the bread and wine, the celebrant places on the corporal the paten with host and the chalice, omitting the signs of the cross with paten and with chalice.

He leaves the paten, with the host on it, on the corporal both before and after the consecration.

10.   In Masses celebrated with a congregation, even when not concelebrated, the celebrant may say the canon aloud. In sung Masses he may sing those parts of the canon that the rite for concelebration allows.

11.   In the canon, the celebrant:

a. begins the *Te igitur* standing erect and with hands outstretched;

b. makes one sign of the cross over the offerings at the words *benedicas +
    haec dona, haec munera, haec sancta sacrificia illibata,* in the prayer
    Te igitur. He makes no other sign of the cross over the offerings.

12.   After the consecration, the celebrant need not join thumb and forefinger;
should any particle of the host have remained on his fingers, he rubs his fingers
together over the paten.

13.   The communion rite for priest and people is to have the following arrangement: after he says *Panem caelestem accipiam,* the celebrant takes the host and,
facing the people, raises it, saying the *Ecce Agnus Dei,* then adding three times
with the people the *Domine, non sum dignus.* He then communicates himself
with host and chalice and immediately distributes communion in the usual
way to the people.

14.   The faithful receiving communion at the chrism Mass on Holy Thursday
may receive again at the evening Mass on the same day.

15.   A Mass celebrated with a congregation should include, according to circumstances, either a period of silence or the singing or recitation of a psalm or
canticle of praise, e.g., Ps 33 [34], *I will bless the Lord,* Ps 150, *Praise the Lord
in his sanctuary* or the canticles *Bless the Lord* [Dn 3:35] or *Blessed are you, O
Lord* [1 Chr 29:10].

16.   At the end of Mass the blessing of the people comes immediately before
the dismissal. It is recommended that the priest recite the *Placeat* silently as he
is leaving the altar.

Even Masses for the dead include the blessing and usual dismissal formulary, *Ite, Missa est,* unless the absolution follows immediately; in this case,
omitting the blessing, the celebrant says: *Benedicamus Domino* and proceeds
to the absolution.

IV. SOME SPECIAL CASES

17.   In nuptial Masses the celebrant says the prayers *Propitiare* and *Deus, qui
potestate* not between the *Pater noster* and its embolism, but after the breaking
of bread and the commingling, just before the *Agnus Dei.*

In a Mass celebrated facing the people the celebrant, after the commingling
and a genuflection, may go to the bride and groom and say the prayers just
mentioned. He then returns to the altar, genuflects, and continues the Mass in
the usual way.

18.   A Mass celebrated by a priest with failing sight or otherwise infirm and
having an indult to say a votive Mass, may have the following arrangement.

a. The priest says the prayers and the preface of the votive Mass.

b. Another priest, a deacon, reader, or server is to do the readings from the Mass of the day or from a weekday lectionary. If only a reader or server is present, he has permission also to read the gospel, but without the *Munda cor meum, Iube, domne, benedicere,* and *Dominus sit in corde meo.* The celebrant however says the *Dominus vobiscum* before the reading of the gospel and at the end kisses the book.

c. The choir, the congregation, or even the reader may take the entrance, offertory, and communion antiphons, and the chants between the readings.

V. VARIATIONS IN THE DIVINE OFFICE

19.   Pending complete reform of the divine office, on days of class I and class II with a matins of three nocturns, recitation of any one nocturn with three psalms and three readings is permitted. The hymn *Te Deum,* when called for by the rubrics, comes after the third reading. In the last three days of Holy Week the pertinent rubrics of the Roman Breviary are to be followed.

20.   Private recitation leaves out the absolution and blessing before the readings as well as the concluding *Tu autem.*

21.   In lauds and vespers celebrated with a congregation, in place of the *capitulum* there can be a longer reading from Scripture, taken, for example, from matins or from the Mass of the day, or from a weekday lectionary, and, as circumstances suggest, a brief homily. Unless Mass immediately follows, general intercessions may be inserted before the prayer.

When there are such insertions, there need only be three psalms, chosen in this way: at lauds one of the first three, then the canticle, then the final psalm; at vespers any three of the five psalms.

22.   At compline celebrated with a congregation participating the psalms can always be those of Sunday.

VI. SOME VARIATIONS IN RITES FOR THE DEAD

23.   The color for the office and Mass for the dead may in all cases be violet. But the conferences of bishops have the right to stipulate another color suited to the sensibilities of the people, not out of keeping with human grief, and expressive of Christian hope as enlightened by the paschal mystery.

24.   At the absolution over the coffin and over the grave, other responsories taken from matins for the dead, namely, *Credo quod Redemptor meus vivit, Qui Lazarum resuscitasti, Memento mei, Deus, Libera me, Domine, de viis inferni,* may replace the *Libera me, Domine.*

VII. VESTMENTS

25. The maniple is no longer required.

26. The celebrant may wear the chasuble for the *Asperges* before Mass on Sundays, for the blessing and imposition of ashes on Ash Wednesday, and for the absolution over a coffin or grave.

27. A concelebrant must wear the vestments obligatory for individual celebration of Mass (*Rite of Concelebration* no. 12).

When there is a serious reason, for example, a large number of concelebrants and a lack of vestments, the concelebrants, with the principal celebrant always excepted, may leave off a chasuble but never the alb and stole.

VIII. USE OF THE VERNACULAR

28. The competent territorial authority observing those matters contained in the Constitution on the Liturgy art. 36, § 3 and § 4 may authorize use of the vernacular in liturgies celebrated with a congregation for:

a. the canon of the Mass;

b. all the rites of holy orders;

c. the readings of the divine office, even in choral recitation.

In the audience granted 13 April 1967 to the undersigned Cardinal Arcadio Maria Larraona, Prefect of the Congregation of Rites, Pope Paul VI approved and confirmed by his authority the present Instruction as a whole and in all its parts, ordering its publication and its faithful observance by all concerned, beginning 29 June 1967.

EUCHARISTICUM MYSTERIUM
ON WORSHIP OF
THE EUCHARIST

INSTRUCTION
SACRED CONGREGATION OF RITES
MAY 25, 1967

AN OVERVIEW OF *EUCHARISTICUM MYSTERIUM*

Rev. Gilbert Ostdiek, OFM

PURPOSE OF THE DOCUMENT

Eucharisticum mysterium (EM), dated 25 May 1967, is the fifth major document issued to guide the implementation of *Sacrosanctum Concilium* (SC). The preceding documents were *Sacram Liturgiam* (January 25, 1964), *Inter Oecumenici* (September 26, 1964), *Musicam sacram* (March 5, 1967), and *Tres abhinc annos* (May 4, 1967). These documents had dealt only briefly with the Eucharist. Eucharist is the sole focus of EM. Its purpose is to "formulate practical norms" for celebration of the Eucharist and for worship of the reserved Sacrament "as may be suitable for the present situation."[1]

MAJOR THEMES OF THE DOCUMENT

To lay a foundation for those norms, the introduction[2] briefly recalls seven doctrinal principles about the Eucharist selected from recent documents, especially Pius XII's encyclical *Mediator Dei* (November 20, 1947), *Sacrosanctum Concilium* and other post-Conciliar documents, *Inter Oecumenici*, and Paul VI's encyclical *Mysterium fidei* (September 3, 1965). Along with familiar Eucharistic themes such as sacrifice, memorial, and sacred banquet, the introduction stresses several themes prominent in SC. Eucharist is the source and summit of worship and Christian life. It is the action not only of Christ, but also of the Church. In it the faithful join their self-offering to that of Christ. Sacrifice and sacred meal belong to the same mystery and are closely bound together (preconciliar theology had often separated them). The three major parts of EM then go on to set down practical norms for three aspects of Eucharistic practice.

Part I focuses on catechesis.[3] SC 19 had called for liturgical catechesis as part of the liturgical renewal. Taking up that call, this part of EM lays out general principles for pastors to follow when they catechize people about the meaning of the Eucharist. Eucharist is at the center of the life of the Church. The Eucharist calls Christians to unity and to reconciliation of divisions. In the Eucharist Christ is present to his people in manifold ways. A close connection exists between the Liturgy of the Word and the Liturgy of the Eucharist, a twofold table at which the faithful are nourished. The lay faithful and the ordained both share in the royal priesthood of Christ, though in different ways. Full, conscious, and active participation is the "aim to be considered before all else."[4]

---

1. *Eucharisticum mysterium* (EM), 2, 4.
2. See ibid., 3.
3. See ibid., 5–15.
4. *Sacrosanctum Concilium* (SC), 14.

The faithful's role is to recall the Paschal Mystery, to give thanks to God, to offer Christ's self-offering, through and with the priest celebrant and to join their self-offering to it. Catechesis for children about the Mass is to be suited to their age and ability. Finally, catechesis about the Mass should take the rites and prayers as its starting point.

Part II contains pastoral norms to guide several aspects of the Eucharistic celebration. These norms reflect the growing development of the general structure of the Mass and the rubrical details being worked out at the time. This part is divided into four sections.

The first section focuses on general norms for celebrations with a congregation.[5] Celebrations should show the unity of the assembly, based in the one Bread shared by all. This unity respects the proper roles of each, whether an ordained minister or one of the lay faithful. Nothing, such as simultaneous celebrations at multiple altars, should disrupt the community or divert their attention. Celebrations are to foster awareness of the local and universal Church, show hospitality to strangers, and provide opportunities for people of another language to participate according to their accustomed ways. To encourage active participation of the people, ministers should fulfill their role in a way that conveys an awareness of the meaning of the sacred actions. Other norms concern Mass on radio or TV and photography during celebrations. Attention is also given to other aspects: the arrangement and care of churches, which contribute greatly to worthy celebration and active participation; buildings adapted to the renewed liturgy; a main altar visible at the center of the assembly as a sign of Christ and his saving mysteries; respect for local sacred art treasures; and vestments of noble beauty. SC's concern for full participation is a recurring theme.

The second section treats celebrations on Sundays and weekdays.[6] After noting that Sunday is the "primordial feast day," this section makes recommendations such as: promoting singing to express the active participation; connecting celebrations in local oratories to that of the parish church for a coordinated pastoral effort; and preference that small non-clerical and similar communities take part in the local parish Mass on Sundays and feasts. Anticipated Masses for Sundays and feasts, where permitted by the local Ordinary, are to use the readings and prayers assigned to those days. Weekday celebrations in Advent and Lent deserve special care and participation. Meetings and gatherings of a religious character aptly culminate in celebration of the Eucharist. Themes of active participation and ecclesial unity are prominent.

The third section takes up Communion of the faithful.[7] The first pastoral norm notes that Communion of the faithful is not to take place earlier during Mass (as was a previous practice), but after the priest celebrant's, and they should be able to communicate with hosts consecrated at that Mass. Regarding Communion under both kinds, SC 55 had left discretion to the bishops, giving three cases as examples. The EM's list is expanded to include thirteen occasions, a list that is almost identical with the one that will later appear in *The General*

---

5. See EM, 16–24.
6. See ibid., 25–30.
7. See ibid., 31–41.

Instruction of the Roman Missal.[8] The Episcopal conference may determine the manner of receiving Holy Communion, whether kneeling or standing (with a prior sign of reverence). Next, the norms address particular issues, such as the relation between Holy Communion and the Sacrament of Penance (not to be celebrated during Mass), particular circumstances such as weddings, frequent and daily Communion, Viaticum, Communion of those unable to attend, and Communion under the species of wine alone. Themes threaded through these norms are appropriate reverence for the Eucharist, its connection to life events, and prolonging its effects in a fruitful daily life of continual thanksgiving.

The fourth section looks at the celebration of the Eucharist in the life and ministry of bishops and priests.[9] A number of these norms underline the ecclesial unity embodied in the hierarchic structure of the celebration by "a holy people united and ordered under its bishop." Priests are not only to observe the laws for valid and licit celebration, but also to choose those options which will ensure that the faithful take part consciously, actively, and fruitfully, as SC 11 had required. The norms for concelebration follow those of the *Rite of Concelebration* issued earlier in 1965, stressing that the celebration should symbolize not only the unity of the sacrifice and the priesthood, but also that of the community.

Part III provides norms for the worship of the reserved Eucharist. There are six sections. The first section addresses the reasons for reservation and prayer before the Blessed Sacrament.[10] Viaticum remains the primary purpose for reservation. Christ's presence in the sacrament derives from Mass and is directed toward both sacramental and spiritual communion.

The second section sets norms for the place of reservation.[11] There should be only one tabernacle, prominently placed, preferably in a special chapel suited to private prayer. Regarding tabernacles located on the altar where Mass is celebrated for a congregation, EM 55 notes significantly that the modes of Christ's presence unfold gradually: first in the gathered faithful, then in the Word proclaimed and explained, in the person of the minister, and finally, uniquely under the Eucharistic species.[12] Thus, since the Eucharistic presence is and should be seen as the fruit of consecration, the reserved Sacrament should not be present on the altar from the very beginning of the Mass.

The third section encourages Eucharistic devotions.[13] They "must harmonize with the liturgy, be in some way derived from it and lead the people toward the liturgy."[14]

The fourth section touches briefly on Eucharistic processions.[15] Solemn Eucharistic processions give public witness to the faith and devotion of the people. The local Ordinary is to decide when such processions are opportune today.

---

8. See *General Instruction of the Roman Missal* (GIRM), 242.

9. See EM, 42–48.

10. See ibid., 49–51.

11. See ibid., 52–57.

12. See SC, 7.

13. See EM, 58.

14. SC, 13.

15. See EM, 59.

The fifth section gives norms for exposition of the Blessed Sacrament.[16] "Care must be taken that during these expositions the worship given to the Blessed Sacrament should be seen, by signs, in its relation to the Mass."[17] The remaining norms speak about different forms of exposition and the inclusion of Scripture readings and song, and they prohibit celebration of Mass before the exposed sacrament and Exposition after Mass merely for the purpose of giving Benediction.

The sixth section concerns Eucharistic congresses in which "Christians seek to understand this mystery more deeply through a consideration of its many aspects (cf. above, no. 3). But they should celebrate it in accordance with the norms of the Second Vatican Council and should venerate it through devotions and private prayers, especially by solemn processions, in such a way that all these forms of devotion find their climax in the solemn celebration of Mass."[18]

IMPLEMENTATION OF *SACROSANCTUM CONCILIUM*

EM falls midway within the postconciliar process of renewing the liturgy of the Eucharist, which lasted from 1964 to 1970. *Sacram Liturgiam* (January 25, 1964) was the first official document on implementing the liturgical renewal. Regarding Mass, it had addressed only SC 52, calling for a Homily on Sundays and Holydays of Obligation.[19] At the conclusion of the process several documents established the final shape of the postconciliar celebration of the Eucharist. The apostolic constitution, *Missale Romanum* (April 3, 1969), promulgated *The General Instruction of the Roman Missal* and the new Roman Missal with the fully revised *Order of the Mass*. Shortly thereafter the *Order of Readings* was promulgated (May 25, 1969). The first *editio typica* of *The Roman Missal* was issued on March 26, 1970.

Various elements of the reform of the Mass were prepared by Groups X-XVIII working under the oversight and coordination of the Consilium. Most significant for EM was Group X, on the Order of the Mass. The need for EM had surfaced at the beginning of the process and became even clearer as the liturgical renewal progressed. Two years in the making (1965–1967), EM was developed simultaneously and in coordination with the work of other groups revising the Mass, especially Group X. It thus gives indirect evidence of how the reform was unfolding. In particular, it witnesses to how the very general prescriptions of SC were being worked out in detail, for example, in regard to Holy Communion under both kinds.[20]

AUTHORITY OF THE AOCUMENT

SC provides the fundamental context for interpreting liturgical law. In determining the relative weight of liturgical norms, as with all official pronouncements, it is necessary to distinguish between legislative and executory documents.

---

16. See ibid., 60–66.
17. Ibid., 60.
18. Ibid., 67.
19. See *Sacram Liturgiam* (SL), III.
20. See SC, 32.

Legislative documents, which contain liturgical laws that are binding for the whole Church, include SC, the *Code of Canon Law*, liturgical books, general decrees, and instructions (*institutiones* in Latin).

Executory documents include directories, circular letters, norms, and instructions (*instructiones* in Latin). These documents contain administrative regulations and directives which interpret the law and guide its implementation. These documents are also binding, though less so than legislative documents. But they are also transitional in character and are more readily superseded by later legislation.

EM is an executory document. Its authority is thus determined by its status as an executory document and the ways in which subsequent documents may have either affirmed or superseded it.

IMPACT OF THE DOCUMENT

The impact of EM is consistent with its intermediary place in the revision of the Mass. One important contribution early on was to root the pastoral norms of the reform in the doctrinal principles of preceding documents. Part I, on liturgical catechesis of the Eucharist, had a modest impact and surfaces only briefly in subsequent documents.[21] Part II, on the celebration of the Eucharist, reflects developments in the Order of Mass, but it does not yet have the same breadth and detail. Part III, on worship of the Eucharist, was to have greater impact. *Holy Communion and Worship of the Eucharist outside Mass* was issued six years later by the Sacred Congregation for Divine Worship (June 21, 1973). Though the later document is much longer [112 articles compared to 67], it owes much to EM, referenced in half of its footnotes. All in all, its goal was to ensure that "the mystery of the Eucharist is the true center of the sacred liturgy and indeed of the whole Christian life. Consequently the Church, guided by the Holy Spirit, continually seeks to understand and to live the Eucharist more fully."[22]

---

21. For example, the 1971 *General Catechetical Directory*, 58 and the 1978 *National Catechetical Directory* (United States), 120–121

22. EM, 1.

EUCHARISTICUM MYSTERIUM
ON WORSHIP OF THE EUCHARIST
INSTRUCTION

SACRED CONGREGATION OF RITES
MAY 25, 1967

INTRODUCTION

MORE RECENT DOCUMENTS ON THE EUCHARISTIC MYSTERY

1.   The eucharistic mystery is truly the center of the liturgy and indeed of the whole Christian life. Consequently the Church, guided by the Holy Spirit, continually seeks to understand this mystery more fully and more and more to derive its life from it.

In our day Vatican Council II has stressed several important aspects of this mystery.[1]

Through the Constitution on the Liturgy, after first recalling certain realities about the nature and importance of this sacrament, the Council established the norms for the reform of the rites of the sacrifice of the Mass so that the celebration of this mystery would further the active and full participation of the faithful.[2] In addition, the Constitution broadened the practice of concelebration and communion under both kinds.[3]

In the Constitution on the Church the Council set forth the close connection between the eucharist and the mystery of the Church.[4] In other documents the Council frequently stressed the important place of the eucharistic mystery in the life of the faithful[5] and its power to shed light on the meaning of human labor and indeed of all creation insofar in it "natural elements, after being fashioned by human hands, are changed into the glorious body and blood of Christ."[6]

For many of these pronouncements of the Council Pius XII had prepared the way, especially by his encyclical *Mediator Dei*.[7] In his encyclical *Mysterium*

---

1. See SC art. 2, 41, 47.

2. See SC art. 48–54, 56.

3. See SC art. 55, 57.

4. See LG nos. 3, 7, 11, 26, 28, 50.

5. See UR nos. 2, 15; CD nos. 15, 30; PO nos. 2, 5–8, 13–14, 18.

6. See GS 38.

7. See Pius XII, Encycl. *Mediator Dei*: AAS 39 (1947) 547–572; *idem*, Address to International Meeting on Pastoral Liturgy, Assisi, 22 Sept. 1956: AAS 48 (1956) 715–724.

fidei[8] Pope Paul VI has recalled the importance of certain aspects of eucharistic teaching, especially on the real presence of Christ and the worship due to this sacrament outside Mass.

NEED TO ATTEND SIMULTANEOUSLY TO THE COMPLETE TEACHING OF THESE DOCUMENTS

2.   In recent times certain aspects of the traditional teaching on this mystery have been considered more thoroughly and have been presented with new zeal to the devotion of the faithful. Research and practical measures of various kinds, especially in the field of liturgy and Scripture, have provided assistance.

There is, consequently, a need to draw out practical norms from the total teaching of such documents, in order to indicate what the relationship of the Christian people toward this mystery should be so that they may achieve that understanding and holiness which the Council set before the Church as an ideal.

It is important that the eucharistic mystery, fully considered under the many facets of its own reality, appear with the clarity it should have before the minds of the faithful; and also that the relationships that are recognized in church teaching as existing objectively between the various facets of the mystery become reflected in the life and mind of the faithful.

THE MOST NOTEWORTHY DOCTRINAL THEMES IN THE RECENT DOCUMENTS

3.   Among the doctrinal principles formulated in the Church's recent documents concerning the eucharist, it is useful to cite those that follow: they address the attitude of Christians toward this mystery and, therefore, have direct bearing on the purpose of this Instruction.

a. "In the human nature united to himself the Son of God, by overcoming death through his own death and resurrection, redeemed us and refashioned us into a new creation (see Gal 6:15; 2 Cor 5:17). By communicating his Spirit, Christ made us his brothers and sisters, called together from all nations, to be mystically his own Body. In that Body the life of Christ is bestowed on believers, who through the sacraments are united in a hidden and real way with Christ who suffered and was glorified."[9]

Therefore, "at the Last Supper, on the night he was betrayed, our Savior instituted the eucharistic sacrifice of his body and blood. He did this in order to perpetuate the sacrifice of the cross throughout the centuries until he should come again and so to entrust to his beloved Bride, the Church, a memorial of his death and resurrection: a sacrament of love, a sign of unity, a bond of charity, a paschal banquet in which Christ is eaten, the heart filled with grace, and a pledge of future glory given to us."[10]

Hence the Mass, the Lord's Supper, is at once and inseparably:

---

8. See Paul VI, Encycl. *Mysterium fidei.*
9. LG no. 7.
10. SC art. 47.

- the sacrifice in which the sacrifice of the cross is perpetuated;

- the memorial of the death and resurrection of the Lord who said: "Do this in memory of me" (Lk 22:19);

- the sacred banquet in which, through the communion of the body and blood of the Lord, the people of God share the benefits of the paschal sacrifice, renew the New Covenant with us made once and for all by God in Christ's blood, and in faith and hope foreshadow and anticipate the eschatological banquet in the Father's kingdom as they proclaim the death of the Lord "until he comes."[11]

b. In the Mass, therefore, the sacrifice and sacred meal form part of the same mystery in such a way that the closest bond conjoins the one with the other.

In the sacrifice of the Mass the Lord is offered when "he begins to be sacramentally present as the spiritual food of the faithful under the appearance of bread and wine."[12] The reason that Christ entrusted this sacrifice to the Church was that the faithful might share in it both spiritually, by faith and charity, and sacramentally, through the sacred meal of communion. A sharing in the Lord's Supper is always a communion with Christ offering himself to the Father for us as a sacrifice.[13]

c. The celebration of the eucharist at Mass is the action not only of Christ but also of the Church. It is Christ's act because, perpetuating in an unbloody way the sacrifice consummated on the cross,[14] he offers himself to the Father for the salvation of the world through the ministry of priests.[15] It is the Church's act because, as the Bride and minister of Christ exercising together with him the role of priest and victim, the Church offers him to the Father and at the same time completely offers itself together with him.[16]

In this way, especially in the great eucharistic prayer, the Church gives thanks together with Christ to the Father in the Holy Spirit for all the benefits he gives us in creation and in a singular way in the paschal mystery and asks the Father for the coming of his kingdom.

d. Hence no Mass, in fact no liturgical service, is a merely private act, but the celebration of the Church as a society composed of different orders and ministries in which all the members have an active part in keeping with their proper order and office.[17]

---

11. See SC art. 6, 10, 47, 106; PO no. 4.

12. Paul VI, Encycl. *Mysterium fidei.*

13. See Pius XII, Encycl. *Mediator Dei*: AAS 39 (1947) 564–566.

14. See SC art. 47.

15. See Council of Trent, sess. 22, *Decr. de Missa* cap. 1: Denz-Schön 1741.

16. See LG no. 11; SC art. 47–48; PO nos. 2, 5. Pius XII, loc. cit.: 552. Paul VI Encycl. *Mysterium fidei.*

17. See SC art. 26–28 and no. 44 of this Instruction.

e. The celebration of the eucharist in the sacrifice of the Mass is truly the origin and the purpose of the worship that is shown to the eucharist outside Mass. For the sacred elements that remain after Mass come from the Mass and they are reserved after Mass so that the faithful who cannot be present at Mass may be united to Christ and the celebration of his sacrifice through sacramental communion received with the right dispositions.[18]

Hence the eucharistic sacrifice is the source and the summit of all the Church's worship and of the entire Christian life.[19] The faithful participate more fully in this sacrifice of thanksgiving, expiation, petition, and praise not only when they wholeheartedly offer the sacred victim and in him offer themselves to the Father with the priest, but also when they receive the same victim in the sacrament.

f. It should be absolutely clear "that all the faithful show this holy sacrament the worship of adoration that is due to God himself, as has always been the practice recognized in the Catholic Church. Nor is the sacrament to be less the object of adoration on the grounds that it was instituted by Christ the Lord to be received as food."[20] For even in the reserved sacrament he is to be adored,[21] because he is substantially present there through the conversion of the bread and wine that, following the Council of Trent,[22] is most accurately termed transubstantiation.

g. Therefore, the eucharistic mystery must be considered in its entirety, both in the celebration of Mass and in the worship of the sacred elements reserved after Mass in order to extend the grace of the sacrifice.[23]

The principles stated must be the source of the norms on the practical arrangement of the worship of this sacrament even after Mass and of its correlation with the proper arrangement of the Mass in conformity with the directives of Vatican Council II and of other pertinent documents of the Apostolic See.[24]

GENERAL INTENT OF THIS PRESENT INSTRUCTION

4.   For this reason Pope Paul VI ordered the Consilium for the Implementation of the Constitution on the Liturgy to prepare a special instruction that would issue such practical norms, fitted to contemporary circumstances.

---

18. See no. 49 of this Instruction.

19. See LG no. 11; SC art. 41; PO nos. 2, 5, 6; UR no. 15.

20. Council of Trent, sess. 13, *Decr. de Eucharistia* cap. 5: Denz-Schön 1643.

21. See Paul VI, Encycl. *Mysterium fidei*. Pius XII, loc. cit.: 569

22. See Council of Trent, loc. cit. cap. 4: Denz-Schön 1652.

23. See the treatment of the Mass in the documents already cited; all of them deal with the twofold aspect of the eucharist: PO nos. 5, 18. Paul VI, Encycl. *Mysterium fidei*. Pius XII, Encycl. *Mediator Dei*: AAS 39 (1947) 547–572; *idem*, Address at Assisi: AAS 48 (1956) 715–723.

24. See Paul VI, Encycl. *Mysterium fidei*. Pius XII, Encycl. *Mediator Dei*: AAS 39 (1947) 547–572. SCR, Instr. de musica sacra, 3 Sept. 1958: AAS 50 (1958) 630–663; *idem*, Instr. InterOec, 26 Sept 1964.

The purpose intended for these norms is both to provide the broad principles for catechesis of the faithful about the eucharistic mystery and to make more understandable the signs through which the eucharist is celebrated as the memorial of the Lord and worshiped in the Church as a lasting sacrament.

For although this mystery has a supreme and unique excellence, namely, the presence of the very author of holiness, nevertheless in common with the other sacraments, it too is the symbol of a sacred reality and the visible expression of an invisible grace.[25] Hence the more pertinent and clear the signs involved in its celebration and worship, the more surely and effectively will it penetrate the minds and lives of the faithful.[26]

PART I
GENERAL PRINCIPLES TO BE GIVEN PROMINENCE IN CATECHIZING THE PEOPLE ON THE EUCHARISTIC MYSTERY

REQUIREMENTS OF PASTORS WHO ARE TO GIVE INSTRUCTION ABOUT THIS MYSTERY

5.   Effective catechesis is necessary so that the eucharistic mystery might suffuse the minds and lives of the faithful.

To hand on this instruction properly, pastors should not only keep in mind the integral teaching of faith, which is contained in the documents of the magisterium, but also with heart and life enter deeply into the spirit of the Church on this matter.[27] Then they will more readily judge which of the many aspects of this mystery best suits the faithful in any given situation.

In view of what was said in no. 3, the following points, among others, deserve special attention.

THE EUCHARISTIC MYSTERY AS CENTER OF THE WHOLE LIFE OF THE CHURCH

6.   Catechesis on the eucharistic mystery should aim at helping the faithful realize deeply that its celebration is the true center of the whole Christian life, both for the universal Church and for the local congregations of that Church. For "the other sacraments, like every ministry of the Church and every work of the apostolate, are linked with the holy eucharist and have it as their end. For the most blessed eucharist contains the Church's entire spiritual wealth, that is, Christ himself. He is our Passover and living bread; through his flesh, made living and life-giving by the Holy Spirit, he is giving people life and thereby inviting and leading them to offer themselves together with him, as well as their labors and all created things."[28]

---

25. See Council of Trent, sess. 13, *Decr. de SS. Eucharistia* cap. 3: Denz-Schön 1639. See also ST 3a, 60.1.

26. See SC art. 33, 59.

27. See SC art. 14, 17–18.

28. PO no. 5.

The eucharist is the effective sign and sublime cause of the sharing in divine life and the unity of the people of God by which the Church exists.[29] It is the culmination both of God's action sanctifying the world in Christ and of the worship we offer to Christ and through him to the Father in the Holy Spirit.[30] Its celebration "is the outstanding means whereby the faithful may express in their lives and manifest to others the mystery of Christ and the real nature of the true Church."[31]

THE EUCHARISTIC MYSTERY AS THE CENTER OF THE LOCAL CHURCH

7.   Through the eucharist "the Church continually lives and grows. This Church of Christ is truly present in all lawful, local congregations of the faithful, which, united with their bishops, are themselves called Churches in the New Testament. For in their own locality these Churches are the new people called by God in the Holy Spirit and in great fullness (see 1 Thes 1:5). In them the faithful are gathered together through the preaching of Christ's Gospel and the mystery of the Lord's Supper is celebrated, so that 'through the meal of the body and blood of the Lord the whole brotherhood is joined together.'[32] Any community of the altar, under the sacred ministry of the bishop,"[33] or of a priest who takes his place,[34] "stands out clearly as a symbol of that charity and 'unity of the Mystical Body without which there can be no salvation.'[35] In these communities, though frequently small and poor or living in isolation, Christ is present and the power of his presence gathers together the one, holy, catholic, and apostolic Church. For 'the sharing of the body and blood of Christ does nothing less than transform us into what we receive.'"[36, 37]

THE EUCHARISTIC MYSTERY AND THE UNITY OF CHRISTIANS

8.   In addition to those things that concern the ecclesial community and the individual faithful, pastors should pay special attention to that part of the doctrine in which the Church teaches that the memorial of the Lord, celebrated in accord with his will, signifies and brings about the unity of all who believe in him.[38]

In compliance with the Decree on Ecumenism of Vatican Council II,[39] the faithful should be led to a proper appreciation of the values that are preserved in the eucharistic tradition through which their brothers and sisters in other Christian Confessions have continued to celebrate the Lord's Supper. For "when

---

29. See LG no. 11; UR nos. 2, 15.
30. See SC art. 10.
31. SC art. 2; see also art.
32. Prayer from the Mozarabic Rite: PL 96, 759 B.
33. LG no. 26.
34. See SC art. 42.
35. See ST 3a, 73.3
36. Leo the Great, *Serm.* 63, 7: PL 54, 357 C.
37. LG no. 26.
38. See LG nos. 3, 7, 11, 26; UR no. 2.
39. See UR nos. 15 and 22.

in the Lord's Supper they commemorate his death and resurrection, they attest to the sign of their life in communion with Christ and they await his glorious Second Coming."[40] Those, moreover, who have preserved the sacrament of orders in the celebration of the eucharist, "united with the bishop and having access to God the Father through the Word incarnate, crucified and glorified, attain communion with the Trinity by the outpouring of the Holy Spirit as people who have become 'partakers in the divine nature' (2 Pt 1:4). In each of these Churches, therefore, the celebration of the eucharist builds up and gives increase 'to the Church of God and its concelebration shows forth the communion of these Churches with each other.'"[41]

Above all in the celebration of the mystery of unity all Christians should be filled with sadness over the divisions separating them. Therefore, they should fervently pray to God that all Christ's disciples may daily come to a deeper understanding of the eucharistic mystery conformed to his own mind. They should celebrate it in such a way that, made partakers in the body of Christ, they may become the one Body (see 1 Cor 10:17), "linked by those same bonds with which he himself desired it to be joined."[42]

THE DIFFERENT MODES OF CHRIST'S PRESENCE

9.   In order to achieve a deeper understanding of the eucharistic mystery, the faithful should be instructed in the principal modes by which the Lord is present to his Church in liturgical celebrations.[43]

He is always present in an assembly of the faithful gathered in his name (see Mt 18:20). He is also present in his word, for it is he who is speaking as the sacred Scriptures are read in the Church.

In the eucharistic sacrifice he is present both in the person of the minister, "the same now offering through the ministry of the priest who formerly offered himself on the cross,"[44] and above all under the eucharistic elements.[45] For in that sacrament, in a unique way, Christ is present, whole and entire, God and man, substantially and continuously. This presence of Christ under the elements "is called the real presence not to exclude the other kinds, as though they were not real, but because it is real par excellence."[46]

CONNECTION BETWEEN THE LITURGY OF THE WORD AND THE LITURGY OF THE EUCHARIST

10.   Pastors should, therefore, "insistently teach the faithful to take their part in the entire Mass," by showing the close connection that exists between the liturgy of the word and the celebration of the Lord's Supper, so that they may

---

40. UR no. 22.
41. UR no. 15: AAS 57 (1965) 102; ConstDecrDecl 265.
42. Paul VI, Encycl. *Mysterium fidei.*
43. See SC art. 7.
44. Council of Trent, *Decr. de Missa* cap. 2: Denz-Schön 1743.
45. See SC art. 7.
46. Paul VI, Encycl. *Mysterium fidei.*

clearly perceive how the two constitute a single act of worship.[47] "The preaching of the word is necessary for the administration of the sacraments. For the sacraments are sacraments of faith and faith has its origin and sustenance in the word."[48] This is especially true of the celebration of Mass, in which the purpose of the liturgy of the word is to develop in a specific way the close link between the proclamation and hearing of the word of God and the eucharistic mystery.[49]

The faithful, therefore, hearing the word of God, should realize that the wonders it proclaims achieve their summit in the paschal mystery, whose memorial is celebrated sacramentally in the Mass. In this way, the faithful, receiving the word of God and nourished by it, will be led in a spirit of thanksgiving to a fruitful participation in the mysteries of salvation. In this way the Church feeds upon the bread of life as it comes from the table of both the word of God and the body of Christ.[50]

THE UNIVERSAL PRIESTHOOD AND THE MINISTERIAL PRIESTHOOD IN THE CELEBRATION OF THE EUCHARIST

11. The more clearly the faithful recognize the place they have in the liturgical assembly and the parts they are to fulfill in the eucharistic celebration the more conscious and fruitful will be the active participation that belongs to a community.[51]

Catechesis, then, should explain the teaching on the royal priesthood, which consecrates the faithful through their rebirth and the anointing of the Holy Spirit.[52]

There should also be further explanation both of the role of the ministerial priesthood in the celebration of the eucharist, which differs from the universal priesthood of the faithful in essence and not merely in degree,[53] and of the parts fulfilled by others who exercise some ministry.[54]

THE NATURE OF ACTIVE PARTICIPATION IN THE MASS

12. It should be explained that all who gather for the eucharist are that holy people who, together with the ministers, have a part in the sacred rites. The priest alone, insofar as he acts in the person of Christ, consecrates the bread and wine. Nevertheless the active part of the faithful in the eucharist consists in: giving thanks to God as they are mindful of the Lord's passion, death, and resurrection; offering the spotless victim not only through the hands of the priest but also together with him; and, through the reception of the body of the Lord,

---

47. See SC art. 56.
48. PO no. 4.
49. See PO no. 4; see also no. 3 of this Instruction.
50. See DV no. 21.
51. See SC art. 14, 26, 30, 38.
52. See LG no. 10; PO no. 2. Paul VI, Encycl. *Mysterium fidei*.
53. See LG no. 10; PO nos. 2, 5.
54. See SC art. 28–29.

entering into the communion with God and with each other that participation is meant to lead to.[55] For there is a fuller share in the Mass when the people, properly disposed, receive the body of the Lord sacramentally in the Mass itself, out of obedience to his own words: "Take and eat."[56]

Like Christ's own passion, this sacrifice, though offered for all, "has no effect except in those who are united to Christ's passion by faith and charity. . . . Even for these, its benefits are greater or less in proportion to their devotion."[57]

All these things should be explained to the faithful in such a way that in consequence they share actively in the celebration of the Mass by both their inner affections and the outward rites, in keeping with the principles laid down by the Constitution on the Liturgy,[58] which have been further specified by the Instruction *Inter Oecumenici* of 26 September 1964, the Instruction *Musicam sacram* of 5 March 1967,[59] and the Instruction *Tres abhinc annos* of 4 May 1967.

INFLUENCE OF THE EUCHARISTIC CELEBRATION ON THE DAILY LIFE OF THE FAITHFUL

13. What the faithful have received through faith and the sacrament in the celebration of the eucharist they should hold to by the way they live. They should strive to live their whole lives joyfully in the strength of this heavenly food, as sharers in the death and resurrection of the Lord. After taking part in the Mass therefore all should be "eager to do good works, to please God, and to live rightly, devoted to the Church, putting into practice what they have learned and growing in devotion."[60] They will seek to fill the world with the Christian spirit and "in all things, even in the midst of human affairs," to become witnesses of Christ.[61]

For "no Christian community is ever built up unless it has its roots and center in the eucharistic liturgy, which, therefore, is the indispensable starting point for leading people to a sense of community."[62]

CATECHESIS FOR CHILDREN ON THE MASS

14. Those who take care of the religious instruction of children, especially parents, pastors, and teachers, should be careful, when introducing them gradually to the mystery of salvation,[63] to give catechesis on the Mass the importance it deserves. This catechesis, suited to children's age and capacities, should, by means of the main rites and prayers of the Mass, aim at conveying its meaning, including what relates to taking part in the Church's life.

---

55. See SC art. 28–29.

56. See SC art. 55.

57. ST 3a, 79.7 ad 2.

58. See SC art. 26–32.

59. See SCR, Instr. *Musicam sacram*, 5 March 1967.

60. Hippolytus, *Traditio Apostolica* 21: B. Botte, ed., 58–59. See SC art. 9, 10; AA no. 3; AG no. 39; PO no. 5.

61. See GS no. 43: AAS 58 (1966) 1063; ConstDecrDecl 746.

62. PO no. 6.

63. See GE no. 2: AAS 58 (1966) 730–731; ConstDecrDecl 391–392.

All these things should be kept in mind in the special situation of preparing children for first communion, so that it will be very clear to them that this communion is their complete incorporation into the Body of Christ.[64]

15.   The Council of Trent prescribes that pastors should frequently "either themselves or through others, elaborate on some part of what is read at Mass and, among other things, explain something of the mystery of this sacrament."[65]

Pastors should therefore guide the faithful to a full understanding of this mystery of faith by suitable catechesis, which should take as its starting point the mysteries of the liturgical year and the rites and prayers that are part of the celebration. Pastors should do this by explaining the meaning of these rites and prayers, especially those of the great eucharistic prayer, and lead the people to grasp the mystery that the rites and prayers signify and accomplish.

PART II
CELEBRATION OF THE MEMORIAL OF THE LORD

I. SOME GENERAL NORMS ON STRUCTURING CELEBRATION OF THE MEMORIAL OF THE LORD IN THE COMMUNITY OF THE FAITHFUL

UNITY OF THE COMMUNITY SHOWN IN THE CELEBRATION

16.   In virtue of baptism "there is neither Jew nor Greek, slave nor freeman, male nor female," but all are one in Christ Jesus (see Gal 3:28). Therefore the assembly that most fully manifests the nature of the Church in the eucharist is one in which the faithful of every class, age, and condition are joined together.

Nevertheless the unity of the community, which is derived from the one bread in which all share (see 1 Cor 10:17), has a hierarchic structure. For this reason it requires that "each one, minister or layperson, who has an office to perform, should do all of, but only, those parts which pertain to that office by the nature of the rite and the principles of liturgy."[66]

The best example of this unity is found "in the full, active participation of all God's holy people . . . in the same eucharist, in a single prayer, at one altar at which the bishop presides, surrounded by his college of priests and by his ministers."[67]

AVOIDING THE SCATTERING AND DISTRACTING OF THE COMMUNITY

17.   In liturgical celebrations, any breakup or distraction of the community must be avoided. Care must be taken, accordingly, not to have two liturgical

---

64. See PO no. 5.
65. Council of Trent, sess. 22, Decr. de Missa cap. 8: Denz
66. SC art. 28.
67. SC art. 41; see also LG no. 26.

celebrations going on in the same church at the same time, since this would distract the attention of the people.

Above all this must be stressed in regard to the celebration of the eucharist. Hence the scattering of the people that generally occurs when Masses are celebrated at the same time in the same church should be carefully avoided on Sundays and holydays of obligation when Mass is celebrated for the people.

The same rule should be applied as far as possible on other days as well. The best way of achieving this is concelebration, in conformity with the law, by priests who want to celebrate Mass at the same time.[68]

Similar precautions must be taken against the communal or choral recitation of the office, sermons, the administration of baptisms, and the celebration of marriages at the same time and in the same church as a scheduled Mass for the people is being celebrated.

SENSE OF THE LOCAL AND UNIVERSAL COMMUNITY FOSTERED

18.   In the celebration of the eucharist, a sense of community should be fostered so that all will feel united with their brothers and sisters in the communion of the local and universal Church and even in a certain way with all humanity. For in the sacrifice of the Mass Christ offers himself for the salvation of the whole world and the congregation of the faithful is the type and sign of the unity of the human family in Christ its Head.[69]

WELCOMING VISITORS INTO THE LOCAL CELEBRATION OF THE EUCHARIST

19.   The faithful who take part in the celebration of the eucharist outside their own parish should join in the form of the sacred services that the local community uses.

Pastors have the responsibility of providing suitable ways to assist the faithful from other regions to join with the local community. This should be of particular concern in the churches of large cities and in places where many of the faithful gather for vacations.

Where there are many visitors or expatriates of another language, pastors should provide them with the opportunity, at least occasionally, to participate in the Mass celebrated in the way customary for them. "Nevertheless steps should be taken enabling the faithful to say or to sing together in Latin those parts of the Ordinary of the Mass belonging to them."[70]

CAREFULNESS ABOUT THE MANNER OF CELEBRATING

20.   To ensure that the celebration is conducted properly and that the faithful take an active part, the ministers should not only fulfill their role correctly

---

68. See no. 47 of this Instruction.
69. See LG no. 3.
70. SC art. 54.

according to the norms of liturgical laws, but their very bearing should communicate a sense of the sacred.

The people have the right to be nourished by the word of God proclaimed and explained. Accordingly priests are to give a homily whenever it is prescribed or seems advisable; but they are also to see to it that anything that their functions require them and the ministers to pronounce is said or sung so distinctly that the people hear it clearly, grasp its meaning, and are thus drawn to respond and participate willingly.[71] To this end ministers should be prepared through the right kind of training, especially in seminaries and religious houses.

CANON OF THE MASS

21.   a. According to the provisions of the Instruction *Tres abhinc annos*, 4 May 1967, no. 10, in Masses celebrated with a congregation, even when not concelebrated, the priest celebrant may say the canon aloud. In sung Masses he may sing those parts of the canon that may be sung according to the *Rite of Concelebration*.

b. In printing the words of consecration the custom of setting them in type different from the general text should be maintained in order that they may stand out more clearly.

RADIO AND TELEVISION BROADCASTS OF MASS

22.   Where, according to the intent of the Constitution on the Liturgy art. 20, the Mass is televised or broadcast, local Ordinaries should see that the prayer and participation of the faithful in attendance are not disturbed; furthermore, the celebration should be marked with such care and dignity that it is a model of celebrating the sacred mysteries according to the laws of the liturgical reform.[72]

PHOTOGRAPHS DURING THE CELEBRATION OF THE EUCHARIST

23.   Strict care should be taken to ensure that liturgical celebrations, especially of the Mass, are not disturbed by the practice of taking photographs. Where a reasonable cause for them exists, everything should be done with great restraint and according to the norms established by the local Ordinary.

IMPORTANCE OF THE ARRANGEMENT OF CHURCHES FOR WELL-ORDERED CELEBRATIONS

24.   "The church, the house of prayer, must be well cared for and suited to prayer and liturgy. There the eucharist is celebrated and reserved and the faithful gather for worship. There the presence of the Son of God, our Savior, offered on the altar of sacrifice for us, is treasured and revered as the aid and solace of the faithful."[73]

---

71. See SC art. 11.
72. See SCR, Instr. MusSacr, 5 March 1967, nos. 6, 8, and 11.
73. PO no. 5.

Pastors should understand, therefore, that the becoming arrangement of the place of worship contributes much to a right celebration and to the active participation of the faithful.

For this reason the rules and directives given in the Instruction *Inter Oecumenici* (nos. 90–99) should be followed regarding: the building of churches and their adaptation to the reformed liturgy; the construction and appointment of altars; the suitable placement of chairs for the celebrant and ministers; the provision of a proper place for the proclamation of the readings; the arrangement of places for the faithful and the choir.

Above all, the main altar should be so placed and constructed that it always appears as a sign of Christ himself, as the place in which the sacred mysteries are carried out, and as the focal point for the gathered faithful, which demands the highest respect.

Care should be taken against destroying treasures of sacred art in the course of remodeling churches. On the judgment of the local Ordinary, after consulting experts and, when applicable, with the consent of other concerned parties, the decision may be made to relocate some of these treasures in the interest of the liturgical reform. In such a case this should be done with good sense and in such a way that even in their new locations they will be set up in a manner befitting and worthy of the works themselves.

Pastors should remember that the material and the design of vestments greatly contribute to the dignity of liturgical celebrations. Vestments should be designed "for a noble beauty rather than mere sumptuous display."[74]

II. CELEBRATIONS ON SUNDAYS AND WEEKDAYS

CELEBRATION OF THE EUCHARIST ON SUNDAY

25.   Whenever the community gathers to celebrate the eucharist, it shows forth the death and resurrection of the Lord in the hope of his glorious coming. But the Sunday assembly shows this best of all for this is the day of the week on which the Lord rose from the dead and on which, from apostolic tradition, the paschal mystery is celebrated in the eucharist in a special way.[75]

In order that the faithful may willingly fulfill the precept to keep this day holy and may understand why the Church calls them together to celebrate the eucharist every Sunday, right from the beginning of their Christian formation it should be set before them and instilled into them that Sunday is the original holyday.[76] On this day above all, gathered as one, they are to hear the word of God and share in the paschal mystery.

Futhermore, all measures should be encouraged that are designed to make Sunday "a day of joy and freedom from work."[77]

---

74. SC art. 124.
75. See SC art. 6 and 106.
76. See SC art. 106.
77. SC art. 106.

26.   It is fitting that the sense of ecclesial community, fostered and expressed especially by the shared celebration of Mass on Sunday, should be carefully developed. This applies to assemblies with the bishop, above all in the cathedral church, and to the parish assembly, whose pastor takes the place of the bishop.[78]

It is of great advantage to promote that active participation of the whole people in the Sunday celebration which is expressed in singing. In fact as far as possible the sung form of celebration should be the first choice.[79]

Especially on Sundays and holydays the celebrations that take place in other churches and oratories must be coordinated with the celebrations in the parish church so that they contribute to the overall pastoral program. It is indeed advantageous that small, nonclerical, religious communities and other such communities, especially those that work in the parish, take part in the parish Mass on those days.

As to the hours and the number of Masses to be celebrated in parishes, the convenience of the parish community must be kept in mind and the number of Masses not so multiplied as to harm pastoral effectiveness. Such would be the case, for example, if because there were too many Masses, only small groups of the faithful would attend each one in churches that can hold many people; or if, also because of the number of Masses, the priests were to be so overwhelmed with work that they could fulfill their ministry only with great difficulty.

MASSES WITH PARTICULAR GROUPS

27.   So that the unity of the parish community may stand out in the eucharist on Sundays and holydays, Masses for such particular groups as parish societies should, if possible, preferably be held on weekdays. If they cannot be transferred to weekdays, care should be taken to maintain the unity of the parish community by incorporating these particular groups into the parish celebrations.

SUNDAY AND HOLYDAY MASSES ANTICIPATED ON THE PREVIOUS EVENING

28.   Where indult of the Apostolic See permits fulfillment on the preceding Saturday evening of the obligation to participate in the Sunday Mass, pastors should carefully teach the faithful the meaning of this favor and should take steps to prevent its lessening in any way the sense of what Sunday is. This concession is meant to enable the faithful in today's conditions to celebrate more easily the day of the Lord's resurrection.

All concessions and contrary customs notwithstanding, this Mass may be celebrated only on Saturday evening, at hours to be determined by the local Ordinary.

---

78. See SC art. 41–42; LG no. 28; PO no. 5.
79. SCR. Instr. MusSacr, 5 March 1967, nos. 16 and 27.

On the Saturday evening, the Mass is to be celebrated as assigned in the calendar for the Sunday and the homily and general intercessions are not to be omitted.

All these points apply also to the celebration of Mass that, for the same reason, is anywhere allowed on the evening before a holyday of obligation.

The evening Mass before Pentecost Sunday is the Mass of the Saturday vigil with the *Credo*. Likewise the evening Mass before Christmas is the Mass of the vigil celebrated in a festal way with white vestments and with the *Alleluia* and the preface from the Mass of the Nativity. The evening Mass before Easter may not be started before dusk or certainly not before sunset. This Mass is always the Mass of the Easter Vigil, which by reason of its special significance in the liturgical year and in the whole Christian life must be celebrated with the liturgical rites for this holy night according to the rite for the Easter Vigil.

The faithful who begin to celebrate the Sunday or holyday of obligation on the evening of the preceding day may go to holy communion even if they have already done so that morning. Those who "receive communion during the Mass of the Easter Vigil or during the Mass of the Lord's Nativity may receive again at the second Mass of Easter and at one of the Day Masses of Christmas."[80] Likewise "the faithful receiving communion at the chrism Mass on Holy Thursday may receive again at the evening Mass on the same day," in accordance with the norm of the Instruction *Tres abhinc annos*, 4 May 1967, no. 14.

MASSES CELEBRATED ON WEEKDAYS

29. The faithful should be invited to take part in Mass often on weekdays as well, even daily.

This is especially recommended for those weekdays that should be celebrated with particular attention, above all in Lent and Advent; also on lesser feasts of the Lord and on certain feasts of the Blessed Virgin Mary or of the saints that are held in special honor in the universal or the local Church.

MASS AT GATHERINGS TO FOSTER THE CHRISTIAN LIFE

30. It is very fitting that meetings or congresses aimed at fostering the Christian life or the apostolate or at promoting religious studies, as well as spiritual retreats of various kinds, should be planned in such a way that the eucharistic celebration is their high point.

III. COMMUNION OF THE FAITHFUL

COMMUNION OF THE FAITHFUL AT MASS

31. The faithful share more fully in the celebration of the eucharist through sacramental communion. It is strongly recommended that they should receive

---

80. InterOec no. 60.

it as a rule in the Mass itself and at that point in the celebration which is prescribed by the rite, that is, right after the communion of the priest celebrant.[81]

In order that the communion may stand out more clearly even through signs as a participation in the sacrifice actually being celebrated, steps should be taken that enable the faithful to receive hosts consecrated at that Mass.[82]

It is proper for the priest celebrant especially to be the minister of communion; nor should he continue the Mass until the communion of the faithful has been completed. Other priests or deacons may, if need be, assist the priest celebrant.[83]

COMMUNION UNDER BOTH KINDS

32.   Holy communion has a more complete form as a sign when it is received under both kinds. For in this manner of reception (without prejudice to the principles laid down by the Council of Trent,[84] that under each element Christ whole and entire and the true sacrament are received), a fuller light shines on the sign of the eucharistic banquet. Moreover there is a clearer expression of that will by which the new and everlasting covenant is ratified in the blood of the Lord and of the relationship of the eucharistic banquet to the eschatological banquet in the Father's kingdom (see Mt 26:27–29).

From now on, therefore, at the discretion of the bishops and preceded by the required catechesis, communion from the chalice is permitted in the following cases, granted already by earlier law[85] or granted now by this Instruction:

1. to newly baptized adults in the Mass following their baptism; to confirmed adults in the Mass of their confirmation; to baptized persons who are received into the communion of the Church;

2. to the spouses in the Mass of their wedding;

3. to those ordained in the Mass of their ordination;

4. to an abbess in the Mass of her blessing; to the consecrated in the Mass of their consecration to a life of virginity; to religious in the Mass of their first profession or of renewal of religious profession, provided they take or renew their vows within the Mass;

5. to lay missionaries in the Mass at which they are publicly sent out on their mission and to others in the Mass in which they receive an ecclesiastical mission;

---

81. See SC art. 55.

82. See SC art. 55. [SCR] *Missale Romanum*, Ritus servandus in celebration Missae, 27 Jan. 1965, no. 7.

83. SCR, Rubricae Breviarii et Missalis Romani, 26 July 1960, no. 502: AAS 52 (1960) 680.

84. See Council of Trent, sess. 21, *Decr. de communion eucharistica* cap. 1–3: Denz-Schön 1726–29.

85. See [SCR], *Rite of Communion under Both Kinds*, 7 March 1965, no. 1.

6. in the administration of viaticum, to the sick person and to all who are present when Mass is celebrated, with conformity to the requirements of the law, in the house of the sick person;

7. to the deacon, subdeacon, and ministers exercising their proper office in a pontifical or solemn Mass;

8. when there is a concelebration:

    a. to all exercising a genuine liturgical ministry in that concelebration, even lay people, and to all seminarians present;

    b. in their own churches, to all members of institutes professing the evangelical counsels and members of other societies in which the members dedicate themselves to God either through religious vows or oblation or promise, and also to all who reside in the house of the members of these institutes and societies;

9. to priests present at large celebrations and unable to celebrate or concelebrate;

10. to all groups making retreats, in a Mass celebrated especially for those actually participating; to all taking part in the meeting of some pastoral commission, at the Mass they celebrate in common;

11. to those listed under nos. 2 and 4, in the Mass of their jubilee;

12. to the godfather, godmother, parents, and spouse of baptized adults, and to the laypersons who have catechized them, in the Mass of initiation;

13. to the relatives, friends, and special benefactors taking part in the Mass of a newly ordained priest.

COMMUNION OUTSIDE MASS

33.   a. The faithful are to be led to the practice of receiving communion in the actual eucharistic celebration.[86] But priests are not to refuse to give communion to those who request it for a just reason even outside Mass. This is permissible even in the afternoon hours with the permission of the local bishop, in keeping with the norm of the Motu Proprio *Pastorale munus* no. 4, or by permission of the supreme moderator of a religious institute, in keeping with the norm of the Rescript *Cum admotae* art. 1, no. 1.[87]

    b. When communion is distributed outside Mass at the prescribed hours, a short celebration of the word of God may, if opportune, precede it, in accordance with the provisions of the Instruction *Inter Oecumenici* (nos. 37, 39).

    c. When Mass cannot be celebrated because there is no priest available and communion is distributed by a minister with the faculty to do this in virtue of

---

86. See Pius XII, Encycl. *Mediator Dei*: AAS 39 (1947) 565–566.

87. See Paul VI, Motu Proprio *Pastorale munus* [I] no. 4. Secretariat of State, Pontifical Rescript *Cum admotae* I, no. 1.

an indult of the Apostolic See, the rite laid down by the competent authority is to be followed.

THE WAY OF RECEIVING COMMUNION

34.   a. In accordance with the custom of the Church, the faithful may receive communion either kneeling or standing. One or the other practice is to be chosen according to the norms laid down by the conference of bishops and in view of the various circumstances, above all the arrangement of the churches and the number of the communicants. The faithful should willingly follow the manner of reception indicated by the pastors so that communion may truly be a sign of familial union among all those who share in the same table of the Lord.

b. When the faithful communicate kneeling, no other sign of reverence toward the most holy sacrament is required, because the kneeling itself expresses adoration.

When they receive communion standing, it is strongly recommended that, approaching in line, they make a sign of reverence before receiving the sacrament. This should be done at a designated moment and place, so as not to interfere with the coming and going of the other communicants.

SACRAMENT OF PENANCE AND COMMUNION

35.   The eucharist should also be proposed to the faithful "as a remedy that frees us from our daily faults and preserves us from mortal sins."[88] They should also receive an explanation of how to make use of the penitential parts of the Mass.

"Those wishing to receive communion should be reminded of the precept 'let them examine themselves' (1 Cor 1:28). Ecclesiastical custom shows that this examination is necessary so that none who are conscious of having committed mortal sin, no matter how contrite they believe themselves to be, should approach the holy eucharist without first making a sacramental confession."[89] "In a case of necessity, however, and when no confessor is available, a person should first make an act of perfect contrition."[90]

The faithful are to be constantly encouraged in the practice of receiving the sacrament of penance outside Mass, especially at the scheduled hours, so that the administration of the sacrament may be unhurried and genuinely useful and that people will not be impeded from active participation in the Mass. Daily or frequent communicants should be instructed to go to confession regularly, depending on their individual needs.

COMMUNION ON SPECIAL OCCASIONS

36.   It is most fitting that whenever the faithful are beginning a new state or a new way of working in the vineyard of the Lord, they take part in the sacrifice

---

88. Council of Trent, sess. 13, *Decr. de Eucharistia* cap. 2: Denz-Schön 1638; see also sess. 22, *Decr. de Missa* cap. 1 and 2: Denz-Schön 1740 and 1743.

89. Council of Trent, sess. 13, *Decr. de Eucharistia* cap. 7: Denz-Schön 1740 and 1743.

90. CIC can. 859.

through sacramental communion, thereby dedicating themselves again to God and renewing their covenant with him.

This may well be done, for example, by the assembly of the faithful when they renew their baptismal vows at the Easter Vigil; by young people when they do the same thing in the presence of the Church, in a manner in keeping with their age; by the bride and groom when they are united by the sacrament of marriage; by those who dedicate themselves to God when they pronounce their vows or other forms of commitment; by the faithful when they are to devote themselves to apostolic service.

FREQUENT AND DAILY COMMUNION

37.   Since "it is clear that the frequent or daily reception of the most blessed eucharist increases union with Christ, nurtures the spiritual life more richly, forms the soul in virtue, and gives the communicant a stronger pledge of eternal happiness, pastors, confessors, and preachers . . . will frequently and zealously exhort the Christian people to this devout and salutary practice."[91]

PRIVATE PRAYER AFTER COMMUNION

38.   On those who partake of the body and blood of Christ the gift of the Spirit is poured out abundantly like living water (see Jn 7:37–39), provided communion is received both sacramentally and spiritually, that is, in living faith that works through love.[92]

But the union with Christ that is the reason for the sacrament itself is to be sought not only at the time of the eucharistic celebration but is also to be prolonged all during the Christian's life. This means that the faithful of Christ, dwelling constantly on the gift they have received, should live their daily lives in continual thanksgiving under the Holy Spirit's guidance and should produce more abundant fruits of charity.

In order to continue more surely in the thanksgiving that in the Mass is offered to God in an eminent way, those who have been nourished by communion should be encouraged to remain for some time in prayer.[93]

VIATICUM

39.   Communion received as viaticum should be considered as a special sign of sharing in the mystery celebrated in the Mass, the mystery of the death of the Lord and his return to the Father. Viaticum seals the faithful in their passage from life with the pledge of the resurrection as they are strengthened by Christ's body.

Therefore, the faithful who are in danger of death from any cause whatever are bound by precept to receive communion;[94] pastors must guard against delay

---

91. SC Council, *Decr. de quotidiana Ss. Eucharistiae sumptione,* 20 Dec. 1905, no. 6: *Acta Sanctae Sedis* 38 (1905–06) 401ff. Pius XII, Encycl. *Mediator Dei*: AAS 39 (1947) 565.

92. See Council of Trent, sess. 13, *Decr. de Eucharistia* cap. 8: Denz-Schön 1648.

93. See Pius XII, Encycl. *Mediator Dei*: AAS 39 (1947) 566.

94. See CIC can. 864, 1.

in the administration of this sacrament and see to it rather that the faithful receive it while still in full possession of their faculties.[95]

Even if the faithful have already communicated on the same day, and then the danger of death arises, it is strongly recommended that they receive communion again.

COMMUNION OF THOSE UNABLE TO COME TO CHURCH

40.   It is right for those prevented from being present at the celebration of the community eucharist to receive the eucharist often; in this way they will also realize that they are part of the eucharistic community, borne up by its charity.

Pastors should take care that the sick and the elderly be given the opportunity, even if they are not gravely ill or in danger of death, to receive the eucharist often, even daily if possible, especially during the Easter season. They may receive communion at any hour of the day.

COMMUNION UNDER THE FORM OF WINE ALONE

41.   In case of necessity and at the discretion of the bishop, it is permissible for the eucharist to be given under the form of wine alone to those who are unable to receive it under the form of bread.

In this case the celebration of Mass in the presence of the sick person is permissible, at the discretion of the local Ordinary.

If, however, Mass is not celebrated in the presence of the sick person, the blood of the Lord should be preserved in a properly covered chalice and placed in the tabernacle after Mass; it should not be carried to the sick person unless it is enclosed in a container that prevents any danger of spilling. In administering the sacrament, the method best suited to the individual case should be chosen from among those indicated in the rites for use in distributing communion under both kinds. If, after communion has been given, some of the precious blood remains, the minister is to consume it; he is also to see to the required ablutions.

IV. CELEBRATION OF THE EUCHARIST IN THE LIFE AND MINISTRY OF THE BISHOP AND PRIEST

CELEBRATION OF THE EUCHARIST IN THE LIFE AND MINISTRY OF THE BISHOP

42.   The celebration of the eucharist expresses in a special way the public and social nature of the liturgical celebrations of the Church, "which is the sacrament of unity, namely, the holy people united and ordered under their bishops."[96]

Hence "marked with the fullness of the sacrament of orders, a bishop is the steward of the grace of the supreme priesthood, especially in the eucharist, which he offers or causes to be offered. . . . Every lawful celebration of the

---

95. See ibid. can. 865.
96. SC art. 26.

eucharist is regulated by the bishop, to whom is committed the office of offering the worship of Christian religion to the divine majesty and of administering it in accordance with the Lord's commandments and the Church's laws, as further defined by his particular judgment for his diocese."[97] The celebration of the eucharist at which the bishop presides, surrounded by his college of priests and ministers, with the whole people of God actively taking part, is the preeminent manifestation of the hierarchically constituted Church.[98]

APPROPRIATENESS OF THE PARTICIPATION OF PRIESTS IN THE EUCHARIST, EXERCISING THEIR PROPER OFFICE

43.   In the celebration of the eucharist, priests also are deputed, by reason of a special sacrament, namely, orders, to fulfill the office proper to them. For they too "as ministers of the sacred, especially in the sacrifice of the Mass, . . . represent the person of Christ in a particular way."[99] Because of the sign value, it is therefore right that they take part in the eucharist by exercising the order proper to them,[100] that is, by celebrating or concelebrating the Mass and not simply by receiving communion like the laity.

DAILY CELEBRATION OF MASS

44.   "In the mystery of the eucharistic sacrifice, the fulfillment of the priest's chief office, the work of redemption is continually actual. Hence, daily celebration is urged upon priests; it remains the act of Christ and the Church even when the faithful cannot attend";[101] in it the priest always acts for the salvation of the people.

FAITHFUL OBSERVANCE OF THE LAWS OF THE CHURCH IN CELEBRATING MASS

45.   Especially in the celebration of the eucharist, only the supreme authority of the Church and, according to the norm of law, the bishops and the conferences of bishops, no one else, not even a priest, may, on his own initiative add, leave out, or change anything in the liturgy.[102] Therefore, priests should be intent on presiding over the celebration of the eucharist in such a way that the faithful know that they are participating not in a rite decided on by private authority,[103] but in the public worship of the Church, the direction of which has been entrusted by Christ to the apostles and their successors.

PRIORITY OF PASTORAL EFFECTIVENESS IN THE CHOICE OF THE DIFFERENT FORMS OF CELEBRATION

46.   "When the liturgy is celebrated, something more is required than the mere observance of the laws governing valid and lawful celebration; it is also their

---

97. LG no. 26.

98. See SC art. 41.

99. PO no. 13; see also LG no. 28.

100. See SC no. 28.

101. PO no. 13. See also Paul VI, Encycl. *Mysterium fidei.*

102. See SC art. 22.

103. See ST 2a2ae, 93, 1.

duty to ensure that the faithful take part fully aware of what they are doing, actively engaged in the rite, and enriched by its effect."[104] Hence, from among the forms of celebration permitted by law priests should take care to choose those that in each situation seem best suited to the needs or well-being of the faithful and to their taking part actively.

CONCELEBRATION

47.   Concelebration of the eucharist aptly expresses the unity of the sacrifice and the priesthood; whenever the faithful take an active part, the unity of the people of God stands out in a special way,[105] particularly if the bishop presides.[106]

Concelebration also symbolizes and strengthens the fraternal bond between priests, because "by virtue of the ordination to the priesthood that they share all are linked together in a close bond of brotherhood."[107]

Unless the needs of the faithful (which always must be regarded with a deep pastoral concern) rule it out, then, and without prejudice to the option of every priest to celebrate Mass individually, this excellent way for priests to celebrate Mass is preferable in the case of communities of priests, their periodic meetings, or in other similar circumstances. Those who live in community or serve the same church should gladly welcome visiting priests to concelebrate with them.

The authorized superiors should therefore facilitate and encourage concelebration whenever pastoral needs or another reasonable cause does not demand otherwise.

The faculty to concelebrate also applies to the principal Masses in churches and public and semipublic oratories of seminaries, colleges, and ecclesiastical institutions, as well as in those of religious orders and societies of common life without vows. Where there are a great many priests, the authorized superior can allow several concelebrations to take place on the same day, but at different times or in different places of worship.

BAKING OF THE BREAD FOR CONCELEBRATION

48.   If a large host is baked for concelebration, as permitted in the *Rite of Concelebration* no. 17, care must be taken that, in keeping with traditional usage, it is of a form and appearance worthy of the eucharistic mystery.

---

104. SC art. 11; also art. 48.
105. See SC art. 57. SCR, Decr. generale *Ecclesiae semper*, 7 March 1965.
106. See SC art. 41; LG no. 28; PO no. 7.
107. LG no. 28: AAS 57 (1965) 35; ConstDecrDecl 148; see also PO no. 8.

PART III
WORSHIP OF THE EUCHARIST AS A PERMANENT SACRAMENT

I. REASONS FOR RESERVING THE EUCHARIST OUTSIDE MASS

REASONS FOR RESERVING THE EUCHARIST OUTSIDE MASS

49. "It is pertinent to recall that the primary and original purpose of reserving the sacred elements in church outside Mass is the administration of viaticum; secondary ends are the distribution of communion outside Mass and the adoration of our Lord Jesus Christ hidden beneath these same elements."[108] For "the reservation of the sacred elements for the sick . . . led to the praiseworthy custom of adoring the heavenly food that is reserved in churches. This worship of adoration has a sound and firm foundation,"[109] especially since faith in the Lord's real presence has as its natural consequence the outward and public manifestation of that belief.

PRAYER IN THE PRESENCE OF THE BLESSED SACRAMENT

50. When the faithful adore Christ present in the sacrament, they should remember that this presence derives from the sacrifice and has as its purpose both sacramental and spiritual communion.

Therefore, the devotion prompting the faithful to visit the blessed sacrament draws them into an ever deeper share in the paschal mystery and leads them to respond gratefully to the gift of him who through his humanity constantly pours divine life into the members of his Body.[110] Abiding with Christ the Lord, they enjoy his intimate friendship and pour out their hearts before him for themselves and for those dear to them and they pray for the peace and salvation of the world. Offering their entire lives with Christ to the Father in the Holy Spirit, they derive from this sublime colloquy an increase of faith, hope, and charity. Thus they foster those right dispositions that enable them with due devotion to celebrate the memorial of the Lord and receive frequently the bread given us by the Father.

The faithful should therefore strive to worship Christ the Lord in the blessed sacrament in a manner fitting in with their own way of life. Pastors should by example show the way and by word encourage their people.[111]

---

108. SC Sacraments, Instr. *Quam plurimum* 1 Oct. 1949: AAS 41 (1949) 509–510. See also Council of Trent, sess. 13, *Decr. de Eucharistia* cap. 6; Denz-Schön 1645. St. Pius X, Decr. *Sacra Tridentina Synodus*, 20 Dec. 1905: Denz-Schön 3375.
109. Pius XII, Encycl. *Mediator Dei*: AAS 39 (1947) 569.
110. See PO no. 5.
111. See PO no. 18.

51.   Pastors should see to it that all churches and public oratories where the blessed sacrament is reserved are open at least several hours in the morning and evening so that the faithful may easily pray before the blessed sacrament.

II. PLACE FOR EUCHARISTIC RESERVATION

THE TABERNACLE

52.   Where the eucharist is allowed to be reserved in keeping with the provisions of law, only one altar or location in the same church may be the permanent, that is, regular place of reservation.[112] As a general rule, therefore, there is to be but one tabernacle in each church and it is to be solid and absolutely secure.[113]

CHAPEL OF RESERVATION

53.   The place in a church or oratory where the eucharist is reserved in a tabernacle should be truly a place of honor. It should also be suited to private prayer so that the faithful may readily and to their advantage continue to honor the Lord in this sacrament by private worship.[114] Therefore, it is recommended that as far as possible the tabernacle be placed in a chapel set apart from the main body of the church, especially in churches where there frequently are marriages and funerals and in places that, because of their artistic or historical treasures, are visited by many people.

TABERNACLE IN THE MIDDLE OF ALTAR OR IN ANOTHER PART OF THE CHURCH

54.   "The eucharist is to be reserved in a solid and secure tabernacle, placed in the middle of the main altar or on a minor, but truly worthy altar, or else, depending on lawful custom and in particular cases approved by the local Ordinary, in another, special, and properly adorned part of the church.

     "It is also lawful to celebrate Mass facing the people even on an altar where there is a small but becoming tabernacle."[115]

TABERNACLE ON AN ALTAR WHERE MASS IS CELEBRATED WITH A CONGREGATION

55.   In the celebration of Mass the principal modes of Christ's presence to his Church[116] emerge clearly one after the other: first he is seen to be present in the assembly of the faithful gathered in his name; then in his word, with the reading and explanation of Scripture; also in the person of the minister; finally, in a singular way under the eucharistic elements. Consequently, on the grounds

---

112. See CIC can. 1268, § 1.
113. See SCR, Instr. InterOec, 26 Sept. 1964, no. 95. SC Sacraments, Instr. *Nullo unquam tempore*, 28 May 1938, no. 4: AAS 30 (1938) 199–200.
114. See PO no. 18. Paul VI, Encycl. *Mysterium fidei*.
115. SCR, Instr. InterOec no. 95.
116. See no. 9 of this Instruction.

of the sign value, it is more in keeping with the nature of the celebration that, through reservation of the sacrament in the tabernacle, Christ not be present eucharistically from the beginning on the altar where Mass is celebrated. That presence is the effect of the consecration and should appear as such.

THE TABERNACLE IN THE CONSTRUCTION OF NEW CHURCHES AND IN THE REMODELING OF EXISTING CHURCHES AND ALTARS

56.   It is fitting that the principles stated in nos. 52 and 54 be taken into account in the building of new churches.

Remodeling of already existing churches and altars must be carried out in exact compliance with no. 24 of this Instruction.

MEANS OF INDICATING THE PRESENCE OF BLESSED SACRAMENT IN THE TABERNACLE

57.   Care should be taken that the faithful be made aware of the presence of the blessed sacrament in the tabernacle by the use of a veil or some other effective means prescribed by the competent authority.

According to the traditional practice, a lamp should burn continuously near the tabernacle as a sign of the honor shown to the Lord.[117]

III. EUCHARISTIC DEVOTIONS

58.   Devotion, both private and public, toward the sacrament of the altar even outside Mass that conforms to the norms laid down by lawful authority and in the present Instruction is strongly advocated by the Church, since the eucharistic sacrifice is the source and summit of the whole Christian life.[118]

In structuring these devotional exercises, account should be taken of the norms determined by Vatican Council II concerning the relationship to be observed between the liturgy and other, nonliturgical sacred services. Particular attention should be paid to this one: "These devotions should be so fashioned that they harmonize with the liturgical seasons, accord with the liturgy, are in some way derived from it, and lead the people to it, since, in fact, the liturgy by its very nature far surpasses any of them."[119]

IV. EUCHARISTIC PROCESSIONS

59.   In processions in which the eucharist is carried through the streets solemnly with singing, especially on the feast of Corpus Christi, the Christian people give public witness to their faith and to their devotion toward this sacrament.

---

117. See CIC can. 1271.
118. See LG no. 11.
119. SC art. 13.

However, it is for the local Ordinary to decide on both the advisability of such processions in today's conditions and on a place and plan for them that will ensure their being carried out with decorum and without any loss of reverence toward this sacrament.

V. EXPOSITION OF THE BLESSED SACRAMENT

60.   Exposition of the blessed sacrament, either in a ciborium or a monstrance, draws the faithful to an awareness of the sublime presence of Christ and invites them to inner communion with him. Therefore, it is a strong encouragement toward the worship owed to Christ in spirit and in truth.

In such exposition care must be taken that the signs of it bring out the meaning of eucharistic worship in its correlation with the Mass. This end is served in the case of solemn and prolonged exposition by having it take place at the end of the Mass in which the host to be exposed for adoration has been consecrated. The Mass itself ends with the *Benedicamus Domino*, without the blessing. In the surroundings of exposition,[120] anything must be carefully avoided that could in any way obscure Christ's intention of instituting the holy eucharist above all in order to be near us to feed, to heal, and to comfort us.[121]

PROHIBITION OF MASS BEFORE THE EXPOSED BLESSED SACRAMENT

61.   The celebration of Mass is prohibited within the body of the church during exposition of the blessed sacrament, all contrary concessions and traditions hitherto in force, even those worthy of special mention, notwithstanding.

For, in addition to the reasons given in no. 55 of this Instruction, the celebration of the eucharistic mystery includes in a higher way that inner communion to which exposition is meant to lead the faithful and does not need the support of exposition.

If exposition of the blessed sacrament goes on for a day or for several successive days, it should be interrupted during the celebration of Mass, unless it is celebrated in a chapel separate from the area of exposition and at least some of the faithful remain in adoration.

In those places where a break with long-established, contrary custom would upset the faithful, the local Ordinary should fix a sufficient but not overly long period for instructing them before the present norm takes effect.

ARRANGEMENT OF THE RITE OF EXPOSITION

62.   For brief exposition, the ciborium or monstrance should be placed on the altar table; for a longer exposition a throne can be used and set in a prominent, but not too elevated or distant position.

---

120. See no. 62 of this Instruction.
121. See St. Pius X, Decr. *Sacra Tridentina Synodus*, 20 Dec. 1905: Denz-Schön 3375.

During the exposition everything should be so arranged that the faithful can devote themselves attentively in prayer to Christ the Lord.

To foster intimate prayer, readings from sacred Scripture, together with a homily or brief inspirational words that lead to a better understanding of the eucharistic mystery, are permitted. It is proper for the people to respond to the word of God with singing. There should also be suitable intervals of silence. At the end of the exposition, benediction is given.

When the vernacular is used, another eucharistic hymn, at the discretion of the conference of bishops, may be substituted for the *Tantum ergo* as the hymn to be sung before the benediction.

ANNUAL SOLEMN EXPOSITION

63. In churches where the eucharist is regularly reserved, there may be an annual, solemn exposition of the blessed sacrament for an extended period of time, even if not strictly continuous, so that the local community may meditate on this mystery more deeply and adore.

Exposition of this kind may take place only if the participation of a reasonable number of the faithful is ensured, the local Ordinary consents, and the established norms are followed.

PROLONGED EXPOSITION

64. For any serious and general need, the local Ordinary may order prayer before the blessed sacrament exposed over a longer period (which may be strictly continuous) in those churches to which the faithful come in large numbers.

INTERRUPTION OF EXPOSITION

65. Where there cannot be uninterrupted exposition, because there is not a sufficient number of worshipers, it is permissible to replace the blessed sacrament in the tabernacle at fixed hours that are announced ahead of time. But this may not be done more than twice a day, for example, at midday and at night.

This reposition can be simple and without singing: the priest vested in surplice and stole, after a brief adoration of the blessed sacrament, places it in the tabernacle. At a set time, the exposition is resumed in a similar way, following which the priest, after a brief period of adoration, leaves.

EXPOSITION FOR SHORT PERIODS

66. Even short expositions of the blessed sacrament, conducted in accord with the norms of the law, must be so arranged that before the benediction reasonable time is provided for readings of the word of God, hymns, prayers, and silent prayer, as circumstances permit.

Local Ordinaries will make certain that these expositions of the blessed sacrament are always and everywhere marked with proper reverence.

Exposition merely for the purpose of giving benediction after Mass is prohibited.

VI. EUCHARISTIC CONGRESSES

67.   In eucharistic congresses, the faithful seek to understand this holy mystery more deeply through a consideration of its various aspects (see no. 3 of this Instruction). Their celebration of the eucharist should, moreover, be in keeping with the norms of Vatican Council II and they should offer their worship through private prayers and devotions, especially in solemn processions, in such a way that all these forms of devotion have their culmination in the solemn celebration of Mass.

All during a eucharistic congress of at least an entire region, it is proper to designate some churches for continuous adoration.

In the audience granted 13 April 1967 to Cardinal Arcadius M. Larraona, Prefect of this Congregation, Pope Paul VI by his authority approved and confirmed this Instruction and ordered it to be published, fixing the feast of the Assumption of the Blessed Virgin Mary, 15 August 1967, as its effective date.

COMME LE PRÉVOIT
ON THE TRANSLATION OF
LITURGICAL TEXTS FOR CELEBRATIONS
WITH A CONGREGATION

INSTRUCTION
CONSILIUM FOR IMPLEMENTING THE
CONSTITUTION ON THE SACRED LITURGY
JANUARY 25, 1969

AN OVERVIEW OF *COMME LE PRÉVOIT*

Rev. Paul Turner

When Pope Paul VI authorized the experimental use of the Roman Canon in vernacular languages in 1967, he asked Conferences of Bishops to prepare translations and to submit them for confirmation to his Consilium for implementing *Sacrosanctum Concilium* (SC).[1] The Consilium, realizing that this and other sections of the soon-to-be-released *Missale Romanum* would provoke unprecedented work for translators, issued guidelines. Its members "thought fit in this declaration to lay down, in common and nontechnical terms, some of the more important theoretical and practical principles for the guidance of all who are called upon to prepare, to approve, or to confirm liturgical translations"[2] The Catholic Church thus received the most influential document in the history of sacred or secular translation, *Comme le prévoit* (CP). The title is the first words of the French original, and it refers to the *Sacrosanctum Concilium*'s permission in paragraph 36 for the use of the vernacular. The opening phrase means, "As [the Constitution] foresees it."

SC foresaw in 1963 that the vernacular would allow people to participate more broadly in the celebration of Mass and the sacraments. This document—the first approved by the Second Vatican Council—preserved the Latin language in the liturgy, but it permitted a broader use of the vernacular especially in readings, directives, prayers, and chants—favoring in particular the parts pertaining to the people. Conferences of Bishops were to decide whether and to what extent the vernacular would be used.[3] Although the Council desired that the faithful be familiar with Latin for their parts in the Order of Mass, it gave provisions for a more extended use of the mother tongue,[4] which the Vatican granted in later years.

Shortly after SC established a framework for liturgical reform, the Sacred Congregation of Rites issued its first instruction on carrying out the vision of SC. The document, prepared by the Consilium and approved by the Congregation, was the first instruction from the Curia to advance the liturgical reforms envisioned by the Council.[5] The instruction *Inter Oecumenici* (IO) noted that the Latin liturgical text formed the basis of translations, that experts in various fields should be consulted, that neighboring Conferences of Bishops using the same language should consult when possible, that nations of several languages should provide for each, and that the books should be of high quality. Pilgrims from other lands should be permitted to use their own language. Melodies should

---

1. Pope Paul VI, "Concession, allowing, ad experimentum, use of the vernacular in the canon of the Mass and in ordinations," 31 January 1967 Notitiae 3 (1967) 154; DOL 117.

2. *Comme le prévoit* (CP), 4.

3. See *Sacrosanctum Concilium* (SC), 36.

4. See ibid., 54.

5. For a discussion on the authorizing source of this instruction, see Piero Marini, *A Challenging Reform: Realizing the Vision of the Liturgical Renewal* (Collegeville, MN: Liturgical Press, 2007), pp. 67 and 76.

be approved. Liturgical books were to remain in force until further reform of the liturgy.[6]

One month later, Cardinal Giacomo Lercaro, president of the Consilium, wrote the presidents of the Conferences of Bishops to stress the point that one translation should be approved for countries sharing the same language.[7] Apparently he was already receiving multiple versions of translations for approval, but insisted on having a single version per language. Doing otherwise "would be detrimental both to the importance of the texts themselves and to the dignity of the liturgical books."[8]

The following year, Pope Paul VI gave initial guidelines for liturgical translations in his address to translators gathered in Rome.[9] He asked that the translation "be within the grasp of all, even children and the uneducated."[10] Yet it should "be worthy of the noble realities it signifies, set apart from the everyday speech of the street and the marketplace, so that it will affect the spirit and enkindle the heart with love of God."[11] He noted that different genres required different types of translation: biblical texts, prayers, and hymns, for example. Translators should know Christian Latin and their own modern language, and take into account the rules of music for those parts to be sung. The pope asked for "a spotless and graceful vesture of speech"[12] to clothe the community. He wanted from translations the clarity of language and dignity of expression that exist in the Latin originals.

In 1966, the Consilium wrote to the presidents of episcopal conferences about texts for the Mass of Jubilee authorized by Pope Paul VI for January 1 to May 29 of that year.[13] The period for using these special texts had already begun, so the letter instructed the conferences to work on the translations and use them without submitting them to the Consilium for confirmation.

Paul VI made history when he authorized experimental vernacular translations of the Roman Canon in 1967. The Roman Canon had been prayed only in Latin since the fourth century. SC did not specifically call for this usage of the vernacular, but it left the door open for such developments. With the news, the Consilium realized it needed to supply guidelines for all the work that lay ahead. Secretary Annibale Bugnini sent preliminary recommendations immediately: the version should be a faithful rendering of the Latin original; the language should avoid exaggerated classical and modern forms; and the style should have some rhythm for speaking and singing. Conferences were permitted to

---

6. See *Inter Oecumenici* (IO), 40–43.

7. Consilium, "Letter *Consilium ad exsequendum* of Cardinal G. Lercaro to presidents of the conferences of bishops, on uniform translation in a language common to several countries," 16 October 1964: *Notitiae* 1 (1965) 195–196; DOL 108.

8. Ibid.

9. Paul VI, "Address to translators of liturgical texts," 10 November 1965: AAS 57 (1965) 967–970; *Notitiae* 1 (1965) 378–381; DOL 113.

10. Ibid.

11. Ibid.

12. Ibid.

13. Consilium, "Communication *Per Litteras Apostolicas* to presidents of the conferences of bishops, on norms for the translation of the Mass of the Jubilee," 21 January 1966: *Notitiae* 2 (1966) 43; DOL 115.

allow an interim translation, published in books with double-columned pages of Latin and English.[14]

In 1968 the Consilium issued a communication to the presidents of national liturgical commissions giving norms for the translation of the *Graduale simplex*, a book of simplified chants for Mass parts in Latin.[15] Although the book is little used in Latin or the vernacular today, the rules for its translation fore-shadowed the forthcoming major document. First, the Consilium handed authority to the Conferences of Bishops to allow the use of the vernacular for all or some of the chants, and to approve the text in keeping with SC. In arranging the formularies, the bishops were to use an approved translation suitable for singing, even with its own division of verses. The Consilium also authorized modifying the antiphons to better interpret the liturgical season or feast and to match musical requirements. It permitted an adaptation of the melodies to the styles of music of individual peoples. It even authorized the conferences to choose different texts, outlining principles for the procedure.

Then came the release of *Comme le prévoit* simultaneously in six modern languages. Having issued shorter directives to help anxious translators meet smaller immediate needs, this larger work virtually accompanied the release of the entire *Missale Romanum*, providing a much needed architecture to bear the weight of the work ahead.[16] In later years, it surprised people that the guidelines for translation came from the Consilium and not from the Sacred Congregation of Rites. However, Paul VI had invested the Consilium with considerable authority, and because this special body had developed all the postconciliar liturgical texts, it was best positioned to offer the guidelines on their translation. Bugnini called *Comme le prévoit* a "working tool," and notes that it was never published in Latin, nor in the official Vatican gazette, *Acta Apostolica Sedis* (AAS), but rather in the fifth publication of the Congregation's journal *Notitiae*.[17] Some later interpreters thought that this diminished the authority of the instruction, but at the time, the pope relied on the Consilium, and the Consilium relied on *Notitiae*.

The instruction opens with a brief introduction laying out the task, and then presents three main sections: "General Principles," "Some Particular Circumstances," and "Committees for Translating."

The introduction[18] reviews some of the norms already in place and lays out the task of the present instruction. The "General Principles" open with reflections

---

14. Consilium, "Communication *Aussitôt après* of A. Bugnini to presidents of the conferences of bishops and, for their information, presidents of national liturgical commissions, on the translation of the Roman Canon," 10 August 1967: *Notitiae* 3 (1967) 326–327; DOL 118.

15. Consilium, "Communication *Instantibus pluribus* to presidents of the national liturgical commissions, on norms for translation of the *Graduale Simplex*," 23 January 1968: *Notitiae* 4 (1968) 10; DOL 120.

16. See John F. Baldovin, *Reforming the Liturgy: A Response to the Critics* (Collegeville, MN: Liturgical Press, 2008), p. 118.

17. Annibale Bugnini, *The Reform of the Liturgy 1948–1975* (Collegeville, MN: Liturgical Press, 1990), p. 236.

18. See CP, 1–4.

on the nature of a liturgical text[19] and the purpose of translation.[20] This paragraph, often quoted, summarizes the thinking of the Church in the years after the Council:

It is not sufficient that a liturgical translation merely reproduce the expressions and ideas of the original text. Rather it must faithfully communicate to a given people, and in their own language, that which the Church by means of this given text originally intended to communicate to another people in another time. A faithful translation, therefore, cannot be judged on the basis of individual words: the total context of this specific act of communication must be kept in mind, as well as the literary form proper to the respective language.[21]

There follows more practical advice on communicating the meaning,[22] and then a summary of scientific methods[23]: Establish a critical text.[24] Consider the historical and cultural uses of Latin terms.[25] Treat the whole passage as the unit of meaning, which may call for reducing the number of adjectives and superlatives.[26] Use words in their proper historical, social, and ritual meanings.[27]

The instruction then summarized points to aid communication.[28] The vocabulary should be that of common usage, yet able to express the highest realities.[29] Revealed truths should be expressed clearly,[30] taking care of "the so-called sacral vocabulary,"[31] dealing with words unique to the Bible and liturgy,[32] and infusing a Christian meaning into common words.[33] The words will communicate well if they are "the prayer of some actual community."[34]

It then promotes "cautious adaptation."[35] Some texts can be translated word for word,[36] but sometimes metaphors must be changed.[37] Translation of phrases contrary to modern Christian ideas or having less relevance today should be changed with "the greatest care."[38]

---

19. Pope Paul VI himself added the second half of the last sentence to paragraph 5: "By spoken words Christ himself speaks to his people and the people, through the Spirit in the Church, answer their Lord." Bugnini, p. 236n.
20. See CP, 6.
21. Ibid.
22. See ibid., 7–8.
23. See ibid., 9.
24. See ibid., 10.
25. See ibid., 11.
26. See ibid., 12.
27. See ibid., 13.
28. See ibid., 14.
29. See ibid., 15.
30. See ibid., 16.
31. Ibid., 17.
32. See ibid., 18.
33. See ibid., 19.
34. Ibid., 20.
35. Ibid., 21.
36. See ibid., 22.
37. See ibid, 23.
38. Ibid., 24.

Spoken communication should be considered.[39] Translators should keep in mind the literary genre,[40] and make distinctions between written and spoken style.[41] The general principles conclude with a reminder that some rules are less important than others.[42]

The second main division of the instruction treats particular considerations. Biblical texts, for example, are "the written voice of God."[43] Translations of them should conform with the Latin liturgical text,[44] possibly worked out with Christians of other traditions.[45] Some formulas, such as consecratory prayers, should be translated "integrally and faithfully, without variations, omissions, or insertions."[46] However, some of the traditional orations are "succinct and abstract" and may be rendered "somewhat more freely."[47] Texts such as acclamations should "be expressed by sound and rhythm."[48]

Regarding texts to be sung, they should match the liturgical action; psalms arranged into stanzas like hymns; responsories and antiphons may be adapted to help singing; episcopal conferences may replace difficult texts; and texts for recitation should be duly prepared.[49] Finally, liturgical hymns may need "a new rendering"[50] to accord with popular poetry in each language.

The last section of *Comme le prévoit* takes up the formation of diverse experts for translating,[51] as well as experimentation with the translations "by selected congregations in different places."[52] Experts and authorities should work together from beginning to end.[53] Countries with a common language should prepare a single text.[54] Procedures for the production of these translations are explained.[55] Finally, and most broadly, the Consilium recommends "the creation of new texts"[56] because those translated from another language are insufficient to celebrate "a fully renewed liturgy."[57]

Many have summarized *Comme le prévoit* as an explanation of "dynamic equivalence," as opposed to "formal equivalence." The instruction never uses those terms. Surely, it did not call for a strict adherence to each word of the

---

39. See ibid., 25.
40. See ibid., 26.
41. See ibid, 27.
42. See ibid., 28–29.
43. Ibid., 30.
44. See ibid., 31.
45. See ibid., 32.
46. Ibid., 33.
47. Ibid., 34.
48. Ibid., 35.
49. Ibid., 36.
50. Ibid., 37.
51. See ibid., 38.
52. See ibid., 39.
53. Ibid., 40. Pope Paul VI added the final sentence to this paragraph: "Otherwise, it should give the task to a new committee which is more suitable, but also composed of qualified people." Bugnini, p. 238n.
54. See ibid., 41.
55. See ibid., 42.
56. Ibid., 43.
57. Ibid.

original Latin, but it did aim to supply ways that the meaning of the original would be fully and beautifully conveyed in the results. The universal Church benefited greatly from this "working tool." The first English translation took particular advantage of the liberties permitted in the instruction. The results veered further from the Latin than those of other languages. Nonetheless, all the translations formed a generation of committed, prayerful Catholics, who participated actively and simultaneously in the Mass using their own diverse languages for the very first time.

COMME LE PRÉVOIT

ON THE TRANSLATION OF LITURGICAL TEXTS
FOR CELEBRATIONS WITH A CONGREGATION

CONSILIUM FOR IMPLEMENTING THE CONSTITUTION ON
THE SACRED LITURGY
JANUARY 25, 1969

1.   The Constitution on the Sacred Liturgy foresees that many Latin texts of the Roman liturgy must be translated into different languages (art. 36). Although many of them have already been translated, the work of translation is not drawing to a close. New texts have been edited or prepared for the renewal of the liturgy. Above all, after sufficient experiment and passage of time, all translations will need review.

2.   In accordance with art. 36 of the Constitution *Sacrosanctum Concilium* and no. 40 of the Instruction of the Congregation of Rites *Inter Oecumenici*, the work of translation of liturgical texts is thus laid down: It is the duty of the episcopal conferences to decide which texts are to be translated, to prepare or review the translations, to approve them, and "after approval, that is, confirmation, by the Holy See" to promulgate them.

When a common language is spoken in several different countries, international commissions should be appointed by the conferences of bishops who speak the same language to make one text for all (letter of Cardinal Lercaro to the presidents of episcopal conferences, dated 16 October 1964).

3.   Although these translations are the responsibility of the competent territorial authority of each country, it seems desirable to observe common principles of procedure, especially for texts of major importance, in order to make confirmation by the Apostolic See easier and to achieve greater unity of practice.

4.   The Consilium has therefore thought fit in this declaration to lay down, in common and non-technical terms, some of the more important theoretical and practical principles for the guidance of all who are called upon to prepare, to approve, or to confirm liturgical translations.

I. GENERAL PRINCIPLES

5.   A liturgical text, inasmuch as it is a ritual sign, is a medium of spoken communication. It is, first of all, a sign perceived by the senses and used by men to communicate with each other. But to believers who celebrate the sacred rites

a word is itself a "mystery." By spoken words Christ himself speaks to his people and the people, through the Spirit in the Church, answer their Lord.

6.   The purpose of liturgical translations is to proclaim the message of salvation to believers and to express the prayer of the Church to the Lord: "Liturgical translations have become . . . the voice of the Church" (address of Paul VI to participants in the congress on translations of liturgical texts, 10 November 1965). To achieve this end, it is not sufficient that a liturgical translation merely reproduce the expressions and ideas of the original text. Rather it must faithfully communicate to a given people, and in their own language, that which the Church by means of this given text originally intended to communicate to another people in another time. A faithful translation, therefore, cannot be judged on the basis of individual words: the total context of this specific act of communication must be kept in mind, as well as the literary form proper to the respective language.

7.   Thus, in the case of liturgical communication, it is necessary to take into account not only the message to be conveyed, but also the speaker, the audience, and the style. Translations, therefore, must be faithful to the art of communication in all its various aspects, but especially in regard to the message itself, in regard to the audience for which it is intended, and in regard to the manner of expression.

8.   Even if in spoken communication the message cannot be separated from the manner of speaking, the translator should give first consideration to the meaning of the communication.

9.   To discover the true meaning of a text, the translator must follow the scientific methods of textual study as used by experts. This part of the translator's task is obvious. A few points may be added with reference to liturgical texts:

10.   a. If need be, a critical text of the passage must first be established so that the translation can be done from the original or at least from the best available text.

11.   b. Latin terms must be considered in the light of their uses—historical or cultural, Christian or liturgical. For example, the early Christian use of *devotio* differs from its use in classical or more modern times. The Latin *oratio* means in English not an oration (one of its senses in classical Latin) but a *prayer*—and this English word bears different meanings, such as prayer of praise or prayer in general or prayer of petition. *Pius* and *pietas* are very inadequately rendered in English as *pious* and *piety*. In one case the Latin *salus* may mean *salvation* in the theological sense; elsewhere it may mean *safety*, *health* (physical health or total health), or *well-being*. *Sarx-caro* is inadequately rendered in English as *flesh*. *Doulos-servus* and *famula* are inadequately rendered in English by *slave*, *servant*, *handmaid*. The force of an image or metaphor must also be considered, whether it is rare or common, living or worn out.

12.   c. The translator must always keep in mind that the "unit of meaning" is not the individual word but the whole passage. The translator must there be

careful that the translation is not so analytical that it exaggerates the importance of particular phrases while it obscures or weakens the meaning of the whole. Thus, in Latin, the piling up of *ratam, rationabilem, acceptabilem* may increase the sense of invocation. In other tongues, a succession of adjectives may actually weaken the force of the prayer. The same is true of *beatissima Virgo* or *beata et glorisa* or the routine addition of *sanctus* or *beatus* to a saint's name, or the too casual use of superlatives. Understatement in English is sometimes the more effective means of emphasis.

13.   d. To keep the correct signification, words and expressions must be used in their proper historical, social, and ritual meanings. Thus, in prayers for Lent, *ieiunium* now has the sense of *lenten* observance, both liturgical and ascetic; the meaning is not confined to abstinence from food. *Tapeinos-humilis* originally had "class" overtones not present in the English *humble* or even *lowly*. Many of the phrases of approach to the Almighty were originally adapted from forms of address to the sovereign in the courts of Byzantium and Rome. It is necessary to study how far an attempt should be made to offer equivalents in modern English for such words as *Quaesumus, dignare, clementissime, maiestas*, and the like.

14.   The accuracy and value of a translation can only be assessed in terms of the purpose of the communication. To serve the particular congregations who will use it, the following points should be observed in translating.

15.   a. The language chosen should be that in "common" usage, that is, suited to the greater number of the faithful who speak it in everyday use, even "children and persons of small education" (Paul VI in the allocution cited). However, the language should not be "common" in the bad sense, but "worthy of expressing the highest realities" (ibid.). Moreover, the correct biblical or Christian meaning of certain words and ideas will always need explanation and instruction. Nevertheless no special literary training should be required of the people; liturgical texts should normally be intelligible to all, even to the less educated. For example, *temptation* as a translation of *tentatio* in the Lord's Prayer is inaccurate and can only be misleading to people who are not biblical scholars. Similarly, *scandal* in the ordinary English sense of gossip is a misleading translation of the scriptural *scandalum*. Besides, liturgical texts must sometimes possess a truly poetic quality, but this does not imply the use of specifically "poetic diction."

16.   b. Certain other principles should be observed so that a translation will be understood by the hearers in the same sense as the revealed truths expressed in the liturgy.

17.   1. When words are taken from the so-called sacral vocabulary now in use, the translator should consider whether the everyday common meaning of these words and phrases bears or can bear a Christian meaning. These phrases may carry a pre-Christian, quasi-Christian, Christian, or even anti-Christian meaning. The translator should also consider whether such words can convey the exact Christian liturgical action and manifestation of faith. Thus in the Greek Bible, the word *hieros (sacer)* was often avoided because of its connection with

the pagan cults and instead the rarer word *hagios (sanctus)* was substituted. Another example. The proper meaning of the biblical *hesed-eleos-misericordia*, is not accurately expressed in English by *mercy* or *pity*. Again, the word *mereri* in classical Latin often signifies *to be worthy of something*, but in the language of the liturgy it carries a meaning very different from the ancient meaning: "I do something because of which I am worthy of a prize or a reward." In English the word *to deserve* when used by itself retains the stricter sense. A translation would lead to error if it did not consider this fact, for example, in translating *Quia quem meruisti portare* in the hymn *Regina caeli* as *Because you deserved to bear. . . .*

18.   2. It often happens that there is no word in common use that exactly corresponds to the biblical or liturgical sense of the term to be translated, as in the use of the biblical *iustitia.* The nearest suitable word must then be chosen which, through habitual use in various catechetical texts and in prayer, lends itself to take on the biblical and Christian sense intended by the liturgy. Such has been the evolution of the Greek word *doxa* and the Latin *gloria* when used to translate the Hebrew *kabod.* The expression *hominibus bonae voluntatis* literally translated as *to men of good will* (or *good will to men* in order to stress divine favor) will be misleading; no single English word or phrase will completely reflect the original Latin or the Greek which the Latin translates. Similarly in English there is no exact equivalent for *mysterium.* In English, *mystery* means something which cannot be readily explained or else a type of drama or fiction. Nor can the word *venerabilis* (as in *sanctas et venerabiles manus*) be translated as *venerable*, which nowadays means *elderly*.

19.   3. In many modern languages a biblical or liturgical language must be created by use. This will be achieved rather by infusing a Christian meaning into common words than by importing uncommon or technical terms.

20.   c. The prayer of the Church is always the prayer of some actual community, assembled here and now. It is not sufficient that a formula handed down from some other time or region be translated verbatim, even if accurately, for liturgical use. The formula translated must become the genuine prayer of the congregation and in it each of its members should be able to find and express himself or herself.

21.   A translation of the liturgy therefore often requires cautious adaptation. But cases differ:

22.   a. Sometimes a text can be translated word for word and keep the same meaning as the original, for example, *pleni sunt caeli et terra gloria tua.*

23.   b. Sometimes the metaphors must be changed to keep the true sense, as in *locum refrigerii* in northern regions.

24.   c. Sometimes the meaning of a text can no longer be understood, either because it is contrary to modern Christian ideas (as in *terrena despicere* or *ut inimicos sanctae Ecclesiae humiliare digneris*) or because it has less relevance

today (as in some phrases intended to combat Arianism) or because it no longer expresses the true original meaning "as in certain obsolete forms of lenten penance." In these cases, so long as the teaching of the Gospel remains intact, not only must inappropriate expressions be avoided, but others found which express a corresponding meaning in modern words. The greatest care must be taken that all translations are not only beautiful and suited to the contemporary mind, but express true doctrine and authentic Christian spirituality.

25. A particular form of expression and speech is required for spoken communication. In rendering any liturgical text, the translator must keep in mind the major importance of the spoken or rhetorical style or what might, by extension of the term, be called the literary genre. On this matter several things should be noted:

26. 1. The literary genre of every liturgical text depends first of all on the nature of the ritual act signified in the words—acclamation or supplication, proclamation or praying, reading or singing. Each action requires its proper form of expression. Moreover a prayer differs as it is to be spoken by one person alone or by many in unison; whether it is in prose or in verse; spoken or sung. All these considerations affect not only the manner of delivery, but also the choice of words.

27. 2. A liturgical text is a "linguistic fact" designed for celebration. When it is in written form (as is usually the case), it offers a stylistic problem for translators. Each text must therefore be examined to discover the significant elements proper to the genre, for example, in Roman prayers the formal structure, cursus, dignity, brevity, etc.

28. Among the separate elements are those which are essential and others which are secondary and subsidiary. The essential elements, so far as is possible, should be preserved in translation, sometimes intact, sometimes in equivalent terms. The general structure of the Roman prayers can be retained unchanged: the divine title, the motive of the petition, the petition itself, the conclusion. Other cannot be retained: the oratorical cursus, rhetorical-prose cadence.

29. It is to be noted that if any particular kind of quality is regarded as essential to a literary genre (for example, intelligibility of prayers when said aloud), this may take precedence over another quality less significant for communication (for example, verbal fidelity).

II. SOME PARTICULAR CONSIDERATIONS

30. Among liturgical texts, sacred Scripture has always held a special place because the Church recognizes in the sacred books the written voice of God (DV no. 9). The divine word has been transmitted to us under different historical forms or literary genres and the revelation communicated by the documents cannot be entirely divorced from these forms or genres. In the case of biblical translations intended for liturgical readings, the characteristics of speech or writing are proper to different modes of communication in the sacred books and

should be preserved with special accuracy. This is particularly important in the translations of psalms and canticles.

31.   Biblical translations in the Roman liturgy ought to conform "with the Latin liturgical text" (instruction *Inter Oecumenici*, 26 September 1964, no. 40 a). In no way should there be a paraphrasing of the biblical text, even if it is difficult to understand. Nor should words or explanatory phrases be inserted. All this is the task of catechesis and the homily.

32.   In some cases it will be necessary that "suitable and accurate translations be made into the different languages from the original texts of the sacred books. And if, given the opportunity and the approval of church authority, these translations are produced in cooperation with the separated brethren as well, all Christians will be able to use them" (DV no. 22). Translations approved for liturgical used should closely approximate the best versions in a particular language.

33.   Some euchological and sacramental formularies like the consecratory prayers, the anaphoras, prefaces, exorcisms, and those prayers which accompany an action, such as the imposition of hands, the anointing, the signs of the cross, etc., should be translated integrally and faithfully, without variations, omissions, or insertions. These texts, whether ancient or modern, have a precise and studied theological elaboration. If the text is ancient, certain Latin terms present difficulties of interpretation because of their use and meaning, which are much different from their corresponding terms in modern language. The translation will therefore demand an astute handling and sometimes a paraphrasing, in order to render accurately the original pregnant meaning. If the text is a more recent one, the difficulty will be reduced considerably, given the use of terms and a style of language which are closer to modern concepts.

34.   The prayers (opening prayer, prayer over the gifts, prayer after communion, and prayer over the people) from the ancient Roman tradition are succinct and abstract. In translation they may need to be rendered somewhat more freely while conserving the original ideas. This can be done by moderately amplifying them or, if necessary, paraphrasing expressions in order to concretize them for the celebration and the needs of today. In every case pompous and superfluous language should be avoided.

35.   All texts which are intended to be said aloud follow the laws proper to their delivery and, in the case of written texts, their literary genre. This applies especially to the acclamations where the act of acclaiming by voice is an essential element. It will be insufficient to translate only the exact meaning of an idea unless the text can also be expressed by sound and rhythm.

36.   Particular care is necessary for texts which are to be sung.

    a. The form of singing which is proper to every liturgical action and to each of its parts should be retained (antiphon alternated with the psalm, responsory, etc. See Instruction *Musicam sacram*, 5 March 1967, nos. 6 and 9).

b. Regarding the psalms, in addition to the division into versicles as given in Latin, a division into stanzas may be particularly desirable if a text is used which is well known by the people or common to other Churches.

c. The responses (versicles, responsories) and antiphons, even though they come from Scripture, become part of the liturgy and enter into a new literary form. In translating them it is possible to give them a verbal form which, while preserving their full meaning, is more suitable for singing and harmonizes them with the liturgical season or a special feast. Examples of such adaptations which include minor adaptations of the original text are numerous in ancient antiphonaries.

d. When the content of an antiphon or psalm creates a special difficulty, the episcopal conferences may authorize the choice of another text which meets the same needs of the liturgical celebration and the particular season or feast.

e. If these same texts are likewise intended for recitation without singing, the translation should be suitable for that purpose.

37. Liturgical hymns lose their proper function unless they are rendered in an appropriate verse rhythm, suitable for singing by the people. A literal translation of such texts is therefore generally out of the question. It follows that hymns very often need a new rendering made according to the musical and choral laws of the popular poetry in each language.

III. COMMITTEES FOR TRANSLATING

38. To make the translations, committees should be formed of experts in the various disciplines, namely, liturgy, Scripture, theology, pastoral study, and especially languages and literature, and according to circumstances, music. If several committees are concerned with the different parts of liturgical texts, their work should be coordinated.

39. Before a text is promulgated, sufficient opportunity should be allowed for experiment by selected congregations in different places. An *ad interim* translation should be properly approved by the liturgical commission of the conference of bishops.

40. Close collaboration should be established between the committee of experts and the authorities who must approve the translations (such as a conference of bishops), so that:

a. the same people, for the most part, share in the work from beginning to end;

b. when the authority asks for emendations, these should be made by the experts themselves and a new text then submitted for the judgment of the authority. Otherwise, it should give the task to a new committee which is more suitable, but also composed of qualified people.

41.   Those countries which have a common language should employ a "mixed commission" to prepare a single text. There are many advantages to such a procedure: in the preparation of a text the most competent experts are able to cooperate; a unique possibility for communication is created among these people; participation of the people is made easier. In this joint venture between countries speaking the same language it is important to distinguish between the texts which are said by one person and heard by the congregation and those intended to be recited or sung by all. Uniformity is obviously more important for the latter category than for the former.

42.   In those cases where a single text is prepared for a large number of countries, the text should satisfy the "different needs and mentalities of each region" (letter of Cardinal Lercaro to the presidents of episcopal conferences, 16 October 1964). Therefore:

1. Each episcopal conference sharing the same language should examine the translation program or the first draft of a text.

2. Meanwhile, to avoid anxiety and unnecessary delay for priests and people, the coordinating secretariat should provide a provisional text which, with the consent of the proper authority (see no. 39), can be published and printed as an *ad interim* text in each country. It is preferable that the same provisional text be used everywhere since the result will contribute to a better final text for all the countries.

3. Each of the countries will receive the definitive text at the same time. If a particular episcopal conference requires a change or substitution for specific local needs, it should propose the change to the "mixed commission," which must first agree. This is necessary in order to have a single text which remains substantially unchanged and under the supervision of the "mixed commission."

4. Each country can publish texts which are provisional as well as texts which are officially approved by the Holy See, but ought to contribute, on a prorated basis according to the extent it publishes, to the expenses of the "mixed commission," which must pay the periti and bishops of the commission. National liturgical commissions should make prior arrangements with the secretariat regarding these publications.

5. In the publications of works from the "mixed commissions," the appropriate notice should appear on the first page: "A provisional text prepared by the 'mixed commission' . . ." or "Text approved by the 'mixed commission' . . . and confirmed by the Consilium for the Implementation of the Constitution on the Sacred Liturgy." If a change or substitution is desirable in an individual country, as indicated in no. 42, 3, a further notice is necessary, namely: "with adaptations authorized by the episcopal conference of . . . and the 'mixed commission'."

43.   Texts translated from another language are clearly not sufficient for the celebration of a fully renewed liturgy. The creation of new text will be necessary. But translation of texts transmitted through the tradition of the Church

is the best school and discipline for the creation of new text so "that any new forms adopted should in some way grow organically from forms already in existence" (SC no. 23).

LITURGICAE INSTAURATIONES
THIRD INSTRUCTION ON THE
ORDERLY CARRYING OUT OF
THE CONSTITUTION ON THE LITURGY

SACRED CONGREGATION FOR DIVINE WORSHIP
SEPTEMBER 5, 1970

AN OVERVIEW OF *LITURGICAE INSTAURATIONES*

Rev. Daniel J. Merz

The Congregation for Rites and its successors (now known as the Congregation for Divine Worship and the Discipline of the Sacraments) have published five instructions on the correct implementation of *Sacrosanctum Concilium*. The third instruction, *Liturgicae instaurationes* (LI), was published on September 5, 1970 in *forma commune*, meaning that it is a document of the Congregation and not of the Holy Father himself. In other words, it was issued as binding norms for interpreting and carrying out the liturgical reform as envisioned by *Sacrosanctum Concilium*. An instruction seeks to "clarify the prescriptions of laws and elaborate on and determine an approach to be followed in implementing them."[1]

Whereas the first two instructions announced specific changes to the rite for celebrating the Eucharist, *Liturgicae instaurationes* was published after the *Ordo Missae* (1969), the *Ordo lectionum Missae* (1969), the *Institutio Generalis Missalis Romani* (1970), and the *Missale Romanum* itself (1970). The third instruction, then, was not concerned with preparing for the English translation of the *Missale Romanum*, but rather with clarifying certain aspects of the reform in light of the Missal's publication. More precisely, its main purpose was to bring to an end those experimentations regarding the Eucharist that were being carried out up to that point, and to provide strict limits on any future experimentation. Annibale Bugnini provides some explanation for this purpose of the instruction: "As the reform advanced, so did the number of reports increase that were sent to the Consilium from all sides on the arbitrary activities of individuals and groups. The result was a sizeable file on which the secretary of the Consilium had written: 'Abuses to be eliminated.'"[2]

A proper interpretation of *Liturgicae instaurationes* requires grasping the situation of the Church around the world at that time. Even more important, however, is to understand the situation of the Church as perceived by various personalities in Rome—personalities often at odds with one another. Pope Paul VI established the Consilium in his 1964 *motu proprio, Sacram Liturgiam*, with the mission to carry out the mandates of *Sacrosanctum Concilium*. In practice, the Consilium operated loosely under the umbrella of the Congregation for Rites, but Paul VI created the body independent of the curia and worked with it directly. On May 8, 1969 (just sixteen months before *Liturgicae instaurationes*), the Holy Father divided the Congregation for Rites into two: one for Divine Worship and the other for the Causes of Saints. The Consilium itself was thereby absorbed into the Congregation for Divine Worship. The last meeting of the Consilium

---

1. *Code of Canon Law*, canon 34 §1.

2. Annibale Bugnini, *The Reform of the Liturgy 1948–1975*, (Collegeville, MN: The Liturgical Press, 1990), p. 840.

took place during the thirteenth plenary session of the Congregation for Rites, April 8–10, 1970. The first plenary meeting of the reorganized Congregation for Worship was held November 3–6, 1970. This marked the more formal entry of the liturgical reform into the world of the Roman Curia.

Fr. Annibale Bugnini, secretary for the Consilium, was appointed secretary for the new Congregation for Divine Worship. The Consilium's program for revision was strengthened by this move, though it was short-lived. More and more the work of the Consilium (and now the Congregation for Divine Worship and the Discipline of the Sacraments) was being put to review by other Congregations within the Roman Curia, notably the Congregation for the Doctrine of the Faith. The same year (1969) is said to mark "the beginning of organized opposition against the reform and against the new Congregation."[3] In just over five years, in 1975, the newly established Congregation for Divine Worship would be merged with the Congregation for the Discipline of the Sacraments, its staff halved, and Archbishop Bugnini sent to Iran as Pro-Nuncio Apostolic.[4]

The third instruction certainly had an effect in minimizing some liturgical abuses, in encouraging greater episcopal oversight of the liturgy within the local Churches, and even in easing the troubled conscience of those concerned about the state of the Church and her liturgical reforms. Given the background within Rome described above, however, its greater significance was less the impact on the wider Church, than the psychological message it sent in signaling an end to one stage of the reform and the beginning of a new attitude within the Roman Curia. This shift was somewhat dramatic and was experienced not only in the strong tone calling for an end to experimentation and for fidelity to the hierarchical communion, but also in the very manner the document was composed. Unlike other documents drafted by the Consilium, this one had not followed the usual course of development and review, "by experts, relators, and members. Few persons had been consulted, and therefore few were kept abreast of the developing instruction. But this was in fact a different kind of document, one that involved the responsibility of the central authority."[5] *Liturgicae instaurationes* signaled that the process of liturgical reform—at least in Rome—was about to become more cautious and more centralized.

The idea for this instruction receives its first written mention in a letter dated February 18, 1968, from the Consilium to the Secretariat of State:

> We are . . . preparing a short but strongly worded instruction that is to be published at the same time as the *Ordo Missae*. The emphasis in it will be on ten or so areas (all covered in the General Instruction of the Roman Missal) that are subject to the greatest abuses . . . The instruction is to be sent only to the *bishops* in an effort to get them involved and let them know clearly the mind of the Holy See on what is permissible and what is not. . . .[6]

---

3. Piero Marini, *A Challenging Reform: Realizing the Vision of the Liturgical Renewal 1963–1975*, (Collegeville, MN: The Liturgical Press, 2007), p. 142.

4. Incidentally, while in Iran, Archbishop Bugnini played a major international role in helping to negotiate the release of the American hostages from the United States Embassy taken during the Islamic revolution in that country.

5. Bugnini, *The Reform of the Liturgy*, p. 843, footnote 27.

6. Ibid., p. 840.

Other influences on the development of the instruction came from the Congregation for the Doctrine of the Faith as well as Pope Paul VI himself. According to Bugnini, for example, the instruction had initially advocated for a limited use of dialogue within the Homily at Mass, but at the request of the pope (dated November 8, 1969), dialogue in the Homily was forbidden (n. 2a). Further corrections were made in light of the instructions *Memoriale Domini* (on the manner of distributing Holy Communion) and *Sacramentali Communione* (on extension of the permission to distribute Holy Communion under two kinds).

The instruction was greeted with strong negative reactions from a number of corners,[7] who wished not only the experimentation to continue, but the regulation of the liturgy to become a predominantly local affair. Bugnini, himself, however, observed that, "the pressures being brought to bear from within the Curia and from outside [upon the Congregation's need to respond firmly to abuses] were many, strong, and justified."[8]

The instruction begins with an introduction that sketches some of the theological underpinnings for the work of the liturgy and of liturgical reform. This provides the rationale for the thirteen paragraphs, which follow. The introduction includes an exhortation for the diocesan bishop to seek constantly to be engaged in the life of the diocese in order better to engage the work of the reform and respond to authentic needs for adaptations, while stopping abuses. In summary, then, the document opens with some positive vision and encouragement, and then continues with a list of mostly abuses, which should be corrected.

The opening line of the instruction states that the "reforms put into effect thus far . . . have to do primarily with the celebration of the mystery of the eucharist." This is true in that all the changes mandated in the first two instructions affected the Eucharist. It should be kept in mind, however, that the Consilium had been hard at work with other liturgical rites as well: in 1969, the Congregation for Rites published the *Rite of Marriage* (March 19); the *General Roman Calendar* (March 21); the *Rite of Infant Baptism* (May 15); and the funeral rite (August 15). Also in the same year, instructions were published on celebrations for special groups (*Actio pastorali*, May 15) and on the manner of giving Communion (*Memoriale Domini*, May 29).

In the first paragraph, the aim of the whole liturgical reform is succinctly summed up: "the purpose of the ritual renewal is to inspire a pastoral ministry that has the liturgy as its crown and source and that is a living-out of the paschal mystery of Christ." In other words, the goal is a *pastoral ministry* that is nothing else than the continuation of the glorified life of Christ, energized and enabled by the sacred liturgy. This reform is said to be "a new path for pastoral-liturgical life, permitting great achievements."

As justification for its call to cease experimentation, the instruction states in its opening paragraphs that within the revised Lectionary and Missal the options and flexibility "are a great advantage to a living, pointed, and spiritually beneficial celebration, that is, one adapted to local conditions and to the character

---

7. See, for example, G.P., "*La terza Istruzione mortifica l'iniziativa,*" *Notitiae* 7 (1971) 85–88; and Aelred Tegels, "Chronicle: A Third Instruction." *Worship* 44, no. 10 (1970) 623–627; and *ibid.*, "Chronicle: More on the Third Instruction." *Worship* 45, no. 4 (1971) 237–241.

8. See Bugnini, *The Reform of the Liturgy*, pp. 842–844.

and culture of the faithful." For these reasons, "personal improvisations" serve to the detriment of the liturgy's unity and fail to respect the dignity of the assembly. Indeed, such improvisations "only trivialize the liturgy."

Sacrosanctum Concilium called for the rites to be "marked by a noble simplicity; they should be short, clear, and unencumbered by useless repetitions; they should be within the people's powers of comprehension and as a rule not require much explanation."[9] The work of the Consilium, especially as directed by *Tres abhinc annos*, translated this call by the Council into liturgical rites that are sometimes criticized for being overly intellectual or rational, overly simple and devoid of mystery, or lacking intuitive imagination. It is not that the previous rites were exemplary with such intuitive imagination and genuine mystery. Some of their "mystery" was simple mysteriousness as opposed to the ritual splendor that opens both the mind and the spirit to transcendence. There was real beauty in the earlier rites, but they were also lacking the kind of intuitive richness that catechizes while it inspires. The Enlightenment had given birth to rationalism, which desired to remove all transcendence from the world, making logic the supreme deity, and mathematics the attendant at its throne to shed light on anything and everything in the world. The Fathers of the Second Vatican Council rejected such rationalism, seeking the proper balance of faith and reason. Western culture, however, was fairly saturated with the Enlightenment and the Council's reforms were sometimes perceived through that lens. *Liturgicae instaurationes* tried to address this reality directly by stating that, "The liturgical reform bears absolutely no relation to what is called 'desacralization' and in no way intends to lend support to the phenomenon of 'secularizing the world.' Accordingly the rites must retain their dignity, spirit of reverence, and sacred character."[10]

There are four markers of a specifically Catholic liturgy, which have been highlighted as the principles the instruction used to make its case against particular abuses. They are:

- Its communitarian nature;

- Its hierarchical structure;

- Its fidelity to living Tradition;

- Its sense of the sacred.[11]

Taken together, such principles seek to engage the right balance of mystery, transcendence, and immanence. It is easy to see these four principles at work in the commendations and concerns given throughout the document. *Liturgicae instaurationes* contravenes a "continuous reductionism" with the exhortation to enter "more deeply into the word of God and the mystery being celebrated," as given by the Church and not by one's "own preferences."[12]

---

9. *Sacrosanctum Concilium* (SC), 4.

10. *Liturgicae instaurationes* (LI), 1.

11. See, Sandro Maggiolini, "Una *Instructio* e il suo Sottofondo Teologico." *Notitiae* 7 (1971) 27–31.

12. LI, 1.

What follows may serve as an outline or brief summary of the material covered in articles 2–13 of the document:

- LI safeguards the Bible in the liturgy and the proper exercise of the Homily.[13]

- LI highlights the many options available in the newly reformed books.[14]

- LI emphatically reserves the Eucharistic Prayer to the priest alone,[15] and gives regulations regarding the matter of the hosts for Mass and on Communion under both kinds.[16]

- LI extends the ministerial role of women, while preserving some strictures.[17]

- LI provides criteria for sacred vessels, vestments, and church furnishings, stipulating that the normal place for worship is within the church building.[18]

- LI calls for a "fixed and worthy arrangement" for churches, especially sanctuaries.[19]

- The style and means of liturgical translations is laid out, including the competence of the Conferences of Bishops.[20]

- Procedures for any further liturgical experimentation are strictly laid out, requiring oversight of a competent local authority with any such plans to be submitted to the Congregation for permission to proceed.[21]

Lastly, the instruction concludes with an exhortation to obedience as well as to deepen the reform by studying its fruits in the revised rituals. Its concluding remarks still affect us today:

> . . . it must be remembered that the liturgical reform decided on by the Council affects the universal Church. It thus requires in pastoral meetings a study of its meaning and practice for the Christian education of the people to the end that the liturgy may become vital, touch the soul, and meet its needs.[22]

---

13. See ibid., 2.
14. See ibid., 3.
15. See ibid., 4.
16. See ibid., 5–6.
17. See ibid., 7.
18. See ibid., 8–9.
19. Ibid., 10.
20. See ibid., 11.
21. See ibid., 12.
22. Ibid., 13.

LITURGICAE INSTAURATIONES
ON THE ORDERLY CARRYING OUT OF THE CONSTITUTION ON THE LITURGY

INSTRUCTION
SACRED CONGREGATION FOR DIVINE WORSHIP
SEPTEMBER 5, 1970

The liturgical reforms put into effect thus far as applications of Vatican Council II's Constitution on the Liturgy have to do primarily with the celebration of the mystery of the eucharist. "For the eucharist contains the Church's entire spiritual wealth, that is, Christ himself. He is our Passion and living bread; through his flesh, made living and life-giving by the Holy Spirit, he is bringing life to people and thereby inviting them to offer themselves together with him, as well as their labors and all created things."[1] The repeated celebration of the sacrifice of the Mass in our worshiping communities stands as evidence that the Mass is the center of the Church's entire life, the focal point of all other activities, and that the purpose of the ritual renewal is to inspire a pastoral ministry that has the liturgy as its crown and source and that is a living-out of the paschal mystery of Christ.[2]

The work of reform, accomplished step by step over the past six years, has served as a passage from the earlier to a new liturgy, presented, since publication of the Roman Missal with its Order of Mass and General Instruction, in such a clearer and fuller form that it truly opens a new path for pastoral-liturgical life, permitting great achievements. In addition, the recently published Mass Lectionary together with the wealth of prayer forms contained in the Roman Missal provide a wide range of options for celebrations of the eucharist.

The many options regarding texts and the flexibility of the rubrics are a great advantage to a living, pointed, and spiritually beneficial celebration, that is, one adapted to local conditions and to the character and culture of the faithful. There is, then, no need for purely personal improvisations, which can only trivialize the liturgy.

Measured transition to new and fresh forms of worship, conducted with both the overall work of renewal and the wide range of local conditions as its criteria, has been welcomed by the majority of clergy and faithful.[3] Still, there have been here and there both resistance and impatience. In the cause of holding on to the old tradition, some have received the changes grudgingly. Alleging

---

1. PO no. 5.
2. See SCR, Instr. InterOec, 26 Sept. 1964, nos. 5–6.
3. See Paul VI, Addr. to a general audience, 21 Aug. 1969.

pastoral needs, others became convinced that they could not wait for promulgation of the definitive reforms. In consequence, they have resorted to personal innovations, to hasty, often ill-advised measures, to new creations and additions or to the simplification of rites. All of this has frequently conflicted with the most basic liturgical norms and upset the consciences of the faithful. The innovators have thus obstructed the cause of genuine liturgical renewal or made it more difficult.

The result is that many bishops, priests, and laity have asked the Apostolic See to bring its authority to bear on the preservation and growth in the liturgy of the effective union of spirit that is to be expected as the right and the characteristic of the family of Christians gathered in God's presence.

What seemed untimely during the process of the Consilium's assiduous work on the reform has now become possible in view of all that has now been solidly and clearly established.

The first appeal must be made to the authority of the individual bishops; the Holy Spirit has chosen them to rule the Church of God[4] and they are "the chief stewards of the mysteries of God, and the overseers, promoters, and guardians of all liturgical life in the particular Churches entrusted to their care."[5] They have the duty of governing, guiding, encouraging, or sometimes reproving, of lighting the way for the carrying out of true reform, and also of taking counsel, so that the whole Body of the Church may be able to move ahead single-mindedly and with the unity of charity in the diocese, the nation, and the entire world. Such efforts of the bishops are the more necessary and urgent because the link between liturgy and faith is so close that service to the one redounds to the other.

With the cooperation of their liturgical commissions, bishops should have complete information on the religious and social condition of the faithful in their care, of their spiritual needs, and of the ways most likely to help them; bishops should also use all the options the new rites provide. They will then be able to evaluate what favors or hampers true reform and with care and discernment to suggest and control courses of action in such a way that, all genuine needs being given their due, the entire undertaking will nevertheless evolve in accord with the norms set by the new liturgical laws.

The bishops' mastery of the knowledge needed greatly assists priests in the ministry they exercise in due hierarchic communion[6] and facilitates that obedience required as a fuller sign of worship and for the sanctification of souls.

With a view to making the bishop's function more effective for an exact application of liturgical norms, especially those of the General Instruction of the Roman Missal, as well as for the sake of restoring discipline and order in the celebration of the eucharist, center of the Church's life, "a sign of unity and

---

4. See Acts 20:28.
5. CD no. 15; see SC art. 22.
6. See PO no. 15: AAS 58 (1966) 1014–15; ConstDecrDecl 660.

a bond of charity,"[7] it seems worthwhile to review the following principles and suggestions.

1.   The new norms have made liturgical formularies, gestures, and actions much simpler, in keeping with that principle established in the Constitution on the Liturgy: "The rites should be marked by a noble simplicity; they should be short, clear, and unencumbered by useless repetitions; they should be within the people's powers of comprehension and as a rule not require much explanation."[8] No one should go beyond these defined limits; to do so would be to strip the liturgy of its sacred symbolism and proper beauty, so needed for the fulfillment of the mystery of salvation in the Christian community and, with the help of an effective catechesis, for its comprehension under the veil of things that are seen.

The liturgical reform bears absolutely no relation to what is called "desacralization" and in no way intends to lend support to the phenomenon of "secularizing the world." Accordingly the rites must retain their dignity, spirit of reverence, and sacred character.

The effectiveness of liturgy does not lie in experimenting with rites and altering them over and over, nor in a continuous reductionism, but solely in entering more deeply into the word of God and the mystery being celebrated. It is the presence of these two that authenticates the Church's rites, not what some priest decides, indulging his own preferences.

Keep in mind, then, that the private recasting of ritual introduced by an individual priest insults the dignity of the believer and lays the way open to individual and idiosyncratic forms in celebrations that are in fact the property of the whole Church.

The ministry of the priest is the ministry of the universal Church: its exercise is impossible without obedience, hierarchic communion, and the will to serve God and neighbor. The hierarchic character and sacramental power of the liturgy as well as the respectful service owed to the believing community demand that the priest fulfill his role in worship as the "faithful servant and steward of the mysteries of God,"[9] without imposing any rite not decreed and sanctioned by the liturgical books.

2.   Of all the texts read in the liturgical assembly the books of sacred Scripture possess the primacy of a unique dignity: in them God is speaking to his people; Christ, in his own word, continues to proclaim his Gospel.[10] Therefore:

a. The liturgy of the word demands cultivation with the utmost attention. In no case is it allowed to substitute readings from other sacred or profane authors, ancient or modern. The homily has as its purpose to explain to the faithful the word of God just proclaimed and to adapt it to the mentality of the times. The priest, therefore, is the homilist; the congregation is

---

7. SC art. 47.
8. SC art. 34.
9. See 1 Cor 4:1.
10. See SC art. 7 and 33.

to refrain from comments, attempts at dialogue, or anything similar. To have only a single reading is never allowed.

b. The liturgy of the word prepares and leads up to the liturgy of the eucharist, forming with it the one act of worship.[11] To separate the two, therefore, or to celebrate them at different times or places is not permitted. As for integrating some liturgical service or part of the divine office before Mass with the liturgy of the word, the guidelines are the norms laid down in the liturgical books for the case in question.

3.   The liturgical texts themselves, composed by the Church, are to be treated with the highest respect. No one, then, may take it on himself to make changes, substitutions, deletions, or additions.[12]

a. There is special reason to keep the Order of Mass intact. Under no consideration, not even the pretext of singing the Mass, may the official translations of its formularies be altered. There are, of course, optional forms, noted in the context of the various rites, for certain parts of the Mass: the penitential rite, the eucharistic prayers, acclamations, final blessing.

b. Sources for the entrance and communion antiphons are: the *Graduale romanum*, *The Simple Gradual*, the Roman Missal, and the compilations approved by the conferences of bishops. In choosing chants for Mass, the conferences should take into account not only suitability to the times and differing circumstances of the liturgical services, but also the needs of the faithful using them.

c. Congregational singing is to be fostered by every means possible, even by use of new types of music suited to the culture of the people and to the contemporary spirit. The conferences of bishops should authorize a list of songs that are to be used in Masses with special groups, for example, with youth or children, and that in text, melody, rhythm, and instrumentation are suited to the dignity and holiness of the place and of divine worship.

The Church does not bar any style of sacred music from the liturgy.[13] Still, not every style or the sound of every song or instrument deserves equal status as an aid to prayer and an expression of the mystery of Christ. All musical elements have as their one purpose the celebration of divine worship. They must, then, possess sacredness and soundness of form,[14] fit in with the spirit of the liturgical service and the nature of its particular parts; they must not be a hindrance to an intense participation of the assembly[15] but must direct the mind's attention and the heart's sentiments toward the rites.

---

11. See SC art. 56.
12. See SC art. 22, § 3.
13. See SCR, Instr. MusSacr, 5 March 1967, no. 9.
14. See MusSacr no. 4.
15. See SC art. 119–120.

More specific determinations belong to the conferences of bishops or, where there are no general norms as yet, to the bishop within his diocese.[16] Every attention is to be given to the choice of musical instruments; limited in number and suited to the region and to community culture, they should prompt devotion and not be too loud.

d. Broad options are given for the choice of prayers. Especially on weekdays in Ordinary Time the sources are any one of the Mass prayers from the thirty-four weeks of Ordinary Time or the prayers from the Masses for Various Occasions[17] or from the votive Masses.

For translations of the prayers the conferences of bishops are empowered to use the special norms in no. 34 of the Instruction on translations of liturgical texts for celebrations with a congregation, issued by the Consilium, 25 January 1969.[18]

e. As for readings, besides those assigned for every Sunday, feast, and weekday, there are many others for use in celebrating the sacraments or for other special occasions. In Masses for special groups the option is granted to choose texts best suited to the particular celebration, as long as they come from an authorized lectionary.[19]

f. The priest may say a very few words to the congregation at the beginning of the Mass and before the readings, the preface, and the dismissal,[20] but should give no instruction during the eucharistic prayer. Whatever he says should be brief and to the point, thought out ahead of time. Any other instructions that might be needed should be the responsibility of the "moderator" of the assembly, who is to avoid going on and on and say only what is strictly necessary.

g. The general intercessions in addition to the intentions for the Church, the world, and those in need may properly include one pertinent to the local community. That will forestall adding intentions to Eucharistic Prayer I (Roman Canon) in the commemorations of the living and the dead. Intentions for the general intercessions are to be prepared and written out beforehand and in a form consistent with the genre of the prayer.[21] The reading of the intentions may be assigned to one or more of those present at the liturgy.

Used intelligently, these faculties afford such broad options that there is no reason for resorting to individualistic creations. Accordingly priests are instructed to prepare their celebrations with their mind on the actual circumstances and the spiritual needs of the people and with faithful adherence to the limits set by the General Instruction of the Roman Missal.

---

16. See MusSacr no.9.
17. See GIRM no. 323
18. See Consilium Instr. *Comme le prévoit*, 25 Jan. 1969, no. 34, also nos. 21–24.
19. See SCDW, Instr. *Actio pastoralis*, 15 May 1969, no. 6 e.
20. See GIRM no. 11.
21. See GIRM nos. 45–46.

4. The eucharistic prayer more than any other part of the Mass is, by reason of his office, the prayer of the priest alone.[22] Recitation of any part by a lesser minister, the assembly, or any individual is forbidden. Such a course conflicts with the hierarchic character of the liturgy in which all are to do all but only those parts belonging to them.[23] The priest alone, therefore, is to recite the entire eucharistic prayer.

5. The bread for eucharistic celebration is bread of wheat and, in keeping with the age-old custom of the Latin Church, unleavened.[24]

Its authenticity as sign requires that the bread have the appearance of genuine food to be broken and shared in together. At the same time the bread, whether the small host for communion of the faithful or the larger hosts to be broken into parts, is *always* to be made in the traditional shape, in keeping with the norm of the General Instruction of the Roman Missal.[25]

The need for greater authenticity relates to color, taste, and thickness rather than to shape. Out of reverence for the sacrament the eucharistic bread should be baked with great care, so that the breaking can be dignified and the eating not offensive to the sensibilities of the people. Bread that tastes of uncooked flour or that becomes quickly so hard as to be inedible is not to be used. As befits the sacrament, the breaking of the consecrated bread, the taking of the consecrated bread and wine in communion, and the consuming of leftover hosts after communion should be done with reverence.[26]

6. In its sacramental sign value communion under both kinds expresses a more complete sharing by the faithful.[27] Its concession has as limits the determinations of the General Instruction of the Roman Missal (no. 242) and the norm of the Instruction of the Congregation for Divine Worship, *Sacramentali Communione*, on the extension of the faculty for administering communion under both kinds, 29 June 1970.

a. Ordinaries are not to grant blanket permission but, within the limits set by the conference of bishops, are to specify the instances and celebrations for this form of communion. To be excluded are occasions when the number of communicants is great. The permission should be for specific, structured, and homogeneous assemblies.

b. A thorough catechesis is to precede admittance to communion under both kinds so that the people will fully perceive its significance.

c. Priests, deacons, or acolytes who have received institution should be present to offer communion from the chalice. If there are none of these present, the rite is to be carried out by the celebrant as it is set out in the General Instruction of the Roman Missal no. 245.

---

22. See GIRM no. 10.
23. See SC art. 28.
24. See GIRM no. 282.
25. See GIRM no. 283.
26. See SCR, Instr. EuchMyst, 25 May 1967, no. 48.
27. See GIRM no. 240.

c. The method of having the communicants pass the chalice from one to another or having them go directly to the chalice to receive the precious blood does not seem advisable. Instead of this, communion should be by intinction.

d. The first minister of communion is the priest celebrant, next deacons, then acolytes, in particular cases to be determined by the competent authority. The Holy See has the power to permit the appointment of other known and worthy persons as ministers, if they have received a mandate. Those lacking this mandate cannot distribute communion or carry the vessels containing the blessed sacrament.

The manner of distributing communion is to conform to the directives of the General Instruction of the Roman Missal (nos. 244–252) and of the 29 June 1970 Instruction of this Congregation. Should there be any concession of a manner of distribution differing from the usual, the conditions the Apostolic See lays down are to be observed.

e. Wherever, for want of priests, other persons—for example, catechists in mission areas—receive from the bishop, with the concurrence of the Apostolic See, the right to celebrate the liturgy of the word and distribute communion, they are to refrain absolutely from reciting the eucharistic prayer. Should it seem desirable to read the institution narrative, they should make it a reading in the liturgy of the word. In the kind of assemblies in question, then, the recitation of the Lord's Prayer and the distribution of holy communion with the prescribed rite immediately follow the liturgy of the word.

f. Whatever the manner of distributing, great care is to be taken for its dignified, devout, and decorous administration and for forestalling any danger of irreverence. There is to be due regard for the character of the liturgical assembly and for the age, circumstances, and degree of preparation of the recipients.[28]

7. In conformity with norms traditional in the Church, women (single, married, religious), whether in churches, homes, convents, schools, or institutions for women, are barred from serving the priest at the altar.

According to the norms established for these matters, however, women are allowed to:

a. proclaim the readings, except the gospel. They are to make sure that, with the help of modern sound equipment, they can be comfortably heard by all. The conferences of bishops are to give specific directions on the place best suited for women to read the word of God in the liturgical assembly.

b. announce the intentions in the general intercessions;

c. lead the liturgical assembly in singing and play the organ or other instruments;

---

28. See SCDW, Instr. *Sacra Communione*, 29 June 1970, no. 6.

d. read the commentary assisting the people toward a better understanding of the rite;

e. attend to other functions, customarily filled by women in other settings, as a service to the congregation, for example, ushering, organizing processions, taking up the collection.[29]

8.   Sacred vessels, vestments, and furnishings are to be treated with proper respect and care. The greater latitude granted with regard to their material and design is intended to give the various peoples and artisans opportunity to devote the full power of their talents to sacred worship.

But the following points must be kept in mind.

a. Objects having a place in worship must always be "of high quality, durable, and well suited to sacred uses."[30] Anything that is trivial or commonplace must not be used.

b. Before use, chalices and patens are to be consecrated by the bishop, who will decide whether they are fit for their intended function.

c. "The vestment common to ministers of every rank is the alb."[31] The abuse is here repudiated of celebrating or even concelebrating Mass with stole only over the monastic cowl or over ordinary clerical garb, to say nothing of street clothes. Equally forbidden is the wearing of the stole alone over street clothes when carrying out other ritual acts, for example, the laying on of hands at ordinations, administering other sacraments, giving blessings.

d. It is up to the conferences of bishops to decide whether it is advisable to choose materials other than the traditional for the sacred furnishings. They are to inform the Apostolic See about their decisions.[32]

As to the design of vestments, the conferences of bishops have the power to decide on and to propose to the Holy See adaptations consistent with the needs and customs of the respective regions.[33]

9.   The eucharist is celebrated as a rule in a place of worship.[34] Apart from cases of real need, as adjudged by the Ordinary for his jurisdiction, celebration outside a church is not permitted. When the Ordinary does allow this, there must be care that a worthy place is chosen and that the Mass is celebrated on a suitable table. If at all possible, the celebration should not take place in a dining room or on a dining-room table.

10.   In applying the reform of the liturgy, bishops should have special concern about the fixed and worthy arrangement of the place of worship, especially the

---

29. See GIRM no. 68.
30. See GIRM no. 288.
31. See GIRM no. 298.
32. See SC art. 128.
33. See GIRM no. 304.
34. See GIRM no. 260.

sanctuary, in conformity with the norms set forth in the General Instruction of the Roman Missal[35] and the Instruction *Eucharisticum mysterium.*[36]

Arrangements begun in recent years as temporary have tended in the meantime to take on a permanent form. Even some repudiated by the Consilium continue, though in fact they are in conflict with the sense of the liturgy, aesthetic grace, and the smoothness and dignity of liturgical celebration.[37]

Through the collaboration of diocesan commissions on liturgy and on sacred art and, if necessary, through consultation with experts or even with civil authorities, there should be a complete review of the blueprints for new constructions and of the existing adaptations. The aim is to ensure a fixed arrangement in all churches that will preserve ancient monuments where necessary and to the fullest extent possible meet new needs.

11.　An understanding of the reformed liturgy still demands an intense effort for accurate translations and editions of the revised liturgical books. These must be translated in their entirety and other, particular liturgical books in use must be suppressed.

Should any conference of bishops judge it necessary and timely to add further formularies or to make particular adaptations, these are to be incorporated after the approval of the Holy See and by means of a distinctive typeface are to be clearly set off as separate from the original Latin text.

In this matter it is advisable to proceed without haste, enlisting the help not only of theologians and liturgists, but of people of learning and letters. Then the translations will be documents of tested beauty; their grace, balance, elegance, and richness of style and language will endow them with the promise of lasting use; they will match the requirements of the inner richness of their content.[38]

The preparation of vernacular liturgical books is to follow the traditional norms for publishing texts: translators or authors are to remain anonymous; liturgical books are for the service of the Christian community and editing and publication is by mandate and authority of the hierarchy, which under no consideration is answerable to outsiders. That would be offensive to the freedom of church authority and the dignity of liturgy.

12.　Any liturgical experimentation that may seem necessary or advantageous receives authorization from this Congregation alone, in writing, with norms clearly set out, and subject to the responsibility of the competent local authority.

All earlier permissions for experimentation with the Mass, granted in view of the liturgical reform as it was in progress, are to be considered as no longer in effect. Since publication of the *Missale Romanum* the norms and forms of

---

35. See GIRM nos. 153–280.

36. See SCR, Instr. EuchMyst nos. 52–57.

37. See Consilium, Letter of Card. G. Lercaro to presidents of the conferences of bishops, 30 June 1965.

38. See Paul VI, Addr. to liturgical commissions of Italy, 7 Feb. 1969.

eucharistic celebration are those given in the General Instruction and the Order of Mass.

The conferences of bishops are to draw up in detail any adaptations envisioned in the liturgical books and submit them for confirmation to the Holy See.

Should further adaptations become necessary, in keeping with the norm of the Constitution *Sacrosanctum Concilium* art. 40, the conference of bishops is to examine the issue thoroughly, attentive to the character and traditions of each people and to specific pastoral needs. When some form of experimentation seems advisable, there is to be a precise delineation of its limits and a testing within qualified groups by prudent and specially appointed persons. Experimentation should not take place in large-scale celebrations nor be widely publicized. Experiments should be few and not last beyond a year. A report then is to be sent to the Holy See. While a reply is pending, use of the petitioned adaptation is forbidden. When changes in the structure of rites or in the order of parts as set forth in the liturgical books are involved, or any departure from the usual, or the introduction of new texts, a point-by-point outline is to be submitted to the Holy See prior to the beginning of any kind of experiment.

Such a procedure is called for and demanded by both the Constitution *Sacrosanctum Concilium*[39] and the importance of the issue.

13. In conclusion: it must be remembered that the liturgical reform decided on by the Council affects the universal Church. It thus requires in pastoral meetings a study of its meaning and practice for the Christian education of the people to the end that the liturgy may become vital, touch the soul, and meet its needs.

The contemporary reform aims at making available liturgical prayer that has its origin in a living and honored tradition. Once available this prayer must appear clearly as the work of the entire people of God in all their orders and ministries.[40]

The effectiveness and authenticity of this reform has as its sole guarantee the unity of the whole ecclesial organism.

Prompted by a ready obedience to church laws and precepts and by a spirit of faith, and putting aside purely personal preferences or idiosyncracies, pastors especially should be ministers of the community liturgy through personal example, study, and an intelligent, persistent catechesis. They will thus prepare for that flowering spring expected from this liturgical reform, which looks to the needs of the age and which repudiates the secular and arbitrary as lethal to itself.

Pope Paul VI has approved this Instruction, prepared at his mandate by the Congregation for Divine Worship, and confirmed it with his authority on 3 September 1970, ordering its publication and its observance by all concerned.

---

39. See SC art. 40.
40. See GIRM no. 58.

THE CHURCH AT PRAYER
A HOLY TEMPLE OF THE LORD

STATEMENT
NATIONAL CONFERENCE OF CATHOLIC BISHOPS
DECEMBER 4, 1983

AN OVERVIEW OF *THE CHURCH AT PRAYER: A HOLY TEMPLE OF THE LORD*

Mary Elizabeth Sperry

At their November 1983 general meeting, the National Conference of Catholic Bishops (now the United States Conference of Catholic Bishops) approved *The Church at Prayer: A Holy Temple of the Lord* (CHP). The statement was formally published on December 4, 1983, exactly twenty years after *Sacrosanctum Concilium* (SC) was approved.

At the same November 1983 general meeting, the bishops approved their landmark pastoral letter on war and peace, *The Challenge of Peace: God's Promise, Our Response*. Thus, it is not surprising that *The Church at Prayer* gives particular attention to the relationship between liturgy, particularly the Eucharist, and the work of peace and justice to which God calls all the faithful.

The Bishops' Committee on the Liturgy (now the Bishops' Committee on Divine Worship) prepared the statement over the course of a year, with extensive consultation and three drafts. The purpose of the statement was not simply to recognize the anniversary, but to recall the key principles of SC, to evaluate its implementation after twenty years, and to foster continued promotion of good liturgy. The statement noted instances where the reform had been particularly successful, identified places where additional work or further reform seemed warranted, and expressed caution about abuses that had crept into some liturgical celebrations, because of an abundance of "unbridled zeal without theological formation, sometimes through personal whim or neglect."[1] Despite these abuses, the bishops make clear that the work of liturgical reform is not to be abandoned.

Because *The Church at Prayer* is intended as a reflection on SC, it makes no new laws nor offers any guidelines for liturgical celebration. Thus, its significance was limited, even in the years immediately following its release. In more recent years, its significance rests in its snapshot portrayal of the state of the reform in the first generation after the introduction of the revised rites.

The structure of *The Church at Prayer* mirrors that of SC, dedicating sections to general liturgical principles, the Eucharist, the other sacraments and sacramentals, liturgical prayer, the liturgical year, and liturgical music, art, and architecture. It examines how each chapter of SC has been implemented in the United States and identifies possible next steps.

The bishops state that the ultimate purpose of SC was not simply to reform the liturgical rites, but "protects and proclaims the core of our Christian tradition so that authentic tradition might grow in the lives of present-day Catholics and bear fruit in the future."[2] Eleven of *The Church at Prayer*'s fifty-five paragraphs deal with liturgical principles, highlighting themes that carry through

---

1. *The Church at Prayer: A Holy Temple of the Lord* (CHP), 4.
2. Ibid., 8.

the remainder of the text. These key themes include the unbreakable link between the liturgy and Christian living; the need for continuing formation; and the importance of developing among all people, clergy and laity, an authentic liturgical spirituality.

The Church at Prayer balances carefully the earthly and the heavenly dimensions of liturgy. Despite its focus on liturgy's power to transform the lives of the faithful, it makes clear that we worship God not because that worship will transform our lives, but because God deserves our wholehearted worship. Still our worship of God is not limited to the liturgical celebration:

> The worship that is given to God does not consist simply in the externals of liturgical rites but rather includes the very lives of those who celebrate the liturgy—lives which should manifest what the liturgy expresses, which reveal the life and love of Christ to others and which call them to share in the Spirit of God and in the work of building up God's Kingdom on earth.[3]

Similarly, it makes clear that inculturation of the liturgy is a theological imperative, not a political concession.[4] It is interesting to note that the initial publication of *The Church at Prayer* was a bilingual English-Spanish edition. Thirty years after its publication, the need for liturgical and other pastoral resources in Spanish and other languages continues to grow.

In articles 19 and 20, the document calls the Eucharist both "the preeminent celebration of the paschal mystery" and a "school of active love for neighbor." *The Church at Prayer* highlights some of the successes of the preceding twenty years, most notably the deepened theological reflection on all aspects of the Eucharistic mystery, the broader use of Scripture in the *Lectionary for Mass*, and the renewed emphasis on liturgical preaching. It cautions that the simpler structure of the Order of Mass requires attention to ensure that liturgical celebrations retain reverence and mystery. While lauding the use of the vernacular in the liturgy and its positive impact on liturgical participation, the bishops emphasize the need to preserve the Latin treasures of the Church's patrimony.

Turning their attention to the other sacraments and sacramentals, the bishops noted that the renewed rites more clearly express the relationship of these celebrations to key points of life, to the Church, and to the Eucharist. The broader use of Scripture continues in the rites for the sacraments with the restoration of a Liturgy of the Word "as an integral view of the sacraments and sacramentals as related components of Christian liturgy and as manifestations of the Church which is itself a sacramental community."[5]

The document calls particular attention to the increased pastoral sensitivity of the funeral liturgy and the Anointing of the Sick, the ecclesial context for the Baptism of children, and the strong theological underpinning of the Rites for Marriage and Holy Orders. Particular note is made of the restoration of the permanent diaconate and the emergence of lay liturgical ministries. Special attention is given to the then still new *Rite of Christian Initiation of Adults*.

---

3. Ibid., 9.
4. See ibid., 16.
5. Ibid., 24.

This rite highlights the importance of the community to Christian living and the intrinsic relationship between doctrine, life, and liturgy.

On the other hand, the bishops note that the revised *Rite of Confirmation* did not address successfully the concerns and questions raised about that sacrament. In addition, the bishops note the pastoral problems surrounding the Sacrament of Penance. Though "the new rites of reconciliation emphasize the reality of both personal and social sin in the Christian community and affirm that Christians are reconciled with God through the ministry of the Church,"[6] such recognition has not halted the decline in people's recourse to this sacrament.

The section on liturgical prayer focuses on the Liturgy of the Hours, stating that their "theological and liturgical thrust . . . should be a model and an ideal for the way in which all Catholic Christians pray."[7] The bishops note that the revised Breviary is not being used as intended by most priests and religious. Because the revised Breviary is designed for communal celebration, it is best used by those who live in community. As many parish priests and religious do not live in community, the revision is less helpful. The bishops call for better formation for clergy and religious to help them appreciate the bounty of scriptural and Patristic readings provided in the Breviary. Finally, the bishops recognize the need for further revision of the Liturgy of the Hours to facilitate their celebration by the laity in parish settings.

The Church at Prayer offers a positive evaluation of the revision of the liturgical calendar, giving special attention to its placement of the Paschal Triduum at the heart of the Church's liturgical year. The centrality of the Sunday celebration and the re-establishment of Lent as a time of preparation for the Easter sacraments and Advent as a joyous time of preparation for the coming of Christ are lauded as is the simplification of the calendar to limit the celebration of the saints so as to maintain focus on the mystery of Christ. The celebrations of Mary in the calendar highlight her role "both as the Mother of the Church and as a model for Christian discipleship."[8]

The bishops highlight several challenges that remain, including the need for a secularized society to recapture a sense of Sunday as the Lord's Day; the need to prepare all liturgical seasons, including Ordinary Time, well; the need to balance the observances of the liturgical year with popular piety; and the need to relate the liturgical calendar and the secular calendar. In addition, the bishops call for study of the potential for a common calendar with other Christian churches and ecclesial communities.

The chapter on liturgical music, art, and architecture highlights the documents on those topics issued by the United States bishops, namely *Music in Catholic Worship, Liturgical Music Today,* and *Environment and Art in Catholic Worship,* encouraging pastors and liturgical artists to follow the guidelines in these documents.[9] The bishops call for formation for artists so that their work will be formed by a strong theological sensibility. The liturgical arts should

---

6. Ibid., 27.

7. Ibid., 34.

8. Ibid., 40.

9. These three documents have since been superseded by *Sing to the Lord: Music in Catholic Worship* and *Built of Living Stones: Art, Architecture and Worship.*

reflect the cultures of the liturgical community. The bishops note the importance of investing in quality liturgical art, even given the other needs of the Church and the world. Even communities with limited means deserve to have liturgical celebrations graced with beauty.

The Church at Prayer sets an agenda for future liturgical efforts. First, it is not sufficient that liturgies be good celebrations. Liturgy must transform lives through the power of Christ's Paschal Mystery, requiring that the faithful "make efforts to appreciate and open our hearts to the spiritual and prayerful dimensions of the liturgy."[10] Second, the faithful must be encouraged to develop a communal liturgical sense to replace the individualistic piety that separates the worshipper from the liturgical community. Third, parishes, dioceses, and seminaries must continue and intensify efforts to provide well-founded liturgical and theological formation for those charged with preparing and celebrating the liturgy. To do otherwise might encourage "a new form of ritualism"[11] as those charged with care of the liturgy become more concerned about the externals of the celebration rather than with the liturgy's ability to call those who participate to conversion and a closer communion with God and others. Parishes and dioceses should make good use of liturgical commissions. Finally, liturgical ministers must be people of prayer, particularly devoted to liturgical prayer. Ministers thoroughly imbued with a liturgical spirituality more effectively lead others to experience Christ in the liturgy—an experience that demands "a willingness to learn from others and to be open to others in generosity and love."[12]

The bishops conclude the document by praising the acceptance of the liturgical changes by the older generations and by encouraging younger generations to allow the liturgy and worship of God to shape their lives and actions in the world. Finally, the bishops commit themselves once again to continuing the work of the liturgical renewal and to renewing prayer, penance, and worship in the life of the Church so as to lead the faithful to the holiness to which they are called.

10. CHP, 46.
11. Ibid., 48.
12. Ibid., 52.

THE CHURCH AT PRAYER

A HOLY TEMPLE OF THE LORD

A PASTORAL STATEMENT COMMEMORATING THE TWENTIETH ANNIVERSARY OF THE CONSTITUTION ON THE SACRED LITURGY

NATIONAL CONFERENCE OF CATHOLIC BISHOPS
DECEMBER 4, 1983

INTRODUCTION

1. Twenty years have passed since the Second Vatican Council solemnly promulgated the Constitution on the Sacred Liturgy (*Sacrosanctum Concilium*) on December 4, 1963. Responding to a deeply felt duty to provide for the renewal and fostering of the liturgy, the Council fathers issued this Constitution as an altogether necessary step in its stated goal "to impart an ever increasing vigor to the Christian life of the faithful" (art. 1). The passage of a score of years now offers us an opportunity not only to commemorate so significant an event in the pilgrim life of our family of faith, but also to evaluate its effect, and to foster its continued importance for the future of the Church in the United States of America.

2. For us as bishops, no work can be more important. As the Council explained, "It is the liturgy through which, especially in the divine sacrifice of the Eucharist, 'the work of our redemption is accomplished'" (art. 2). In this *"Year that is truly Holy,"* this extraordinary Jubilee of the Redemption which coincides with the anniversary we celebrate, we are reminded by Pope John Paul II that the redemption is communicated

> through the proclamation of the Word of God and through the sacraments, in that divine economy whereby the Church is constituted as the Body of Christ, 'as the universal sacrament of salvation.' . . .
>
> *Open the Doors to the Redeemer* 3

3. The generation after the Council is challenged anew to reaffirm God's close and intimate contact with each human life, to stress the importance of prayer, and especially liturgical prayer, as the principal means by which God interacts with his people, to recall the goals of the liturgical reforms mandated by the Council, to assess the strengths and the weaknesses inherent in the implementation of reform measures, to derive encouragement from liturgical achievements,

and to specify the paths that lie before us in the vital work yet to be done in promoting the renewal of Catholic life and worship.

4.   At the same time we are mindful of liturgical abuses that have occurred, sometimes through unbridled zeal without theological formation, sometimes through personal whim or neglect. While lamenting these unhappy instances, we are hopeful that they will not prevent us from seeking with zeal and courage an authentic renewal of our liturgical life. What Pope Paul VI said in 1975 still applies today:

> In the course of our eagerness to rekindle the vitality and authenticity of religion in the life of individuals, but especially in the life of the people of God, we must revere and promote the liturgy in our times, in ecclesial and collective life. . . . For us it suffices here to confirm the liturgical program that the Church has set before itself, to make stable and fruitful the idea and therefore the practice of liturgy. In that program lies the secret of a new vitality for the Church's tradition, the face of the Church's beauty, the expression of the Church's interior and universal unity. . . .
>
> Address to a General Audience, 6 August 1975

This "liturgical program" continues to be our program for the Church in the United States of America, for its growth and vitality, for its participation in the great work of the redemption and reconciliation accomplished in Jesus Christ.

GENERAL LITURGICAL PRINCIPLES

Christ is always present in his Church, especially in her liturgical celebrations.
Article 7

5.   One of the primary concerns of the Second Vatican Council was to affirm the incarnational and the sacramental character of the Church. The Word of God who took flesh of the virgin of Nazareth continues to dwell in the world through the Church. Thus what is central to the life and work of the Church is to build up that union with God made visible in Jesus Christ, a relationship made possible by his life, death, and resurrection. The paschal mystery is at the heart of the life of the Church. It is this mystery that the Church proclaims and shares with her members who are formed into the people of God through the outpouring of the Holy Spirit. The experience of this mystery is made possible through personal prayer but above all in and through the celebration of the liturgy.

6.   The liturgy is a principal means by which God acts upon the Church to make it holy. That sanctification takes place through the presence of Christ in the power of the Holy Spirit, a presence manifested through the word of Sacred Scripture, through the community itself gathered in prayer and song, and above all through the sacraments, especially the Eucharist. The sanctification of the

Church results in the creation of a community capable of continuing the saving work of Jesus Christ in the world.

7.   The liturgy is the chief means by which the Church, through Jesus Christ and in the unity of the Holy Spirit, responds to God's saving presence in thanksgiving, praise, petition, and longing. In the liturgy the members of the worshipping community are united both inwardly and outwardly with Christ: inwardly by being conformed to Christ in his disposition of humble, self-giving service of the Father and his people; outwardly by expressing both in word and action that interior conformity with the attitude of Christ. In responding to God's gift of his life offered in Christ, the Church recognizes the mystery of the Father's love entrusted to "vessels of clay." It is our challenge in faith to live the paradox of this human element which leaves the People of God in this world always an imperfect community, always inadequate in its acceptance of God's love, thus always in need of reform and renewal. In this sense the Church is always a community of penitents.

8.   The primary purpose of the liturgical reforms in which we have been engaged in a special way for the past twenty years has not been simply a change in sacramental rites. Rather the reform of the rites has been distinguished by a noble simplicity which both protects and proclaims the core of our Christian tradition so that authentic tradition might grow in the lives of present-day Catholics and bear fruit in the future. The goal is above all to enrich the Church's life of prayer and worship so that those who believe in Christ and are members of his Church might be empowered and motivated to proclaim the good news that God has offered salvation to all in his Son Jesus Christ.

9.   The worship that is given to God does not consist simply in the externals of liturgical rites but rather includes the very lives of those who celebrate the liturgy—lives which should manifest what the liturgy expresses, which reveal the life and love of Christ to others and which call them to share in the Spirit of God and in the work of building up God's Kingdom on earth. For as we noted in our reflections commemorating the fifteenth anniversary of the Decree on the Apostolate of the Laity in 1980,

> the quality of worship depends in great measure on the spiritual life of all present. As lay women and men cultivate their own proper response to God's call to holiness, this should come to expression in the communal worship of the Church.

Called and Gifted: The American Catholic Laity p. 3

10.   Liturgical renewal, then, implies an ever deeper involvement of the whole Christian community in the paschal mystery of Jesus Christ. The primary means to achieve renewal is that liturgical formation which enables all those who take part in the liturgy to become more and more imbued with its spirit and power. Liturgical formation is as necessary for the laity as it is for the clergy. For

> as lay persons assume their roles in liturgical celebration according to the gifts of the Spirit bestowed on them for that purpose, the ordained celebrant

will be more clearly seen as the one who presides over the community, bringing together the diverse talents of the community as gift to the Father.

Called and Gifted: The American Catholic Laity p. 4

The secondary means is an ongoing reform of the liturgical rites themselves to ensure that the words and actions of the liturgy express more and more adequately the holy realities which these words and actions signify. Liturgical formation and the continued reform of the rites therefore bring about that complete, active and conscious participation in the liturgy required of the assembly and its ministers.

11. Properly trained ministers and programs for such training must be available for liturgical formation. To provide for the future, seminarians and those beginning their lives as religious must be properly formed both academically and spiritually in the spirit of the liturgy. In this regard we direct the attention of those responsible to the norms and guidelines set forth in the Instruction on Liturgical Formation in Seminaries issued by the Sacred Congregation for Catholic Education in 1979. Bishops, priests and deacons must be helped also to understand better what they are doing when they celebrate the liturgy, to live the liturgical life more profoundly, and to share it effectively with others. They have a special responsibility to be formed in the spirit of the liturgy. As leaders in the Christian community and in the liturgical assemblies, bishops and priests have as one of their principal tasks to preside at worship in such a manner that the other members of the assembly are led to pray. In a sense they should be transparent images of what it means for a Christian to die and rise with Jesus.

12. Deacons and other liturgical ministers likewise require a formation that is at once personally profound and directed toward their service within the assembly. The laity must not only be helped to participate fully both internally and externally in the liturgy, but they must also be encouraged to use and develop their various ministerial gifts in the liturgical celebration.

13. In recent years we have seen a renewed interest in traditional and newer forms of prayer, but special effort must be made to assure that the spirituality of individual Catholics is both Christian and liturgical. The way the Church prays and worships should be the way individual Christians pray and worship. In that sense the liturgy is normative for Christian spirituality. The personal prayer of individual Christians is important because it ensures that they will come to the liturgy with the proper dispositions. In liturgical celebrations their minds and hearts will be in tune with what they say and do. Personal prayer, however, does not displace the liturgy nor is it a substitute for it; rather it should lead Christians to the celebration of the paschal mystery and, in turn, be nourished by that mystery.

14. We do not worship God primarily to become better people; the very nature and excellence of God demand worship. But when we worship, by the grace of the redemption, we can be transformed into better people. And so the worship of the Church is a moment in which Christians are formed as moral persons.

The liturgy helps to form Christian character, and, as a result, those who celebrate the liturgy are empowered to relate to one another in justice and peace and to involve themselves in the establishment of God's kingdom on earth.

15.   The Eucharist especially teaches us the meaning of God's peace and justice. For as we have said in another pastoral letter, the Mass is

> a unique means of seeking God's help to create the conditions essential for true peace in ourselves and in the world. In the Eucharist we encounter the risen Lord, who gave us His peace. He shares with us the grace of the redemption, which helps us to preserve and nourish this precious gift.
>
> *The Challenge of Peace: God's Promise and Our Response* 295

God's gifts of justice and peace, indeed all those gifts which strengthen our moral life, are summed up in the liturgy, especially in the Eucharist as a sacrament of reconciliation. As God loves us and shares this new life with us, so we are enabled to love and serve one another. In the liturgy the divine story of creation and redemption is told and retold; that revelation is reinforced by ritual patterns which communicate Christian meaning and values in verbal and non-verbal ways. As a result a Christian vision of life is shared. It is a vision framed and permeated by faith. In celebrating the liturgy, Christians do not leave their everyday world and responsibilities behind; rather they enter into God's real world and see it as it actually is in Jesus—a place where God's providence and love are indeed at work.

16.   In order that the Christian vision may be available to all members of the Church, efforts have been made in the past twenty years to adapt the liturgical rites and symbols to the diverse cultures of the world. If the Church is to become incarnate in every culture, the liturgy must express the paschal mystery, which lies at the heart of the Church, in some symbols derived from these diverse cultures. In our own country, special care must be taken to adapt the liturgy so that it is perceived as inclusive of women and responsive to the needs of persons of diverse ages, races and ethnic groups. Liturgical adaptation is not simply a concession granted by the Constitution on the Sacred Liturgy; it is rather a theological imperative of liturgical renewal that the paschal mystery may be celebrated for all people and that all may be able to bring their talents to the service of the liturgy.

17.   A renewed appreciation of the centrality of worship in the life of the Church with its emphasis on God's initiative in offering unity and peace to his people through his Son has increased our sensitivity to the need for greater ecumenical activity among all Christians. While working to overcome doctrinal and structural differences, Christians have been encouraged to pray together and to celebrate those rites which have been authorized for common celebration, especially celebrations of the Word of God, so that Christian unity might be more readily and effectively achieved.

18.   In our own country the rediscovery by other churches and ecclesial communities of liturgical sources and traditions common to our Christian heritage

encourages all Christians. Recent liturgical reforms in many churches of North America, especially in the rites of the Eucharist, already point to a convergence and unity of liturgical prayer that gives hope for eventual doctrinal agreement. That many churches now use a similar three-year cycle of Scripture readings for the Eucharist based on The Roman Lectionary means that the majority of American Christians hear the same Word proclaimed each Sunday. The liturgy has already become a source of unity and a sign of hope for even greater unity.

THE EUCHARISTIC MYSTERY

At the Last Supper, on the night he was betrayed, our Savior instituted the eucharistic sacrifice of his Body and Blood. This he did in order to perpetuate the sacrifice of the Cross throughout the ages until he should come again, and so to entrust to his beloved Spouse, the Church, a memorial of his death and resurrection: a sacrament of love, a sign of unity, a bond of charity, a paschal banquet in which Christ is consumed, the mind is filled with grace, and a pledge of future glory is given to us.

Article 47

19. It is by means of the liturgy that the Church touches its members at the principal moments in their lives. Baptism and confirmation, penance and anointing, orders and marriage each reveal and reflect for Catholic Christians a particular facet of the paschal mystery of Christ and make possible a vital transforming relationship with Christ in his Church. However, it is the Eucharist which is the preeminent celebration of the paschal mystery. In the Eucharist the victory of Christ over death is made manifest, enabling the community to be one with Christ and to give to the Father, in the unity of the Holy Spirit, all honor and glory.

20. The revised liturgical books, along with numerous decrees relating to the Eucharist have been issued in the past twenty years. These documents have resulted in a renewed appreciation of all aspects of eucharistic theology and spirituality: the celebration of the sacrifice of the Mass, the reception of Holy Communion, and the reservation of the Blessed Sacrament whether for the communion of the sick and dying or for devotion on the part of the faithful. Just as there has been a renewed appreciation of the Eucharist as both sacrifice and meal, so too the Eucharist is the "school of active love for neighbor," as Pope John Paul II stated in his letter *On the Mystery and Worship of the Eucharist*: "The Eucharist educates us to this love in a deeper way; it shows us, in fact, what value each person, our brother or sister, has in God's eyes, if Christ offers himself equally to each one, under the species of bread and wine" (no. 6). The Eucharist is therefore the bond of charity and unity which unites Christians in God's love.

21. The revised Order of Mass sets out a rite that is simple and uncluttered, a rite which underscores the unity and bond of the assembly. This enables the symbols to speak with clarity but also necessitates great care on the part of the

ministers so that the celebrating community will be drawn to a reverent experience of the mysterious presence of Christ in word and sacrament. A recent evaluation project, centered on the structural elements of the Order of Mass, was sponsored by our Committee on the Liturgy and the Federation of Diocesan Liturgical Commissions. It provided an excellent opportunity both for liturgical formation concerning the Eucharist and for suggesting ways to improve the celebration.

22.   Certainly for Roman Catholics one of the most significant achievements of the contemporary liturgical reform has been a retrieval of the riches of Sacred Scripture and the breadth of exposure to the Word of God set out in the new lectionary. The importance of the homily as an effective way of relating that Word to the contemporary lives of the community has been stressed by our Committee on Priestly Life and Ministry in its document *Fulfilled in Your Hearing: The Homily in the Sunday Assembly*. We urge those charged with the ministry of preaching the homily to study that document carefully and to make even greater efforts to preach a well-prepared homily at both Sunday and daily celebrations. Likewise the restoration of the general intercessions has offered an opportunity to relate the Eucharist to the universal Church and the world.

23.   The introduction of vernacular languages into the liturgy has enabled the faithful to make the liturgy truly their own through greater understanding of the rites. We must also continue our efforts to preserve the treasures of our liturgical patrimony in Latin. Regular reception of Holy Communion as an integral part of the eucharistic celebration, a more frequent availability of Communion under both kinds, and the extension of the practice of concelebration have also contributed to the desired effect of greater participation in the eucharistic liturgy. Nevertheless, as bishops charged with the promotion and custody of the liturgy, we urge priests, deacons and lay people to give more of their energy to an even greater and more profound participation in the Church's eucharistic mystery.

THE SACRAMENTS AND SACRAMENTALS

For well-disposed members of the faithful the liturgy of the sacraments and sacramentals sanctifies almost every event of their lives with the divine grace which flows from the paschal mystery of the passion, death, and resurrection of Christ. From this source all sacraments and sacramentals draw their power. There is scarcely any proper use of material things which cannot thus be directed toward the sanctification of men and the praise of God.
Article 61

24.   In revising other aspects of the liturgy, efforts have been made to help the faithful develop an integral view of the sacraments and sacramentals as related components of Christian liturgy and as manifestations of the Church which is itself a sacramental community. The rites have been carefully related to the paschal mystery of Christ, to the Eucharist as the principal celebration of that

mystery, and to the critical experiences of individual Christians and communities. The Liturgy of the Word has been restored as an integral component in all sacramental celebrations and other liturgical rites.

25.   The Rite of Christian Initiation of Adults is only gradually being implemented and appreciated in our country, but already many parishes have discovered the benefits that are available not only to the newly initiated members of the Church but also to the parish community as a whole. Above all, the rites of initiation have affirmed the importance of a vital ecclesial community in the life of Christians and have shown the essential relationship among the doctrines Christians believe, the worship they carry out, and the responsible moral lives they live. The Rite of Baptism for Children also has stressed the importance of the faith community as the essential environment in which the infant grows toward a personal faith commitment as well as the primary responsibility of both parents and godparents for nurturing that faith in the life of the child.

26.   Although pastoral, liturgical and theological questions continue to be raised about the sacrament of confirmation, the introduction of a new rite for this sacrament of initiation has contributed to a renewed appreciation of the role of the Holy Spirit in Christian life. As pastors and theologians continue to study the sacrament, it should be stressed that although the sacrament of confirmation may be an occasion for giving testimony to a religious commitment, it is above all the outpouring of the Holy Spirit, "the seal of the gift of the Holy Spirit," who operates in a powerful transforming way in the life of the baptized Christian.

27.   Although intensive study and discussion preceded formulation of the revised Rite of Penance, pastoral problems continue to surround the sacrament. The new rites of reconciliation emphasize the reality of both personal and social sin in the Christian community and affirm that Christians are reconciled with God through the ministry of the Church. The fact is, however, that the importance of this sacrament has declined in the lives of many Christians, who are not likely to recover appreciation for it unless they are once again convinced of its role in their lives. In spite of the evil so obviously rampant in our world, a genuine sense of sin in our lives is often absent. Greater pastoral efforts must be directed toward a recovery of that sense of sin joined to a more profound understanding of the merciful forgiveness and reconciliation offered to us in Christ Jesus.

28.   We urge our priests and those who have charge of catechesis to greater efforts in leading all of us toward a deeper faith in the healing power of God who, in his Son Jesus Christ, has reconciled us. That faith can only be deepened if we understand the existence of sin in our lives, "for the members of the Church . . . are exposed to temptation and often fall into the wretchedness of sin" (*Rite of Penance* 3). As individuals and as a people we must come before God seeking pardon and reconciliation. As individuals we need to experience healing, reconciliation and forgiveness, an experience that comes preeminently through the ministry of the Church. And as a people we must experience this same forgiveness:

In fact, people frequently join together to commit injustice. But it is also true that they help each other in doing penance; freed from sin by the grace of Christ, they become, with all persons of good will, agents of justice and peace in the world.

Rite of Penance 5

Therefore, not only should great attention be given to celebrations of the sacrament with individuals, but pastors should also assure communal celebrations of penance, especially in Advent and Lent, according to the norms of the rite, remembering that inner conversion embraces sorrow for sin and the intent to lead a new life.

29.   The revised rites for the sick and the dying, known as Pastoral Care of the Sick: Rites of Anointing and Viaticum, convey with sensitivity and power the Lord's healing love. These rites have been deeply appreciated because of their pastoral sensitivity and the consolation and strength they have brought not only to the sick and dying but also to their families and friends in time of crisis. In keeping with the revised ritual, priests, deacons, other ministers and those engaged in any ministry to the sick in homes, hospitals and hospices should avail themselves of the riches and variety of these liturgical texts and rites, never contenting themselves with brief or "emergency" forms unless absolutely necessary. The sick and the dying are members of the Body of Christ, greatly in need of the Church's pastoral care.

30.   That same consolation has been experienced through the revised Rite of Funerals which carefully relates the death of Christians to the death and resurrection of Christ. Although the funeral rites honestly acknowledge the dread of death as a result of sin and evil in the world, above all they stress the right of Christians to hope for triumph over death because of Christ's resurrection. In that trust we wish to make clear our responsibility to pray for the deceased so that freed fully from their sins they may experience the joy of God's light and love. At the same time we urge continued effort by pastors, deacons, musicians, and other ministers toward better celebrations of the funeral rites so that these will console the living and demonstrate the community's faith in the saving death and resurrection of Christ.

31.   In the revised rites of ordination emphasis has been clearly placed on the candidate's responsibility for proclaiming the Word of God, presiding over the liturgy and ministering the sacraments. An unclouded understanding of these basic ministries sets a firm foundation for other pastoral and liturgical services, fosters commitment on the part of the laity, and cultivates the development of Christian community. Of special significance has been the restoration of the permanent diaconate and the emergence of lay involvement in a number of ministries which were until recently performed only by the ordained clergy. Continuing education and formation in the liturgy is therefore all the more important for priests, deacons and lay ministers. Liturgical renewal and spiritual growth need "mystagogues," men and women themselves well-versed in the ways of the Lord, to lead others to drink more deeply from the refreshing

waters of divine life, always eager to live the Christian life as though newly-baptized.

32.   The revised rites for the sacrament of marriage acknowledge human friendship as one of the most basic symbols of God's loving presence to human life. In marriage Christian men and women sacramentalize the covenant relationship of commitment between Christ and his Church, between God and humankind. Their love is expressed in their self-gift to each other, in children who manifest the creative nature of love, and in their witness of fidelity in a world where life-time commitments are increasingly rare. The revised rites and liturgical texts for Christian marriage underscore the totality of the mutual gift involved in this sacrament which St. Paul calls a "great mystery" and Pope John Paul II recently called a "memorial," for marriage calls to mind the great works of God in creation. Likewise marriage is a communion which specifically represents Christ's incarnation and the mystery of the covenant. For all that is human in marital love signifies the intimacy of our relationship with God (Address to a General Audience, 3 November 1979). When couples are preparing for marriage, their attention should be directed toward the proper choice of liturgical texts, music and rites. They should also be shown how the Rite of Marriage itself expresses the bond and covenant into which they are about to enter.

33.   In the Church, the vocation to Christian marriage is complemented and strengthened by the vocation to celibacy ratified in the revised Rites of Religious Profession and the Rites of Consecration to a Life of Virginity. These rites, so little known to most Catholics, reflect the positive value of celibate love.

LITURGICAL PRAYER

The Church, by celebrating the Eucharist and by other means, especially the celebration of the divine office, is ceaselessly engaged in praising the Lord and interceding for the salvation of the entire world.
Article 83

34.   By both word and example, the Lord Jesus taught his disciples that prayer is necessary for Christian believers. Like the prayer of Jesus himself, it should flow from the experience of living intimately in the presence of God. Such a communion is one in which we, as God's people, share in the divine life and love and, in turn, respond to these gifts with praise and thanksgiving, petition and longing. To foster that spirit of prayer the Liturgy of the Hours or Divine Office has been reformed. Although a special mandate has been given to bishops, priests and deacons to celebrate the Liturgy of the Hours, it is also clearly desired that all the faithful take part in this liturgical prayer of the Church, especially Morning and Evening Prayer. The theological and liturgical thrust of the Liturgy of the Hours should be a model and an ideal for the way in which all Catholic Christians pray.

35.   This communal experience of liturgical prayer will be new for many; its effectiveness will depend to a great extent on liturgical formation and the experience of well-structured and prayerfully executed celebrations. Unfortunately it must be acknowledged that the revised Liturgy of the Hours, which has been designed especially for communal celebration, has not yet become a vital prayer form for many priests and religious who do not reside in liturgically-structured communities. In order that extended psalmody and patristic readings be experienced as inspiring sources of strength for ministry, it is necessary to provide adequate scriptural, theological and liturgical background. Similarly, more realistic efforts must be made to adapt the Liturgy of the Hours to the actual situations which prevail in parishes. Where the responsibility to pray in the spirit of the Church has been taken seriously and time and effort have been put into the preparation and celebration of the Liturgy of the Hours, the experience has been very rewarding. This is an area which calls for much more attention on the part of pastors and prayer leaders in our Catholic communities.

LITURGICAL TIME

Once each week, on the day which she has called the Lord's Day, Holy Mother Church keeps the memory of the Lord's resurrection. She also celebrates it once every year, together with his blessed passion, at Easter, that most solemn of all feasts.

In the course of the year, moreover, she unfolds the whole mystery of Christ from the incarnation and nativity to the ascension, to Pentecost and the expectation of the blessed hope of the coming of the Lord. Thus recalling the mysteries of the redemption, she opens up to the faithful the riches of her Lord's powers and merits.

Article 102

36.   The life of the Church is sanctified not only by the Liturgy of the Hours but also by the celebration of the liturgical year. In revising the liturgical calendar, each liturgical season is focused on the paschal mystery of Christ as the center of all liturgical worship. Hence the feasts of the Lord, especially the celebration of his death and resurrection, have been given preference. These mysteries are celebrated in a special way during the Paschal Triduum but also on Sunday which, since early centuries, has been observed as the "Lord's Day."

37.   Lent has been restored to its proper observance as a preparation for the celebration of the paschal mystery. The primary features of this season are the purification and enlightenment of catechumens and works of prayer, almsgiving or service to others, and penance, especially fasting and abstinence. Through the celebration of the forty days of Lent and the fifty days of Easter, the main lines of the Church's Year of the Lord are clearly established; it is essentially a celebration of the saving work of Christ.

38.   Throughout the rest of the year the various aspects of that saving mystery unfold. Of special importance is the celebration of Christmas. During the

Christmas season the mysteries highlighted in the gospel infancy narratives are celebrated. The solemnity of the Epiphany of the Lord reveals the universal saving mission of Christ the Messiah. The feast of the Baptism of the Lord, which marks the beginning of Christ's public ministry, brings the Christmas season to an end. The season of Advent is celebrated with joyful expectancy as a reminder of God's fidelity and care culminating in the first coming of Christ, and as preparation for his second coming at the end of time.

39. The Sundays of the Year ("Ordinary Time") and the feasts and solemnities of the Lord are always celebrations of the same paschal mystery commemorated in the "great seasons." Yet all too often little attention is given to these "ordinary times." In view of the increasing secularization of the Lord's Day, we suggest that full celebration of the Sundays of the Year be promoted, since they are essential and crucial to the development and deepening of the Christian life. In addition, we urge our people and pastors to make greater efforts in planning the whole liturgical year in such a way that each season, memorial, feast and solemnity is given its proper significance and importance. Furthermore, we must all be reminded of the close link between liturgy and devotion, liturgy and popular piety. The devotion which surrounds the solemnity of Corpus Christi, for example, is a model of the proper relationship between liturgy and popular piety in the liturgical year. True and authentic piety can only help us to be more devoted to the liturgy.

40. Special care has been taken to stress the role of Mary, the Mother of God, in the life of the Church, as we have stated many times, especially in our pastoral letter on the Blessed Virgin Mary. (*Behold Your Mother: Woman of Faith*, 21 November 1973). The great Marian feasts and solemnities of the revised calendar relate the life of Mary to the mystery of her Son; in this way she is honored both as the Mother of the Church and as a model for Christian discipleship.

41. The new calendar significantly reduces the number of saints' days so that the mystery of Christ may not be overshadowed. The Constitution on the Sacred Liturgy prescribed that only saints of universal importance should be proposed to the whole Church for obligatory commemoration. Every nation, indeed every diocese, has its own particular and proper calendar celebrating certain mysteries, saints and days of prayer.

42. In the United States, for example, the Church honors Mary in a special way under the title of the Immaculate Conception as patroness of the United States and under the title of Our Lady of Guadalupe as patroness of the Americas. American holy men and women such as Isaac Jogues and companions, Kateri Tekakwitha, Elizabeth Ann Seton, John Neumann, Frances Cabrini and others testify to holiness in America. Thanksgiving Day, while not a liturgical feast, nevertheless is celebrated liturgically by American Catholics as a day of prayer and thanksgiving for the gifts God has bestowed upon us.

43. Efforts must also be made to relate the liturgical year to the secular calendar so that the ordinary lives of Christians may be sanctified. Ecumenical discussions have raised a number of important questions concerning the

possibility of a fixed date for Easter and a common calendar shared by various churches and ecclesial communities; these are questions that require and deserve further study by the whole Church.

LITURGICAL MUSIC, ART AND ARCHITECTURE

Holy Mother Church has always been the patron of the fine arts and has ever sought their noble ministry, to the end especially that all things set apart for use in divine worship should be worthy, becoming, and beautiful, signs and symbols of things supernatural.

Article 122

44. In matters of liturgical music, art and architecture, only directives of a very general nature have been issued in the past twenty years, and rightly so, for the creation of art is something that can be neither clearly defined nor readily mandated. In this regard, our Committee on the Liturgy has issued statements which have been well received and proven very useful, especially *Music in Catholic Worship, Liturgical Music Today and Environment and Art in Catholic Worship.* The norms and guidelines of these documents should be followed by pastors and all those engaged in the liturgical arts. Our churches must be homes for the arts and houses pleasing to the Lord.

45. Artists, architects, artisans and musicians who work for the Church should be competent in their own right and should have a clear understanding of the theology of the liturgy and the role of their proper arts in liturgical celebrations. We must continue to search for appropriate ways to enrich our liturgies both by retrieving our artistic tradition and using it appropriately, being open to new forms of the artistic imagination, and by utilizing the cultural heritage of the diverse ethnic and racial groups of the Church in America. While we continue to make efforts to alleviate world poverty, it is important that some of the Church's material resources, even in the case of financially impoverished communities, be allocated to the development of the liturgical arts because they nourish the human spirit and bear witness to the preeminence of the sacred in human life. They enable Christians to grow more and more into that holy temple wherein God can dwell and empower people to transform the world in his name.

CONCLUSIONS

Mother Church earnestly desires that all the faithful should be led to that full, conscious, and active participation in liturgical celebrations which is demanded by the very nature of the liturgy, and to which the Christian people, "a chosen race, a royal priesthood, a holy nation, a redeemed people" (1 Pet. 2:9, 4–5) have a right and obligation by reason of their baptism.

Article 14

46.   There have been many significant liturgical gains in the past twenty years, but there remain many areas of unfinished liturgical business. Liturgical reform must move more and more toward genuine Christian renewal. That means above all that we must continue to make efforts to appreciate and open our hearts to the spiritual and prayerful dimensions of the liturgy.

47.   Much progress has been made over the past generation through great personal and pastoral effort to help people develop a sense of communal prayer. Yet, in many cases, piety continues to be individualistic and untouched by the richness and treasures of the liturgy. Even specialized programs in spiritual renewal are at times only minimally related to experience of Christian worship and sacraments.

48.   The liturgy should be the primary school for Christian prayer and spirituality, enabling Christians to live justly, peacefully, and charitably in the world. Often we fail to understand that the celebration of the liturgy is the Church's ministry of worship and prayer, calling people to conversion and contemplation, inviting them into communion with God and with each other. And the more professional we become in the area of liturgy, the more we may be tempted to become preoccupied with external forms and aesthetic experiences. The end result may simply be a new form of ritualism.

49.   Liturgical ministers themselves must be people of prayer. If sometimes there is a gap between liturgical ministers and the larger Christian community, it may be because the ministers may not appear to be praying people. Liturgical ministers must be spiritually and personally involved in the mystery of Christ, and they must show outwardly this involvement if they are to lead people into that same experience.

50.   If in the last analysis a great part of the responsibility for liturgical formation and renewal falls on the individual Christian, there is nevertheless a need for help from others in this regard. Parish liturgy committees, diocesan liturgical commissions and offices of worship also have a great task before them to continue the work begun twenty years ago when the Constitution on the Sacred Liturgy was first promulgated. Parish liturgy committees should assist priests, deacons and other liturgical ministers such as readers and ministers of communion in fulfilling their roles. At the same time, through planning and careful attention to the norms of each of the rites they will help lead the assembly toward a more profound worship of God and communion with Christ and one another.

51.   The diocesan liturgical commission or office of worship must assist the bishop in carrying out his functions as promoter and guardian of the liturgical life of the diocese. First convened by our Committee on the Liturgy in 1968, the Federation of Diocesan Liturgical Commissions, especially through the annual national meeting of liturgical commissions and worship office personnel, should continue to assist us on a national level. In this way, all those engaged in the great work of liturgical renewal will ensure not only the continuation of "that full, conscious, and active participation in liturgical celebrations," but also help

the Church always to be a Church of pilgrims, ever renewed and ever being renewed in its life and worship.

52.   We must continue to struggle to overcome our selfishness, our closed-mindedness, our indifference, our timidity, and our lack of trust in God and one another. Both Christian life and worship presuppose community—a willingness to learn from others and to be open to others in generosity and love. Only on such a base can liturgy really be said to affect and deepen the sense of community. In its language, symbol, style and spirit today's liturgy is a growing sign and instrument of community, people at one with each other and with God.

53.   This score of years has witnessed the most sweeping changes in liturgical life that the Catholic Church has known in centuries. When we observe similar shifts in culture, values and attitudes elsewhere throughout the world, we can have no doubt that the Council acted under the guidance of the Holy Spirit. Liturgical flexibility and adaptation have made it possible for the Church's proclamation of the Good News to challenge our times with a realistic chance for a hearing and an impact. Above all, the liturgical reform has helped the Church to come into the presence of the all-holy God in languages, signs and gestures spoken and made by contemporary Catholics without loss of its tradition—truly a gift of the Holy Spirit.

54.   For older generations acceptance of liturgical changes has been a true venture in faith; it is a sign of the Church's vitality that the vast majority has endorsed and taken to heart the reforms initiated by the Council. For a newer generation the provisions of the Constitution on the Sacred Liturgy have offered hope that worship and world, liturgy and life, can be harmonized and truly become the gift of the Father who has loved us through the Son and empowers us to return that love in the Spirit.

55.   Mindful of our own responsibilities as bishops to carry out the office of sanctification in the Church, we pledge renewed efforts to continue the great work of the Council in liturgical renewal and in the renewal of prayer, penance and worship in the life of the Church. This anniversary and this holy year of the redemption must lead us all to a "renewed and deepened Spirit of Advent," a prayerful spirit of expectation, as our Holy Father John Paul II reminds us (*Open the Doors to the Redeemer* 9). We urge, therefore, our helpers in the ministry, priests and deacons, our lay ministers in the liturgy, our liturgists, but above all our liturgical assemblies to engage themselves continually with faith and trust in that holy work which is the liturgy, and always to remember these words of the Constitution on the Sacred Liturgy as we await the coming of the Lord:

> In the earthly liturgy we take part in a foretaste of that heavenly liturgy which is celebrated in the holy city of Jerusalem toward which we journey as pilgrims, where Christ is sitting at the right hand of God, minister of the holies and of the true tabernacle. With all the warriors of the heavenly army we sing a hymn of glory to the Lord; venerating the memory of the saints, we hope for some part and fellowship with them; we eagerly await

the Savior, our Lord Jesus Christ, until he our life shall appear and we too will appear with him in glory.

Article 8

VICESIMUS QUINTUS ANNUS
ON THE 25TH ANNIVERSARY
OF THE PROMULGATION
OF THE CONCILIAR CONSTITUTION
"SACROSANCTUM CONCILIUM"
ON THE SACRED LITURGY

APOSTOLIC LETTER
POPE JOHN PAUL II
DECEMBER 4, 1988

AN OVERVIEW OF *VICESIMUS QUINTUS ANNUS*

S. Joyce Ann Zimmerman, CPPS

On December 4, 1988, the very day of the twenty-fifth anniversary of the promulgation of *Sacrosanctum Concilium* (SC), Pope John Paul II issued *Vicesimus quintus annus*, an apostolic letter[1] extolling the vision of this first fruit of Vatican II. This rather short document[2] is divided into six sections dealing with liturgical renewal principles, guidelines, application, the future, and competent liturgical authority. Although the document is addressed "To all my Brothers in the episcopate and the Priesthood," most of its content is pertinent for all the faithful—clergy and laity alike.

OPENING PARAGRAPHS

In the two opening paragraphs the Holy Father makes three critical points that set the tone for the whole document. First, he clearly supports the work of renewal that the Council set out to do, specifically mentioning the Council Fathers' "authoritative teaching and pastoral decisions."[3] His endorsement includes the work of "a great liturgical and pastoral movement."[4] This pre-Council scholarship and practice not only prepared for SC, but also set an agenda for liturgical renewal that the liturgy constitution would take up and further. Second, renewing liturgy is renewing the whole Church. Pope John Paul II specifically mentions the effect of SC on *Lumen gentium*. Third, the pope hints at emerging problems concerning liturgical renewal,[5] but at the same time he emphasizes "the enduring value of its principles."[6] Immediately after the promulgation of SC, a sort of liturgical euphoria had set in. By the 1980s the climate had begun to shift. The pope is well aware of this situation as he writes this apostolic letter.

I. RENEWAL IN ACCORD WITH TRADITION

The next two paragraphs comprise the first major section of the document and address the issue of continuity with Tradition. Beginning with a brief statement about the liturgical renewal undertaken by the Council of Trent, the pope next commends the renewal work of two popes of the twentieth century, Pius X and Pius XII, and briefly lists their accomplishments, among them, setting up liturgical renewal commissions, reforming *The Roman Breviary*, issuing the encyclical

---

1. An apostolic letter is issued by a pope or by a Roman congregation in the pope's name and concerns some important topic. It carries the authority of the papal office, but is not primarily legislative in intent.

2. The apostolic letter consists of only twenty-three paragraphs.

3. *Vicesimus quintus annus*, (VQA), 2.

4. Ibid., 1.

5. See ibid., 2.

6. Ibid.

Mediator Dei, changing the time for the Eucharistic fast to encourage the faithful to receive Holy Communion, and revising the Easter Vigil and Holy Week.[7] Pope John Paul II again comes back to the theme of the relationship of liturgical and ecclesial renewal and quotes from his own Holy Thursday letter to the clergy, *Dominicae cenae*: "A very close and organic bond exists between the renewal of the liturgy and the renewal of the whole life of the Church."[8] This clearly echoes a core principle from SC: "The liturgy is the summit toward which the activity of the Church is directed; at the same time it is the fount from which all the Church's power flows."[9]

The very last sentence of this first section might easily be missed, but it is of paramount importance for contemporary liturgical discussions and tensions. Pope John Paul II says, "This work [of renewal immediately after the Council] was undertaken in accordance with the conciliar principles of fidelity to tradition and openness to legitimate development;[10] and so it is possible to say that the reform of the Liturgy is strictly traditional and in accordance with 'the ancient usage of the holy Fathers.'"[11] Thus, the Holy Father is affirming SC's organic unity with previous liturgical practice. What becomes clear later in this apostolic letter is that it is not the *principles* of SC that are causing difficulties, but the *manner* in which they are sometimes implemented. It is important to keep this distinction in mind.

II. THE GUIDING PRINCIPLES OF THE CONSTITUTION

The Holy Father only makes reference to three principles in this second section of the document: the Paschal Mystery, proclaiming God's Word, and the self-manifestation of the Church. The first two are to be expected and familiar; the last echoes his insistence on the relationship of liturgical and ecclesial renewal.

Two paragraphs underscore the basic principle that liturgy reenacts the Paschal Mystery. This language reminds us that we are not merely recalling the historical event of the mystery of Christ at liturgy, but rather that "Liturgy is the privileged place for the encounter of Christians with God and the one whom he has sent, Jesus Christ (cf Jn 17:3)."[12] To flesh out what he means by this encounter, Pope John Paul II refers to the four liturgical presences of Christ: Christ is present in the Church assembled for prayer; in the ordained minister who acts *"in persona Christi"*; in the Word proclaimed; and, "by the power of the Holy Spirit," in every one of the sacraments but "in a special and preeminent fashion (*sublimiori modo*), in the Sacrifice of the Mass under the Eucharistic Species."[13] By adjoining the Paschal Mystery with these presences of Christ, the Holy Father is implying that the Paschal Mystery is a lived reality in both the sacraments where we encounter Christ and in our daily Christian living where we also

---

7. Ibid., 3.

8. *Dominicae cenae*, (DC) 13.

9. *Sacrosanctum Concilium* (SC), 10. Pope John Paul II specifically cites this relationship in the first paragraph of the conclusion; VQA, 22.

10. Note 17 in the text references SC, 23.

11. VQA, 4; Note 18 in the text references, SC, 23.

12. VQA, 7.

13. Ibid.

encounter Christ. Christ and his mystery are ever present to us. The self-offering of Christ in his life, ministry, suffering, and death and his passing over to risen life is enacted in our liturgical celebrations as an ongoing self-offering of Christ to which we unite our own self-offering. As our presence encounters divine presence in liturgy, we are imbued with a liturgical spirituality that compels us to live that same mystery of self-offering in all we do each day.

The second principle on the proclamation of God's Word is just one short paragraph, the major thrust of which is the invitation to come to a deeper appreciation for Sacred Scripture and its authentic interpretation. The pope alludes to the revised Lectionary with its greater use of Scripture, especially with the addition of readings from the Old Testament. He hints at the call for a restoration of a Liturgy of the Word in every sacrament that is celebrated, and quotes SC as an important challenge: so that "the intimate link between rite and word" might be more easily seen.[14] In a very lengthy sentence John Paul II associates growth in liturgical life with a greater appreciation of the Scriptures and makes some very practical points: the importance of authentically translating and interpreting Sacred Scripture, the importance of how the Scriptures are proclaimed, the disposition of the proclaiming ministers, and the importance of the Homily, to name a few.

The third principle the Holy Father addresses concerns the reality that the Church is manifested when the members of the Body of Christ gather to pray liturgically. This principle is explained by briefly commenting on each of the four marks of the Church. The Church is *one* and *holy* because of the unity of the Trinity and the holiness of Christ who is encountered in Liturgy. The Church is catholic, that is, universal, because the Spirit "gathers together people of all languages in the profession of the same faith."[15] Finally, the Church is apostolic because, first, she is founded on the Apostles and, second, because the Church is sent forth from liturgy to live and proclaim the Gospel to the entire world.

III. GUIDELINES FOR THE RENEWAL OF LITURGICAL LIFE

Having laid down the principles, Pope John Paul II next derives norms and guidelines for applying these principles to liturgical renewal. Thus, the principle of enacting the Paschal Mystery gives us a share (by our Baptism) in the priesthood of Christ through the power of the Holy Spirit. The proclamation of the Word cautions us to use only words during liturgy that accord with that inspired Word of God. Since liturgy makes present the Church, liturgy itself is an act of the whole Church and can be regulated only by competent authorities. Further, since liturgy is an act of the Church, liturgy requires the full, conscious, and active participation by all present,[16] each person according to what is proper to them. Other pastoral matters include the need for liturgical education, use of the vernacular, increase of the number of Prefaces and Eucharistic Prayers, adaptation that is open to various peoples and cultures, and fuller use of sacramental signs. Much of this, of course, has already been implemented, but this twenty-

---

14. Ibid., 8; quoting SC, 35.
15. VQA, 9.
16. See ibid., 10; see also SC, 14.

fifth anniversary letter might stand as both a critique and encouragement of the renewal we have embraced.

IV. THE PRACTICAL APPLICATION OF THE REFORM

Three paragraphs in this section essentially offer a critique of the renewal process by the end of the 1980s. The first paragraph[17] points to the difficulties the liturgical renewal has precipitated, and here the Holy Father is very forthright in categorizing people's response to renewal: from indifference to being reactionary to implementing innovations contrary to the norms. The next paragraph points to positive outcomes: a spirit of obedience on the part of clergy and faithful alike in responding to the "movement of the Holy Spirit,"[18] a greater realization of and appreciation for the table of the Word,[19] the new translations available, greater participation by all, and greater joy and vitality in the liturgy. The third paragraph[20] in this section returns to concerns the pope has about renewal. These include liturgical leadership implementing practices outside the norms with examples such as omitting or adding to the rites; blurring the lines between the universal and ministerial priesthood; composing original texts; and substituting readings other than the ones appointed from Sacred Scripture.

V. THE FUTURE OF THE RENEWAL

Next, John Paul II projects four areas in which liturgical renewal needs to advance greater biblical and liturgical formation;[21] cultural adaptation;[22] attention to new challenges such as liturgical celebrations with children, youth, and those who are developmentally challenged;[23] and attending to the relationship of liturgy and popular devotions.[24] Twenty-five years after the pope has written this letter, these areas still call for our attention.

VI. THE ORGANISMS RESPONSIBLE FOR LITURGICAL RENEWAL

Liturgical practice is governed only by competent authorities because liturgy is the right and privilege of the whole Church. John Paul II mentions three levels of authority in this final section of his letter: the Congregation for Divine Worship and the Discipline of the Sacraments,[25] the various bishops' conferences,[26] and

---

17. See VQA, 11.

18. Ibid., 12.

19. The Holy Father does not discuss the relationship of the tables of Word and Sacrament, although scholarship in this area is still much needed.

20. See VQA, 13.

21. See ibid., 15.

22. See ibid., 16.

23. See ibid., 17.

24. See ibid., 18. A document that has been immensely helpful in this last area is the *Directory on Popular Piety and the Liturgy: Principles and Guidelines* issued by the Congregation for Divine Worship and the Discipline of the Sacraments in 2002.

25. See ibid., 19.

26. See ibid., 20.

diocesan bishops.[27] The bishop is the chief liturgist in his diocese but, curiously, no mention is made of the authority of pastors with respect to liturgy.

VII. CONCLUSION

In two brief concluding paragraphs, the Holy Father comments on the liturgy as the source and summit of the Church's life[28] and once again calls for a spirit of renewal.[29] There can be no doubt for anyone reading this anniversary letter that Pope John Paul II supported with great enthusiasm and vigor authentic liturgical renewal.

---

27. See ibid., 21.
28. See ibid., 22; see footnote 9 above.
29. See ibid., 23.

VICESIMUS QUINTUS ANNUS

ON THE TWENTY-FIFTH ANNIVERSARY OF THE PROMULGATION OF THE CONCILIAR CONSTITUTION *"SACROSANCTUM CONCILIUM"* ON THE SACRED LITURGY

APOSTOLIC LETTER
JOHN PAUL II
DECEMBER 4, 1988

To all my Brothers in the Episcopate and the Priesthood,
greetings and the Apostolic Blessing

1.   Twenty-five years ago on 4 December 1963 the Supreme Pontiff Paul VI promulgated the Constitution *Sacrosanctum Concilium* on the Sacred Liturgy, which the Fathers of the Second Vatican Council, gathered in the Holy Spirit, had approved but a short time before.[1] It was a memorable event on several accounts. Indeed, it was the first fruit of the Council, called by Pope John XXIII, to update the Church. The moment had been prepared for by a great liturgical and pastoral movement and was a source of hope for the life and the renewal of the Church. In putting into practice the reform of the Liturgy, the Council achieved in a special way the fundamental aim which it had set itself: "To impart an ever increasing vigor to the Christian life of the faithful; to adapt more suitably to the needs of our own times those institutions that are subject to change; to foster whatever can promote union among all who believe in Christ; to strengthen whatever can help to call the whole of humanity into the household of the Church".[2]

2.   From the beginning of my pastoral ministry in the See of Peter, I have taken care to "state the lasting importance of the Second Vatican Council" calling attention to "our clear duty to devote our energies to putting it into effect". Our efforts have been directed towards "bringing to maturity in the sense of movement and of life the fruitful seeds which the Fathers of the Ecumenical Council, nourished by the word of God, cast upon the good soil (cf. Mt 13:8, 23), that is, their authoritative teaching and pastoral decisions".[3] On several occasions I have developed various aspects of the conciliar teaching on the Liturgy[4] and have

---

1. AAS 56 (1964), pp. 97–134.

2. Second Vatican Council, Constitution on the Sacred Liturgy *Sacrosanctum Concilium*, 1.

3. First message to the world (17 October 1978): AAS 70 (1978), pp. 920–921.

4. Cf. especially: Encyclical Letter *Redemptor Hominis* (4 March 1979), 7, 18–22: AAS 71 (1979), pp. 268–269, 301–324; Apostolic Exhortation *Catechesi Tradendae* (16 October 1979), 23, 27–30, 33, 37, 48, 53–55, 66–68: AAS 71 (1979), pp. 1296–1297, 1298–1303, 1305–1306,

emphasized the importance of the Constitution *Sacrosanctum Concilium* for the life of the people of God: in it "the substance of that ecclesiological doctrine which would later be put before the conciliar Assembly is already evident. The Constitution *Sacrosanctum Concilium*, the first conciliar document, anticipated"[5] the Dogmatic Constitution *Lumen Gentium* on the Church and amplified, in its turn, the teaching of the Constitution. After a quarter of a century, during which both the Church and society have experienced profound and rapid changes, it is a fitting moment to throw light on the importance of the Conciliar Constitution, its relevance in relation to new problems and the enduring value of its principles.

I
RENEWAL IN ACCORD WITH TRADITION

3.   In response to the requests of the Fathers of the Council of Trent, concerned with the reform of the Church in their time, Pope Saint Pius V saw to the reform of the liturgical books, above all the Breviary and the Missal. It was towards this same goal that succeeding Roman Pontiffs directed their energies during the subsequent centuries in order to ensure that the rites and liturgical books were brought up to date and when necessary clarified. From the beginning of this century they undertook a more general reform. Pope Saint Pius X established a special Commission for this reform and he thought that it would take a number of years for it to complete its work; however he laid the foundation stone of this edifice by renewing the Roman Breviary.[6] "In fact this all demands" he affirmed, "according to the views of the experts, a work both detailed and extensive; and therefore it is necessary that many years should pass, before this liturgical edifice, so to speak, . . . reappears in new splendor in its dignity and harmony, once the marks of old age have been cleared away".[7]

Pope Pius XII took up again the great project of liturgical reform by issuing the Encyclical *Mediator Dei*[8] and by establishing a new Commission.[9] He likewise decided important matters for example: authorizing a new version of the Psalter to facilitate the understanding of the Psalms;[10] the modification of the Eucharistic fast in order to facilitate access to Holy Communion; the use of

---

1308–1309, 1316; Letter *Dominicae Cenae*, On the mystery and worship of the Holy Eucharist (24 February 1980): AAS 72 (1980). pp. 113–148; Encyclical Letter *Dives in Misericordia* (30 November 1980), 13–15: AAS 72 (1980), pp. 1218–1232; Apostolic Exhortation *Familiaris Consortio* (22 November 1981), 13, 15, 19–21, 33, 38–39, 55–59, 66–68: AAS 74 (1982), pp. 93–96, 97, 101–106, 120–123, 129–131, 147–152, 159–165; Post Synodal Apostolic Exhortation *Reconciliatio et Paenitentia* (2 December 1984): AAS 77 (1985), pp. 185–275, especially nos. 23–33, pp. 233–271.

    5. Address to the Congress of Presidents and Secretaries of National Liturgical Commissions (27 October 1984), 1: *Insegnamenti*, VII, 2 (1984), p. 1049.

    6. Apostolic Constitution *Divino Afflatu* (1 November 1911): AAS 3 (1911), p. 633–638.

    7. Motu Proprio *Abhinc Duos Annos* (23 October 1913): AAS 5 (1913), pp. 449–450.

    8. 20 November 1947: AAS 39 (1947), pp. 521–600.

    9. Sacred Congregation of Rites, Historical Section no. 71, *Memoria sulla riforma liturgica* (1946).

    10. Pius XII, Motu Proprio *In Cotidianis Precibus* (24 March 1945): AAS 37 (1945), pp. 65–67.

contemporary language in the Ritual; and, above all, the reform of the Easter Vigil[11] and Holy Week.[12] The introduction to the Roman Missal of 1963 was preceded by the declaration of Pope John XXIII, according to which "the fundamental principles, related to the general reform of the Liturgy, were to be entrusted to the Fathers in the forthcoming Ecumenical Council".[13]

4.   Such an overall reform of the Liturgy was in harmony with the general hope of the whole Church. In fact, the liturgical spirit had become more and more widespread together with the desire for an "active participation in the most holy mysteries and in the public and solemn prayer of the Church",[14] and a wish to hear the word of God in more abundant measure. Together with the biblical renewal, the ecumenical movement, the missionary impetus and ecclesiological research, the reform of the Liturgy was to contribute to the overall renewal of the Church. I draw attention to this in the Letter *Dominicae Cenae*: "A very close and organic bond exists between the renewal of the Liturgy and the renewal of the whole life of the Church. The Church not only acts but also expresses herself in the Liturgy and draws from the Liturgy the strength for her life".[15]

The reform of the rites and the liturgical books was undertaken immediately after the promulgation of the Constitution *Sacrosanctum Concilium* and was brought to an effective conclusion in a few years thanks to the considerable and selfless work of a large number of experts and bishops from all parts of the world.[16]

This work was undertaken in accordance with the conciliar principles of fidelity to tradition and openness to legitimate development;[17] and so it is possible to say that the reform of the Liturgy is strictly traditional and in accordance with "the ancient usage of the holy Fathers".[18]

II
THE GUIDING PRINCIPLES OF THE CONSTITUTION

5.   The guiding principles of the Constitution which were the basis of the reform, remain fundamental in the task of leading the faithful to an active celebration of the mysteries, "the primary and indispensable source of the true Christian spirit".[19] Now that the greater part of the liturgical books have been

---

11. Sacred Congregation of Rites, Decree *Dominicae Resurrectionis* (9 February 1951): AAS 43 (1951), pp. 123–129.

12. Sacred Congregation of Rites, Decree *Maxima Redemptionis* (16 November 1955): AAS 47 (1955), pp. 838–841.

13. John XXIII, Apostolic Letter *Rubricarum Instructum* (25 July 1960): AAS 52 (1960), p. 594.

14. Pius X, Motu Proprio *Tra le sollecitudini dell'officio pastorale* (22 November 1903): *Pii X Pontificis Maximi Acta*, I, p. 77.

15. Letter *Dominicae Cenae* (24 February 1980), 13: AAS 72 (1980), p. 146.

16. Cf. Second Vatican Council, Constitution on the Sacred Liturgy *Sacrosanctum Concilium*, 25.

17. Cf. ibid., 23.

18. Cf. ibid., 50; Roman Missal, Preface, 6.

19. Second Vatican Council, Constitution on the Sacred Liturgy *Sacrosanctum Concilium*, 14.

published, translated and brought into use, it is still necessary to keep these principles constantly in mind and to build upon them.

A) THE RE-ENACTMENT OF THE PASCHAL MYSTERY

6.   The first principle is the reenactment of the Paschal Mystery of Christ in the Liturgy of the Church, based on the fact that "it was from the side of Christ as he slept on the Cross that there issued forth the sublime sacrament of the whole Church".[20] The whole of liturgical life gravitates about the Eucharistic Sacrifice and the other sacraments in which we draw upon the living springs of salvation (cf. Is 13:3).[21] Hence we must have a sufficient awareness that through the "Paschal Mystery we have been buried with Christ in Baptism, so that we may rise with him to new life".[22] When the faithful participate in the Eucharist they must understand that truly "each time we offer this memorial sacrifice the work of our redemption is accomplished",[23] and to this end bishops must carefully train the faithful to celebrate every Sunday the marvelous work that Christ has wrought in the mystery of his Passover, in order that they likewise may proclaim it to the world.[24] In the hearts of all, bishops and faithful, Easter must regain its unique importance in the liturgical year, so that it really is the Feast of feasts.

Since Christ's Death on the Cross and his Resurrection constitute the content of the daily life of the Church[25] and the pledge of his eternal Passover,[26] the Liturgy has as its first task to lead us untiringly back to the Easter pilgrimage initiated by Christ, in which we accept death in order to enter into life.

7.   In order to reenact his Paschal Mystery, Christ is ever present in his Church, especially in liturgical celebrations.[27] Hence the Liturgy is the privileged place for the encounter of Christians with God and the one whom he has sent, Jesus Christ (cf. Jn 17:3).

Christ is present in the Church assembled at prayer in his name. It is this fact which gives such a unique character to the Christian assembly with the consequent duties not only of brotherly welcome but also of forgiveness (cf. Mt 5:23–24), and of dignity of behavior, gesture and song.

Christ is present and acts in the person of the ordained minister who celebrates.[28] The priest is not merely entrusted with a function, but in virtue of the

---

20. Second Vatican Council, Constitution on the Sacred Liturgy *Sacrosanctum Concilium*, 5; Roman Missal, The Easter Vigil; Prayer after the 7th Reading.

21. Second Vatican Council, Constitution on the Sacred Liturgy *Sacrosanctum Concilium*, 5–6, 47, 61, 102, 106–107.

22. Roman Missal, The Easter Vigil, Renewal of Baptismal Promises.

23. Ibid., Evening Mass "In *Cena Domini*", Prayer over the Gifts.

24. Cf. ibid., Preface of Sundays In Ordinary Time, 1.

25. Cf. Encyclical Letter *Redemptor Hominis* (4 March 1979), 7: AAS 71 (1979), .pp. 268–270.

26. Cf. Letter *Dominicae Cenae* (24 February 1980), 4: AAS 72 (1980), pp. 119–121.

27. Cf. Second Vatican Council, Constitution on the Sacred Liturgy *Sacrosanctum Concilium*, 7; cf. Paul VI, Encyclical Letter *Mysterium Fidei* (3 September 1965): AAS 57 (1965), pp. 762, 764.

28. Cf. Sacred Congregation of Rites, Instruction *Eucharisticum Mysterium* (25 May 1967), 9: AAS 59 (1967), p. 547.

Ordination received he has been consecrated to act *"in persona Christi"*. To this consecration there must be a corresponding disposition, both inward and outward, also reflected in liturgical vestments, in the place which he occupies and in the word which he utters.

Christ is present in his word as proclaimed in the assembly and which, commented upon in the homily, is to be listened to in faith and assimilated in prayer. All this must derive from the dignity of the book and of the place appointed for the proclamation of the word of God, and from the attitude of the reader, based upon an awareness of the fact that the reader is the spokesman of God before his or her brothers and sisters.

Christ is present and acts by the power of the Holy Spirit in the sacraments and, in a special and preeminent fashion (*sublimiori modo*), in the Sacrifice of the Mass under the Eucharistic Species,[29] also when these are reserved in the tabernacle apart from the celebration with a view to Communion of the sick and adoration by the faithful.[30] With regard to this real and mysterious presence, it is the duty of pastors to recall frequently in their catechetical instruction the teaching of the faith, a teaching that the faithful must live out and that theologians are called upon to expound. Faith in this presence of the Lord involves an outward sign of respect towards the church, the holy place in which God manifests himself in mystery (cf. Ex. 3:5), especially during the celebration of the sacraments: holy things must always be treated in a holy manner.

B) THE READING OF THE WORD OF GOD.

8.   The second principle is the presence of the word of God.

The Constitution *Sacrosanctum Concilium* sets out likewise to restore a "more abundant reading from Holy Scripture, one more varied and more appropriate".[31] The basic reason for this restoration is expressed both in the Constitution on the Liturgy, namely, so that "the intimate link between rite and word" may be manifested,[32] and also in the Dogmatic Constitution on Divine Revelation, which teaches: "The Church has always venerated the divine Scriptures, just as she has venerated the very body of the Lord, never ceasing above all in the Sacred Liturgy to nourish herself on the bread of life and the table both of the word of God, and of the Body of Christ, and to minister it to the faithful".[33]

Growth in liturgical life and consequently progress in Christian life cannot be achieved except by continually promoting among the faithful, and above all among priests, a "warm and living knowledge of Scripture".[34] The word of God is now better known in the Christian communities, but a true renewal sets further and ever new requirements: fidelity to the authentic meaning of the

---

29. Cf. Paul VI, Encyclical Letter *Mysterium Fidei* (3 September 1965): AAS 57 (1965), p. 763.

30. Cf. ibid., pp. 769–771.

31. Second Vatican Council, Constitution on the Sacred Liturgy *Sacrosanctum Concilium*, 35.

32. Ibid.

33. Second Vatican Council, Constitution on Divine Revelation *Dei Verbum*, 21.

34. Second Vatican Council, Constitution on the Sacred Liturgy *Sacrosanctum Concilium*, 24.

Scriptures which must never be lost from view, especially when the Scriptures are translated into different languages; the manner of proclaiming the word of God so that it may be perceived for what it is; the use of appropriate technical means; the interior disposition of the ministers of the Word so that they carry out properly their function in the liturgical assembly;[35] careful preparation of the homily through study and meditation; effort on the part of the faithful to participate at the table of the word; a taste for prayer with the Psalms; a desire to discover Christ—like the disciples at Emmaus—at the table of the word and the bread.[36]

c) THE SELF-MANIFESTATION OF THE CHURCH

9.   Finally the Council saw in the Liturgy an epiphany of the Church: it is the Church at prayer. In celebrating Divine Worship the Church gives expression to what she is: One, Holy, Catholic and Apostolic.

The Church manifests herself as one, with that unity which comes to her from the Trinity,[37] especially when the holy people of God participates "in the one Eucharist, in one and the same prayer, at the one altar, presided over by the bishop surrounded by his presbyterate and his ministers".[38] Let nothing in the celebration of the Liturgy disrupt or obscure this unity of the Church! The Church expresses the holiness that comes to her from Christ (cf. Eph 5:26–27) when, gathered in one body by the Holy Spirit[39] who makes holy and gives life,[40] she communicates to the faithful by means of the Eucharist and the other sacraments all the graces and blessings of the Father.[41]

In liturgical celebration the Church expresses her catholicity, since in her the Spirit of the Lord gathers together people of all languages in the profession of the same faith[42] and from East to West presents to God the Father the offering of Christ, and offers herself together with him.[43]

In the Liturgy the Church manifests herself as apostolic, because the faith that she professes is founded upon the witness of the apostles; because in the celebration of the mysteries, presided over by the bishop, successor of the apostles, or by a minister ordained in the apostolic succession, she faithfully hands on what she has received from the Apostolic Tradition; and because the worship which she renders to God commits her to the mission of spreading the Gospel in the world.

---

35. Cf. Letter *Dominicae Cenae* (24 February 1980), 10: AAS 72 (1980), pp. 134–137.
36. Cf. Liturgy of the Hours, Monday of Week IV, Prayer at Evening Prayer.
37. Cf. Roman Missal, Preface of Sundays In Ordinary Time, VIII.
38. Second Vatican Council, Constitution on the Sacred Liturgy Sacrosanctum Concilium, 41.
39. Cf. Roman missal, Eucharistic Prayers II and IV.
40. Cf. ibid., Eucharistic Prayer III; Nicene-Constantinopolitan Creed.
41. Cf. Ibid., Eucharistic Prayer I.
42. Cf. ibid., Solemn Blessing on Pentecost Sunday.
43. Cf. ibid., Eucharistic Prayer III.

Thus it is especially in the Liturgy that the Mystery of the Church is proclaimed, experienced and lived.[44]

III
GUIDELINES FOR THE RENEWAL OF LITURGICAL LIFE

10.   From these principles are derived certain norms and guidelines which must govern the renewal of liturgical life. While the reform of the Liturgy desired by the Second Vatican Council, can be considered already in progress, the pastoral promotion of the Liturgy constitutes a permanent commitment to draw ever more abundantly from the riches of the Liturgy that vital force which spreads from Christ to the members of his Body which is the Church.

Since the Liturgy is the exercise of the priesthood of Christ, it is necessary to keep ever alive the affirmation of the disciple faced with the mysterious presence of the Lord: "It is the Lord!" (Jn 21:7). Nothing of what we do in the Liturgy can appear more important than what in an unseen but real manner Christ accomplishes by the power of his Spirit. A faith alive in charity, adoration, praise of the Father and silent contemplation will always be the prime objective of liturgical and pastoral care.

Since the Liturgy is totally permeated by the word of God, any other word must be in harmony with it, above all in the homily, but also in the various interventions of the minister and in the hymns which are sung. No other reading may supplant the Biblical word, and the words of men must be at the service of the word of God without obscuring it.

Since liturgical celebrations are not private acts but "celebrations of the Church, the 'sacrament of unity'",[45] their regulation is dependent solely upon the hierarchical authority of the Church.[46] The Liturgy belongs to the whole body of the Church.[47] It is for this reason that it is not permitted to anyone, even the priest, or any group, to subtract or change anything whatsoever on their own initiative.[48] Fidelity to the rites and to the authentic texts of the Liturgy is a requirement of the *Lex orandi*, which must always be in conformity with the *Lex credendi*. A lack of fidelity on this point may even affect the very validity of the sacraments.

Since it is a celebration of the Church, the Liturgy requires the active, conscious and full participation of all, according to the diversity of Orders and of office.[49] All the ministers and the other faithful, in the accomplishment of their particular function, do that and only that which is proper to them.[50] It is for this

---

44. Cf. Address to the Congress of Presidents and Secretaries of National Liturgical Commissions (27 October 1984), 1: *Insegnamenti*, VII, 2 (1984), p. 1049.
45. Second Vatican Council, Constitution on the Sacred Liturgy *Sacrosanctum Concilium*, 26.
46. Cf. ibid., 22 and 26.
47. Cf. ibid., 26.
48. Cf. ibid., 22.
49. Cf. ibid., 26.
50. Cf. ibid., 28.

reason that the Church gives preference to celebrations in common, when the nature of the rites implies this;[51] she encourages the formation of ministers, readers, cantors and commentators, who carry out a true liturgical ministry;[52] she has restored concelebration,[53] and she recommends the common celebration of the Liturgy of the Hours.[54]

Given that the Liturgy is the school of the prayer of the Church, it has been considered good to introduce and develop the use of the vernacular—without diminishing the use of Latin, retained by the Council for the Latin Rite[55]—so that every individual can understand and proclaim in his or her mother tongue the wonders of God (cf. Acts 2:11). It has likewise been considered good to increase the number of Prefaces and Eucharistic Prayers, so as to enrich the Church's treasury of prayer and an understanding of the mystery of Christ.

Since the Liturgy has great pastoral value, the liturgical books have provided for a certain degree of adaptation to the assembly and to individuals, with the possibility of openness to the traditions and cultures of different peoples.[56] The revision of the rites has sought a noble simplicity[57] and signs that are easily understood, but the desired simplicity must not degenerate into an impoverishment of the signs. On the contrary, the signs, above all the sacramental signs, must be easily grasped but carry the greatest possible expressiveness. Bread and wine, water and oil, and also incense, ashes, fire and flowers, and indeed almost all the elements of creation have their place in the Liturgy as gifts to the Creator and as a contribution to the dignity and beauty of the celebration.

IV
THE PRACTICAL APPLICATION OF THE REFORM

A) DIFFICULTIES

11. It must be recognized that the application of the liturgical reform has met with difficulties due especially to an unfavorable environment marked by a tendency to see religious practice as something of a private affair, by a certain rejection of institutions, by a decrease in visibility of the Church in society, and by a calling into question of personal faith. It can also be supposed that the transition from simply being present, very often in a rather passive and silent way, to a fuller and more active participation has been for some people too demanding. Different and even contradictory reactions to the reform have resulted from this. Some have received the new books with a certain indifference, or without trying to understand the reasons for the changes; others, unfortunately, have turned back in a one-sided and exclusive way to the previous liturgical forms

---

51. Cf. ibid., 27.

52. Cf. ibid., 29.

53. Cf. ibid., 57; cf. Sacred Congregation of Rites, General Decree *Ecclesiae Semper* (7 March 1965): AAS 57 (1965), pp. 410–412.

54. Second Vatican Council, Constitution on the Sacred Liturgy *Sacrosanctum Concilium*, 99.

55. Cf. ibid., 36.

56. Cf. ibid., 37–40.

57. Cf. ibid., 34.

which some of them consider to be the sole guarantee of certainty in faith. Others have promoted outlandish innovations, departing from the norms issued by the authority of the Apostolic See or the bishops, thus disrupting the unity of the Church and the piety of the faithful and even on occasion contradicting matters of faith.

B) POSITIVE RESULTS

12.   This should not lead anyone to forget that the vast majority of the pastors and the Christian people have accepted the liturgical reform in a spirit of obedience and indeed joyful fervor. For this we should give thanks to God for that movement of the Holy Spirit in the Church which the liturgical renewal represents;[58] for the fact that the table of the word of God is now abundantly furnished for all;[59] for the immense effort undertaken throughout the world to provide the Christian people with translations of the Bible, the Missal and other liturgical books; for the increased participation of the faithful by prayer and song, gesture and silence, in the Eucharist and the other sacraments; for the ministries exercised by lay people and the responsibilities that they have assumed in virtue of the common priesthood into which they have been initiated through Baptism and Confirmation; for the radiant vitality of so many Christian communities, a vitality drawn from the wellspring of the Liturgy.

These are all reasons for holding fast to the teaching of the Constitution *Sacrosanctum Concilium* and to the reforms which it has made possible: "the liturgical renewal is the most visible fruit of the whole work of the Council".[60] For many people the message of the Second Vatican Council has been experienced principally through the liturgical reform.

C) ERRONEOUS APPLICATIONS

13.   Side by side with these benefits of the liturgical reform, one has to acknowledge with regret deviations of greater or lesser seriousness in its application.

On occasion there have been noted illicit omissions or additions, rites invented outside the framework of established norms; postures or songs which are not conducive to faith or to a sense of the sacred; abuses in the practice of general absolution; confusion between the ministerial priesthood, linked with Ordination, and the common priesthood of the faithful, which has its foundation in Baptism.

It cannot be tolerated that certain priests should take upon themselves the right to compose Eucharistic Prayers or to substitute profane readings for texts from Sacred Scripture. Initiatives of this sort, far from being linked with the liturgical reform as such, or with the books which have issued from it, are in

---

58. Cf. ibid., 43.

59. Cf. Second Vatican Council, Dogmatic Constitution on Divine Revelation *Dei Verbum*, 21; Constitution *Sacrosanctum Concilium*, 51.

60. Final Report of the Extraordinary Assembly of the Synod of Bishops (7 December 1985), II, B, b, 1.

direct contradiction to it, disfigure it and deprive the Christian people of the genuine treasures of the Liturgy of the Church.

It is for the bishops to root out such abuses, because the regulation of the Liturgy depends on the bishop within the limits of the law[61] and because "the life in Christ of his faithful people in some sense is derived from and depends on him".[62]

V
THE FUTURE OF THE RENEWAL

14.   The Constitution *Sacrosanctum Concilium* is the expression of the unanimous voice of the College of Bishops gathered around the Successor of Peter and with the help of the Spirit of Truth promised by the Lord Jesus (cf. Jn 15:26). The Constitution continues to sustain the Church along the paths of renewal and of holiness by fostering genuine liturgical life.

The principles enunciated in that document are an orientation also for the future of the Liturgy, in such a way that the liturgical reform may be ever better understood and implemented. "It is therefore necessary and urgent to actuate a new and intensive education in order to discover all the riches contained in the Liturgy".[63]

The Liturgy of the Church goes beyond the liturgical reform. We are not in the same situation as obtained in 1963: a generation of priests and of faithful which has not known the liturgical books prior to the reform now acts with responsibility in the Church and society. One cannot therefore continue to speak of a change as it was spoken of at the time of the Constitution's publication; rather one has to speak of an ever deeper grasp of the Liturgy of the Church, celebrated according to the current books and lived above all as a reality in the spiritual order.

A) BIBLICAL AND LITURGICAL FORMATION

15.   The most urgent task is that of the biblical and liturgical formation of the people of God, both pastors and faithful. The Constitution had already stressed this: "There is no hope that this may come to pass unless pastors of souls themselves become imbued more deeply with the spirit and power of the liturgy so as to become masters of it".[64] This is a long-term program, which must begin in the seminaries and houses of formation[65] and continue throughout their priestly

---

61. Second Vatican Council, Constitution on the Sacred Liturgy *Sacrosanctum Concilium*, 22, 1.

62. Ibid., 41.

63. Letter *Dominicae Cenae*, (24 February 1980), 9: AAS 72 (1980), p. 133.

64. Second Vatican Council, Constitution on the Sacred Liturgy *Sacrosanctum Concilium*, 14.

65. Cf. Sacred Congregation of Rites, Instruction *Inter Oecumenici* (26 September 1964), 11–13: AAS 56 (1964), pp. 879–880; Sacred Congregation for Catholic Education, *Ratio Fundamentalis* on Priestly Formation (6 January 1970), cap. VIII: AAS 62 (1970), pp. 351–361; Instruction *In Ecclesiasticam Futurorum* on Liturgical Formation in Seminaries (3 June 1979), Rome 1979.

life.[66] A formation suited to their state is indispensable also for lay people,[67] especially since in many regions they are called upon to assume ever more important responsibilities in the community.

B) ADAPTATION

16.   Another important task for the future is that of the adaptation of the Liturgy to different cultures. The Constitution set forth the principle, indicating the procedure to be followed by the bishops' conferences.[68] The adaptation of languages has been rapidly accomplished, even if on occasion with some difficulties. It has been followed by the adaptation of rites, which is a more delicate matter but equally necessary. There remains the considerable task of continuing to implant the Liturgy in certain cultures, welcoming from them those expressions which are compatible with aspects of the true and authentic spirit of the Liturgy, in respect for the substantial unity of the Roman Rite as expressed in the liturgical books.[69] The adaptation must take account of the fact that in the Liturgy, and notably that of the sacraments, there is a part which is unchangeable, because it is of divine institution, and of which the Church is the guardian. There are also parts open to change, which the Church has the power and on occasion also the duty to adapt to the cultures of recently evangelized peoples.[70] This is not a new problem for the Church. Liturgical diversity can be a source of enrichment, but it can also provoke tensions, mutual misunderstandings and even divisions. In this field it is clear that diversity must not damage unity. It can only gain expression in fidelity to the common Faith, to the sacramental signs that the Church has received from Christ and to hierarchical communion. Cultural adaptation also requires conversion of heart and even, where necessary, a breaking with ancestral customs incompatible with the Catholic faith. This demands a serious formation in theology, history and culture, as well as sound judgment in discerning what is necessary or useful and what is not useful or even dangerous to faith. "A satisfactory development in this area cannot but be the fruit of a progressive maturing in faith, one which encompasses spiritual discernment, theological lucidity, and a sense of the universal Church, acting in broad harmony".[71]

C) ATTENTION TO NEW PROBLEMS

17.   The effort towards liturgical renewal must furthermore respond to the needs of our time. The Liturgy is not disincarnate.[72] In these twenty-five years new problems have arisen or have assumed new importance, for example: the

---

66. Cf. Sacred Congregation of Rites, Instruction *Inter Oecumenici* (26 September 1964), 14–17: AAS 56 (1964), pp. 880–881.

67. Second Vatican Council, Constitution on the Sacred Liturgy *Sacrosanctum Concilium*, 19.

68. Cf. ibid., 39.

69. Cf. ibid., 37–40.

70. Cf. ibid., 21.

71. Address to a group of bishops from the Episcopal Conference of Zaire (12 April 1983), 5: AAS 75 (1983), p. 620.

72. Cf. Address to the Congress of Presidents and Secretaries of National Liturgical Commissions (27 October, 1984), 2: *Insegnamenti*, VII, 2 (1984), p. 1051.

exercise of a diaconate open to married men; liturgical tasks in celebrations which can be entrusted to lay people; liturgical celebrations for children, for young people and the disabled; the procedures for the composition of liturgical texts appropriate to a particular country.

In the Constitution *Sacrosanctum Concilium* there is no reference to these problems, but the general principles are given which serve to coordinate and promote liturgical life.

d) LITURGY AND POPULAR DEVOTIONS

18.   Finally, to safeguard the form and ensure the promotion of the Liturgy[73] it is necessary to take account of popular Christian devotion and its relation to liturgical life.[74] This popular devotion should not be ignored or treated with indifference or contempt, since it is rich in values,[75] and per se gives expression to the religious attitude towards God. But it needs to be continually evangelized, so that the faith which it expresses may become an ever more mature and authentic act. Both the pious exercises of the Christian people[76] and also other forms of devotion are welcomed and encouraged provided that they do not replace or intrude into liturgical celebrations. An authentic pastoral promotion of the Liturgy will build upon the riches of popular piety, purifying and directing them towards the Liturgy as the offering of the peoples.[77]

VI
THE ORGANISMS RESPONSIBLE FOR LITURGICAL RENEWAL

a) THE CONGREGATION FOR DIVINE WORSHIP AND THE DISCIPLINE OF THE SACRAMENTS

19.   The task of promoting the renewal of the Liturgy pertains in the first place to the Apostolic See.[78] It was four hundred years ago that Pope Sixtus V created the Sacred Congregation of Rites and entrusted it with responsibility for keeping watch over the exercise of Divine Worship, reformed after the Council of Trent. Pope Saint Pius X instituted another Congregation for the Discipline of the Sacraments. With a view to the practical implementation of the Second Vatican Council's Constitution *Sacrosanctum Concilium* on the Liturgy, Pope Paul VI instituted a *Consilium*[79] later the Sacred Congregation for Divine Worship[80] and

---

73. Cf. Second Vatican Council, Constitution on the Sacred Liturgy *Sacrosanctum Concilium*, 1.

74. Cf. ibid., 12–13.

75. Cf. Paul VI Apostolic Exhortation *Evangelii Nuntiandi* (8 December 1975), 48: AAS 68 (1976), pp. 37–38.

76. Cf. Second Vatican Council, Constitution on the Sacred Liturgy *Sacrosanctum Concilium*, 13.

77. Cf. Address to the Episcopal Conference of Abruzzo and Molise (24 April 1986), 3–7: AAS 78 (1986), pp. 1140–1143.

78. Cf. Second Vatican Council, Constitution on the Sacred Liturgy *Sacrosanctum Concilium*, 22, 1.

79. Apostolic Letter *Sacram Liturgiam* (25 January 1964): AAS 56 (1964), pp. 139–144.

80. Apostolic Constitution *Sacra Rituum Congregatio* (8 May 1969): AAS 61 (1989), pp. 297–305.

they carried out the task entrusted to them with generosity, competence and promptness. In accordance with the new structure of the Roman Curia as laid down by the Apostolic Constitution *Pastor Bonus*, the whole area of Sacred Liturgy is brought together and placed under the responsibility of a single Dicastery: the Congregation for Divine Worship and the Discipline of the Sacraments. Always taking into account the area of competence of the Congregation for the Doctrine of the Faith[81] it pertains to this Congregation to regulate and promote the Liturgy of which the Sacraments are the essential part, by encouraging pastoral liturgical activities,[82] supporting the various Organisms devoted to the liturgical apostolate, music, song and sacred art,[83] and keeping watch over sacramental discipline.[84] This is a work of importance for it concerns above all the faithful preservation of the great principles of the Catholic Liturgy, as illustrated and developed in the Conciliar Constitution. It is likewise a question of drawing upon these principles for inspiration and promoting and deepening throughout the Church the renewal of liturgical life.

The Congregation will assist diocesan bishops in their efforts to offer to God true Christian worship and to regulate it according to the precepts of the Lord and the laws of the Church.[85] It will be in close and trusting contact with the bishops' conferences for all that pertains to their competence in the liturgical field.[86]

B) THE BISHOPS' CONFERENCES

20. The Bishops' Conferences have had the weighty responsibility of preparing the translations of the liturgical books.[87] Immediate need occasionally led to the use of provisional translations, approved ad interim. But now the time has come to reflect upon certain difficulties that have subsequently emerged, to remedy certain defects or inaccuracies, to complete partial translations, to compose or approve chants to be used in the Liturgy, to ensure respect for the texts approved and lastly to publish liturgical books in a form that both testifies to the stability achieved and is worthy of the mysteries being celebrated.

For the work of translation, as well as for the wider implications of liturgical renewal for whole countries, each bishops' conference was required to establish a national commission and ensure the collaboration of experts in the various sectors of liturgical science and pastoral practice.[88] The time has come to evaluate this commission, its past activity, both the positive and negative aspects, and the guidelines and the help which it has received from the bishops' conference

---

81. Apostolic Constitution *Pastor Bonus* (28 June 1988), 62: AAS 80 (1988), p. 876.

82. Cf. ibid., 64: I. c, pp. 876–877.

83. Cf. ibid., 65: I. c, pp. 877.

84. Cf. ibid., 63 and 66: I. c, pp. 876 and 877.

85. Cf. Dogmatic Constitution on the Church *Lumen Gentium*, 26; Constitution on the Sacred Liturgy *Sacrosanctum Concilium*, 22, 1.

86. Cf. Apostolic Constitution *Pastor Bonus*, 63, 3: AAS 80 (1988), p. 877.

87. Second Vatican Council, Constitution on the Sacred Liturgy *Sacrosanctum Concilium*, 36 and 63.

88. Cf. ibid., 44.

regarding its composition and activity. The role of this commission is much more delicate when the conference wishes to introduce measures of adaptation or inculturation:[89] this is one reason for making sure that the commission contains people who are truly competent.

D) THE DIOCESAN BISHOP

21.   In every diocese the bishop is the principal dispenser of the mysteries of God, and likewise the governor, promoter and guardian of the entire liturgical life of the Church entrusted to him.[90] When the bishop celebrates in the midst of his people, it is the very mystery of the Church which is manifested. Therefore it is necessary that the bishop should be strongly convinced of the importance of such celebrations for the Christian life of his faithful. Such celebrations should be models for the whole diocese.[91] Much still remains to be done to help priests and the faithful to grasp the meaning of the liturgical texts, to develop the dignity and beauty of celebrations and the places where they are held, and to promote, as the Fathers did, a "mystagogic catechesis" of the sacraments. In order to bring this task to a successful conclusion, the bishop should set up one or more diocesan commissions which help him to promote liturgical activity, music and sacred art in his diocese.[92] The diocesan commission, for its part, will act according to the mind and directives of the bishop and should be able to count upon his authority and his encouragement to carry out its particular task properly.

CONCLUSION

22.   The Liturgy does not exhaust the entire activity of the Church, as the Constitution *Sacrosanctum Concilium* pointed out.[93] It is, however, a source and summit.[94] It is a source, because above all from the sacraments the faithful draw abundantly the water of grace which flows from the side of the Crucified Christ. To use an image dear to Pope John XXIII, it is like the village fountain to which every generation comes to draw water ever living and fresh. It is also a summit, both because all the activity of the Church is directed towards the communion of life with Christ, and because it is in the Liturgy that the Church manifests and communicates to the faithful the work of salvation, accomplished once and for all by Christ.

23.   The time has come to renew that spirit which inspired the Church at the moment when the Constitution *Sacrosanctum Concilium* was prepared, discussed,

---

89. Cf. ibid., 40.
90. Cf. Second Vatican Council, Decree on the Bishop's Office in the Church *Christus Dominus*, 15.
91. Cf. Address to Italian bishops (12 February 1988), 1: L'Osservatore Romano on 13 February 1988, p. 4.
92. Cf. Second Vatican Council, Constitution on the Sacred Liturgy *Sacrosanctum Concilium*, 45–46.
93. Cf. ibid., 9.
94. Cf. ibid., 10.

voted upon and promulgated, and when the first steps were taken to apply it. The seed was sown; it has known the rigors of winter, but the seed has sprouted, and become a tree. It is a matter of the organic growth of a tree becoming ever stronger the deeper it sinks its roots into the soil of tradition.[95] I wish to recall what I said at the Congress of Liturgical Commissions in 1984: in the work of liturgical renewal, desired by the Council, it is necessary to keep in mind "with great balance the part of God and the part of man, the hierarchy and the faithful, tradition and progress, the law and adaptation, the individual and the community, silence and choral praise. Thus the Liturgy on earth will fuse with that of heaven where . . . it will form one choir . . . to praise with one voice the Father through Jesus Christ".[96]

With this confident hope, which in my heart becomes a prayer, I impart to all my Apostolic Blessing. Given at the Vatican, on the fourth day of December in the year 1988, the eleventh of my Pontificate.

IOANNES PAULUS PP. II

---

95. Cf. ibid., 23.

96. Address to the Congress of Presidents and Secretaries of National Liturgical Commissions (27 October 1984), 6: *Insegnamenti*, VII, 2 (1984), p. 1054.

VARIETATES LEGITIMAE
INCULTURATION AND
THE ROMAN LITURGY

FOURTH INSTRUCTION FOR THE RIGHT APPLICATION OF THE
CONCILIAR CONSTITUTION ON THE LITURGY (NOS. 37–40)

CONGREGATION FOR DIVINE WORSHIP AND
THE DISCIPLINE OF THE SACRAMENTS
MARCH 29, 1994

AN OVERVIEW OF *VARIETATES LEGITIMAE*

Richard E. McCarron

The Congregation for Divine Worship and the Discipline of the Sacraments issued the instruction *Varietates legitimae* on January 25, 1994.[1] It was promulgated on March 29, 1994. Its full title, *Varietates legitimae:* Inculturation and the Roman Liturgy, Fourth Instruction for the Right Application of the Conciliar Constitution on the Liturgy (nos. 37–40), situates its theological and liturgical themes and its relation to liturgical renewal in line with the three previous instructions.[2] *Varietates legitimae* (VL) presents the complex and dynamic process of the interaction of the Roman liturgy with local cultures opened by *Sacrosanctum Concilium* (SC) 37–40 and offers ecclesiastical procedures for oversight. This introduction traces the context and process of VL's development, offers an overview of the document, and concludes with some brief assessment of its influence.

CONTEXT OF DEVELOPMENT

The issue of cultural adaptation of the liturgy had arisen prior to the Second Vatican Council and gained momentum on the eve of the council as witnessed by the First International Congress on Pastoral Liturgy at Assisi in 1956. Following the promulgation of SC where cultural adaptation was given particular attention in articles 37–40, local Churches sought to bring the Roman liturgy into dialogue with their local cultures. In line with SC 39, the *praenotanda* of the revised rites included sections entitled "Adaptations (*aptationes*) by Conferences of Bishops or by Bishops" and "Adaptations (*accommodationes*) by the Minister," or even—as in the case of the Rite of Marriage—"Preparation of Local Rituals." *The General Instruction of the Roman Missal* likewise included a section, "Accommodation (*accomodatio*) to New Conditions," in its various editions since 1970 (translated as "Adaptation to Modern Conditions" prior to 2002).

It is important to note here the use of terminology. SC uses the terms *aptatio* and *accommodatio*; the term *inculturation* (*inculturatio*) does not appear. There is a certain fluidity of use of the two terms in SC. While SC 1 speaks of the whole project of liturgical renewal with *accommodare*, this term is also used to speak of the revision of the sacramental rites.[3] In SC 37–40, the term *aptatio* is used.[4] Following the council, *aptatio* (adaptation) is used in liturgical books to refer to the permanent introduction of local elements approved by the bishops and confirmed by Rome. *Accommodatio* is used to refer to the options

---

1. *De Liturgia Romana et Inculturatione: Instructio Quarta "Ad Exsecutionem Constitutionis Concilii Vaticani Secundi De Sacra Liturgia Recte Ordinandam" (Ad Const. art. 37–40).* The official Latin text appears in *Acta Apostolica Sedes* 87 (1995): 288–314 and *Notitiae* 30 (1994): 80–115.

2. See pages 313–340, 363–374, and 427–442 in this collection.

3. See *Sacrosanctum Concilium* (SC), 63–68.

4. See ibid., 1, 34, 62, 63b, 65, 67, 68, 75, 89c, 90, 107, 119, 128.

a particular minister may use "as the circumstances" of a particular celebration may require.

During the period of the implementation of SC, a number of bishops asked for permission to introduce local cultural gestures, symbols, and expressions in the liturgy: Thailand (1967), Pakistan (1968), India (1969), Laos-Cambodia (1970), and Zambia, Congo-Brazzaville, and Zaire (1969–1970). The Consilium for the Implementation of the Constitution on the Sacred Liturgy and then the Congregation for Divine Worship (formed in 1970) considered cultural adaptation of the liturgy as part of a third phase of liturgical renewal after the promulgation of the revised liturgical books and their translation and implementation.[5]

Development in theological and missiological fields went together with the liturgical developments. It is from these fields that the term and concept of *inculturation* come. Most scholars trace the first use of the term inculturation in theological circles to an article published by Belgian Jesuit Joseph Masson in 1962. The term and concept would come to figure in the November 3, 1977, Message of the Synod of Bishops to the People of God, which used inculturation in relation to catechesis to name the process whereby "the Christian message must find its roots in human cultures and must also transform these cultures."[6]

Further impetus for the use of inculturation and its operative definition in theological contexts come from Pedro Arrupe, SJ, in his 1978 letter to the Society of Jesus following the Thirty-second General Congregation of the Society of Jesus held 1974–1975:

> Inculturation is the incarnation of Christian life and of the Christian message in a particular cultural context, in such a way that this experience not only finds expression through elements proper to the culture in question, but becomes a principle that animates, directs and unifies the culture, transforming and remaking it so as to bring about a "new creation."[7]

John Paul II would formally introduce the term into papal teaching in an address to the Pontifical Biblical Commission, also linking inculturation to Incarnation.[8] John Paul II quotes from this statement in his 1979 post-synodal exhortation, *Catechesi trandendae*, article 53. He offers a fuller presentation of inculturation in *Redemptoris missio* (1985), especially at article 52. The pope continues the analogy of Incarnation and speaks of the lengthy process of the mutual interaction of Church, Gospel, and culture. In 1988 the International Theological Commission issued a statement on "Faith and Inculturation." John Paul II, also in 1988, addressed liturgical adaptation and diversity in his apostolic letter *Vicesimus quintus annus* on the twenty-fifth anniversary of the promulgation of SC at article 16.

---

5. Annibale Bugnini, *La Riforma Liturgica (1948–1975)*, 2d ed., *Bibliotheca Ephemerides Liturgicae Subsidia*, 30 (Rome: CLV *Edizione Liturgiche*, 1997), p. 268. He treats liturgical adaptation on 268–277.

6. Message of the Synod of Bishops to the People of God, 5.

7. Pedro Arrupe, "Letter on Inculturation to the Whole Society of Jesus," in *Other Apostolates Today: Selected Letters and Addresses of Pedro Arrupe, SJ*, ed. J. Aixala, 2nd ed. (St Louis: Institute of Jesuit Sources, 1981), Volume 3, pp. 172–181.

8. AAS 71 (1979): 607.

Further discussion of inculturation comes from the assemblies of the Latin American Episcopal Conference (CELAM), in particular the meetings of Puebla in 1979 and Santo Domingo in 1992. The concept of culture was given a dynamic, social-historical presentation at Puebla, for example, and liturgy and popular religiosity were highlighted at Santo Domingo. The work of CELAM also called attention to the violence and damage done to indigenous cultures in the missionary effort.

A watershed moment came in April 30, 1988, with the approval of *The Roman Missal* for the Dioceses of Zaire (named Democratic Republic of Congo since 1997). The Order of Mass draws on historical expressions (for example, the Ethiopian Rite) and from the social-cultural context of the local congregations. Discussion of cultural adaptation and development of liturgical rites would figure prominently in the discussions around the Synod for Africa. This synod opened in Rome on April 10, 1994, in St. Peter's Basilica with a liturgy that reflected the various liturgical styles of the regions of Africa. In addition to consideration of liturgical rituals for Marriage, Anointing of the Sick, and funerals, the question of new ritual families was raised for the synod. Cardinal Hyacinthe Thiandoum of Dakar would speak of "a right not a concession" for new rites to emerge:

> *Worship and liturgy* are specially privileged fields for inculturation. The ancient rites of the Church, including those of Africa, in Egypt and in Ethiopia, are fruits of liturgical inculturation. More attention should be paid to these ancient African rites as we try to evolve new ones in other parts of Africa. In this regard, the experience of Zaire, approved by the Holy See, is a step in the right direction. The emergence of such rites is as *of right* not as concession.[9]

PROCESS OF DEVELOPMENT

VL would come to be elaborated as these wider developments and discussions in theology, liturgy, and pastoral care were taking place. In 1984 the Congregation of Divine Worship engaged the work of Filipino Benedictine liturgical scholar Anscar Chupungco and an initial working group to draft a text on the "adaptation of the liturgy to various cultures."[10] A new working group was formed in 1985, again under the direction of Chupungco, which presented a new text for discussion at the congregation consultors' meeting in April and then in October at the plenary meeting. As work continued on the document, many consultors proposed a more robust understanding of inculturation rather than the frame of adaptation, taking cognizance of the theological developments noted above. In 1987 the document was revised and presented again to the congregation. The draft was remanded for further development. In 1988 the congregation examined

---

9. Hyacinthe Thiandoum, *"Relatio ante Disceptationem"* (First Report of Cardinal Hyacinthe Thiandoum), no. 17, in *The African Enchiridion: Documents and Texts of the Church in the African World.* Available at http://emi.it/AfricanEnchiridion/ae/docs/dp936.htm; accessed September 10, 2012.

10. This sketch relies on Mauro Paternoster, *"Varietates legitimae": Liturgia Romana e Inculturazione,* Monumenta Studia Instrumenta Liturgica 33 (Vatican City: Libreria Editrice Vaticana, 2004), pp. 37–40.

a new draft in French. By 1991 the draft had undergone further revision and development and would come to bear the title "Inculturation and the Roman Liturgy." The change in title should be understood as the result of a considered reflection and appropriation of the theological and missiological development of inculturation beyond the language of adaptation. It was then reviewed by the Congregation for the Doctrine of the Faith, the Congregation for Evangelization, the Pontifical Council for Culture, and the Pontifical Council for Legislative Texts.[11]

PROMULGATION

The fourth instruction was approved by John Paul II on January 25, 1994, the Feast of the Conversion of St. Paul the Apostle. It was released just a few days before the Synod for Africa—where liturgical inculturation was to be discussed—opened on April 10, 1994. As an instruction, VL is alligned with stipulations of canon 34 of the 1983 *Code of Canon Law*. The instruction was prepared at the order of Pope John Paul II[12] and confirmed and published at his direction.[13] Article 3 of VL makes its purpose explicit: VL defines the norms to govern "adaptation of the liturgy" given in SC 37–40 and the procedures to be followed. VL remains the most complete magisterial statement on cultural adaptation of the liturgy for "those countries which do not have a Christian tradition or where the Gospel has been proclaimed in modern times by missionaries who brought the Roman Rite with them," countries "with a long-standing Western Christian tradition," and countries with "a culture marked by indifference or disinterest in religion."[14]

OVERVIEW OF THE DOCUMENT

VL consists of seventy articles, divided into four parts with an introduction and conclusion. After the introduction,[15] part one[16] takes up scriptural foundations and the historical process of inculturation. The issue of terminology is addressed in article 4, presenting John Paul II's definition of inculturation from *Redemptoris missio*. VL understands inculturation as a double movement of the Incarnation of the Gospel (and thus by extension the liturgy) into culture and the assimilation of the people's spiritual gifts and values by the Church.

A key theological theme that is highlighted is the centrality of the Paschal Mystery of Christ, "which constitutes the essential element of Christian

---

11. For further analysis, see Paternoster, pp. 9–49. See also Kenneth Martin, *The Forgotten Instruction: The Roman Liturgy, Inculturation, and Legitimate Adaptations* (Chicago, IL: Liturgy Training Publications, 2007), esp. pp. 95–134. An "official" commentary was issued in 1994: Congregation for Divine Worship and Discipline of the Sacraments, "'Commentarium' alla Quarta Istruzione per una Corretta Applicazione della Costituzione Conciliare sulla Sacra Liturgia," *Notitiae* 332, vol. 30, no. 3 (1994): 152–166. See also the important comments of Anscar Chupungco, "Remarks on 'The Roman Liturgy and Inculturation,' *Ecclesia Orans* 11, no. 3 (1994): pp. 269–277.

12. See VL, 3.

13. See ibid., 70.

14. Ibid., 6–8.

15. See ibid., 1–8.

16. See ibid., 9–20.

worship."[17] After a cursory historical summary, VL notes that the "liturgy, like the Gospel, must respect cultures, but at the same time invite them to purify and sanctify themselves."[18] This theme of embrace of culture together with purification is threaded through the instruction (taking a lead from SC 37–40).

Part two[19] opens with analysis of the nature of liturgy and the Church. VL stresses that liturgy is "at once the action of Christ . . . and the action of the church which is his body."[20] Further, VL explains, "In the liturgy the faith of the church is expressed in a symbolic and communitarian form."[21] Because of this ecclesial expression, VL explains the need for legislative oversight and organization of worship.[22] After consideration of the importance of the translation of the Bible as the necessary "first necessary step in the process of inculturation,"[23] VL takes up the question of agency in the process—people competent in liturgical studies as well as local cultures, people with pastoral experience, and "'wise people' of the country."[24] The role of the Conferences of Bishops is introduced at 31–32, which should be read together with 62 and 64–69.

Part three[25] reviews the goal and process of liturgical inculturation. SC 21 is invoked as the goal, which highlights the importance of the liturgical texts and rites to express the holy things they signify and of the full and active participation of the faithful in the liturgical celebration.[26] The process is given clear parameters: the "substantial unity" of the Roman Rite is to be preserved, inculturation "does not foresee the creation of new families of rites";[27] inculturation leads to "adaptations which still remain part of the Roman rite." The substantial unity of the Roman Rite is not defined. Rather, VL explains that this unity is expressed in the approved liturgical books—both the authoritative Latin editions *and* in the vernacular books approved by the conferences of bishops and confirmed by the Apostolic See. The process is overseen by the authority of the Church—"inculturation is not left to the personal initiative of celebrants"[28] or the liturgical assembly.

Part three then outlines categories of adaptations: language, music, gestures and postures, rhythmic bodily expressions, and article 45 notes the importance of popular devotional practices.[29] The more open stance toward inculturation is juxtaposed with a call for prudence in the process. VL cautions against an artificial grafting of new forms onto existing forms, syncretism, diminishment of the Christian rites by local customs, and ambiguity regarding

---

17. Ibid., 12.
18. Ibid., 19.
19. See ibid., 21–32.
20. Ibid., 21.
21. Ibid., 27.
22. See ibid.
23. See ibid., 28.
24. See ibid., 30.
25. See ibid., 33–51.
26. See also SC, 14.
27. Ibid., 36.
28. VL, 37.
29. The *Directory for Popular Piety and the Liturgy: Principles and Guidelines* was issued in 2001 as a guide for these matters.

the status of traditional usages. On the one hand, VL calls for attention to "minority cultures"[30] that may be neglected, yet it cautions against extremes of localization in regions with many languages and tribes. VL upholds a certain ritual uniformity in larger cultural areas and regions that may border one another.[31]

More profound adaptations are treated in part four.[32] It is important to note that the terminology used in the latter parts of VL shifts from *inculturation* to *adaptation*. VL 4 identifies *adaptation* with external, transitory modifications and *inculturation* with a deeper, inner transformation. Articles 53–62 take up translation and adaptations of the rites (sacraments, blessings, liturgical year) in the existing liturgical books (the adaptations that are envisioned by the law as set out in the *praenotanda* and general instructions). More "radical adaptation"[33] is discussed in 63–69, that is, that which goes beyond what is envisaged in the general instructions or *praenotanda*. VL sets a limit on these: "Adaptations of this kind do not envisage a transformation of the Roman Rite, but are made within the context of the Roman Rite."[34] As several commentators have noted, VL asserts the centralized authority of the dicastery in the process over the diocesan bishop and Conferences of Bishops.[35]

The fourth instruction concludes with a call that the work of liturgical inculturation of the Roman Rite should be "carefully integrated into a pastoral plan for the inculturation of the Gospel into the many different human situations."[36]

ASSESSMENT

While VL does not introduce any new liturgical changes, it guides implementation of existing liturgical books and future questions of more profound cultural adaptation of the liturgy with a theological and liturgical foundation and procedural direction.

VL remains significant in its embrace of the terminology of inculturation and aligning liturgical inculturation with wider ecclesial reflection on the interaction of Gospel, Church, and local cultures. It marks an advance in the years since the publication of SC by situating inculturation as a goal that comes through adaptations of the Roman Rite. It also puts the work of liturgical inculturation in the broader frame of inculturation of the Gospel in a given cultural context. Yet, inculturation of the faith cannot be equated simply with liturgical inculturation. Rather, inculturation of the liturgy follows from the process of the incarnation of the Gospel in a local culture.

There also remain open questions for reflection. The process of inculturation does envision a "new creation" that is mutually enriching of both local culture and Church. Yet, VL is reluctant to envision an inner transformation of the Roman Rite. In the fifty years since the publication of SC, there have been

---

30. VL, 50.
31. See ibid., 51.
32. See ibid., 52–69.
33. *Profundior aptatio,* citing SC, 40.
34. VL, 63.
35. See VL ,64–68; cf. *Code of Canon Law,* canon. 838 § 3–4.
36. VL, 70.

a number of shifts in understanding of culture and context in theological and anthropological research. These insights should be integrated into an appropriation of VL. For example, VL does not offer a clear definition of culture: at times it embraces a modern approach, at others a more classicist approach. However, theology and anthropology have come to engage more postmodern understandings of culture and cultural diversity and attend to the forces of globalization and the effects of colonial conditions. Cultures are far more porous and fragmented than the rather stable and bounded nature that is presented by VL. Further, many theologians have turned to the more integrative category of context rather than culture in order to account for shared experience and social-historical location and change. It has been acknowledged that the process of inculturation should also come to include recognition of the violence done to peoples—both physically and psychologically— in planting the Gospel and liturgical practices in local cultures.

In terms of an ongoing reception of VL, scholars of liturgy and culture should continue to nuance what is meant by substantial unity of the Roman Rite, why any transformation of the Roman Rite is delimited, how the relation of ecclesiology and liturgy raised in the document can be extended and advanced, how cultural analysis of the liturgy is as necessary as cultural analysis of the local people, and what appropriate methodologies might be enlisted in the process.

Varietates legitimae has rightly been called a milestone in the liturgical renewal advanced by *Sacrosanctum Concilium*. The Church's continued reception, appropriation, and extension of its insights remain important twenty years later.

VARIETATES LEGITIMAE
INCULTURATION AND THE ROMAN LITURGY

FOURTH INSTRUCTION FOR THE RIGHT APPLICATION OF THE CONCILIAR CONSTITUTION ON THE LITURGY (NOS. 37–40)

CONGREGATION FOR DIVINE WORSHIP AND THE
DISCIPLINE OF THE SACRAMENTS
MARCH 29, 1994

INTRODUCTION

1.   Legitimate differences in the Roman rite were allowed in the past and were foreseen by the Second Vatican Council in the Constitution on the Sacred Liturgy *Sacrosanctum Concilium*, especially in the missions.[1] "Even in the liturgy the church has no wish to impose a rigid uniformity in matters that do not affect the faith or the good of the whole community."[2] It has known and still knows many different forms and liturgical families, and considers that this diversity, far from harming her unity, underlines its value.[3]

2.   In his apostolic letter *Vicesimus Quintus Annus*, the Holy Father Pope John Paul II described the attempt to make the liturgy take root in different cultures as an important task for liturgical renewal.[4] This work was foreseen in earlier instructions and in liturgical books, and it must be followed up in the light of experience, welcoming where necessary cultural values "which are compatible with the true and authentic spirit of the liturgy, always respecting the substantial unity of the Roman rite as expressed in the liturgical books."[5]

A) NATURE OF THIS INSTRUCTION

3.   By order of the supreme pontiff, the Congregation for Divine Worship and the Discipline of the Sacraments has prepared this instruction: The norms for the adaptation of the liturgy to the temperament and conditions of different peoples, which were given in Articles 37–40 of the constitution *Sacrosanctum Concilium*, are here defined; certain principles expressed in general terms in

---

1. Cf. SC, 38; cf. also no. 40.
2. SC, 37.
3. Cf. OE, 2; SC, 3 and 4; CCC, 1200–1206, especially 1204–1206.
4. Cf. VQA, 16: AAS 81 (1989), 912.
5. Ibid.

those articles are explained more precisely, the directives are set out in a more appropriate way and the order to be followed is clearly set out, so that in the future this will be considered the only correct procedure. Since the theological principles relating to questions of faith and inculturation have still to be examined in depth, this congregation wishes to help bishops and episcopal conferences to consider or put into effect, according to the law, such adaptations as are already foreseen in the liturgical books; to re-examine critically arrangements that have already been made; and if in certain cultures pastoral need requires that form of adaptation of the liturgy which the constitution calls "more profound" and at the same time considers "more difficult," to make arrangements for putting it into effect in accordance with the law.

B) PRELIMINARY OBSERVATIONS

4.   The constitution *Sacrosanctum Concilium* spoke of the different forms of liturgical adaptation.[6] Subsequently the magisterium of the church has used the term *inculturation* to define more precisely "the incarnation of the Gospel in autonomous cultures and at the same time the introduction of these cultures into the life of the church."[7] Inculturation signifies "an intimate transformation of the authentic cultural values by their integration into Christianity and the implantation of Christianity into different human cultures."[8]

The change of vocabulary is understandable, even in the liturgical sphere. The expression *adaptation*, taken from missionary terminology, could lead one to think of modifications of a somewhat transitory and external nature.[9] The term *inculturation* is a better expression to designate a double movement: "By inculturation, the church makes the Gospel incarnate in different cultures and at the same times introduces peoples, together with their cultures, into her own community."[10] On the one hand the penetration of the Gospel into a given sociocultural milieu "gives inner fruitfulness to the spiritual qualities and gifts proper to each people . . . , strengthens these qualities, perfects them and restores them in Christ."[11]

On the other hand, the church assimilates these values, when they are compatible with the Gospel, "to deepen understanding of Christ's message and give it more effective expression in the liturgy and in the many different aspects of the life of the community of believers."[12] This double movement in the work of inculturation thus expresses on the component elements of the mystery of the incarnation.[13]

---

6. SC, 37–40.

7. John Paul II, Encyclical *Slavorum Apostoli*, June 2,1985, no. 21: AAS 77 (1985), 802–803; discourse to the Pontifical Council for Culture, plenary assembly, January 17, 1987, no. 5: AAS 79 (1987), 1204–1205.

8. RM, 52: AAS 83 (1991), 300.

9. Cf. *ibid.*, and Synod of Bishops, Final Report *Exeunte Coetu Secundo*, December 7, 1985, D 4.

10. RM, 52.

11. GS, 58.

12. GS, 58.

13. Cf. CT, 53: AAS 71 (1979), 1319.

5.   Inculturation thus understood has its place in worship as in other areas of the life of the church.[14] It constitutes one of the aspects of the inculturation of the Gospel, which calls for true integration[15] in the life of faith of each people of the permanent values of a culture rather than their transient expressions. It must, then, be in full solidarity with a much greater action, a unified pastoral strategy which takes account of the human situation.[16] As in all forms of the work of evangelization, this patient and complex undertaking calls for methodical research and ongoing discernment.[17] The inculturation of the Christian life and of liturgical celebrations must be the fruit of a progressive maturity in the faith of the people.[18]

6.   The present instruction has different situations in view. There are in the first place those countries which do not have a Christian tradition or where the Gospel has been proclaimed in modern times by missionaries who brought the Roman rite with them. It is now more evident that "coming into contact with different cultures, the church must welcome all that can be reconciled with the Gospel in the tradition of a people to bring to it the riches of Christ and to be enriched in turn by the many different forms of wisdom of the nations of the earth."[19]

7.   The situation is different in the countries with a long-standing Western Christian tradition, where the culture has already been penetrated for a long time by the faith and the liturgy expressed in the Roman rite. That has helped the welcome given to liturgical reform in these countries, and the measures of adaptation envisaged in the liturgical books were considered, on the whole, sufficient to allow for legitimate local diversity (cf. below nos. 53–61). In some

---

14. Cf. CCEC, c. 584.2: *"Evangelizatio gentium ita fiat, ut servata integritate fidei et morum Evangelium se in cultura singulorum populorum exprimere possit, in catechesi scilicet, in ritibus propriis liturgicis, in arte sacra in iure particulari ac demum in tota vita ecclesiali."*

15. Cf. CT, 53: "concerning evangelization in general, we can say that it is a call to bring the strength of the Gospel to the heart of culture and cultures. . . . It is in this way that it can propose to cultures the knowledge of the mystery hidden and help them to make of their own living tradition original expressions of life, celebration and Christian thought."

16. Cf. RM, 52: "Inculturation is a slow process covering the whole of missionary life and involves all who are active in the mission *ad gentes* and Christian communities in the measure that they are developing." Discourse to Pontifical Council for Culture plenary assembly: "I strongly reaffirm the need to mobilize the whole church into a creative effort toward a renewed evangelization of both people and cultures. It is only by a joint effort that the church will be able to bring the hope of Christ into the heart of cultures and present-day ways of thinking."

17. Cf. Pontifical Biblical Commission, *Foi et culture a la lumiere de la Bible*, 1981; and International Theological Commission, "Faith and Inculturation," 1988.

18. Cf. John Paul II, discourse to the bishops of Zaire, April 12, 1983, no. 5: AAS 75 (1983), 620: "How is it that a faith which has truly matured, is deep and firm, does not succeed in expressing itself in a language, in a catechesis, in theological reflection, in prayer, in the liturgy, in art, in the institutions which are truly related to the African soul of your compatriots? There is the key to the important and complex question of the liturgy, to mention just one area. Satisfactory progress in this domain can only be the fruit of a progressive growth in faith, linked with spiritual discernment, theological clarity, a sense of the universal church."

19. Discourse to Pontifical Council for Culture, 5: "In coming into contact with the cultures, the church must welcome all that in the traditions of peoples is compatible with the Gospel, to give all the riches of Christ to them and to enrich itself of the varied wisdom of the nations of the earth."

countries, however, where several cultures coexist, especially as a result of immigration, it is necessary to take account of the particular problems which this poses (cf. below no. 49).

8.　It is necessary to be equally attentive to the progressive growth both in countries with a Christian tradition and in others of a culture marked by indifference or disinterest in religion.[20] In the face of this situation, it is not so much a matter of inculturation, which assumes that there are pre-existent religious values and evangelizes them, but rather a matter of insisting on liturgical formation[21] and finding the most suitable means to reach spirits and hearts.

I. PROCESS OF INCULTURATION THROUGHOUT THE HISTORY OF SALVATION

9.　Light is shed upon the problems being posed about the inculturation of the Roman rite in the history of salvation. The process of inculturation was a process which developed in many ways.

The people of Israel throughout its history preserved the certain knowledge that it was the chosen people of God, the witness of his action and love in the midst of the nations. It took from neighboring peoples certain forms of worship, but its faith in the God of Abraham, Isaac and Jacob subjected these borrowings to profound modifications, principally changes of significance but also often changes in the form, as it incorporated these elements into its religious practice in order to celebrate the memory of God's wonderful deeds in its history.

The encounter between the Jewish world and Greek wisdom gave rise to a new form of inculturation: the translation of the Bible into Greek introduced the word of God into a world that had been closed to it and caused, under divine inspiration, and enrichment of the Scriptures.

10.　"The law of Moses, the prophets and the psalms" (cf. Luke 24:27 and 44) was a preparation for the coming of the Son of God upon earth. The Old Testament, comprising the life and culture of the people of Israel, is also the history of salvation.

On coming to the earth the Son of God, "born of a woman, born under the law" (Galatians 4:4), associated himself with social and cultural conditions of the people of the alliance, with whom he lived and prayed.[22] In becoming a man he became a member of a people, a country and an epoch "and in a certain way, he thereby united himself to the whole human race."[23] For "we are all one in Christ, and the common nature of our humanity takes life in him. It is for this that he was called the 'new Adam.'"[24]

---

20. Cf. discourse to the Pontifical Council for Culture, 5; cf. also VQA, 17.

21. Cf. SC, 19 and 35.

22. Cf. AG, 10.

23. GS, 22.

24. St. Cyril of Alexandria, *In Ioannem*, I 14: PG, 73, 162C.

11.   Christ, who wanted to share our human condition (cf. Hebrews 2:14), died for all in order to gather into unity the scattered children of God (cf. John 11:52). By his death he wanted to break down the wall of separation between mankind, to make Israel and the nations one people. By the power of his resurrection he drew all people to himself and created out of them a single new man (cf. Ephesians 2:14–16; John 12:32). In him a new world has been born (cf. 2 Corinthians 5:16–17), and everyone can become a new creature. In him, darkness has given place to light, promise became reality and all the religious aspirations of humanity found their fulfillment. By the offering that he made of his body, once for all (cf. Hebrews 10:10), Christ Jesus brought about the fullness of worship in spirit and in truth in the renewal which he wished for his disciples (cf. John 4:23–24).

12.   "In Christ . . . the fullness of divine worship has come to us."[25] In him we have the high priest, taken from among men (cf. Hebrews 5:15; 10:19–21), put to death in the flesh but brought to life in the spirit (cf. 1 Peter 3;18). As Christ and Lord, he has made out of the new people "a kingdom of priests for God his Father" (cf. Revelation 1:6; 5:9 –10).[26] But before inaugurating by the shedding of his blood the paschal mystery,[27] which constitutes the essential element of Christian worship,[28] Christ wanted to institute the eucharist, the memorial of his death and resurrection, until he comes again. Here is to be found the fundamental principle of Christian liturgy and the kernel of its ritual expression.

13.   At the moment of his going to his Father, the risen Christ assures his disciples of his presence and sends them to proclaim the Gospel to the whole of creation, to make disciples of all nations and baptize them (cf. Matthew 28:15; Mark 16:15; Acts 1:8). On the day of Pentecost, the coming of the Holy Spirit created a new community with the human race, uniting all in spite of the differences of language, which were a sign of division (cf. Acts 2:1–11). Henceforth the wonders of God will be made known to people of every language and culture (cf. Acts 10:44–48). Those redeemed by the blood of the Lamb and united in fraternal communion (cf. Acts 2:42) are called from "every tribe, language, people and nation" (cf. Revelation 5:9).

14.   Faith in Christ offers to all nations the possibility of being beneficiaries of the promise and of sharing in the heritage of the people of the covenant (cf. Ephesians 3:6), without renouncing their culture. Under the inspiration of the Holy Spirit, following the example of St. Peter (cf. Acts 10), St. Paul opened the doors of the church, not keeping the Gospel within the restrictions of the Mosaic law but keeping what he himself had received of the tradition which came from the Lord (cf. 1 Corinthians 11:23). Thus, from the beginning, the church did not demand of converts who were uncircumcised "anything beyond what was necessary" according to the decision of the apostolic assembly of Jerusalem (cf. Acts 15:28).

---

25. SC, 5.

26. Cf. LG, 10.

27. Cf. RomM, Fifth Weekday of the Passion of the Lord, 5: Prayer One: ". . . *per suum cruorem instituit paschale mysterium.*"

28. Cf. Paul VI, apostolic letter *Mysterii Paschalis*, February 14, 1969: AAS 61 (1969), 222–226.

15.   In gathering together to break the bread on the first day of the week, which became the day of the Lord (cf. Acts 20:7; Revelation 1:10), the first Christian communities followed the command of Jesus who, in the context of the memorial of the Jewish pasch, instituted the memorial of his passion. In continuity with the unique history of salvation, they spontaneously took the forms and texts of Jewish worship and adapted them to express the radical newness of Christian worship.[29] Under the guidance of the Holy Spirit, discernment was exercised between what could be kept and what was to be discarded of the Jewish heritage of worship.

16.   The spread of the Gospel in the world gave rise to other types of ritual in the churches coming from the gentiles, under the influence of different cultural traditions. Under the constant guidance of the Holy Spirit, discernment was exercised to distinguish those elements coming from "pagan" cultures which were incompatible with Christianity from those which could be accepted in harmony with apostolic tradition and in fidelity to the gospel of salvation.

17.   The creation and the development of the forms of Christian celebration developed gradually according to local conditions in the great cultural areas where the good news was proclaimed. Thus were born distinct liturgical families of the churches of the West and of the East. Their rich patrimony preserves faithfully the Christian tradition in its fullness.[30] The church of the West has sometimes drawn elements of its liturgy from the patrimony of the liturgical families of the East.[31] The church of Rome adopted in its liturgy the living language of the people, first Greek and then Latin, and, like other Latin churches, accepted into its worship important events of social life and gave them a Christian significance. During the course of the centuries, the Roman rite has known how to integrate texts, chants, gestures and rites from various sources[32] and to adapt itself in local cultures in mission territories,[33] even if at certain periods a desire for liturgical uniformity obscured this fact.

18.   In our own time, the Second Vatican Council recalled that the church "fosters and assumes the ability, resources and customs of each people. In assuming them, the church purifies, strengthens and ennobles them. . . . Whatever good lies latent in the religious practices and cultures of diverse peoples, it is not only saved from destruction but it is also cleansed, raised up and made perfect unto

---

29. Cf. CCC, 1096.

30. Cf. CCC, 1200–1203.

31. Cf. UR, 14–15.

32. Texts: cf. the sources of the prayers, the prefaces and the eucharistic prayers of the RomM; chants: for example the antiphons for Jan. 1, baptism of the Lord; Sept. 8, the *Improperia* of Good Friday, the hymns of the Liturgy of the Hours; gestures: for example the sprinkling of holy water, use of incense, genuflection, hands joined; rites: for example Palm Sunday procession, the adoration of the cross on Good Friday, the rogations.

33. Cf. in the past St. Gregory the Great, Letter to Mellitus: Reg. XI, 59: CIC 140A, 961–962; John VIII, Bull *Industriae Tuae*, June 26, 880: PL, 126, 904; Congregation for the Propagation of the Faith, Instruction to the Apostolic Vicars of China and Indochina (1654): *Collectanea S.C. de Propaganda Fide*, I 1 Rome, 1907, no. 135; instruction *Plane Compertum*, December 8, 1939: AAS 32 (1940), 2426.

the glory of God, the confounding of the devil, and the happiness of mankind."[34] So the liturgy of the church must not be foreign to any country, people or individual, and at the same time it should transcend the particularity of race and nation. It must be capable of expressing itself in every human culture, all the while maintaining its identity through fidelity to the tradition which comes to it from the Lord.[35]

19.   The liturgy, like the Gospel, must respect cultures, but at the same time invite them to purify and sanctify themselves.

In adhering to Christ by faith, the Jews remained faithful to the Old Testament, which led to Jesus, the Messiah of Israel; they knew that he had fulfilled the Mosaic alliance, as the mediator of the new and eternal covenant, sealed in his blood on the cross. They knew that, by his one perfect sacrifice, he is the authentic high priest and the definitive temple (cf. Hebrews 6–10), and the prescriptions of circumcision (cf. Galatians 5:1–6), the Sabbath (cf. Matthew 12:8 and similar),[36] and the sacrifices of the temple (cf. Hebrews 10) became of only relative significance.

In a more radical way Christians coming from paganism had to renounce idols, myths, superstitions (cf. Acts 19:18–19; 1 Corinthians 10:14–22; 2:20–22; 1 John 5:21) when they adhered to Christ.

But whatever their ethnic or cultural origin, Christians have to recognize the promise, the prophecy and the history of their salvation in the history of Israel. They must accept as the word of God the books of the Old Testament as well as those of the New.[37] They welcome the sacramental signs, which can only be understood fully in the context of Holy Scripture and the life of the church.[38]

20.   The challenge which faced the first Christians, whether they came from the chosen people or from a pagan background, was to reconcile the renunciations demanded by faith in Christ with fidelity to the culture and traditions of the people to which they belonged.

And so it will be for Christians of all times, as the words of St. Paul affirm: "We proclaim Christ crucified, scandal for the Jews, foolishness for the pagans" (1 Corinthians 1:23).

The discernment exercised during the course of the church's history remains necessary, so that through the liturgy the work of salvation accomplished by

---

34. LG, 17 also 13.

35. Cf. CT, 52–53; RM, 53– 54; CCC 1204–1206.

36. Cf., also St. Ignatius of Antioch, Letter to the Magnesians, 9: Funk 1, 199: "We have seen how former adherents of the ancient customs have since attained to a new hope; so that they have given up keeping the sabbath, and now order their lives by the Lord's day instead."

37. Cf. DV, 14–16; *Ordo Lectionum Missae ed. typica altera Praenotanda*, 5: "It is the same mystery of Christ that the church announces when she proclaims the Old and New Testament in the celebration of the liturgy. The New Testament is, indeed, hidden in the Old and, in the New the Old is revealed. Because Christ is the center and fullness of all Scripture, as also of the whole liturgical celebration"; CCC, 120–123, 128–130, 1093–1095.

38. Cf. CCC, 1093–1096.

Christ may continue faithfully in the church by the power of the Spirit in different countries and times and in different human cultures.

II. REQUIREMENTS AND PRELIMINARY CONDITIONS FOR LITURGICAL INCULTURATION

A) REQUIREMENTS EMERGING FROM THE NATURE OF THE LITURGY

21.   Before any research on inculturation begins, it is necessary to keep in mind the nature of the liturgy. It "is, in fact the privileged place where Christians meet God and the one whom he has sent, Jesus Christ" (cf. John 17:3).[39] It is at once the action of Christ the priest and the action of the church which is his body, because in order to accomplish his work of glorifying God and sanctifying mankind, achieved through visible signs, he always associates with himself the church, which, through him and in the Holy Spirit, gives the Father the worship which is pleasing to him.[40]

22.   The nature of liturgy is intimately linked up with the nature of the church; indeed, it is above all in the liturgy that the nature of the church is manifested.[41] Now the church has specific characteristics which distinguish it from every other assembly and community.

It is not gathered together by a human decision, but is called by God in the Holy Spirit and responds in faith to his gratuitous call (*ekklesia* derives from *klesis*, "call"). This singular characteristic of the church is revealed by its coming together as a priestly people, especially on the Lord's day, by the word which God addresses to his people and by the ministry of the priest, who through the sacrament of orders acts in the person of Christ the head.[42]

Because it is catholic, the church overcomes the barriers which divide humanity: By baptism all become children of God and form in Christ Jesus one people where "there is neither Jew nor Greek, neither slave nor free, neither male nor female" (Galatians 3:28). Thus church is called to gather all peoples, to speak the languages, to penetrate all cultures.

Finally, the church is a pilgrim on the earth far from the Lord (cf. 2 Corinthians 5:6): It bears the marks of the present time in the sacraments and in its institutions, but is waiting in joyful hope for the coming of Jesus Christ (cf. Titus 2:13).[43] This is expressed in the prayers of petition: It shows that we are citizens of heaven (cf. Philippians 3:20), at the same time attentive to the needs of mankind and of society (cf. 1 Timothy 2:1–4).

23.   The church is nourished on the word of God written in the Old and New Testaments. When the church proclaims the word in the liturgy, it welcomes it

---

39. VQA, 7.
40. Cf. SC, 5–7.
41. Cf. SC, 2; VQA, 9.
42. Cf. PO, 2.
43. Cf. LG, 48; SC, 2 and 8.

as a way in which Christ is present: "It is he who speaks when the sacred Scriptures are read in church."[44] For this reason the word of God is so important in the celebration of the liturgy[45] that the holy Scripture must not be replaced by any other text, no matter how venerable it may be.[46] Likewise the Bible is the indispensable source of the liturgy's language, of its signs and of its prayer, especially in the psalms.[47]

24.   Since the church is the fruit of Christ's sacrifice, the liturgy is always the celebration of the paschal mystery of Christ, the glorification of God the Father and the sanctification of mankind by the power of the Holy Spirit.[48] Christian worship thus finds its most fundamental expression when every Sunday throughout the whole world Christians gather around the altar under the leadership of the priest, celebrate the eucharist, listen to the word of God, and recall the death and resurrection of Christ, while awaiting his coming in glory.[49] Around this focal point, the paschal mystery is made present in different ways in the celebration of each of the sacraments.

25.   The whole life of the liturgy gravitates in the first place around the eucharistic sacrifice and the other sacraments given by Christ to his church.[50] The church has the duty to transmit them carefully and faithfully to every generation. In virtue of its pastoral authority, the church can make dispositions to provide for the good of the faithful, according to circumstances, times and places.[51] But it has no power over the things which are directly related to the will of Christ and which constitute the unchangeable part of the liturgy.[52] To break the link that the sacraments have with Christ, who instituted them, and with the very beginnings of the church,[53] would no longer be to inculturate them, but to empty them of their substance.

26.   The church of Christ is made present and signified in a given place and in a given time by the local or particular churches, which through the liturgy reveal the church in its true nature.[54] That is why every particular church must be united with the universal church not only in belief and sacramentals, but also

---

44. SC, 7.

45. Cf. SC, 24.

46. Cf. *Ordo Lectionem Missae Praenotanda*, 12: "It is not allowed to suppress or reduce either the biblical readings in the celebration of Mass or the chants that are drawn from sacred Scripture. It is absolutely forbidden to replace these readings by other nonbiblical readings. It is through the word of God in the Scriptures that 'God continues to speak to his people' (SC, 33), and it is through familiarity with the Holy Scripture that the people of God, made docile by the Holy Spirit in the light of faith, can by their life and way of living witness to Christ before the whole world."

47. Cf. CCC, 2585–2589.

48. Cf. SC, 7.

49. Cf. SC, 6, 47, 56, 102, 106; cf. GIRM, 1, 7, 8.

50. Cf. SC, 6.

51. Cf. Council of Trent, Session 21, Chap. 2: Denz-Schonm. 1728; SC, 48ff; 62ff.

52. Cf. SC, 21.

53. Cf. CDF, *Inter Insigniores*, October 15, 1976: AAS 69 (1977), 107–108.

54. Cf. LG, 28; also no. 26.

in those practices received through the church as part of the uninterrupted apostolic tradition.[55] This includes, for example, daily prayer,[56] sanctification of Sunday and the rhythm of the week, the celebration of Easter and the unfolding of the mystery of Christ throughout the liturgical year,[57] the practice of penance and fasting,[58] the sacraments of Christian initiation, the celebration of the memorial of the Lord and the relationship between the Liturgy of the Word and the eucharistic liturgy, the forgiveness of sins, the ordained ministry, marriage and the anointing of the sick.

27.   In the liturgy the faith of the church is expressed in a symbolic and communitarian form: This explains the need for a legislative framework for the organization of worship, the preparation of texts and the celebration of rites.[59] The reason for the preceptive character of this legislation throughout the centuries and still today is to ensure the orthodoxy of worship; that is to say, not only to avoid errors, but also to pass on the faith in the integrity so that the "rule of prayer" (*lex orandi*) of the church may correspond to the "rule of faith" (*lex credendi*).[60]

However deep inculturation may go, the liturgy cannot do without legislation and vigilance on the part of those who have received this responsibility in the church: the Apostolic See and, according to the prescriptions of the law, the episcopal conference for its territory and the bishop for his diocese.[61]

B) PRELIMINARY CONDITIONS FOR INCULTURATION OF THE LITURGY

28.   The missionary tradition of the church has always sought to evangelize people in their own language. Often indeed, it was the first apostles of a country who wrote down languages which up till then had only been oral. And this is right, as it is by the mother language, which conveys the mentality and the culture of a people, that one can reach the soul, mold it in the Christian spirit and allow to share more deeply in the prayer of the church.[62]

After the first evangelization, the proclamation of the word of God in the language of a country remains very useful for the people in their liturgical cele-

---

55. Cf. St. Irenaeus, *Against the Heresies*, III, 2, 1–3; 3, 1–2: SCh, 211, 24–31; cf. St. Augustine, *Letter to Januarius* 54, 1: PL 33, 200: "But regarding those other observances which we keep and all the world keeps, and which do not derive from Scripture but from tradition, we are given to understand that they have been ordained or recommended to be kept by the apostles themselves or by the plenary councils, whose authority is well founded in the church"; cf. RM, 53– 4; cf. CDF, *Letter to Bishops of the Catholic Church on Certain Aspects of the Church Understood as Communion*, May 28, 1992, nos. 7–10.

56. Cf. SC, 83.

57. Cf. SC, 102, 106 and App.

58. Cf. Paul VI, apostolic constitution Paenitemini, February 17, 1966: AAS 58 (1966), 177–198.

59. Cf. SC, 22; 26; 28; 40, 43 and 128; CIC, c. 2 and *passim*.

60. Cf. GIRM, 2; Paul VI, *Discourse to the Consilium for the Application of the Constitution on the Liturgy*, October 13, 1966: AAS 58 (1966), 1146; October 14, 1968: AAS 60 (1968), 734.

61. Cf. SC, 22; 36; 40; 44–46; CIC, cc. 47ff and 838.

62. Cf. RM, 53.

brations. The translation of the Bible, or at least of the biblical texts used in the liturgy, is the first necessary step in the process of the inculturation of the liturgy.[63]

So that the word of God may be received in a right and fruitful way, "it is necessary to foster a taste for holy Scripture, as is witnessed by the ancient traditions of the rites of both East and West."[64] Thus inculturation of the liturgy presupposes the reception of the sacred Scripture into a given culture.[65]

29. The different situations in which the church finds itself are an important factor in judging the degree of liturgical inculturation that is necessary. The situation of countries that were evangelized centuries ago and where the Christian faith continues to influence the culture is different from countries which were evangelized more recently or where the Gospel has not penetrated deeply into cultural values.[66] Different again is the situation of a church where Christians are a minority of the population. A more complex situation is found when the population has different languages and cultures. A precise evaluation of the situation is necessary in order to achieve satisfactory solutions.

30. To prepare an inculturation of the liturgy, episcopal conferences should call upon people who are competent both in the liturgical tradition of the Roman rite and in the appreciation of local cultural values. Preliminary studies of a historical, anthropological, exegetical and theological character are necessary. But these need to be examined in the light of the pastoral experience of the local clergy, especially those born in the country.[67] The advice of "wise people" of the country, whose human wisdom is enriched by the light of the Gospel, would also be valuable. Liturgical inculturation should try to satisfy the needs of traditional culture[68] and at the same time take account of the needs of those affected by an urban and industrial culture.

c) THE RESPONSIBILITY OF THE EPISCOPAL CONFERENCE

31. Since it is a question of local culture, it is understandable that the constitution *Sacrosanctum Concilium* assigned special responsibility in this matter to the "various kinds of competent territorial bodies of bishops legitimately established."[69] In regard to this, episcopal conferences must consider "carefully and prudently what elements taken from the traditions and cultures of individual peoples may properly be admitted into divine worship."[70] They can sometimes introduce "into the liturgy such elements as are not bound up with superstition and error . . . provided they are in keeping with the true and authentic spirit of the liturgy."[71]

---

63. Cf. SC, 35 and 36; CIC, c. 825.1.
64. SC, 24.
65. Cf. SC; CT, 55.
66. In SC, attention is drawn to nos. 38 and 40: "above all in the missions."
67. Cf. AG, 16 and 17.
68. Cf. AG, 19.
69. SC, 22; cf. AG, 39 and 40; CIC, cc. 447–448ff.
70. SC, 40.
71. SC, 37.

32.   Conferences may determine, according to the procedure given below (cf. nos. 62 and 65–69), whether the introduction into the liturgy of elements borrowed from the social and religious rites of a people, and which form a living part of their culture, will enrich their understanding of liturgical actions without producing negative effects on their faith and piety. They will always be careful to avoid the danger of introducing elements that might appear to the faithful as the return to a period before evangelization (cf. below, no. 47).

In any case, if changes in rites or texts are judged to be necessary, they must be harmonized with the rest of the liturgical life and, before being put into practice, still more before being made mandatory, they should first be presented to the clergy and then to the faithful in such a way as to avoid the danger of troubling them without good reason (cf. below, nos. 46 and 69).

III. PRINCIPLES AND PRACTICAL NORMS FOR INCULTURATION OF THE ROMAN RITE

33.   As particular churches, especially the young churches, deepen their understanding of the liturgical heritage they have received from the Roman church which gave them birth, they will be able in turn to find in their own cultural heritage appropriate forms which can be integrated into the Roman rite where this is judged useful and necessary.

The liturgical formation of the faithful and the clergy, which is called for by the constitution *Sacrosanctum Concilium*,[72] ought to help them to understand the meaning of the texts and the rites given in the present liturgical books. Often this will mean that elements which come from the tradition of the Roman rite do not have to be changed or suppressed.

A) GENERAL PRINCIPLES

34.   In the planning and execution of the inculturation of the Roman rite, the following points should be kept in mind: 1) the goal of inculturation; 2) the substantial unity of the Roman rite; 3) the competent authority.

35.   The goal which should guide the inculturation of the Roman rite is that laid down by the Second Vatican Council as the basis of the general restoration of the liturgy: "Both texts and rites should be so drawn up that they express more clearly the holy things they signify and so that the Christian people, as far as possible, may be able to understand them with ease and to take part in the rites fully, actively and as befits a community."[73]

Rites also need "to be adapted to the capacity of the faithful and that there should not be a need for numerous explanations for them to be understood."[74] However, the nature of the liturgy always has to be borne in mind, as does the

---

72. Cf. SC, 14–19.
73. SC, 21.
74. Cf. SC, 34.

biblical and traditional character of its structure and the particular way in which it is expressed (cf. above, nos. 21–27).

36.   The process of inculturation should maintain the substantial unity of the Roman rite.[75] This unity is currently expressed in the typical editions of liturgical books, published by authority of the supreme pontiff and in the liturgical books approved by the episcopal conferences for their areas and confirmed by the Apostolic See.[76] The work of inculturation does not foresee the creation of new families of rites; inculturation responds to the needs of a particular culture and leads to adaptations which still remain part of the Roman rite.[77]

37.   Adaptations of the Roman rite, even in the field of inculturation, depend completely on the authority of the church. This authority belongs to the Apostolic See, which exercises it through the Congregation for Divine Worship and the Discipline of the Sacraments;[78] it also belongs, within the limits fixed by law, to episcopal conferences[79] and to the diocesan bishop.[80] "No other person, not even if he is a priest, may on his own initiative add, remove or change anything in the liturgy."[81] Inculturation is not left to the personal initiative of celebrants or to the collective initiative of an assembly.[82]

Likewise concessions granted to one region cannot be extended to other regions without the necessary authorization, even if an episcopal conference considers that there are sufficient reasons for adopting such measures in its own area.

B) ADAPTATIONS WHICH CAN BE MADE

38.   In an analysis of a liturgical action with a view to its inculturation, it is necessary to consider the traditional value of the elements of the action and in

---

75. Cf. SC, 37–40.

76. Cf. VQA, 16.

77. Cf. John Paul II, discourse to the plenary assembly of the Congregation for Divine Worship and the Discipline of the Sacraments, January 26, 1991, no. 3: AAS 83 (1991), 940: "This is not to suggest to the particular churches that they have a new task to undertake following the application of liturgical reform, that is to say, adaptation or inculturation. Nor is it intended to mean inculturation as the creation of alternative rites. . . . It is a of collaborating so that the Roman rite, maintaining its own identity, may incorporate suitable adaptations."

78. Cf. SC, 22; CIC, cc. 838.1 and 838.2; John Paul II, apostolic constitution Pastor Bonus, 62, 64.3: AAS 80 (1988), 876 – 877; VQA, 19.

79. Cf. SC, 22 and cc. 447ff and 838.1 and 838.3; VQA, 20.

80. Cf. SC, 22, and CIC, cc. 838.1 and 838.4; VQA, 21.

81. Cf. SC, 22.

82. The situation is different when, in the liturgical books published after the constitution, the introductions and the rubrics envisaged adaptations and the possibility of leaving a choice to the pastoral sensitivity of the one presiding, for example, when it says "if it is opportune," "in these or similar terms," "also," "according to circumstances," "either . . . or," "if convenient," "normally," "the most suitable form can be chosen." In making a choice, the celebrant should seek the good of the assembly, taking into account the spiritual preparation and mentality of the participants rather than his own or the easiest solution. In celebrations for particular groups, other possibilities are available. Nonetheless, prudence and discretion are always called for in order to avoid the breaking up of the local church into little "churches" or "chapels" closed in upon themselves.

particular their biblical or patristic origin (cf. above, nos. 21–26), because it is not sufficient to distinguish between what can be changed and what is unchangeable.

39. Language, which is a means of communication between people; in liturgical celebrations its purpose is to announce to the faithful the good news of salvation[83] and to express the church's prayer to the Lord. For this reason it must always express, along with the truths of the faith, the grandeur and holiness of the mysteries which are being celebrated.

Careful consideration therefore needs to be given to determine which elements in the language of the people can properly be introduced into liturgical celebrations, and in particular whether it is suitable or not to use expressions from non-Christian religions. It is just as important to take account of the different literary genres used in the liturgy: biblical texts, presidential prayers, psalmody, acclamations, refrains, responsories, hymns and litanies.

40. Music and singing, which express the soul of people, have pride of place in the liturgy. And so singing must be promoted, in the first place singing the liturgical text, so that the voices of the faithful may be heard in the liturgical actions themselves.[84] "In some parts of the world, especially mission lands, there are people who have their own musical traditions, and these play a great part in their religious and social life. Due importance is to be attached to their music and a suitable place given to it, not only in forming their attitude toward religion, but also in adapting worship to their native genius."[85]

It is important to note that a text which is sung is more deeply engraved in the memory than when it is read, which means that it is necessary to be demanding about the biblical and liturgical inspiration and the literary quality of texts which are meant to be sung.

Musical forms, melodies and musical instruments could be used in divine worship as long as they "are suitable, or can be made suitable, for sacred use, and provided they are in accord with the dignity of the place of worship and truly contribute to the uplifting of the faithful."[86]

41. The liturgy is an action, and so gesture and posture are especially important. Those which belong to the essential rites of the sacraments and which are required for their validity must be preserved just as they have been approved or determined by the supreme authority of the church.[87]

The gestures and postures of the celebrating priest must express his special function: He presides over the assembly in the person of Christ.[88]

---

83. Cf. CIC, cc. 762–772, esp. c. 769.

84. Cf. SC, 118; also no. 54: While allowing that "a suitable place be allotted to the language of the country" in the chants, "steps should be taken so that the faithful may also be able to say or sign together in Latin those parts of the ordinary of the Mass which pertain to them," especially the Our Father, cf. GIRM, 19.

85. SC, 119.

86. SC., 120.

87. Cf. CIC, c. 841.

88. Cf. SC, 33; CIC, c. 899.2.

The gestures and postures of the assembly are signs of its unity and express its active participation and foster the spiritual attitude of the participants.[89] Each culture will choose those gestures and bodily postures which express the attitude of humanity before God, giving them a Christian significance, having some relationship if possible, with the gestures and postures of the Bible.

42.   Among some peoples, singing is instinctively accompanied by hand clapping, rhythmic swaying and dance movements on the part of the participants. Such forms of external expression can have a place in the liturgical actions of these peoples on condition that they are always the expression of true communal prayer of adoration, praise, offering and supplication, and not simply a performance.

43.   The liturgical celebration is enriched by the presence of art, which helps the faithful to celebrate, meet God and pray. Art in the church, which is made up of all peoples and nations, should enjoy the freedom of expression as long as it enhances the beauty of the buildings and liturgical rites, investing them with the respect and honor which is their due.[90] The arts should also be truly significant in the life and tradition of the people.

The same applies to the shape, location and decoration of the altar,[91] the place for the proclamation of the word of God[92] and for baptism,[93] all the liturgical furnishings, vessels, vestments and colors.[94] Preference should be given to materials, forms and colors which are in use in the country.

44.   The constitution *Sacrosanctum Concilium* has firmly maintained the constant practice of the church of encouraging the veneration by the faithful of images of Christ, the Virgin Mary and the saints,[95] because the honor "given to the image is given to its subject."[96] In different cultures believers can be helped in their prayer and in their spiritual life by seeing works of art which attempt, according to the genius of the people, to express the divine mysteries.

45.   Alongside liturgical celebrations and related to them, in some particular churches there are various manifestations of popular devotion. These were sometimes introduced by missionaries at the time of the initial evangelization, and they often develop according to local custom.

The introduction of devotional practices into liturgical celebrations under the pretext of inculturation cannot be allowed "because by its nature, (the liturgy) is superior to them."[97]

---

89. Cf. SC, 30.
90. Cf. SC, 123–124; CIC, c. 1216.
91. Cf. GIRM, 259–270; CIC, cc. 1235–1239, esp. c. 1236.
92. Cf. GIRM, 272.
93. Cf. *De Benedictionibus Ordo Benedictionis Baptisterii seu Fontis Baptismalis*, 832–837.
94. Cf. GIRM, 287–310.
95. Cf. SC, 125; LG, 67; CIC, c. 1188.
96. Council of Nicea II: Denz.-Schonm. 601; cf. St. Basil, "On the Holy Spirit," XVIII, 45; SCh 17, 194.
97. SC, 13.

It belongs to the local ordinary[98] to organize such devotions, to encourage them as supports for the life and faith of Christians, and to purify them when necessary, because they need to be constantly permeated by the Gospel.[99] He will take care to ensure that they do not replace liturgical celebrations or become mixed up with them.[100]

c) NECESSARY PRUDENCE

46.   "Innovations should only be made when the good of the church genuinely and certainly requires them; care must be taken that any new forms adopted should in some way grow organically from forms already existing."[101] This norm was given in the constitution *Sacrosanctum Concilium* in relation to the restoration of the liturgy, and it also applies, in due measure, to the inculturation of the Roman rite. In this field changes need to be gradual and adequate explanation given in order to avoid the danger of rejection or simply an artificial grafting onto previous forms.

47.   The liturgy is the expression of faith and Christian life, and so it is necessary to ensure that liturgical inculturation is not marked, even in appearance, by religious syncretism. This would be the case if the places of worship, the liturgical objects and vestments, gestures and postures let it appear as if rites had the same significance in Christian celebrations as they did before evangelization. The syncretism will be still worse if biblical readings and chants (cf. above, no. 26) or the prayers were replaced by texts from other religions, even if these contain an undeniable religious and moral value.[102]

48.   The constitution *Sacrosanctum Concilium* envisaged the admission of rites or gestures according to local custom into rituals of Christian initiation, marriage and funerals.[103] This is a stage of inculturation, but there is also the danger that the truth of the Christian rite and the expression of the Christian faith could be easily diminished in the eyes of the faithful. Fidelity to traditional usages must be accompanied by purification and, if necessary, a break with the past. The same applies, for example, to the possibility of Christianizing pagan festivals or holy places, or to the priest using the signs of authority reserved to the heads of civil society or for the veneration of ancestors. In every case it is necessary to avoid any ambiguity. Obviously the Christian liturgy cannot accept magic rites, superstition, spiritism, vengeance or rites with a sexual connotation.

---

98. Cf. CIC, c. 839.2.

99. VQA, 18.

100. Cf. *ibid.*

101. SC, 23.

102. These texts can be used profitably in the homily because it is one of the tasks of the homily "to show the points of convergence between revealed divine wisdom and noble human thought, seeking the truth by various paths" (John Paul II, apostolic letter *Dominicae Cenae*, February 24, 1980, no. 10: AAS 72 (1980), 137.

103. SC, 65, 77, 81. Cf. , 30–31, 79–81, 88–89; *Ordo Celebrandi Matrimonium, editio typica altera, Praenotanda,* 41–44; *Ordo Exsequiarum, Praenotanda,* 21–22.

49.   In a number of countries there are several cultures which coexist and sometimes influence each other in such a way as to lead gradually to the formation of a new culture, while at times they seek to affirm their proper identity or even oppose each other in order to stress their own existence. It can happen that customs may have little more than folkloric interest. The episcopal conference will examine each case individually with care: They should respect the riches of each culture and those who defend them, but they should not ignore or neglect a minority culture with which they are not familiar. They should weigh the risk of a Christian community becoming inward looking and also the use of inculturation for political ends. In those countries with a customary culture, account must also be taken of the extent to which modernization has affected the people.

50.   Sometimes there are many languages in use in the one country, even though each one may be spoken only by a small group of persons or a single tribe. In such cases a balance must be found which respects the individual rights of these groups or tribes but without carrying to extremes the localization of the liturgical celebrations. It is also sometimes possible that a country may be moving toward the use of a principal language.

51.   To promote liturgical inculturation in a cultural area bigger than one country, the episcopal conferences concerned must work together and decide the measures which have to be taken so that "as far as possible, there are not notable ritual differences in regions bordering on one another."[104]

IV. AREAS OF ADAPTATION IN THE ROMAN RITE

52.   The constitution *Sacrosanctum Concilium* had in mind an inculturation of the Roman rite when it gave norms for the adaptation of the liturgy to the mentality and needs of different peoples, when it provided for a degree of adaptation in the liturgical books (cf. below, nos. 53– 61), and also when it envisaged the possibility of more profound adaptations in some circumstances, especially in mission countries (cf. below, nos. 63–64).

A) ADAPTATIONS IN THE LITURGICAL BOOKS

53.   The first significant measure of inculturation is the translation of liturgical books into the language of the people.[105] The completion of translations and their revision, where necessary, should be effected according to the directives given by the Holy See on this subject.[106] Different literary genres are to be respected, and the content of the texts of the Latin typical edition is to be preserved; at the same time the translations must be understandable to participants (cf. above, no. 39), suitable for proclamation and singing, with appropriate responses and acclamations by the assembly.

---

104. SC, 23.
105. Cf. SC, 36; 54; 63.
106. Cf. VQA, 20.

All peoples, even the most primitive, have a religious language which is suitable for expressing prayer, but liturgical language has its own special characteristics: It is deeply impregnated by the Bible; certain words in current Latin use (memoria, sacramentum) took on a new meaning in the Christian faith. Certain Christian expressions can be transmitted from one language to another, as has happened in the past, for example in the case of ecclesia, evangelium, baptisma, eucharistia.

Moreover, translators must be attentive to the relationship between the text and the liturgical action, aware of the needs of oral communication and sensitive to the literary qualities of the living language of the people. The qualities needed for liturgical translations are also required in the case of new compositions, when they are envisaged.

54.   For the celebration of the eucharist, the Roman Missal, "while allowing . . . for legitimate differences and adaptations according to the prescriptions of the Second Vatican Council," must remain "a sign and instrument of unity"[107] of the Roman rite in different languages. The General Instruction on the Roman Missal foresees that "in accordance with the constitution on the liturgy, each conference of bishops has the power to lay down norms for its own territory that are suited to the traditions and character of peoples, regions and different communities."[108] The same also applies to the gestures and postures of the faithful,[109] the way in which the altar and the book of the gospels are venerated,[110] the texts of the opening chants,[111] the song at the preparation of the gifts[112] and the communion song,[113] the rite of peace,[114] conditions regulating communion with the chalice,[115] the materials for the construction of the altar and liturgical furniture,[116] the material and form of sacred vessels,[117] liturgical vestments.[118] Episcopal conferences can also determine the manner of distributing communion.[119]

55.   For the other sacraments and for sacramentals, the Latin typical edition of each ritual indicates the adaptations which pertain to the episcopal conferences[120]

---

107. Cf. Paul VI, apostolic constitution *Missale Romanum*, April 3, 1969: AAS 61 (1969), 221.
108. GIRM, 6; cf. also *Ordo Lectionum Missae, editio typica altera, Praenotanda*, 111–118.
109. GIRM, 22.
110. Cf. GIRM, 232.
111. Cf. GIRM, 26.
112. Cf. GIRM, 50.
113. Cf. GIRM, 56 i.
114. Cf. GIRM, 56 b.
115. Cf. GIRM, 242.
116. Cf. GIRM, 263 and 288.
117. Cf. GIRM, 290.
118. Cf. GIRM, 304, 305, 308.
119. Cf. *De Sacra Communione et de Cultu Mysterii Eucharistici Extra Missam, Praenotanda*, 21.
120. Cf. *Ordo Initiationis Christianae Adultorum, Praenotanda Generalia*, 30–33; *Praenotanda*, 12, 20,47, 64–65; *Ordo*, 312; Appendix, 12; *Ordo Baptismi Parvulorum, Praenotanda*, 8, 23–25; *Ordo Confirmationis, Praenotanda*, 11–12, 16–17; *De Sacra Communione et de Cultu Mysterii Eucharistici Extra Missam, Praenotanda*, 12; *Ordo Paenitentiae, Praenotanda*, 35b, 38; *Ordo Unctionis Infirmorum Eorumque Pastoralis Curae, Praenotanda*, 38–39; *Ordo Celebrandi Matrimonium, editio typica altera, Praenotanda*, 39–44;

or to individual bishops in particular circumstances.[121] These adaptations concern texts, gestures and sometimes the ordering of the rite. When the typical edition gives alternative formulas, conferences of bishops can add other formulas of the same kind.

56. For the rites of Christian initiation, episcopal conferences are "to examine with care and prudence what can properly be admitted from the traditions and character of each people"[122] and "in mission countries to judge whether initiation ceremonies practiced among the people can be adapted into the rite of Christian initiation and to decide whether they should be used."[123] It is necessary to remember, however, that the term *initiation* does not have the same meaning or designate the same reality when it is used of social rites of initiation among certain people or when it is contrary to the process of Christian initiation, which leads through the rites of the catechumenate to incorporation into Christ in the church by means of the sacraments of baptism, confirmation and eucharist.

57. In many places it is the marriage rite that calls for the greatest degree of adaptation so as not to be foreign to social customs. To adapt it to the customs of different regions and peoples, each episcopal conference has the "faculty to prepare its own proper marriage rite, which must always conform to the law which requires that the ordained minister or the assisting layperson,[124] according to the case, must ask for and obtain the consent of the contracting parties and give them the nuptial blessing."[125] This proper trite must obviously bring out clearly the Christian meaning of marriage, emphasize the grace of the sacrament and underline the duties of the spouses.[126]

58. Among all peoples, funerals are always surrounded with special rites, often of great expressive value. To answer to the needs of different countries, the Roman Ritual offers several forms of funerals.[127] Episcopal conferences must choose those which correspond best to local customs.[128] They will wish to preserve all that is good in family traditions and local customs, and ensure that funeral rites manifest the Christian faith in the resurrection and bear witness to the true values of the Gospel.[129] It is in this perspective that funeral rituals can incorporate the customs of different cultures and respond as best they can to the needs and traditions of each region.[130]

De Ordinatione Episcopi Presbyterorum et Diaconorum, editio typica altera, Praenotanda, 11; *De Benedictionibus, Praenotanda Generalia,* 39.

121. Cf. *Ordo Initiationis Christianae Adultorum, Praenotanda,* 66; *Ordo Baptismi Parvulorum, Praenotanda,* 26; *Ordo Paenitentiae, Praenotanda,* 39; *Ordo Celebrandi Matrimonium, editio typica altera, Praenotanda,* 36.

122. *Ordo Initiationis Christianae Adultorum, Praenotanda Generalis,* 30.2.

123. Ibid., 31; cf. SC, 65.

124. Cf. CIC, cc. 1108 and 1112.

125. SC, 77; *Ordo Celebrandi Matrimonium, editio typica altera, Praenotanda,* 42.

126. Cf. SC, 77.

127. Cf. Ordo *Exsequiarum Praenotanda,* 4.

128. Cf. ibid., 9 and 21.1–21.3.

129. Cf. ibid., 2.

130. Cf. SC, 81.

59.   The blessing of persons, places or things touches the everyday life of the faithful and answers their immediate needs. They offer many possibilities for adaptation, for maintaining local customs and admitting popular usages.[131] Episcopal conferences will be able to employ the foreseen dispositions and be attentive to the needs of the country.

60.   As regards the liturgical year, each particular church and religious family adds its own celebrations to those of the universal church, after approval by the Apostolic See.[132] Episcopal conferences can also, with the prior approval of the Apostolic See, suppress the obligation of certain feasts or transfer them to a Sunday.[133] They also decide the time and manner of celebrating rogationtide and ember days.[134]

61.   The Liturgy of the Hours has as its goal the praise of God and the sanctification by prayer of the day and all human activity. Episcopal conferences can make adaptations in the second reading of the office of readings, hymns and intercessions and in the final Marian antiphons.[135]

procedure

62.   When an episcopal conference prepares its own edition of liturgical books, it decides about the translations and also the adaptations which are envisaged by the law.[136] The acts of the conference, together with the final vote, are signed by the president and secretary of the conference and sent to the Congregation for Divine Worship and the Discipline of the Sacraments, along with two copies of the approved text.

Moreover along with the complete dossier should be sent:

a) A succinct and precise explanation of the reasons for the adaptations that have been introduced.

b) Indications as to which sections have been taken from other already approved liturgical books and which are newly composed.

After the recognition by the Apostolic See has been received according to the law,[137] the episcopal conference promulgates the decree and determines the date when the new text comes into force.

---

131. Cf. SC, 79; *De Benedictionibus, Praenotanda Generalia,* 39; *Ordo Professionis Religiosae, Praenotanda,* 12–15.
132. Cf. GNLY, 49, 55; CDW, *Instruction Calendaria Particularia,* June 24, 1970: AAS, 62 (1970), 349–370.
133. Cf. CIC, c. 1246.2.
134. Cf. GNLY, 46.
135. GILOH, 92, 162, 178, 184.
136. Cf. CIC, cc. 455.2 and 838.3; that is also the case for a new edition, cf. VQA, 20.
137. CIC, c. 838.3

63.   Apart from the adaptations provided for in the liturgical books, it may be that "in some places and circumstances an even more radical adaptation of the liturgy is needed, and this entails greater difficulties."[138] This is more than the sort of adaptations envisaged by the general instructions and the *praenotanda* of the liturgical books.

It presupposes that an episcopal conference has exhausted all the possibilities of adaptation offered by the liturgical books; that it has made an evaluation of the adaptations already introduced and maybe revised them before proceeding to more far-reaching adaptations.

The desirability or need for an adaptation of this sort can emerge in one of the areas mentioned above (cf. nos. 53–61) without the others being affected. Moreover, adaptations of this kind do not envisage a transformation of the Roman rite, but are made within the context of the Roman rite.

64.   In some places when there are still problems about the participation of the faithful, a bishop or several bishops can set out their difficulties to their colleagues in the episcopal conferences and examine with them the desirability of introducing more profound adaptations, if the good of souls truly requires it.[139]

It is the function of episcopal conferences to propose to the Apostolic See the modifications it wishes to adopt following the procedure set out below.[140]

The Congregation for Divine Worship and the Discipline of the Sacraments is ready to receive the proposals of episcopal conferences and examine them, keeping in mind the good of the local churches concerned and the common good of the universal church, and to assist the process of inculturation where it is desirable or necessary. It will do this in accordance with the principles laid down in this instruction (cf. above, nos. 33–51), and in a spirit of confident collaboration and shared responsibility.

procedure

65.   The episcopal conference will examine what has to be modified in liturgical celebrations because of the traditions and mentality of peoples. It will ask the national or regional liturgical commission to study the matter and examine the different aspects of the elements of local culture and their eventual inclusion in the liturgical celebrations. The commission is to ensure that it receives the appropriate expert advice. It may be sometimes opportune to ask the advice of members of non-Christian religions about the religious or civil value of this or that element (cf. above, nos. 30–32).

---

138. SC, 40.

139. Cf. Congregation for Bishops, *Directory on the Pastoral Ministry of Bishops*, February 22, 1973, no. 84.

140. Cf. SC, 40.

If the situation requires it, this preliminary examination will be made in collaboration with the episcopal conferences of neighboring countries or those with the same culture (cf. above, nos. 33–51).

66.   The episcopal conference will present the proposal to the congregation before any experimentation takes place. The presentation should include a description of the innovations proposed, the reasons for their adoption, the criteria used, the times and places chosen for a preliminary experiment and an indication which groups will make it, and finally the acts of the discussion and the vote of the conference.

After an examination of the proposal carried out together by the episcopal conference and the congregation, the latter will grant the episcopal conference a faculty to make an experiment for a definite period of time, where this is appropriate.[141]

67.   The episcopal conference will supervise the process of experimentation,[142] normally with the help of the national or regional liturgical commission. The conference will also take care to ensure that the experimentation does not exceed the limits of time and place that were fixed. It will also ensure pastors and the faithful know about the limited and provisional nature of the experiment, and it will not give it publicity of a sort which could have an effect on the liturgical practice of the country. At the end of the period of experimentation, the episcopal conference will decide whether it matches up to the goal that was proposed or whether it needs revision, and it will communicate its conclusions to the congregation along with full information about the experiment.

68.   After examining the dossier, the congregation will issue a decree giving its consent, possibly with some qualifications, so that the changes can be introduced into the territory covered by the episcopal conference.

69.   The faithful, both lay people and clergy, should be well informed about the changes and prepared for their introduction into the liturgical celebrations. The changes are to be put into effect as circumstances require, with a transition period if this is appropriate (cf. above, no. 61).

CONCLUSION

70.   The Congregation for Divine Worship and the Discipline of the Sacraments presents these rules to the episcopal conferences to govern the work of liturgical inculturation envisaged by the Second Vatican Council as a response to the pastoral needs of peoples of different cultures. Liturgical inculturation should be carefully integrated into a pastoral plan for the inculturation of the Gospel into the many different human situations that are to be found. The Congregation for Divine Worship and the Discipline of the Sacraments hopes that each particular church, especially the young churches, will discover that the diversity

---

141. Cf. SC, 40.
142. Cf. SC, 40.

of certain elements of liturgical celebrations can be a source of enrichment, while respecting the substantial unity of the Roman rite, the unity of the whole church and the integrity of the faith transmitted to the saints for all time (cf. Jude 3).

The present instruction was prepared by the Congregation for Divine Worship and the Discipline of the Sacraments, by order of His Holiness Pope John Paul II, who approved it and ordered that it be published.

From the Congregation for Divine Worship and the Discipline of the Sacraments, January 25, 1994.

LITURGIAM AUTHENTICAM
ON THE USE OF
VERNACULAR LANGUAGES
IN THE PUBLICATION OF THE BOOKS
OF THE ROMAN LITURGY

FIFTH INSTRUCTION FOR THE
"RIGHT IMPLEMENTATION OF THE CONSTITUTION
ON THE SACRED LITURGY OF THE SECOND VATICAN COUNCIL"
(*SACROSANCTUM CONCILIUM*, ART. 36)

CONGREGATION FOR DIVINE WORSHIP AND
THE DISCIPLINE OF THE SACRAMENTS
MARCH 28, 2001

AN OVERVIEW OF *LITURGIAM AUTHENTICAM*

Christopher Carstens

AN AUTHENTIC LITURGY

It has been the long-standing practice of the Roman Catholic Church to identify her documents, especially those emanating from the Holy See, by the first words of the Latin text. In the present document, these words are *Liturgiam authenticam*.

But beyond naming the document and, at times, giving some insight into the document's content, the usefulness of these initial Latin words ceases. Indeed, for most of us today, the education needed to navigate the sea of Latin grammar and vocabulary is absent. What the reader needs, therefore, is a translation.

What does *liturgiam authenticam*—these particular words, as well as the document as a whole—mean? Literally, *liturgiam authenticam* means "authentic liturgy." A cursory look to the roots of these respective words helps make their meaning clear. "Authentic" has as a root the word *auto*, which means "self," and the word as a whole means "an action according to one's own power," in this case, Jesus's power. *Liturgy*, as many a Catholic student has come to know, means "a work done on behalf of the people," or, in the Christian sense, the Paschal work of Jesus that saved his people. An "authentic liturgy," then, is one where Jesus himself carries on his saving work for the entire world.

The meaning of the words *liturgiam authenticam* captures well the purpose of the document as a whole, for it gives translators of liturgical texts the guidelines for translating Latin liturgical texts into the many vernacular languages used in the celebration of the Roman Rite. And it does so with the aim of an "authentic liturgy"—where Jesus acts for our salvation—in each tongue.

PRAYING IN TONGUES

St. Peter is the founding Apostle of the Roman Church. Having preached in Rome and, in the year 67, died in Rome, his message of Jesus's saving work spread and took root throughout the Roman Empire. While the educated classes of Rome spoke the Greek language, the more common tongue was Latin. The early centuries of liturgical worship reflect these two languages: Greek was used in the city of Rome until about the fourth century when it was replaced by Latin. (At this same time, St. Jerome was commissioned to translate many of the Greek texts of the Sacred Scriptures into the more common, or *vulgar*, Latin tongue, which came to be known as the *Vulgate*.)

Latin liturgical and scriptural texts went where Rome went: first throughout Europe and North Africa, and later to the mission lands of greater Africa and the Americas. It was, then, a Roman Rite with a Latin language about which the Council Fathers directed the following in the year 1963:

Particular law remaining in force, the use of the Latin language is to be preserved in the Latin rites. But since the use of the mother tongue, whether in the Mass, the administration of the sacraments, or other parts of the liturgy, frequently may be of great advantage to the people, the limits of its use may be extended.[1]

Coming after 1,600 years of a nearly exclusive Latin-language liturgy, this grant is nothing short of revolutionary. These words—again, after sixteen centuries of Latin—are also not much in the way of practical advice about *how* to translate. Such a terse statement of principle is just that—a principle from which to work. It was, consequently, only the beginning of a long translation process of trial, error, confirmation, and prayer in the years and decades to follow.

A STRANGER IN A STRANGE LAND

Anyone having traveled to a foreign country, whose inhabitants speak a language different from his or her own, knows firsthand some of the challenges posed by communicating. For this very reason, there are a number of resources to help future travelers translate between their own languages and that of their international destinations. And while such resources—pocket dictionaries, phrase sheets, audio files for study—provide only a minimal amount of aid, nevertheless, the traveler finds that at the end even of a short visit, understanding and communicating in the other language is easier than at the beginning.

The Church's journey during the years following the Second Vatican Council was not unlike our travels to foreign lands. Like the traveler to another country, the Church has had to learn to translate from a liturgical language that she had been speaking for 1,600 years into the many vernacular languages of her children. And just as it is with some difficulty, some errors, and some small victories that the foreigner navigates in a strange land, so, too, the Church's translators have learned to translate over the course of time.

Part of the challenge is that translating is not simply a matter of uncovering and relating information. Rather, a *liturgical* translation must not only be accurate, but also suitable for public proclamation and singing, while being beautiful and memorable. From the start, it was recognized that translating in this way would take time.

After *Sacrosanctum Concilium's* (SC) norms on the use of Latin and vernacular languages (a mere four paragraphs!), the first significant document that expanded upon SC and gave more precise guidelines was the (roughly) eight-page document *Comme le prévoit* (CP). At bottom, and informing the directives of this Vatican document, is the translation principle known as "dynamic equivalence."[2] This translation principle places special emphasis on the receptor language (rather than the original language) and on the message conveyed (rather than the means used to convey it):

A faithful translation cannot be judged on the basis of individual words: the total context of this specific act of communication must be kept in mind, as well as the literary form proper to the respective language. . . .

---

1. *Sacrosanctum Concilium* (SC), 36.
2. See Rev. Paul Turner's article regarding this document on pages 409–425 in this collection.

Translations, therefore, must be faithful to the art of communication in all its various aspects, but especially in regard to the message itself, in regard to the audience for which it is intended, and in regard to the manner of expression. Even if in spoken communication the message cannot be separated from the manner of speaking, the translator should give first consideration to the meaning of the communication.[3]

Comme le prévoit was a necessary first step in the new work of translating liturgical texts, and it gave to the Church her initial translations in various vernacular languages.

FROM INITIAL STEPS TO STABLE TEXTS

The Church's first translations were good, but they needed to be better. Twenty-five years after *Sacrosanctum Concilium*, Pope John Paul II acknowledged the difficult and important job of bishops in producing the Church's first translations. He then continues:

But now the time has come to reflect upon certain difficulties that have subsequently emerged, to remedy certain defects or inaccuracies, to complete partial translations, to compose or approve chants to be used in the Liturgy, to ensure respect for the texts approved and lastly to publish liturgical books in a form that both testifies to the stability achieved and is worthy of the mysteries being celebrated.[4]

The first of two key tools for cultivating a mature liturgical language as John Paul II directed is the 1994 document on inculturation, *Varietates legitimae* (VL); the second is the 2001 instruction on translation itself, *liturgiam authenticam* (LA). It is necessary to take a first, albeit brief, look at *Varietates legitimae*, for it is in conjunction with this document that the norms found in *Liturgiam authenticam* are understood.[5]

Varietates legitimae is the fourth instruction for the proper implementation of *Sacrosanctum Concilium* and is an elaboration on the norms concerning liturgical adaptation or (as it came to be called) inculturation. The Council Fathers directed that "Provisions shall also be made, even in the revision of liturgical books, for legitimate variations and adaptations to different groups, regions, and peoples, especially in mission lands, provided the substantial unity of the Roman Rite is preserved; this should be borne in mind when rites are drawn up and rubrics devised."[6]

Adapting liturgical rites and texts to various cultures takes as its model the Incarnation of Christ himself.[7] In the one divine Person of Christ there exists the perfect harmony of the human and the divine natures. In him, the best of human nature meets the divine nature of God; this union undoes the fall, purifying and even divinizing human nature. All types of liturgical inculturation—music, gestures, art—follow the incarnate model. In the liturgy, the human

---

3. *Comme le prévoit* (CP), 7–8.
4. *Vicesimus quintus annus* (VQA), 20.
5. See *Liturgiam authenticam* (LA), 8.
6. SC, 38.
7. See *Varietates legitimae* (VL), 4.

elements meet the divine and, while retaining their own inherent goodness, are perfected. In terms of language, in the liturgy, our vernacular, cultural language encounters the heavenly language of the new and eternal Jerusalem, and in so doing, it harmonizes with the angels and saints around God's throne.

"WE HEAR THEM SPEAKING IN OUR OWN TONGUES OF THE MIGHTY ACTS OF GOD."[8]

In 2001, Pope John Paul II authorized the publication *Liturgiam authenticam*, the *Fifth Instruction "for the Right Implementation of the Constitution on the Sacred Liturgy of the Second Vatican Council."* Promulgated through the Congregation for Divine Worship and the Discipline of the Sacraments, the instruction opens:

> The Second Vatican Council strongly desired to preserve with care the authentic Liturgy [*liturgiam authenticam*], which flows forth from the Church's living and most ancient spiritual tradition, and to adapt it with pastoral wisdom to the genius of the various peoples so that the faithful might find in their full, conscious, and active participation in the sacred actions— especially the celebration of the Sacraments—an abundant source of graces and a means for their own continual formation in the Christian mystery.[9]

From the start, therefore, the document sees liturgical translations as a type of inculturation, the meeting and mutual enrichment of, on the one hand, the supernatural and spiritual tradition of the Church and, on the other hand, the genius of a particular people and culture. A liturgical translation, in short, ought to balance and reveal the substance of the Church's learned, Latin tongue with the beauty and accessibility of today's modern languages.

It must be noted that *Liturgiam authenticam* gives principles and directives applicable to modern languages as a whole. For example, when the document directs that "the translations should be characterized by a kind of language which is easily understandable, yet which at the same time preserves these texts' dignity, beauty, and doctrinal precision,"[10] such a norm applies to *any and all* modern tongues. A subsequent document—called the *Ratio translationis*[11]— may be composed that applies the Church's more universal norms on translations to each particular language used in the Roman Rite.

THE MEDIUM IS THE MESSAGE

Unlike *Comme le prévoit's* emphasis on "the meaning of the communication,"[12] *Liturgiam authenticam* gives more attention to the actual *medium* of the communication:

> [I]t is to be kept in mind in mind from the beginning that the translation of the liturgical texts of the Roman liturgy is not so much a work of creative innovation as it is of rendering the original texts faithfully and accurately

---

8. Acts of the Apostles 2:11.
9. LA, 1.
10. Ibid., 25.
11. See ibid., 9.
12. CP, 8.

into the vernacular language. . . . [T]he original text, insofar as possible, must be translated integrally and in the most exact manner, without omissions or additions in terms of their content, and without paraphrases or glosses.[13]

Put another way, the medium is an essential element in communicating the meaning. Such emphasis on the medium itself is often called "formal equivalence."

In paying closer attention to the particular words, syntax, and sentence structure of the Latin original, the translations subsequent to *Liturgiam authenticam* capture more accurately that balance between the traditional language and the modern tongue. In fact, each of *Liturgiam authenticam's* principles for translation can be seen through the model of the Incarnation where the supernatural and natural unite in balanced harmony.

Some norms, for example, are designed to safeguard and express divine and ecclesial dimension of an incarnate and inculturated liturgy. Translations, for example, should reflect transcendent and divine truths,[14] should be doctrinally precise,[15] must signify the unity of the Roman Rite,[16] and express that particularly Roman way of praying.[17]

Still other norms foster the other dimension of inculturation, that is, the human and cultural element. Consequently, translations need also to be easily understandable,[18] promote a sacred language in each of the vernacular tongues,[19] and promote the active participation of the people who worship.[20]

OVERVIEW

In total, the document is 133 articles in length, which, in itself, indicates the development in liturgical translation and practice since *Sacrosanctum Concilium's* few paragraphs nearly forty years earlier. After the introduction,[21] in which the progress subsequent to *Sacrosanctum Concilium* is recalled, the unity of the Roman Rite is emphasized, and the concepts of inculturation put forward, the document gives a brief, but significant, treatment of the "Choice of Languages to be Introduced into Liturgical Use."[22] Here, caution is put forward lest the number of languages introduced into the Roman Rite serve to fragment groups united by the one Roman Rite.[23]

The bulk of *Liturgiam authenticam* follows in Section II, "On the Translation of Liturgical Texts into Vernacular Languages."[24] This section gives translation

---

13. LA, 20.
14. See ibid., 19.
15. See ibid., 26.
16. See ibid., 5.
17. See ibid., 57.
18. See ibid., 25.
19. See ibid., 47.
20. See ibid., 28.
21. See ibid., 1–9.
22. See ibid., Section I, 10–18.
23. See ibid., 10, 12.
24. See ibid., 19–69.

principles for liturgical texts and scriptural texts (including Lectionaries); in both cases, the Latin editions of the liturgical books and the Latin Neo Vulgate are to serve as a basis and reference point for translation.[25] It also gives particular attention to the different types of texts found in a ritual book: prayers, introductions (also called *preanotanda*), rubrics, and texts meant to be said by the assembly as a whole. At bottom is the objective to make the traditional, supernatural content of the faith of the Roman Rite accessible to the men and women of today's modern culture.

Sections III-V of the document direct bishops and translators on the procedures to be followed for producing and publishing translations. Mention is made concerning the qualities that a translator ought to possess[26] and of the Mixed Commission[27] the translator may be a part of.[28] While bishops themselves may not do the actual translations, it is their responsibility—individually[29] and collectively[30]—to oversee their production, approve the texts, and submit them for approval to the Apostolic See. Detailed instructions are put forward to episcopal conferences on voting and submitting texts.[31] For its own part, the Congregation for Divine Worship and the Discipline of the Sacraments, in the name of the Holy Father, has the authority to approve translations that have been submitted.[32]

EVER OLD, EVER NEW

Before the Second Vatican Council's *Sacrosanctum Concilum* allowed for the liturgy in the mother tongue, Pope John XXIII, when opening the Council on October 11, 1962, gave in broad terms the mission of the Council. In short: "The substance of the ancient doctrine of the deposit of faith is one thing, and the way in which it is presented is another. And it is the latter that must be taken into great consideration."

Liturgiam authenticam embodies this very sentiment. The principles and guidelines now used to translate liturgical texts seek to convey the ancient substance of the faith in a language that today's Roman Rite Catholics can benefit from. The result of uniting the old and the new, the traditional and the modern, is a new and vigorous Christian life.

Such renewal—in liturgy, learning, and life—is the common desire of *Sacrosanctum Concilium* and *Liturgiam authenticam*. Early in the latter document, it announces that the instruction "envisions and seeks to prepare for a new era of liturgical renewal,"[33] while its final word is of catechetical renewal: "It is to be hoped that this new effort will provide stability in the life of the

---

25. See ibid., 23–24, 37.

26. See ibid., 75.

27. A Mixed Commission is a translation body employed by multiple, same-language Episcopal Conferences.

28. See LA, 92–105.

29. See ibid., 70.

30. See ibid., 71.

31. See ibid., 79.

32. See ibid., 80.

33. Ibid., 7.

Church, so as to lay a firm foundation for supporting the liturgical life of God's people and bringing about a solid renewal of catechesis."[34]

Will such a renewal happen? At this writing, the majority of liturgical books have yet to be translated according to the principles and methods outlined in *Liturgiam authenticam*. But if the Word of the Trinity can resound more clearly in today's culture—and if there are ears to hear—the new heavens and new earth will be remade after the image of Jesus, the Word, himself.

---

34. Ibid., 133.

LITURGIAM AUTHENTICAM

ON THE USE OF VERNACULAR LANGUAGES IN THE PUBLICATION OF THE BOOKS OF THE ROMAN LITURGY

FIFTH INSTRUCTION "FOR THE RIGHT IMPLEMENTATION OF THE CONSTITUTION ON THE SACRED LITURGY OF THE SECOND VATICAN COUNCIL" (*SACROSANCTUM CONCILIUM*, ART. 36)

CONGREGATION FOR DIVINE WORSHIP AND
THE DISCIPLINE OF THE SACRAMENTS
MARCH 20, 2001

1.   The Second Vatican Council strongly desired to preserve with care the authentic Liturgy, which flows forth from the Church's living and most ancient spiritual tradition, and to adapt it with pastoral wisdom to the genius of the various peoples so that the faithful might find in their full, conscious, and active participation in the sacred actions—especially the celebration of the Sacraments—an abundant source of graces and a means for their own continual formation in the Christian mystery.[1]

2.   Thereupon there began, under the care of the Supreme Pontiffs, the great work of renewal of the liturgical books of the Roman Rite, a work which included their translation[2] into vernacular languages, with the purpose of bringing about in the most diligent way that renewal of the sacred Liturgy which was one of the foremost intentions of the Council.

3.   The liturgical renewal thus far has seen positive results, achieved through the labor and the skill of many, but in particular of the Bishops, to whose care and zeal this great and difficult charge is entrusted. Even so, the greatest pru-

---

1. Second Vatican Council, Const. on the Sacred Liturgy *Sacrosanctum Concilium*, nn. 1, 14, 21, 33; cf. Council of Trent, Sess. XXII, 17 September 1562, Doctr. *De ss. Missae sacrif.*, c. 8: Denz.-Schönm. n. 1749.

2. The notion of the act of rendering a given text into another language is often expressed in Latin by the words *versio, conversio, interpretatio, redditio*, and even *mutatio, transductio* or similar words. Such is also the case in the Constitution *Sacrosanctum Concilium* and many other recent documents of the Holy See. Nevertheless, the sense often attributed to these terms in modern languages involves some variation or discrepancy from the original text and its meaning. For the purpose of excluding any ambiguity in this Instruction, which treats explicitly of the same theme, the word *translatio*, with its cognates, has been preferred. Even if their use presents some difficulty as regards Latin style or is redolent of a "neologism", such terms nevertheless have a certain international character and are able to communicate the present intent of the Apostolic See, as they are able to be employed in many languages without the danger of error.

dence and attention is required in the preparation of liturgical books marked by sound doctrine, which are exact in wording, free from all ideological influence, and otherwise endowed with those qualities by which the sacred mysteries of salvation and the indefectible faith of the Church are efficaciously transmitted by means of human language to prayer, and worthy worship is offered to God the Most High.[3]

4.   The Second Vatican Ecumenical Council in its deliberations and decrees assigned a singular importance to the liturgical rites, the ecclesiastical traditions, and the discipline of Christian life proper to those particular Churches, especially of the East, which are distinguished by their venerable antiquity, manifesting in various ways the tradition received through the Fathers from the Apostles.[4] The Council asked that the traditions of each of these particular Churches be preserved whole and intact. For this reason, even while calling for the revision of the various Rites in accordance with sound tradition, the Council set forth the principle that only those changes were to be introduced which would foster their specific organic development.[5] Clearly, the same vigilance is required for the safeguarding and the authentic development of the liturgical rites, the ecclesiastical traditions, and the discipline of the Latin Church, and in particular, of the Roman Rite. The same care must be brought also to the translation of the liturgical texts into vernacular languages. This is especially true as regards the Roman Missal, which will thus continue to be maintained as an outstanding sign and instrument of the integrity and unity of the Roman Rite.[6]

5.   Indeed, it may be affirmed that the Roman Rite is itself a precious example and an instrument of true inculturation. For the Roman Rite is marked by a signal capacity for assimilating into itself spoken and sung texts, gestures and rites derived from the customs and the genius of diverse nations and particular Churches—both Eastern and Western—into a harmonious unity that transcends the boundaries of any single region.[7] This characteristic is particularly evident in its orations, which exhibit a capacity to transcend the limits of their original situation so as to become the prayers of Christians in any time or place. In preparing all translations of the liturgical books, the greatest care is to be taken to maintain the identity and unitary expression of the Roman Rite,[8] not as a sort

3. Cf. S. Congr. for Divine Worship, Letter to the Presidents of the Conferences of Bishops *De linguis vulgaribus in S. Liturgiam inducendis*, 5 June 1976: *Notitiae* 12 (1976) 300–302.

4. Cf. Second Vatican Council, Decr. On Eastern Catholic Churches *OrientaliumEcclesiarum*, n. 1.

5. Cf. Second Vatican Council, Const. *Sacrosanctum Concilium*, n. 4; Decr. *OrientaliumEcclesiarum*, nn. 2, 6.

6. Cf. Second Vatican Council, Const. *Sacrosanctum Concilium*, n. 38; Pope Paul VI, Apost. Const. *Missale Romanum*: AAS 61 (1969) 217–222. Cf. *Missale Romanum*, editio typica tertia: *Institutio Generalis*, n. 399.

7. Congr. for Divine Worship and the Discipline of the Sacraments, Instr. IV "for the right implementation of the Second Vatican Council's Constitution on the Sacred Liturgy" *Varietates legitimae*, n. 17: AAS 87 (1995) 294–295; *Missale Romanum*, editio typica tertia: *Institutio Generalis*, n. 397.

8. Second Vatican Council, Const. *Sacrosanctum Concilium*, n. 38; *Missale Romanum*, editio typica tertia: *Institutio Generalis*, n. 397.

of historical monument, but rather as a manifestation of the theological realities of ecclesial communion and unity.[9] The work of inculturation, of which the translation into vernacular languages is a part, is not therefore to be considered an avenue for the creation of new varieties or families of rites; on the contrary, it should be recognized that any adaptations introduced out of cultural or pastoral necessity thereby become part of the Roman Rite, and are to be inserted into it in a harmonious way.[10]

6. Ever since the promulgation of the Constitution on the Sacred Liturgy, the work of the translation of the liturgical texts into vernacular languages, as promoted by the Apostolic See, has involved the publication of norms and the communication to the Bishops of advice on the matter. Nevertheless, it has been noted that translations of liturgical texts in various localities stand in need of improvement through correction or through a new draft.[11] The omissions or errors which affect certain existing vernacular translations—especially in the case of certain languages—have impeded the progress of the inculturation that actually should have taken place. Consequently, the Church has been prevented from laying the foundation for a fuller, healthier and more authentic renewal.

7. For these reasons, it now seems necessary to set forth anew, and in light of the maturing of experience, the principles of translation to be followed in future translations—whether they be entirely new undertakings or emendations of texts already in use—and to specify more clearly certain norms that have already been published, taking into account a number of questions and circumstances that have arisen in our own day. In order to take full advantage of the experience gained since the Council, it seems useful to express these norms from time to time in terms of tendencies that have been evident in past translations, but which are to be avoided in future ones. In fact, it seems necessary to consider anew the true notion of liturgical translation in order that the translations of the Sacred Liturgy into the vernacular languages may stand secure as the authentic voice of the Church of God.[12] This Instruction therefore envisions and seeks to prepare for a new era of liturgical renewal, which is consonant with the qualities and the traditions of the particular Churches, but which safeguards also the faith and the unity of the whole Church of God.

8. The norms set forth in this Instruction are to be substituted for all norms previously published on the matter, with the exception of the Instruction *Varietates legitimae*, published by the Congregation for Divine Worship and the Discipline of the Sacraments on 25 January 1994, in conjunction with which

---

9. Pope Paul VI, Address to the Consilium "for the implementation of the Constitution on the Sacred Liturgy," 14 October 1968: AAS 60 (1968) 736.

10. Cf. Congr. for Divine Worship and the Discipline of the Sacraments, Instr. *Varietates legitimae*, n. 36: AAS 87 (1995) 302; cf. also *Missale Romanum*, editio typica tertia: *Institutio Generalis*, n. 398.

11. Cf. Pope John Paul II, Apost. Letter *Vicesimus quintus annus*, 4 December 1988, n. 20: AAS 81 (1989) 916.

12. Cf. Pope Paul VI, Address to translators of liturgical texts into vernacular languages, 10 November 1965: AAS 57 (1965) 968.

the norms in this present Instruction are to be understood.[13] The norms contained in this Instruction are to be considered applicable to the translation of texts intended for liturgical use in the Roman Rite and, *mutatis mutandis*, in the other duly recognized Rites of the Latin Church.

9. When it may be deemed appropriate by the Congregation for Divine Worship and the Discipline of the Sacraments, a text will be prepared after consultation with Bishops, called a *"ratio translationis"*, to be set forth by the authority of the same Dicastery, in which the principles of translation found in this Instruction will be applied in closer detail to a given language. This document may be composed of various elements as the situation may require, such as, for example, a list of vernacular words to be equated with their Latin counterparts, the setting forth of principles applicable specifically to a given language, and so forth.

I
ON THE CHOICE OF VERNACULAR LANGUAGES TO BE INTRODUCED INTO LITURGICAL USE

10. To be considered first of all is the choice of the languages that it will be permissible to put into use in liturgical celebrations. It is appropriate that there be elaborated in each territory a pastoral plan that takes account of the spoken languages there in use, with a distinction being made between languages which the people spontaneously speak and those which, not being used for natural communication in pastoral activity, merely remain the object of cultural interest. In considering and drafting such a plan, due caution should be exercised lest the faithful be fragmented into small groups by means of the selection of vernacular languages to be introduced into liturgical use, with the consequent danger of fomenting civil discord, to the detriment of the unity of peoples as well as of the unity of the particular Churches and the Church universal.

11. In this plan, a clear distinction is to be made also between those languages, on the one hand, that are used universally in the territory for pastoral communication, and those, on the other hand, that are to be used in the Sacred Liturgy. In drawing up the plan, it will be necessary to take account also of the question of the resources necessary for supporting the use of a given language, such as the number of priests, deacons and lay collaborators capable of using the language, in addition to the number of experts and those trained for and capable of preparing translations of all of the liturgical books of the Roman Rite in accord with the principles enunciated here. Also to be considered are the financial and technical resources necessary for preparing translations and printing books truly worthy of liturgical use.

12. Within the liturgical sphere, moreover, a distinction necessarily arises between languages and dialects. In particular, dialects that do not support common academic and cultural formation cannot be taken into full liturgical use,

---

13. Congr. for Divine Worship and the Discipline of the Sacraments, Instr. *Varietates legitimae*: AAS 87 (1995) 288–314.

since they lack that stability and breadth that would be required for their being liturgical languages on a broader scale. In any event, the number of individual liturgical languages is not to be increased too greatly.[14] This latter is necessary so that a certain unity of language may be fostered within the boundaries of one and the same nation.

13.   Moreover, the fact that a language is not introduced into full liturgical use does not mean that it is thereby altogether excluded from the Liturgy. It may be used, at least occasionally, in the Prayer of the Faithful, in the sung texts, in the invitations or instructions given to the people, or in parts of the homily, especially if the language is proper to some of Christ's faithful who are in attendance. Nevertheless, it is always possible to use either the Latin language or another language that is widely used in that country, even if perhaps it may not be the language of all—or even of a majority—of the Christian faithful taking part, provided that discord among the faithful be avoided.

14.   Since the introduction of languages into liturgical use by the Church may actually affect the development of the language itself and may even be determinative in its regard, care is to be taken to promote those languages which—even while perhaps lacking a long literary tradition—seem capable of being employed by a greater number of persons. It is necessary to avoid any fragmentation of dialects, especially at the moment when a given dialect may be passing from spoken to written form. Instead, care should be taken to foster and to develop forms of speech that are common to human communities.

15.   It will be the responsibility of the Conference of Bishops to determine which of the prevailing languages are to be introduced into full or partial liturgical use in its territory. Their decisions require the *recognitio* of the Apostolic See before the work of translation is undertaken in any way.[15] Before giving its decision on this matter, the Conference of Bishops should not omit to seek the written opinion of experts and other collaborators in the work; these opinions, together with the other acts, are to be sent in written form to the Congregation for Divine Worship and the Discipline of the Sacraments, in addition to the *relatio* mentioned below, in art. n. 16.

16.   As regards the decision of the Conference of Bishops for the introduction of a vernacular language into liturgical use, the following are to be observed (cf. n. 79):[16]

---

14. S. Congr. for the Sacraments and Divine Worship, Letter to the Presidents of the Conferences of Bishops *De linguis vulgaribus in S. Liturgiam inducendis*, 5 June 1976: *Notitiae* 12 (1976) 300–301.

15. Cf. Second Vatican Council, Const. *Sacrosanctum Concilium*, n. 36 § 3; S. Congr. for the Sacraments and Divine Worship, Letter to the Presidents of the Conferences of Bishops *De linguis vulgaribus in S. Liturgiam inducendis*, 5 June 1976: *Notitiae* 12 (1976) 300–301.

16. Cf. Second Vatican Council, Const. *Sacrosanctum Concilium*, n. 36 § 3; Pope Paul VI, Apost. Letter *Sacram Liturgiam*, 25 January 1964: AAS 56 (1964) 143; S. Congr. of Rites, Inst. *Inter Oecumenici*, 26 September 1964, nn. 27–29: AAS 56 (1964) 883; cf. S. Congr. for the Sacraments and Divine Worship, letter to the Presidents of the Conferences of Bishops *De linguis vulgaribus in S. Liturgiam inducendis*, 5 June 1976: *Notitiae* 12 (1976) 300–302.

a) For the legitimate passage of decrees, a two-thirds vote by secret ballot is required on the part of those in the Conference of Bishops who have the right to cast a deliberative vote;

b) All of the acts to be examined by the Apostolic See, prepared in duplicate, signed by the President and Secretary of the Conference and duly affixed with its seal, are to be sent to the Congregation for Divine Worship and the Discipline of the Sacraments. In these acts are to be contained the following:

i) the names of the Bishops, or of those equivalent to them in law, who were present at the meeting,

ii) a report of the proceedings, which should contain the outcome of the votes pertaining to the individual decrees, including the number of those in favor, the number opposed, and the number abstaining;

iii) a clear exposition of the individual parts of the Liturgy into which the decision has been made to introduce the vernacular language;

c) In the *relatio* is to be included a clear explanation of the language involved, as well as the reasons for which the proposal has been made to introduce it into liturgical use.

17.　As for the use of "artificial" languages, proposed from time to time, the approval of texts as well as the granting of permission for their use in liturgical celebrations is strictly reserved to the Holy See. This faculty will be granted only for particular circumstances and for the pastoral good of the faithful, after consultation with the Bishops principally involved.[17]

18.　In celebrations for speakers of a foreign language, such as visitors, migrants, pilgrims, etc., it is permissible, with the consent of the diocesan Bishop, to celebrate the Sacred Liturgy in a vernacular language known to these people, using a liturgical book already approved by the competent authority with the subsequent *recognitio* of the Apostolic See.[18] If such celebrations recur with some frequency, the diocesan Bishop is to send a brief report to the Congregation for Divine Worship and the Discipline of the Sacraments, describing the circumstances, the number of participants, and the editions used.

---

17. Cf., for example, Congr. for Divine Worship and the Discipline of the Sacraments, *Normae de celebranda Missa in "esperanto"*, 20 March 1990: *Notitiae* 26 (1990) 693–694.

18. Cf. S. Congr. of Rites, Instr. *Inter Oecumenici*, n. 41: AAS 56 (1964) 886.

II
ON THE TRANSLATION OF LITURGICAL TEXTS INTO VERNACULAR LANGUAGES

1. GENERAL PRINCIPLES APPLICABLE TO ALL TRANSLATION

19.   The words of the Sacred Scriptures, as well as the other words spoken in liturgical celebrations, especially in the celebration of the Sacraments, are not intended primarily to be a sort of mirror of the interior dispositions of the faithful; rather, they express truths that transcend the limits of time and space. Indeed, by means of these words God speaks continually with the Spouse of his beloved Son, the Holy Spirit leads the Christian faithful into all truth and causes the word of Christ to dwell abundantly within them, and the Church perpetuates and transmits all that she herself is and all that she believes, even as she offers the prayers of all the faithful to God, through Christ and in the power of the Holy Spirit.[19]

20.   The Latin liturgical texts of the Roman Rite, while drawing on centuries of ecclesial experience in transmitting the faith of the Church received from the Fathers, are themselves the fruit of the liturgical renewal, just recently brought forth. In order that such a rich patrimony may be preserved and passed on through the centuries, it is to be kept in mind from the beginning that the translation of the liturgical texts of the Roman Liturgy is not so much a work of creative innovation as it is of rendering the original texts faithfully and accurately into the vernacular language. While it is permissible to arrange the wording, the syntax and the style in such a way as to prepare a flowing vernacular text suitable to the rhythm of popular prayer, the original text, insofar as possible, must be translated integrally and in the most exact manner, without omissions or additions in terms of their content, and without paraphrases or glosses. Any adaptation to the characteristics or the nature of the various vernacular languages is to be sober and discreet.[20]

21.   Especially in the translations intended for peoples recently brought to the Christian Faith, fidelity and exactness with respect to the original texts may themselves sometimes require that words already in current usage be employed in new ways, that new words or expressions be coined, that terms in the original text be transliterated or adapted to the pronunciation of the vernacular language,[21] or that figures of speech be used which convey in an integral manner the content of the Latin expression even while being verbally or syntacti-

---

19. Cf. Second Vatican Council, Const. *Sacrosanctum Concilium*, n. 33; Dogm. Const. on Divine Revelation *Dei Verbum*, n. 8; cf. *Missale Romanum*, editio typica tertia: *Institutio Generalis*, n. 2.

20. Cf. The Consilium "For the Implementation of the Constitution on the Sacred Liturgy", Letter to the Presidents of the Conferences of Bishops, 21 June 1967: *Notitiae* 3 (1967) 296; Card. Secr. of State, Letter to the Pro-Prefect of the Congr. for Divine Worship and the Discipline of the Sacraments, 1 February 1997.

21. Cf. Congr. for Divine Worship and the Discipline of the Sacraments, Instr. *Varietates legitimae*, 25 January 1994, n. 53: AAS 87 (1995) 308.

cally different from it. Such measures, especially those of greater moment, are to be submitted to the discussion of all the Bishops involved before being inserted into the definitive draft. In particular, caution should be exercised in introducing words drawn from non-Christian religions.[22]

22.   Adaptations of the texts according to articles 37–40 of the Constitution *Sacrosanctum Concilium* are to be considered on the basis of true cultural or pastoral necessity, and should not be proposed out of a mere desire for novelty or variety, nor as a way of supplementing or changing the theological content of the *editiones typicae*; rather, they are to be governed by the norms and procedures contained in the above-mentioned Instruction *Varietates legitimae.*[23] Accordingly, translations into vernacular languages that are sent to the Congregation for Divine Worship and the Discipline of the Sacraments for the *recognitio* are to contain, in addition to the translation itself and any adaptations foreseen explicitly in the *editiones typicae*, only adaptations or modifications for which prior written consent has been obtained from the same Dicastery.

23.   In the translation of texts of ecclesiastical composition, while it is useful with the assistance of historical and other scientific tools to consult a source that may have been discovered for the same text, nevertheless it is always the text of the Latin *editio typica* itself that is to be translated.

Whenever the biblical or liturgical text preserves words taken from other ancient languages (as, for example, the words *Alleluia* and *Amen*, the Aramaic words contained in the New Testament, the Greek words drawn from the *Trisagion* which are recited in the *Improperia* of Good Friday, and the *Kyrie eleison* of the Order of Mass, as well as many proper names) consideration should be given to preserving the same words in the new vernacular translation, at least as one option among others. Indeed, a careful respect for the original text will sometimes require that this be done.

24.   Furthermore, it is not permissible that the translations be produced from other translations already made into other languages; rather, the new translations must be made directly from the original texts, namely the Latin, as regards the texts of ecclesiastical composition, or the Hebrew, Aramaic, or Greek, as the case may be, as regards the texts of Sacred Scripture.[24] Furthermore, in the preparation of these translations for liturgical use, the *Nova Vulgata Editio*, promulgated by the Apostolic See, is normally to be consulted as an auxiliary tool, in a manner described elsewhere in this Instruction, in order to maintain the tradition of interpretation that is proper to the Latin Liturgy.

25.   So that the content of the original texts may be evident and comprehensible even to the faithful who lack any special intellectual formation, the translations should be characterized by a kind of language which is easily understandable, yet which at the same time preserves these texts' dignity, beauty, and doctrinal

---

22. Ibid., n. 39: AAS 87 (1995) 303.

23. Ibid.: AAS 87 (1995) 288–314; cf. *Missale Romanum*, editio typica tertia, *Institutio Generalis*, n. 397.

24. Cf. S. Congr. of Rites, Instr. *Inter Oecumenici*, n. 40 a: AAS 56 (1964) 885.

precision.[25] By means of words of praise and adoration that foster reverence and gratitude in the face of God's majesty, his power, his mercy and his transcendent nature, the translations will respond to the hunger and thirst for the living God that is experienced by the people of our own time, while contributing also to the dignity and beauty of the liturgical celebration itself.[26]

26.   The liturgical texts' character as a very powerful instrument for instilling in the lives of the Christian faithful the elements of faith and Christian morality,[27] is to be maintained in the translations with the utmost solicitude. The translation, furthermore, must always be in accord with sound doctrine.

27.   Even if expressions should be avoided which hinder comprehension because of their excessively unusual or awkward nature, the liturgical texts should be considered as the voice of the Church at prayer, rather than of only particular congregations or individuals; thus, they should be free of an overly servile adherence to prevailing modes of expression. If indeed, in the liturgical texts, words or expressions are sometimes employed which differ somewhat from usual and everyday speech, it is often enough by virtue of this very fact that the texts become truly memorable and capable of expressing heavenly realities. Indeed, it will be seen that the observance of the principles set forth in this Instruction will contribute to the gradual development, in each vernacular, of a sacred style that will come to be recognized as proper to liturgical language. Thus it may happen that a certain manner of speech which has come to be considered somewhat obsolete in daily usage may continue to be maintained in the liturgical context. In translating biblical passages where seemingly inelegant words or expressions are used, a hasty tendency to sanitize this characteristic is likewise to be avoided. These principles, in fact, should free the Liturgy from the necessity of frequent revisions when modes of expression may have passed out of popular usage.

28.   The Sacred Liturgy engages not only man's intellect, but the whole person, who is the "subject" of full and conscious participation in the liturgical celebration. Translators should therefore allow the signs and images of the texts, as well as the ritual actions, to speak for themselves; they should not attempt to render too explicit that which is implicit in the original texts. For the same reason, the addition of explanatory texts not contained in the *editio typica* is to be prudently avoided. Consideration should also be given to including in the vernacular editions at least some texts in the Latin language, especially those from the priceless treasury of Gregorian chant, which the Church recognizes as proper to the Roman Liturgy, and which, all other things being equal, is to be given

---

25. Cf. Pope Paul VI, Address to translators of liturgical texts into vernacular languages, 10 November 1965: AAS 57 (1965) 968; Congr. for Divine Worship and the Discipline of the Sacraments, Instr. *Varietates legitimae*, n. 53: AAS 87 (1995) 308.

26. Cf. Pope John Paul II, Address to a group of Bishops from the United States of America on their *Ad limina* visit, 4 December 1993, n. 2: AAS 86 (1994) 755–756.

27. Cf. Second Vatican Council, Const. *Sacrosanctum Concilium*, n. 33.

pride of place in liturgical celebrations.[28] Such chant, indeed, has a great power to lift the human spirit to heavenly realities.

29. It is the task of the homily and of catechesis to set forth the meaning of the liturgical texts,[29] illuminating with precision the Church's understanding regarding the members of particular Churches or ecclesial communities separated from full communion with the Catholic Church and those of Jewish communities, as well as adherents of other religions—and likewise, her understanding of the dignity and equality of all men.[30] Similarly, it is the task of catechists or of the homilist to transmit that right interpretation of the texts that excludes any prejudice or unjust discrimination on the basis of persons, gender, social condition, race or other criteria, which has no foundation at all in the texts of the Sacred Liturgy. Although considerations such as these may sometimes help one in choosing among various translations of a certain expression, they are not to be considered reasons for altering either a biblical text or a liturgical text that has been duly promulgated.

30. In many languages there exist nouns and pronouns denoting both genders, masculine and feminine, together in a single term. The insistence that such a usage should be changed is not necessarily to be regarded as the effect or the manifestation of an authentic development of the language as such. Even if it may be necessary by means of catechesis to ensure that such words continue to be understood in the "inclusive" sense just described, it may not be possible to employ different words in the translations themselves without detriment to the precise intended meaning of the text, the correlation of its various words or expressions, or its aesthetic qualities. When the original text, for example, employs a single term in expressing the interplay between the individual and the universality and unity of the human family or community (such as the Hebrew word 'adam, the Greek *anthropos,* or the Latin *homo*), this property of the language of the original text should be maintained in the translation. Just as has occurred at other times in history, the Church herself must freely decide upon the system of language that will serve her doctrinal mission most effectively, and should not be subject to externally imposed linguistic norms that are detrimental to that mission.

31. In particular: to be avoided is the systematic resort to imprudent solutions such as a mechanical substitution of words, the transition from the singular to

---

28. Cf., ibid., n. 116; S. Congr. of Rites, Instr. *Musicam sacram,* 5 March 1967, n. 50: AAS 59 (1967) 314; S. Congr. for Divine Worship, Letter sent to the Bishops with the volume *Iubilate Deo,* 14 April 1974: *Notitiae* 10 (1974) 123–124; Pope John Paul II, Letter *Dominicae Cenae,* 24 February 1980, n. 10: AAS 72 (1980) 135; Address to a group of Bishops from the United States of America on their *Ad limina* visit, 9 October 1998, n. 3: AAS 91 (1999) 353–354; cf. *Missale Romanum,* editio typica tertia, *Institutio Generalis,* n. 41.

29. Cf. Second Vatican Council, Const. *Sacrosanctum Concilium,* n. 35, 52; S. Congr. of Rites, Instr. *Inter Oecumenici,* n. 54: AAS 56 (1964) 890; cf. Pope John Paul II, Apost. Exhortation *Catechesi tradendae,* 16 October 1979, n. 48: AAS 71 (1979) 1316; *Missale Romanum,* editio typica tertia: *Institutio Generalis,* n. 65.

30. Cf., Second Vatican Council, Decr. on Ecumenism *Unitatis redintegratio;* Decl. on the Relationship of the Church to Non-Christian Religions *Nostra aetate.*

the plural, the splitting of a unitary collective term into masculine and feminine parts, or the introduction of impersonal or abstract words, all of which may impede the communication of the true and integral sense of a word or an expression in the original text. Such measures introduce theological and anthropological problems into the translation. Some particular norms are the following:

a) In referring to almighty God or the individual persons of the Most Holy Trinity, the truth of tradition as well as the established gender usage of each respective language are to be maintained.

b) Particular care is to be taken to ensure that the fixed expression "Son of Man" be rendered faithfully and exactly. The great Christological and typological significance of this expression requires that there should also be employed throughout the translation a rule of language that will ensure that the fixed expression remain comprehensible in the context of the whole translation.

c) The term "fathers", found in many biblical passages and liturgical texts of ecclesiastical composition, is to be rendered by the corresponding masculine word into vernacular languages insofar as it may be seen to refer to the Patriarchs or the kings of the chosen people in the Old Testament, or to the Fathers of the Church.

d) Insofar as possible in a given vernacular language, the use of the feminine pronoun, rather than the neuter, is to be maintained in referring to the Church.

e) Words which express consanguinity or other important types of relationship, such as "brother", "sister", etc., which are clearly masculine or feminine by virtue of the context, are to be maintained as such in the translation.

f) The grammatical gender of angels, demons, and pagan gods or goddesses, according to the original texts, is to be maintained in the vernacular language insofar as possible.

g) In all these matters it will be necessary to remain attentive to the principles set forth above, in nn. 27 and 29.

32.   The translation should not restrict the full sense of the original text within narrower limits. To be avoided on this account are expressions characteristic of commercial publicity, political or ideological programs, passing fashions, and those which are subject to regional variations or ambiguities in meaning. Academic style manuals or similar works, since they sometimes give way to such tendencies, are not to be considered standards for liturgical translation. On the other hand, works that are commonly considered "classics" in a given vernacular language may prove useful in providing a suitable standard for its vocabulary and usage.

33.   The use of capitalization in the liturgical texts of the Latin *editiones typicae* as well as in the liturgical translation of the Sacred Scriptures, for honorific or

otherwise theologically significant reasons, is to be retained in the vernacular language at least insofar as the structure of a given language permits.

2. OTHER NORMS PERTAINING TO THE TRANSLATION OF THE SACRED SCRIPTURES AND THE PREPARATION OF LECTIONARIES

34.   It is preferable that a version of the Sacred Scriptures be prepared in accordance with the principles of sound exegesis and of high literary quality, but also with a view to the particular exigencies of liturgical use as regards style, the selection of words, and the selection from among different possible interpretations.

35.   Wherever no such version of the Sacred Scriptures exists in a given language, it will be necessary to use a previously prepared version, while modifying the translation wherever appropriate so that it may be suitable for use in the liturgical context according to the principles set forth in this Instruction.

36.   In order that the faithful may be able to commit to memory at least the more important texts of the Sacred Scriptures and be formed by them even in their private prayer, it is of the greatest importance that the translation of the Sacred Scriptures intended for liturgical use be characterized by a certain uniformity and stability, such that in every territory there should exist only one approved translation, which will be employed in all parts of the various liturgical books. This stability is especially to be desired in the translation of the Sacred Books of more frequent use, such as the Psalter, which is the fundamental prayer book of the Christian people.[31] The Conferences of Bishops are strongly encouraged to provide for the commissioning and publication in their territories of an integral translation of the Sacred Scriptures intended for the private study and reading of the faithful, which corresponds in every part to the text that is used in the Sacred Liturgy.

37.   If the biblical translation from which the Lectionary is composed exhibits readings that differ from those set forth in the Latin liturgical text, it should be borne in mind that the *Nova Vulgata Editio* is the point of reference as regards the delineation of the canonical text.[32] Thus, in the translation of the deuterocanonical books and wherever else there may exist varying manuscript traditions, the liturgical translation must be prepared in accordance with the same manuscript tradition that the *Nova Vulgata* has followed. If a previously prepared translation reflects a choice that departs from that which is found in the *Nova Vulgata Editio* as regards the underlying textual tradition, the order of verses, or similar factors, the discrepancy needs to be remedied in the preparation

---

31. Cf. Pope Paul VI, Apost. Const. *Laudis canticum*, 1 November 1970, n. 8: AAS 63 (1971) 532–533; *Officium Divinum*, Liturgia Horarum iuxta Ritum romanum, editio typica altera 1985: *Institutio Generalis de Liturgia Horarum*, n. 100; Pope John Paul II, Apost. Letter *Vicesimus quintus annus*, n. 8 : AAS 81 (1989) 904–905.

32. Cf. Council of Trent, Session IV, 8 April 1546, *De libris sacris et de traditionibus recipiendis*, and *De vulgata editione Bibliorum et de modo interpretandi s. Scripturarum*: Denz.–Schönm., nn. 1501–1508; Pope John Paul II, Apost. Const. Scripturarum thesaurus,25 April 1979: AAS 71 (1979) 558–559.

of any Lectionary so that conformity with the Latin liturgical text may be maintained. In preparing new translations, it would be helpful, though not obligatory, that the numbering of the verses also follow that of the same text as closely as possible.

38.   It is often permissible that a variant reading of a verse be used, on the basis of critical editions and upon the recommendation of experts. However, this is not permissible in the case of a liturgical text where such a choice would affect those elements of the passage that are pertinent to its liturgical context, or whenever the principles found elsewhere in this Instruction would otherwise be neglected. For passages where a critical consensus is lacking, particular attention should be given to the choices reflected in the approved Latin text.[33]

39.   The delineation of the biblical *pericopai* is to conform entirely to the *Ordo lectionum Missae* or to the other approved and confirmed liturgical texts, as the case may be.

40.   With due regard for the requirements of sound exegesis, all care is to be taken to ensure that the words of the biblical passages commonly used in catechesis and in popular devotional prayers be maintained. On the other hand, great caution is to be taken to avoid a wording or style that the Catholic faithful would confuse with the manner of speech of non-Catholic ecclesial communities or of other religions, so that such a factor will not cause them confusion or discomfort.

41.   The effort should be made to ensure that the translations be conformed to that understanding of biblical passages which has been handed down by liturgical use and by the tradition of the Fathers of the Church, especially as regards very important texts such as the Psalms and the readings used for the principal celebrations of the liturgical year; in these cases the greatest care is to be taken so that the translation express the traditional Christological, typological and spiritual sense, and manifest the unity and the inter-relatedness of the two Testaments.[34] For this reason:

a) it is advantageous to be guided by the *Nova Vulgata* wherever there is a need to choose, from among various possibilities [of translation], that one which is most suited for expressing the manner in which a text has traditionally been read and received within the Latin liturgical tradition;

b) for the same purpose, other ancient versions of the Sacred Scriptures should also be consulted, such as the Greek version of the Old Testament

---

33. Cf. Pope Paul VI, Address to the Cardinals and Prelates of the Roman Curia, 23 December 1966, n. 11: AAS 59 (1967) 53–54; cf. Address to the Cardinals and Prelates of the Roman Curia, 22 December 1977: AAS 70 (1978) 43; cf. Pope John Paul II, Apost. Const. *Scripturarum thesaurus*, 25 April 1979: AAS 71 (1979) 558; *Nova Vulgata Bibliorum Sacrorum*, editio typica altera, 1986, Praefatio ad Lectorem.

34. Cf. Officium Divinum, Liturgia Horarum iuxta Ritum romanum, editio typica altera 1985: Institutio Generalis de Liturgia Horarum, nn. 100–109.

commonly known as the "Septuagint", which has been used by the Christian faithful from the earliest days of the Church;[35]

c) in accordance with immemorial tradition, which indeed is already evident in the above-mentioned "Septuagint" version, the name of almighty God expressed by the Hebrew *tetragrammaton* (YHWH) and rendered in Latin by the word Dominus, is to be rendered into any given vernacular by a word equivalent in meaning.

Finally, translators are strongly encouraged to pay close attention to the history of interpretation that may be drawn from citations of biblical texts in the writings of the Fathers of the Church, and also from those biblical images more frequently found in Christian art and hymnody.

42. While caution is advisable lest the historical context of the biblical passages be obscured, the translator should also bear in mind that the word of God proclaimed in the Liturgy is not simply an historical document. For the biblical text treats not only of the great persons and events of the Old and New Testaments, but also of the mysteries of salvation, and thus refers to the faithful of the present age and to their lives. While always maintaining due regard for the norm of fidelity to the original text, one should strive, whenever there is a choice to be made between different ways of translating a term, to make those choices that will enable the hearer to recognize himself and the dimensions of his own life as vividly as possible in the persons and events found in the text.

43. Modes of speech by which heavenly realities and actions are depicted in human form, or designated by means of limited, concrete terminology—as happens quite frequently in biblical language (i.e., anthropomorphisms)—often maintain their full force only if translated somewhat literally, as in the case of words in the *Nova Vulgata Editio* such as *ambulare, brachium, digitus, manus,* or *vultus* [*Dei*], as well as *caro, cornu, os, semen,* and *visitare.* Thus it is best that such terms not be explained or interpreted by more abstract or general vernacular expressions. As regards certain terms, such as those translated in the *Nova Vulgata* as *anima* and *spiritus,* the principles mentioned in above nn. 40–41 should be observed. Therefore, one should avoid replacing these terms by a personal pronoun or a more abstract term, except when this is strictly necessary in a given case. It should be borne in mind that a literal translation of terms which may initially sound odd in a vernacular language may for this very reason provoke inquisitiveness in the hearer and provide an occasion for catechesis.

44. In order for a translation to be more easily proclaimed, it is necessary that any expression be avoided which is confusing or ambiguous when heard, such that the hearer would fail to grasp its meaning.

45. Apart from that which is set forth in the *Ordo lectionum Missae,* the following norms are to be observed in the preparation of a Lectionary of biblical readings in a vernacular language:

---

35. Second Vatican Council, Const. *Dei Verbum,* n. 22.

a) Passages of Sacred Scripture contained in the *Praenotanda* of the *Ordo lectionum Missae* are to conform completely to the translation of the same passages as they occur within the Lectionary.

b) Likewise the titles, expressing the theme of the readings and placed at the head of them, are to retain the wording of the readings themselves, wherever such a correspondence exists in the *Ordo lectionum Missae*.

c) Finally, the words prescribed by the *Ordo lectionum Missae* for the beginning of the reading, called the *incipits*, are to follow as closely as possible the wording of the vernacular biblical version from which the readings are generally taken, refraining from following other translations. As regards those parts of the *incipits* that are not part of the biblical text itself, these are to be translated exactly from the Latin when preparing Lectionaries, unless the Conference of Bishops shall have sought and obtained the prior consent of the Congregation for Divine Worship and the Discipline of the Sacraments authorizing a different procedure for introducing the readings.

3. NORMS CONCERNING THE TRANSLATION OF OTHER LITURGICAL TEXTS

46.   The norms set forth above, and those regarding Sacred Scripture, should be applied, mutatis mutandis, in like manner to the texts of ecclesiastical composition.

47.   While the translation must transmit the perennial treasury of orations by means of language understandable in the cultural context for which it is intended, it should also be guided by the conviction that liturgical prayer not only is formed by the genius of a culture, but itself contributes to the development of that culture. Consequently it should cause no surprise that such language differs somewhat from ordinary speech. Liturgical translation that takes due account of the authority and integral content of the original texts will facilitate the development of a sacral vernacular, characterized by a vocabulary, syntax and grammar that are proper to divine worship, even though it is not to be excluded that it may exercise an influence even on everyday speech, as has occurred in the languages of peoples evangelized long ago.

48.   The texts for the principal celebrations occurring throughout the liturgical year should be offered to the faithful in a translation that is easily committed to memory, so as to render them usable in private prayers as well.

A. VOCABULARY

49.   Characteristic of the orations of the Roman liturgical tradition as well as of the other Catholic Rites is a coherent system of words and patterns of speech, consecrated by the books of Sacred Scripture and by ecclesial tradition, especially the writings of the Fathers of the Church. For this reason the manner of translating the liturgical books should foster a correspondence between the biblical text itself and the liturgical texts of ecclesiastical composition which

contain biblical words or allusions.[36] In the translation of such texts, the translator would best be guided by the manner of expression that is characteristic of the version of the Sacred Scriptures approved for liturgical use in the territories for which the translation is being prepared. At the same time, care should be taken to avoid weighting down the text by clumsily over-elaborating the more delicate biblical allusions.

50. Since the liturgical books of the Roman Rite contain many fundamental words of the theological and spiritual tradition of the Roman Church, every effort must be made to preserve this system of vocabulary rather than substituting other words that are alien to the liturgical and catechetical usage of the people of God in a given cultural and ecclesial context. For this reason, the following principles in particular are to be observed:

a) In translating words of greater theological significance, an appropriate degree of coordination should be sought between the liturgical text and the authoritative vernacular translation of the Catechism of the Catholic Church, provided that such a translation exists or is being prepared, whether in the language in question or in a very closely related language;

b) Whenever it would be inappropriate to use the same vocabulary or the same expression in the liturgical text as in the Catechism, the translator should be solicitous to render fully the doctrinal and theological meaning of the terms and of the text itself;

c) One should maintain the vocabulary that has gradually developed in a given vernacular language to distinguish the individual liturgical ministers, vessels, furnishings, and vesture from similar persons or things pertaining to everyday life and usage; words that lack such a sacral character are not to be used instead;

d) In translating important words, due constancy is to be observed throughout the various parts of the Liturgy, with due regard for n. 53 below.

51. On the other hand, a variety of vocabulary in the original text should give rise, insofar as possible, to a corresponding variety in the translations. The translation may be weakened and made trite, for example, by the use of a single vernacular term for rendering differing Latin terms such as *satiari, sumere, vegetari*, and *pasci*, on the one hand, or the nouns *caritas* and *dilectio* on the other, or the words *anima, animus, cor, mens*, and *spiritus*, to give some examples. Similarly, a deficiency in translating the varying forms of addressing God, such as *Domine, Deus, Omnipotens aeterne Deus, Pater*, and so forth, as well as the various words expressing supplication, may render the translation monotonous and obscure the rich and beautiful way in which the relationship between the faithful and God is expressed in the Latin text.

---

36. Cf. Pope Paul VI, Apost. Exhortation *Marialis cultus*, 11 February 1974, n. 30: AAS 66 (1974) 141–142.

52.   The translator should strive to maintain the denotation, or primary sense of the words and expressions found in the original text, as well as their connotation, that is, the finer shades of meaning or emotion evoked by them, and thus to ensure that the text be open to other orders of meaning that may have been intended in the original text.

53.   Whenever a particular Latin term has a rich meaning that is difficult to render into a modern language (such as the words *munus, famulus, consubstantialis, propitius*, etc.) various solutions may be employed in the translations, whether the term be translated by a single vernacular word or by several, or by the coining of a new word, or perhaps by the adaptation or transcription of the same term into a language or alphabet that is different from the original text (cf. above, n. 21), or the use of an already existing word which may bear various meanings.[37]

54.   To be avoided in translations is any psychologizing tendency, especially a tendency to replace words treating of the theological virtues by others expressing merely human emotions. As regards words or expressions conveying a properly divine notion of causality (e.g., those expressed in Latin by the words "*praesta, ut . . .*"), one should avoid employing words or expressions denoting a merely extrinsic or profane sort of assistance instead.

55.   Certain words that may appear to have been introduced into the Latin liturgical text for reasons of meter or other technical or literary reasons convey, in reality, a properly theological content, so that they are to be preserved, insofar as possible, in the translation. It is necessary to translate with the utmost precision those words that express aspects of the mysteries of faith and the proper disposition of the Christian soul.

56.   Certain expressions that belong to the heritage of the whole or of a great part of the ancient Church, as well as others that have become part of the general human patrimony, are to be respected by a translation that is as literal as possible, as for example the words of the people's response *Et cum spiritu tuo*, or the expression *mea culpa, mea culpa, mea maxima culpa* in the Act of Penance of the Order of Mass.

B. SYNTAX, STYLE AND LITERARY GENRE

57.   That notable feature of the Roman Rite, namely its straightforward, concise and compact manner of expression, is to be maintained insofar as possible in the translation. Furthermore, the same manner of rendering a given expression is to be maintained throughout the translation, insofar as feasible. These principles are to be observed:

   a) The connection between various expressions, manifested by subordinate and relative clauses, the ordering of words, and various forms of parallelism, is

---

37. Cf. Congr. for Divine Worship and the Discipline of the Sacraments, Instr. *Varietates legitimae*, n. 53: AAS 87 (1995) 308.

to be maintained as completely as possible in a manner appropriate to the vernacular language.

b) In the translation of terms contained in the original text, the same person, number, and gender is to be maintained insofar as possible.

c) The theological significance of words expressing causality, purpose or consequence (such as *ut, ideo, enim,* and *quia*) is to be maintained, though different languages may employ varying means for doing so.

d) The principles set forth above, in n. 51, regarding variety of vocabulary, are to be observed also in the variety of syntax and style (for example, in the location within the Collect of the vocative addressed to God).

58.   The literary and rhetorical genres of the various texts of the Roman Liturgy are to be maintained.[38]

59.   Since liturgical texts by their very nature are intended to be proclaimed orally and to be heard in the liturgical celebration, they are characterized by a certain manner of expression that differs from that found in everyday speech or in texts intended be read silently. Examples of this include recurring and recognizable patterns of syntax and style, a solemn or exalted tone, alliteration and assonance, concrete and vivid images, repetition, parallelism and contrast, a certain rhythm, and at times, the lyric of poetic compositions. If it is sometimes not possible to employ in the translation the same stylistic elements as in the original text (as often happens, for example, in the case of alliteration or assonance), even so, the translator should seek to ascertain the intended effect of such elements in the mind of the hearer as regards thematic content, the expression of contrast between elements, emphasis, and so forth. Then he should employ the full possibilities of the vernacular language skillfully in order to achieve as integrally as possible the same effect as regards not only the conceptual content itself, but the other aspects as well. In poetic texts, greater flexibility will be needed in translation in order to provide for the role played by the literary form itself in expressing the content of the texts. Even so, expressions that have a particular doctrinal or spiritual importance or those that are more widely known are, insofar as possible, to be translated literally.

60.   A great part of the liturgical texts are composed with the intention of their being sung by the priest celebrant, the deacon, the cantor, the people, or the choir. For this reason, the texts should be translated in a manner that is suitable for being set to music. Still, in preparing the musical accompaniment, full account must be taken of the authority of the text itself. Whether it be a question of the texts of Sacred Scripture or of those taken from the Liturgy and already duly confirmed, paraphrases are not to be substituted with the intention of making them more easily set to music, nor may hymns considered generically equivalent be employed in their place.[39]

---

38. Cf. ibid.; cf. *Missale Romanum,* editio typica tertia: *Institutio Generalis,* n. 392.

39. Cf. *Missale Romanum,* editio typica tertia: *Institutio Generalis,* nn. 53, 57.

61.   Texts that are intended to be sung are particularly important because they convey to the faithful a sense of the solemnity of the celebration, and manifest unity in faith and charity by means of a union of voices.[40] The hymns and canticles contained in the modern *editiones typicae* constitute a minimal part of the historic treasury of the Latin Church, and it is especially advantageous that they be preserved in the printed vernacular editions, even if placed there in addition to hymns composed originally in the vernacular language. The texts for singing that are composed originally in the vernacular language would best be drawn from Sacred Scripture or from the liturgical patrimony.

62.   Certain liturgical texts of ecclesiastical composition are associated with ritual actions expressed by a particular posture, gesture, or the use of signs. Thus, in preparing appropriate translations it will be advantageous to consider such factors as the time required for reciting the words, their suitability for being sung or continually repeated, etc.

4. NORMS PERTAINING TO SPECIAL TYPES OF TEXTS

A. THE EUCHARISTIC PRAYERS

63.   The high point of all liturgical action is the celebration of the Mass, in which the Eucharistic Prayer or Anaphora in turn occupies a pre-eminent place.[41] For this reason, the approved translations of the approved Eucharistic Prayers require the utmost care, especially as regards the sacramental formulae, for which a particular procedure is prescribed below, in nn. 85–86.

64.   Without real necessity, successive revisions of translations should not notably change the previously approved vernacular texts of the Eucharistic Prayers which the faithful will have committed gradually to memory. Whenever a completely new translation is necessary, the principles given below, in n. 74, are to be observed.

B. THE CREED OR PROFESSION OF FAITH

65.   By means of the Creed (*Symbolum*) or profession of faith, the whole gathered people of God respond to the word of God proclaimed in the Sacred Scriptures and expounded in the homily, recalling and confessing the great mysteries of the faith by means of a formula approved for liturgical use.[42] The Creed is to be translated according to the precise wording that the tradition of the Latin Church has bestowed upon it, including the use of the first person singular, by which is clearly made manifest that "the confession of faith is handed down in the Creed, as it were, as coming from the person of the whole Church, united by means of

---

40. Cf. Pope John Paul II, Apost. Letter *Dies Domini*, n. 50: AAS 90 (1998) 745.

41. *Missale Romanum*, editio typica tertia: *Institutio Generalis*, n. 78.

42. Cf. ibid., n. 67.

the Faith."[43] In addition, the expression *carnis resurrectionem* is to be translated literally wherever the Apostles' Creed is prescribed or may be used in the Liturgy.[44]

C. THE "PRAENOTANDA" AND THE TEXTS OF A RUBRICAL OR JURIDICAL NATURE

66.   All parts of the various liturgical books are to be translated in the same order in which they are set forth in the Latin text of the *editio typica*, including the *institutiones generales*, the *praenotanda*, and the instructions supplied in the various rites, which function as a support for the whole structure of the Liturgy.[45] The distinction between the various liturgical roles and the designation of the liturgical ministers by their proper titles is to be maintained in the translation precisely as it is in the rubrics of the *editio typica*, maintaining due regard for the principles mentioned in n. 50c above.[46]

67.   Wherever such *praenotanda* or other texts of the *editiones typicae* explicitly call for adaptations or specific applications to be introduced by the Conferences, as for example the parts of the Missal that are to be defined more specifically by the Conference of Bishops,[47] it is permissible to insert these prescriptions into the text, provided that they have received the *recognitio* of the Apostolic See. It is not required in such cases, by their very nature, to translate these parts verbatim as they stand in the *editio typica*. Nevertheless, a mention is to be made of the decree of approbation of the Conference of Bishops and of the *recognitio* granted by the Congregation for Divine Worship and the Discipline of the Sacraments.

68.   At the beginning of the vernacular editions are to be placed the decrees by which the *editiones typicae* have been promulgated by the competent Dicastery of the Apostolic See, with due regard for the prescriptions found in n. 78. Also to be placed there are the decrees by means of which the *recognitio* of the Holy See has been granted for the translations, or at least the mention of the *recognitio* is to be made together with the date, month, year, and protocol number of the decree issued by the Dicastery. Since these are also historical documents, the names of the Dicasteries or other organ of the Apostolic See are to be translated exactly as they appeared on the date of promulgation of the document, rather than being altered to reflect the present name of the same or equivalent body.

69.   The editions of the liturgical books prepared in the vernacular language are to correspond in every part to the titles, the ordering of texts, the rubrics, and the system of numbering that appears in the *editio typica*, unless otherwise directed in the *praenotanda* of the same books. Furthermore, any additions

---

43. St. Thomas Aquinas, *Summa Theologiae*, IIa IIae, I, 9.

44. Cf. S. Congr. for the Doctrine of the Faith, *Communicatio*, 2 December 1983: *Notitiae* 20 (1984) 181.

45. Cf. Second Vatican Council, Const. *Sacrosanctum Concilium*, n. 63b; S. Congr. for Divine Worship, Decl. *De interpretationibus popularibus novorum textuum liturgicorum*, 15 September 1969: *Notitiae* 5 (1969) 333–334.

46. Cf. Congr. for the Clergy et al., Instr. *Ecclesiae de mysterio*, 15 August 1997, art. 1–3, 6–12: AAS 89 (1997) 861–865, 869–874.

47. Cf. *Missale Romanum*, editio typica tertia: *Institutio Generalis*, n. 389.

approved by the Congregation for Divine Worship and the Discipline of the Sacraments are to be inserted either in a supplement or appendix, or in their proper place in the book, as the Apostolic See shall have directed.

III
ON THE PREPARATION OF TRANSLATIONS AND THE ESTABLISHMENT OF COMMISSIONS

1. THE MANNER OF PREPARING A TRANSLATION

70.   On account of the entrusting to the Bishops of the task of preparing liturgical translations,[48] this work is committed in a particular way to the liturgical commission duly established by the Conference of Bishops. Wherever such a commission is lacking, the task of preparing the translation is to be entrusted to two or three Bishops who are expert in liturgical, biblical, philological or musical studies.[49] As regards the examination and approbation of the texts, each individual Bishop must regard this duty as a direct, solemn and personal fiduciary responsibility.

71.   In nations where many languages are used, the translations into individual vernacular languages are to be prepared and submitted to the special examination of those Bishops involved.[50] Nevertheless, it is the Conference of Bishops as such that retains the right and the power to posit all of those actions mentioned in this Instruction as pertaining to the Conference; thus, it pertains to the full Conference to approve a text and to submit it for the *recognitio* of the Apostolic See.

72.   The Bishops, in fulfilling their mission of preparing translations of liturgical texts, are carefully to ensure that the translations be the fruit of a truly common effort rather than of any single person or of a small group of persons.

73.   Whenever a Latin *editio typica* of a given liturgical book is promulgated, it is necessary that it be followed in a timely manner by the preparation of a translation of the same book, which the Conference of Bishops is to send, after having duly approved it, to the Congregation for Divine Worship and the Discipline of the Sacraments, to whom it pertains to grant the *recognitio* according to the norms set forth in this Instruction, and also in keeping with others established by the law.[51] However, when it is a question of a change affecting only a part of the Latin *editio typica* or the insertion of new elements, these new elements are to be maintained fully and faithfully in all succeeding editions produced in the vernacular language.

---

48. Cf. Second Vatican Council, Const. *Sacrosanctum Concilium*, n. 36; cf. *Code of Canon Law*, can 838 § 3.

49. Cf. Second Vatican Council, Const. *Sacrosanctum Concilium*, n. 44; S. Congr. of Rites, Instr. *Inter Oecumenici*, nn. 40 b, 44: AAS (1964) 885–886.

50. Cf. S. Congr. of Rites, Instr. *Inter Oecumenici*, n. 40 d: AAS 56 (1964) 886.

51. Cf., *Code of Canon Law*, can. 838.

74.   A certain stability ought to be maintained whenever possible in successive editions prepared in modern languages. The parts that are to be committed to memory by the people, especially if they are sung, are to be changed only for a just and considerable reason. Nevertheless, if more significant changes are necessary for the purpose of bringing the text into conformity with the norms contained in this Instruction, it will be preferable to make such changes at one time, rather than prolonging them over the course of several editions. In such case, a suitable period of catechesis should accompany the publication of the new text.

75.   The translation of liturgical texts requires not only a rare degree of expertise, but also a spirit of prayer and of trust in the divine assistance granted not only to the translators, but to the Church herself, throughout the whole process leading to the definitive approbation of the texts. The readiness to see one's own work examined and revised by others is an essential trait that should be evident in one who undertakes the translation of liturgical texts. Furthermore, all translations or texts prepared in vernacular languages, including those of the *praenotanda* and the rubrics, are to be anonymous with respect to persons as well as to institutions consisting of several persons, as in the case of the *editiones typicae*.[52]

76.   In implementing the decisions of the Second Vatican Council, it has become evident from the mature experience of the nearly four decades of the liturgical renewal that have elapsed since the Council that the need for translations of liturgical texts—at least as regards the major languages—is experienced not only by the Bishops in governing the particular Churches, but also by the Apostolic See, for the effective exercise of her universal solicitude for the Christian faithful in the City of Rome and throughout the world. Indeed, in the Diocese of Rome, especially in many of the Churches and institutes of the City that depend in some way on the Diocese or the organs of the Holy See, as well as in the activity of the Dicasteries of the Roman Curia and the Pontifical Representations, the major languages are widely and frequently employed even in liturgical celebrations. For this reason, it has been determined that in the future, the Congregation for Divine Worship and the Discipline of the Sacraments will be involved more directly in the preparation of the translations into these major languages.

77.   Furthermore, as regards the major languages, an integral translation of all of the liturgical books is to be prepared in a timely manner. Translations heretofore approved *ad interim* are to be perfected or thoroughly revised, as the case requires, and afterwards submitted to the Bishops for definitive approbation in accordance with the norms set forth in this Instruction. Finally, they are to be sent to the Congregation for Divine Worship and the Discipline of the Sacraments with a request for the *recognitio*.[53]

78.   In the case of the less diffused languages that are approved for liturgical use, the larger or more important liturgical books, in particular, may be translated, according to pastoral necessity and with the consent of the Congregation

---

52. Cf. S. Congr. for Divine Worship, Decl., 15 May 1970: *Notitiae* 6 (1970) 153.
53. Cf. Pope John Paul II, Apost. Letter *Vicesimus quintus annus*, n. 20: AAS 81(1989) 916.

for Divine Worship and the Discipline of the Sacraments. The individual books thus selected are to be translated integrally, in the manner described in n. 66 above. As for the decrees, the *institutio generalis*, the *praenotanda* and the instructions, it is permissible to print them in a language that is different from the one used in the celebration, but nevertheless intelligible to the priest or deacon celebrants in the same territory. It is permissible to print the Latin text of the decrees, either in addition to the translation or instead of it.

2. THE APPROBATION OF THE TRANSLATION AND THE PETITION FOR THE *RECOGNITIO* OF THE APOSTOLIC SEE

79. The approbation liturgical texts, whether definitive, on the one hand, or *ad interim* or *ad experimentum* on the other, must be made by decree. In order that this be legitimately executed, the following are to be observed:[54]

a) For the legitimate passage of decrees, a two-thirds vote by secret ballot is required on the part of all who enjoy the right to a deliberative vote of the Conference of Bishops.

b) All acts to be examined by the Apostolic See, prepared in duplicate, signed by the President and Secretary of the Conference, and duly affixed with its seal, are to be sent to the Congregation for Divine Worship and the Discipline of the Sacraments. In these acts are to be contained:

i) the names of the Bishops or of those equivalent in law who were present at the meeting,

ii) a *relatio* of the proceedings, which should contain the results of the voting for each individual decree, including the number in favor, the number opposed, and the number abstaining.

c) Two copies are to be sent of the liturgical texts prepared in the vernacular language; insofar as possible, the same text should be sent on computer diskette;

d) In the particular *relatio*, the following should be explained clearly:[55]

i) the process and criteria followed in the work of translation.

ii) a list of the persons participating at various stages in the work, together with a brief note describing the qualifications and expertise of each.

---

54. Cf. Second Vatican Council, Const. *Sacrosanctum Concilium*, n. 36; Pope Paul VI, Apost. Letter *Sacram Liturgiam*, IX: AAS 56 (1964) 143; S. Congr. of Rites, Instr. *Inter Oecumenici*, nn. 27–29: AAS 56 (1964) 883; Centr. Comm. for Coordinating Post-Conciliar Works and Interpreting the Decrees of the Council, Response to Dubium: AAS 60 (1968) 361; cf. S. Congr. for the Sacraments and Divine Worship, Letter to thePresidents of the Conferences of Bishops *De linguis vulgaribus in S. Liturgiam inducendis*, 5 June 1976: Notitiae 12 (1976) 300–302.

55. Cf. S. Congr. of Rites, Instr. *Inter Oecumenici*, n. 30: AAS 56 (1964) 883; S. Congr. for the Sacraments and Divine Worship, Letter to the Presidents of the Conferences of Bishops *De linguis vulgaribus in S. Liturgiam inducendis*, 5 June 1976: Notitiae 12 (1976) 302.

iii) any changes that may have been introduced in relation to the previous translation of the same edition of the liturgical book are to be indicated clearly, together with the reasons for making such changes;

iv) an indication of any changes with respect to the content of the Latin *editio typica* together with the reasons which they were necessary, and with a notation of the prior consent of the Apostolic See for the introduction of such changes.

80.   The practice of seeking the *recognitio* from the Apostolic See for all translations of liturgical books[56] accords the necessary assurance of the authenticity of the translation and its correspondence with the original texts. This practice both expresses and effects a bond of communion between the successor of blessed Peter and his brothers in the Episcopate. Furthermore, this *recognitio* is not a mere formality, but is rather an exercise of the power of governance, which is absolutely necessary (in the absence of which the act of the Conference of Bishops entirely in no way attains legal force); and modifications—even substantial ones—may be introduced by means of it.[57] For this reason it is not permissible to publish, for the use of celebrants or for the general public, any liturgical texts that have been translated or recently composed, as long as the *recognitio* is lacking. Since the *lex orandi* must always be in harmony with the *lex credendi* and must manifest and support the faith of the Christian people, the liturgical translations will not be capable of being worthy of God without faithfully transmitting the wealth of Catholic doctrine from the original text into the vernacular version, in such a way that the sacred language is adapted to the dogmatic reality that it contains.[58] Furthermore, it is necessary to uphold the principle according to which each particular Church must be in accord with the universal Church not only as regards the doctrine of the Faith and the sacramental signs, but also as regards those practices universally received through Apostolic and continuous tradition.[59] For these reasons, the required *recognitio* of the Apostolic See is intended to ensure that the translations themselves, as well as any variations introduced into them, will not harm the unity of God's people, but will serve it instead.[60]

81.   The *recognitio* granted by the Apostolic See is to be indicated in the printed editions together with the *concordat cum originali* signed by the chairman of the liturgical commission of the Conference of Bishops, as well as the *imprimatur*

---

56. Cf. Second Vatican Council, Const. *Sacrosanctum Concilium*, n. 36; S. Congr. of Rites, Instr. *Inter Oecumenici*, nn. 20–21, 31: AAS (1964) 882, 884; *Code of Canon Law*, can. 838.

57. Cf. Pont. Comm. for the Revision of the Code of Canon Law, Acta: *Communicationes* 15 (1983) 173.

58. Cf. Pope Paul VI, Address to the Members and Experts of the Consilium "for the implementation of the Constitution on the Sacred Liturgy", 13 October 1966: AAS 58 (1966) 1146; Address to the Members and Experts of the Consilium "for the implementation of the Constitution on the Sacred Liturgy", 14 October 1968: AAS 60 (1968) 734.

59. *Missale Romanum*, editio typica tertia, *Institutio Generalis*, n. 397.

60. Cf. Second Vatican Council, Dogm. Const. On the Church *Lumen Gentium*, n. 13; cf. Pope John Paul II, Apost. Letter (Motu proprio) *Apostolos suos*, 21 May 1998, n. 22: AAS 90 (1998) 655–656.

undersigned by the President of the same Conference.[61] Afterwards, two copies of each printed edition are to be sent to the Congregation for Divine Worship and the Discipline of the Sacraments.[62]

82. Any alteration of a liturgical book that has already been approved by the Conference of Bishops with the subsequent *recognitio* of the Apostolic See, as regards either the selection of texts from liturgical books already published or the changing of the arrangement of the texts, must be done according to the procedure established above, in n. 79, with due regard also for the prescriptions set forth in n. 22. Any other manner of proceeding in particular circumstances may be employed only if it is authorized by the Statutes of the Conference of Bishops or equivalent legislation approved by the Apostolic See.[63]

83. As regards the editions of liturgical books prepared in vernacular languages, the approbation of the Conference of Bishops as well as the *recognitio* of the Apostolic See are to be regarded as valid only for the territory of the same Conference, so that these editions may not be used in another territory without the consent of the Apostolic See, except in those particular circumstances mentioned above, in nn. 18 and 76, and in keeping with the norms set forth there.

84. Wherever a certain Conference of Bishops lacks sufficient resources or instruments for the preparation and printing of a liturgical book, the President of that Conference is to explain the situation to the Congregation for Divine Worship and the Discipline of the Sacraments, to whom it pertains to establish or to approve any different arrangement, such as the publication of liturgical books together with other Conferences or the use of those already employed elsewhere. Such a concession shall only be granted by the Holy See *ad actum*.

3. ON THE TRANSLATION AND APPROBATION OF SACRAMENTAL FORMULAE

85. As regards the translation of the sacramental formulae, which the Congregation for Divine Worship must submit to the judgment of the Supreme Pontiff, the following principles are to be observed besides those required for the translation of other liturgical texts:[64]

a) In the case of the English, French, German, Italian, Portuguese and Spanish languages, all of the acts are to be presented in that language;

---

61. Cf. *Code of Canon Law*, can. 838 § 3.

62. Cf. S. Congr. for the Sacraments and Divine Worship, Letter to the Presidents of the Conferences of Bishops *De linguis vulgaribus in S. Liturgiam inducendis*, 5 June 1976: *Notitiae* 12 (1976) 302.

63. Cf. ibid., 300–302.

64. Cf., S. Congr. for Divine Worship, Letter to the Presidents of the Conferences of Bishops *De normis servandis quoad libros liturgicos in vulgus edendos, illorum translatione in linguas hodiernas peracta*, 25 October 1973: AAS 66 (1974) 98–99; S. Congr. for the Sacraments and Divine Worship, Letter to the Presidents of the Conferences of Bishops *De linguis vulgaribus in S. Liturgiam inducendis*, 5 June 1976: *Notitiae* 12 (1976) 300–302.

b) If the translation differs from a vernacular text already prepared and approved in the same language, it is necessary to explain the reason for the introduction of the change;

c) The President and Secretary of the Conference of Bishops should testify that the translation has been approved by the Conference of Bishops.

86. In the case of the less widely diffused languages, everything shall be prepared as set forth above. The acts, however, are to be prepared with great care in one of the languages mentioned above as more widely known, rendering the meaning of each individual word of the vernacular language. The President and Secretary of the Conference of Bishops, after any necessary consultation with trustworthy experts, are to testify to the authenticity of the translation.[65]

4. ON A UNIFIED VERSION OF THE LITURGICAL TEXTS

87. It is recommended that there be a single translation of the liturgical books for each vernacular language, brought about by means of coordination among the Bishops of those regions where the same language is spoken.[66] If this proves truly impossible because of the circumstances, the individual Conferences of Bishops, after consultation with the Holy See, may decide either to adapt a previously existing translation or to prepare a new one. In either case, the *recognitio* of their acts is to be sought from the Congregation for Divine Worship and the Discipline of the Sacraments.

88. In the case of the Order of Mass and those parts of the Sacred Liturgy that call for the direct participation of the people, a single translation should exist in a given language,[67] unless a different provision is made in individual cases.

89. Texts which are common to several Conferences, as mentioned above in nn. 87–88, are ordinarily to be approved by each of the individual Conferences of Bishops which must use them, before the confirmation of the texts is granted by the Apostolic See.[68]

90. With due regard for Catholic traditions and for all of the principles and norms contained in this Instruction, an appropriate relationship or coordination is greatly to be desired, whenever possible, between any translations intended for common use in the various Rites of the Catholic Church, especially as regards

---

65. Cf. S. Congr. for Divine Worship, Letter to the Presidents of the Conferences of Bishops *De normis servandis quoad libros liturgicos in vulgus edendos, illorum translatione in linguas hodiernas peracta*, 25 October 1973: AAS 66 (1974) 98–99; S. Congr. for the Sacraments and Divine Worship, Letter to the Presidents of the Conferences of Bishops *De linguis vulgaribus in S. Liturgiam inducendis*, 5 June 1976: *Notitiae* 12 (1976) 300–302.

66. Cf. S. Congr. for Divine Worship, Norms *De unica interpretatione textuum liturgicorum*, 6 February 1970: *Notitiae* 6 (1976) 84–85; cf. S. Congr. of Rites, Instr. *Inter Oecumenici*, n. 40 c: AAS 56 (1964) 886.

67. Cf. S. Congr. for Divine Worship, Norms *De unica interpretatione textuum liturgicorum*, 6 February 1970: *Notitiae* 6 (1970) 84–85.

68. Cf. ibid., 85.

the text of Sacred Scripture. The Bishops of the Latin Church are to foster the same in a spirit of respectful and fraternal cooperation.

91. A similar agreement is desirable also with the particular non-Catholic Eastern Churches or with the authorities of the Protestant ecclesial communities,[69] provided that it is not a question of a liturgical text pertaining to doctrinal matters still in dispute, and provided also that the Churches or ecclesial communities involved have a sufficient number of adherents and that those consulted are truly capable of functioning as representatives of the same ecclesial communities. In order completely to avoid the danger of scandal or of confusion among the Christian faithful, the Catholic Church must retain full liberty of action in such agreements, even in civil law.

5. ON "MIXED" COMMISSIONS

92. So that there might be unity in the liturgical books even as regards vernacular translations, and so that the resources and the efforts of the Church might not be consumed needlessly, the Apostolic See has promoted, among other possible solutions, the establishment of "mixed" commissions, that is, those in whose work several Conferences of Bishops participate.[70]

93. The Congregation for Divine Worship and the Discipline of the Sacraments erects such "mixed" commissions at the request of the Conferences of Bishops involved; afterwards the commission is governed by statutes approved by the Apostolic See.[71] It is ordinarily to be hoped that each and every one of the Conferences of Bishops will have deliberated the matter of the above-mentioned establishment of the commission as well as of the composition of its statutes before the petition is submitted to the Congregation for Divine Worship and the Discipline of the Sacraments. Even so, if it is judged opportune by that Dicastery due to the great number of Conferences, or the protracted period of time required for a vote, or particular pastoral necessity, it is not excluded that the statutes be prepared and approved by the same Dicastery, after consultation, insofar as possible, with at least some of the Bishops involved.

94. A "mixed" commission, by its very nature, provides assistance to the Bishops rather than substituting for them as regards their pastoral mission and their

---

69. Cf. Second Vatican Council, Const. *Dei Verbum*, n. 22; *Code of Canon Law*, can. 825 § 2; Pont. Council for Promoting Christian Unity, *Directorium Oecumenicum*, 25 March 1993, nn. 183–185, 187: AAS 85 (1993) 1104–1106; cf. *Code of Canons of the Eastern Churches*, can. 655 § 1.

70. Cf. Consilium "For the Implementation of the Constitution on the Sacred Liturgy", Letter of the President, 16 October 1964: *Notitiae* 1 (1965) 195; Pope Paul VI, Address to translators of liturgical texts into vernacular languages, 10 November 1965: AAS 57 (1965) 969; S. Congr. for Divine Worship, Norms *De unica interpretatione textuum liturgicorum*, 6 February 1970: *Notitiae* 6 (1970) 84–85.

71. Cf. S. Congr. of Rites, Instr. *Inter Oecumenici*, n. 23 c: AAS 56 (1964) 882; *Code of Canon Law*, cann. 94, 117, 120; Cf. Pope John Paul II, Apost. Const. *Pastor Bonus*, 28 June 1988, art. 65: AAS 80 (1988) 877.

relations with the Apostolic See.[72] For a "mixed" commission does not constitute a *tertium quid* place between the Conferences of Bishops and the Holy See, nor is it to be regarded as a means of communication between them. The Members of the Commission are always Bishops, or at least those equivalent in law to Bishops. It pertains to the Bishops, furthermore, to direct the Commission as its Members.

95.   It would be advantageous that among the Bishops who participate in the work of each "mixed" commission, there be at least some who are responsible for dealing with liturgical matters in their respective Conferences, as, for example, the chairman of the liturgical commission of the Conference.

96.   Such a commission, in fact, insofar as possible, should exercise its office by means of the resources of the liturgical commissions of the individual Conferences involved, using their experts, their technical resources, and their secretarial staff. For example, the work undertaken is coordinated in such a way that a first draft of the translation is prepared by the liturgical commission of one Conference and then improved by the other Conferences, even in light of the diversity of expression prevailing in the same language in the individual territories.

97.   It is preferable that at least some Bishops participate at the various stages of work on a given text, until the time when the mature text is submitted to the Plenary Assembly of the Conference of Bishops for its examination and approval and is then sent immediately by the Conference President, with the signature also of the Secretary General, to the Apostolic See for the *recognitio*.

98.   In addition, the "mixed" commissions are to limit themselves to the translation of the *editiones typicae*, leaving aside all theoretical questions not directly related to this work, and not involving themselves either in relations with other "mixed" commissions or in the composition of original texts.

99.   In fact, the necessity remains for establishing commissions dealing with the Sacred Liturgy as well as sacred art and sacred music according to the norm of law in each diocese and territory of the Conference of Bishops.[73] These commissions shall work in their own right for the purposes proper to them, and shall not cede the matters entrusted to them to any "mixed" commission.

100. All of the principal collaborators of any "mixed" commission who are not Bishops, and to whom a stable mission is entrusted by such commissions, require the *nihil obstat* granted by the Congregation for Divine Worship and the Discipline of the Sacraments before beginning their work. The *nihil obstat* will be granted after consideration of their academic degrees and testimonies regarding their

---

72. Cf. Pope John Paul II, Apost. Letter *Apostolos suos*, 21 May 1998, nn. 18–19: AAS 90 (1998) 653–654.

73. Cf. Pope Pius XII, Encycl. Letter *Mediator Dei*, 20 November 1947: AAS 39 (1947) 561–562; Second Vatican Council, Const. *Sacrosanctum Concilium*, nn. 44–46; Pope Paul VI, Apost. Letter *Sacram Liturgiam*: AAS 56 (1964) 141; S. Congr. of Rites, Instr. *Inter Oecumenici*, nn. 44–46: AAS 56 (1964) 886–887.

expertise, and a letter of recommendation submitted by their own diocesan Bishop. In the preparation of the statutes mentioned above, in n. 93, the manner in which the request for the *nihil obstat* is to be made shall be described with greater precision.

101. All, including the experts, are to conduct their work anonymously, observing confidentiality to which all who are not Bishops are to be bound by contract.

102. It is also advantageous that the terms of office of the members, collaborators and experts be renewed periodically in a manner defined by the Statutes. On account of a need on the part of the Commissions that may become evident in the course of the work, the Congregation for Divine Worship and the Discipline of the Sacraments may grant, upon request, a prolongation by indult of the term of office established for a particular member, collaborator or expert.

103. In the case of previously existing "mixed" Commissions, their statutes are to be revised within two years from the date that this Instruction enters into force, according to the norms of n. 93 and of the other norms prescribed by this Instruction.

104. For the good of the faithful, the Holy See reserves to itself the right to prepare translations in any language, and to approve them for liturgical use.[74] Nevertheless, even if the Apostolic See, by means of the Congregation for Divine Worship and the Discipline of the Sacraments, may intervene from time to time out of necessity in the preparation of translations, it still belongs to the competent Conference of Bishops to approve their assumption into liturgical use within the boundaries of a given ecclesiastical territory, unless otherwise explicitly indicated in the decree of approbation of the translation promulgated by the Apostolic See. Afterwards, for the purpose of obtaining the *recognitio* of the Holy See, the Conference shall transmit the decree of approbation for its territory together with the text itself, in accordance with the norms of this Instruction and of the other requirements of the law.

105. For reasons such as those set forth in nn. 76 and 84 above or for other urgent reasons of pastoral need, commissions, councils, committees, or work groups depending directly on the Apostolic See are established by decree of the Congregation for Divine Worship and the Discipline of the Sacraments for the purpose of working on the translation either of individual liturgical books or of several. In this case, insofar as possible, at least some of the Bishops involved in the matter will be consulted.

---

74. *Code of Canon Law*, cann. 333, 360; Pope John Paul II, Apost. Const. *Pastor Bonus*, 28 June 1988, art. 62–65: AAS 80 (1988) 876–877; cf. S. Congr. for Divine Worship, Letter to the Presidents of the Conferences of Bishops *De normis servandis quoad libros liturgicos in vulgus edendos, illorum translatione in linguas hodiernas peracta*, 25 October 1973, n. 1: AAS 66 (1974) 98.

6. THE COMPOSITION OF NEW LITURGICAL TEXTS
IN A VERNACULAR LANGUAGE

106. Regarding the composition of new liturgical texts prepared in vernacular languages, which may perhaps be added to those translated from the Latin *editiones typicae*, the norms currently in force are to be observed, in particular those contained in the Instruction *Varietates legitimae*.[75] An individual Conference of Bishops shall establish one or more Commissions for the preparation of texts or for the work involved in the suitable adaptation of texts. The texts are then to be sent to the Congregation for Divine Worship and the Discipline of the Sacraments for the *recognitio*, prior to the publication of any books intended for the celebrants or for the general use of the Christian faithful.[76]

107. It is to be borne in mind that the composition of new texts of prayers or rubrics is not an end in itself, but must be undertaken for the purpose of meeting a particular cultural or pastoral need. For this reason it is strictly the task of the local and national liturgical Commissions, and not of the Commissions treated in nn. 92–104 above. New texts composed in a vernacular language, just as the other adaptations legitimately introduced, are to contain nothing that is inconsistent with the function, meaning, structure, style, theological content, traditional vocabulary or other important qualities of the texts found in the *editiones typicae*.[77]

108. Sung texts and liturgical hymns have a particular importance and efficacy. Especially on Sunday, the "Day of the Lord", the singing of the faithful gathered for the celebration of Holy Mass, no less than the prayers, the readings and the homily, express in an authentic way the message of the Liturgy while fostering a sense of common faith and communion in charity.[78] If they are used widely by the faithful, they should remain relatively fixed so that confusion among the people may be avoided. Within five years from the publication of this Instruction, the Conferences of Bishops, necessarily in collaboration with the national and diocesan Commissions and with other experts, shall provide for the publication of a directory or repertory of texts intended for liturgical singing. This document shall be transmitted for the necessary *recognitio* to the Congregation for Divine Worship and the Discipline of the Sacraments.

IV
THE PUBLICATION OF LITURGICAL BOOKS

109. Of the liturgical books of the Roman Rite containing only Latin texts, only the one published by decree of the Congregation having competency at the time

---

75. Cf. Congr. for Divine Worship and the Discipline of the Sacraments, Instr. *Varietates legitimae*, 25 January 1994: AAS 87 (1995) 288–314.

76. Cf. ibid., n. 36: AAS 87 (1995) 302.

77. Cf. *Missale Romanum*, editio typica tertia: *Institutio Generalis*, n. 398.

78. Pope John Paul II, Apost. Letter *Dies Domini*, 31 May 1998, nn. 40, 50: AAS 90 (1998) 738, 745.

is designated the *"editio typica"*.[79] The *editiones typicae* published prior to this Instruction were issued either *Typis Polyglottis Vaticanis* or by the *Libreria Editrice Vaticana*; in the future, they are usually to be printed by the *Tipografia Vaticana*, while the right of publication is reserved to the *Libreria Editrice Vaticana*.

110. The norms of this Instruction, as regards all rights, refer to the *editiones typicae* that have been or will be published, whether of a whole book or of a part: namely, the editions of the *Missale Romanum*, the *Ordo Missae*, the Lectionary of the *Missale Romanum*, the Evangeliary of the *Missale Romanum*, the *Missale parvum* extracted from the *Missale Romanum* and *Lectionarium*, the *Passio Domini Nostri Iesu Christi*, the *Liturgia Horarum*, the *Rituale Romanum*, the *Pontificale Romanum*, the *Martyrologium Romanum*, the *Collectio Missarum de Beata Maria Virgine* and its Lectionary, the *Graduale Romanum*, the *Antiphonale Romanum*, as well as the other books of Gregorian chant and the editions of the books of the Roman Rite promulgated by decree as *editiones typicae*, such as the *Caeremoniale Episcoporum* and the *Calendarium Romanum*.

111. As regards the liturgical books of the Roman Rite promulgated in an *editio typica* either before or after the Second Vatican Council by decree of the Congregations competent at the time, the Apostolic See, through the *Administratio Patrimonii* or, in its name and by its mandate, through the *Libreria Editrice Vaticana*, possesses and reserves to itself the right of ownership commonly known as "copyright". The granting of permission for a reprinting pertains to the Congregation for Divine Worship and the Discipline of the Sacraments.

112. Of the liturgical books of the Roman Rite, those prepared in the Latin language by an editor after the publication of the *editio typica*, with the permission of the Congregation for Divine Worship and the Discipline of the Sacraments, are said to be *"iuxta typicam"*.

113. As regards the editions *iuxta typicam* intended for liturgical use: the right of printing liturgical books containing only the Latin text is reserved to the *Libreria Editrice Vaticana* and to those editors to whom the Congregation for Divine Worship and the Discipline of the Sacraments will have chosen to grant contracts, unless a different provision is made in the norms inserted into the *editio typica* itself.

114. The right of translating the liturgical books of the Roman Rite in a vernacular language, or at least the right of approving them for liturgical use and of printing and publishing them in their own territory, remains uniquely that of the Conference of Bishops, with due regard, however, to the rights of *recognitio*[80] and the proprietary rights of the Apostolic See, also set forth in this Instruction.

115. As regards the publication of liturgical books translated into the vernacular which are the property of a given Conference of Bishops, the right of publication is reserved to those editors to whom the Conference of Bishops shall have given

---

79. Cf. *Code of Canon Law*, can. 838 § 2.
80. Cf. ibid., can. 838 § 3.

this right by contract, with due regard for the requirements both of civil law and of juridical custom prevailing in each country for the publication of books.

116. In order for an editor to be able to proceed to the printing of editions *iuxta typicam* intended for liturgical use, he must do the following:

a) in the case of books containing only the Latin text, obtain, in each single instance, the consent of the Congregation for Divine Worship and the Discipline of the Sacraments, and then enter into an agreement with the *Administratio Patrimonii Sedis Apostolicae* or with the *Libreria Editrice Vaticana*, which acts in the name and by the mandate of the same body, regarding the conditions for the publication of such books;

b) in the case of books containing texts in a vernacular language, obtain the consent, according to the circumstances, of the President of the Conference of Bishops, the Institute or the Commission that manages the matter in the name of several Conferences by license of the Holy See, and enter at the same time into an agreement with this body regarding the conditions for publication of such books, with due regard for the norms and laws in force in that country;

c) in the case of books containing principally a vernacular text but also containing extensive use of the Latin text, the norms of n. 116 a are to be observed for the Latin part.

117. The rights of publication and the copyright for all translations of liturgical books, or at least the rights in civil law necessary for exercising complete liberty in publishing or correcting texts, is to remain with the Conferences of Bishops or their national liturgical Commissions.[81] The same body shall possess the right of taking any measures necessary to prevent or correct any improper use of the texts.

118. Wherever the copyright for translated liturgical texts is common to several Conferences, a licensing agreement is to be prepared for the individual Conferences, such that, insofar as possible, the matter may be administrated by the individual Conferences themselves, according to the norm of law. Otherwise, a body shall be established for such administration by the Apostolic See, after consultation with the Bishops.

119. The correspondence of the liturgical books with the *editiones typicae* approved for liturgical use, in the case of a text prepared only in the Latin language, must be established by the attestation of the Congregation for Divine Worship and the Discipline of the Sacraments; however, in the case of a text prepared in a vernacular language or in the case described above, in n. 116 c, it must be established by attestation of the local Ordinary in whose diocese the books are published.[82]

---

81. S. Congr. for Divine Worship, Decl., 15 May 1970: *Notitiae* 6 (1970) 153.
82. Cf. *Code of Canon Law*, can. 826 § 2; cf. also below, n. 111.

120. The books from which the liturgical texts are recited in the vernacular with or on behalf of the people should be marked by such a dignity that the exterior appearance of the book itself will lead the faithful to a greater reverence for the word of God and for sacred realities.[83] Thus it is necessary as soon as possible to move beyond the temporary phase characterized by leaflets or fascicles, wherever these exist. All books intended for the liturgical use of priest or deacon celebrants are to be of a size sufficient to distinguish them from the books intended for the personal use of the faithful. To be avoided in them is any extravagance which would necessarily lead to costs that would be unaffordable for some. Pictures or images on the cover and in the pages of the book should be characterized by a certain noble simplicity and by the use of only those styles that have a universal and perennial appeal in the cultural context.

121. Even in the case of pastoral aids published for the private use of the faithful and intended to foster their participation in the liturgical celebrations, the publishers must observe the proprietary rights:

a) of the Holy See, in the case of the Latin text, or of the Gregorian music in books of chant published either before or after the Second Vatican Council—with the exception, however, of those rights conceded universally, or those to be thus conceded in the future;

b) of the Conference of Bishops or of several Conferences of Bishops simultaneously, in the case of a text prepared in a vernacular language or of the music printed in the same text, which is the property of the Conference or Conferences.

For these aids, especially if published in the form of books, the consent of the diocesan Bishop is required, according to the norm of law.[84]

122. Care is to be taken to ensure that the choice of publishers for the printing of the liturgical books be made in such a way as to exclude any whose publications are not readily seen to conform to the spirit and norms of Catholic tradition.

123. Regarding texts produced by agreement with the particular Churches and ecclesial communities separated from the communion of the Holy See, it is necessary that the Catholic Bishops and the Apostolic See retain full rights for introducing any changes or corrections that may be deemed necessary for their use among Catholics.

124. According to the judgment of the Conference of Bishops, leaflets or cards containing liturgical texts for the use of the faithful may be excepted from the general rule by which liturgical books prepared in a vernacular language must contain everything that is in the Latin *textus typicus* or *editio typica*. As for the official editions, namely those for the liturgical use of the priest, deacon or

---

83. Cf. Second Vatican Council, Const. *Sacrosanctum Concilium*, n. 122; S. Congr. of Rites, Instr. *Inter Oecumenici*, n. 40 e: AAS 56 (1964) 886.
84. *Code of Canon Law*, can. 826 § 3.

competent lay minister, the norms mentioned above, in nn. 66–69, are to be maintained.[85]

125. Besides what is contained in the *editio typica* or foreseen or set forth specifically in this Instruction, no text is to be added in the vernacular edition without prior approbation granted by the Congregation for Divine Worship and the Discipline of the Sacraments.

V
THE TRANSLATION OF PROPER LITURGICAL TEXTS

1. DIOCESAN PROPERS

126. In the preparation of a translation of texts of a diocesan liturgical approved by the Apostolic See as *textus typici*, the following are to be observed:

a) The translation is to be done by the diocesan liturgical Commission[86] or by another body designated by the diocesan Bishop for this purpose, and then it must be approved by the diocesan Bishop, after consultation with his clergy and with experts;

b) The translation is to be sent to the Congregation for Divine Worship and the Discipline of the Sacraments for the *recognitio*, along with three copies of the *textus typicus* together with the translation;

c) A *relatio* is to be prepared as well, which is to contain:

i) the decree by which the *textus typicus* has been approved by the Apostolic See,

ii) the process and criteria followed in the translation;

iii) a list of the persons who have participated at various stages of the work, together with a brief description of their experience or abilities, and of their academic degrees;

d) In the case of the less widely diffused languages, the Conference of Bishops should testify that the text is accurately translated into the language in question, as mentioned above, in n. 86.

127. In the printed text are to be contained the decrees by means of which the *recognitio* of the Holy See is granted for the translations; or at least a mention is to be made of the *recognitio*, including the date, the month, the year, and the protocol number of the decree published by the Dicastery, in keeping with the

---

85. Second Vatican Council, Const. Sacrosanctum Concilium, n. 63 b; S. Congr. for Divine Worship, Decl. *De interpretationibus popularibus novorum textuum liturgicorum*, 15 September 1969: *Notitiae* 5 (1969) 333–334.

86. Cf. Pope Pius XII, Encycl. Letter *Mediator Dei*, 20 November 1947: AAS 39 (1947) 561–562; SECOND VATICAN COUNCIL , Const. Sacrosanctum Concilium, n. 45.

same norms as above, in n. 68. Two copies of the printed text are to be sent to the Congregation for Divine Worship and the Discipline of the Sacraments.

2. PROPERS OF RELIGIOUS FAMILIES

128. In the preparation the translation of texts approved by the Apostolic See as *textus typici* for religious families, that is, Institutes of Consecrated Life or Societies of Apostolic Life, or other approved associations or organizations having the rights to their use, the following are to be observed:

a) The translation is to be made by the general liturgical Commission or by another body constituted for the purpose by the Supreme Moderator or at least by his mandate given to the Provincial Superior, and then it is to be approved by the Supreme Moderator with the deliberative vote of his Council, after any necessary consultation with experts and with appropriate members of the Institute or Society;

b) The translation is to be sent to the Congregation for Divine Worship and the Discipline of the Sacraments for the *recognitio*, together with three copies of the *textus typicus*;

c) A *relatio* is also to be prepared, which is to contain:

i) the decree by which the *textus typicus* has been approved by the Apostolic See,

ii) the process and criteria followed in the translation,

iii) a list of the persons who have participated at various stages of the work, together with a brief description of their experience or abilities, and of their academic degrees;

d) In the case of the less widely diffused languages, the Conference of Bishops should testify that the text is accurately translated into the language in question, as mentioned above, in n. 86.

e) As regards religious families of diocesan right, the same procedure is to be followed, but in addition, the text is to be sent by the diocesan Bishop, together with his judgment of approbation, to the Congregation for Divine Worship and the Discipline of the Sacraments.

129. In the liturgical Propers of religious families, the translation of the Sacred Scriptures to be employed for liturgical use is to be the same one approved for liturgical use according to the norm of law for the same territory. If this proves difficult, the matter is to be referred to the Congregation for Divine Worship and the Discipline of the Sacraments.

130. In the printed text are to be contained the decrees by means of which the *recognitio* of the Holy See is granted for the translations, or at least a mention is to be made of the *recognitio*, including the date, the month, the year, and the

protocol number of the decree published by the Dicastery, in keeping with the same norms as above, in n. 68. Two copies of the printed text are to be sent to the Congregation for Divine Worship and the Discipline of the Sacraments.

CONCLUSION

131. Approbation granted in the past for individual liturgical translations remains in effect even if a principle or criterion has been followed which differs from those contained in this Instruction. Nevertheless, from the day on which this Instruction is published, a new period begins for the making of emendations or for undertaking anew the consideration of the introduction of vernacular languages or idioms into liturgical use, as well as for revising translations heretofore made into vernacular languages.

132. Within five years from the date of publication of this Instruction, the Presidents of the Conferences of Bishops and the Supreme Moderators of religious families and institutes equivalent in law are bound to present to the Congregation for Divine Worship and the Discipline of the Sacraments an integral plan regarding the liturgical books translated into the vernacular in their respective territories or institutes.

133. In addition, the norms established by this Instruction attain full force for the emendation of previous translations, and any further delay in making such emendations is to be avoided. It is to be hoped that this new effort will provide stability in the life of the Church, so as to lay a firm foundation for supporting the liturgical life of God's people and bringing about a solid renewal of catechesis.

After the preparation of this Instruction by the Congregation for Divine Worship and the Discipline of the Sacraments in virtue of the mandate of the Supreme Pontiff transmitted in a letter of the Cardinal Secretary of State dated 1 February 1997 (Prot. n. 408.304), the same Supreme Pontiff, in an audience granted to the Cardinal Secretary of State on 20 March 2001, approved this Instruction and confirmed it by his own authority, ordering that it be published, and that it enter into force on the 25th day of April of the same year.

From the offices of the Congregation for Divine Worship and the Discipline of the Sacraments, 28 March, the year 2001.

JORGE A. CARD. MEDINA ESTÉVEZ

PREFECT

FRANCESCO PIO TAMBURRINO

ARCHBISHOP SECRETARY

CHIROGRAPH
OF THE
SUPREME PONTIFF JOHN PAUL II
FOR THE
CENTENARY
OF THE
MOTU PROPRIO
"TRA LE SOLLECITUDINI"
ON SACRED MUSIC

POPE JOHN PAUL II
NOVEMBER 22, 2003

OVERVIEW OF *CHIROGRAPH OF THE SUPREME PONTIFF JOHN PAUL II FOR THE CENTENARY OF THE MOTU PROPRIO "TRA LE SOLLECITUDINI" ON SACRED MUSIC*

Steven R. Janco

The lengthy pontificate of Blessed John Paul II saw the publication of a wide variety of documents that have significantly impacted the Church's liturgical life. One that has received relatively little attention, however, is the *Chirograph of the Supreme Pontiff John Paul II for the Centenary of the Motu Proprio "Tra le Sollecitudini" On Sacred Music* (CSM), issued on the hundreth anniversary of St. Pius X's influential encyclical. In fact, *Sing to the Lord: Music in Divine Worship* (STL), issued by the United States Conference of Catholic Bishops in 2007, includes just one quote from this 2003 document, even though it was the most recent papal statement on liturgical music at the time STL was drafted. John Paul uses the centenary of *Tra le sollecitudini* (TLS) as an opportunity "to recall the important role of sacred music . . ."[1] and expresses hope that the *Chirograph* will serve as "an encouragement and incentive to those who are involved in this important aspect of liturgical celebrations."[2] The document is fairly brief at 3,500 words, but has some interesting, perhaps even surprising things to say.

That John Paul's document was issued as a chirograph, a little-used Vatican classification, left many unsure how to contextualize and interpret it. On the other hand, the authority of TLS was clear. Issued *motu proprio*, Pius X described TLS as a "juridical code of sacred music" and imposed its "scrupulous observance on all."[3] The term "chirograph" suggests that the 2003 document was handwritten, or at least signed, by John Paul II. While nothing in the document explains its classification, its location on the Vatican website offers a bit of clarification. CSM is listed among John Paul's "letters," many of which are personal missives written to specific individuals, for specific occasions, or to acknowledge significant anniversaries. John Paul's better-known 1999 *Letter to Artists* is located similarly. Viewed in this context, CSM is a kind of personal reflection by the pope, written to encourage and challenge those responsible for liturgical music.

As one would expect in a document commemorating the anniversary of another, John Paul II pays tribute to Pius X and other twentieth-century pontiffs who devoted attention "to this delicate sector."[4] He offers a ceremonial affirmation of principles articulated in TLS, but then notes that the fathers of the Second

---

1. *Chirograph of the Supreme Pontiff John Paul II on the Motu Proprio "Tra le sollecitudini" On Sacred Music* (CSM), 1.
2. Ibid., 15.
3. *Tra le sollecitudini* (TLS), introduction.
4. CSM, 2.

Vatican Council reasserted earlier principles "with a view to their application in the changed conditions of the times."[5] In light of the writings of his predecessors, but "taking into account in particular the pronouncements of the Second Vatican Council," John Paul II desires to "re-propose several fundamental principles . . . with the intention of ensuring that liturgical music corresponds ever more closely to its specific function."[6] Though he offers a number of customary cautions concerning quality and appropriateness, his creative interpretation of earlier principles and his pastoral approach to certain issues lead me to believe that this document, written near the end of his pontificate, reflects John Paul's extensive travels and his experience of celebrating liturgy with people of many cultures.

John Paul begins his reflections by referencing an early section of TLS that lists three qualities required "to guarantee dignity and excellence to liturgical compositions."[7] However, John Paul provides new interpretations for all three.

First, music for liturgy must have *holiness* as its reference point. For Pius X, this meant distinguishing sacred music, especially chant, from profane music, including music of the opera and theater. John Paul's contemporary interpretation does not reassert that holiness is a quality inherent in the music itself. Rather he quotes *Sacrosanctum Concilium* (SC), which indicates that holiness is connected to ritual context: "sacred music will be the more holy the more closely it is joined to the liturgical rite, whether by adding delight to prayer, fostering oneness of spirit, or investing the rites with greater solemnity."[8]

Second, music for liturgy must exhibit *sound form*. For Pius X this meant that sacred music must be "true art." John Paul suggests, however, "this quality alone does not suffice. Indeed, liturgical music must meet the specific prerequisites of the Liturgy. . . ."[9] He then elaborates on this requirement by raising two issues: the *expressive* and *mystagogical* function of music in the liturgy and the "legitimate demands of adaptation and inculturation."[10] We will explore these two issues in more detail shortly.

Third, borrowing a principle from TLS, music for liturgy must exhibit *universality*. Pius X believed that musical pieces used anywhere in the world, including each nation's "native music," must be subordinated to the "general characteristics of sacred music," so that that "nobody of any nation may receive an impression other than good on hearing them."[11] John Paul provides a much narrower interpretation, suggesting that the principle of universality implies that new "forms of composition and performance" must not be "introduced without careful review."[12]

In his discussion about the need for music to meet liturgical requirements, John Paul raises two significant issues. First, he talks about music having an expressive and mystagogical function in the liturgy:

---

5. Ibid.

6. Ibid., 3.

7. Ibid.

8. *Sacrosanctum Concilium* (SC), 112.

9. CSM, 5.

10. Ibid.

11. TLS, 2.

12. CSM, 6.

Music must . . . appropriately reflect the gestures proposed by the rite. The various moments of the liturgy require a musical expression of their own. From time to time this must fittingly bring out the nature proper to a specific rite, now proclaiming God's marvels, now expressing praise, supplication or even sorrow for the experience of human suffering. . . .[13]

To say that each ritual moment of the liturgy *requires* a musical expression to "bring out" its proper nature is an extraordinary affirmation that music is *necessary* for effective liturgical celebration. The gestures proposed by the liturgy (praise, proclamation, supplication, sorrow) are not readily communicated through words and symbols alone. They require a *musical* expression. More specifically, John Paul indicates that each ritual moment requires *its own* particular kind of musical expression, one that effectively brings out its proper nature. Here he seems to suggest that no single genre or style of music can adequately meet every ritual need.

Following his discussion of music's expressive and mystagogical function, John Paul explores a second and related prerequisite: "The music and song requested by the liturgical reform—it is right to stress this point—must comply with the legitimate demands of adaptation and inculturation."[14] He goes on to stress that the "necessary involvement of the assembly" must be respected and that "concessions to frivolity or superficiality" must be avoided. He concludes this section by saying that "elitist forms of 'inculturation'" should be avoided, especially pieces that are "of possible artistic value, but that indulge in a language that is incomprehensible to the majority."[15] The context suggests that incomprehensibility refers to *music* as well as text. In order for music to effectively express the nature of particular ritual moments, it must "speak" the musical language of the local culture and be accessible to the assembly.

Worthy of mention are two aspects of the document's treatment of Gregorian chant. The first concerns the status of Gregorian chant in the postconciliar liturgy. Rather than quoting *Sacrosanctum Concilium*, which says that "other things being equal," Gregorian chant "should be given pride of place in liturgical services,"[16] John Paul relies on a clarification provided in the 1967 document *Musicam sacram* when he asserts that "Gregorian chant . . . should be given, other things being equal, pride of place in liturgical services sung *in Latin*."[17] That John Paul reasserts this narrower interpretation in 2003 is significant.

John Paul also refers to Gregorian chant when discussing new compositions of liturgical music. He makes his own the "general rule of Pius X," which suggests that "the more closely a composition for the church approaches in its movement, inspiration and savor, the Gregorian melodic form, the more sacred and liturgical it becomes."[18] But then he reinterprets TLS once again, indicating that this rule is not a question of "imitating Gregorian chant, but rather of

---

13. Ibid., 5.
14. Ibid., 6.
15. Ibid.
16. SC, 116.
17. CSM, 7; see also *Musicam sacram* (MS), 50, emphasis mine.
18. TLS, 3.

ensuring that new compositions are imbued with the same spirit that inspired and little by little came to shape it."[19]

What surprises me most about this document, and what serves to put much of it in perspective, is that John Paul reserves his greatest praise and warmest language for comments on "popular religious song." Coupled with this is a concern that new musical expressions are not receiving adequate attention and proper consideration.[20] Though he offers a customary acknowledgement that "not all forms of music can be considered suitable for liturgical celebrations,"[21] John Paul points out that the "renewal introduced by the Second Vatican Council" inspired a "special development in popular religious song," which is "particularly suited to the participation of the faithful." Popular singing constitutes "a bond of unity and a joyful expression of the community at prayer, fosters the proclamation of the one faith and imparts to large liturgical assemblies an incomparable and recollected solemnity." Near the end of the document, he notes, "contemporary compositions often use a diversity of musical forms that have a certain dignity of their own. To the extent that they are helpful to the prayer of the church they can prove a precious enrichment."[22]

John Paul's positive comments about popular song make clear that he is not targeting "new musical expressions" or the music of particular cultures when he discusses the need to "purify worship from ugliness of style, from distasteful forms of expression, from uninspired musical texts. . . ." Indeed, he suggests that many new musical expressions have the potential to "express the inexhaustible riches of the Mystery proposed in the Liturgy and thereby encourage the active participation of the faithful in celebrations."[23]

Forty years after the promulgation of *Sacrosanctum Concilium*, promoting the active participation of the liturgical assembly remained a priority for John Paul II, who in CSM celebrates the Church's heritage of singing and affirms the integral role of music in liturgical celebration. But he also issues some challenges to current and future liturgical musicians: Respect and serve the liturgical assembly. Regard popular religious song as a gift of local cultures. And discover the dignity of new musical expressions, which may indeed be capable of expressing inexhaustible riches, even as they promote active participation.

---

19. CSM, 12.
20. See ibid., 7.
21. Ibid., 4.
22. Ibid., 11 and 14.
23. Ibid., 7 and 3.

CHIROGRAPH OF THE
SUPREME PONTIFF JOHN PAUL II
FOR THE CENTENARY OF
THE *MOTU PROPRIO "TRA LE SOLLECITUDINI"*
ON SACRED MUSIC

1.   Motivated by a strong desire "to maintain and promote the decorum of the House of God," my Predecessor St Pius X promulgated the Motu Proprio *Tra le Sollecitudini* 100 years ago. Its purpose was to renew sacred music during liturgical services. With it he intended to offer the Church practical guidelines in that vital sector of the Liturgy, presenting them, as it were, as a "juridical code of sacred music."[1] This act was also part of the program of his Pontificate which he summed up in the motto: "*Instaurare omnia in Cristo.*"

The centenary of the Document gives me the opportunity to recall the important role of sacred music, which St Pius X presented both as a means of lifting up the spirit to God and as a precious aid for the faithful in their "active participation in the most holy mysteries and in the public and solemn prayer of the Church."[2]

The holy Pontiff recalls that the special attention which sacred music rightly deserves stems from the fact that, "being an integral part of the solemn Liturgy, [it] participates in the general purpose of the Liturgy, which is the glory of God and the sanctification and edification of the faithful."[3] Since it interprets and expresses the deep meaning of the sacred text to which it is intimately linked, it must be able "to add greater efficacy to the text, in order that through it the faithful may be . . . better disposed for the reception of the fruits of grace belonging to the celebration of the most holy mysteries."[4]

2.   The Second Vatican Council followed up this approach in chapter VI of the Constitution *Sacrosanctum Concilium* on the Sacred Liturgy, in which the ecclesial role of sacred music is clearly defined: "The musical tradition of the universal Church is a treasure of inestimable value, greater even than that of any other art. The main reason for this preeminence is that, as sacred melody united to words, it forms a necessary or integral part of the solemn Liturgy."[5] The Council also recalls that "Sacred Scripture, indeed, has bestowed praise upon sacred song. So have the Fathers of the Church and the Roman Pontiffs

---

1. *Pii X Pontificis Maximi Acta,* Vol. I, p. 77.

2. *Ibid.*

3. *Ibid.,* n. 1, p. 78.

4. *Ibid.*

5. *Ibid.,* n. 112.

who in more recent times, led by St Pius X, have explained more precisely the ministerial function exercised by sacred music in the service of the Lord."[6]

In fact, by continuing the ancient biblical tradition to which the Lord himself and the Apostles abided (cf. Mt 26: 30; Eph 5: 19; Col 3: 16), the Church has encouraged song at liturgical celebrations throughout her history, providing wonderful examples of melodic comment to the sacred texts in accordance with the creativity of every culture, in the rites of both West and East.

The attention my Predecessors thus paid to this delicate sector was constant. They recalled the fundamental principles that must enliven the composition of sacred music, especially when it is destined for the Liturgy. Besides Pope St Pius X, other Popes who deserve mention are Benedict XIV with his Encyclical *Annus Qui* (19 February 1749), Pius XII with his Encyclicals *Mediator Dei* (20 November 1947) and *Musicae sacrae disciplina* (25 December 1955), and lastly Paul VI, with the luminous statements that punctuated many of his Speeches.

The Fathers of the Second Vatican Council did not fail to reassert these principles with a view to their application in the changed conditions of the times. They did so specifically in chapter six of the Constitution *Sacrosanctum Concilium*. Pope Paul VI then saw that those principles were translated into concrete norms, in particular with the Instruction *Musicam sacram*, promulgated on 5 March 1967 with his approval by the Congregation then known as the Sacred Congregation for Rites. In this same context, it is necessary to refer to those principles of conciliar inspiration to encourage a development in conformity with the requirements of liturgical reform and which will measure up to the liturgical and musical tradition of the Church. The text of the Constitution *Sacrosanctum Concilium* in which it is declared that the Church "approves of all forms of true art which have the requisite qualities,[7] and admits them into divine worship," finds satisfactory criteria for application in nn. 50-53 of the above-mentioned Instruction *Musicam sacram*.[8]

3.   On various occasions I too have recalled the precious role and great importance of music and song for a more active and intense participation in liturgical celebrations.[9] I have also stressed the need to "purify worship from ugliness of style, from distasteful forms of expression, from uninspired musical texts which are not worthy of the great act that is being celebrated,"[10] to guarantee dignity and excellence to liturgical compositions.

In this perspective, in the light of the Magisterium of St Pius X and my other Predecessors and taking into account in particular the pronouncements of the Second Vatican Council, I would like to re-propose several fundamental principles for this important sector of the life of the Church, with the intention of ensuring that liturgical music corresponds ever more closely to its specific function.

---

6. *Ibid.*

7. *Ibid.*

8. Cf. *AAS* 59 (1967), 314–316.

9. Cf. e.g., *Address to the Pontifical Institute of Sacred Music for its 90th Anniversary* (19 January 2001), 1: *L'Osservatore Romano* English Edition *[ORE]*, 7 February 2001, p. 7.

10. *General Audience*, 26 February 2003, n. 3: *[ORE]*, 5 March 2003, p. 11.

4.   In continuity with the teachings of St Pius X and the Second Vatican Council, it is necessary first of all to emphasize that music destined for sacred rites must have *holiness* as its reference point: indeed, "sacred music increases in holiness to the degree that it is intimately linked with liturgical action."[11] For this very reason, "not all without distinction that is outside the temple (*profanum*) is fit to cross its threshold," my venerable Predecessor Paul VI wisely said, commenting on a Decree of the Council of Trent.[12] And he explained that "if music—instrumental and vocal—does not possess at the same time the sense of prayer, dignity and beauty, it precludes the entry into the sphere of the sacred and the religious."[13] Today, moreover, the meaning of the category "sacred music" has been broadened to include repertoires that cannot be part of the celebration without violating the spirit and norms of the Liturgy itself.

St Pius X's reform aimed specifically at purifying Church music from the contamination of profane theatrical music that in many countries had polluted the repertoire and musical praxis of the Liturgy. In our day too, careful thought, as I emphasized in the Encyclical *Ecclesia de Eucharistia*, should be given to the fact that not all the expressions of figurative art or of music are able "to express adequately the mystery grasped in the fullness of the Church's faith."[14] Consequently, not all forms of music can be considered suitable for liturgical celebrations.

5.   Another principle, affirmed by St Pius X in the Motu Proprio *Tra le Sollecitudini* and which is closely connected with the previous one, is that of *sound form*. There can be no music composed for the celebration of sacred rites which is not first of all "true art" or which does not have that efficacy "which the Church aims at obtaining in admitting into her Liturgy the art of musical sounds."[15]

Yet this quality alone does not suffice. Indeed, liturgical music must meet the specific prerequisites of the Liturgy: full adherence to the text it presents, synchronization with the time and moment in the Liturgy for which it is intended, appropriately reflecting the gestures proposed by the rite. The various moments in the Liturgy require a musical expression of their own. From time to time this must fittingly bring out the nature proper to a specific rite, now proclaiming God's marvels, now expressing praise, supplication or even sorrow for the experience of human suffering which, however, faith opens to the prospect of Christian hope.

6.   The music and song requested by the liturgical reform–it is right to stress this point–must comply with the legitimate demands of adaptation and inculturation. It is clear, however, that any innovation in this sensitive matter must respect specific criteria such as the search for musical expressions which respond to the necessary involvement of the entire assembly in the celebration and which,

---

11. Second Vatican Council, Constitution on the Sacred Liturgy *Sacrosanctum Concilium*, n. 112.

12. *Address to the Participants in the General Assembly of the Italian Association Santa Cecilia* (18 September 1968): *Insegnamenti* VI (1968), 479.

13. *Ibid.*

14. *Ibid.*, n. 50: *AAS* 95 (2003), 467.

15. *Ibid.*, n. 2, p. 78.

at the same time, avoid any concessions to frivolity or superficiality. Likewise, on the whole, those elitist forms of "inculturation" which introduce into the Liturgy ancient or contemporary compositions of possible artistic value, but that indulge in a language that is incomprehensible to the majority, should be avoided.

In this regard St Pius X pointed out–using the term *universal*–a further prerequisite of music destined for worship: " . . . while every nation," he noted, "is permitted to admit into its ecclesiastical compositions those special forms which may be said to constitute its native music, still these forms must be subordinate in such a manner to the general character of sacred music, that nobody of any nation may receive an impression other than good on hearing them."[16] In other words, the sacred context of the celebration must never become a laboratory for experimentation or permit forms of composition and performance to be introduced without careful review.

7.   Among the musical expressions that correspond best with the qualities demanded by the notion of sacred music, especially liturgical music, Gregorian chant has a special place. The Second Vatican Council recognized that "being specially suited to the Roman Liturgy"[17] it should be given, other things being equal, pride of place in liturgical services sung in Latin.[18] St Pius X pointed out that the Church had "inherited it from the Fathers of the Church," that she has "jealously guarded [it] for centuries in her liturgical codices" and still "proposes it to the faithful" as her own, considering it "the supreme model of sacred music."[19] Thus, Gregorian chant continues also today to be an element of unity in the Roman Liturgy.

Like St Pius X, the Second Vatican Council also recognized that "other kinds of sacred music, especially polyphony, are by no means excluded from liturgical celebrations."[20] It is therefore necessary to pay special attention to the new musical expressions to ascertain whether they too can express the inexhaustible riches of the Mystery proposed in the Liturgy and thereby encourage the active participation of the faithful in celebrations.[21]

8.   The importance of preserving and increasing the centuries-old patrimony of the Church spurs us to take into particular consideration a specific exhortation of the Constitution *Sacrosanctum Concilium*: "Choirs must be assiduously developed, especially in cathedral churches."[22] In turn, the Instruction *Musicam Sacram* explains the ministerial task of the *choir*: "Because of the liturgical ministry it exercises, the choir (*cappella musicale* or *schola cantorum*) should be mentioned here explicitly. The conciliar norms regarding the reform of the

16. *Ibid.*, pp. 78–79.

17. Constitution on the Sacred Liturgy *Sacrosanctum Concilium*, n. 116.

18. Cf. Sacred Congregation for Rites, Instruction on Music in the Sacred Liturgy *Musicam Sacram* (5 March 1967), 50: *AAS* 59 (1967), 314.

19. Moto Proprio *Tra le Sollecitudini*, n. 3, p. 79.

20. Constitution on the Sacred Liturgy *Sacrosanctum Concilium*, n. 116.

21. Cf. *ibid.*, n. 30.

22. *Ibid.*, n. 114.

Liturgy have given the choir's function greater prominence and importance. The choir is responsible for the correct performance of its part, according to the differing types of song, to help the faithful to take an active part in the singing. Therefore, . . . choirs are to be developed with great care, especially in cathedrals and other major churches, in seminaries and in religious houses of study."[23] The *schola cantorum's* task has not disappeared: indeed, it plays a role of guidance and support in the assembly and, at certain moments in the Liturgy, has a specific role of its own.

From the smooth coordination of all—the priest celebrant and the deacon, the acolytes, the altar servers, the readers, the psalmist, the *schola cantorum*, the musicians, the cantor and the assembly—flows the proper spiritual atmosphere which makes the liturgical moment truly intense, shared in and fruitful. The musical aspect of liturgical celebrations cannot, therefore, be left to improvisation or to the arbitration of individuals but must be well conducted and rehearsed in accordance with the norms and competencies resulting from a satisfactory liturgical formation.

9.   In this area, therefore, the urgent need to encourage the sound formation of both pastors and the lay faithful also comes to the fore. St Pius X insisted in particular on the musical training of clerics. The Second Vatican Council also recalled in this regard: "Great importance is to be attached to the teaching and practice of music in seminaries, in the novitiate houses of studies of Religious of both sexes, and also in other Catholic institutions and schools."[24] This instruction has yet to be fully implemented. I therefore consider it appropriate to recall it, so that future pastors may acquire sufficient sensitivity also in this field.

In the task of training, a special role is played by schools of sacred music, which St Pius X urged people to support and encourage[25] and which the Second Vatican Council recommended be set up wherever possible.[26] A concrete result of the reform of St Pius X was the establishment in Rome in 1911, eight years after the Motu Proprio, of the "Pontificia Scuola Superiore di Musica Sacra" (Pontifical School for Advanced Studies in Sacred Music), which later became the "Pontificio Istituto di Musica Sacra" (Pontifical Institute of Sacred Music). As well as this academic institution, which has now existed for almost a century and has rendered a high-quality service to the Church, the particular Churches have established many other schools that deserve to be supported and reinforced by an ever better knowledge and performance of good liturgical music.

10.   Since the Church has always recognized and fostered progress in the arts, it should not come as a surprise that in addition to Gregorian chant and polyphony she admits into celebrations even the most modern music, as long as it respects both the liturgical spirit and the true values of this art form. In compositions written for divine worship, therefore, the particular Churches in the various nations are permitted to make the most of "those special forms which

---

23. *Ibid.*, n. 19: *AAS* 59 (1967), 306.

24. Constitution on the Sacred Liturgy *Sacrosanctum Concilium*, n. 115.

25. Cf. Moto Proprio *Tra le Sollecitudini*, n. 28, p. 86.

26. Cf. Constitution on the Sacred Liturgy *Sacrosanctum Concilium*, n. 115.

may be said to constitute the special character of [their] native music."[27] On the lines of my holy Predecessor and of what has been decreed more recently by the Constitution *Sacrosanctum Concilium*,[28] I have also intended in the Encyclical *Ecclesia de Eucharistia* to make room for new musical contributions, mentioning in addition to the inspired Gregorian melodies, "the many, often great composers who sought to do justice to the liturgical texts of the Mass."[29]

11.   The last century, with the renewal introduced by the Second Vatican Council, witnessed a special development in popular religious song, about which *Sacrosanctum Concilium* says: "Religious singing by the faithful is to be intelligently fostered so that in devotions and sacred exercises as well as in liturgical services, the voices of the faithful may be heard . . . "[30] This singing is particularly suited to the participation of the faithful, not only for devotional practices "in conformity with the norms and requirements of the rubrics,"[31] but also with the Liturgy itself. Popular singing, in fact, constitutes "a bond of unity and a joyful expression of the community at prayer, fosters the proclamation of the one faith and imparts to large liturgical assemblies an incomparable and recollected solemnity."[32]

12.   With regard to compositions of liturgical music, I make my own the "general rule" that St Pius X formulated in these words: "The more closely a composition for church approaches in its movement, inspiration and savor the Gregorian melodic form, the more sacred and liturgical it becomes; and the more out of harmony it is with that supreme model, the less worthy it is of the temple."[33] It is not, of course, a question of imitating Gregorian chant but rather of ensuring that new compositions are imbued with the same spirit that inspired and little by little came to shape it. Only an artist who is profoundly steeped in the *sensus Ecclesiae* can attempt to perceive and express in melody the truth of the Mystery that is celebrated in the Liturgy.[34] In this perspective, in my *Letter to Artists* I wrote: "How many sacred works have been composed through the centuries by people deeply imbued with the sense of mystery! The faith of countless believers has been nourished by melodies flowing from the hearts of other believers, either introduced into the Liturgy or used as an aid to dignified worship. In song, faith is experienced as vibrant joy, love and confident expectation of the saving intervention of God."[35]

Renewed and deeper thought about the principles that must be the basis of the formation and dissemination of a high-quality repertoire is therefore

---

27. Pius X, Motu Proprio *Tra le Sollecitudini*, n. 2, p. 79.

28. Cf. n. 119.

29. N. 49: *AAS* 95 (2003), 466.

30. N. 118.

31. *Ibid.*

32. John Paul II, *Address to the International Congress on Sacred Music* (27 January 2001), n. 4: *ORE*, 7 February 2001, p. 4.

33. Moto Proprio *Tra le Sollecitudini*, n. 3, p. 79.

34. Cf. Second Vatican Council, Constitution on the Sacred Liturgy *Sacrosanctum Concilium*, n. 112.

35. N. 12: *Insegnamenti* XXII/1 (1999), 718.

required. Only in this way will musical expression be granted to serve appropriately its ultimate aim, which is "the glory of God and the sanctification of the faithful."[36]

I know well that also today there are numerous composers who are capable of making their indispensable contribution in this spirit, increasing with their competent collaboration the patrimony of music at the service of a Liturgy lived ever more intensely. To them I express my confidence, together with the most cordial exhortation to put their every effort into increasing the repertoire of compositions worthy of the exalted nature of the mysteries celebrated and, at the same time, suited to contemporary sensibilities.

13. Lastly, I would like to recall what St Pius X disposed at the practical level so as to encourage the effective application of the instructions set out in his Motu Proprio. Addressing the Bishops, he prescribed that they institute in their Dioceses "a special Commission of qualified persons competent in sacred music."[37] Wherever the papal disposition was put into practice, it has yielded abundant fruit. At the present time there are numerous national, diocesan and interdiocesan commissions which make a precious contribution to preparing local repertoires, seeking to practice a discernment that takes into account the quality of the texts and music. I hope that the Bishops will continue to support the commitment of these commissions and encourage their effectiveness in the pastoral context.[38]

In the light of the experience gained in recent years, the better to assure the fullfilment of the important task of regulating and promoting the sacred Liturgy, I ask the Congregation for Divine Worship and the Discipline of the Sacraments to increase its attention, in accordance with its institutional aims,[39] in the sector of sacred liturgical music, availing itself of the competencies of the various commissions and institutions specialized in this field as well as of the contribution of the Pontifical Institute of Sacred Music. Indeed, it is important that the musical compositions used for liturgical celebrations correspond to the criteria appropriately set down by St Pius X and wisely developed by both the Second Vatican Council and the subsequent Magisterium of the Church. In this perspective, I am confident that the Bishops' Conferences will carefully examine texts destined for liturgical chant[40] and will devote special attention to evaluating and encouraging melodies that are truly suited to sacred use.[41]

14. Again at the practical level, the Motu Proprio whose centenary it is also deals with the question of the musical instruments to be used in the Latin Liturgy. Among these, it recognizes without hesitation the prevalence of the

---

36. Second Vatican Council, Constitution on the Sacred Liturgy *Sacrosanctum Concilium*, n. 112.

37. Moto Proprio *Tra le Sollecitudine*, n. 24, p. 85.

38. Cf. John Paul II, Apostolic Letter *Vicesimus Quintus Annus* (4 December 1987), n. 20: *AAS* 81 (1989), 916.

39. Cf. John Paul II, Apostolic Constitution *Pastor Bonus* (28 June 1988), 65: *AAS* 80 (1988), 877.

40. Cf. John Paul II, Encyclical Letter *Dies Domini* (31 May 1998), 50: *AAS* 90 (1988), 745; Congregation for Divine Worship and the Discipline of the Sacraments, Instruction *Liturgiam Authenticam* (28 March 2001), 108: *AAS* 93 (2001), 719.

41. Cf. *Institutio Generalis Missalis Romani*, editio typica III, 393.

pipe organ and establishes appropriate norms for its use.[42] The Second Vatican Council fully accepted my holy Predecessor's approach, decreeing: "The pipe organ is to be held in high esteem in the Latin Church, for it is the traditional musical instrument, the sound of which can add a wonderful splendor to the Church's ceremonies and powerfully lifts up people's minds to God and to higher things."[43]

Nonetheless, it should be noted that contemporary compositions often use a diversity of musical forms that have a certain dignity of their own. To the extent that they are helpful to the prayer of the Church they can prove a precious enrichment. Care must be taken, however, to ensure that instruments are suitable for sacred use, that they are fitting for the dignity of the Church and can accompany the singing of the faithful and serve to edify them.

15.   I hope that the centenary commemoration of the Motu Proprio *Tra le Sollecitudini*, through the intercession of their holy Author together with that of St Cecilia, patroness of sacred music, may be an encouragement and incentive to those who are involved in this important aspect of liturgical celebrations. Sacred music lovers, by dedicating themselves with renewed impetus to a sector of such vital importance, will contribute to the spiritual growth of the People of God. The faithful, for their part, in expressing their faith harmoniously and solemnly in song, will experience its richness ever more fully and will abide by the commitment to express its impulses in their daily life. In this way, through the unanimous agreement of pastors of souls, musicians and faithful, it will be possible to achieve what the Constitution *Sacrosanctum Concilium* describes as the true "purpose of sacred music," that is, "the glory of God and the sanctification of the faithful."[44]

May your example and model in this be the Virgin Mary, whose praise in the *Magnificat* of the marvels God works in human history remains beyond compare. With this hope, I impart my Blessing to everyone with affection.

Given in Rome at St Peter's on 22 November, the Memorial of St Cecilia, in the year 2003, the 26th of the Pontificate.

JOHN PAUL II

---

42. Cf. Motu Proprio *Tra le Sollecitudini*, nn. 15-18, p. 84.
43. Second Vatican Council, Constitution on the Sacred Liturgy *Sacrosanctum Concilium*, n. 120.
44. *Ibid.*, n. 112.

SPIRITUS ET SPONSA
ON THE
40TH ANNIVERSARY
OF THE
CONSTITUTION
ON THE SACRED LITURGY
"SACROSANCTUM CONCILIUM"

APOSTOLIC LETTER
POPE JOHN PAUL II
DECEMBER 4, 2003

AN OVERVIEW OF *SPIRITUS ET SPONSA*

S. Joyce Ann Zimmerman, CPPS

The apostolic letter, *Spiritus et Sponsa* (SS), is very short, comprised of only six-teen paragraphs, but we ought not be fooled by its brevity into thinking that Pope John Paul II is offering nothing new here. Written on the fortieth anniver-sary of the promulgation of *Sacrosanctum Concilium* (SC), the Holy Father does reiterate some of the points he made in his apostolic letter *Vicesimus quintus annus* (VQA). which was written fifteen years earlier on the twenty-fifth anni-versary of SC. But he also does much more than retell previous content. Even the division of the letter is deceiving in its simplicity: There are five opening paragraphs, five paragraphs under the heading "From renewal to deepening," five paragraphs under the heading "Future prospects," and a brief one-paragraph conclusion. Thus, evenly divided, the letter exhibits a marvelous balance between principle and application, praise and caution, "dare" and assurance, present real-ity and future possibilities.

As in the previous document, the pope seeks in this 2003 letter to empha-size the importance of guiding principles for the liturgy, to evaluate their imple-mentation, and to look to the future renewal of liturgy.[1] He uses the term *themes* rather than the word *principles*. The former word aptly describes how the Holy Father weaves together what is on his mind liturgically at the beginning of this new millennium. Rather than developing at length key themes, he teases us by reemphasizing points he made in *Vicesimus quintus annus* at the same time that he brings in wholly new topics.

THEMES PREVIOUSLY EMPHASIZED

With respect to what Pope John Paul II reemphasizes, we find such themes (prin-ciples) as Paschal Mystery;[2] liturgy as the summit and font of the whole Christian life;[3] inculturation;[4] being faithful to liturgical tradition;[5] all the faithful wit-nessing to and living what we celebrate;[6] and the need for ongoing liturgical formation.[7] A theme he previously addressed but now develops in the 2003 let-ter a bit more is that of popular devotions and their relationship to liturgy.[8] Since 1988, when he wrote his first letter on an anniversary of SC, two documents have been promulgated about devotional prayer: the *Directory on Popular Piety*

---

1. *Spirtus et Sponsa* (SS), 1.

2. Ibid., 2 , 3, 16.

3. Ibid., 2 (where he quotes SC 10) and 6 (where he uses his own words, "origin and summit").

4. SS, 4; hinted at in the context of music.

5. Ibid. 7; in 15 he decries "grave forms of abuse."

6. Ibid., 3.

7. Ibid., 7, 12, 15. In paragraph 12 the pope calls for a rediscovery of "the *art of 'mystagogic catechesis.'"

8. Ibid., 10 and 14.

and the Liturgy: Principles and Guidelines (DPPL) and his apostolic letter
Rosarium Virginis Mariae (RVM).[9]

This latter document on the Rosary is particularly helpful for understanding the relationship of liturgical and devotional prayer. Not only did this apostolic letter announce the "Year of the Rosary,"[10] but in it, the Holy Father also proposed five new mysteries of the Rosary. He acknowledges that the traditional fifteen mysteries, grouped in sets of five and known as the joyful, sorrow, and glorious mysteries, are associated with 150 Hail Marys, equal to the number of psalms; his new set of five mysteries weakens this rich symbolism. Nevertheless, he is quite clear about why he is suggesting these new mysteries. While the traditional mysteries all deal with Christ, they do not lead us to meditate on important aspects of Jesus's public ministry. Hence, the "mysteries of light"[11] refer to Gospel events that show forth Christ as the Light of the World: Jesus's baptism, his first public miracle at Cana, his proclamation of the Kingdom of God, his Transfiguration, and his institution of the Holy Eucharist. The Holy Father *suggests* that these mysteries be inserted between the joyful mysteries with their meditations on Jesus's Incarnation and hidden life and the events at the end of his earthly life: the sorrowful mysteries with their meditations on Jesus's suffering and Death, and the glorious mysteries with their meditations on the Resurrection and his subsequent risen life.

We can tease two important points about the relationship of devotional and liturgical prayer out of the pope's reference in SS to his apostolic letter on the Rosary. First, the Holy Father makes clear that there is no mandate to use these mysteries at all, nor in the way he suggests. The Rosary is devotional prayer and so it is not regulated by competent authorities as liturgy is regulated. There is no "must" about it.[12] Further, as a devotional prayer, the Rosary will always take second place to liturgy[13] and serve it. This brings us to a second important point. In *Rosarium Virginis Mariae* the pope stresses that all of the Rosary's mysteries focus on the person and ministry of Jesus Christ. While we think of the Rosary as a Marian prayer, it is, nonetheless, a prayer truly focused on Christ. When our personal prayer focuses in a special way on Christ, it is the kind of devotional prayer that most definitely leads us back to liturgy. This is not to say there is no value in devotions to the saints or other kinds of devotions. The Holy Father is, however, clearly stressing the value of a prayer life focused on Christ and encountering him in all the beauty and vastness of his saving mystery.

The 1988 apostolic letter *Vicesimus quintus annus* placed a heavy emphasis on Sacred Scripture, the Word of God. This 2003 letter does not ignore this important theme. When the Holy Father speaks of deepening our celebration of liturgy, he asks an important question: "Has the rediscovery of the value of the Word of God brought about by liturgical reform met with a positive confirmation

---

9. Issued on 16 October 2002, at the beginning of Pope John Paul II's twenty-fifth year as our Holy Father.

10. *Rosarium Virginis Mariae* (RVM), 19.

11. Ibid., 21.

12. Although we shall see below how the pope emphasizes the importance of personal (that is, devotional) prayer.

13. SS, 3 speaks to the preeminence of the liturgy over all other activity of the Church.

in our celebrations?"[14] He points to the wider exposure to Sacred Scripture made possible by the revised *Lectionary for Mass*.[15] In both these paragraphs speaking to the Word of God, the Holy Father stresses that we simply do not hear the Word, but we also must internalize it, must live it. This theme of living and witnessing to liturgy was also prominent in the twenty-fifth anniversary letter.

THEMES NEWLY EMPHASIZED

The Holy Father introduces new themes in this letter. He begins SS by quoting from the Apocalypse—the Book of Revelation—that last book of the New Testament that gives us a glimpse of the glory of the heavenly liturgy. Thus, he begins and ends with an eschatological theme. He reflects on how liturgy "opens a glimpse of Heaven on earth"[16] and how, whenever we raise our hearts and minds to God in praise, we do so with the whole heavenly court.

Placing the Liturgy of the Hours in its rightful place as the daily prayer of all the baptized, John Paul II offers a refreshing stimulus for taking up a regular habit of praying this liturgical prayer. By it we can offer continual praise to God while we pray for the salvation of the whole world.[17] Later, when he is speaking of the future of renewal, the pope uses a strong and bold word: "dare."[18] We must call forth and teach the faithful the celebration of the Liturgy of the Hours and dare them to pray this beautiful liturgical prayer. We do this because, as does all liturgy, the Liturgy of the Hours makes visible the Church as well as celebrates the whole mystery of Christ.

Aesthetics was a theme dear to John Paul II, and it comes out in two ways in SS. The pope mentions that SC "pays special attention to the importance of *sacred music*.[19] He relates music in the liturgy to active participation and leaves open the possibility of adaptations for our times and the use of various musical traditions of different cultures. In the next paragraph he extols sacred art, which enables the "splendor of worship"[20] to shine forth. Sacred art is an especially important consideration when building and renovating sacred spaces. Beautiful art created for the service of liturgy reflects the "infinite beauty of God."[21]

In an all too brief paragraph the Holy Father mentions that Sunday is at the "heart of liturgical life."[22] This is the special day of the week on which we commemorate and celebrate the Resurrection. Jesus's being raised to new life on the first day of the week is the reason why Sunday is a day of Eucharistic liturgy obligation for Catholics. Sunday helps us to enter more fully into the liturgical year, during which we celebrate the fullness of Christ's mystery. The pope does not mention Sunday as a day of rest, but this theme is implied when he speaks of Sunday as necessary for living the Christian life well every day. It is

---

14. Ibid., 6.
15. Ibid., 8.
16. Ibid., 16.
17. Ibid., 3.
18. Ibid., 14.
19. Ibid., 4; emphasis in original.
20. Ibid., 5.
21. Ibid.
22. Ibid., 9.

only by taking time out of our busy and challenging lives to rest both physically and spiritually in the Lord that we can keep a proper balance between work and leisure, between ministry and prayer.[23]

If Sunday is, indeed, to be a day of rest and rejuvenation, then an ongoing *"experience of silence"*[24] is necessary both as part of liturgy and as a part of daily living. The Holy Father introduces this theme by mentioning "an increasingly frenetic pace"[25] of society and our daily living. He uses again the word "dare" when he calls for specific education in silence for both our daily living and liturgy. Liturgy has both obligatory silences[26] and optional silences.[27] All too often our Eucharistic celebrations go lickety-split from the opening Sign of the Cross to the concluding blessing and dismissal. If liturgy is to be prayer that is internalized in order to make a difference in how we live, then we need pauses, we need silences to pass from frenetic to peacefully attentive stances before God.

The opening paragraph of the section on future prospects for liturgical renewal mentions that now "is the time for *new evangelization.*"[28] This, too, is a theme dear to Pope John Paul II's heart. We can hear his heart bleed for "a world in which the signs of the Gospel are dying out."[29] On the one hand he decries that "spirituality seems to have been put aside by a broadly secularized society"[30]; on the other hand he points to a thirst for an encounter with God, a thirst that always brings us back to the celebration of liturgy during which we encounter Christ in the fullness of his saving mystery.

Toward the end of his conclusion the Holy Father mentions liturgical spirituality.[31] This brings together in a single phrase all his yearnings for liturgy and all his support for SC. Liturgical spirituality is a way of daily Christian living derived from celebrating the liturgy well. Liturgical spirituality is possible when we have deeply encountered Christ during liturgy and have surrendered ourselves to being faithful disciple members of the Body of Christ. Through our love relationship with the divine Word, we can be faithful witnesses to the saving presence and power in the Spirit of our loving God for all those we meet each day of our lives.

---

23. See also the pope's 1998 apostolic letter, *Dies domini: On Keeping the Lord's Day Holy.*

24. Ibid., 13; emphasis in original.

25. Ibid.

26. For example, at the beginning of Mass, after the invitation to pray for the collect and prayer after Communion, after the Communion procession is completed if there is no communal hymn of praise.

27. For example, after the readings and Homily, as part of the Universal Prayer (Prayer of the Faithful).

28. SS, 11.

29. Ibid.

30. Ibid.

31. Ibid., 16.

SPIRITUS ET SPONSA

ON THE FORTIETH ANNIVERSARY OF THE CONSTITUTION ON THE SACRED LITURGY "SACROSANCTUM CONCILIUM"

APOSTOLIC LETTER
JOHN PAUL II
DECEMBER 4, 2003

1.   "The Spirit and the Bride say 'Come'. And let him who hears say, 'Come'. And let him who is thirsty come, let him who desires take the water of life without price" (Apoc 22:17). These words from the Apocalypse echo in my heart as I remember that 40 years ago today, exactly on 4 December 1963, my venerable Predecessor, Pope Paul VI, promulgated the Constitution *Sacrosanctum Concilium* on the Sacred Liturgy. What, indeed, is the Liturgy other than the voice of the Holy Spirit and of the Bride, holy Church, crying in unison to the Lord Jesus: "Come"? What is the Liturgy other than that pure, inexhaustible source of "living water" from which all who thirst can freely draw the gift of God (cf. Jn 4:10)?

Indeed, in the Constitution on the Sacred Liturgy, the first fruit of the Second Vatican Council, that "great grace bestowed on the Church in the 20th century"[1], the Holy Spirit spoke to the Church, ceaselessly guiding the disciples of the Lord "into all the truth" (Jn 16:13). The commemoration of the 40th anniversary of this event is a good opportunity to rediscover the basic themes of the liturgical renewal that the Council Fathers desired, to seek to evaluate their reception, as it were, and to cast a glance at the future.

2.   With the passing of time and in the light of its fruits, the importance of *Sacrosanctum Concilium* has become increasingly clear. The Council brilliantly outlined in it the principles on which are based the liturgical practices of the Church and which inspire its healthy renewal in the course of time[2]. The Council Fathers set the Liturgy within the horizon of the history of salvation, whose purpose is the redemption of humanity and the perfect glorification of God. The wonders wrought by God in the Old Testament were but a prelude to the redemption brought to completion by Christ the Lord, especially through the Paschal Mystery of his blessed Passion, his Resurrection from the dead and his glorious

---

1. John Paul II, Apostolic Letter *Novo Millennio Ineunte* (6 January 2001), n. 57: AAS 93 (2001), 308; cf. Apostolic Letter *Vicesimus Quintus Annus* (4 December 1988), n. 1 [ORE, 22 May 1989, p. 7]; AAS 81 (1989), 897.
   2. Cf. ibid., n. 3.

Ascension[3]. However, it needs not only to be proclaimed but also to be accomplished; this "is set in train through the sacrifice and sacraments, around which the entire liturgical life revolves"[4]. Christ makes himself present in a special way in the liturgical gestures associating the Church with himself. Every liturgical celebration, therefore, is the work of Christ the Priest and of his Mystical Body, "full public worship"[5] in which the faithful take part, with a foretaste in it of the Liturgy of the heavenly Jerusalem[6]. This is why the "Liturgy is the summit toward which the activity of the Church is directed" and at the same time, "the fount from which all her power flows"[7].

3.   The liturgical outlook of the Council did not keep to interchurch relations, but was open to the horizons of all humanity. Indeed, in his praise to the Father, Christ attaches to himself the whole community of men and women. He does so specifically through the mission of a praying Church which, "by celebrating the Eucharist and by other means, especially the celebration of the Divine Office, is ceaselessly engaged in praising the Lord and interceding for the salvation of the entire world"[8].

In the perspective of *Sacrosanctum Concilium*, the liturgical life of the Church acquires a cosmic and universal scope that makes a deep mark on human time and space. It is also possible to understand in this perspective the renewed attention that the Constitution pays to the liturgical year through which the Church journeys, commemorating and reliving the Paschal Mystery of Christ[9].

If the Liturgy consists in all of this, the Council rightly affirms that every liturgical action "is a sacred action surpassing all others. No other action of the Church can equal its efficacy by the same title and to the same degree"[10]. At the same time, the Council recognizes that "the Sacred Liturgy does not exhaust the entire activity of the Church"[11]. Indeed, on the one hand the Liturgy presupposes the proclamation of the Gospel, and on the other, it demands a Christian witness in history. The mystery proposed in preaching and catechesis, listened to with faith and celebrated in the Liturgy, must shape the entire life of believers who are called to be its heralds in the world[12].

4.   Then with regard to the different elements involved in liturgical celebration, the Constitution pays special attention to the importance of *sacred music*. The Council praises it, pointing out as its objective: "the glory of God and the sanctification of the faithful"[13]. In fact, sacred music is a privileged means to

---

3. Cf. ibid., n. 5.

4. Second Vatican Council, *Sacrosanctum Concilium* [SC], n. 6.

5. Ibid., n. 7.

6. Cf. ibid., n. 8.

7. Ibid., n. 10.

8. Ibid., n. 83.

9. Cf. ibid., n. 5.

10. Ibid., n. 7.

11. Ibid., n. 9.

12. Cf. ibid., n. 10.

13. Ibid., n. 112.

facilitate the active participation of the faithful in sacred celebration, as my venerable Predecessor St. Pius X desired to highlight in his Motu Proprio On the Restoration of Sacred Music *Tra le Sollecitudini*, whose centenary occurs this year. It was this very anniversary that recently gave me an opportunity to reassert the need to preserve and to emphasize the role of music at liturgical celebrations, in accordance with the directives of *Sacrosanctum Concilium*[14] and mindful of the Liturgy's real character as well as the sensibility of our time and the musical traditions of the world's different regions.

5.   *Sacred art* was another fruitful topic addressed by the conciliar Constitution. It gave rise to many developments. The Council gives clear instructions to continue to leave considerable room for it in our day too, so that the splendor of worship will shine out through the fittingness and beauty of liturgical art. To this end it will be appropriate to make provision for projects to train the various craftsmen and artists who are commissioned to build and decorate places destined for liturgical use[15]. At the root of these guidelines is a vision of art, and sacred art in particular, that relates it to "the infinite beauty of God in works made by human hands"[16].

FROM RENEWAL TO DEEPENING

6.   Forty years later, it is appropriate to review the ground covered. I have already suggested on former occasions a sort of examination of conscience concerning the reception given to the Second Vatican Council[17]. Such an examination must also concern the liturgical and sacramental life. "Is the Liturgy lived as the 'origin and summit' of ecclesial life, in accordance with the teaching of *Sacrosanctum Concilium*?"[18]. Has the rediscovery of the value of the Word of God brought about by liturgical reform met with a positive confirmation in our celebrations? To what extent does the Liturgy affect the practice of the faithful and does it mark the rhythm of the individual communities? Is it seen as a path of holiness, an inner force of apostolic dynamism and of the Church's missionary outreach?

7.   The Council's renewal of the Liturgy is expressed most clearly in the publication of *liturgical books*. After a preliminary period in which the renewed texts were little by little incorporated into the liturgical celebrations, a deeper knowledge of their riches and potential has become essential.

The mainspring of this deepening must be a principle of *total fidelity* to the Sacred Scriptures and to Tradition, authoritatively interpreted in particular by the Second Vatican Council, whose teachings have been reasserted and developed in the ensuing Magisterium. This fidelity engages in the first place the Bishop "to whom is committed the office of offering the worship of Christian

---

14. Cf. ibid., n. 6.
15. Cf. ibid., n. 127.
16. Ibid., n. 122.
17. Cf. Apostolic Letter *Tertio Millennio Adveniente* (10 November 1994), n. 36; AAS 87 (1995), 28.
18. Ibid.

religion to the divine Majesty and of administering it in accordance with the Lord's commandments and with the Church's laws"[19]; at the same time, it involves the entire ecclesial community "in different ways, depending on their orders, their role in the liturgical services and their actual participation in them"[20].

In this perspective, it is more necessary than ever to intensify liturgical life within our communities by means of an *appropriate formation* of the pastors and of all the faithful with a view to the active, conscious and full participation in liturgical celebrations desired by the Council[21].

8.   Consequently, what is needed is a *pastoral care of the Liturgy* that is totally faithful to the new *ordines*. Through these, renewed interest in the *Word of God* has gradually developed as the Council desired, hoping for a return to a "more ample, more varied and more suitable reading from Sacred Scripture"[22]. The new lectionaries, for example, offer a broad choice of passages from Scripture which constitute an inexhaustible source from which the People of God can and must draw. Indeed, we cannot forget that "in listening to the Word of God the Church grows and is built, and the wonderful works God once wrought in many different ways in the history of salvation are represented in their mystical truth through the signs of the liturgical celebration"[23]. In this celebration, the Word of God expresses the fullness of their meaning, inciting Christian life to continuous renewal, so that "what is heard at the liturgical celebration may also be put into practice in life"[24].

9.   *Sunday*, the Lord's Day, on which the Resurrection of Christ is especially commemorated, is at the heart of liturgical life as the "foundation and nucleus of the whole liturgical year"[25]. There is no doubt that considerable pastoral effort has been expended to bring people to rediscover the value of Sunday. Yet it is essential to make a point of this, for "the spiritual and pastoral riches of Sunday, as it has been handed on to us by tradition, are truly great. When its significance and implications are understood in their entirety, Sunday in a way becomes a synthesis of the Christian life and a condition for living it well"[26].

10.   Liturgical celebration nourishes the spiritual life of the faithful. The principle I formulated in my Apostolic Letter *Novo Millennio Ineunte*: "calling for a Christian life distinguished above all *in the art of prayer*"[27], stems from the Liturgy. *Sacrosanctum Concilium* interprets this urgency prophetically, spurring

---

19. Second Vatican Council, Dogmatic Constitution on the Church *Lumen Gentium*, n. 26.

20. Second Vatican Council, Constitution on the Sacred Liturgy *Sacrosanctum Concilium*, n. 26.

21. Cf. n. 14; John Paul II, Apostolic Letter *Vicesimus Quintus Annus* (4 December 1988), n. 15; AAS 81 (1989), 911–912.

22. SC, n. 35 (1).

23. *Ordo Lectionum Missae*, n. 7.

24. Ibid., n. 6.

25. Second Vatican Council, Constitution on the Sacred Liturgy *Sacrosanctum Concilium*, n. 106; cf. John Paul II, Apostolic Letter *Vicesimus Quintus Annus* (4 December 1988), n. 22: AAS 81 (1989), 917.

26. John Paul II, Apostolic Letter *Dies Domini* (31 May 1998), n. 81: AAS 90 (1998), 763.

27. Ibid., n. 32; AAS 93 (2001), 288.

the Christian community to intensify its prayer life, not only through the Liturgy but also in "popular devotions", for as long as these are in harmony with the Liturgy, they are in some way derived from it and lead to it[28]. The pastoral experience in recent decades has reinforced this insight. In this regard, the *Congregation for Divine Worship and the Discipline of the Sacraments* has made a valuable contribution with its *Directory on Popular Piety, Liturgy, Principles, Guidelines*[29]. Then, with the Apostolic Letter *Rosarium Virginis Mariae*[30] and the announcement of the Year of the Rosary, I myself wanted to make explicit the contemplative treasure of this traditional prayer that has spread far and wide among the People of God. I therefore recommended its rediscovery as a privileged path to contemplation of the Face of Christ at the school of Mary.

FUTURE PROSPECTS

11.   Looking to the future we see various challenges that the Liturgy is called to confront. During the past 40 years, in fact, society has undergone profound changes, some of which have put ecclesial commitment severely to the test. We have before us a world in which the signs of the Gospel are dying out, even in regions with an ancient Christian tradition. Now is the time for new evangelization. This challenge calls the Liturgy directly into question.

At first sight, spirituality seems to have been put aside by a broadly secularized society; but it is certain that despite secularization, a renewed need for it is re-emerging in different ways in our day.

How can we not see this as proof that the thirst for God cannot be uprooted from the human heart? Some questions find an answer only in personal contact with Christ. Only in intimacy with him does every existence acquire meaning and succeed in experiencing the joy that prompted Peter to exclaim on the mountain of the Transfiguration: "Master, it is well that we are here" (Lk 9:33).

12.   The Liturgy offers the deepest and most effective answer to this yearning for the encounter with God. It does so especially in the Eucharist, in which we are given to share in the sacrifice of Christ and to nourish ourselves with his Body and his Blood. However, Pastors must ensure that the sense of mystery penetrates consciences, making them rediscover the art of "mystagogic catechesis", so dear to the Fathers of the Church[31]. It is their duty, in particular, to promote dignified celebrations, paying the proper attention to the different categories of persons: children, young people, adults, the elderly, the disabled. They must all feel welcome at our gatherings, so that they may breathe the atmosphere of the first community of believers who "devoted themselves to the Apostles' teaching and fellowship, to the breaking of bread and the prayers" (Acts 2:42).

---

28. Cf. SC, n. 13.

29. Vatican City, 2002.

30. Cf. AAS 95 (2003), 5–36.

31. John Paul II, Apostolic Letter *Vicesimus Quintus Annus* (4 December 1988), 21: AAS (1989), 917.

13.   One aspect that we must foster in our communities with greater commitment is the experience of silence. We need silence "if we are to accept in our hearts the full resonance of the voice of the Holy Spirit and to unite our personal prayer more closely to the Word of God and the public voice of the Church"[32]. In a society that lives at an increasingly frenetic pace, often deafened by noise and confused by the ephemeral, it is vital to rediscover the value of silence. The spread, also outside Christian worship, of practices of meditation that give priority to recollection is not accidental. Why not start, with pedagogical daring, a specific education in silence within the coordinates of personal Christian experience? Let us keep before our eyes the example of Jesus, who "rose and went out to a lonely place, and there he prayed" (Mk 1:35). The Liturgy, with its different moments and symbols, cannot ignore silence.

14.   Pastoral attention to the Liturgy through the introduction to the various celebrations must instill a taste for prayer. To do so, it will of course take into account the ability of individual believers and their different conditions of age and culture; but in doing so it will not be content with the "minimum".

The Church's teaching must be able to "dare". It is important to introduce the faithful to the celebration of the Liturgy of the Hours "which, as the public prayer of the Church, is a source of piety and nourishment for personal prayer"[33]. It is an action that is neither individual nor "private, but is proper to the entire Body of the Church. . . . Thus, if the faithful are summoned for the Liturgy of the Hours and gather together, joining heart and voice, they make manifest the Church, which celebrates the mystery of Christ"[34]. Priority attention to liturgical prayer does not vie with personal prayer but indeed implies and demands it[35], and harmonizes well with other forms of community prayer, especially when it is recognized and recommended by the ecclesiastic Authority[36].

15.   Pastors have the indispensable task of educating in prayer and more especially of promoting liturgical life, entailing a duty of discernment and guidance. This should not be seen as an uncompromising attitude that is incompatible with the need of Christian souls to abandon themselves to the action of God's Spirit who intercedes in us and "for us with sighs too deep for words" (Rom 8:26). Rather, the guidance of Pastors constitutes a principle of "guarantee", inherent in God's plan for his Church that is governed by the assistance of the Holy Spirit. The liturgical renewal that has taken place in recent decades has shown that it is possible to combine a body of norms that assure the identity and decorum of the Liturgy and leave room for the creativity and adaptation that enable it to correspond closely with the need to give expression to their respective situation and culture of the various regions. Lack of respect for the liturgical norms can sometimes even lead to grave forms of abuse that obscure the truth of the mystery

---

32. *Institutio Generalis Liturgiae Horarum*, 202.
33. Second Vatican Council, Constitution on the Sacred Liturgy *Sacrosanctum Concilium*, n. 90.
34. *Institutio Generalis Liturgiae Horarum*, 20, 22.
35. Cf. Second Vatican Council, Constitution on the Sacred Liturgy *Sacrosanctum Concilium*, n. 12.
36. Cf. ibid., n. 13.

and give rise to dismay and stress in the People of God[37]. This abuse has nothing to do with the authentic spirit of the Council and should be prudently and firmly corrected by Pastors.

CONCLUSION

16.   The promulgation of the Constitution on the Liturgy marked a stage of fundamental importance in the life of the Church for the promotion and development of the Liturgy. It is in the Liturgy that the Church, enlivened by the breath of the Spirit, lives her mission as "sacrament—a sign and instrument, that is, of communion with God and of unity among all men"[38], and finds the most exalted expression of her mystical reality.

In the Lord Jesus and in his Spirit the whole of Christian existence becomes "a living sacrifice, holy and acceptable to God", genuine "spiritual worship" (Rom 12:1). The mystery brought about in the Liturgy is truly great. It opens a glimpse of Heaven on earth, and the perennial hymn of praise rises from the community of believers in unison with the hymn of heavenly Jerusalem: "Sanctus, Sanctus, Sanctus, Dominus Deus Sabaoth. Pleni sunt caeli et terra gloria tua. Hosanna in excelsis!".

At the beginning of this millennium, may a "liturgical spirituality" be developed that makes people conscious that Christ is the first "liturgist" who never ceases to act in the Church and in the world through the Paschal Mystery continuously celebrated, and who associates the Church with himself, in praise of the Father, in the unity of the Holy Spirit.

Together with this wish, I impart my Blessing to everyone from the depths of my heart.

From the Vatican, 4 December 2003, 26th Year of the Pontificate of John Paul PP. II.

JOHN PAUL II

---

37. John Paul II, Encyclical Letter *Ecclesia de Eucharistia* (17 April 2003), n. 52: AAS 95 (2003), 468; Apostolic Letter *Vicesimus Quintus Annus*, n. 16 (4 December 1988), AAS 81 (1989), 910–911.
38. Second Vatican Council, Dogmatic Constitution on the Church *Lumen Gentium*, n. 1.

INDEX

The following is a general index of primary themes, insights, and terminology from Sacrosanctum Concilium. *These same themes, insights, and terminology are also indexed from the pre–Conciliar and post–Conciliar documents. Please note that documents without article numbers have not been included in this index.*

ACCLAMATION
MD 149; SC 30; IO 57; MS 15–16, 29, 34, 58; CP 26, 35; LI 3; VL 39, 53

ADAPTATION
MSD 43, 112; SC 24, 38–39, 40, 44, 62, 107, 128; MS 65; EM 24; CP 21, 36, 42; LI 8, 10–12; CHP 16, 53; VQA 10, 16, 20; VL 3–4, 7, 38–45, 52–69; LA 5, 20, 22, 53, 67, 106–107; CSP 6; SS 15

ANTIPHONS
TLS 10–11; MSSL 27; SC 30; IO 57; MS 16; TAA 18; CP 36; LI 3; VL 61

ARTISTS
MD 195–196; MSD 22–23, 26–29, 39; MSSL 48; SC 122, 124, 127, 129; CHP 45; CSP 12; SS 5

ASSEMBLY
MCC 27; MD 204; SC 33, 114, 121; MS 10, 14, 26, 19, 26, 33–34, 45, 47, 53, 64; EM 9, 11, 16, 25–26, 36, 55; LI 2, 3, 4, 6, 7; CHP 10–12, 21, 50; VQA 7, 8, 10; VL 14, 22, 37, 41, 53; CSP 6, 8

BAPTISM
MCC 17–18, 22, 27, 30, 101, 108; MD 43, 88, 104; LHSOI 12, 14, 16; MSSL 93; SC 6, 10, 14, 55, 66–71, 109; IO 6, 61, 65, 99; MS 15; EM 16–17, 32, 36; CHP 19, 25, 38; VQA 6, 12–13; VL 22, 43, 53, 56

CATECHESIS
SC 35, 56, 109; IO 4, 7; MS 16, 39; EM 4–6, 11, 14–15, 32; CP 31; LI 1, 6, 13; CHP 28; VQA 21; LA 29–30, 40, 43, 74, 133; SS 3, 12

CHARITY
MC 1, 8, 11–13, 15, 20–21; MCC 5–6, 23–24, 51, 65, 70, 73–75, 83, 91, 96–98, 102, 105–106; MD 23, 33, 47–48, 99, 117, 137, 167; LHSOI 2; MSD 83, 85; MSSL 101; SC 9, 47, 59; EM 3, 7, 12, 38, 40, 50; CHP 18, 20; VQA 10; LA 61, 108

CHOIR/*SCHOLA CANTORUM*
TLS 8, 11–14, 25, 27; DCS 2–9; MD 145, 191–192, 195; LHSOI 5–6; MSD 11, 35, 74; MSSL 14, 16–18, 21, 25, 27, 35–37, 40, 42–43, 71, 93, 97, 99–103, 114; SC 29, 89, 95–96, 99, 101, 114, 121; IO 32, 36, 48, 78, 85, 97; MS 7, 9, 13, 15–16, 19–26, 34, 37–38, 53, 65; TAA 18; EM 24; VQA 23; LA 60; CSP 8

COMMENTATOR
MSSL 14, 72, 78, 96; SC 29; IO 13; MS 13, 26; VQA 10

COMMISSION (INTERNATIONAL, DIOCESAN, LITURGICAL)
TLS 24; MSSL 48, 50, 55, 64, 69, 102, 118; SC 44–46, 126; SL II; IO 39–40, 44–47; MS 54, 68–69; CP 2, 39, 41–42; LI 10; CHP 21, 50–51; VQA 3, 20–21, 23; VL 65, 67; LA 70, 81, 92–108, 116–117, 126, 128; CSP 13

COMPOSERS
MSD 14, 43, 54; MSSL 10, 97–98; SC 121; MS 4, 54, 56, 59; CSP 10, 12

CONCELEBRATION
MD 83; MSSL 38; SC 57–58; IO 15; MS 34; TAA 10, 27; EM 1, 8, 17, 21, 32, 47–48; CHP 23; VQA 10

10, 13, 16, 19, 24, 36–37, 39; VQA 6–7;
VL 12, 24; SS 2–3, 16

PRESENCE, CHRIST'S
MC 4, 7, 13; MCC 57, 75, 79, 82; MD 18,
20, 70, 92, 126, 131, 134, 203; SC 7, 35;
EM 1,3–4, 7, 9, 24, 49–50, 55, 60; LI 1;
CHP 6–7, 21, 32, 34, 53; VQA 7–8, 10;
VL 13

RADIO AND TELEVISION
MSSL 71, 74–79; SC 20; MS 8; EM 22

REDEMPTION
MC 1, 4; MCC 12, 31, 44, 51, 65, 74–75;
MD 1, 17, 29, 31, 36, 73, 77–79, 118, 135,
148, 151, 164, 183, 192; SC 2, 5,
102–103, 107; IO 55; EM 3, 44; CHP 2,
4, 14–15, 35, 55; VQA 6; VL 13; SS 2

RELIGIOUS MUSIC AND SONGS
MSD 13, 36, 70, 78; MSSL 4, 10, 20,
51–55; MS 4, 46; CSP 11
Responses
DCS 9; MSSL 22, 25, 31, 96; SC 30; MS
15–16, 33, 58; CP 36; VL 53

SACRED ART
TLS 26, 28; MD 109; MSD 22, 27–28;
MSSL 118; SC 122–130; EM 24; LI 10;
CHP 44; VQA 19, 21; LA 99; SS 5

SACRIFICE
MC 7, 10–13, 16–19; MCC 20, 27, 29, 47,
54, 69, 82, 90, 106; MD 1–3, 5–6, 12,
16–21, 27, 29, 31–32, 35, 37, 47, 52, 59,
67–68, 70–72, 75–83, 86–87, 89, 91–93,
95–96, 98–101, 103–104, 106, 112–115,
118–119, 122, 124, 129, 131, 138–139,
152, 169, 192, 200–201, 204–205; MSD
34, 47–48, 64; MSSL 2, 14, 22, 25, 30,
37–38, 93, 106; SC 2, 6, 7, 10, 12, 47, 49,
55; EM 1, 3, 9, 12, 18, 24, 31, 36, 43–44,
47, 50, 58; CHP 2, 20; VQA 6–7, 19,
24–25; SS 2, 12, 16

SERVER
MD 97; MSSL 14; MSSL 31, 111, 113; SC
29; IO 50; MS 13, 26; TAA 18; CSP 8

SILENCE
MCC 17, 99; MD 28, 156, MSSL 14, 27, 73,
85; SC 30; MS 17; TAA 15; EM 62; VQA
12, 23; SS 13

SOURCE
MC 4–6, 9, 15; MCC 12, 51, 56, 59, 63, 77,
84, 87, 110; MD 1, 24, 34, 163, 165, 201;
SC 10, 14, 35, 90; IO 5; EM 3, 58; CHP
18, 35; VQA 1, 5, 16, 22; LA 1; SS 1, 8,
14

STUDY
DCS 1–2; MCC 1, 8, 10–11, 25, 78; MD 4,
62, 94, 161, 202, 206; MSD 2, 14, 16, 38,
75–76, 79; SC 15–16, 115; SL I; MS 19,
37, 52–53, 56, 59; CP 9, 13, 38; LI 13;
CHP 22, 26, 27, 43; VQA 8; VL 65; LA
36; CSP 8

SUMMIT
MSSL 35; SC 10; IO 5; EM 3, 10, 58; VQA
22; SS 2, 6

WOMEN
TLS 13; DCS 10; MCC 39, 101; MSD 74;
MSSL 96, 100, 110; SC 101; IO 18; MS
22, 23; TAA 4; LI 7; CHP 9, 16, 31–32,
42; SS 3

VERNACULAR
TLS 7, 21; DCS 9; MD 59, 108, 192; MSD
13, 49; MSSL 13–14, 16, 32, 36, 96; SC
36, 63, 76, 78, 101; SL V, IX; IO 30, 37,
40–42, 48, 51, 57–59, 61, 74, 82–83, 86,
89; MS 35, 41, 45, 47–49, 51, 54–61;
TAA 2, 28; EM 62; LI 11; CHP 23; VQA
10; See *Comme le prévoit* and
Liturgiam authenticam

ABOUT THE AUTHORS

Authors are listed in the order in which their articles appear in this publication.

Rev. Robert L. Tuzik is a special assistant to His Eminence Francis Cardinal George, OMI. Father Tuzik serves as a consultant to the Congregation for Divine Worship and the Discipline of the Sacraments, the Chicago Office for Divine Worship, and Liturgy Training Publications. He holds a doctorate in Liturgical Theology from the University of Notre Dame and a Licentiate in Sacred Theology from Mundelein Seminary.

Jakob K. Rinderknecht is a doctoral student in Systematic Theology at Marquette University. He has been involved with parish liturgical ministry across the country and coordinated liturgical environment for the 2011 Southwest Liturgical Conference. His research interests include sacramental and ecumenical theology and their expression in the life of the local church.

Rev. Anthony Ruff, OSB, is a monk of Saint John's Abbey and professor of liturgy at Saint John's University / School of Theology•Seminary. He headed the committee that wrote English chant for the 2010 Roman Missal and was on the committee that drafted the United States Conference of Catholic Bishops' document *Sing to the Lord: Music in Divine Worship.* He is founding director of the National Catholic Youth Choir.

Michael R. Prendergast, MTS, MA, is a seasoned pastoral musician and liturgist with experience at the parish, cathedral, and diocesan levels. He is a frequent speaker and clinician for conferences, dioceses, and parishes. He has edited and authored numerous books and articles, including *The Liturgical Ministry Series: Guide for Liturgy Committees* (LTP), coauthored with Paul Turner. Michael holds advanced degrees in theological studies and liturgy. Michael is coordinator of liturgy at St. Andrew Church in Portland, Oregon; an instructor in the Lay Ministry Formation program for the Archdiocese of Portland; and an instructor in the theology department at the University of Portland. He is also a team member for the North American Forum on the Catechumenate. Michael is founder and executive director of Sacred Liturgy Ministries, a liturgical consulting firm.

S. Judith M. Kubicki, CSSF, PHD, is Associate Professor of Theology at Fordham University in New York City. She has served as Chair of the Board of Directors of the National Association of Pastoral Musicians and as President of the North American Academy of Liturgy. Her books include *Liturgical Music as Ritual Symbol: A Case Study of Jacques Bethier's Taizé Music* (1999) and *The Presence of Christ in the Gathered Assembly* (2006). Dr. Kubicki has published articles in *Worship, Theological Studies, Studia Liturgica, New Theology Review, The Living Light, Pastoral Music, Pastoral Liturgy, GIA Quarterly, Aim,* and *INTAMS review.*

Rev. Richard Fragomeni is a presbyter of the Diocese of Albany, New York and has been a member of the faculty of the Chicago Theological Union since 1990. His teaching involves him in Roman Catholic theology, interpretation theory, and poetry. His current work is in the field of word and sacrament: the intersection of symbolic activity and language as it creates insights into the Christian proclamation of grace. Central to this work is a fascination with the power of liturgy and preaching in the transformation of the human heart.

Richard is an adjunct faculty member in the Department of Religious Studies at DePaul University. He also serves as the Rector of The Shrine of Our Lady of Pompeii, an Italian American spiritual center in Chicago's historic Little Italy. In addition to his teaching duties he is a preacher of parish missions and gives presentations nationally and internationally on liturgical, sacramental, and catechetical topics.

He is author of *Come to the Feast* and coauthor with Br. Michael McGrath, OCFS, of both *Blessed Art Thou Mother, Lady, Mystic, Queen*, and *At the Name of Jesus: The Way, The Truth and The Light*. He has published *In Shining Splendor: Fifty Eastertime Meditations*, and *The Eucharist: 50 Questions from the Pews*.

David W. Fagerberg is associate professor in the Department of Theology at the University of Notre Dame. He holds an MDIV from Luther Northwestern Seminary; an MA from St. John's University, Collegeville; an STM from Yale Divinity School; and the PHD from Yale University. His work explores how the Church's *lex credendi* (law of belief) is founded upon the Church's *lex orandi* (law of prayer). He is the author of *The Size of Chesterton's Catholicism* (Notre Dame Press, 1998), *Theologia Prima* (Liturgy Training Publications, 2003), and *On Liturgical Asceticism* (Catholic University Press, 2013).

Corinna Laughlin, PHD, is the director of liturgy for St. James Cathedral in Seattle. She also serves on the Liturgical Commission for the Archdiocese of Seattle. She coauthored *The Liturgical Ministry Series: Guide for Sacristans* and *The Liturgical Ministry Series: Guide for Servers* (both LTP), and is a frequent contributor to *Sourcebook for Sundays, Seasons, and Weekdays: The Almanac for Parish Liturgy*. Corinna has also written articles for *Pastoral Liturgy, Today's Liturgy, Ministry & Liturgy*, and *AIM: Liturgy Resources*. She holds a doctorate in English from the University of Washington and a bachelor's degree in English from Mount Holyoke College.

Deacon Francis L. Agnoli, OFS, MD, DMIN, was ordained for the Diocese of Lexington, Kentucky, in 2002, and currently serves as the Director of Liturgy and the Director of Deacon Formation for the Diocese of Davenport, Iowa. Frank is married to Marianne, and they have two children. He worked as a family physician in rural Kentucky for a number of years before returning to school to earn a Master of Divinity and Master of Arts in Theology degrees from Saint John's University / School of Theology•Seminary. He and his family then returned to Kentucky where he served for five years as the primary pastoral caregiver for two parishes that did not have a resident priest. He earned the Doctor of Ministry in Preaching degree from the Aquinas Institute of Theology in 2009 and is currently completing a certificate program in homiletic supervision at the St. Meinrad School of Theology and Seminary. In addition to his diocesan responsibilities, he has taught in the deacon formation programs sponsored by Brescia University and by St. Meinrad's.

Steven R. Janco, MCM, STL, DMIN, is Director of the Rensselaer Program of Church Music and Liturgy at Saint Joseph's College in Rensselaer, Indiana, which offers summer study leading to master's degrees in church music and pastoral liturgy, as well as a number of three-day intensives—including its long-standing Gregorian Chant Institute. A composer of liturgical music, his published works include three Mass settings written for the texts of third edition of *The Roman Missal*. He has had articles and reviews published in a number of liturgy and liturgical music journals. He is a member of the North American Academy of Liturgy, the Catholic Academy of Liturgy, the National Association of Pastoral Musicians, and the National Association for Lay Ministry. He is also a life member of the Hymn Society in the United States and Canada and has served on the Society's Executive Committee.

Rev. Msgr. Joseph DeGrocco, pastor of Our Lady of Perpetual Help Church, Lindenhurst, New York, and former professor of liturgy and director of liturgical formation at the Seminary of the Immaculate Conception in Huntington, New York, holds an MA in theology (liturgical studies) from the University of Notre Dame and a Doctor of Ministry from the Seminary of the Immaculate Conception. He is the author of *A Pastoral Commentary on the General Instruction of the Roman Missal*, the *Dictionary of Liturgical Terms*, *The Church at Worship: Theology, Spirituality and Practice of Parish Liturgy*, the "Q & A" column in *Pastoral Liturgy* (all from LTP), and is a member of his diocese's Liturgical Commission.

Rev. Msgr. Kevin Irwin is a priest of the Archdiocese of New York and has served on the faculty of the School of Theology and Religious Studies at The Catholic University of America since 1986. He holds the Walter J. Schmitz Chair of Liturgical Studies, and served as dean from 2005 until 2011.

Msgr. Irwin is the author of fifteen books on liturgy and sacraments including *Liturgy, Prayer and Spirituality* (Paulist, 1984), *Liturgical Theology: A Primer* (Liturgical Press, 1990), *Context and Text: Method in Liturgical Theology* (Liturgical Press, 1994), the three-volume commentary on the liturgical seasons entitled *Advent-Christmas, Lent, and Easter: A Guide to Eucharist and Hours* (Pueblo/Liturgical Press,1985-91), *Models of the Eucharist* (Paulist Press, 2005), and *101 Questions and Answers on the Mass* (Paulist, 1999, 2012).

He is the author of over fifty articles and sixty reviews in such journals as *Worship, The Thomist, Pastoral Music, Eglise et théologie, La Maison-Dieu, American Benedictine Review, Theological Studies, Louvain Studies, Liturgical Ministry, The Jurist, New Theology Review, Studia Liturgica,* and *American Catholic Historical Review* as well as the *New Catholic Encyclopedia, New Dictionary of Theology,* and *New Dictionary of Catholic Spirituality.*

He is a member of the North American Academy of Liturgy, the Catholic Academy of Liturgy, the Society for Catholic Liturgy and the Catholic Theological Society of America.

In addition to his academic work, Msgr. Irwin regularly celebrates Mass and preaches at the Basilica of the National Shrine in Washington, DC, during the week and on weekends at the Church of Saint Bridget, Richmond, Virginia, where he is involved in parish education and liturgy programs.

Rev. Msgr. Richard B. Hilgartner is the Executive Director of the Secretariat of Divine Worship at the United States Conference of Catholic Bishops. A priest of the Archdiocese of Baltimore, Msgr. Hilgartner has worked in parish ministry and campus ministry and has taught theology and homiletics. He completed his mdiv/stb at St. Mary's Seminary and University, Baltimore, and an stl in Sacramental Theology at the Pontifical Athenaeum of Saint Anselm in Rome, where he is currently engaged in doctoral studies. In his work with the Bishops' Committee on Divine Worship, he helped prepare for the implementation of the third edition of *The Roman Missal* and is a frequent presenter on a variety of liturgical matters.

Rev. Gilbert Ostdiek, OFM, an ordained Franciscan, is Professor of Liturgy at Catholic Theological Union. In addition, Gil has conducted numerous adult education workshops on liturgy. He holds an STL and STD from the Pontifical Athenaeum Antonianum (Rome) and has done postdoctoral studies at Harvard Divinity School and the University of California/GTU. He served on the International Committee on the Liturgy for fifteen years, chairing the Subcommittee on the Translation and Revision of Texts. Gil is a former president of the North American Academy of Liturgy and a member of the Catholic Academy of Liturgy (CAL). The Notre Dame Center for Pastoral Liturgy and the Georgetown Center for Liturgy have given him awards for contributions to the liturgical life of the Church. His publications include *Catechesis for Liturgy* and entries in the CAL commentaries on the *General Instruction of the Roman Missal* and the *Order of Mass* in the *Third Edition of Roman Missal*.

Rev. Paul Turner is pastor of St. Anthony Parish in Kansas City, Missouri. A priest of the Diocese of Kansas City–St. Joseph, he holds a doctorate in sacred theology from Sant'Anselmo in Rome.

His publications include *At the Supper of the Lamb* (Chicago: Liturgy Training Publications, 2011); *Glory in the Cross* (Collegeville: Liturgical Press, 2011); *ML Bulletin Inserts* (San Jose: Resource Publications, 2012); and *Celebrating Initiation: A Guide for Priests* (Chicago: World Library Publications, 2008).

He is a former President of the North American Academy of Liturgy and a team member for the North American Forum on the Catechumenate. He is a member of Societas Liturgica and the Catholic Academy of Liturgy. He serves as a facilitator for the International Commission on English in the Liturgy.

Rev. Daniel J. Merz, a priest of the Diocese of Jefferson City, holds a doctorate in Sacred Liturgy from the Pontifical Institute of Liturgy in Rome. He has served in a parish, as professor and formator at Conception Seminary College, and currently works as the Associate Director for the Divine Worship Secretariat at the United States Conference of Catholic Bishops. He has published several articles on the liturgy, and coauthored with Abbot Marcel Rooney, osb, a pastoral commentary on the orations of the new Roman Missal: *Essential Presidential Prayers and Texts: A Roman Missal Study Edition and Workbook*.

Mary Elizabeth Sperry, MA, holds a master's degree in liturgical studies from The Catholic University of America. She has worked for the USCCB since 1994 in the Secretariat for the Liturgy, United States Conference of Catholic Bishops' Publishing, and the Department of Communications. She is the author of *Bible Top Tens* and *Ten: How the Commandments Can Change Your Life* (both 2012). Her articles have appeared in *The Liguorian, Emmanuel Magazine, Today's Parish Minister,* and other publications. She has been interviewed about the Bible on National Public Radio, CBS Radio, NBC News, the *Drew Mariani Show*, and *Seize the Day*.

S. Joyce Ann Zimmerman, CPPS, PHD, STD, is the director of the Institute for Liturgical Ministry in Dayton, Ohio; adjunct professor of liturgy at the Athenaeum of Ohio; a liturgical consultant; frequent speaker and facilitator of workshops on liturgy, spirituality, and other related topics; and an award-winning author of numerous books and articles on liturgy and spirituality. She is the recipient of the Notre Dame Center for Liturgy 2008 Michael Mathis Award and the 2010 Georgetown Center for Liturgy National Award for Outstanding Contributions to the Liturgical Life of the American Church. She is a theological consultant to the United States Conference of Catholic Bishops' Committee on Divine Worship.

Richard E. McCarron, PHD, is associate professor of liturgy and chair of the department of Word and Worship at Catholic Theological Union, Chicago, Illinois. He currently serves as editor of the *Proceedings of the North American Academy of Liturgy*.

Christopher Carstens holds a BA from the Oratory of St. Philip in Toronto, an MA in Philosophy from the University of Dallas, and an MA (Liturgical Studies) from The Liturgical Institute. He is currently the Director of the Office of Sacred Worship for the Diocese of La Crosse, Wisconsin, where he serves as Coordinator of Pontifical Liturgies, liturgical coordinator for the Permanent Deacon formation program, and diocesan Director of RCIA. He is an adjunct faculty member at the Liturgical Institute and a frequent presenter in liturgical conferences and parish education. He is a member of the Society for Catholic Liturgy and is married with seven children. Mr. Carstens is one of the presenters of *Mystical Body, Mystical Voice* program for understanding the English-language texts of the third edition of *The Roman Missal*.

Jason J. McFarland, MMUS, PHD, is a scholar of music and liturgy, and a frequent presenter at academic conferences and workshops on liturgical music and theology. He is a member of the North American Academy of Liturgy, *Societas Liturgica*, the Catholic Theological Society of America, and the National Association of Pastoral Musicians. Jason has authored articles and reviews in *Pastoral Music, Catholic Studies*, and the *Proceedings of the North American Academy of Liturgy* (2012). His book *Announcing the Feast: The Entrance Song in the Mass of the Roman Rite* was published by Liturgical Press in 2011 and he was a contributing author to *The Liturgy Documents, Volume One: Fifth Edition* (Liturgy Training Publications, 2012). Jason sang as a member of the professional choir at the Basilica of the National Shrine of the Immaculate Conception from 1997–2011. For the past six years Jason has worked as the Assistant Editor at the International Commission on English in the Liturgy (ICEL), where he was involved in the preparation of the third edition of *The Roman Missal*, and has been a lecturer in Liturgical Studies at The Catholic University of America. From 2012–2014, he is working as a professor at Zunyi Normal College, Guizhou, China. His home parish is St. Joseph the Workman, Huntimer, South Dakota.